INTERNATIONAL LAW IN
HISTORICAL PERSPECTIVE

NOVA ET VETERA IURIS GENTIUM

PUBLICATIONS OF THE INSTITUTE FOR INTERNATIONAL LAW
OF THE UNIVERSITY OF UTRECHT

EDITOR: PROFESSOR DR. M. BOS

SERIES A. MODERN INTERNATIONAL LAW
NUMBER 7

A.W. SIJTHOFF-LEYDEN
1970

INTERNATIONAL LAW
IN HISTORICAL
PERSPECTIVE

BY

Dr. J. H. W. VERZIJL

Emeritus Professor of International Law
Utrecht University

PART III

STATE TERRITORY

A.W.SIJTHOFF-LEYDEN

1970

© A. W. SIJTHOFF'S UITGEVERSMAATSCHAPPIJ, N.V. 1970
LIBRARY OF CONGRESS CATALOG CARD NUMBER: 68-26728
ISBN 90 218 9050 X

FOREWORD

Part III of this work is devoted to State Territory. It follows Parts I and II, the publication of which commenced in 1968.

The work has been carried out in exactly the same manner and with the same aims as its predecessors. I have endeavoured, wherever possible to bring the subject matter up-to-date although events in some fields are moving so rapidly that any work is almost bound to be comprehensive only up to the point at which the manuscript goes to the printers.

In conclusion I have only to offer my heartfelt gratitude to those who continue to assist me in completing the task I have undertaken, a task which I might well have never commenced had I fully realised its formidable extent at the outset. Had the vastness of the canvas to be covered been fully revealed to me at my first glance I might well have quailed. However, "fools rush in where angels fear to tread" and it is now too late for repentance!

December 1969   J. H. W. VERZIJL

TABLE OF CONTENTS

CHAPTER I

THE LEGAL NATURE OF STATE TERRITORY
(HISTORICAL AND THEORETICAL)
THE CONCEPT OF TERRITORIAL SOVEREIGNTY

The legal nature of territory as an "element of the State" and as the object of (territorial) sovereignty under modern international law can best be defined after a preliminary survey of its historical development, on the one hand, and a brief analysis of certain juridical facts affecting it, such as cession, on the other.

For many centuries territory has exhibited distinctly patrimonial features in the sense that it was generally considered as being the property, or at least within the possession and the legal disposal, of the person vested with the supreme authority, Emperor, King or Prince of lower rank. It would be going too far afield to retrace here the development in this respect since the Merovingian epoch (from the middle of the 5th century onwards) via the days of Charlemagne (circa 800) and the Carolingian period, which followed the division of his empire, through the rise, flowering, and decline of feudalism up to the birth of the modern sovereign State. The old idea of the "eminent domain" or the supreme authority of the Prince over the whole of his territory, although now having become completely obsolete, has lingered in legal parlance up to the present day.

The concept of *dominium eminens* has been developed by older writers on public law who attributed to the State an overriding right to the real property of its subjects; a right which was, however, distinguished from the right of ownership according to the adage: "Omnia rex imperio possidet, singuli dominio". This *dominium eminens* was in fact *imperium* by its nature, not *dominium* in the sense of a proprietary right. The term still plays a certain part in the doctrinal foundation of the right of expropriation appertaining to the modern State. The confusion between *imperium* and *dominium* up to the present time is shown by the use of the incorrect term of *condominium* where *co-imperium* or co-sovereignty is meant. Comp. on this right of "eminent domain" and its origin, *inter alios:* VATTEL, *Le droit des gens, ou principes de la loi naturelle, etc.*, I, 20, 235, 244; II, 7, 81; J.S.PÜTTER, *Litteratur des teutschen Staatsrechts* (Göttingen, 1776-1791), III, p. 378.

Obsolete notions of this kind were still reflected in the terminology of many international instruments at the beginning of the 19th century. Comp., *e.g.*, Articles IV and VII of the Peace Treaty of Kiel between Sweden and Denmark of 14 January 1814 (Martens, N.R., I, 666):

(IV) "S.M. le Roi de Danemarc, pour lui et ses successeurs, renonce irrévocablement et à jamais, en faveur de S.M. le Roi de Suède et de ses successeurs, à tous les droits et prétentions au Royaume de Norvège …; tous les droits et émolumens appartiendront dorénavant *en propriété entière et souveraine* à S.M. le Roi de Suède …;" (VII) "… Ces provinces (la Pomeranie suédoise et la principauté de l'île de Rugen, cédées par la Suède) … appartiendront dorénavant, *comme pleine propriété*, à la couronne de Danemarc …" (italics applied).

This obsolete terminology can still be found in treaties of much later date.

It was adumbrated in the time when the King-Emperor installed a system of enfeoffment of his chief judicial and civil servants appointed for the administration of the different regions of his Kingdom-Empire— the "graves" or counts—with feuds (fiefs) and *beneficia* held on the condition that they rendered military service in return. It reached its fullest development during the time when the administrative and judicial offices and the fiefs thus created became hereditary and the great vassals imitated and complemented the feudal system by the creation of vavasories or sub-vassalages, and when such feudal tenures, of whatever rank in the tier of feudal hierarchy they might be, often lapsed on the extinction of the male line of succession of the vassal, or could still be forfeited on the ground of felony. The system survived to, indeed still flourished in, the days of the Congress of Westphalia (1648) in spite of the fact that the liegemen of the Holy Roman Empire were on that occasion vested with the *Landeshoheit* (territorial supremacy) and thus became real territorial sovereigns *(Landesherren)*, subject only to a last residuum of the paramount power of the Emperor and the Empire.[1]

The Peace Congress even sanctioned the grant of a number of new lands "in perpetuum et immediatum (haereditarium) Imperii feudum": Article X, §§ 2 and 3 (Pomerania citerior, with the island of Rügen; parts of Pomerania ulterior, including Stettin, the island of Wollin and the Frische Haff), §§ 6 (Wismar *c.a.*) and 7 (the archbishopric of

---

1. A distinction between the King (Emperor) and the Kingdom (Empire) as two separate juridical persons had already developed in very early days and would seem to date back to the reign of Conrad II (1024-1039). Comp. H. MITTEIS, *Deutsche Rechtsgeschichte*, 3rd ed. (1954), p. 93. It has continued to be observed as a practical political reality until the very end of the existence of the Holy Roman Empire. Comp., *e.g.*, the introduction to the Peace Treaty of Lunéville between the Emperor and the First Consul of the French Republic of 9 February 1801 (Martens, R², VII, 296):

"Sa dite Majesté impériale et royale ne désirant pas moins vivement de faire participer l'empire germanique aux bienfaits de la paix et les conjonctures présentes ne laissant pas le temps nécessaire pour que l'empire soit consulté …, susdite Majesté … a résolu, à l'example de ce qui a eu lieu dans des circonstances semblables, de stipuler au nom du corps germanique".

Bremen and the bishopric of Verden), all to Sweden; Article XI, §§ 1, 4 and 5 (the archbishoprics of Halberstadt, Minden and Cammin), all to Brandenburg, which was moreover granted the "expectative" (comp. *infra*, Chapter III, section 1, § 2, *sub* (*d*), p. 310) with regard to the archbishopric of Magdeburg in perpetual fief in case it should fall vacant.

In those centuries territories, whether feudal or allodial, were susceptible of deliberate transfer and automatic transition from one tenant to another by sale, gift, exchange, compromise, endowment, matrimonial grant, will, dynastic inheritance or hereditary partition. They could likewise be granted by their tenants to others on temporary terms, such as: mortgage, usufruct, life rent, emphyteusis and the like,—types of temporary disposal which were only too often, explicitly or tacitly, transformed by a gradual "novation" into definitive tenures in the course of the years or centuries. All these institutions and transactions dating from feudal times, many of which are directly responsible for part of the actual territorial division of Europe, belong to a past which is already remote. It is curious to state, however, that feudal territorial claims have continued to show their possible juridical relevancy as late as 1815, and even beyond (comp. below).

Although the feudal system has since long ceased to operate, nevertheless fossilized feudal survivals are still extant in modern Europe, in particular in certain enclaves or condominia, such as:

the mountainous region of Andorra and other areas in the Franco-Spanish borderland of the Pyrenees:

The legal status of Andorra is still that of a fossilized medieval *pariagium*, a special kind of *condominium*, which was not uncommon in Southern France in the 13th century. This *pariagium* of Andorra was established by an arbitral award of 1278 between the Count of Foix and the Bishop of Urgel. A *pariagium* could also be set up by agreement. Comp. further on Andorra the French Presidential Decree of 3 June 1882 (Martens, N.R.G.[2], IX, 214), and below, Chapter III, section 1, § 4, p. 325,

the British Channel Islands on the coast of France:

The somewhat unusual fact that a number of islands off the coast of France, the so-called Channel Islands or Îles normandes: Jersey, Guernsey, Alderney, Sark, Herm, Jethou and the Ecrehos and Minquiers groups—the latter two, still nearer to the French coast, definitively recognized as British by the International Court of Justice (Judgment of 17 November 1953, *I.C.J. Reports* 1953, p. 47)—appertain to Great Britain is an historical consequence of the fact that continental Normandy was once an area held by the Kings of England in fief from the Kings of France. When the English forces were driven out of the continent in 1204, the Channel Islands remained under English rule and this has continued up to the present time. Comp. on this subject my *The Jurisprudence of the World Court*, vol. II, p. 169;

the Baarle-Nassau and Baarle-Hertog enclaves near the Netherlands-Belgian boundary between the two Brabant provinces:

3

The Baarle enclaves date from the 13th century when, in consequence of the division of the holdings of the Berthout family, some small areas passed in fief to the Nassau dynasty in their capacity of barons of Breda—hence their name of Baarle-Nassau—, while others—Baarle Duc or Baarle-Hertog—fell to the Dukes of Brabant. Their continued existence as enclaves is due to the fact that all successive attempts or opportunities to liquidate them have either failed or been lost. It was only two minute plots of land among the, otherwise undisputed, respective Belgian and Netherlands enclaved border areas which gave rise to proceedings before the International Court of Justice in 1959 (*I.C.J. Reports* 1959, p. 209). Even after its Judgment of 20 June of that year, which adjudicated those two plots to Belgium, the enclaves themselves continue to exist as feudal survivals, a status which will last perhaps for a few more centuries. Comp. on this case my *The Jurisprudence of the World Court*, vol. II, p. 353 and on the history of these enclaves: F. A. BREKELMANS, *De Belgische enclaves in Nederland* in *Bijdragen tot de geschiedenis van het Zuiden van Nederland*, vol. IV (Tilburg, 1965),

the Italian enclave of Campione on the Lake of Lugano:

The Italian enclave of Campione on the eastern bank of the Lake of Lugano had been since the 8th century a fief of the Abbey of Sant'Ambrogio of Milan. It later fell with the Duchy of Milan to Austria (Lombardy), in 1859 to Sardinia and in the final event to the new Kingdom of Italy. Comp. further on this curious enclave below Chapter V, section 2, p. 450,

and others. The Federal Republic of Germany up to the present day still upholds wholly obsolete claims to sovereignty over the entire surface of the Ems estuary between the Netherlands province of Groningen and the ex-county (principality) of Eastern-Friesland, which she asserts she derives from a 15th century bill of enfeoffment of the Emperor Frederick III, spuriously dated 1454, but which is in fact only a forged edition of a genuine later feudal instrument of 1464 that affords no support whatsoever for this far-fetched claim.

A bill of enfeoffment of 1454 never existed. It was only fabricated at a later date after a genuine feudal grant had been given in 1464 to the then local "Häuptling" of Norden. The latter grant, which created a "County in East-Friesland", was subsequently by, or at the instigation of, the Counts antedated to 1454 and on important points forged at consecutive periods, the last time shortly before 1558 when five additional words were intercalated in the body of the instrument ("auch dem Wasser die Embse") which had never been in the original text but which were intended to provide a late but spurious legal foundation for the East-Frisian claim to sovereignty over the whole breadth of the Ems estuary. Even German historians and lawyers no longer maintain the authenticity of the pretended basic instrument of 1454. Comp. in particular the elaborate studies of W. VON BIPPEN in (Sybel's) *Historische Zeitschrift*, 1880 (vol. 44), pp. 299 *et seq.*, and *Hansische Geschichtsblätter*, 1883, pp. 43 *et seq.*; H. REIMERS, "Edzard der Grosse" in *Abhandlungen und Vorträge zur Geschichte Ostfrieslands*, vol. XIII/XIV, with passages quoted in support in *Emder Jahrbuch*, 1913/1914 (XVIII). See below Chapter VI, section 4, p. 599.

Moreover, the traditional medieval conceptions which underlay the

4

institutions alluded to, or originated from them, have never entirely lost their influence on legal theory and have proved their tenacity by the survival of a number of obsolete terms, concepts and types of legal transaction long after the decline of the feudal system.

It is, therefore, not surprising that such old historic patrimonial notions have left their traces in the conceptual and terminological storehouse of the sources and doctrine of public international law even up to modern times.

The same observation may be made with regard to the gradual evolution of the concept of territorial sovereignty from its original meaning of the superiority of one authority over another and its initial appearance as a large cluster of separate *regalia* or royal rights, to their eventual symbiosis in the modern indissoluble and all-embracing notional unity of State sovereignty.[2] Thus the modern idea of territorial sovereignty is weighed down with a mass of legal history, most of which is, nowadays, merely dead weight, and the situation therefore calls for the discarding of all those supererogatory elements which have long since lost their relevance to contemporary conditions.

The international community was indeed already approaching the twilight of the feudal system when the law of nations still remained partly embedded in it. Hence the many international treaties in which feudal relationships and cognate institutions still played an unmistakable rôle. I will only cite a few more of these below as an illustration of the peculiarities of this period of transition from the remnants of feudalism in inter-state relations to the emergence of a law of nations purged of such feudal admixtures, in particular in the last quarter of the 18th and the first quarter of the 19th century.

The usual term to indicate territorial sovereignty was in earlier times and continued to be up to the second half of the 18th century: *superioritas territorialis* or its French equivalent, and in German: *Territorial-Oberherrschaft* (later replaced by *Gebietshoheit*).

> See, *e.g.*, the treaties between France and Lorraine of 21 January 1718 (Rousset, *Receuil*, I, 103), Article 14; between Milan and Grisons of 8 February 1763 (Martens, R[2], I, 175), Article 4; between Austria and Poland of 18 September 1773 (*ibid.*, R[2], II, 109), Article 2; and between Austria and the Palatinate, at Teschen, of 13 May 1779 (*ibid.*, R[2], II, 669), Article 6.

Some older treaties made a sharp distinction in respect of the domination over landed estates between *superioritas territorialis, plenum jus dominii privati* and *Lehnherrlichkeit*.

> See for example Article 4 of the convention of 27 May 1768 (*ibid.*, R[2], I, 597) regarding the cession of the "Elb-pertinentia" (certain islands off the mouth of the river Elbe) by Holstein to the City of Hamburg.

2. Comp. on this vexed notion of sovereignty in general my analysis in Part I of this publication, Chapter VI, p. 256.

Other diplomatic instruments opposed certain "droits régaliens" to the "pleine supériorité territoriale".

On the reunion of Alsace with the French Crown part of those *regalia*, enumerated in a series of 45 Articles, were reserved by Letters Patent of the French King of May 1779 (*ibid.*, R², II, 690) for the former seigniors in so far as they did not impair the "autorité souveraine".

A curious list of such "droits régaliens" was also drawn up in the *Lettres patentes* of June 1768 (*ibid.*, R², I, 615) by which King Louis XV of France confirmed the Duke of Württemberg in the rights or estates in Alsace which he had enjoyed under the German Empire as an "unmittelbarer Reichsstand" and which he would be allowed to continue to exercise under the sovereignty of France: high, median and low jurisdiction, subject to an appeal to the *Conseil supérieur d'Alsace*, *e.g.*, by a "forest chamber"; the appointment and deposition of officials; the execution of judgments; the issue of police by-laws; a limited right to levy contributions; the further exercise of feudal rights in case of the vacation of a fief, or of the felony of vassals, to be judged by a feudal court, and of the right of "retrait féodal et seigneurial"; hunting, fishing and foresting rights; the right to impose certain fatigue duties; "droits de péage et de pontenage"; the right to sell salt and iron to the inhabitants; the right of "déshérence et de biens vacans"; *dixmes novales* (tithes to be levied from lands which were going to be cultivated for the first time); the extraction of minerals and fossils, hidden treasure and saltpetre; the right of emigration (*Abzug*) and mainmorte, that of *Umgeld* or *Liegergeld*, and of the "taille" and other rents in money, wine, grains, etc.; *Judengeld* of twelve *écus* per person and per family and the right to expel Jews; existing markets,—all these rights being maintained subject to the condition that the Duke should recognize that he held them in fief from the King of France, bring him "foi et hommage", and render him "aveu et dénombrement" on each occasion. A catalogue such as this throws a vivid light on the complicated nature of the legal relations of the period and their impact even on inter-state relations.

In Article 28 of her treaty of exchange of certain enclaves in the Southern Netherlands with Austria, dated 16 May 1769 (Martens, R², I, 661), France expressly renounced her existing right of protection of the abbey of St. Hubert in the territory ceded.

Poland was forced by Prussia in Articles 3 and 4 of their treaty of 18 September 1773 which finalized Poland's first partition (*ibid.*, R², II, 149), to acquiesce in the abolition of all her feudal claims and right of reversion relative to Prussia and Lauenburg which were based on their treaties of Velan of 19 September 1654 (Dumont, VI², 192) and of Bydgośc of 6 November 1657. Prussia's counterclaims against Poland had been set out in detail in Letters Patent of the King of Prussia of 13 September 1772 (Martens, R², II, 98). Comp. on this case also Part II of this publication, Chapter VI, section 1, pp. 351, 358, and below Chapter III, section 1, § 2, *sub (e)*, p. 314, on Reversibility.

In the boundary treaty between France and the Electorate of Trier of 1 July 1778 (*ibid.*, R², II, 268) reservation or cession was made of all sorts of "droits honorifiques et utiles", "fiefs", "droits de sauvegarde", "sauvemens", "prérogatives de paturage et d'affouage", etc.; these provisions were further elaborated in Letters Patent of the King of France of August 1780 (*ibid.*, II, 278), mentioning a number of other peculiar rights, such as those of mill rents, the felling of trees, of "terrage", "sevrage", "thonlieu et hutage", etc.

6

By their peace treaty of Teschen of 13 May 1779 (*ibid.*, II, 661) Maria Theresia and Friedrich II of Prussia reciprocally renounced the still existing feudal ties between Bohemia and the principalities of Baireuth and Anspach (Articles 10 and 11) and insisted upon the Emperor conferring the fiefs of the Empire in Bavaria and Swabia upon the Elector of the Palatinate and his house (Article 13).

Article 11 of the secret Convention additional to the Peace Treaty of Campo Formio of 17 October 1797 (Martens, R², VI, 426) still dealt with the once famous "fiefs Impériaux" in Italy.

The transition from feudal rights, or from territorial sovereignty restricted by such rights, and from the idea of an aggregate of separate sovereign rights to complete, all-embracing sovereignty was still taking place even as late as the first part of the 19th century.

The decisive onslaught on the remnants of the feudal system, in the international sphere also, was started at the end of the 18th century by the leaders of the French Revolution. It was on the initiative of the Constituent National Assembly that these lingering vestiges of a dying past were abolished. Its relevant decrees of different dates in August 1789, 15 March and 28 October 1790, and 9 June 1791, still sanctioned by King Louis XVI, suppressed all "droits seigneuriaux et féodaux" in France, also in the *départements* of the Upper and Lower Rhine and to the detriment of German princes, such as those of Salm-Salm and Löwenstein-Wertheim, who were, however, initially still promised adequate compensation for the losses thus suffered. Comp. the decrees of 1790-1792, inserted in Martens, R², V, 138-144. However, the suppression of feudal and seigniorial rights was much slower in Germany and northern Italy. The major instruments of 1803 *(Reichsdeputations-Hauptschluss)*, 1806 (Act of the Confederation of the Rhine) and 1815 (Final Act of the Congress of Vienna) were still thick with references to existing feudal rights, "droits de suzeraineté" and some more specific rights of a kindred nature, and a number of them, such as the "droit de réversion", have survived even the Peace Congress of Vienna.

The *Reichsdeputations-Hauptschluss* of 25 February 1803 (*ibid.*, R², VII, 435) still mentioned in its § 29 (2) the "suzerainty" of German princes even over certain Swiss territories, and *vice versa*.

One of the most characteristic international instruments to show the gradual transition from the old to the new concepts is the treaty of 12 July 1806 which established the Confederation of the Rhine (*ibid.*, R², VIII, 480). Whereas it was stipulated in Articles 24 and 25 that a certain number of German kings, grand dukes, princes and dukes "exerceront tous les droits de souveraineté" over a great number of territories constituting until then (parts of) other, minor principalities, counties, seigniories, margraviates, burggraviates, landgraviates, baronies, bailiwicks and knightly domains (terres équestres), and Article 26 defined these "droits de souveraineté" as "ceux de législation, de juridiction

7

suprême, de haute-police, de conscription militaire ou de recrutement et d'impôt", Article 27 expressly reserved for these minor ex-rulers —besides their former demesnes, thenceforward to be held as "patrimonial and private property"—"tous les droits seigneuriaux et féodaux non essentiellement inhérans à la souveraineté, et notamment le droit de basse et moyenne juridiction en matière civile et criminelle, de juridiction et de police forestière, de chasse, de pêche, de mines, d'usines, des dîmes et prestations féodales, de pâturage et autres semblables revenus provenans des dits domaines et droits".

It was only in 1806 that *Landeshoheit* became sovereignty, at least in the construction which was put upon the legal-political events, reviewed by two *Austrägal-Entscheidungen* of the Court of Appeal of the Grand Duchy of Baden between Lippe-Detmold and Lippe-Schaumburg of 25 January 1839 (Martens, N.R., XVI[1], 432 *et seq.*), which are very interesting from the legal-historical point of view. There one reads at pp. 482-483 the following passage:

> "Dazu kommt, dass die Rechte des Erstgeborenen nicht bloss "Superiorität, Hoheit und Regierung" (1614) sonder auch "hohe Landesobrigkeit" (1616) und im Vergleich von 1621 sogar "Landeshoheit" genannt sind, welche letztere gerade der allgemeine Ausdruck für dasjenige ist, was Lippe-Detmold vor 1806 gehabt zu haben behauptet und was durch die Rheinbundsacte zur Souverainetät geworden ist".

Almost all diplomatic instruments of this period of transition relating to German lands still mirror the lasting feudal relationships of those days. A few further examples from Martens, R[2], VIII may suffice:

> In the Convention of 30 August 1806 between the Grand Duke of Hesse and the Prince of Nassau-Weilburg (p. 514) the former recognized the latter's *dominium directum* over certain *Lehnherrschaften* (Article II), whereas a controversy concerning the *Hoheit oder Souverainetät* over a certain march (border area) was left in suspense (Article III).
>
> Articles IV, VI and VII of the Convention between the same Grand Duke and the Prince-Primate of 26 September 1806 (p. 519) mentioned certain fiefs of the principality of Aschaffenburg, which were ceded to the Grand Duke, while the *Lehnherrlichkeit* remained unaltered, and a cession *mit voller Souverainetät* to the Grand Duke of certain localities over which the Prince-Primate had had up to then the *Landeshoheit*.

The former elector, thenceforward Grand Duke, of Baden, in his Edict of 12 July 1806 (Martens, R[2], VIII, 501), still felt it necessary to define his newly acquired "souveraineté illimitée" as comprising legislation, supreme jurisdiction, high police, the right of conscription and that of the levying of taxes.

And even Napoleon, in his self-styled capacity of Protector of the Confederation of the Rhine, in his letter to the Prince-Primate of 11 September 1806 (*ibid.*, R[2], VIII, 506), declared in express terms that he laid no claim to "la portion de souveraineté qu'exerçait l'empereur d'Allemagne comme suzerain".

8

Various provisions of the Final Act of the Congress of Vienna also contained reminiscences of old feudal relations. Comp. Article 18 (renunciation by the Emperor in favour of the King of Prussia of the rights of suzerainty over the margraviates of the Upper and Lower Lausitz which belonged to him in his capacity of King of Bohemia), 19 *in fine* (mutual waiver by the Kings of Prussia and Saxony of "tout droit ou prétention de féodalité qu'ils exerceraient ou qu'ils auraient exercés" beyond their newly fixed frontiers; comp. also Article 6 (2) of their bilateral treaty of 18 May 1815, Martens, N.R., II, 272), 23, last paragraph (re-instatement of the King of Prussia in the "droits de souveraineté et suzeraineté" over the county of Wernigerode), and 100, paragraph 3, *sub* 2 and 3 (dealing with suzerainty over part of Elba and over the principality of Piombino). The latter provision is characteristic of the terminological and conceptual confusion between widely differing rights:

> "Il sera en outre réuni au Grand-Duché (de Toscane), pour être possédé en toute *propriété* et *souveraineté* (par le Grand-Duc):
> ...
> 3. la *suzeraineté* et *souveraineté* de la Principauté de Piombino et ses dépendances" (italics applied).

The bracketing together of sovereignty and property was, for the rest, very current at the time, also in the Final Act. Comp. among many other provisions:

> Article 23 by which the King of Prussia was restored not only to the sovereignty, but also in the "property" of all the lands which he had lost at Tilsit (1807);
> Article 47 which made a clear distinction between property and sovereignty of the salt mines of Kreuznach on the left bank of the Nahe (the former allotted to Hesse, the latter remaining with Prussia), whereas, on the other hand, it awarded to Hesse certain territory on the left bank of the Rhine "en toute souveraineté et propriété",
> and Article 67 by which part of the old Duchy of Luxembourg was ceded to the Sovereign Prince, thenceforward King, of the Netherlands, "pour être possédée à perpétuité par Lui et Ses successeurs en toute propriété et souveraineté" as a compensation for the loss by his dynasty of the principalities of Nassau-Dillenburg, Siegen, Hadamar and Dietz in Germany.

Articles 85, 89, 98 and 100, *in fine*, *sub* 4, still recalled the old "fiefs impériaux", now incorporated into Sardinia, Massa-Carrara and Tuscany. Comp. on these Imperial fiefs Part II of this publication, p. 357.

Article XIV of the Act of the German Confederation of 8 June 1815 (Martens, N.R., II, 353) reserved for the German Princes who had been mediatized in 1806 and the following years a certain number of rights which had formerly accrued to them in their capacity of *Reichsstände*. Excepted from that reservation were (under *c*) those rights which belonged to the "Staatsgewalt" and the "höhere Regierungsrechte", but the mediatized Princes (under 4) remained under certain specified

9

conditions possessed of "die Ausübung der bürgerlichen and peinlichen Gerechtigkeitspflege in erster, und wo die Besitzung gross genug ist, in zweiter Instanz, der Forstgerichtsbarkeit, Ortspolizei und Aufsicht in Kirchen- und Schulsachen, auch über milde Stiftungen ..." An echo can still be heard in that provision of the ancient concept of sovereignty as an aggregate of distinct public powers.

A most curious and much later echo of the said Article XIV has still sounded in The Netherlands in the period 1952-1957 when Fürst Nicolaus zu Salm-Salm invoked that Article in order to be exempted from the confiscation of certain of his estates, situated in The Netherlands, as enemy property. His action was dismissed in three instances, comp. *Ned. Jur.* 1957, Nos. 82 and 492 (*N.T.I.R.*, 1957 (IV), 209 and 1958 (V), 94).

Another relic of the feudal past was at issue in the arbitral proceedings which were instituted in virtue of Article 69 of the Final Act of Vienna with regard to the Duchy of Bouillon, the rights to which were disputed between Prince Charles de Rohan and vice-admiral Philippe d'Auvergne:

"Dans l'intervalle S.M. le Roi des Pays-Bas, Grand-Duc de Luxembourg, prendra en dépôt la propriété de ladite partie du Duché de Bouillon, pour la restituer, ensemble le produit de cette administration intermédiaire, à celui des compétiteurs en faveur duquel le jugement arbitral sera prononcé ...".

The award of 1 July 1816 was in favour of the Prince of Rohan. Comp. on this arbitration: DE LAPRADELLE-POLITIS, *Recueil des arbitrages internationaux*, vol. I, pp. 256-268.

Various other provisions still dealt with the cognate institution of "reversibility" of a number of countries—the margraviates of the Lausitz (Article 18, § 2), the duchy of Modena, Reggio and Mirandola and the principalities of Massa and Carrara (Article 98, § 3), the duchies of Parma, Piacenza and Guastalla (Article 99) and the duchy of Lucca (Article 102)—to other princely houses (comp. on this "droit de réversion" below, Chapter III, section 1, § 2 (*e*), pp. 314 *et seq.*).

From all this appears that feudal relations have for centuries played a prominent rôle in international affairs. As far as their effects have made themselves immediately felt upon the acquisition or loss of State territory, a few further details will be given below in the relevant Chapter III, section 1.

As far as the phenomenon of "vassal States" in the sense of international law is concerned, they have been dealt with in Part II of this publication on International Persons, Chapter VI, section 1, pp. 339 *et seq.*, 355 *et seq.*

What then is the conceptual content of territorial sovereignty at the present time? Scholarly theories have been devoted to this subject. VON LISZT in his *Völkerrecht*, 12th ed. (Berlin, 1925), p. 129, note 2, summarized the doctrinal controversy by opposing the "Raumtheorie" to the "Objekttheorie":

10

"Gegenstand der Staatsgewalt als Gebietshoheit ist nicht das Staatsgebiet; ihren Gegenstand bilden vielmehr stets die Menschen, die sich auf dem Gebiete aufhalten oder durch Vermittlung dinglicher Rechte an unbeweglichen im Staatsgebiet gelegenen Gütern in Beziehung zu dem Staatsgebiet treten (sog. "Raumtheorie")."

Territorial sovereignty (Gebietshoheit) is, according to RANITZKY,[3] equivalent to "örtliche Kompetenzsphäre" (local sphere of competence). Many writers, in particular German and Italian, have displayed their ingenuity in developing doctrinal constructions, among others: C.V. FRICKER, *Vom Staatsgebiet* (1867) and *Gebiet und Gebietshoheit* (Tübingen, 1901); C.GHIRARDINI, *La sovranità territoriale nel diritto internazionale* (Cremona, 1913) and D.DONATI, *Stato e territorio* (*R.D.I.*, 1923 (15), p. 349 and 1924 (16), p. 47). Joseph L.KUNZ has dealt with the controversy in the context of the right of option, F.GAUTIER in that of the institution of co-sovereignty.[4] Comp. also W.SCHOENBORN, *La nature juridique du territoire* in *Recueil des Cours* 1929-V, t. 30, p. 81.

I would like to approach the question from the purely practical angle of a simple analysis, from the point of view of an international lawyer, of what happens in the case of a cession of territory. Different juridical constructions have been put upon this elementary transaction between States. The main antithesis regarding this subject centers on the question as to whether in the case of cession of territory there is any real transfer at all. According to whether the answer to this central question is negative or positive, further queries arise. If there is no genuine transfer of anything, what then is the essence of the transaction? And if there is, what exactly is the object of the transfer?

Those who deny that cession of territory involves any real transfer generally argue in support of their view that the idea of transfer in this field is an obsolete doctrinal remnant of the "patrimonial" past when territory was still, and could correctly be considered as, the object of private, feudal or public rights *in re*, a notion irreconcilable with modern conditions. In their opinion, the transaction essentially consists in the unilateral withdrawal by the "ceding" State of its public authority over the territory "ceded", accompanied either by the immediate automatic filling of the territorial vacuum thus created, as if through the force of a law of juridical physics, with the public authority of the "cessionary" State, or by the, immediate or subsequent, corresponding unilateral extension by the latter of its authority over the "cessum", as if through a new occupation of a just created no man's land. Apart from the objection that if, in the latter way of presenting the juridical events, the

3. In *Archiv des öffentlichen Rechts* 1905 (XX), p. 340 and 1912 (XXVIII), p. 454.
4. J.L.KUNZ, *Die völkerrechtliche Option* (Breslau, 1925), I, pp. 18 *et seq.*; F. GAUTIER, *Das Wesen des Staatsgebiets dargestellt am Kondominat*, thesis Heidelberg, 1906.

correlative occupation by the cessionary State fails to be performed immediately, a covetous third State might find a god-sent opportunity thrown in its way of filling the territorial vacuum itself by occupation of such a no man's land, the entire presentation of these events would seem to be highly artificial. The wish, understandable in itself, to eliminate obsolete relics of the past here only results in a theory which bears no relation to what occurs in reality, and therefore makes no sense.

There is, in fact, no objection of any weight to adduce against the idea of the transfer of territory, provided that the object of the transfer be defined correctly and adapted to modern conditions and notions. What is transferred in the case of cession of State territory is no longer a "real" right (*jus in re*) of a proprietary or patrimonial nature, not even a right of "public domain" in the sense of the "domaine public" according to French administrative law, which indeed only comprises that State property which is destined for the public use, such as public roads and waterways. The object of the transfer is rather the aggregate of public competencies respecting the territory and its inhabitants which the ceding State used, or was entitled under international law, to exercise until the cession. What is in reality transferred is the total of State competencies inherent in the concept of territorial sovereignty. This construction again allows of two variations: the cession may be regarded as the transfer of nothing more than an "empty" competence lacking any substantial content until it is filled by the cessionary State according to its own free sovereign will, or it may be regarded as the transfer of a competence which preserves the substantial contents that the ceding State had given it in the exercise of its territorial sovereignty, until the cessionary State alters it in accordance with its own constitutional processes. Although the cessionary State cannot be denied the sovereign right to substitute immediately a new content of the territorial competence, thus transferred to it, for the old, and although the differences in political regime and legal conceptions between the ceding and the cessionary State may be so profound that maintenance of at least part of the old contents cannot be reasonably assumed, the necessity or desirability of the greatest possible degree of continuity in the exercise of sovereignty for the benefit of the population of the *cessum* would generally and with due reservations seem to tell in favour of the second variant of the theory propounded above. This particular aspect of the object of territorial sovereignty will be further discussed under the heading of State succession. See Part VII of this publication.

Other juridical acts in regard of State territory, such as occupation, lease, the establishment of State servitudes, etc. can appropriately be explained in the same way.

In the light of the observations above territorial sovereignty would seem to be adequately defined as being—not so much the sum total of an aggregate of various separate rights, as—the plenitude of exclusive competencies appertaining to a State under public international law within the boundaries of a definite portion of the globe, or in the words of A.N.SACK, *Les effets des transformations des Etats sur leurs dettes publiques et autres obligations financières* (Paris, 1927), I, p. 43:

"Le rôle du territoire d'Etat consiste à ce qu'il détermine les limites matérielles dans lesquelles s'exerce le pouvoir suprême du gouvernement",

and of L.DUGUIT, *Traité de droit constitutionnel*, 2nd. ed., t. II, p. 47, quoted by SACK at p. 44:

"Le territoire est ainsi la partie du globe sur laquelle le gouvernement peut exercer sa puissance de contrainte, organiser et faire fonctionner les différents services publics", the rôle of the territory being "cela, tout cela et (rien) que cela".

CHAPTER II

EXTENT AND ELEMENTS OF STATE TERRITORY

Introduction: Constituent Elements

Until relatively recently State territory could suitably be described as a (slightly convex) plane confined within definite geographical linear boundaries. This description would, however, nowadays be completely inadequate. State territory, conceived as the earthly space within which a State is entitled to exercise exclusive competencies, has gradually developed from a bi-dimensional, slightly spherical, plane into a tri-dimensional body, extremely irregular and complicated in shape and, as far as coastal States with a continental shelf are concerned, showing to the eye of the imagination the peculiar configuration of a huge aerial skyscraper with a constantly soaring and broadening top structure, mounted partly on a thin terrestrial socle or pedestal and partly on an adjoining iceberg-like submarine terrace.[1] Astounding technical developments have in actual fact expanded the extent of State territory in its old traditional planimetrical conception into an immense, more or less amorphous, stereometrical polyhedral structure.

Let us therefore now look at that structure more closely. Both from the angle of historical development and from that of logical priority the nucleus of State territory will always remain a defined portion of the surface of the earth. All other elements of it are dependent on, and inconceivable without, such a basic territorial substratum. No subsoil sovereignty, no State authority over the territorial sea or the continental shelf, no claims to air space are imaginable without that indispensable layer. Any discussion of this subject must accordingly start from the undisputed element (1) the land territory of the State—including also, somewhat inconsistently, its (inland) water territory: lakes, rivers, canals, ports—and can continue with—in their historical order—(2) the subsoil, (3) the territorial sea and (4) the air column, all three of which

1. My colleague of the (Municipal) University of Amsterdam A.J.P.TAMMES has employed a striking metaphor for the aerial part of the territory of a State by comparing it to the beam of light sent out by a lighthouse and sweeping round through the immensity of space.

14

are nowadays equally undisputed elements of State territory. The exposition must then proceed with an examination of more doubtful component parts such as (5) the continental shelf and (6) the contiguous zone in its delimitation towards the high seas. Still farther distant from State territory proper, both from the geographical and the theoretical point of view, are (7) exclusive fishery protection zones, (8) the so-called epicontinental waters and (9) assertedly exclusive fishery zones. The most problematical of all objects of conceivable State sovereignty, or at least State jurisdiction, are (10) the higher spheres of space. (11) Celestial bodies, still further away from the territorial substratum, are entirely alien to or outside the framework of State territory. If, contrary to all expectations, any "sovereign rights" over certain belts of space or over heavenly bodies should ever be recognized by the common consent of States, this new spatial and celestial imperialism or colonialism would be a subject of discussion lying wholly outside the normal limits of State territory. Earthly rules do not apply to space or to heavenly bodies.

When, starting from this general picture, one makes a vertical section across the territory of a State which from this aspect presents the most complicated type, namely, a maritime State with a fringe of islands along its coast, that section may in a horizontal direction seaward successively pass through the following areas: land territory, maritime internal waters, island territory, territorial sea, continental shelf, contiguous zone and a fishery protection zone. The degree of intensity of the powers to be exercised by the State concerned, in particular in the latter four of these successive zones, decreases steadily towards the high seas, from full territorial sovereignty (over the land and insular territory and the intermediate water territory) via limited territorial sovereignty (territorial sea), an aggregate of functional sovereign rights (continental shelf) and certain limitatively defined powers of selfprotection (contiguous zone), to a mere right of supervision of fishing, the latter as a rule jointly with specific other States.

When, on the other hand, such a vertical section is made in the length of the coastal belt or territorial sea by erecting a perpendicular plane on the line which separates that belt from the high seas, that section shows from the depth upward two completely different faces: to the landward side, the following series of areas: the subsoil of the sea and the seabed, the body of water covering the latter, the surface of the territorial sea, the air column over it, all falling under the overall sovereignty of the State concerned, and finally above them the immensity of stateless space; to the seaward side: the subsoil of the sea and the seabed, over which the coastal State only exercises certain functional sovereign rights, but which remain for the rest *regio nullius*, surmounted by the epicontinental waters and the air column above them, both stateless domain, subject only to certain limited rights of control of the coastal State, in so far as it thinks fit to lay claim to a limited contiguous zone, and above them again the infinity of space.

A successive examination of all the possible territorial elements of a State, enumerated above, leads to the conclusion that if, from a systematic point of view, the element under (5) can still, perhaps, with some reservations be held to fall under the territorial sovereignty of the (coastal) State, the elements under (6)-(11) certainly cannot. They do not, therefore, properly belong to this Chapter and will be treated elsewhere, those under (6)-(9), together with the high seas, in Part IV-A of this publication on Stateless Earthly Domain and those under (10) and (11) in Part IV-B on Space and Heavenly Bodies.

As to the element (1) I propose to deal with it in this way that I will first describe its general status cursorily. Since, however, a closer analysis or description of that status from an historical and a juristic point of view would burden this Chapter II unduly, I intend to enter into more detail with regard to this element in a separate monographic Annex which follows, *infra* pp. 94-296. Similar considerations induce me to refrain from dealing in section 1 of this Chapter with the frontiers of State land territory, a subject which also deserves a more elaborate monographic analysis. For this subject I may therefore be allowed to refer to a separate Chapter VI, *infra* pp. 513 *et seq.* The same considerations do not apply to the elements (2)-(5).

Section 1. LAND TERRITORY INCLUDING INLAND WATERWAYS

The territorial substratum of the State consists of land and water.

General. Nothing special needs to be said of the land territory of a State in general, but its inland waters call for some discussion from the point of view of international law. These waters are again of different types: inland lakes or seas, rivers, canals, ports and, in the case of coastal States, inlets from the sea on the landside of their general coastline. Side by side with canals, other artificial structures, such as railways and roads, telegraph- and telephone lines, pipelines and cables, and hydroelectric and similar systems also call for some comment.

It is, of course, possible to differentiate from a legal aspect between different parts of the land territory in general, *e.g.*, between the mother country and its colonies or overseas dominions, provinces and other dependencies, or between various regions of a State according to their differing constitutional status—the *regioni autonome* of Italy, the so-called "State fragments", etc.—, but such an internal differentiation has only in exceptional cases a direct bearing on the legal status of the different parts concerned, viewed in their general capacity of State territory under international law. However, the distinction between the mother

16

country and dependent territories has since World War II become the sport of politics under Chapter XI of the Charter of the United Nations on Non-Selfgoverning Territories. Many of these have increasingly developed from simple overseas possessions, in the old patrimonial conception, of the mother country into integral parts of its territory with an at first embryonic but gradually fully emerging personality of their own. Others have been prematurely blessed with a devastating independence. And for the rest the United Nations General Assembly is constantly engaged in a somewhat ludicrous hunt for non-selfgoverning territories which can still be "decolonized", but many of which are so minute and undeveloped, that they are unable under any conceivable circumstances to stand on their own feet and, therefore, are much better left in their present status. Comp. on the status of colonies: A. N. SACK, *Les effets des transformations des Etats sur leurs dettes publiques et autres obligations financières* (Paris, 1927), pp. 135 *et seq.*

The manner in which the General Assembly has in the course of the years gradually changed its construction of Article 73 within the context of the whole of the Charter, correlatively to the increase in number of the anti-colonialist Member States, in fact amounts to a complete twisting of its original meaning. Whatever one may think of Portugal's attitude vis-à-vis her African provinces, it can hardly be denied that Franco Nogueira's criticism of the progressive misconstruction of Articles 73 and 74[2] is perfectly justified. It has indeed denatured General Assembly recommendations under those Articles into binding decisions which can be adopted by a simple majority. It has progressively transformed into an anticolonialist slogan a set of provisions which expressly foresaw the possible desirability of maintaining dependent territories, incapable of a viable independent existence, under the guidance of a guardian State. It has, as a result, in fact amended the Charter by an entirely unauthorized and irregular method. And, moreover and still worse, it has done so with a strong bias and without taking into account that, on the one hand, certain ex-colonies are in fact already entirely self-governing and so have no claim to be involved in this anti-colonialist campaign and, on the other hand, there are various other regions in the world—outside the colonial sphere—in which peoples are still "non-selfgoverning" without finding a favourable hearing from the organized community.

I will not enter into that aspect in this context. Nor do I embark here upon a peculiar type of overseas possessions, designated in the imperialist

---

2. Comp. his *The United Nations and Portugal, a study of anti-colonialism* (London, 1963). Comp. on the concept of colonies in international law in general: Giov. M. UBERTAZZI "Il concetto giuridico di colonia nel diritto internazionale" in *Studi Economico-Giuridici pubblicati per cura della Facoltà di Giurisprudenza della Università di Cagliari*, 1962 (XLII) (Padova).

era by such names as "spheres of interest" or "zones of influence". They could not be considered to be State territory proper as long as they had not yet been effectively brought under the actual control of the States concerned. Their establishment provisionally only gave an "inchoate title"—to use a term coined in another context by Max Huber in his arbitral award of 4 April 1928 concerning sovereignty over the island of Palmas (*A.A.*, II, 845). However, as between the parties to agreements intended to delimit their respective zones of influence—I refer here, among many others, to the Anglo-German Arrangement of 1 July 1890 (Martens, N.R.G.², XVI, 894), Article 7—such delimitations created strict legal obligations. Third States could not be held to be definitely bound thereby. Comp. on this type of territorial expansion Chapter V, section 9, and on the concept of an "inchoate title", Chapter III, section 1, *sub* A, § 5 below, p. 326.

In the present section, I will confine myself to a brief survey (in §§ 1-8) of the inland water territory of a State and a few remarks on the artificial structures referred to above. Their complicated international status will, as remarked above, be further set out separately and more elaborately in an Annex to this Chapter, *infra* pp. 94 *et seq.*, and so also will the topic of State land boundaries in Chapter VI *infra*, pp. 513 *et seq.*

§ 1. *Inland Lakes or Seas.* These are not generally of much interest as far as international law is concerned. Exclusive jurisdiction over them appertains to the State, just as over its land territory. They only occasionally enter the province of the law of nations. This is the case, *e.g.*, when they have a vital interest for neighbouring States, such as the Ethiopian Lake Tana for both the Sudan and Egypt (comp. on this lake below, p. 99), and the Lake of Mont Cénis after its cession to France by the Italian Peace Treaty of Paris of 10 February 1947, Articles 2(2) and 9 (comp. section 7 of the Annex below, p. 291), or when they happen to be bounded by two or more States. In the first case international conventions may be concluded with the object of safeguarding such interest; in the latter case frontier problems or controversies over their exact legal regime or common use may arise. Inland frontier lakes may belong exclusively to one of the adjacent States; they may conceivably form a *condominium*, or be endowed with some other exceptional legal status under which, for example, one of the riparian States enjoys a preferential position. Their status will, however, in general be that of an area belonging to the neighbouring States *pro diviso*.

Purely national inland lakes are, *e.g.*, the endiked Netherlands IJsselmeer which has replaced the former open Zuiderzee, the Swiss lakes of Luzern and Zürich, the Italian lakes of Como and Garda, the Hungarian Balaton lake, the Russian lake of Onega and the Aral and Baikal seas, the Japanese Biwa-ko, the Ethiopian lake Tana, the Canadian Great

Bear and Great Slave lakes and the North-American Lake Michigan and Great Salt lake.

Frontier lakes which belong exclusively to one of the adjacent States are rather rare. This is, *inter alia*, the case of the Israeli lake of Tiberias and the lake of Nicaragua. On these cases comp. below in Chapter VI on State frontiers (pp. 587 *et seq.*).

Lakes placed under the joint sovereignty *(co-imperium)* of two or more riparian States do not to my knowledge actually exist. There are, however, a few examples of lakes in undeveloped regions which were, at least for the time being, placed under a regime which might be called co-sovereignty.[3] The status of a lake under *co-imperium* has, it is true, been attributed to the Lake of Konstanz (Bodensee) by H. RETTICH[4] but this was legally incorrect. The fact that fishing on it is common to all three surrounding States: Germany (at present Land Württemberg-Baden), Switzerland (Cantons of Thurgau and St.Gallen) and Austria (Land Vorarlberg) does not imply anything as to its territorial status, nor surely does the lake participate over its entire surface in the permanent neutrality of Switzerland. It is, therefore, quite normal that Article 3 of the multilateral Convention of 22 September 1867 (Martens, N.R.G.[1], XX, 117) laid down that the five contracting parties should be responsible for the prevention of obstacles to navigation on the lake, "jeder längs seiner Uferstrecke und auf dem dazu gehörigen Wassergebiete", and that Article 17 of the Convention of 9 December 1869 between Baden and Switzerland (*ibid.*, N.R.G.[1], XX, 166) reserved for those other Governments "in deren Gebiet Theile des Bodensees und Zuflüsse zu demselben gelegen sind", the right to accede to that Convention. The Bodensee has, for the rest, since the middle of the 19th century been the object of a long series of international conventions dealing with common interests of the riparian States, on which comp. section 1 of the Annex at pp. 95 *et seq.* below.

A curious case of an inland sea with regard to which one of the riparian States was placed in a preferential position was that of the Caspian Sea from 1828 to 1921. Comp. on this sea below section 1 of the Annex, *sub* (*j*) (i), at p. 102 and Chapter VI, section 1, p. 587.

A few further particulars may be mentioned in respect of the legal status of frontier lakes. Thus, it is questionable whether they can lawfully be considered a theatre of war for the purpose of the exercise of the right

---

3. Thus it was agreed between France (for Equatorial Africa) and Great Britain (for the Anglo-Egyptian Sudan) in their exchange of notes of 10/21 January 1924 (Martens, N.R.G.[3], XVII, 420), section VI *in fine* under 2, that the waters of Lake Undur (Oumdour) would be "common to the tribes living on either bank".

4. *Die völker- und staatsrechtlichen Verhältnisse des Bodensees* (Tübingen, 1884).

of capture under the international law of maritime prize. On this special question comp. my *Le droit des prises de la Grande Guerre* (Leiden, 1924), pp. 258-260.

Frontier lakes can also be made the object of demilitarization or neutralization. On this subject, comp. the Annex to this Chapter, section 1, *sub* (*j*)(ii) and (iii), pp. 102 and 103.

§ 2. *Rivers*. These doubtless belong nowadays to State territory, even if they constitute the frontier between two neighbouring States. In the latter case either of them has, as a rule, territorial sovereignty over that stretch of river which is adjacent to its land territory. It is still conceivable that, deviating from this rule, boundary rivers are placed under the exceptional regime of co-sovereignty, or that they belong entirely to one of the riparian States to the exclusion of the other(s). They may also give rise to border disputes respecting the exact *tracé* of the frontier in the river bed. But the time has gone when the main rivers did not as yet fall under the authority of the riparian territorial power(s) but were still endowed with the old status of *regalia*, being reserved, as *stratae regiae*, for the King or the Holy Roman Empire to be disposed of by royal or imperial grants, or when they were still treated as winding strips of no man's land between the adjoining States, each of which extended its sovereignty only to the river bank. Comp. further in Chapter VI on State frontiers, below p. 537.

The use that can be made of rivers and the interests involved in such a use for the riparian State(s) are so varied that a very large number of international conventions have been concluded with the object of dealing with such interests. The conclusion of conventions of this kind dates back many centuries, in particular as far as freedom of riverine navigation is concerned. The number and the detailedness of treaties on fluvial matters depend to a large extent on the specific features of the rivers concerned, according to whether they are national or "international", navigable or non-navigable, and according to the degree to which they happen to be further "internationalized", again an ambiguous term. In view of the extreme intricacy and vastness of this subject, however, I will discuss these aspects and the various international regulations on rivers separately below in section 2 of the Annex, pp. 103 *et seq.*

Before entering into an exposition of international river law, whether relating to national or to international rivers, one must first be able to define what a river is. This will not in general be doubtful, but international practice serves to show that there are situations in which the characterization of a watercourse as a river may be open to question. This remark applies, in particular, to estuaries through which a river empties itself into the sea, and still more especially to those estuaries which are encircled by a chain of islands between which the open sea is

20

reached. I intend to deal with these parts of rivers under the heading Inlets from the sea, pp. 27 *et seq.* and 293 *et seq.*

Umpire E.P. Alexander was once faced with the problem of the essentials of a river in regard to a practical case submitted to his arbitration: a controversy between Costa Rica and Nicaragua of 1896, subsequent to the failure of the parties to carry out an earlier award by President Cleveland of 1888. The case is reported in La Fontaine's *Pasicrisie Internationale* (p. 529), and is the subject of the first of Alexander's five awards concerning the boundary in the San Juan de Nicaragua, dated 30 September 1897. Doubts will arise, in particular, in cases where a river widens into, or ends in a vast inundated area or marsh, and so loses its identity as a river. This was what the Joint Argentine-Paraguayan Frontier Commission had to state in its Final Report of 16 August 1944 with respect to the River Pilcomayo in the sector between Salto Palmar and Horqueta (See *U.N. Legislative Series ST/LEG/SER.B/12*, pp. 153-154), where it described the unique nature of that river sector as follows:

"The waters of the River Pilcomayo throughout (that area), whether they form watercourses, or only marshes, lack permanent stability both as watercourses and as marshes. On the contrary, they are liable to change and shift constantly under the influence of various forces. Hence nothing could be gained by stipulating only one frontier line between the two adjacent countries. Such a frontier line would be little more than a line on paper. Nature would very soon make it meaningless by sending a large part of the waters in one direction or another, unexpectedly and capriciously".

§ 3. *Canals.* These are only to a lesser extent of interest to international law. They may, *e.g.*, be endowed with a special regime in their capacity of lateral canals, constructed with the object of creating an alternative shipping route to stretches of an international river which are difficult or dangerous for navigation and then they usually follow the general status of such a river. Lateral canals of this kind exist, among others, along the rivers Rhine, Meuse and Ems.

Rhine: lateral canal near Kembs, the project of which was adopted by Germany, France and Switzerland in their agreement of 10 May 1922 (Martens, N.R.G.[3], XX, 194) with a subsequent convention of 27 August 1926 (*ibid.*, XX, 202) for the regulation of Franco-Swiss relations in respect of certain clauses of the legal regime of this future diversion of the Rhine.— Comp. also on possible future lateral canals Article 358 of the Peace Treaty of Versailles.

Maas (Meuse): lateral canal between Liège and Maastricht under a treaty of 12 July 1845 (Martens, N.R.G.[1], VIII, 383); Juliana Canal between Maastricht and Maasbracht, constructed at a much later stage (1934) by the Netherlands alone on her own territory without previous agreement with Belgium, constituting together the elements of a complicated Netherlands-Belgian case of 1937 before the Permanent Court of International Justice (comp. the Judgment of 28 June 1937, *Publications P.C.I.J.*, series A/B, No. 70, commented upon in my *The Jurisprudence of the World Court*, vol. I, pp. 458 *et seq.*).

Ems: lateral canal past Lingen towards Meppen, constructed in accordance with § 2-c of an agreement reached at Berlin between expert commissioners of Hanover and Prussia on 26 April 1820 (Hanoverian *Actenstücke, Zweite Diät, Heft IV, Litt. B. zur Anlage No. 23*) for the implementation of Article 5 of the Prusso-Hanoverian treaty of 29 May 1815 (Martens, N.R., II, 316), annexed under No. 6 to the Final Act of the Congress of Vienna (*ibid.*, II, 379 *et seq.*, at p. 429—Article 118).

Canals may in their turn be international in the sense of connecting two or more countries and having been constructed for that purpose jointly by the countries concerned. Their regime necessarily rests on an agreement between such States. Something similar applies to cases in which a canal, originally purely national, becomes divided into different national sections as a result of State succession.

Comp. the case of the intersection of the initially entirely French Rhine-Rhône Canal and a new intersection of the Marne-Rhine Canal by the new Franco-German frontier as a consequence of the cession of Alsace-Lorraine to Germany in 1871: Article 14 of the Franco-German treaty of 11 December 1871 (Martens, N.R.G.[1], XX, 847), additional to the Peace Treaty to Frankfurt.—The southern provinces of the Netherlands present similar intersections as a consequence of the separation of Belgium from Holland in 1830-1839.—Other more recent cases are those of a number of canals in the eastern part of the former German Reich, and of the Einser Canal in the now Hungarian Burgenland.

International canals of this type, also, have given rise to treaty regulation, albeit on a considerably smaller scale than have international rivers.

By and large, however, such international canals are not subject to any mandatory rules of general international law, for example in respect of the principles of freedom of navigation and non-discrimination, although their use may in fact be declared by the States concerned to be free and equal to vessels under the flags of other States. This difference in status is easily explained by the fact that canals are artificial waterways dug by the territorial State(s) at great financial cost.

The first General Conference of the League of Nations Organization on Communications and Transit of March/April 1921, held in Barcelona, made a cautious attempt to bring canals under the regime, established at that Conference for a special category of rivers which it designated by a new description "navigable waterways of international concern", by opening for separate signature an Additional Protocol dealing with *all* navigable waterways, even those naturally not navigable, including canals. See on that attempt and its result: Martens, N.R.G.[3], XVIII, 738/739.

However, the greatest, and a special, interest has been aroused by a few merely national (or, in the case of the Panama Canal, pseudo-national)[5] canals, *i.e.*, canals constructed across the territory of one single

5. The Panama Canal Zone, although in fact under United States control, is still formally part of Panamanian territory. The latest developments make this

State, but which connect two different oceans or seas. Even these are not necessarily endowed with a genuinely international regime: thus, the Canal of Corinth between the Gulfs of Corinth and Aighina is a national Greek canal in respect of which the territorial State is not obliged by international law to allow passage to all flags, although such passage is in fact free. There are only three such inter-oceanic or sea-connecting canals which present a distinctly international legal character, namely, those of Suez, Panama and Kiel.

Since a more detailed discussion of the rôle of canals in international law requires too much room to be inserted in this section on Territory, I refer for this subject also, just as for that of rivers, to section 3 of the Annex, below pp. 221 *et seq.*

The frontier in a boundary canal will, as a rule, follow its median line.

§ 4. *Ports.* Ports also form areas of the inland water territory of a State which are endowed with a special legal status, so far as they either lie on an international river or canal and thus constitute an integral part thereof, or answer to the definition of a sea-port as given in Article 1 of the Statute annexed to the Convention of Geneva on the International Regime of Sea-Ports of 9 December 1923 (Martens, N.R.G.[3], XIX, 250). Comp. on river ports section 2 of the Annex on International Rivers below, p. 123.

Seaports in the sense of the Statute of Geneva are "all ports which are normally frequented by seagoing vessels and used for foreign trade". (Barcelona, Article 9).

Such seaports may lie in an inlet from the sea without any essential connection with a river, such as Oslo, Piraios, Cape Town, Trieste, Tokyo. They may also be situated on a river which is itself devoid of any "international" character in the sense of international law, as is the case of London (Thames), New York (Hudson), Bordeaux (Gironde), or on a canal that is not itself "internationalized", such as is the situation of Amsterdam (North Sea Canal), another canal (Amsterdam-Rhine Canal) linking it up with the river Rhine.

Some confusion may arise in the case of sea-ports within the meaning of the Statute of Geneva which equally lie on an international river, sometimes at a considerable distance from the mouth inland, such as is, or was, the case of Bremen (Weser), Hamburg (Elbe), Rotterdam (connected with the sea through an artificial waterway, the Hollandse Waterweg, dating from 1862), Buenos Aires (Río de la Plata).

In the latter cases the legal nature of the port as a seaport prevails over its character as a port on an international river. Comp. on the

abundantly clear: *A.J.I.L.* 1966 (60), p. 397 and *Dep. of State Bulletin* 1967 (57), p. 65.

23

possible collision between rules covering the status of ports falling under both of these descriptions: declaration No. 12 in the Final Act of the General Conference of Barcelona of 10 March 1921:

"12. The Conference declares that in laying down in Article 9 of the Statute relating to the regime of navigable waterways of international concern the regime for ports situated on such waterways, there was no intention of settling any question of principle relating to the regime of national sea-ports". (L. of N., Doc. 20/31/58, *Official instruments approved by the Conference*, under No. 9 Final Act (at p. 43).

In some such cases the fluvial regime is expressly declared to end, at least as far as certain features thereof are concerned, at a specified inland port: thus, the regime of the "conventional Rhine", pursuant to Article 2 of the Revised Convention of Mannheim of 17 October 1868 (Martens, N.R.G.[1], XX, 355) ends at the inland towns of Krimpen on the river Lek and Dordrecht on the river Noord.

When a port lies on a river which bears no "international" character, *e.g.*, London, the port itself can nevertheless be endowed with an international regime as a sea-port.

A special, also historically interesting, place among the international ports is taken by the so-called free ports.

A "free" port is historically a port, usually a sea-port, to which ships of all flags have free access without being subject to the payment of customs duties and to customs control. They constitute, therefore, a special category of "open" ports, *i.e.*, ports to which, in contradistinction to "closed" ports, foreign vessels have free access. Their establishment—which dates back to the Middle Ages—served to stimulate international trade and to direct it to places favourably situated on a coast, especially at the mouth of a river, which could thus be made flourishing commercial centers. One of the oldest free ports was that of Livorno (1547), with regard to which Article V of the Quadruple Alliance Treaty between England, France, the Emperor and The Netherlands of 22 July/2 August 1718 (Rousset, *Recueil*, I, 180) could truthfully dispose that Livorno was to remain a free port as of yore. Many other free ports have since been established in what is now Italy, in France, in what was once Austria and in other countries. However, a later development has terminated the older practice of placing entire ports under the regime of customs-free access for all foreign shipping and limited that freedom to strictly demarcated port areas equipped with storage yards and warehouses for the benefit of intermediate and transit trade, as was the English system.

Comp. for further details concerning the regime of sea-ports section 4 of the Annex to this Chapter.

§ 5. *Roads and railways.* Most of the general remarks made in respect of national and international canals in § 3 apply equally to roads and railways, because these also are man-made forms of communication which may have international importance.

Thus, elaborate international conventions have often been needed in preparing the construction of railways and railway tunnels connecting neighbouring States, and to regulate their juridical regime once they had been built. I refer in particular to the series of treaties concerning the St. Gothard and Simplon lines. To a minor extent this also applies to international roads.

Since a more detailed exposition of this subject of roads and railways in international law would again overburden the present section on land territory too much, I will discuss it, just as that of rivers and canals, in section 5 of the Annex, pp. 247 and 251, where I will also insert some particulars concerning the legal aspects and the successive stages of international road and railway connections, and the attempts made to codify the main principles of international railway law.

Attention will be drawn there also to the rôle which railways especially have played in diplomatic history. Their construction has in fact often served imperialist and not exclusively commercial aims.

§ 6. *Telegraph and telephone lines, cables and pipelines.* The construction of telegraph and telephone lines and the laying of cables or pipelines has likewise been prompted by economic as well as political motives. Since these installations are comparable to railways and roads in that they are equally linked with the soil, I may be justified in making a few general remarks regarding them in the present paragraph while referring for further particulars to the corresponding section 6 of the Annex below, p. 274.

Telegraph lines have not become the concern of international law until the middle of the 19th century. They started their career as new overhead means of communication, without any direct political importance, but they have subsequently shown their increasing value as concomitant instruments of political expansion in the imperialist era. Hence the construction of telegraph and telephone lines along politically important roads and railways wherever empire building demanded the construction of the latter, or simply in regions where the rapid transmission of orders or information was in the interest of the expansion of western control over, or the tightening of an initial grip on, "spheres of interest" or "zones of influence", or prospective colonies, colonial protectorates, or vassal States. This development from an originally a-political device to one of the greatest political importance lately reached its acme in the construction of "hot" telephone lines between Moscow on the one hand, and Washington, Paris and London on the other, with the object of use in time of extreme international tension and as a safeguarding against the sudden outbreak of a devastating nuclear war. Comp. for the text of the Convention relative to the Soviet-American line of 20 June 1963: *U.N.T.S.*, vol. 472, p. 163.

What is remarked here applies also *mutatis mutandis* to underground cables intended for the transmission of messages. Cables for the transport of electricity ("houille blanche") from one country to another serve rather an economic purpose. I may refer for this subject also to section 6 of the Annex below, p. 274.

Pipelines are the most recent addition to this series of devices for long distance international transport. Oleoducts have already played an important rôle in international politics in the Middle East and North Africa; they have been extremely effective in support of modern warfare (the famous Pluto pipeline from the Isle of Wight to the French coast laid in preparation of the Allied invasion in Normandy in 1944); they are increasingly employed as a cheaper means of oil transport also in Western Europe, and they will presumably remain of great economic and political importance also in the future. The same applies to the present pipelines for the transportation of natural gas.—I again refer to section 6 of the Annex below, p. 281.

§ 7. *Hydraulic systems.* A special area of land territory may be formed by a coherent hydraulic or hydrodynamic system (for the purposes of canalization, inundation, irrigation, drainage, the generation of electric power, etc.) astride an international frontier. Such systems may originally have been built by adjacent States in common. They may also, however, owe their existence to a shift in the territorial sovereignty over the region concerned which caused it to fall under the power of two or more contiguous States without, however, attaining thereby the status of a *co-imperium.*

In the first case, the common system is naturally governed by the conventions which preceded its construction or establishment. Comp., *e.g.,* the Franco-Swiss conventions of 4 October 1913 (Martens, N.R.G.[3], X, 290) "pour l'aménagement de la puissance hydraulique du Rhône" and of 19 November 1930 (*ibid.*, XXVI, 312) "concernant l'aménagement de la chute du Doubs près de Châtelot".

In the second case, the States concerned must necessarily, if they are not prepared to simply leave their relations to the play of an uncertain customary law, lay down new rules for the future international regime of the system thus disrupted. This has been done repeatedly in the first half of this century in the many peace settlements. Comp. for example, Article 44[1] of the Peace Treaty of St. Germain (1919) by which it was laid down that the furnishing of electric power from Austrian territory would continue also to those territories which were transferred to Italy.

Further details on these regulations will be given in the corresponding section 7 of the Annex to this Chapter, at p. 282.

26

At the second Conference of the International Organization of Communications and Transit at Geneva of 1923 an attempt was made to formulate general principles to govern cases of this nature in the absence of relevant treaty regulations. Its efforts did lead to the conclusion of a Convention, of 9 December 1923 (Martens, N.R.G.[3], XIX, 290) concerning the Management of Hydraulic Forces interesting several States, but that Convention did not lay down any mandatory rules for the solution of the problem, nor has it until now received more than a small number of ratifications, and there only by States which are not *inter se* contiguous. For the rest, I may refer, on this subject also, to the Annex to this Chapter, at p. 282.

§ 8. *Inlets from the sea.* I deliberately choose such a vague term to comprise a variety of widely differing aqueous formations which have one feature in common, namely, that they are all situated on the inner side of the general coastline, base-line of the territorial sea, and are in open communication with the sea, whatever denomination is applied to them: bays, gulfs, fiords, seas, haffs, firths, lagoons, limans, estuaries, and so on. However, in order to qualify as parts of State territory proper—in contradistinction to the territorial sea of a State—they must satisfy certain legal requirements which have only recently been defined more precisely and uniformly at the first Conference of Geneva on the Law of the Sea of 1958, and even then only incompletely and in certain respects ambiguously. While referring for this subject to a special study on the results and failures of that Conference (annexed as an Excursus to Part IV-A of this publication), I will confine myself here to giving a general survey of the problems involved and to making a few additional observations.

It is characteristic for the work of the Conference that it has dealt exclusively with bays, and similar inlets from the sea, which are surrounded by one single State. All problems concerning pluristatal bays were deliberately eliminated because it was deemed impossible to reach any measure of consensus with regard to the legal status of this type of inlet from the sea from the point of view of territorial sovereignty. The only subject that was discussed and resolved was the right of innocent passage from the high seas into such pluristatal bays—and *vice versa*—through the territorial sea of one or more States which dominate their entrance, and even that only in the somewhat disguised formula of a general principle couched in the following terms (Article 16, paragraph 4, of Convention I on the Territorial Sea and the Contiguous Zone):

"There shall be no suspension of the innocent passage of foreign ships through straits which are used for international navigation between one part of the high seas and another part of the high seas or the territorial sea of a foreign State", a provision which in its final words clearly covers situations such as that of the Gulf of Aqaba.

The practical outcome of this international abstention from attempts to lay down general principles concerning bays surrounded by more than one State was that no legal solution of any kind was reached

either as regards the closing line of such bays towards the high seas,

or as regards their possible legal status of either themselves forming part of the high seas, or, alternatively, of being subject to a co-imperium of the riparian States,

or as regards the frontier delimitation between the latter inside the bay concerned, should it neither belong to the high seas nor fall under their co-sovereignty.

Since this aggregate of problems is closely related to the subject of State boundaries and to the territorial sea, respectively, I further refer to the relevant Chapter VI, section 4, and this Chapter, section 8, below, pp. 293 *et seq.*

Suffice it simply to state here that the solution which the first Conference on the Law of the Sea of 1958, after empassioned discussion, adopted in respect of inlets from the sea surrounded by one single State amounts to this that such inlets are internal waters, and consequently belong to State territory proper, if the closing line does not exceed twenty-four nautical miles[6], but that otherwise they form part of the high seas, subject to the territorial sovereignty of the riparian State concerned over the traditional belt of territorial sea running along its coast inside the bay.

This solution adopted by the Geneva Conference had been preceded by a Judgment of the International Court of 18 December 1951 (*I.C.J. Reports* 1951, p. 116 *et seq.*, at p. 131), in which the Court had denied the force of a general rule of customary international law to a rule which had occasionally been accepted with regard to specified bays, fixing the closing line at ten nautical miles.

A closing line of this length had been adopted, for example, in a number of treaties regarding the North Sea, entered into by Great Britain, with France on 2 August 1839, Article 9 (Martens, N.R., XVI, 954; de Clerq, IV, 497; *B.F.S.P.*, vol. 27, p. 988); 24 May 1843, Article 2 (N.R.G.[1], IX, 527; *B.F.S.P.*, vol. 31, p. 166); 11 November 1876, Article 1 (N.R.G.[1], XX, 465; *B.F.S.P.*, vol. 57, p. 9); and with Denmark on 24 June 1901 (*B.F.S.P.*, vol. 94, p. 29); with the North-German Federation and the German Empire in November 1868 and December 1874; and with the North Sea States in general in the North Sea Fisheries Convention of 6 May 1882 (*ibid.*, N.R.G.[2], IX, 556), Article 2. The same ten-miles rule was embodied in the—unratified—Bayard-Chamberlain Treaty between Great Britain and the United States of 1888 (cited

6. The alternatives discussed at Geneva were: twice three; ten; or some other more or less arbitrary number of fifteen or twenty-five miles.

by J. BROWN SCOTT in his article on the North Atlantic Fisheries dispute in SCHÜCKING's *Das Werk vom Haag*, 2nd series, 1st *Band*, 2nd Teil, p. 342; comp. also p. 506). The five-member arbitral tribunal in that same Fisheries dispute also adopted the rule in its award of 7 September 1910 (Martens, N.R.G.³, IV, 89; *A.A.*, XI, 173) relative to Question V, but only as a recommendation to the parties. Comp. on this subject the dissenting opinion of Luís DRAGO (*Das Werk vom Haag*, *ibid.*, pp. 498-511, resp. *A.A.*, XI, p. 203).

Excursus

ISLANDS IN DIPLOMATIC HISTORY AND INTERNATIONAL LAW

A special category of territory involved in treaty regulation or arbitral adjudication is that of islands. A large number of them scattered all over the earth have been the object of cession, exchange or restitution by treaty, of adjudication by arbitral or judicial decision, or of a declaration of independence. In the alphabetic table below I summarize in brief the fortunes of the most important of them which one comes across when going through collections of treaties (when not specified, de Martens) or awards covering a very wide span of time.

Ada Kaleh, small Danubian fortress island downstream of Orsowa, under Austrian occupation 1878-1913; see on its legal status Chapter IV, section 3, p. 411.

Admiralty Islands. See under Bismarck archipelago.

Adriatic, Islands in the—. Were for a long time Venetian. Fell to Austria pursuant to Article 6 of her treaty with France of Campo Formio of 17 October 1797 (Martens, R², VI, 420) and remained Austrian until the Peace Treaty of St. Germain of 10 September 1919 (*ibid.* N.R.G.³, XI, 691). Were divided between Italy and the Serb-Croat-Slovene State by their treaty of Rapallo of 12 November 1920 (N.R.G.³, XII, 821). Those still belonging to Italy ceded to Yugoslavia by Article 11 of the Italian Peace Treaty of Paris of 10 February 1947 (*U.N.T.S.*, vol. 49, p. 3).

Aegean Islands. Comp. in particular: Dodecanese; Imbros and Tenedos; Rhodes.

Åland Islands. As part of Finland recognized Swedish territory ever since the Peace Treaty of Nöteborg (1323). Ceded to Russia in 1809 (Frederikshamn, 17 September, Martens, N.R., I, 19); demilitarized in 1856 (Paris, 30 March, *ibid.*, N.R.G.¹, XV, 788); fell to independent Finland in 1918 (League of Nations Council proceedings); renewal of demilitarization in 1921 (Convention of Geneva, 20 October 1921, *ibid.*, N.R.G.[3], XII, 65), maintained by Article 5 of the Finnish Peace Treaty of Paris of 10 February 1947 (*U.N.T.S.*, vol. 48, p. 203).

Andamanes, see Nicobares.

Anguilla. United with St. Kitts and Nevis in a federation which in 1967 became an "associated State" within the Commonwealth; seceded from that federation in 1967 and made itself "independent"; occupied by British forces in March 1969.

Anjouan. See Comores.

Annabon or Annobom. Ceded by Portugal to Spain together with Fernando Póo, Article 13 of their Pardo treaty of 1 March 1778 (R[2], II, 612). Became part of independent Equatorial Guinea in 1969.

Antigua. First colonized by England; after its conquest by France restituted to England by Article 12 of their Peace Treaty of Breda of 31 July 1667 (Dumont, VII[1], 40).

Arguin, off the west coast of Africa. See Franco-Netherlands Convention of Commerce of 13 January 1727 (S.,I, 176).

Aruba, see Curaçao.—The Spanish State Archives still contain an elaborate exposition in support of the sovereignty of Spain over the island (Isla de Vrue), dating from 1779 (Bussemaker, *Verslag van een voorloopig onderzoek te Lissabon, Sevilla, Madrid, Escorial, Simancas en Brussel naar archivalia belangrijk voor de geschiedenis van Nederland, op last der Regeering ingesteld.* (The Hague, 1905), p. 136).

Ashmore and Cartier Islands. Transferred to Australia in 1931.

Aves Island. Adjudicated to Venezuela by Queen Isabel II of Spain by arbitral award between Venezuela and the Netherlands of 30 June 1865 (*Pas.int.*, 152).

Azores, (re)discovered by the Portuguese in the middle of the 15th century; have remained up to the present a province of Portugal (temporarily under Spanish rule from 1580-1640).

Bahamas. After their discovery by Columbus in 1492, first occupied by Spain, later by England; after temporary conquests by the United States and Spain, returned to Great Britain by the Peace Treaty of Versailles of 3 September 1783 (Martens, R[2], III, 519).

Banka. After the Napoleonic era ceded by Great Britain to the Netherlands by Article 2 of their treaty of 13 August 1814 (Martens, N.R., II, 57). Since 1949 part of Indonesia.

Barbados. After its discovery by the Portuguese in 1519 occupied by England in 1605. Independent since 1966.

Bay Islands, in the Bay of Honduras; a British colony from 1852 to 1859, but recognized as part of Honduras by the treaty of Comayagua of 28 November 1859 (Martens, N.R.G.[1], XVI[2], 370; *B.F.S.P.*, vol. 49, p. 13).

Belle Isle. Originally French; after its capture by Great Britain restituted

30

to France by Articles 8 and 24 of their Peace Treaty of Paris of 10 February 1763 (R^2, I, 104).

Bermudas Islands, after their discovery by Spain in 1502 colonized by England as from 1612.

Billiton. British objection to the occupation of the island by the Netherlands withdrawn by Article 11 of their treaty of 17 March 1824 respecting territory and commerce in the East-Indies (Martens, N.S., I, 628). Since 1949 part of Indonesia.

Bismarck archipelago (Neupommern, Neumecklenburg and Neuhannover) and Admiralty Islands. Colonized by the NeuGuinea-Kompagnie since 1885 (Martens, N.R.G.^{2}, XI, 476). Fell as a Mandated Territory of the C-type to Australia in 1920 and became a Trust Territory in 1946. Comp. vol. II of this publication, pp. 102-103.

Bonin Islands. Southeast of Hondo (Japan), with Rosario and Volcano Islands, Pareca Vela and Marcus Island. To be placed under the Trusteeship of the United States as Administering Authority in virtue of Article 3 of the Japanese Peace Treaty of San Francisco of 8 September 1951 (U.N.T.S., vol. 136, p. 45).

Borneo. Divided between the Netherlands (until 1949) and Great Britain (until 1963); now between Indonesia, the Federation of Malaysia and the Sultanate of Brunei. Sovereignty of the Malaysian Federation over Sabah disputed by the Philippines.

Bornholm. Conquered by and ceded to Sweden by the Dano-Swedish Peace Treaty of Röskilde of 26 February-8 March 1658 (Dumont, VI^2, 205), but restituted to Denmark by that of Copenhagen of 27 May-6 June 1660 (Dumont, VI^2, 319).

Bougainville. See Salomon Islands.

Bourbon or Réunion. Near Madagascar, restored by Great Britain to France by Article 8 of the (first) Peace Treaty of Paris of 30 May 1814 (N.R., II, 1).

Bulama off the coast of Guinea. Adjudicated to Portugal by President Grant as Arbitrator between her and Great Britain, 21 April 1870 (Pas. Int., 83).

Canaries. Attributed under the name of Isolae Fortunatae to a Spanish prince by a Papal bull of 15 November 1344 (Magn. Bull., IV, 474). Comp. vol. II of this publication, p. 331.

Canton and Enderbury Islands. Under Anglo-American joint administration and control under agreement of 6 April 1939 (Martens, N.R.G.^{3}, XXXVII, 371).

Cape Breton. Early possession of France (29 March 1632, Dumont, VI^1, 31), remained French in 1678 and 1713, was ceded to Great Britain by Articles 4 and 5 of their Peace Treaty of Paris of 10 February 1763 (Martens, R^2, I, 104).

Capraia. Island near Corsica, to be restituted by France to Genova by their treaty of 15 May 1768 (R², I, 591); at a later stage allotted to Sardinia by Article 85 *in fine* of the Final Act of Vienna of 9 June 1815 (N.R., II, 379).

Caribbean Islands, in the colonial era occupied by various European powers, Spain, England, France, the Netherlands, Denmark and Sweden. Now in different stages of political evolution. See the separate islands.

Carolines. After protests by Spain against their occupation by Germany in 1885, adjudicated to Spain by a mediatory pronouncement of the Pope of 22 October, accepted by the parties (N.R.G.², XII, 283, 287). Afterwards acquired by Germany in virtue of a treaty of sale of 30 June 1899 (N.R.G.², XXXII, 66), together with the Marianas and the Palaos. Fell after World War I to Japan as a Mandated Territory of the C-type (1920); were assigned to the United States as a strategic Trust area in 1947 (comp. Article 2 (*d*) of the Peace Treaty of San Francisco of 8 September 1951, *U.N.T.S.*, vol. 136, p. 45).

Cartier Islands. See Ashmore Islands.

Castellorizo, off the coast of Anatolia. Under Italian occupation since 1911-1912; ceded by Turkey to Italy by Article 15 of the Peace Treaty of Lausanne of 24 July 1923 (N.R.G.³, XIII, 338); controversy between Italy and Turkey on the frontier in the strait between it and Turkey, brought before the Permanent Court of International Justice in 1929 (*Publications P.C.I.J.*, series A/B, No. 51), in the event settled by agreement (comp. my *The Jurisprudence of the World Court*, vol. II, pp. 535/536). Ceded to Greece by Article 14 of the Italian Peace Treaty of Paris of 10 February 1947 (*U.N.T.S.*, vol. 49, p. 3).

Cephalonia. See Kephalonia.

Cerigo. See Ionian Islands.

Ceylon. First colonized by Portugal; in the hands of the United Netherlands since the middle of the 17th century; ceded to Great Britain by Article 5 of the Treaty of Amiens of 25/27 March 1802 (R², VII, 404). Independent since 1948.

Chafarinas. Belonged to the Spanish Presidios on the coast of Morocco, since 6 January 1848 (N.R.G.¹, XIII, 631).

Chagos archipelago, north of Mauritius (Aldabra, Tarquhar, Desroches), under the administration of the Seychelles; also used by the United States for military installations.

Channel Islands. Remained English after the loss of the duchy of Normandy in 1204 up till the present time. They comprise the islands of Jersey, Alderney, Guernsey, Sark, Herm and Jethou.

Chausey Islands, the only French possession off the coast of Normandy.

Cherso and Lussin, in the Adriatic. Would become Italian together with the islands in the Istria district, in virtue of Article 4 of the secret

32

treaty of London of 26 April 1915 (Martens, N.R.G.³, X, 329), and they were so allotted by Article III of the boundary treaty of Rapallo of 12 November 1920 (N.R.G.³, XII, 821).

Chincha Islands. Group of guano islands, belonging to Peru.

Chios or Chio, demilitarized pursuant to Article 13 of the Peace Treaty of Lausanne of 24 July 1923 (N.R.G.³, XIII, 338).

Christmas Islands. Transferred to Australia in 1958.

Clipperton. Adjudicated to France by an arbitral award of the king of Italy between her and Mexico of 28 January 1931 (A.A., II, 1105), in virtue of a *compromis* of 2 March 1909 (N.R.G.³, V, 8).

Cocos (Keeling) Islands. Transferred from the Straits Settlements (Singapore) to Australia by the *Cocos Islands Act, 1955* (3 & 4 Eliz. 2, c.5).

Colón Archipelago. See Galápagos Islands.

Comino. See Gozo.

Comores. Occupied by France March 1843 (N.R.G.¹, V, 52); treaty between Great Britain and the Sultan of Johanna (or Anjouan) of 3 June 1850 (*ibid.*, XV, 415); declaration of 8 March 1873 (*ibid.*, XX, 522).

Cook's Islands. Under New Zealand since 1901.

Corfu. Has long belonged to Venice, since 1387. Fell to France on the strength of Article 5 of the Franco-Austrian treaty of Campo Formio of 17 October 1797 (R², VI, 420). Became later the main island of the Seven United Ionian Islands. See under Ionian Islands.

Corn Islands (Great and Little). Leased by Nicaragua to the United States for a term of 99 years, 5 August 1914 (N.R.G.³, IX, 350), Article 2.

Corsica. Component part of Genua, at her request occupied by France in 1764 (R², I, 265); pledged to France in 1786 (R², I, 591); incorporated into France in 1789 (R², V, 145).

Crete. Vassal State of the Ottoman Empire as from 1899 (Constitution of 29 April 1899); acquired by Greece after the Balkan Wars of 1913.

Cuba. Old Spanish colony, temporarily conquered in part by Great Britain, but restored to Spain by Articles 19 and 24 of the Peace Treaty of Paris of 10 February 1763 (R², I, 104). Severed from Spain by her Peace Treaty with the United States of Paris of 10 December 1898 (N.R.G.², XXXII, 74); independent since 1903, subject to certain limitations upon her sovereignty.

Curaçao. Former Netherlands colony in the Antilles; equal partner in the Kingdom of the Netherlands since 1954 together with Aruba, Bonaire, Saba, St. Eustatius and (half) St. Maarten (comp. vol. II of this publication, p. 205).

Cyclades. See Aegean Islands.

Cyprus. Transferred in "occupation and administration" to Great

33

Britain in 1878; annexed by her on 5 November 1914; annexation recognized by Turkey in Article 20 of the Peace Treaty of Lausanne of 24 July 1923 (N.R.G.³, XIII, 338); granted independence in 1960 subject to different limitations (comp. vol. II of this publication, p. 116).

Dagelet. See Quelpart.

Dagö, off the Gulf of Riga. Ceded by Denmark to Sweden by their Peace Treaty of Brömsebro of 13 August 1645 (Dumont, VI¹, 314); ceded by Sweden to Russia by their Peace Treaty of Nystad of 30 August 1721 (Rousset, *Recueil* I, 327; Dumont, VI¹, 36).

Daito Islands. See Ryukyu Islands.

Danish Caribbean Islands, St.Thomas, St.John and St.Croix. See Virgin Islands.

Delagoa Bay, Inyack and Elephants Islands. Adjudicated to Portugal by President Mac Mahon as Arbitrator between Great Britain and Portugal, 24 July 1875 (Martens, N.R.G.², III, 517; *Pas Int.*, 172).

Desirade. French since 1728; after its capture by Great Britain returned to France by Articles 8 and 24 of their Peace Treaty of Paris of 10 February 1763 (R², I, 104).

Dodecanese. Archipelago in the Aegean, occupied by Italy during the Tripoli War of 1911-1912; remained under her occupation, first as a pledge (Article 2 of the Peace Treaty of Ouchy-Lausanne of 18 October 1912, N.R.G.³, VII, 7); promised to Italy by Article 8 of the secret treaty of London of 26 April 1915 (N.R.G.³, X, 329); acquired by her in virtue of a formal cession by Article 15 of the Peace Treaty of Lausanne of 24 July 1923 (N.R.G.³, XIII, 338), until 10 February 1947, when Italy was forced to cede them to Greece; Article 14 of the Italian Peace Treaty of Paris (*U.N.T.S.*, vol. 49, p. 3). Comp. on these islands Chapter IV, section 1 *infra*, p. 395.

Dominica. One of the "neutral" islands in the Caribbean, allotted to Great Britain by Article 9 of the Anglo-French Peace Treaty of 10 February 1763 (R², I, 104); restituted to Great Britain, after its conquest by France, by Articles 8 and 20 of that of Versailles of 3 September 1783 (R², III, 519).

Doumeírah *et al.* "Neutral" islets off the coast of the Red Sea and the Gulf of Aden, France-Italy 24 January 1900 (N.R.G.³, II, 830): no occupation; joint resistance to usurpation of rights by others.

Ecrehos and Minquiers. Belonging to the British Channel Islands; proceedings before the I.C.J. in 1953 (*I.C.J. Reports*, p. 47).

Elba. Long disputed between Genua and Pisa. In the second half of the 16th century divided between Tuscany (Porto Ferraio) and Sicily (Porto Longone). Complicated legal status, see Article V (3) of the Qua-

34

druple Alliance Treaty of 2 August 1718 (Rousset, *Receuil*, I, 180) and Article 100, 3rd para., *sub* 2 and para. 4 of the Final Act of Vienna of 9 June 1815 (N.R., II, 379). Temporarily independent under Napoleon as sovereign.

Elb-pertinentia. Islands in the mouth of the river Elbe, ceded by Holstein to the city of Hamburg, 27 May 1768 (R^2, I, 597).

Elephants Island. See Delagoa Bay.

Enderbury Island. See Canton Island.

Falkland Islands or Islas Malvinas. Occupation by a British force (Port Egmont in Saunders Island) dates back to 1765; disputed by France and Spain; evacuated by the British in 1774 without *animus derelinquendi* (see on the period 1771-1774: R^2, II, 1-4); evacuation by Spain in 1811; after new clashes, between independent Argentina and the United States, in 1831, reoccupation by Great Britain in 1833.

Farøer. Old Danish archipelago, endowed with autonomous regime.

Fernando Póo. Ceded by Portugal to Spain, together with Annabon, by Article 13 of their Pardo treaty of 1 March 1778 (R^2, II, 612). Became part of independent Equatorial Guinea in 1969.

Fiji Islands. British possession since 1874 (N.R.G.^{2}, II, 529).

Formosa (Tai-Wan). Originally Chinese; ceded to Japan by Article II (*b*) of the Peace Treaty of Shimonoseki of 17 April 1895 (N.R.G.^{2}, XXI, 642). All right, title and claim to it renounced by Japan in Article 2 (*b*) of the Peace Treaty of San Francisco of 8 September 1951 (*U.N.T.S.*, vol. 136, p. 45). Now the seat of Nationalist China.

Fundy Bay islands. See Passamaquoddy Bay islands.

Galápagos Islands, belong to Ecuador.

Gorée Island, on the Senegal coast; after its capture by England restituted to France, first by Articles 10 and 24 of their Peace Treaty of Paris of 10 February 1763 (R^2, I, 104) and at a later stage by Article 9 of that of Versailles of 3 September 1783 (R^2, III, 519).

Gotland, ceded by Denmark to Sweden by their Peace Treaty of Brömsebro of 13 August 1645 (Dumont, VI^1, 314).

Gozo and Comino. Belonged to Malta and shared its fortunes. Comp. *e.g.*, Article 10 of the Peace Treaty of Amiens of 25/27 March 1802 (R^2, VII, 404).

Grand Menan island in the Bay of Fundy, adjudicated to Great Britain by an arbitral award of 24 November 1817 (Martens, N.R., V, vol. suppl., 397; *Pas. Int.*, 8).

Grenade and Grenadines. Ceded by France to Great Britain by Article 9 of their Peace Treaty of Paris of 10 February 1763 (R^2, I, 104), restored to her after their conquest by France by Articles 8 and 20 of the Peace Treaty of Versailles of 3 September 1783 (R^2, III, 519).

35

Guadeloupe. Originally French; after its conquest by Great Britain returned to France by Articles 8 and 24 of their Peace Treaty of Paris of 10 February 1763 (R², I, 104); conquered by Great Britain and ceded by her to Sweden by a treaty of subsidies of 3 March 1813 (N.R., I, 558), strongly denounced by France (*sénatusconsulte* of 14 October 1813, *ibid.*, 563); ultimately restituted to France by Sweden by Article 9 of the (first) Peace Treaty of Paris of 30 May 1814 (N.R., II, 1). The compensation which Sweden should receive for this retrocession was originally to be paid by The Netherlands in connection with the enlargement of its territory, but was shortly afterwards taken over by Great Britain. See her treaties of 13 August 1814 with Sweden (N.R., II, 55) and the Netherlands (N.R., II, 57).

Guam in the Marianas. Ceded by Spain to the United States by Article 2 of their Peace Treaty of Paris of 10 December 1898 (N.R.G.², XXXII, 74).

Hainan, Chinese island in the Kwang-tung province.

Hawaii Islands. Resolution concerning the annexation of the Islands by the United States, 7 July 1898 (N.R.G.², XXXII, 72). See Part II of this publication, pp. 129 and 183.

Heard Islands and McDonald Islands. Transferred to Australia in 1947/1950.

Hebrides. Once in the past a separate Kingdom of the Isles, first under Norwegian, later under Scottish suzerainty. See Part II, p. 342.

Heligoland. Originally Danish; conquered by England in 1807; formally retained by Great Britain by Article 3 of their Peace Treaty of Kiel of 14 January 1814 (N.R., I, 678); ceded to Germany by Article 12 of their Agreement of 1 July 1890 (N.R.G.², XVI, 894; *B.F.S.P.*, vol. 82, p. 35).

Hispaniola. See Santo Domingo.

Hong-Kong, ceded to Great Britain in 1841. See the proclamation of 29 January-1 February in N.R.G.¹, II, 6, 7.

Hwen, in the Baltic. Danish till 1658; since then Swedish. See Peace Treaties of Röskilde, Dumont, VI², 205 (26-27 Februari 1658) and 218 (7 May 1658) and Copenhagen (1660), Dumont VI², 319.

Ile de France. See Mauritius.

Imbros and Tenedos, off the entrance to the Dardanelles. Remained under Turkish sovereignty in virtue of the resolution of the Ambassadors' Conference of 13 February 1914 (*British Documents on the Origins of the War (1898-1914)*, vol. X, Part I, pp. 231-232; *Documents diplomatiques français (1871-1914)*, 3e série (1911-1914), t. IX), on the strength of Article 5 of the Peace Treaty of London of 30 May 1913 (N.R.G.³, VIII, 16); would have fallen to Greece under Article 84 of the (abortive) Peace Treaty of Sèvres of 10 August 1920 (N.R.G.³, XII, 664), but remained Turkish pursuant to Article 14 of that of Lausanne of 24 July 1923 (N.R.G.³, XIII, 338).

Inyack Island. See Delagoa Bay.

Ionian Islands, in particular Corfu, Zanthe, Kephalonia, St.Maura. Have for a long time belonged to Venice.

Iturup and islands further south. Assigned to Japan by Article 2 of the Russo-Japanese treaty of Simoda of 26 January 1855 (N.R.G.¹, XVI², 454).

Jamaica. Occupied by England since 1655; left to her pursuant to the rule of *uti possidetis* by the Anglo-Spanish treaty of Madrid of 18 July 1670 (Dumont, VII¹, 137), interpreting an earlier treaty of 12/23 May 1667 (*ibid.*, VII¹, 27). Independent since 1962.

Jan Mayen Island. Declared to be under the sovereignty of Norway by a Royal Decree of 8 May 1929 (comp. *A. D.* 1933-1934, Case No. 42).

Kamaran, in the Red Sea. Occupied by Great Britain in 1915; belongs to Southern Yemen since 30 November 1967.

Karrack. In the Persian Gulf, occupied by Great Britain in 1838 (N.R., XI, 567-580).

Keeling Island. See Cocos Islands.

Kephalonia. See Ionian Islands.

Kuria Muria Islands. Ceded by the Sultan of Muscat to Great Britain, 14 July 1854 (N.R.G.¹, XVI² 126); retroceded to Muscat-Oman, 15 November 1967 (Treaty Series No. 8 (1968), Cmd. 3505).

Kurile Islands. Assigned to Russia by Article 2 of her treaty with Japan of 26 January 1855 (N.R.G.¹, XVI², 454); acquired by Japan from Russia in exchange for her half of Sakhalin, 7 May 1875 (N.R.G.², II, 285); all right, title and claim renounced by Japan by Article 2 (*c*) of the Treaty of San Francisco of 8 September 1951 (*U.N.T.S.*, vol. 136, p. 45).

Ladrones. See Marianas.

Lagosta and Pelagosa in the Adriatic. Were to become Italian in virtue of Article 5 of the secret treaty of London of 26 April 1915 (N.R.G.³, X, 329), and became in fact Italian by Art. III of the treaty of Rapallo of 12 November 1920 (N.R.G.³, XII, 821), but were finally ceded to Yugoslavia by Art. II of the Italian Peace Treaty of 1947.

Lampedusa and Linosa, south of Sicily, belong to Italy.

Lamu, off the east coast of Africa. Certain disputes, having arisen between Germany and Great Britain, were adjudicated upon by an arbitral award of 17 August 1889 of Baron Lambermont (Martens, N.R.G.², XXII, 101).

Lesbos. See Mytilene.

Linosa. See Lampedusa.

Los Islands. Ceded by Great Britain to France by their Convention of 8 April 1904 (N.R.G.², **XXXII**, 12).

Lussin. See Cherso.

Lyukyu Islands. See Ryukyu Islands.

Macdonald Island. See Heard Islands.

Madagascar, protectorate of France since 1885; independent Malagasy since 1960. Comp. vol. II of this publication, pp. 438-439.

Madeira, has belonged to Portugal ever since the division of the oceans in 1493-1494. See Part IV-A of this publication. Comp. on the Napoleonic period the Treaty of Alliance between England and Portugal of 19 February 1810 (R², I, 245), Article III, referring to an earlier treaty of 15 March 1808.

Mafia, off the east coast of Africa, formerly German, now under Tanzania.

Maldives, fell to Great Britain, together with Ceylon, as a separate sultanate under British protection. Independent since 1965.

Malta. Granted in fief by Charles V to the Order of the Johannites in 1530. Conquered by the French in 1798, by the British in 1800; promised back to the Order in 1802 (Article 10 of the Peace Treaty of Amiens, 25/27 March 1802, R², VII, 404); but finally allotted to Great Britain by Article 7 of the (first) Peace Treaty of Paris of 30 May 1814 (N.R., II, 1). Independent since 1964.

Malvinas. See Falkland Islands.

Man. Once in the past a separate kingdom, first under Norwegian, later under Scottish suzerainty.

Mandated Islands in the Pacific. See Pacific Islands north and south of the Equator.

Marcus Island. See: Bonin Islands.

Marianas or Ladrones. Recognized by Portugal as belonging to Spain by Article 21 of their treaty of 1 October 1777 (R², II, 545). After her war with the United States of 1898 sold by Spain to Germany, together with the Carolines and Palaos, but with the exception of Guam, by their treaty of 30 June 1899 (N.R.G.², **XXXII**, 66). Were after World War I placed under Japan as a Mandated Territory of the C-type (1920), but withdrawn from her after World War II (1947) and assigned as a Trust Territory (strategic area) to the United States (comp. Article 2 (d) of the Peace Treaty of San Francisco of 8 September 1951 (*U.N.T.S.*, vol. 136, p. 45).

Marie Galante. Occupied by France; after its conquest by England returned to France by Articles 8 and 24 of their Peace Treaty of 10 February 1763 (R², I, 104).

Marmara, Islands in the Sea of—. Belong to Turkey.

Marquises Islands. French *Ordonnance* of 28 April 1843 (N.R.G.[1], V, 277).

Martinique. Originally French; after its capture by Great Britain restored to France by Articles 8 and 24 of their Peace Treaty of Paris of 10 February 1763 (R[2], I, 104).

Mauritius (or Ile de France). Ceded by France to Great Britain by Article 8 of the (first) Peace Treaty of Paris of 30 May 1814 (N.R., II, 1). Anglo-American treaty relative to military bases. Independent since 1968.

Miangas Island. See Palmas Island.

Midway in the Pacific. Belongs to the United States.

Minorca. Spanish since the 14th century; conquered by Great Britain in 1708 and ceded to her by Spain by Article 11 of their Peace Treaty of Utrecht of 13 July 1713 (Dumont VIII[1], 393). After its conquest by France in 1756 restored to Great Britain by Articles 12 and 24 of their Peace Treaty of Paris of 10 February 1763 (R[2], I, 104); occupied by France and Spain jointly in 1782, but recaptured by Great Britain in 1798; ceded by her to Spain by Article 11 of the Peace Treaty of Amiens of 25/27 March 1802 (R[2], VII, 404).

Minquiers. See: Ecrehos.

Miquelon and St.-Pierre. Originally insular possessions of England, ceded to France by Articles 6 and 24 of their Peace Treaty of Paris of 10 February 1763 (R[2], I, 104), returned to her after their conquest by Articles 4 and 20 of that of Versailles of 3 September 1783 (R[2], III, 519; comp. also 529-520) and Article 15 of that of Amiens of 25/27 March 1802 (R[2], VII, 404).

Montserrat. After its conquest by France returned to Great Britain first by Article 12 of their Peace Treaty of Breda of 31 July 1667 (Dumont, VII[1], 40) and at a later stage by Articles 8 and 20 of that of Versailles of 3 September 1783 (R[2], III, 519).

Mushah Island, off the coast of Somalia; first ceded to the United Kingdom (under the administration of India); French protectorate recognized in an exchange of Notes of February 1888 (*Hertslet Treaties,* vol. 19, p. 204).

Mytilene (Lesbos), demilitarized pursuant to Article 13 of the Peace Treaty of Lausanne of 24 July 1923 (N.R.G.[3], XIII, 338).

Nauru or Pleasant Island. Originally cocupied by Germany as a colony. Placed under a League of Nations Mandate in 1920, to be exercised for the British Empire by Australia. Transformed into a Trust Territory in 1947. Independent since 1968. Comp. Part II of this publication pp. 102-103.

Netherlands Antilles. See Curaçao.

Nevis. After its conquest by France restored to Great Britain by Articles 8 and 20 of their Peace Treaty of Versailles of 3 September 1783 (R², III, 519). See further under St. Kitts.

Newfoundland. After its conquest by France guaranteed with adjoining islands to Great Britain by Article 13 of their Peace Treaty of Utrecht of 11 April 1713 (Dumont, VIII¹, 339) and Article 4 of that of Versailles of 3 September 1783 (R², III, 519).

New Guinea. Divided into three parts, first between the Netherlands (West), Germany (Kaiser Wilhelms-Land, Northeast) and Australia (Papua, Southeast), later (since 1920) between the Netherlands, Australia as Mandatory Power (since 1946 under Trust administration) and Australia as colonial power. Western New Guinea (Irian) part of Indonesia since 1962; consultation of its Papua people in 1969.

New Hebrides. Under Franco-British co-sovereignty since 1887, comp. Chapter V, section 1 below, p. 437.

New Zealand. British in virtue of the so-called treaty of Waitangi with the Maori Chiefs of 6 February 1840.

Nicobares, on the southeast side of the Gulf of Bengal. Temporarily Danish (1756; 1846) and Austrian (1778). Since 1869 British, in administrative union with the Andamans.

Nikaria, demilitarized by Article 13 of the Peace Treaty of Lausanne of 24 July 1923 (N.R.G.³, XIII, 338).

Niue. Under New Zealand since 1961 (with the Cook's Islands).

Norfolk Island. Transferred to Australia in 1914 (*Norfolk Island Act No. 15 of 1913*).

Novaya Zemlya, under Russian sovereignty.

Okinawa. In the central group of the Ryukyu Islands, under Trust administration by the United States as a strategic area (Article 3 of the Japanese Peace Treaty of San Francisco of 8 September 1951 (*U.N.T.S.*, vol. 136, p. 45). Negotiations over its return to Japan in progress.

Orkney Islands. Fell to Scotland as a consequence of a pledge by Norway in 1496 for a debt which was never since redeemed; comp. Chapter IV, section 1, below, p. 391.

Ösel, off the Gulf of Riga, Danish since 1559. After its cession to Sweden by the Dano-Swedish Peace Treaty of Brömsebro of 13 August 1645 (Dumont, VI¹, 314), ceded to Russia by Article 4 of their Peace Treaty of Nystad of 30 August 1721 (Dumont, VIII², 36; Rousset, *Recueil*, I, 327).

Pacific Islands north of the Equator (Marianas, Carolines, Yap, Palaos, Marshall Islands) came under the Mandate System of the League of Nations in 1920, with Japan as the Mandatory Power; were withdrawn from her and transferred to the United States as a Trust Territory

40

(strategic area) in 1947. Comp. Article 2 (*d*) of the Peace Treaty of San Francisco of 8 September 1951 (*U.N.T.S.*, vol. 136, p. 45) and vol. II of this publication, pp. 102-103.

Pacific Islands south of the Equator (Admiralty Islands, Bismarck archipelago, German part of the Salomon Islands-Bougainville) came under the Mandate System in 1920 and became a Trust Territory in 1947, both under Australia. Comp. *ibid.*

Palaos (Pelew Islands), shared since 1899 the fate of the Carolines (see there).

Palmas (or Miangas) Island. Has long been uninhabited; disputed between the United States and the Netherlands after the former's acquisition of the Philippines from Spain, awarded to the Netherlands by an arbitral award of Max Huber of 4 April 1928 (*A. A.*, vol. III, p. 831).

Papua, see New Guinea.

Paracel Islands. Renounced by Japan by Article 2(*f*) of the Peace Treaty of San Francisco of 8 September 1951 (*U.N.T.S.*, vol. 136, p. 45).

Parece Vela. See Bonin Islands.

Passamaquoddy Bay Islands. Adjudicated partly to the United States and partly to Great Britain by an arbitral award of 24 November 1817 (Martens, N.R., V, vol. suppl., 397; *Pas. Int.*, 8).

Pelagosa. See Lagosta.

Pemba, belonged to Zanzibar, now to Tanzania.

Penang. Was one of the Straits Settlements, now under the Federation of Malaysia.

Perim. Occupied by Great Britain from Aden in 1857 (under India).

Pescadores. Originally Chinese; ceded to Japan by Article II(*c*) of the Peace Treaty of Shimonoseki of 17 April 1895 (N.R.G.², XXI, 642); all right, title and claim to them renounced by Japan by Article 2(*b*) of the Peace Treaty of San Francisco of 8 September 1951 (*U.N.T.S.*, vol. 136, p. 45).

Philippines. Recognized by Portugal as belonging to Spain by Article 21 of their treaty of 1 October 1777 (R², II, 545). Ceded by Spain to the United States by Article 3 of their Peace Treaty of Paris of 10 December 1898 (N.R.G.², XXXII, 74). Independent since 1946.

Pines Island, near Cuba, provisionally left outside Cuban territory by Article 6 of the treaty of 22 May 1903 (N.R.G.², XXXII, 79); separate agreement of 2 March 1904 (N.R.G.³, XIV, 3): relinquished to Cuba.

Pleasant Island. See Nauru.

Port Hamilton island. See Quelpart.

Pratas Islands. Recognized by Japan as appertaining to China: treaty of 11 October 1909 (N.R.G.³, VI, 853).

Prince Edward Island, in the St.Lawrence Bay. First colonized by France (Saint-Jean), conquered by the British in 1745 and ceded to

Great Britain by the Peace Treaty of Paris of 10 Februari 1763 (R^2, I, 104).

Prince Island (Küzül-Adalar) in the sea of Marmora, see there.

Príncipe, off the coast of Guinea. Occupied by the Portuguese and retained by Portugal in Article 13 of her Pardo Treaty with Spain of 1 March 1778 (R^2, II, 612).

Puerto Rico. Ceded by Spain to the United States by Article 2 of their Peace Treaty of Paris of 10 December 1898 (N.R.G.^{2}, XXXII, 74); later endowed with a regime of regional autonomy.

Quelpart. Belongs to South Korea; renounced by Japan in Article 2 (*a*) of the Peace Treaty of San Francisco of 8 September 1951 (*U.N.T.S.*, vol. 136, p. 45), together with Port Hamilton and Dagelet.

Quemoy. Under the actual authority of Formosa.

Rabbits Islands. Remained Turkish under the resolution of the Ambassadors' Conference of 13 February 1914 (see under Imbros and Tenedos) and Article 12 of the Peace Treaty of Lausanne of 24 July 1923 (N.R.G.^{3}, XIII, 338).

Réunion. See Bourbon.

Rhodes. See Dodecanese.

Rockall. West of the Outer Hebrides. Officially occupied by Great Britain in 1955 (*The Times*, 24 September 1955).

Rodrigo. See Seychelles.

Rosario Island. See Bonin Islands.

Rügen. Acquired by Sweden "in perpetuum pro haereditario feudo", in virtue of Article X, §§ 2 and 3 of the Peace Treaty of Osnabrück of 24 October 1648 (Dumont, VI^1, 469; Zeumer, 2nd ed., II, pp. 395-434); after its conquest by Denmark restored to Sweden by their Peace Treaty of Lund of 26 September 1679 (Dumont, VII^1, 425; comp. also the treaty of Fontainebleau, 2 September 1679, *ibid.*, 419), and at a later stage by that of Fredriksborg of 3 June 1720 (Dumont, VIII^2, 29; Rousset, *Recueil*, I, 357); conquered by France in 1807, but restituted to Sweden in virtue of Article 4 of their treaty of 6 January 1810 (N.R., I, 232); allotted to Denmark by Articles 7 and 15 (*b*) of the Peace Treaty of Kiel of 14 January 1814 (N.R., I, 666), but ceded by her to Prussia in exchange for Lauenburg by their treaty of 4 June 1815 (N.R. II, 349).

Ryukyu (or Lyukyu) Islands, consisting of three groups between Kyu-shu (Japan) and Formosa (Tai-Wan), the middle group comprising Okinawa. To be placed under Trusteeship, together with the Daito Islands, under the United States as Administering Authority in virtue of Article 3 of the Japanese Peace Treaty of San Francisco of 8 September 1951 (*U.N.T.S.*, vol. 136, p. 45).

42

Saba. See Curaçao.

Saint. See St.

Sakhalin. An old Nippo-Russian condominium: Article 2 of the treaty of Simoda of 26 January 1855 (N.R.G.^{1}, XVI^2, 454); Japan waives her claims to it in exchange for the Kuriles, 7 May 1875 (N.R.G.^{2}, II, 582); southern half returns to Japan 5 September 1905 (treaty of Portsmouth) (N.R.G.^{2}, XXXIII, 3); all right, title and claim renounced by Japan by Article 2 (c) of the Peace Treaty of San Francisco of 8 September 1951 (*U.N.T.S.*, vol. 136, p. 45).

Salomon Islands, in 1885/1899 divided between Germany and Great Britain (Solomon Islands). German part shared the fate of Germany's Pacific Islands south of the Equator (see there).

Samoa Islands. Under a joint protectorate of Germany, Great Britain and the United States as from 14 June 1889 (Protocols of the Conference of Berlin and its General Act in N.R.G.^{2}, XVI, 301 and XV, 571), dissolved 12 December 1899: allocation of Western Samoa to Germany and of Eastern Samoa (Tutuila) to the Uinted States (N.R.G.^{2}, XXX, 683). German (West) Samoa after World War I placed under a British Mandate of the C type, later transformed into a Trust Territory. Became independent in 1962.

Samos. Made an Ottoman vassal State in 1832; comp. vol. II of this publication, p. 386. Incorporated into Greece in 1914: decision of the Ambassadors' Conference of 13 February 1914, confirmed by Article 12 of the Peace Treaty of Lausanne of 24 July 1923 (N.R.G.^{3}, XIII, 338); demilitarized by Article 13 of the same treaty.

Sandwich Islands. See Hawaii.

Santa Catarina. On the border between Brazil and Argentina, restituted by Spain to Portugal by Article 22 of their Pardo Convention of 1 October 1777 (R^2, II, 545).

Santo Domingo. Old Spanish possession; cession of western half to France, Article 25 of their Peace Treaty of Rijswijk of 20 September 1697 (Dumont, VII^2, 408); entirely in French hands pursuant to Article 9 of their treaty of Basel of 22 July 1795 (R^2, VI, 124); emergence of two independent Negro States under "emperors"; retrocession of the western half to Spain by Article 8 of the (first) Peace Treaty of Paris of 30 May 1814 (N.R., II, 1); defection of the island from Spain in 1821; union of the two halves under President Boyer, deposed in 1843; emergence of two sovereign States, Haïti and Dominican Republic, repeatedly at war together.

São Tomé. Off the coast of Guinea, discovered by Portugal in 1470 and retained by her in Article 13 of her Pardo Treaty with Spain of 1 March 1778 (R^2, II, 612).

Saseno. Was to become Italian under the secret treaty of London of 26 April 1915 (N.R.G.^{3}, X, 329); remained an apple of discord with

43

Albania, until Italy renounced all claims by Article 28 of the Peace Treaty of Paris of 10 February 1947 (*U.N.T.S.*, vol. 49, p. 3).

Serpents Island off the mouth of the Danube. Was not mentioned either in the Russo-Turkish Peace Treaty of Adrianople of 14 September 1829 (N.R., VIII, 143) or in the Peace Treaty of Paris of 30 March 1856 (N.R.G.[1], XV, 770), but was in 1857 assigned, as a dependency of the delta, to the Ottoman Empire (16 January and 19 June, N.R.G.[1], XV, 793 and XVI[2], 11); its cession to Russia by Article 19*a* of her preliminary peace treaty with Turkey of San Stefano (N.R.G.[2], III, 246) was reversed by Article 46 of the definitive Peace Treaty of Berlin (N.R.G.[2], III, 449); assignment to Romania.

Seychelles and Rodrigo. Ceded by France to Great Britain by Article 8 of the (first) Peace Treaty of Paris of 30 May 1814 (N.R., II, 1), as dependencies of the Ile de France (Mauritius), herself independent since 1960.

Shetland Islands. Fell to Scotland as a consequence of a pledge by Norway in 1496 for a debt which was never since redeemed: comp. Chapter IV, section 1, below, p. 391.

Singapore. Netherlands objections to its occupation by subjects of His Britannic Majesty withdrawn by Article 12 of their treaty of 17 March 1824 respecting territory and commerce in the East-Indies (Martens, N.S. I, 628). Acceded to the Federation of Malaysia in 1963, but seceded again in 1965, to become independent. See Part II of this publication, p. 78.

Solomon Islands. See Salomon Islands.

South Georgia. See Falkland Islands.

South Orkneys. See Falkland Islands.

South Shetlands. See Falkland Islands.

Spitzberg. Destined at first to become a no-man's land, insusceptible of occupation; in the event allotted to Norway under an international regime. Comp. Chapter V, section 6 below, p. 483.

Sporades. See Aegean Islands.

Spratly Islands. Renounced by Japan by Article 2 (*f*) of the Peace Treaty of San Francisco of 8 September 1951 (*U.N.T.S.*, vol. 136, p. 45).

Staaten Island, off the eastern point of Tierra del Fuego; discovered by the Dutch; belongs to Chile.

St. Andrea. Severed from the virreinato of Guatemala and added to that of Nueva Granada by a Spanish Royal Ordinance of 20/30 November 1803 (N.R.G.[1], XV, 166); recognized as Nicaraguan in a treaty with Colombia of 24 March 1928 (N.R.G.[3], XXXVI, 806).

St. Barthélemy. Colonized by a French Company since 1648; ceded by France to Sweden by Article 8 of their treaty of 1 July 1784 (R[2], III, 743); capitulated to the English forces in March 1801 (R[2], VII, 252-255); retroceded by Sweden to France by treaty of 10 August 1877

44

(N.R.G.², IV, 366), with Protocol of 31 October 1877 (*ibid.*, 367).

St. Christopher = St. Kitts.

St. Croix. See Virgin Islands.

St. Eustatius. See Curaçao.

St. Helena, acquired by the English East India Company from the Dutch in 1650. Place of exile of Napoleon from 1815 to 1821.

St. Jean, see Prince Edward Island.

St. John. See Virgin Islands.

St. Kitts (or St. Christopher). Once divided between England and France; old English part after its conquest by France restituted by her to England by Article 7 of their Peace Treaty of Breda of 31 July 1667 (Dumont, VII¹, 40); cession to England of the old French half, also, by Article 11 of their Peace Treaty of Utrecht of 11 April 1713 (*ibid.*, VIII¹, 339); after its reconquest by France, together with Nevis, restored to Great Britain by Articles 8 and 20 of their Peace Treaty of Versailles of 3 September 1783 (R², III, 519). Combined with Nevis and Anguilla in a federation, which was given in 1967 the status of an "associated State" of the Commonwealth. Anguilla seceded in 1967.

St. Lucia. One of the "neutral" islands in the Caribbean, allotted to France by Articles 9 and 24 of the Anglo-French Peace Treaty of Paris of 10 February 1763 (R², I, 104); returned to her, after its conquest by Great Britain, by Articles 7 and 20 of that of Versailles of 3 September 1783 (R², III, 519), but eventually ceded to Great Britain by Article 8 of the (first) Peace Treaty of Paris of 30 May 1814 (N.R., II, 1).

St. Martin (St. Maarten). Divided between the Netherlands and France since 1648; the Netherlands half now with Curaçao, Bonaire, Aruba, St. Eustatius and Saba component parts of the Kingdom of the Netherlands; the French half now an overseas department of France.

St. Maura. See Ionian Islands.

St. Pierre. See Miquelon.

St. Thomas. See Virgin Islands.

St. Vincent. One of the "neutral" islands in the Caribbean, allotted to Great Britain by Article 9 of the Franco-British Peace Treaty of Paris of 10 February 1763 (R², I, 104), restored to Great Britain, after its conquest by France, by Articles 8 and 20 of that of Versailles of 3 September 1783 (R², III, 519).

Sulu Archipelago. Recognition of Spain's sovereignty by Germany and Great Britain: protocol of 7 March 1885 (N.R.G.², X, 642); fell later to the Philippines.

Sumatra. Parts of this once Netherlands island remained in British hands until their colonial treaty of 17 March 1824 (N.R., VI, 415 = N.S., I, 628).

Taïti. A French protectorate since 1843: N.R.G.[1], V, 56-66; 452-459; VI, 58-101; comp. also the earlier documents of 1838 and 1842: II, 548; III, 560, and the subsequent ones of 1847: X, 473-477.

Tai-Wan. See Formosa.

Tenedos. See Imbros.

Tigre Island. Temporary cession by Honduras to the United States, 28 September 1849 (N.R.G.[1], XV, 186).

Timor. Divided between the Netherlands (Indonesia) and Portugal; object of a boundary dispute in 1914 (*A.A.*, XI, 481) and of a pre-emption clause in a declaration of 1 July 1893, additional to their Convention of 10 June 1893 (N.R.G.[2], XXII, 463, 465).

Tobago. After Dutch occupation 1632-1677, alternating occupation by France and England, interspersed with colonization attempts by Curlandia; one of the "neutral" islands in the Caribbean allotted to Great Britain by Article 9 of the Anglo-French Peace Treaty of Paris of 10 February 1763 (R[2], I, 104), ceded by Great Britain to France by Article 7 of that of 3 September 1783 of Versailles (R[2], III, 519), but retroceded by France to Great Britain by Article 8 of the (first) Peace Treaty of Paris of 30 May 1814 (N.R., II, 1).

Independent since 1962, together with Trinidad.

As appears from an investigation by BUSSEMAKER in the Spanish State Archives (see the *Verslag*, cited under Aruba, p. 126), the ownership (not the sovereignty) of the island was still in 1680 sold by the States General to a Spanish subject, Don Antonio Medrano, but his Government objected to this purchase and ordered him to retrocede the island to them. The States General thereupon sold it to a Dutch nobleman, the Seignior of Sommelsdijk, but this in turn met with objections, this time from the Papal nuncio on the ground that the buyer was a heretic.

Tokelau (or Union) Islands. Under New Zealand since 1925.

Tonga archipelago (or Friendly Islands), under British protection since 8 November 1899. Still a protected State, see Whiteman, I (1963), p. 450.

Trinidad. Initially Spanish (1588); French immigration; conquered by Great Britain in 1797; ceded to her by Article 4 of the Peace Treaty of Amiens of 25/27 March 1802 (R[2], VII, 404). Independent since 1962, together with Tobago.

Trinity Island, at 20°31′ lat. south and 13°47′57″ long. west. Discovered by the Portuguese in 1501; occupied by England in 1700. Diplomatic correspondence Brazil-Great Britain, 20/22 July 1895 (N.R.G.[2], XXI, 633).

Tristan da Cunha, between 37° and 38° lat. south and 12° long. west, British possession.

Turks Islands, southeastern group of the Bahamas (see there).

Union Islands. See Tokelau Islands.

Urup Island. Assigned to Russia by Article 2 of her treaty with Japan of 26 January 1855 (N.R.G.¹, XVI², 454).

Usedom. See Wollin.

Virgin Islands. Colonized by the Danish West India and Guinea Company as from 1672; St. Thomas a free port since 1716; the sugar island St. Croix purchased from France by a treaty of 15 June 1733 which also guaranteed her Denmark's neutrality in the approaching War over the Polish Succession. A United States offer to purchase St. Thomas and St. John in 1867 not accepted; a treaty of sale entered into in 1902 was abortive as a result of a tie vote in the Danish Upper House. New negotiations during World War I finally resulted in their sale by the treaty of 4 August 1916 (Martens, N.R.G.³, X, 357). The Danish flag was lowered on 31 March 1917 (R. RAPHAEL, "Denmark's Caribbean Venture" in *The American-Scandinavian Review*, vol. IV, No. 1, March 1967). Comp. further on this sale Chapter III, section 2, § 4, p. 374.

Volcano Islands. See Bonin Islands.

William's Island. Uninhabited island in the Bahamas, claimed by Great Britain; abused as a base by anti-Castro Cubans in the 1960's.

Wollin. Acquired by Sweden in virtue of Article X, § 2 of the Peace Treaty of Osnabrück of 24 October 1648 (Dumont, VI¹, 469; Zeumer, 2nd ed., II, pp. 395-434); ceded to Prussia, together with Usedom, by Article 3 of the Prusso-Swedish Peace Treaty of Stockholm of 21 January 1720 (Dumont, VIII², 21).

Yap, one of the Carolines (see there).

Zanthe. See Ionian Islands.

Zanzibar. Protectorate of Great Britain since 1890. Independent since 1963 and subsequently merged with Tanganyika in Tanzania.

Section 2. THE SUBSOIL

Barring the special type of subsoil which will be dealt with under the headings Continental Shelf and High Seas, the ordinary subsoil of the surface territory of the State does not give rise to many legal problems.

There is no juridical limit to the exercise of territorial sovereignty downwards. There is no international right of transit for oil or gas pipelines, water mains, electricity cables, sewers, etc., but nothing hinders two or more States from concluding for these purposes bi- or multilateral agreements, as have been in actual fact concluded. The second Conference of the Organization of Communications and Transit of the League of Nations at Geneva in 1923 has made an, unfortunately almost fruitless, attempt to create an international right to transmit electric power in transit from one country to another across the territory of a third State. See the Convention of 9 December 1923 relating to such transmission (Martens, N.R.G.[3], XIX, 276).

> This Convention only established an obligation of any of the parties, at the request of another, to negotiate the conclusion of an agreement for ensuring the transmission in transit without any guarantee that it will in actual fact be concluded. And even that obligation does not exist if the State requested "can represent that the transmission in transit of electric power across its territory would be seriously detrimental to its national economy or security".
> —The Convention further contains certain details concerning what is to be understood by "transmission in transit", about the technical methods to be employed, and about provisions which the agreement applied for may reasonably comprise.

Such agreements can even be directed to the establishment of a so-called State servitude (comp. on this notion Chapter IV, section 4 *infra*, pp. 413 *et seq.*).

The subject of concessions granted to foreigners for the exploitation of mineral riches in the subsoil will be discussed elsewhere, as will, for that matter, the postulated fundamental right of the State freely to dispose of such riches, assertedly even without regard for previously assumed voluntary commitments (see Part V of this publication).

A legally curious subject matter of international concern and which calls for international regulation is the extraordinary and rare phenomenon where the surface frontier between two States does not exactly correspond with their subterranean boundary. The delimitation and demarcation of such a boundary may become necessary mainly on two occasions, when namely: (*a*) a boundary area becomes the scene of underground exploitation of coal, gold, salt or other mines, or becomes involved in a modification of the State frontier after such exploitation has been undertaken; (*b*) a railway or road tunnel is built through a mountain. In the first case it can happen that the mine concerned is about to be extended under the territory of the neighbouring State, or that the frontier modification causes the mine to become situated under foreign territory—eventualities which necessitate an agreement on a subterranean frontier. This will not necessarily have to lie in the same vertical plane with the State boundary on the surface; the two boundaries may indeed be functionally independent. The same can occur in the second case: the boundary line over the mountain crest or watershed has no direct logical connection with that in the tunnel and the two, each determined by specific considerations, may easily lie in different vertical planes.[7]

ad (a) Mining in frontier regions[8]

An example thereof is the Netherlands coal mining industry in the southern part of the province of Limburg: one of the mines extends eastward under German territory, another may extend westward under the river Maas into Belgian underground territory. The former situation dates back to the days of the Congress of Vienna (1815), when the surface boundary between the Netherlands and Prussia was, as a result of a cession of territory to Prussia, drawn in such a way that it came to run to the west of the underground eastern limit of exploration of the Netherlands coal mine then already existing. In view of this special clauses were inserted in Articles 19 and 20 of the Boundary Treaty of Aachen between the Netherlands and Prussia of 26 June 1816 (Martens, N.R., III, 24) with the object of guaranteeing an undisturbed exploitation of the mines located under the ceded territory.[9] By a judgment of 21 April 1914, the *Oberlandesgericht* of Cologne recognized this treaty provision as having established a State servitude (see *Zeitschrift für Völkerrecht* 1914 (VIII), p. 437). This exceptional situation implies that the interior of the mine must be considered, for the purposes not only of mining law proper, but also of criminal law, social provisions and taxation, as being Netherlands territory.[10] In later years the furthermost limits of this subterranean territory towards the river Worms have been fixed by a treaty entered into just before Germany's invasion of the Netherlands in the Second World War: 17 May 1939 (*L.N.T.S.*, vol. 199,

7. A kindred problem relates to the possibility that a boundary line on and in the continental shelf beyond the territorial sea is not a prolongation of the surface boundary line in it. Comp. on this particular problem p. 70 below.
8. See on this subject G. BRAUN, *Die völkerrechtliche Problematik des grenzüberschreitenden Bergwerkbetriebes* (dissertation Cologne, 1967).
9. Article 19: "La cession des parties de Kerkraede et de Rolduc ... ne portera aucun préjudice à l'exploitation des mines de houille, qui, ayant ci-devant appartenu à l'abbaye de Rolduc, se continue aujourd'hui dans les Communes de Kerkraede et de Rolduc pour le compte du Gouvernement des Pays-Bas, de manière que ce Gouvernement ou tout autre concessionnaire, qui le représenterait, pourra faire dans les parties cédées tels ouvrages qu'il trouvera bon, soit pour l'extraction de la houille, soit pour l'épuisement des eaux ...". The Prussian Government must refrain from all hindrance to this exploitation, either by allowing its mining-engineers to give instructions, or by levying an extraction tax, or by granting private concessions in the area. The Netherlands Government was moreover empowered to establish the necessary hydraulic works on the river Worms, whose actual state the Prussian Government shall not change.
10. Netherlands Courts have also had to deal with this unusual territorial situation; see the judgment of the Court of Appeal of 's-Hertogenbosch of 1936 (*A.D.* 1935-1937, Case No. 53), concerning a theft of dynamite from the Kerkrade colliery by a stateless person.

p. 240), by which the underground boundary was straightened so as no longer to follow the meandering course of the river. The latter mining area, under the river Maas (Meuse) on the Belgian side, has equally given rise to the conclusion of treaties, *viz.*, on 23 October 1950 (*U.N.T.S.*, vol. 136, p. 31), 5 April 1963 (*U.N.T.S.*, vol. 507, p. 270) and 27 April 1965 (*U.N.T.S.*, vol. 596, p. 235). In this area a complicated regulation was required in connection with occasional shifts in the thalweg of the river.

A similar situation to that beneath the Netherlands-German boundary existed since 1922 in the German-Polish frontier region in Upper Silesia: see on the so-called *Tiefer Friedrichstollen* the convention of 7 December 1927 (Martens, N.R.G.[3], XXX, 289).

ad (b) Road and railway tunnels

The idea of the construction of a tunnel through a mountain would seem to be already fairly old, as a plan to connect Nizza with Genova under the Col di Tenda is ascribed to Ann of Lusignan in 1450. This project, however, was not approved for execution until 1782 by King Victor Amedeus II of Savoy, who in his turn had to abandon it owing to an invasion of the French in 1794.

Actual attempts to pierce tunnels with international cooperation have only followed in the second half of the 19th century. The first international railway tunnels were those built between Switzerland and her neighbours through the Col de Fréjus (Mont Cenis) (1871), the St. Gotthard (1881), the Arlberg (1885) and the Simplon (1906). Comp. on the legal history of the St. Gotthard tunnel my account in section 5 of the Annex to this Chapter on Roads and Railways, *infra* pp. 263 *et seq.* See further:

on the road and railway tunnel under the Mont Blanc between Chamonix and Courmayeur the Franco-Italian treaty of 14 March 1953, with final *procès-verbal* of 16 May 1953, in *U.N.T.S.*, vol. 284, p. 221.[10a]

> According to this treaty two national companies were to carry out the plan on joint account in equal shares, each on the strength of a national concession for a term of seventy years, and under the supervision of an international commission. The tunnel was to remain the common and indivisible property of both States. Minerals which might be struck were to fall to the State to which the tunnel section concerned belonged;

on the road tunnel under the Grand St. Bernard the Swiss-Italian treaty of 23 May 1958 in *U.N.T.S.*, vol. 363, p. 81. The details of the regulation are generally the same as those of the Mont Blanc treaty.

As I have already remarked earlier, the principles governing the delimitation of State frontiers across mountains or mountain ranges are

---

10a. See P. LAPORTE, *Le tunnel du Mont-Blanc* in *A.F.D.I.* 1963 (IX), p. 259.

in no way necessarily identical to those governing such delimitation in the interior of the mountains. The latter boundary has nothing whatever to do, in principle, with the line over the summit(s) or along the watershed: it may, for example, be practical to delimit the frontier in the heart of a mountain half-way between the two tunnel entrances. Thus, the solution, chosen for the tunnel through the Alps between Nice and Savoy in the Franco-Italian Convention of 10 December 1874 (Martens, N.R.G.², I, 370) was that

> "la limite de la frontière entre la France et l'Italie, à l'intérieur du tunnel des Alpes, est fixée au point de séparation des deux pentes opposées se dirigeant l'une vers l'Italie, l'autre vers la France, à environ 150 mètres au Sud de la verticale passant par la faîte de la montagne".

In the case of the Mont Blanc tunnel the subterranean boundary is determined by the perpendicular dropped from the mountain frontier (Article 11 of the treaty of 1953) although, according to a map reproduced in the *Corriere della Sera* of 15 August 1962, the middle of the tunnel at an equal distance of 5,8 kilometres from its entrances is situated well to the north of that perpendicular. The same regulation applies to the Grand St. Bernard tunnel: the boundary is formed by the intersection of the axis of the tunnel with the perpendicular line from the frontier in the open air.

The piercing of frontier-crossing tunnels raises many other questions, relative to customs and sanitary control, the control of passenger traffic, and of defence. On the latter subject see, *e.g.*, the regulation laid down in the Italo-Swiss agreement concerning the Simplon tunnel of November-December 1908 (Martens, N.R.G.³, IV, 877).

Section 3. THE TERRITORIAL SEA

A. *General, historical*

The concept of a territorial sea and its legal status have in the course of time disengaged themselves from, or developed concurrently with, the notion of the freedom of the high seas. This territorial sea has a centuries old legal history behind it. Extensive historical research in medieval and, for that matter, already in classical sources has revealed to what extent the modern idea of State sovereignty over the littoral belt originates from an extension of public power from the land area seaward or, on the contrary, from a withdrawal of earlier claims to the high seas landward. In the recent past the latter course of events, which is historically demonstrable in specified maritime areas of Europe, has taken the opposite trend of pushing the boundary of the territorial sea seaward, a tendency which holds obvious dangers for the revered principle of the freedom of the seas.

Thorough historical studies have been devoted to this fascinating subject, *inter alios*, by L. E. VISSER, RAESTAD, GIDEL and CIALDEA.[11] There can be no question of writing an independent monograph here on the basis of personal research into the multifarious sources and I must, therefore, confine myself to some general observations and to the occasional insertion of a summary of the results reached by the authors cited.

The two opposite directions taken by the legal development alluded to above can be described as follows.

As long as, or in regions where, the idea of a *dominium maris*, *i.e.*, the exclusive authority over large portions of the high seas which specific maritime States were in a position, and deemed themselves entitled, to rule had not yet penetrated into international practice and the sea was still considered a *res communis omnium*, the notion of a coastal belt subject to the jurisdiction of the State to which the land territory belonged could only arise in the form of an extension of public power from the land territory over the adjacent sea area for limited purposes and for reasons of public policy peculiar to the historical epoch concerned.

When, and where, on the contrary, in particular in the Scandinavian and Mediterranean regions, adjacent States laid claim to rights of jurisdiction over large parts of the sea, there was little scope for a special claim to exclusive authority over a limited coastal belt. It was only after such claims to jurisdiction over vast maritime areas had gradually shrunk or faded away under the growing resistance of other States that the idea of State authority over a limited coastal belt (re)appeared in the form of a retraction of pretentions of that kind in the opposite direction, from the high seas landward, until only a modest residue thereof was, for corresponding reasons of public policy, left at a relatively small distance from the coast.

Since I intend to deal with the tenet of the freedom of the seas separately I will refer on that subject to Part IV of this publication under A.

The idea of a maritime belt along the coast subject to the exclusive jurisdiction of the riparian State was prompted, on the one hand, by the necessity of national defence: the protection of the coast or of coastal shipping against pirates, privateers or foreign attacks or invasion or, in a later period, the prevention of encroachments upon the country's neutrality, and, on the other hand, by economic motives: the tendency to use the authority of the State over the coast, in accordance with the

11. L. E. VISSER, *De territoriale zee* (thesis Utrecht; Amersfoort, 1894); A. RAESTAD, *La mer territoriale* (Paris, 1913); G. GIDEL, *Le droit international public de la mer*. Tome III *La mer territoriale et la zone contiguë* (Paris, 1934); B. CIALDEA, *La formazione dell'ordinamento marittimo nelle relazioni internazionali (secoli XIV-XVIII)* (Milano, 1959).

practice of early days, to levy taxes on passing foreign shipping, or to exclude foreign fishermen from the maritime coastal areas. Comp. on the neutrality aspect of this development Part IV-A of this publication, and on the general content of the rights and duties of a coastal State in respect of foreign navigation through, and fishing in, the territorial sea below under B.

Apart from the substantive contents of the right of a riparian State over its marginal maritime belt, which changed in the course of time, there was the special problem of its breadth and of the baseline from which it must be measured. This vexed problem has remained unsolved until the present day; it was even less controversial in the past than it is nowadays. See on this subject below under C.

A further special subject concerns the lateral delimitation of adjacent stretches of territorial sea, and the delimitation of territorial sea areas in the case of opposite coasts. See below under D.

A still more special subject is that of the territorial sea of archipelagos. See under E.

To begin with a terminological point, in this exposition I will use the official technical term of "territorial sea". It is so called at present since the Conference on the Law of the Sea of 1958 (Geneva). The first and only Codification Conference of the former League of Nations of 1930 still preferred the term of "territorial waters" which, however, was much too wide and was, because of its ambiguity, the direct cause of much confusion with internal waters, in particular those which lie on the land side of the inner baseline of the coastal or littoral belt. These latter terms, however, may equally be used occasionally for the sake of variation without thereby causing any risk of misunderstanding in alternation with the official appellation of "territorial sea".

In the older doctrine of public international law the territorial sea has been conspicious as the result of a double controversy concerning the legal nature of the rights of the coastal State in respect of it, namely, (*a*) their conception either as a fascicle of separate rights or as the fulness of territorial authority or sovereignty, (*b*) their qualification as proprietary rather than as sovereign rights of the coastal State.

The maritime belt nowadays belongs incontestably to the territorial domain of the riparian State. This was different in former days when certain medieval conceptions still survived in respect of the juristic appraisal of sovereignty in general, inclusive of those exercised by a coastal State over the belt of sea running the length of its land territory. Old patrimonial conceptions have persisted for a long time in later doctrine, witness the not uncommon earlier presentation of those rights as State property rather than as territorial sovereignty, and as a collection of separate powers rather than as the fulness of State authority. These vestiges of obsolete notions surviving in subsequent centuries have today wholly vanished. The nature of the jurisdiction of a State over its maritime belt is now universally recognized as genuine territorial sovereignty, although, owing to the special features of the physical milieu where that authority was exerted, it necessarily remained clearly distinguishable from sovereignty over land areas. And that territorial sovereignty is no longer a collection of specified sovereign rights, as was the current line of thought respecting public authority in general in feudal days, but the fulness of rights, only subject to a certain number of limitations determined by public international law.

Since I have at the time written a separate paper on the Conference on the Law of the Sea of 1958, which I wish to maintain as a self-contained article in preference to dissecting it into different parts (see my Excursus to Part IV-A of this publication), I confine myself here in the main to referring to Ch. I of that Excursus dealing with Convention I of that Conference, and for the rest to digressing a little on a few aspects of this subject matter not discussed in that paper.

The first general problem is the following. Assuming as an axiom that any State has the right to claim a territorial sea of at least three nautical miles, must it be held that this breadth also constitutes a minimum? In other words, is a State precluded from either reducing this breadth of its coastal belt, or renouncing it entirely? This latter question has occasionally been discussed and answered: by RAESTAD in his *La mer territoriale* (Paris, 1913), p. 162, in a negative sense, by Sir Arnold McNAIR (as he then was) in his dissenting opinion in the *Norwegian Fisheries case* (United Kingdom *v.* Norway) of 1951 (*I.C.J. Reports* 1951, at p. 160) in a positive sense:

> "To every State whose land territory is at any place washed by the sea, international law attaches a corresponding portion of maritime territory ... International law does not say to a State: "You are entitled to claim territorial waters if you want them". No maritime State can refuse them. International law imposes upon a maritime State certain obligations and confers upon it certain rights arising out of the sovereignty which it exercises over its maritime territory. The possession of this territory is not optional, not dependent upon the will of the State, but compulsory".

This latter opinion is certainly the correct one.—This does not, however, exclude the possibility that a deviation of the minimum rule may be agreed upon by an international Convention, at least *inter partes*, in respect of a specific maritime area. This is evidenced by a special rule inserted in Article 2-II of the Åland Islands Convention of 20 October 1921 (Martens, N.R.G.[3], XII, 65), according to which the territorial waters of those islands "are considered to extend to a distance of three nautical miles from the low-water mark of the islands, islets and reefs not permanently submerged, delimited above (*viz.*, in Article 2-I)", but with the express proviso that "nevertheless, these waters shall at no point extend beyond the lines fixed in paragraph I of the present Article." The lines referred to are two parallels of latitude on the north and the south, and a series of straight lines joining successively specified geographical points on the east and the west, and obviously run in places at a shorter distance from the component elements of the archipelago than three nautical miles.

A second connected question is whether it is juridically possible for a State to transfer part of its territorial sea to another State without any accompanying land territory? The answer must, as a general rule, be negative: the territorial sea has no independent existence as an element of the national territory, severed from the coast which it borders. Should such an isolated transfer in exceptional cases be held legally possible, then this could only be in the variant of a boundary rectification between two adjoining maritime belts. See on lateral frontier delimitation in the territorial sea *infra* under D.

A third question is whether a delimitation of the territorial sea of a State can be relative in the sense that it has a breadth of x miles in respect of State A, but of y miles in respect of State B, or in the sense that it has a breadth of x miles in one respect or case, but of y miles in another? This somewhat surprising question crossed my mind when reading the statement of reasons of the International Court of Justice in the *Norwegian Fisheries case* of 1951 (*I.C.J. Reports* 1951, p. 116) and the dissenting opinion of Judge McNair. The Court started from the *a priori* (at p. 126) that the question of the extent of Norway's territorial sea was not the subject of the dispute because "the 4-mile limit claimed by Norway was acknowledged by the United Kingdom in the course of the proceedings", thus suggesting the, to my mind erroneous, idea that the acknowledgment by two States of whatever limit they choose to adopt for the extent of their territorial sea can, even *inter se*, make law. Judge McNair's summary of the United Kingdom's admissions or concessions (at p. 159) *sub* (*a*), that *for the purposes of that case* (italics applied) Norway was entitled to a four-mile limit, gives rise to still more doubt: is it possible that she would be so entitled in one case and not in another? Comp. my observations in *The Jurisprudence of the World Court*, vol. II, pp. 101-102.

A further question is whether a coastal State is entitled to double its sovereignty over the territorial sea with the ownership of it under municipal private law? I pose this question because the Netherlands Government has indeed in their proposals for a new Civil Code, at present in the making, extended the property rights of the State from the beaches of the sea over the whole of its territorial sea. I do not feel that there is anything illegal in that. If nothing is said about the ownership of this area under civil law, it might conceivably be appropriated by enterprising individuals or companies in accordance with the traditional rules on the acquisition of real property by occupation. It is, therefore, safe to lay down expressly the ownership of the State over this maritime area, as was traditionally done in the past with respect to public rivers, beaches, etc.

> The same conclusion cannot be drawn, however, with regard to the continental shelf because the coastal State has only, with regard to it, limited sovereign rights, which can hardly create a right of full ownership under private law. See thereupon below, p. 80.

B. *The juridical content of sovereignty over the territorial sea*

A hard struggle has taken place over the exact juridical content of this particular type of territorial sovereignty at the first Conference on the Law of the Sea convened by the United Nations at Geneva in 1958, where a determined final effort was made to define the legal status of the coastal belt in concrete treaty provisions. It was not the first time this had been attempted: in fact, twenty-eight years earlier, the Codification Conference of the League of Nations (1930) had already undertaken that task, and with success; that it nevertheless after all failed was due only to unbridgeable disagreement over the breadth of the territorial sea (comp. on the 1930 Codification Conference Part I of this publication, Annex to Chapter I, pp. 20 *et seq.*, at pp. 25-27).

The issue at stake in 1958 was again the striking of a generally acceptable balance between the authority of the coastal State in that belt and the freedom of innocent passage of other States through it. Since I have described that struggle and its outcome in my separate paper on the 1958 Conference mentioned under A, I will not go into that subject here in any detail.

Three of the most important elements of the legal situation in the territorial sea are

(*a*) the right of innocent passage for foreign shipping;

(*b*) the reservation of cabotage (coasting trade) to the national flag of the coastal State;

(*c*) the exclusive right of fishing.

ad(a). The main controversy relative to this right of innocent passage— a notion difficult to define exactly—concerns the passage of foreign warships and, if such right must be acknowledged, the conditions under which it can be exercised. As I have already argued in Part I of this publication at p. 87, normal treaty construction leads to the conclusion that no restrictions are allowed even on the innocent passage of foreign warships through the territorial sea, that therefore, a coastal State is not entitled to make such passage conditional upon its agreement to a previous request for authorization, and that at the utmost previous notification can legally be prescribed. However, the peculiar conditions under which Article 23 of Convention No. I of 1958 was in the event adopted makes this doubtful and may warrant another conclusion, *viz.*, that the Conference has intended to leave the decision of this question to the pre-existing, but entirely uncertain rules of customary law. The Draft prepared by the International Law Commission had in express terms (Article 24) entitled the coastal State to make the passage of warships through the territorial sea subject to both previous authorization or notification, but this Article was struck out. See further below.

ad(b). It is generally admitted that a coastal State is fully entitled to reserve coastwise trade (cabotage) to trading vessels under its own flag. Universal unanimity on this point does not exclude the freedom of coastal States to waive their undisputed right to close their territorial sea for foreign trading vessels for that purpose. The rule (reservation of coasting trade to the national flag) is expressly embodied in a long series of treaties of commerce and navigation, and must generally be held to obtain even when such treaties are silent.

> Comp. for example, Article 5 of the treaty between Tuscany and Sardinia of 5 June 1847 (Martens, N.R.G.[1], X, 590) and Article 4 of that between Germany and Mexico of 5 December 1892 (STRUPP, *Urkunden zur Geschichte des Völkerrechts*, Gotha, 1911, vol. II, p. 292), in the latter case subject to the operation of the most-favoured nation clause.

Exceptions to the rule (where, consequently, cabotage is made free for foreign vessels) are rare.

See, for instance, Articles 3 and 4 of the Anglo-French Convention of 8 April 1904 (Martens, N.R.G.[2], XXXII, 3) which testify to the already existing freedom of cabotage for English vessels plying between Moroccan ports since 1901 and for French vessels plying between Egyptian ports.

As appears from an exchange of notes of 18/20 September 1904 (*ibid.*, N.R.G.[3], VI, 309), a Convention negotiated between Great Britain and Italy guaranteed reciprocally to their respective subjects the advantages of the coasting trade in the ports of the other country. Italy, however, asked for the postponement of its signature, to which England did not object on the condition, accepted by Italy, that the *status quo*, by which British ships had hitherto enjoyed the rights of the coasting trade in Italian ports, be prolonged *sine die*, notwithstanding an Italian law of July 1904 which reserved this privilege in the absence of special international conventions to the Italian flag.

ad(c). Equally undisputed is the right for a coastal State to reserve the right of fishing to its own nationals. Freedom for foreign fishing vessels to exercise their trade in the territorial sea can only rest on a unilateral permission by the coastal State, or on an express treaty provision. The latter can even bear the legal character of a State servitude, as will be further illustrated below in Chapter IV, section 4, p. 422.

For the rest, a coastal State is entitled to regulate and to exercise control on navigation in its territorial sea, to prevent infraction of its customs or quarantine regulations, to avert and, if necessary, exert force against the display of power by foreign States. On the other hand, a coastal State is bound to protect foreign shipping in its littoral belt. There has been much discussion in the past with regard to the exercise of jurisdiction by the coastal State over the occupants of foreign vessels in their territorial sea, in particular when they are only plying along the coast and do not intend to enter a port or to cast anchor.

The two most important controversies, historically, to which passage through the territorial sea has given rise relate to the jurisdiction of the coastal State over merchant ships which only pass through it without anchoring or calling at a port, and to the freedom for warships to pass freely through it.

The first controversy arose on the occasion of the enactment of the British *Territorial Waters Jurisdiction Act of 1878* (41 & 42 Vict. Ch. 73). This Act was intended to remedy an unsatisfactory legal situation which had revealed itself after a collision in Britain's territorial maritime belt in the English Channel in which the German vessel *Franconia* was involved. In that case—penal proceedings of 1876, known as *Reg. v. Keyn* (2 Exch. D. 63)—the Court for Crown Cases Reserved held with a slight majority and on grounds which were indeed very doubtful legally, that no indictment was possible, not because this was contrary to international law, but because there was no rule of British law in force which permitted the prosecution of offenders on foreign vessels seawards of the low-water mark from which the maritime belt is measured. The Act of 1878, which extended British criminal jurisdiction to the territorial sea, conferred upon the Admiralty jurisdiction in respect of offences committed within that sea even on board or by means of a foreign ship and by an alien, although in the case of the latter proceedings would only be permitted with the consent of a Secretary of State.[12] It was the broad wording of this Act which called forth criticism by many international lawyers, in particular because it made no exception for cases in which the offence produced no effect beyond the foreign vessel herself or those on board. Hence the limitations placed upon the criminal jurisdiction of the coastal State over aliens on passing foreign ships, introduced by Article 7 of the draft *Règlement relatif à la mer territoriale en temps de paix*, adopted by the Institut de Droit International at Stockholm on 28 August 1928 *(Annuaire*, vol. 34, p. 757; *Tableau général des Résolutions (1873-1956)*, p. 125):

> "Les crimes et délits commis à bord des navires de commerce de passage dans la mer territoriale ne tombent pas comme tels sous la juridiction de l'Etat riverain.
>
> Par exception les crimes et délits dont l'effet dépasse les bords du navire

12. Comp. *inter alios*, C.J.Colombos, *The international law of the sea*, 3rd ed., London, 1967, §§ 105 and 338 *et seq.*

sont soumis à la juridiction pénale de l'Etat riverain en tant qu'ils sont de nature à troubler la tranquillité publique de ce pays et qu'ils constituent des faits punissables selon ses lois et que ses tribunaux sont compétents pour en connaître,"

and by Article 8 of the Draft Convention of the Codification Conference of the Hague of 1930, which prohibited a coastal State taking any steps on board a foreign vessel passing through its territorial sea to arrest any person or to conduct any investigation by reason of any crime committed on board the vessel during her passage, save only in the following cases: (1) if the consequences of the crime extend beyond the vessel, or (2) if the crime is of a kind to disturb the peace of the country or the good order of the territorial sea, or (3) if the assistence of the local authorities has been requested by the master of the vessel or by the Consul of the country whose flag the vessel flies.

The first Conference of Geneva on the Law of the Sea (1958) adopted this provision in Article 19(1) of Convention No. 1 with only a few minor alterations: under (a) it changed the wording of (1) of 1930 into: "if the consequences of the crime extend to the coastal State" and it further added under (d): "if it is necessary for the suppression of illicit traffic in narcotic drugs". The other paragraphs of Article 19(2-5) laid down a few further additions.

The admissibility of the exercise of civil jurisdiction over foreign ships which only pass through the territorial sea is still more problematic. Articles 8 and 9 of the above-mentioned draft *Règlement* of Stockholm of 1928 exempted juridical acts accomplished on board of a passing vessel from the judicial and legislative competence of the coastal State but reserved the case of collision. The matter was ultimately regulated by Article 20 of Convention I of 1958, which laid down a prohibition to stop or divert a passing foreign ship for the purpose of exercising civil jurisdiction and, subject to two exceptions, to levy execution against or arrest such a ship for the purpose of any civil proceedings.

On certain other legal questions related to the territorial sea, such as the right of hot pursuit and the right of a coastal State to act against foreign vessels which threaten its interests while they are still on the high seas, comp. Part IV-A of this publication, Chapter I.

The other controversy, over the freedom of passage for foreign warships, is still unresolved. It has always been recognized as a matter of course that the passage of warships can be detrimental to the coastal State and therefore deserves special consideration. Article 11 of the above-mentioned draft *Règlement* of 1928 (session of the Institut de Droit International at Stockholm) simply laid down, without further specification, that

"Le libre passage des navires de guerre peut être assujetti à des règles spéciales par l'Etat riverain".

The Codification Conference of The Hague of 1930 elaborated this idea in Article 12 of its draft Convention in the following terms:

> "As a general rule, a coastal State will not forbid the passage of foreign warships in its territorial sea, and will not require a previous authorisation or notification. The coastal State has the right to regulate the conditions of such passage. Submarines shall navigate on the surface".

The International Law Commission, in its sixth session in 1954, still took the view that passage should be granted to warships without prior authorization or notification, but it changed its opinion in its seventh session of 1955 and amended its original provision. This amended version was maintained in 1956 and appeared in Article 24 of the 1956 Draft in the following wording:

> "The coastal State may make the passage of warships through the territorial sea subject to previous authorization or notification. Normally it shall grant innocent passage subject to the observance of the provisions of Articles 17 and 18 [dealing with rights of protection of the coastal State and with duties of foreign ships during their passage]".

When the provision concerned was discussed in the First Committee of the 1958 Conference, it was still maintained as it ran. When, however, in the plenary session the words "authorization or" were put to a separate vote, they failed to gain the support of the necessary two-thirds majority, so that only the admissibility of the requirement of previous notification remained. At the final voting on Article 24 the whole provision failed to be adopted by the required majority and was consequently struck out, as a result of the combined opposition of those States which rejected, and those which upheld the admissibility of both requirements.

I do not go here into the conclusions to be drawn from this course of events because I have already discussed them in another context in Part I of this publication, p. 87.

The legal situation in the coastal belt changes basically in time of war, irrespective of whether the coastal State itself is at war, or is neutral in a war between other powers. This subject belongs to Part IX on war and neutrality. Further restrictions than are allowed in normal times are permissible in periods of international tension.

C. *Baseline and breadth of the territorial sea*

As far as the baseline of the territorial sea is concerned, Convention I of 1958 now defines it with exactitude in its Articles 3 *et seq.* Comp. on this subject also, my separate paper on the 1958 Conference in Part IV-A.

As to the breadth of the territorial sea the following can be said.

In the *Norwegian Fisheries case* of 1951 (*I.C.J. Reports* 1951, pp. 116 *et seq.*, at p. 142) the International Court of Justice assumed that the breadth of the territorial sea along the coasts of Norway was originally determined by the distance to which the eye could see, "the range of vision being, as is recognized by the United Kingdom Government, the principle of delimitation in force at that time (the 17th century)". A fixed breadth in these regions—traditionally of one ordinary sea league, equivalent to four geographical miles of about 1852 metres—was introduced into actual practice only later.

> The Netherlands State Archives still contain a memorial for the use of a deputy of the States General to Denmark, dated 1741, charged with negotiations for the settlement of disputes which had arisen from Netherlands fishing within a distance of four miles from the coast of Iceland.

Professor BASDEVANT, in a contribution in *Symbolae Verzijl* (The Hague, 1958, p. 37 *et seq.*, at pp. 49 and 50), has shown that another famous old criterion of delimitation of the territorial sea, that of the range of a cannon shot, was first formulated by the French Ambassador to the Republic of the United Netherlands, JEANNIN, during the armistice negotiations between that Republic and Spain, in June 1609 (letter of 29 June 1609 to the Governor of Calais in *Négociations diplomatiques et politiques du Président Jeannin, Ambassadeur et Ministre de France*, Paris, 1821/2, vol. V, p. 517), and not, as is usually assumed—by FULTON, RAESTAD, GIDEL and FAUCHILLE—, by the Ambassadors of the Republic in the London Conference on fisheries in 1610.

A very curious distinction was made in the second half of the 18th century in the treaties concluded by Great Britain with the Kingdom of Algier (14 May 1762, Martens, R[2], I, 68) and the State of Tunis (22 June 1762, *ibid.*, I, 72). In the case of a war in which Great Britain would be involved, but these North African States would remain neutral, the latter's littoral belt within which no naval action by British warships or privateers against enemy vessels would be allowed was fixed at a distance determined "by the reach of cannon shot of the shore" if such a war was with other Christian nations. But in case of a war with Mohammedan countries Great Britain should leave their ships unmolested if encountered "within sight of any part of the coast of the Kingdom of Algier (respectively Tunis)". I have been unable to discover the rationale of this distinction.

In the course of time, however, the contrasting practices, based either on the range of vision, or on the distance which a ship can cover in a certain period of time, or on the range of a cannon shot, were to all intents and purposes abandoned and ultimately replaced by one single criterion, *viz.*, that of a certain number of nautical miles of one sixtieth of a degree on the Equator.

According to Luís Drago in his dissenting opinion in the *North Atlantic Fisheries* case (award of 7 September 1910; *A.A.*, XI, 203), quoted *inter alia* in Schücking's *Das Werk vom Haag*, 2nd series, 1st Band, 2nd Teil, pp. 498 *et seq.*, at p. 507, the (unratified) Anglo-American treaty of

61

20 October 1818 has been the first Convention to transform the cannon shot rule into that of a three-mile jurisdiction zone. The Jay treaty of 19 November 1794 (Martens, R², V, 641) had, in the third paragraph of Article 25, still applied the cannon shot rule in matters of prize and neutrality. For a long time this old rule has even continued to be accepted by arbitrators. Comp. the award of the seven-member tribunal in the Anglo-American *Behring Sea Furseals* dispute of 15 August 1893 (Martens, N.R.G.², XXI, 439; English version at p. 449), where reference is made to Russia's recognition in 1824/1825 of her lack of jurisdiction "beyond the reach of cannon shot from shore" as "the ordinary limit of territorial waters", and the award of F. de Martens of 25 February 1897 in the Anglo-Netherlands *Costa Rica Packet* case (*Pas. Int.*, 510; Martens, N.R.G.², XXIII, 808):

> "Considérant que le droit de souveraineté de l'Etat sur la mer territoriale est déterminée par la portée du canon à partir de la laisse de basse mer ...".

The Institut de Droit International had meanwhile in its Paris session of 1894 suggested a breadth of 6 miles.

The exact breadth had also been discussed in earlier arbitral proceedings, *e.g.*, in the (undecided) case of the *William Turner* before the Mixed Commission of Washington between Mexico and the United States in 1842. On that occasion Mexico invoked against the three miles claim of the United States an old Spanish Ordinance fixing the breadth at ten miles from the coast. King Philip II of Spain had at an earlier stage, in a decree of October 1565, still laid down the visual horizon as the outer limit of the coastal belt. Comp. on this case Lapradelle-Politis, I, pp. 494 *et seq.*, and the references in note 2 at p. 496.

Although the most generally accepted breadth was fixed at three sea miles, equivalent to 3 x 1852 metres, or about 5,555 kilometres, the international community has to the present day failed to agree upon the exact number. In several countries different breadths were fixed for different purposes: defence, neutrality, customs, fishing, etc., which only served still further to confound the existing confusion in the determination of the breadth of the territorial sea in general. The fixing of varying widths for various purposes has now become unnecessary as the result of the recognition of a contiguous zone of twelve miles at the utmost from the baseline of the territorial sea, but the outer limit of the latter still remains undefined.

A claim to sovereignty over a territorial sea broader than twelve miles is, however, clearly incompatible with Convention I of Geneva (1958). That Convention indeed recognizes a contiguous zone in addition to the maritime belt proper only up to a distance of twelve miles seaward beyond the baseline of the territorial sea. That provision is obviously intended to assign to the coastal State a contiguous zone of 12 - x miles beyond the x miles of its maritime belt, but absolutely excludes any claim to a territorial sea extending more than 12 miles seaward from that baseline.

Since I have set out the deliberations relative to the admissible breadth of the territorial sea, as it presented itself to the 1958 Conference, in my separate paper on that Conference, I may again be permitted to refer to that paper, inserted in Part IV-A of this publication (also in *N.T.I.R.* 1959 (VI), pp. 1 and 115), and to the postscript added to it, and for the rest only to summarize the net result of the fierce legal struggle over this subject in the Conferences of 1958 and 1960.

The proposal which gathered most favourable votes at the first conference was that of the United States. It was worded in part as follows:

"1. The maximum breadth of the territorial sea of any State shall be six miles.

2. The coastal State shall in a zone having a maximum breadth of twelve miles, measured from the applicable baseline, determined as provided in these rules, have the same rights in respect of fishing and the exploitation of the living resources of the sea as it has in its territorial sea; provided that such rights shall be subject to the right of the vessels of any State whose vessels have fished regularly in that portion of the zone having a continuous baseline and located in the same major body of water for the period of five years immediately preceding the signature of this Convention, to fish in the outer six miles of that portion of the zone, under obligation to observe therein such conservation regulations as are consistent with the rules on fisheries adopted by this Conference and other rules of international law".

This proposal, which was still rejected in Committee I on 19 April 1958 with 38 votes against, 36 in favour and 9 abstentions, was ultimately adopted—the only one among four rival proposals—in the plenary session of 25 April, but only with 45 votes in favour, 33 against and 7 abstentions, so that the majority of two-thirds required was not obtained.

The famous issue which thus had failed to find a solution at the first Conference was discussed again by the second *ad hoc* Conference of 1960, but eventually again failed to be resolved there. The proposal which had the best chances of ultimate success was that introduced by way of a compromise by the delegations of Canada and the United States jointly, in replacement of their original separate proposals. In its final wording it ran in part as follows:

"1. A State is entitled to fix the breadth of its territorial sea up to a maximum of six nautical miles measured from the applicable baseline ...

2. A State is entitled to establish a fishing zone in the high seas contiguous to its territorial sea extending to a maximum of twelve nautical miles from the base line from which the breadth of its territorial sea is measured, in which it shall have the same rights in respect of fishing and the exploitation of the living resources of the sea as it has in its territorial sea.

3. Any State whose vessels have made a practice of fishing in the outer six

63

miles of the fishing zone established by the coastal State, in accordance with paragraph 2 above, for the period of five years immediately preceding January 1, 1958, may continue to do so for a period of ten years from October 31, 1960".

In the Committee stage of the second Conference this joint proposal —still in a slightly different text—obtained a majority of 43 votes (by 33 against and 12 abstentions). This majority vote was at the final voting in the plenary session of 29 April 1960 considerably reinforced, viz., to 54 affirmative votes (by 28 against and 5 abstentions), but it was just one vote too little to constitute the required two-thirds majority. An American proposal to hold a second voting in order to enable hesitant delegations to tip the very delicate balance failed.

Thus the result was again negative, but it showed, especially after the rejection of the rival proposal sponsored by ten countries[13]—pursuant to which, pending the consideration of the question of the breadth of the territorial sea by the General Assembly of the United Nations, any State should be entitled to exercise exclusive fishing rights up to a limit of 12 nautical miles—, that the great majority of States was in favour of a solution consisting in a maximum breadth of the territorial sea of six miles from the baseline, supplemented by additional exclusive fishing rights up to a distance of twelve miles from that same line. One is therefore justified in stating that for the time being this latter solution corresponds most adequately to a widely held common conviction on what, for the sake of unity, the rule of the future should be.

I would have liked to insert here a complete and up-to-date list of breadths of the territorial sea as fixed by successive laws or decrees of the various countries, but I must abandon that idea because such a list would become obsolete before these lines are printed. I am confirmed in that certainty by the fact that just at the moment of writing (April 1969) I hear over the radio that Brazil has extended its latest six-miles zone to one of twelve miles. I must therefore confine myself to referring to a few lists of breadths, comprising not only territorial seas proper, but also additional fishery zones, inserted in recent publications:

U.N.Doc. A/Conf. 19/4 (8 February 1960), reprinted as an annex to the Summary Records of Plenary Meetings and Meetings of the Committee of the Whole, Second United Nations Conference on the Law of the Sea, U.N.Doc. A/Conf. 19/8;

I.L.M. 1963 (II), p. 1122; 1964 (III), pp. 551-552;

M.I. KEHDEN and M.-L. HENKMANN, Die Inanspruchnahme von Meereszonen durch Küstenstaaten (Hamburg, 1967): situation on 1 June 1967; and

FAO Fisheries Technical Paper No. 79 (Rome, 1968) on Limits and

---

13. Introduced by Indonesia, Iraq, Lebanon, Mexico, Morocco, Saudi Arabia, Sudan, the United Arab Republic, Venezuela and Yemen.

Status of the territorial sea, exclusive fishing zones, fishery conservation zones and the continental shelf, also to be found in *I.L.M.* 1969 (VIII), p. 516.

An interesting problem which has arisen in this field relates to the question of the correct legal solution when two divergent national determinations of the breadth of the territorial sea lead to an international dispute between the States concerned. The answer depends, among other things, upon the question as to whether there exists an absolute maximum distance from the coast beyond which no State is entitled to extend its territorial sovereignty: the exercise of State sovereignty beyond that line would be unlawful. As stated above this certainly applies to State activity beyond a distance of twelve nautical miles from the coast. The situation is more doubtful for the maritime area between three and twelve miles, especially for the area between six and twelve miles, in respect of which it can be considered certain that no general new rule of customary law, sanctioning an extension of the coastal belt beyond six miles, has as yet emerged from a general State practice. Considering the measure of agreement reached in favour of a new general maximum of at least six miles, the same can no longer, in my opinion, be sustained with regard to the area between three and six miles. However, irrespective of whether the problem arises from activities performed in the maritime belt between three and six miles or in that between six and twelve miles from the coast, it is essentially the same: is a State which considers the maximum permissible breadth of the territorial sea under positive international law to be only x miles, entitled to disregard the claim of another State which sticks to the greater distance of y miles, or must it acquiesce in that claim?

The problem has presented itself in an interesting variant during World War I between States which still confined their claim to three, respectively four miles. Merchant vessels were occasionally captured by belligerent warships in the maritime area extending between three and four nautical miles from the Swedish or Norwegian coast. Could such captures be declared valid by the prize courts of the belligerent States concerned? The answer which they gave to this problem was typical for the reigning uncertainty: whereas the French prize courts held the captures to be null and void as having been made in neutral waters according to the Swedish and Norwegian view, the British and German prize courts refused to recognize the correctness of that view and declared the captures valid as having been made on the high seas according to their own national view. Comp. on this difference of opinion the data mentioned in my *Le droit des prises de la Grande Guerre* (Leyden, 1922), pp. 271 *et seq.*

The determination of the breadth of the territorial sea can raise domestic controversies in federations. The ultimate power of determining it must in general be held to belong to the federal authorities.

As far as the lateral delimitation of two conterminous stretches of territorial sea is concerned—a problem which, owing to its complexity, had never before permitted the adoption of a general rule, although its importance had already been stressed, *e.g.*, in connection with the Swedish-Norwegian maritime boundary dispute of 1904-1908 concerning the Grisbådarna,[14] the Conference on the Law of the Sea (1958) eventually succeeded in laying down, if not a hard and fast rule, at any rate a general guiding line which may prove useful in the future. It is formulated in Article 12 (1) of Convention I and runs as follows:

> "Where the coasts of two States are opposite or adjacent to each other, neither of the two States is entitled, failing agreement between them to the contrary, to extend its territorial sea beyond the median line every point of which is equidistant from the nearest points on the baselines from which the breadth of the territorial sea of each of the two States is measured. The provisions of this paragraph shall not apply, however, where it is necessary by reason of historic title or other special circumstances to delimit the territorial seas of the two States in a way which is at variance with this provision".

As results from this text, the Conference rightly drew the attention of maritime States to the desirability of fixing the boundary line between two adjacent territorial seas[15] in common accord: the geographical features of a given frontier situation are indeed so varying in different cases that the automatic application of a fixed general rule, whatever it may be, must often reveal itself as inappropriate. Only in default of such an accord, the quoted Article provides its own solution consisting of the

---

14. This was a dispute over the State frontier in a bay, the Oslo fjord, whereupon comp. Chapter VI, section 4, *infra*, p. 596.
15. Unlike the corresponding regulation relative to the delimitation of the respective continental shelves between two States in Article 6 of Convention IV of 1958, which treats the situations separately—see *infra* section 5, pp. 85 *et seq.*—, the text of Article 12 (1) of Convention I combines the situations of two opposite and two adjacent coasts. This discrepancy and other divergences between the texts of the corresponding regulations are not conducive to a correct construction of the provisions concerned.

As to the delimitation of two territorial seas, the International Law Commission had still proposed two separate texts, Article 12 for the case of opposite coasts, Article 14 for that of adjacent coasts, and moreover laid particular stress on the primary necessity of an agreement between the neighbouring States. Its text of Article 14 ran as follows:

"(1) The boundary of the territorial sea between two adjacent States shall be determined by agreement between them. In the absence of such agreement, and unless another boundary line is justified by special circumstances, the boundary is drawn by application of the principle of equidistance from the nearest points on the baseline from which the breadth of the territorial sea of each country is measured".

66

adoption of the principle of "equidistance",[16] sometimes easier to accept in general terms than to apply in actual fact. But even so, the provision makes its applicability in a sense dependent upon the non-existence of a case "where it is necessary by reason of historic title or other special circumstances to delimit the territorial seas" in a different way. I, for one, cannot see how it can ever be *necessary* to do so by reason of an historic title[17] and I, therefore, consider this text as incorrectly drafted. But, worst of all, the initial attempts of the First Committee of the Conference to obviate the inconvenience which the proviso quoted is certain to cause, by a supplementary clause of compulsory adjudication, in the event failed to obtain the required two-thirds majority in the Plenary Session. See for further particulars on the genesis and the deficiency of the provision my more detailed paper on the Conference on the Law of the Sea of 1958 as a whole in Part IV-A of this publication.

> The need for a lateral delimitation of national stretches of adjacent maritime areas also exists with regard to adjoining exclusive fishery zones beyond the territorial sea, discussed in the same paper. The acceptance of corresponding rules for that delimitation is to be recommended.

While I, therefore, refrain from going here further into this subject now, there is, however, scope for two additional digressions, the first concerning the past, the second concerning the future.

(*a*) As to the past, legal history proves that in this field also, the eventual adoption of a (qualified) general rule has been preceded by a series of bilateral maritime boundary agreements, some of them dating back more than a century. It is impossible to give a complete survey, and I must therefore confine myself to a certain number of historical examples.

Delimitation of adjoining sections of the territorial sea was obviously at first held to be hardly necessary, so that many frontier *tracés* stopped at the coast or only took their start from there. The Netherlands, for instance, still in 1845 rejected a Belgian proposal to carry the land frontier in the endiked river Zwin forward through the territorial sea as being needless (GIDEL, *Droit international public de la mer* (Paris, 1934) III, pp. 765-766, note 2). The consequence of such a negative attitude was that it was often left uncertain whether the land frontier, on reaching the sea, (*a*) ran straight on in the same direction in which it struck the coast

16. The use of this term, instead of the simpler, but indeed unsatisfactory, term "median line", already occurs in documents prior to the Conference of 1958. Comp. for example, the Franco-German boundary agreement relative to Dahomey, Upper Volta and Niger, on the one hand, and Togo, on the other, in the lagoon near Bayol of 12/28 September 1912 (Martens, N.R.G.³, VII, 381).
17. The corresponding provision of Article 6 regarding the continental shelf is rightly worded differently, *viz.*, "unless another boundary line is *justified* by special circumstances".

line, possibly at an acute angle with that line, or (*b*) continued in a line perpendicular to the coast, possibly with a sudden sharp bend, or (*c*) passed on following the meridian or the parallel of the point of intersection with the coast, possibly again in a sudden turn aside. And these three variants of a possible lateral delimitation between two adjoining territorial seas are not the only ones which must be taken into account. Apart from the application of the principle of equidistance which was finally adopted as the most reasonable solution in 1958, the suggestion had sometimes been made, in cases where the State boundary reaches the sea through the mouth of a river or an estuary, to continue the land frontier seaward through the littoral belt following the so-called "exterior thalweg", if the existence of any such thalweg in continuation of the fluvial thalweg proper was in fact demonstrable. GIDEL, in his *Droit international public de la mer*, III, pp. 771 *et seq.*, condemned the term of "thalweg extérieur", but was not entirely against the idea in itself. As this writer recalls, de Magalhães suggested during the preparation of the Codification Conference of 1930 the adoption of that "exterior thalweg" as the State frontier off river mouths or estuaries up to the point where it ceases to exist as such, and from there onward to continue by a perpendicular line to the coast. GIDEL, however, stated correctly that there was insufficient authority in favour of the mixed solution suggested and that it could not, therefore, be held to be a rule of common international law. Yet, the idea of adopting a possible continuation of the river thalweg into the territorial sea as the State boundary in the latter might prove in appropriate cases to be acceptable.

Past international practice, if it adopted any concrete rule at all, chose one or the other of the solutions surveyed above. But the exact borderline in the territorial sea was more often than not left drifting in the water. Even in the peace treaties following World War I the many new frontiers still ended, as a rule, at the coast. Comp. in the Peace Treaty of Versailles Articles 27, 7⁰ *in fine* ("to the Baltic Sea"), 28 ("from a point on the coast of the Baltic Sea ... to the western shore of the Kurische Nehrung"), 87 ("bounded by the Baltic Sea"), 99 ("included between the Baltic, etc."), 100 ("from the Baltic Sea southwards ... to the Baltic Sea") and 109 ("leaving the Baltic Sea ... to the North Sea").

However, adjacent maritime States gradually realized the advantage which could be gained from an exact delimitation of their frontier also in the territorial sea, and entered into agreements of this kind.

The express determination of lateral State boundaries in the territorial sea would seem to have occurred in the first instance, and still occurs in the majority of cases off the mouth of a river. See the following examples.

United States-Mexico, Peace Treaty of Guadalupe Hidalgo of 2 February 1848 (Martens, N.R.G.[1], XIV, 7), Article 5: "the boundary line between the two republics shall commence in the Gulf of Mexico, three leagues from land, opposite the mouth of the Río Grande, ... or opposite the mouth of its deepest branch if it should have more than one branch emptying directly into the sea";

Mexico-Guatemala, 27 September 1882 (*ibid.*, N.R.G.², XIII, 670), Article 3: "la línea media del río Suchiate, desde un punto situado en el mar a tres leguas de su desembocadura, río arriba, por su canal más profundo ...";

Spain-Portugal, 2 October 1885 (*ibid.*, N.R.G.², XIV, 77), Article 4, Rio Miño and Rio Guadiana: frontier delimitation in the coastal sea for fishing purposes, see *infra*;[18]

French Guinea-Portuguese Guinea, 12 May 1886 (*ibid.*, N.R.G.², XIV, 108), Article 1: after following first the thalweg of the Río Cajet (or Kasset) the boundary further runs through the Pass of the Pilots;

Norway-Finland, Convention of 28 April 1924 (*ibid.*, N.R.G.³, XXIV, 860), Article 3: frontier between the "government" of Finmark and the bailiwick of Petsamo, where the equidistance line is accepted as the frontier "à partir du point où le chenal (the thalweg) se termine dans la Mer Glaciale hors de l'embouchure du Jakobsälv", a definition which might, but does not necessarily, support the mixed solution suggested by de Magelhães about 1930;

Free Territory of Trieste-Yugoslavia, Italian Peace Treaty of Paris of 10 February 1947 (*U.N.T.S.*, vol. 49, p. 3), Article 22 (iv): "Thence the line follows the main improved channel of the (river) Quieto to its mouth, passing through Porto del Quieto to the high seas by following a line placed equidistant from the coastlines of the Free Territory of Trieste and Yugoslavia" (see the map in Annex I to the treaty);

Free Territory of Trieste-Italy, same treaty, Article 4 (ii and iii): "The line then extends in a southerly direction to a point in the Gulf of Panzano, equidistant from Punta Sdobba at the mouth of the Isonzo (Soca) river and Castello Vecchio at Duino... The line then reaches the high seas by following a line placed equidistant from the coastlines of Italy and the Free Territory of Trieste" (see the same map).

Because of the presence of large numbers of islands in front of the outlet of the rivers concerned into the adjacent bay-like maritime areas, the *tracé*'s of the State frontiers are very complicated both between Sweden and Finland in the so-called Head of Bottenviken (Torneå) (boundary treaty of 20 November 1810, Martens, N.R., I, 313 = IV, 33, Article 1), and between Finland and the Soviet Union in the Virolahti area (Article 2 of their treaty of 14 October 1920, *ibid.*, N.R.G.³, XII, 37, modified by their subsequent Peace Treaty of 12 March 1940, *ibid.*, N.R.G.³, XXXVIII, 323), confirmed on this point by the Finnish Peace Treaty of Paris of 10 February 1947 (*U.N.T.S.*, vol. 48, p. 203), and the treaty of 20 May 1965 (*U.N.T.S.*, vol. 566, p. 31).

On the delimitation between the adjacent and opposite territorial

18. On the maritime frontier between Spain on the one hand, and France and Portugal, on the other, comp. the data contained in the *Colección de los Tratados, convenios y documentos internacionales celebrados por nuestros gobiernos con los estados extranjeros desde el reinado de Doña Isabel II hasta nuestros días*, by the Marqués DE OLIVART (Madrid, 1890-1911).

belts of Finland and the Soviet Union in the Gulf of Finland for the purpose of the maintenance of order see their treaty of 28 July 1923 (Martens, N.R.G.³, XX, 237) and for customs purposes that of 13 April 1929 (*ibid.*, XXVII, 442).

Special difficulties have arisen with regard to the southern section of the Spanish-Portuguese boundary in the mouth of the Río Guadiana. After the frontier, by Article 4 of an Arrangement of 2 October 1885 (*ibid.*, N.R.G.², XIV, 77), had been delimited summarily, namely by a line drawn from the extremity of the axis of the sandbar in the river seaward along the meridian of that point,[19] the commissioners charged with the further demarcation appeared unable to agree on the exact location of the critical point; the deadlock was removed in Article 4, *sub a* of Appendix VI to the subsequent treaty of 27 March 1893 (*ibid.*, XXII, 414 *et seq.*, at p. 432) by a compromise settlement by which the respective maritime zones were "para el efecto de este reglamento" demarcated along a median line between the two different meridians, indicated by the Spanish and Portuguese commissioners respectively.

The boundary line between the territorial seas of Spain and France beyond the "closing line" of the Bay of Higuera follows the meridian running from the middle of that line northward. Comp. on that bay Chapter VI, section 4, *infra* p. 596.

(*b*) As to the future, it remains to be seen how the provisions of Convention I of 1958 will be applied in actual practice. There is the threat of a special complication arising as a consequence of the fact that there is not an exact parallel between the delimitation rules of Convention I regarding the division of the territorial sea and those of Convention IV concerning that of the continental shelf (comp. *infra* section 5, p. 84), so that the second boundary line, which only begins where the territorial sea ends, may not be a simple prolongation seaward of the former and the two lines may in actual fact follow different directions. There would, indeed, seem to be no legal substance in the suggestion of the German delegation at the Conference of 1958 after the voting on Article 6 of Convention IV (*Comptes rendus analytiques*, A/Conf. 13/42, p. 117, 2nd column) that where for special reasons the boundary line in the territorial sea is fixed in deviation from the general rule, the boundary line across the continental shelf must necessarily lie in the prolongation of the other. The two boundary lines, as for that matter the two Conventions, are in principle independent one of the other, and even if they were not, it

19. "Para el efecto de este convenio la separación de las aguas territoriales en las zonas marítimas adyacentes de los dos Países será demarcada por líneas tiradas desde la estremidad del eje de las barras de río Miño y Guadiana prolongadas hacia el mar y coincidiendo en el primer caso con el paralelo y en el segundo con el meridiano de esos puntos".

70

would not be obvious which of the two should be dependent of the other.

Boundary *tracé*'s between the territorial seas of conterminous States must be sharply distinguished from delimitations which occasionally occur between States with respect to parts of the high seas. Comp. on such delimitations, which have nothing to do with territorial sovereignty proper, although they sometimes tended to separate the respective zones of influence, intended to prepare the acquisition of new colonial possessions (comp. Chapter V, section 9, *infra* pp. 494 *et seq.*) Part IV-A of this publication.

E. *The territorial sea of archipelagos*

There remains the special question relative to the territorial sea of archipelagos. There are two Articles in Convention I of 1958 which would seem to have a direct bearing on this question, on the one hand Article 10 (2) providing, after a definition of an island in paragraph 1, that "The territorial sea of an island is measured in accordance with the provisions of these articles",[20] and on the other, Article 4 (1), sanctioning the admissibility of the drawing of straight baselines along a coast which is either sharply indented or surrounded by a fringe of islands. Normal treaty interpretation would lead to the conclusion that apart from the latter situation of coastal archipelagos and in the absence of any corresponding provision concerning outlying archipelagos, the legal status of such archipelagos is governed by the general rule enunciated in Article 10 (2). This would mean that (*a*) an uninterrupted baseline of the territorial sea along the outer islands of such outlying archipelagos can only be admitted where two or more neighbouring islands are situated at a distance *inter se* not greater than the double of the normal breadth of the territorial sea; that (*b*) the maritime area enclosed by the outer string of islands, in so far as that area does not consist of zones of territorial sea around individual islands, can only be recognized as internal waters if it can only be reached through interinsular passages equally not surpassing the double of the normal breadth of the territorial sea; and that (*c*) even in the case of the presence of such an internal sea inside the archipelago, the right of innocent passage through it must be acknowledged in analogy with the case of maritime straits.

There is only one argument which might be adduced to rebut these conclusions from the provisions of the Convention, *viz.*, a statement of the International Law Commission in its commentary *ad* Article 10 (8th session, *ad* Article 10, 1st sentence, *Yearbook I.L.C.* 1956 II, p. 270), that the proposed provision was not intended to settle the difficult

20. The International Law Commission had in Article 10 of its final draft of 1956 introduced a similar definition by the following, differently worded rule: "Every island has its own territorial sea".

question relating to archipelagos, obviously especially outlying archipelagos. Even if this expression of intention of the I.L.C. were sufficient to overrule the simple text of Article 10 (2) of the Convention as finally adopted, and ordinary rules of treaty construction, no other conclusion would be warranted than that the legal status of such outlying archipelagos and their enclosed maritime areas has remained under the sway of traditional customary law. This again would in my opinion mean that the substantive content of Article 10 (2) would continue to apply, *i.e.*, outlying archipelagos must be held to have remained subject to the traditional rule that every island has its own territorial sea, with the result that only in so far as those territorial sea areas overlap or just meet, can there be any question of a common littoral belt along them and, possibly, of an enclosed interior sea of internal water. For though it may be true that a few archipelagic States have put forward the claim that their land and enclosed maritime areas must be considered as one coherent area under their exclusive sovereign control, this claim has never been accepted by other States. This is, *e.g.*, the case of the contention, formulated in a Declaration of the Indonesian Government of 13 December 1957, circulated at the Conference of 1958, according to which the baseline of the territorial sea of Indonesia was to follow without interruption and regardless of the distance between them the outer islands of her archipelago, to the effect that all maritime waters enclosed by them would become internal waters (*Official Records*, vol. III, pp. 15 and 43/44). Its validity, therefore, was rightly disputed by a number of countries and must be denied as nothing more than an unwarranted unilateral assertion.

Comp. on this subject an article by M. Sørensen on "The territorial sea of archipelagos" in *N.T.I.R.* 1959 (VI), special issue (*Liber Amicorum J.P.A. François*), p. 315, with whose argumentation and conclusion I regret to be unable to concur.

An elaborate survey of the delimitation of the territorial waters of archipelagos by Jens Evensen, advocate at the Supreme Court of Norway, was submitted to the first Geneva Conference on the Law of the Sea as Preparatory Document No. 15 (A/Conf. 13/18).[20a] It summarized a number of studies by international bodies and views of international law publicists on the subject, and further offered details relative to State practice in this field concerning, separately, coastal and outlying (midocean) archipelagos.

The Institut de droit international did not seriously deal with the situation in archipelagos until 1927-1928 (session of Stockholm), when the following text was adopted (Article 5, paragraph 2):

> "Where archipelagos are concerned, the extent of the marginal sea shall be measured from the outermost islands or islets provided that the archipelago

[20a]. *U.N. Conference on the Law of the Sea, Official Records*, vol. I, p. 289.

is composed of islands and islets not further apart from each other than twice the breadth of the marginal sea and also provided that the islands and islets nearest to the coast of the mainland are not situated further out than twice the breadth of the marginal sea." (on that occasion proposed at three nautical miles).

Comp. on the treatment of this subject in the Institut: *Annuaire* vol. 11 (1889), pp. 136, 139 *et seq.*; vol. 33-I (1927), p. 81; vol. 34 (1928), p. 673.

During the preparation of the Hague Codification Conference of 1930 there was a great diversity of views, reflected mainly in three currents of opinion: (*a*) a single belt of territorial sea can only be drawn around archipelagos if the constituent islands are not further apart than a certain maximum; (*b*) archipelagos, both coastal and outlying, must be considered as single units, irrespective of the distance between the constituent islands; (*c*) the solution *sub* (*b*) can only be accepted where geographical peculiarities warrant it. Parallel with this difference of views ran the connected question whether the waters enclosed within the group should be regarded as internal waters or as marginal seas.

The compromise suggested by the Preparatory Commission in its Basis of Discussion No. 13 ran as follows:

"In the case of a group of islands which belong to a single State and at the circumference of the group are not separated from one another by more than twice the breadth of territorial waters,[20b] the belt of territorial waters shall be measured from the outermost islands of the group. Waters included within the group shall also be territorial waters.

The same rule shall apply as regards islands which lie at a distance from the mainland not greater than twice the breadth of territorial waters." (L. of N. Document C.74.M.39.1929.V, p. 51).

The discussions led to no definite result: the majority of the 2nd Sub-committee of the 2nd Committee of the Conference suggested a maximum distance of ten miles and did not express any opinion concerning the nature of the enclosed waters. No discussion took place in the plenary sessions of the Conference.

During the preparation of the Geneva Conference of 1958 by the International Law Commission successive and ever changing suggestions were made by the Special Rapporteur Professor François and the Commission itself, but the latter ended by stating that it was unable to overcome the difficulties involved, also in view of the complications caused by the different forms which the problem takes in different archipelagos. Neither did the Conference itself attempt to reach any definite solution.

Publicists on the subject are divided, but they show a certain tendency in favour of considering archipelagos as units, a solution with which I, for one, am unable to agree.

20[b]. In the terminology of those days "territorial waters" meant "territorial sea".

The legal situation of coastal archipelagos was in 1951 clarified or, perhaps more correctly, defined by a *sic volo hoc jubeo* in the *Anglo-Norwegian Fisheries* case by the Judgment of the International Court of Justice of 18 December 1951 (*I.C.J. Reports* 1951, p. 116; comp. my *The Jurisprudence of the World Court*, vol. II, pp. 100-116) concerning the *skjaergaard* of Norway, which held that the Norwegian system of drawing straight baselines along the outer points of the Norwegian coastal archipelago, as laid down in a Royal Decree of 12 July 1935, was not contrary to international law. After the generalization and elaboration of this pronouncement by the Conference on the Law of the Sea in 1958 in Article 4 of Convention I on the Territorial Sea, the same principle as was adopted in regard to Norway must now be held also to apply to such archipelagos as lie around the coasts of Ireland, Denmark, Sweden, Finland, Yugoslavia and Cuba.

The legal status of outlying (mid-ocean) archipelagos is much more doubtful. These can again be subdivided in two groups, the first forming together sovereign insular States, the second being insular dependencies of sovereign States.

Most prominent amongst the first group are the Philippines and Indonesia.

As appears from statements made by the Philippine Government, reproduced in the *Yearbook of the International Law Commission* 1956-II, pp. 69-70, they claim as national or inland waters, subject to the exclusive sovereignty of the Philippines, "all waters around, between and connecting different islands belonging to the Philippine Archipelago, irrespective of their width or dimension." This statement leaves a blank with regard to the Sulu Sea between the Philippines proper and North Borneo. For the rest, the Philippine Government considers all other water areas embraced within the lines described in the treaties of 10 December 1898 (Martens, N.R.G.², XXXII, 74), 7 November 1900 (*ibid.*, N.R.G.², XXXII, 82), 2 January 1930 (*ibid.*, N.R.G.³, XXVII, 58) and 6 July 1932 (*ibid.*, XXVII, 66), and drawn along certain degrees long. E. and lat.N., only as "maritime territorial waters for purposes of protection of its fishing rights, conservation of its fishery resources, enforcement of its revenue and anti-smuggling laws, defence and security, and protection of such interests as the Philippines may deem vital to its national welfare and security."

Analogous claims were advanced by Indonesia during the 1958 Conference on the Law of Sea, but they were immediately rejected by other powers, such as Great Britain.

The second group of outlying archipelagos comprises, *e.g.*, various islands under the sovereignty of Iceland lying far out at sea outside the straight baselines of her main territory (each with its own territorial sea); the Danish Farøer (considered in the Anglo-Danish agreement of 22

April 1955, *U.N.T.S.* vol. 213, p. 318, as a unit, delimited by a mixed system of straight baselines and arcs of circles); the Norwegian Spitzbergen or Svalbard archipelago (defined in the multilateral treaty of 4 February 1920, Martens, N.R.G.³, XIII, 473); the Ecuadorian Galápagos or Colón archipelago (treated as a unit in a Decree of 22 February 1951); and the Hawaiian, Fiji, Solomon and Cook's Islands groups (none of which is considered as a unit). Comp. for further details concerning these various archipelagos the above-mentioned study of Jens Evensen.

Section 4. THE AIR COLUMN

The problem of air sovereignty has for many centuries hardly played a part in international relations. When it was, exceptionally, mentioned, it was disposed of by an analogy to property under private law, said to extend *usque ad coelum*, a rather undefined distance, taking into account the developments of modern technology. Nor was there any serious discussion about a possible right of air transit until the eve of World War I, although a Belgian author, DE NENY, when dealing in the last part of the 18th century, in the French edition of his historical and political *Mémoires* of the Austrian Netherlands (Neuchâtel, 1784), with the postulated right of unhampered transit over the lower stretch of the River Scheldt on behalf of the, then Austrian, southern provinces of the Low Countries, supported this, not yet acknowledged, right of free fluvial transit with an appeal to a right of free air transit which was under the then existing technical possibilities still much more dubious. The problem of air sovereignty only came to the fore when imaginative minds began to fathom the tremendous importance of air traffic for future generations, *inter alios*, FAUCHILLE in his report to the Institut de droit international of 1909/1910. After a short theoretical disputation between three competing doctrines, one on the analogy of private law (sovereignty *usque ad coelum*), another on that of the high seas (freedom of the air), a third on that of the territorial sea (freedom of the air with the exception of a territorial belt of atmosphere), the evolution of positive international law immediately and without hesitance took the first of the three courses (sovereignty of the State over its air column). The formation of customary law has indeed seldom, though with the help of the outbreak of the first World War, taken place at such a quick tempo and with such an overwhelmingly convincing force as in respect of the maxim sanctioning the territorial sovereignty of the State over its air column. And when, for the first time, an international treaty was concluded on this subject—the Convention of Saint-Germain on Aerial Navigation of 13 October 1919 (Martens, N.R.G.³, XIII, 61), Article 1

75

thereof simply registered a principle, which could even be called an axiom of public international law, already sanctioned by customary international practice, *viz.*, the recognition that every State has complete and exclusive sovereignty in the air space above its metropolitan and colonial territory and its territorial waters. This sovereignty only suffers certain legal limitations upon its exercise for the benefit of innocent international air traffic in time of peace. Since the Convention of 1919 has after World War II been replaced by the Convention on International Civil Aviation of Chicago of 7 December 1944 (*U.N.T.S.*, vol. 15, p. 295), I will only deal here with the latter and, in the context of this section, only with those of its provisions which have a bearing upon the legal status of the air column. The Chicago Convention (which only applies between the Contracting States and does not pretend to codify the law of the air) indeed treats in its four Parts and 96 Articles of a great many subjects which do not belong here: the nationality, airworthiness, radio equipment etc. of aircraft, international standards with regard to air navigation, the organization of the I.C.A.O. (International Civil Aviation Organization), international air transport, etc.

What is pertinent to this section is, apart from the principle of complete and exclusive sovereignty over the airspace, laid down again in Article 1, the following:

(Article 3) No State aircraft (in military, customs or police services) shall fly over the territory of another State without authorization.

(Articles 5 and 6) As to civil aircraft a sharp distinction is made between non-scheduled flights and scheduled air services: whereas the former are, under certain conditions, in principle free over foreign territory both in transit non-stop across it and to stop for non-traffic purposes, the latter may not be operated over or into such territory except with special permission.

(Article 7) Air cabotage may be refused to foreign aircraft, and permission may in no case be granted or sought on a discriminatory basis.

(Article 8) Pilotless aircraft shall only be admitted in virtue of a special authorization and subject to such control as to obviate danger to civil aircraft.

Article 9 allows and regulates the establishment of prohibited areas for reasons of military necessity or public safety.

Further Articles (10 and following) deal with customs control, air regulations, the prevention of the spread of disease etc.

Other provisions will be mentioned elsewhere in their appropriate places.

One of the most important, still unresolved, problems concerning the air column is that of its height. It must be contemplated in the combined light of Article 1 of the Convention of Chicago of 1944 and of the impact of the triumphs of contemporary science, at that time still unforeseeable. The correct construction of the provision of Article 1 of the Chicago Convention and the outlook for future agreement on the height of the air column to be adopted as the upper limit of the earthly domain and the starting plane for the fascinating novel domain of space law are more conveniently reserved for discussion or speculation in Part IV-B of this publication on Space Law.

The lateral delimitation between adjoining air columns raises no problem. As already remarked earlier, the air column subject to State sovereignty shows to the eye of the imagination of the legal observer the stereometrical shape of a curious polyhedral spatial body, *viz.*, a truncated aerial cone whose "apex" lies in the centre of the earth, whose "height" is very small in comparison with the total height of the cone, whose very irregularly formed "section" is identical with the, slightly spherical, surface of that part of the earth which is bordered by the State's international frontiers, and whose consequently irregular and parallel spherical "base" hovers in the air at a still uncertain altitude. This part of the "territory" of a State shows the embarrassing feature of swinging round with the speed of the rotation of the earth, like the beam of light sent out by a lighthouse, so that an object which is sent up, rising in the national air column, may in the process penetrate through the latter's "conical surface" into the corresponding air column or cone of a neighbouring State,—an occurrence that increases in frequency and gravity as the object ascends further into the higher spheres of space.

Section 5. THE CONTINENTAL SHELF

Whereas the land territory, subsoil, territorial sea and air column, dealt with in the preceding sections 1-4, are undisputedly integral parts of the territory of a State and, therefore, fall entirely under its territorial sovereignty, this is not, strictly speaking, the case of the continental shelf to be discussed now. This submarine area is indeed situated in a juridical border zone between territory and stateless domain. I will deal first (under A) with its general legal regime and then (under B) with its boundaries.

A. *Legal regime*

When using the term "continental shelf", one must be aware of the fact that it denotes a concept which has two different meanings according to whether one employs it in its general geological or in its present artificial legal sense.

In the former, geological sense the continental shelf of a country, island or continent designates that part of their supporting submarine socle that extends to where its, broadly speaking horizontal, upper plateau slopes down over its edge into the continental abyss where the whole structure is embedded in the bottom of the sea. In this geological connotation the continental shelf begins at the coastline and ends at the edge where the plateau descends into the gulf of the ocean, no matter how far from the coast and at what exact depth below the surface of the sea.

In the latter, strictly technical, present legal sense the continental shelf is restricted to that part of the submarine plateau which extends from the outer limit of the territorial sea to the isobath of 200 metres, being the imaginary line that connects all the points on that plateau along the coast where the sea reaches a depth of 200 metres, or at the utmost to such a further distant, and essentially changeable, line which indicates the outside limits of the—present or future—exploitability of the submarine subsoil from the surface of the sea downwards by means of derricks or other comparable devices.

However, in this section I intend to begin by understanding under "continental shelf" something midway between the two technical concepts, which corresponds neither to the geological nor to the legal meaning of the term, namely, that part of the submarine plateau in its geological sense which stretches from the coastline or other baseline of the territorial sea to the above-mentioned isobath (or exceptional further line), *i.e.*, inclusive of the part thereof extending nearest to the coast underneath the territorial sea between its base line and its outside boundary. There is undoubtedly a certain terminological artificiality in refusing to extend the appellation of continental shelf (in the sense of the new law of nations) to cover that part of the submarine plateau which is situated under the territorial sea, and in reserving it for that part of it which departs seaward from the marginal belt. However, the Conference on the Law of the Sea of 1958 did so for a perfectly valid reason. The definition adopted by that Conference in Article 1 of Convention IV is indeed explained and justified by the consideration that the strip of the continental plateau situate underneath the territorial sea has a legal status which entirely differs from that stretching seaward beyond the littoral belt. The continental plateau is indeed astride on a juridical borderline, *viz.*, the outer boundary of the territorial sea. It is for this reason that the said Article 1 lays down that

> "For the purpose of these articles, the term "continental shelf" is used as referring *a.* to the seabed and subsoil of the submarine areas adjacent to the coast but outside the area of the territorial sea, to a depth of 200 metres or, beyond that limit, to where the depth of the superjacent waters admits of the exploitation of the natural resources of the said areas; *b.* to the seabed and subsoil of similar submarine areas adjacent to the coasts of islands".

Apart from this geographical aspect, the continental shelf constitutes yet another borderzone, related to the substantive contents of the legal regime to which it is subjected, namely, between full territorial sovereignty and a novel form of limited, so to speak "functional", sovereignty. I will enlarge a little on both these aspects.

(i) Little needs to be said about the difference in legal status between the two strips of the continental plateau, one landwards, the other seawards of the outer limit of the territorial sea. The former strip falls entirely and completely under the normal territorial sovereignty of the country concerned. The coastal State is, consequently, subject to no restriction of any kind on the exercise of its sovereignty, either by subterranean activity from the land by tunnelling or operational drilling, or by means of derricks and other devices from the surface of the coastal belt. The latter strip, on the contrary, falls under a very special and restrictive legal regime elaborated in great detail in Geneva.

(ii) This legal regime is so strictly defined and conditioned that it is questionable if it can still be qualified as territorial sovereignty proper. The answer must be that it only gives the coastal State a limited or quasi-sovereignty, confined in contents to such sovereign rights as are, in the terms of Article 2 of the Convention, necessary "for the purpose of exploring (the continental shelf) and exploiting its natural resources". In all other respects the seaward stretch of continental shelf falls outside the authority of the coastal State and is in principle in the same legal position as the bed of the high seas outside the shelf area, or, as Article 3 expresses it:

"The rights of the coastal State over the continental shelf do not affect the legal status of the superjacent waters as high seas, or that of the airspace above those waters".

It must, therefore, in my opinion, be held in other respects to have remained either *territorium nullius*, or *res communis omnium*, according to which of these two doctrinal constructions one is inclined to apply to the legal status of the seabed and subsoil of the open sea. I shall have to return to this subject in Part IV-A of this publication dealing, *inter alia*, with the high seas.

Since the sovereign rights allotted to the coastal State are limited to those required specifically for the exploration of the continental shelf and the exploitation of its natural resources, it is certainly not from *that* aggregate of rights that such a State can derive any authority to display in the waters which cover the continental shelf—the "superjacent" or "epicontinental" waters—or on that shelf itself *other* official activities as if it were the territorial sovereign. I am thinking in this context of the erection by the coastal State itself on its continental shelf of a fortress, a radio station, a weather station, or an aeroport, or, inversely, of hindering other States from proceeding to similar constructions there. Should such other activities be allowed there at all, then other considerations would have to be invoked in support, such as: the right to occupy *territorium nullius*

79

(which would then equally apply to third States), or a preferential position of the coastal State, based on such grounds as propinquity, the need for protection of vital national interests, or an analogy with the contiguous zone in the surface area. The most appropriate place, systematically, to deal with this important problem seems to me to be in a paragraph on the legal status of the superjacent or epicontinental waters in Part IV-A of this publication concerning the High Seas.

It follows from the above considerations that, strictly speaking, the outer zone of the continental shelf does not constitute a part of the State's territory proper, but an exceptional submarine region over which the coastal State is entitled to exercise some very important exclusive sovereign rights. And these rights, according to Article 2, para. 3, appertain to the coastal State without any occupational or other official activity on its side, they accrue to it automatically *ipso jure*:

> "The rights of the coastal State over the continental shelf do not depend on occupation, effective or notional, or on any express proclamation".

The coastal State cannot even disclaim them, although the Convention empowers it in Article 2, para. 2, to permit their exercise by another State by granting a concession for their exploitation:

> "The rights referred to in paragraph 1 of this article are exclusive in the sense that if the coastal State does not explore the continental shelf or exploit its natural resources, no one may undertake these activities, or make a claim to the continental shelf, without the express consent of the coastal State".

The legal situation becomes, however, extremely complicated by the further fact that whereas the sovereign rights of the coastal State, though of a limited *functional* nature, extend to the entire body of the submarine zone, if exercised from the surface of the superjacent waters, that same State is entirely free to extend its *real* territorial sovereignty—in so far as this is imaginable and technically possible—over the interior of that body by the traditional method of effective occupation, if exercised by the digging of tunnels or by operational drilling into the zone from the land, but in that case exclusively over the tunnels which it actually digs and over the bore-holes which it actually drills.

Since I have discussed the results of the (first) Conference on the Law of the Sea of 1958 as a whole in a separate paper, which I prefer not to split up into its component parts, I may be allowed to refer here further to Chapter 4 of that paper, which will be inserted as an Excursus in Part IV-A of this publication on the High Seas, and for the rest to digress a little below on certain basic questions relative to the birth of the new international law concerning the continental shelf.

The importance of the continental shelf—an area long familiar to geologists—for international law has only relatively recently dawned upon statesmen and students of the law of nations. As the regulation of this subject matter has developed during the preparation and discussions of the Geneva Conference of 1958, it shows the confluence of two very dissimilar subjects into one bed. What is now in international law terms the continental shelf is a combination of two entirely different areas of exploitation: the seabed and its subsoil.

The seabed is well known from of old as an exploitation area for the pearl and coral gathering industry and for sedentary fisheries. The subsoil of the seabed only acquired practical importance much later, first from an expansion of the coal mining industry from the land seaward under the territorial sea and beyond, then from similar drilling operations in the subsoil in search of oil or natural gas, directed from the mainland, and eventually from the novel technical devices to extract oil or gas from submarine areas by means of derricks erected on the bottom of the sea, or from floating platforms or ships.

As far as the exploitation of the *seabed* for the fishing of pearls, corals and other sedentary products of the sea is concerned, it was always somewhat controversial whether a State was entitled to the exclusive exploitation of such fisheries outside its territorial sea by diving for pearls (around Ceylon), the collecting of corals or the fishing of sedentary species on other coasts. It was fairly generally held that such fishing operations were indeed reserved for the coastal State and its subjects, at least in so far as they were sanctioned by ancient practice and custom.

As far as the exploitation of the *subsoil* for the mining of coal, oil or natural gas is concerned, there was never any serious opposition from the point of view of international law against the extension of coal mining operations from the mainland under the adjacent submarine areas, whether within or beyond the outer limit of the territorial sea, as no infringement of the principle of the freedom of the sea was involved. There was, however, at first some hesitation from the legal angle when the technique of drilling from derricks erected on the seabed or from floating platforms outside the coastal belt was invented and practised: was this device, or was it not, an encroachment upon the freedom of the sea, and was the coastal State really entitled to the exclusive exploitation of such submarine areas? States whose oil companies had pioneered in this field soon realized that other States did not in fact object and were prepared to follow the example set by the pioneers. This tacit acceptance of the practice thus initiated was in the early years of development evidenced by two series of facts: (*a*) the conclusion by adjoining States of a convention for the mutual delimitation of their submarine shelf areas—comp. on this boundary aspect below, under B—and (*b*) an increasing number of unilateral proclamations or laws extending State sovereignty over the adjacent continental shelf, which remained generally unopposed.

This development is a striking example of a rapid growth of international customary law, although it was not yet quite clear from the outset, as a matter of doctrinal construction, whether the juridical acts concerned—treaty delimitations and unilateral proclamations—testified to the legal conviction that adjoining portions of the submarine subsoil could lawfully be brought under the territorial sovereignty of the coastal State(s) concerned by the traditional constitutive method of occupation of *terra nullius*, or whether they proceeded, rather, from the theory that any State has *ipso jure* territorial sovereignty over its adjacent submarine shelf and, consequently, were of a merely declaratory nature.

The juridical situation on the eve of the Conference of 1958 can accordingly be described as follows.

As to the exploitation of the *seabed* adjacent to the coast, even beyond the outer limit of the territorial sea, for the purpose of the fishing of pearls, corals, and other sedentary species, traditional historical claims were internationally recognized. No clear distinction was yet made between two very different types of "sedentary fisheries", namely, those sedentary on account of the sedentary nature of the objects of the catch, and those sedentary owing to the sedentary nature of the devices used for the catching of non-sedentary species (for example on the shallow coast of Tunisia).

As to the exploitation of the *subsoil*, even beyond the outer limit of the territorial sea, it had already been tacitly admitted that the coastal State was entitled to acquire sovereignty over those portions of that area which it occupied in the traditional sense of that term by allowing its subjects to explore and exploit them, or by itself proceeding to such exploration and exploitation from the adjoining mainland. Apart from that, a rapidly developing custom had sanctioned, as a matter of principle, the admissibility of claims of coastal States to exclusive sovereign rights over the adjacent submarine subsoil area for the purpose of its exploitation from the surface of the sea even outside the coastal belt, without, however, any definite customary rules having matured with regard to the many practical questions of detail to which the adoption of the broad principle gave rise.

The International Law Commission, which had to cope with this general situation when preparing its codificatory draft, chose, unhappily to my mind, to amalgamate the two matters for regulation—seabed and subsoil—, though so widely different in character, and moreover did not deal in its draft with submarine activities in the subsoil, conducted from the land seaward, so that on that point a vacuum remained.

Attempts have sometimes been made to found the claim to sovereignty over the continental shelf on geological grounds: thus, it has been argued that the sovereignty of the coastal State over it must be recognized because the shelf has originated not in the accretion of land from outside areas, but in the grinding-down of coastal areas, once integral parts of the national territory. Such arguments are, however, in my opinion, mere *Spielereien*. They are similar to the theory advanced by Canadians to the effect that Canada has an exclusive right to the salmon in maritime areas far outside her territorial sea because they will swim there from Canadian rivers to mature and then later return to spawn, so that they must be held to be as it were Canadian nationals abroad. Or they recall that other theory, advanced by Peru, to the effect that she has a natural right to the exclusive catch of fish also far distant from her coastline because these move and feed on plankton in the Humboldt current, which in part runs through her territorial sea but for large stretches of its course turns off from the coast into the high seas, implying the proposition that that current may, with its piscifauna, by construction be annexed to the national territory, also where it deviates far from the coast.

Looking for the most readily acceptable construction of the claim to sovereign rights over the continental shelf, one can take different theoretical roads. (*a*) One can invoke the doctrine of effective occupation: the shelf may be considered as *res nullius* and, therefore, susceptible of acquisition by the traditional legal means. (*b*) One can refer to the vicinity of that *res nullius* to the land mass of the State and allow the latter to annex it preferentially by a proclamation, in order to exclude the possibility of other States taking possession. (*c*) One can allege that same closeness of the shelf to the national territory to defend the position that it naturally and *ipso jure* belongs to the land mass on the strength of the principle of contiguity without any special action of the coastal State being required. Anyone who is a protagonist of the idea that the natural resources of the continental shelf should accrue to the benefit of the entire community of States, land-locked States included, may try to support their demand by (*d*) the argument that the shelf forms part of the high seas and is, therefore, by its nature as either *res publica* or *res communis omnium*, incapable of acquisition by any individual State.

There is little sense in enquiring into the validity of the doctrinal foundation of these different theories now that the Geneva Conference of 1958 has unanimously adopted the theory under (*c*). As mentioned above, Article 2, paragraph 3, of Convention IV indeed lays down that "the rights of the coastal State over the continental shelf do not depend on occupation, effective or notional, or on any express proclamation".

The natural appurtenance of the continental shelf to the adjacent coastal State, which cannot even waive it, had in fact by a stupendously quick development achieved the standing of a customary principle of international law even prior to its formal recognition as such in Convention IV of 1958, irrespective of whichever "theory" the acting States may at the time have espoused as the legal basis of their action or claim. The absence of diplomatic protests against the successive unilateral proceedings in this field has witnessed to the fairly general repudiation of the "universalistic" doctrine under (d). The principle of the freedom of the sea has, in fact, hardly anything to do with the status of the seabed or its subsoil, save for the necessity of a basic international agreement to obviate possible obstacles which its exploration or exploitation may cause in different areas to international navigation. It would therefore be overstressing the tenor of that principle to invoke it against the legality of appropriation by individual States of the continental shelf. Yet, the "universalistic" theory has reappeared in legal doctrine and in international discussions in view of the growing probability that even the exploration and exploitation of the subsoil of the open sea outside the shelf areas will at some time in the near future become technically and possibly economically feasible. See on this subject again Part IV-A of this publication dealing, *inter alia*, with the high seas.

B. *Frontiers*

Just as in respect of the territorial sea, two boundaries of the continental shelf are at issue: (i) that towards the bed and subsoil of the high seas and (ii) that between adjoining shelf areas, either lateral or opposite.

As to (i), the unfortunate insertion in Article 1 of Convention IV of 1958 (*U.N.T.S.*, vol. 499, p. 311) of the additional vague criterion of exploitability even beyond the isobath of 200 metres is causing increasing uncertainty with regard to the permissible outer limit of the continental shelf seaward. Not only has this additional criterion made it easy for coastal States, parallel with their technical development, to claim a continually widening extent of their shelf across the edge of the continental plateau proper downwards along the continental slope to constantly increasing depths and up to an indefinite distance from their coast, but it has also as a consequence that it needs only one highly developed and successful national oil or gas mining industry to drag all the continental shelf areas throughout the world with it in an automatic geographical expansion because the criterion of exploitability can hardly be construed as subjective, but must be taken as objective. This entirely undefined elastic formula threatens moreover in the event to efface the borderline, which was clearly contemplated by Convention IV, between the continental shelf and the bottom of the high seas.

As to (ii), the lateral delimitation of adjoining continental shelf areas, the rapid development of a universal rule has been preceded, as is often the case in international law, by incidental bilateral conventions, entered into by coastal States which realized the necessity of a demarcation rule.

Venezuela and Great Britain (for Trinidad) would seem to have been the first States to recognize the need for partition of a common continental shelf, namely, in the gulf of Pariá. As a result they agreed upon a submarine boundary, following a straight line running from the western spit of land bordering the Dragon's Mouth, a strait of access in the north, to the eastern tongue bordering the Serpent's Mouth, another strait of access in the south: comp. their Treaty of Caracas of 26 February 1942 (*L.N.T.S.*, vol. 205, p. 121). This submarine boundary, however, left the general status of the Gulf untouched.

Another of the rare early examples of delimitation was that between Bahrein and Saudi Arabia of 22 February 1958 concerning the Persian Gulf (translation in *I.C.L.Q.* 1958 (VII), pp. 519-521).

In this field also, the Conference of 1958 succeeded in laying down a general rule, formulated as follows in Article 6 of Convention No. IV:

> "1. Where the same continental shelf is adjacent to the territories of two or more States whose coasts are opposite each other, the boundary of the continental shelf appertaining to such States shall be determined by agreement between them. In the absence of agreement, and unless another boundary line is justified by special circumstances, the boundary is the median line, every point of which is equidistant from the nearest points of the baselines from which the breadth of the territorial sea of each State is measured.
> 2. Where the same continental shelf is adjacent to the territory of two adjacent States, the boundary of the continental shelf shall be determined by agreement between them. In the absence of agreement, and unless another boundary line is justified by special circumstances, the boundary shall be determined by application of the principle of equidistance from the nearest points of the baselines from which the breadth of the territorial sea of each State is measured."

This provision, which relates exclusively to exploration and exploitation from the surface of the sea, since an amendment to extend its operation also to the case of tunnelling or operational drilling from the land was rejected, differs in certain respects from that adopted for the delimitation of adjoining or opposite stretches of territorial sea, quoted above, in section 3, p. 66. As I have dealt with this particular point in my separate paper on the 1958 Conference, I may be permitted to merely refer to it here (Part IV-A of this publication).

Very shortly after the adoption of Convention IV new delimitations of adjoining continental shelves have already taken place, either by unilateral proclamation, or by treaty.[21] Comp., e.g., the following series of instruments to that effect.

One of the oldest delimitations after the 1958 Conference is that be-

21. See for many details and texts of recent shelf delimitations *I.C.J. Pleadings, North Sea Continental Shelf*, 1968, vol. I and the FAO Fisheries Technical Paper No. 79 (Rome, December 1968) on the *Limits and Status of the territorial sea, exclusive fishing zones, fishery conservation zones and the continental shelf.*

tween British North Borneo (now Sabah) and Sarawak, and between Sarawak and the Sultanate of Brunei: Orders in Council issued in virtue of the *Colonial Boundaries Act, 1895* (58 & 59 Vict. c. 34), on 11 September 1958 (*Stat. Instr.* 1958, Nos. 1517 and 1518). These delimitations followed upon two other Orders in Council, *viz.*, the *Sarawak (Alteration of Boundaries) O.i.C. 1954* of 24 June of that year (*Stat. Instr.* 1954, No. 839) extending the boundaries of that Colony "to include the area of the continental shelf being the seabed and its subsoil which lies beneath the high seas contiguous to the territorial waters of Sarawak", and a parallel Order of the same date (*ibid.*, No. 838) concerning North Borneo.

A further series of shelf delimitations has been agreed on in the North Sea area between the States bordering on that sea: Great Britain, the Netherlands, the German Federal Republic, Denmark and Norway. See the treaties between

Great Britain and Norway, 10 March 1965 (*U.N.T.S.*, vol. 551, p. 213);

Great Britain and the Netherlands, 6 October 1965 (*U.N.T.S.*, vol. 595, p. 113);

Great Britain and Denmark, 3 March 1966 (*U.N.T.S.*, vol. 592, p. 207);

Denmark and Norway, 8 December 1965 (*Z.a.ö.R.V.* 1966 (26), p. 775);

the Netherlands and Denmark, 31 March 1966 (*Z.a.ö.R.V.* 1966 (26), p. 778). The latter treaty was only concluded after prolonged negotiations between the German Federal Republic and its neighbours Denmark and the Netherlands had failed to reach more than a partial result. The Netherlands-West German treaty of 1 December 1964 (*U.N.T.S.*, vol. 550, p. 123), which had already been preceded by another treaty of 14 May 1962 (*U.N.T.S.*, vol. 509, p. 124) for the determination of a gas exploitation boundary in the estuary of the river Ems from Emden to the outer boundary of the respective territorial seas, had indeed limited the demarcation seaward of the adjacent continental shelf sections from that outer boundary up to a point situated on the degree of 54^0 lat.N., leaving the further boundary *tracé* in suspense. Denmark and the Federal Republic had followed that example by extending their shelf delimitation to a distance of only twenty-five miles seaward, see their treaty of 9 June 1965 (*U.N.T.S.*, vol. 570, p. 91).

Of these North Sea shelf delimitations those between Great Britain, on the one hand, and Norway, Denmark and the Netherlands, on the other, were clearly "median", "opposite" or "frontal", whereas the others (Norway-Denmark, Denmark-West Germany and West Germany-the Netherlands) were "lateral". It was only owing to the special concave configuration of Germany's sea front that a "lateral" boundary between the Netherlands and Denmark, though not being adjacent conterminous States, became nevertheless possible at a considerable distance from the coast. As the International Court rightly remarked in § 4 of its Judgment of 20 February 1969, summarized below, it would have been theoretically possible to draw "median" lines also between West Germany and Norway and between the Netherlands and Norway (with differing delimitation results), but this method would have been artificial and has not been applied in actual fact. Neither has a ("median") delimitation taken place between Great Britain and the German Federal Republic (which would in itself have been quite natural) just because the concave configuration of the German sea coast prevented West Germany's portion of the continental shelf, as normally determined by the ("lateral") equidistance principle, from even reaching the median line, drawn between Great Britain on the west side and her neighbours on the east side of the North Sea.

As Judge Ammoun in his individual opinion (*I.C.J. Reports* 1969, pp. 152-153) rightly states, this median line would not even be reached if the equidistance principle were applied not with the actual coast line of the German Federal Republic as the *basis a qua*, but from a straight line drawn across the *Deutsche Bucht* as a "maritime façade" (coastal front) connecting the outer protruding points of that coast line, the island of Borkum and the northern point of the island of Sylt.

The only disputes which thus remained with regard to the seabed and subsoil of the North Sea, namely, between Germany, on the one hand, and Denmark and the Netherlands, on the other, were after fruitless negotiations submitted in 1968 to the International Court of Justice by a Special Agreement which was drafted in such a way that it left many questions open. Its essential clause ran indeed as follows:

> "1) The International Court of Justice is requested to decide the following question:
> What principles and rules of international law are applicable to the delimitation as between the Parties of the areas of the continental shelf in the North Sea which appertain to each of them beyond the partial boundary determined by the above mentioned Convention of 1 December 1964 (respectively 9 June 1965)?"

This wording of the *compromis* is explained by the fact that Germany had not ratified Convention IV and had refused to accept as against herself the principle of equidistance sanctioned by its Article 6.

The Parties further undertook to subsequently delimit the continental shelf between their countries by means of an agreement concluded in conformity with the decision asked from the Court.

The International Court has just pronounced its Judgment on 20 February 1969 (*I.C.J. Reports* 1969, p. 3).

At the time of writing I am unable to do more than give a general exposition of the Judgment and its reasons, and of the main features of the individual and dissenting opinions. The whole of this new volume in the series of pronouncements of the Court (about 250 pages) is very interesting and deserves a much closer analysis than is possible here, the more so because this case lay outside the political battlefield and the Judgment is accordingly not tainted by extra-juridical considerations of that nature.

It was adopted as to its operative part by 11 votes to 6. Five Judges of the majority (marked below with an asterisk) felt compelled to make shorter or longer reservations to specific paragraphs or to add observations which they considered worth-while to develop. The majority consisted of the Judges President Bustamante y Rivero*, Fitzmaurice, Jessup*, Zafrulla Khan*, Padilla Nervo*, Forster, Gros, Ammoun*, Petrén, Onyeama and Mosler (Judge *ad hoc* for the German Federal Republic). The dissenting minority was formed by the Judges Vice-President Koretskiï, Tanaka, Morelli, Lachs, Bengzon and Sørensen (Judge *ad hoc* for Denmark and the Netherlands jointly).

In the framework of this section 5, I will begin by simply reproducing the operative part of the Judgment (at pages 53-54).[22]

THE COURT,

by eleven votes to six,

finds that, in each case,

(A) the use of the equidistance method of delimitation not being obligatory as between the Parties; and

(B) there being no other single method of delimitation the use of which is in all circumstances obligatory;

(C) the principles and rules of international law applicable to the delimitation as between the Parties of the areas of the continental shelf in the North Sea which appertain to each of them beyond the partial boundary determined by the agreements of 1 December 1964 and 9 June 1965, respectively, are as follows:

(1) delimitation is to be effected by agreement in accordance with equitable principles, and taking account of all the relevant circumstances, in such a way as to leave as much as possible to each Party all those parts of the continental shelf that constitute a natural prolongation of its land territory into and under the sea, without encroachment on the natural prolongation of the land territory of the other;

(2) if, in the application of the preceding sub-paragraph, the delimitation leaves to the Parties areas that overlap, these are to be divided between them in agreed proportions or, failing agreement, equally,

---

22. The English text is authoritative. The French text does not exactly correspond with it. Whereas the words "not being" and "there being" *sub* A and B and their junction by "and" make these two paragraphs an introductory legal statement to the principal dictum *sub* C and its appendix *sub* D, the French text presents A-D as four independent dicta, all in the indicative. I do not see the justification for such unnecessary discrepancies.

unless they decide on a régime of joint jurisdiction, user, or exploitation for the zones of overlap or any part of them;

(D) in the course of the negotiations, the factors to be taken into account are to include:

(1) the general configuration of the coasts of the Parties, as well as the presence of any special or unusual features;

(2) so far as known or readily ascertainable, the physical and geological structure, and natural resources, of the continental shelf areas involved;

(3) the element of a reasonable degree of proportionality, which a delimitation carried out in accordance with equitable principles ought to bring about between the extent of the continental shelf areas appertaining to the coastal State and the length of its coast measured in the general direction of the coastline, account being taken for this purpose of the effects, actual or prospective, of any other continental shelf delimitations between adjacent States in the same region.

From this *dictum* it follows that the reasoning of the Court would certainly have developed along different lines if it had held the German Federal Republic bound by Convention IV, especially by the delimitation principles embodied in its Article 6, and that it might then, perhaps, have reached dissimilar conclusions.

The reasons why the Court held that the use of the equidistance method of delimitation is not obligatory as between the parties to this case were fourfold: (a) although the Federal Republic has signed the Convention No. IV—and without availing herself of the opportunity, opened to her by Article 12, of making a reservation to Article 6—, she has not ratified it and is consequently not bound by its content as a Convention; (b) her conduct, public statements and proclamations after the signature have not created a situation of estoppel precluding her from denying the applicability of the conventional régime; (c) neither is she bound by Article 6 as constituting the embodiment in 1958 of a binding rule of customary law; (d) nor is there sufficient evidence that the legal development since 1958 has transformed the conventional provision into a universally binding rule.

Even before reaching the above conclusions the Court had already rejected, as a matter of principle, the contentions of the German Federal Republic that (§ 15) "the correct rule to be applied, at any rate in such circumstances as those of the North Sea, is one according to which each of the States concerned should have a "just and equitable share" of the available continental shelf, in proportion to the length of its coastline or sea-frontage", and "is entitled to a continental shelf area extending up to a central point situated on the median line of the whole seabed (in effect a sector), or at least extending to the median line at some point or other"; as a means of giving effect to these ideas "the Federal Republic proposed the method of the "coastal front" or façade, constituted by a straight baseline joining the two ends of her inward curving or recessed coast, upon which the necessary geometrical constructions would be erected". The Court rejected these contentions in the particular form they had taken, on the grounds that its task in the proceedings related essentially to the delimitation of the areas concerned, being a process which involves establishing the boundaries of areas already, in principle, appertaining to the coastal States, and not to their apportionment *de novo* by the awarding of a just and equitable share of an as yet undelimited area considered as an integral, still less an undivided whole. The German doctrine of "a just and equitable share" of the whole continental shelf area of the North Sea was held to be "wholly at variance with what the Court entertains no doubt is the most fundamental of all the rules of law relating to the continental shelf, enshrined in Article 2 of the 1958 Geneva Convention, though quite independent of it,— namely that the rights of the coastal State in respect of the area of the continental shelf that constitutes a natural prolongation of its land territory into and under the sea exist *ipso facto* and *ab initio*, by virtue of its sovereignty over the land, and as an extension of it in an exercise of sovereign rights for the purpose of exploring the seabed and exploiting its natural resources",—in short an inherent right.

What is not inherent, however, is the method of delimiting, laid down in Article 6 of the Convention, by means of drawing an equidistance line. This method may be on the whole acceptable and recommend itself because it can be easily applied by any cartographer, but its application can in unusual geographical conditions of the coast result in distinctly inequitable *tracés*. The genesis of Article 6 proves that adoption of the equidistance method has never been conceived as a logical necessity: it was one of various possible solutions and an eminently practical one, but it was made subordinate to negotiations for the conclusion of a direct inter-State agreement, which is primarily recommendable, and further to the existence of special circumstances which may in special cases tell in favour of more equitable *tracés* of the lateral shelf boundary.

It was on the basis of the arguments summarized above that the Court finished by formulating its findings under C and D of the operative part of its Judgment. The parties are obliged to reopen negotiations with the sincere intention to reach an agreement in accordance with "equitable principles", and in the case of the possible overlapping of parts of the continental shelf that constitute a natural prolongation of their respective land territory into and under the sea, either to divide them in agreed proportions or, failing agreement, equally, or to decide on a régime of joint jurisdiction, user, or exploitation. The factors to be taken into account in the negotiations are: the general configuration of the coasts and possible special or unusual geographical features; the physical and geological structure and natural resources of the areas, as far as known or readily ascertainable; and a reasonable degree of proportionality between the shelf areas to be allotted and the length of the coasts in question measured in the general direction of the coastline (maritime frontage).

One of the specific delimitation problems at issue of course relates to the presence of single submarine geological structures which extend across a demarcation line. As the Judgment points out, that problem has already been resolved in a number of conventions, both in the North Sea area and in the Persian Gulf, by agreements for joint exploitation and joint profit sharing.

As to the North Sea mention is made of the agreements of 10 March 1965 between the United Kingdom and Norway and of 6 October 1965 between the United Kingdom and the Netherlands, and also of the corresponding German-Netherlands agreement of 14 May 1962 concerning a joint plan for exploiting the natural resources underlying the Ems estuary.

In the Persian Gulf area the solution has been sought in different directions. Whereas Saudi Arabia and Bahrein had already on the eve of the first Geneva Conference, *viz.*, on 22 February 1958 (*I.C.L.Q.* 1958 (VII), pp. 519-521) delimited their respective shelf zones in accordance with the principle of equidistance, Saudi Arabia, on the contrary, reached agreements with two other neighbour States for shared exploitation and shared profits of the area concerned. This was quite natural in the case of the so-called Neutral Zone between herself and Kuwait extending into the Gulf: treaty of 7 July 1965 (*A.J.I.L.* 1966 (60), p. 744). But it was recently also applied in her treaty with Iran. The latter also refrained from dividing the disputed offshore area in the Gulf by a median line or any other geometrical demarcation and plumped for the economic rather than geographic method of dividing all the recoverable oil contained in the pertinent geological structure into two equal parts. Another delimitation, between Iran and Kuwait, was agreed upon on 13 January 1968 (*R.G.D.I.P.*, 1969 (73), p. 806).

In the Adriatic Italy and Yugoslavia have come to an agreement in a convention of 8 January 1968, dividing it over its whole breadth even where no continental shelf exists (*I.L.M.* 1968 (7), pp. 547-553).

The dissenting Judges attached greater importance to the equidistance rule than did the majority and considered it to be a binding rule, either because its acceptance in 1958 and its subsequent application in a large number of cases had created an *opinio juris*, the more so because the same principle was adopted with respect to the territorial sea and the contiguous zone (Articles 12 and 24 of Convention I) and to the fish conservation zones (Article 7 of Convention III), or because the conduct of the German Federal Republic between 1958 and the proceedings had precluded her from further denying its validity, or because it is an inherent necessary rule without which the lateral delimitation of the shelf areas would be left hanging in the air, contrary to the basic idea of the shelf being an automatic natural prolongation of the land territory into and under the sea. The dissenting view of Judge Morelli is curious: in his opinion the equidistance rule is basic and inherent to such an extent that he even construes Article 6 as a derogation by convention of a pre-existing rule according to which the equidistance principle should be applied, not from the baseline from which the breadth of the territorial sea is measured, but from its outer boundary.

As I have already mentioned in Part II of this publication, p. 284 and note 146, a number of member states of the United States have after World War II become involved in judicial proceedings with the Federal Government. The latter indeed denied the right of six southern coastal states to exploit oil and other national resources of offshore submerged lands, held itself entitled to full dominion and power over the lands, minerals and other natural resources underlying the Pacific Ocean seaward of the low-water mark on the coast of California and the waters of the Gulf of Mexico lying more than three geographical or nautical miles seaward from the coasts of Texas, Louisiana, Mississippi, Alabama and Florida, and required the six States to account to the United States for all sums of money derived by them in the past from natural resources in those submerged areas. The Supreme Court, in the exercise of its original jurisdiction, held in 1947 (*U.S. v. California*, 332 U.S. 19; *A.D.* 1947, Case No. 20, p. 56) that the United States possessed paramount rights in such lands underlying the Pacific Ocean seaward of the low-water mark on the coast, and in 1950 (*U.S. v. Louisiana*, 339 U.S. 699; 340 U.S. 899; *I.L.R.* 1950, Case No. 33, p. 131;—*U.S. v. Texas*, 339 U.S. 707; 340 U.S. 900; *I.L.R.* 1950, Case No. 32, p. 126) that it possessed similar rights with respect to submerged lands in the Gulf of Mexico. However, lengthy discussions ultimately resulted in federal legislation dealing with State and federal rights in these areas: the *Submerged Lands Act* of 22 May 1953 (67 Stat. 29, 43 U.S.C. §§ 1301-1315). This *Act* relinquished to the coastal States all rights of the United States in such lands within specified geographical limits and confirmed its own rights therein beyond those limits seaward. However, the *Act* gave rise to fresh proceedings before the Supreme Court because its wording lent itself to conflicting constructions. The geographical limits concerned were the state boundaries as they existed at the time a State became a member of the Union or as heretofore approved by Congress, not extending, however, seaward from the coast more than three geographical or nautical miles in the Pacific Ocean and the Atlantic, or more than nine such miles (equivalent with three marine leagues) in the Gulf of Mexico. It moreover confirmed to each coastal State a seaward boundary of three nautical miles, without questioning or prejudicing the existence of any boundary beyond that distance if this was so provided by the State's constitution or laws prior to or at the time it became a member of the Union, or if it had been heretofore approved by Congress. On the basis of these provisions the Supreme Court came to conclusions different for Louisiana, Mississippi and Alabama, on the one hand, and for Texas and Florida, on the other. None of the first three states was held to be entitled to any interest in submerged lands more than three geographical miles from their coast, but the two others were, namely, up to a distance of three marine leagues or nine geographical miles. See on the case of Louisiana, Mississippi, Alabama and Texas the judgment of 31 May 1960 (363 U.S. 1; *I.L.R.*, vol. 31, pp. 141-205) and on the case of Florida that reported in 363 U.S. 121 (*I.L.R.*, vol. 31, p. 205). Texas was held to be entitled to the wider three-marine-league (nine-nautical-mile) belt of land under the Gulf on the ground that Texas had as an independent State (1836-1845) established that boundary and that the United States had ratified it on its admission to the Union in 1845; in a supplemental decree of 3 March 1969 (394 U.S. 1) the Court held, however, that jurisdiction should be measured from the modern coast line and not from the coast line as it was in 1845 when Texas was admitted to the Union. And Florida was held to be entitled to a three-marine-league belt on the ground that Congress had "approved" this wider boundary by its approval of the Florida constitution of 1868. These considerations did not, in the opinion of the Court, apply to the States of Louisiana, Mississippi and Alabama.

However, this was not yet the end of the struggle between the States and the federal Government. Almost simultaneously with the *Submerged Lands Act* Congress had enacted another law, the *Outer Continental Shelf Lands Act* of 7 August 1953 (67 *Stat.* 462, 43 *U.S.C.* 1331-1343), which provided that the need for further exploration and development of the oil and gas deposits of the submerged lands of the Outer Continental Shelf should be met by the issuance of mineral leases in that area by the Secretary of the Interior to private operators.

The State of Maine, in particular, asserted that it could claim title to submerged lands extending 100 miles into the Atlantic Ocean on the basis of provisions contained in a number of colonial charters, and, relying on that claim, issued a permit purporting to grant exclusive oil and gas exploration and exploitation rights in approximately 3,3 million acres of these submerged areas in the Atlantic Ocean, more than three miles from the coast. And the other Atlantic coast States—New Hampshire, Massachusetts, Rhode Island, New York, New Jersey, Delaware, Maryland, Virginia, North Carolina, South Carolina and Georgia, and Florida with respect to its claims in the Atlantic Ocean (including the

Florida Straits on the southern side of the Florida Keys)—advanced corresponding claims. Hence the complaint of the United States Government against the thirteen Atlantic coastal States filed in the U.S. Supreme Court on 1 April 1969, which is still pending. See *I.L.M.* 1969 (VIII), pp. 850-866. See the *Study of the outer continental shelf lands of the U.S.* (Public Land Law Review), ed. R. B. KRUEGER (Los Angeles, 1968).

As to the Persian Gulf, the difficulties are caused by the extreme complications met when determining the equidistance line, owing to the fact that it is uncertain what importance and effect must be attributed in that determination to certain minor islands in the gulf. On 24 October 1968 Saudi Arabia and Iran signed an agreement concerning the sovereignty over the Al-'Arabiyah and Farsi islands and the delimitation of the boundary line separating the submarine areas between the two States (*I.L.M.* 1969 (VIII), p. 493). Iran and Qatar were to sign an agreement on the demarcation of the marine boundaries between them on 30 June 1969 (*Bulletin of Legal Developments* 1969, p. 130).

See for further particulars concerning these shelf delimitations F.MÜNCH in the *Zeitschrift für ausländisches öffentliches Recht und Völkerrecht* 1964 (24), pp. 167 and 625, and 1966 (26), p. 761. Comp. also *I.C.L.Q.* 1966 (XV), p. 904.

The Soviet Union has delimited her continental shelf towards that of Finland by an exchange of letters of 20 May 1965 (*I.L.M.* 1967 (VI), p. 727), followed by an agreement of 5 May 1967 (*I.L.M.* 1968 (VII), p. 560). On 23 October 1968 the D.D.R., Poland and the Soviet Union signed a declaration concerning the continental shelf of the Baltic Sea (*I.L.M.* 1968 (VII), p. 1393). On 28 August 1969 Poland and the Soviet Union signed a delimitation agreement in Warsaw for the boundary in the bay of Gdansk and the S.E. Baltic (*Bulletin of Legal Developments* 1969 (4), p. 194).

See on submarine boundaries in general the paper by David J. PADWA in *I.C.L.Q.* 1960 (IX), pp. 628-653.

Annex to Chapter II, section 1

LEGAL SITUATION OF THE LAND TERRITORY

As planned in my introductory remarks to Chapter II above (p. 16), I will in this Annex give a more detailed and systematic survey of the various regulations which have existed in the past or are still in force with respect to the different elements of the land territory of a State, including its territorial internal waters and certain installations linked with its soil. I will not deal in this Annex with State frontiers; these are reserved for a separate Chapter VI, pp. 513 *et seq.*

International regulations on various matters of international concern have been adopted for a great number of boundary lakes—sometimes in combination with rules governing the rivers flowing through them—, or, for that matter, for purely inland lakes with international importance, such as the Ethiopian Lake Tana. Among those regulations there are many, especially in Africa, which date from the colonial period and are mainly of historical interest, but a number of them may still make their influence felt after de-colonization. The survey below shows that they deal, or dealt, among other things, with the following subjects.

(*a*) *Freedom of navigation. Equality of treatment. Interdiction of shipping tolls*

Lago Maggiore and Lake of Lugano. Following a dispute between Austria and Sardinia, caused by the latter's refusal to allow Austrian vessels on the Lago Maggiore to touch at the Piedmontese shore, countered by the former by retorsion measures against Sardinian vessels on the Lombardic shore (notification of 19 January 1852, Martens, N.R.G.[1], XVI[1], 198), a more liberal Swiss-Sardinian treaty of 25 April 1860 (*ibid.*, XX, 161) granted freedom of navigation. A more recent Italo-Swiss treaty is that of 22 October 1923, applicable to both the Lago Maggiore and the Lake of Lugano (*ibid.*, N.R.G.[3], XVIII, 424).

Lake Garda. Peace Treaty of Zürich, 10 November 1859 (*ibid.*, N.R.G.[1], XVI[2], 531), Article 18: freedom of navigation.

Lake of Geneva, France-Switzerland, 9 July 1887 (*ibid.*, N.R.G.[2], XIV, 357): a very elaborate convention (82 Articles) dealing with French, respectively Swiss steamships conducting a public service on the lake (subject to a system of concessions and public control; requirements as to construction and crew, navigational rules to prevent collisions, ports and landing-places, etc.);—10 September 1902 (*Traités de France*, XXII, 207).

Lake of Konstanz (*Bodensee*), Bavaria-Switzerland, 2 May 1853 (Martens, N.R.G.[1], XX, 112): equal treatment of each other's ships in ports, in particular with regard to their use and the levying of duties.

Untersee (*Lower Lake of Konstanz*). A curious echo of older times can still be heard in the express prohibition, in Article 1, paragraphs 3 and 4, of the Convention between Baden and Switzerland of 28 September 1867 (Martens, N.R.G.[1], XX, 139), of the obsolete staple right and the old practice of forcing shippers to break bulk (*Umschlagsrecht*).

Lakes of Maurepas and *Pontchartrain*, Great Britain-France-Spain, 10 February 1763 (*ibid.*, R[2], I, 104), Article 7: implied participation in the freedom of navigation on the Mississippi river.

Caspian Sea, Soviet Union-Persia, 1 October 1927 (*ibid.*, N.R.G.[3], XXI, 842), with Protocol of 31 January 1928 (*ibid.*, 855).

Conventional Congo Basin. General recognition of the principle of freedom without discrimination as regards all important lakes in this area by Article 15 of the General Act of the Congo Conference of Berlin of 26 February 1885 (*ibid.*, N.R.G.[2], X, 414), followed by a series of bilateral treaties between colonial powers, granting freedom of navigation, but—unlike the freedom granted to the flags of all nations on such rivers as the Zambesi and the Shiré—limited to each other's flag, on: *Victoria Nyanza, Lakes Nyasa* and *Tanganyika*, Article VIII, in connection with Article I of the Anglo-German treaty of 1 July 1890 (*ibid.*, N.R.G.[2], XVI, 894: especially, no transit dues on Lake Tanganyika); *Lakes Chiuta* and *Chilwa*, Article XI, in connection with Article I (2) of the Anglo-Portuguese treaty of 20 August 1890 (*ibid.*, XVI, 929 = XVIII, 154); *Lake Chad*, Article II of the Franco-British treaty of 29 May 1906 (*ibid.*, XXXV, 463). This recognition of the freedom of navigation has presumably survived the recent process of decolonization.

(*b*) *Regulation of navigation. Policing in general*

Lake of Konstanz (Bodensee), *Règlement* concerning navigation, adopted at Bregenz, 22 September 1867 by all riparian States, Austria, Baden, Bavaria, Switzerland and Württemberg (*ibid.*, N.R.G.[1], XX, 117), dealing in 27 Articles and a final protocol with port installations, the removal of obstacles, ship certificates, shipping patents, the powers of port authorities, the transport of passengers, safety measures against the transport of dangerous shiploads, navigation proper, etc. This *Règlement* was on 28 September 1867 complemented for the *Untersee (Lower Lake)* by Baden and Switzerland (*ibid.*, XX, 139). These Regulations have been repeatedly amended, completed or replaced by subsequent conventions.[23]

Lakes Tiberias and Hula, France-Great Britain as Mandatory Powers, exchange of Notes of 7 March 1923, confirming a Commission report of 3 February 1922 (*ibid.*, N.R.G.[3], XVII, 208/209, at p. 214): "the inhabitants of Syria and the Lebanon shall have the same fishing and navigation rights ... as the inhabitants of Palestine, but the Government of Palestine shall be responsible for the policing of the lakes."

Lake of Geneva, France-Switzerland, 10 September 1902: control on navigation (*Traités de France*, XXII, 207).

See on the prevention and suppression of smuggling

on *Lago Maggiore*: Austria-Sardinia, 4 December 1834 (Martens, N.R., XII, 198), revised 22 November 1851 (*ibid.*, N.R.G.[2], XVI[1], 189);

on *Lake Garda*:[24] Peace Treaty of Zürich, 10 November 1859 (*ibid.*,

23. 6 May 1892 (Martens, N.R.G.[2], XVIII, 903 = XX, 354); 8 April 1899 (*ibid.*, XXX, 206); 1 January 1910 (*ibid.*, N.R.G.[3], VII, 435); 1 July 1915 (*ibid.*, XX, 513); 1 November 1927 (*ibid.*, XX, 514); etc.
24. Since 1919—Article 27, *sub* 2, of the Austrian Peace Treaty of St. Germain of 1919—an exclusively Italian lake.

XVI², 531), Article 18 (2), providing for the provisional application of the Convention of 1851, just cited, pending the conclusion of a special convention.

(c) Fishing and bird shooting

Lake of Konstanz (Bodensee). Conventions on fishing have been concluded by Switzerland and Bavaria for the main lake on 5 July 1893 (*Eidgen. Gesetzsammlung, n. F.* XIV, 72); by Switzerland and Baden for the Rhine between Konstanz and Basel, inclusive of the Untersee, on 9 December 1869 (Martens, N.R.G.¹, XX, 166), revised at different times.[25]

As is apparent from Article 2 of the boundary treaty between Switzerland (for the Canton of Thurgau) and Baden on 20/31 October 1854 (*ibid.*, N.R.G.¹, XX, 177), a common right of fishing already existed in the second half of the 18th century: mention is there made of Article 114 of a *Fischer-Ordnung* of 22 August 1774.

A special treaty regulating bird-shooting on the lake was concluded by Switzerland and Baden for part of the Untersee on 7/8 December 1897, laying down a *Vogeljagdordnung* for the area of the common *Wasserjagd* on the Lower Lake and the Rhine, amended on 15 November 1927 (*ibid.*, N.R.G.³, XVIII, 400).

Lake Garda, Austria-Italy, 9 August 1883 (*ibid.*, N.R.G.², XI, 598).

Lake of Geneva: France-Switzerland, 9 March 1904 (*ibid.*, XXXIII, 501) and supplementary French regulations of 20 January 1909 (*ibid.*, N.R.G.³, V, 318).

Great Lake of Cambodia (when this was still a Thai-Cambodian boundary lake), France-Siam, 14 July 1870 (*ibid.*, N.R.G.², XII, 630): very complicated regulation on fishing on the lake, with respect to which both States and their subjects have equal rights; no duties will be levied on fishing in boats; but a tax of $8\frac{1}{2}$ % of the value of the catch shall be due in the case of the construction of hangars or other constructions on the banks for the drying or smoking of fish.

Lakes Tiberias and Hula: France-Great Britain as Mandatory Powers, exchange of notes cited under (*b*): equal fishing rights of Syrians and Palestinians.

Caspian Sea: Soviet Union-Persia, Convention of 1927, cited above under (*a*), Article 14: recognition by Persia of the special importance of her fishing industry on the southern banks of the sea for the supply of fish to the Russian population.

Great Lakes forming the boundary between Canada and the United States: Convention of 10 September 1954 (*U.N.T.S.*, vol. 238, p. 99),

25. 25 March 1875 (*ibid.*, N.R.G.², II, 60/63); 21 September 1884 (*ibid.*, X, 523); 16 May 1887 (*ibid.*, XIV, 350); 3 July 1897 (*ibid.*, XXV, 396); 17 November 1908 (*ibid.*, N.R.G.³, IV, 875); 14 November 1911 (*ibid.*, VIII, 898), etc.

97

establishing a Great Lakes Fishery Commission with the task of formulating a research program designed to determine the need for measures to make possible the maximum sustained productivity of any stock of fish in the convention area, and to eradicate or minimize the sea lamprey populations in that area.

Lake Titicaca: Bolivia and Peru have co-operated repeatedly to study and favour fishing on the lake: preliminary convention of 17 July 1935, exchange of notes of 20 April 1955, preliminary convention of 30 July 1955 (see *U.N. Legislative Series ST/LEG/SER.B/12*, pp. 164 *et seq.*).

Lake Nyasa: A relatively recent example in Africa: Article I (3) of the Anglo-Portuguese convention of 18 November 1954 (*U.N.T.S.*, vol. 325, p. 307) by which the Nyasaland (now Malawi)-Mozambique frontier, as fixed in an earlier treaty of 11 June 1891 (Martens, N.R.G.², XVIII, 185), was advanced from the banks of Lake Nyasa to its median line (comp. on this new frontier delimitation Chapter VI, p. 587):

> "The inhabitants of Nyasa Land [now: Malawi] and the inhabitants of Mozambique shall have the right to use all the waters of Lake Nyasa for fishing and other legitimate purposes, provided that the methods of fishing which may be employed shall be only those which are agreed upon by the Government of Nyasa Land and the Government of Mozambique. This provision shall not, however, prevent the said Governments from agreeing that different methods of fishing may be employed in the waters of one Party from those which may be employed in the waters of the other Party. There shall be no discrimination between the inhabitants of Nyasa Land and the inhabitants of Mozambique under the regulations made by the said Governments for this purpose.
>
> In the event of a fishing concession being granted by either Party the area of the concession shall be confined to the waters of that Party".

The above Convention belongs to those which on account of their legal nature as a dispositive regulation of frontier and connected local interests automatically pass from a predecessor to a successor State on the strength of generally recognized principles of State succession, so that it is now binding upon Malawi as the successor State on the British side. It remains to be seen, however, how the 1954 Convention will work out under the new conditions. The prospects would not seem to be too bright.

(d) Construction or common use of jetties. Construction of ports

In *Lake Tiberias* under the Franco-British Agreement of 23 December 1920 (*ibid.*, N.R.G.³, XII, 582), Article 1.

(e) Manipulation of the water level. Diversion. Irrigation

Swedish-Norwegian frontier lakes. See the detailed Convention of 26 October 1905 (*ibid.*, N.R.G.², XXXIV, 710), also extending to boundary rivers:

98

"Article 1. S'il est question, sur le territoire de l'un des deux Etats, d'endiguer un lac, d'en abaisser le niveau ou d'en dériver les eaux ..., c'est la législation de cet Etat qui sera appliquée en ce qui concerne le droit d'entreprendre les travaux, quand même ceux-ci pourraient influencer les eaux situées dans l'autre Etat ...

Article 2. Conformément aux principes généraux du droit international, il est entendu que les travaux mentionnés à l'article 1 ne pourront être exécutés dans l'un des deux Etats sans le consentement de l'autre, chaque fois que ces travaux, en influençant les eaux situées dans l'autre Etat, auraient pour effet soit de mettre des entraves sensibles à l'utilisation d'un cours d'eau pour la navigation ou le flottage, soit d'apporter autrement des changements sérieux aux eaux d'une région d'étendue considérable."

Lake of Konstanz (Bodensee), convention concluded by Austria, Baden, Bavaria, Switzerland and Württemberg on 31 August 1857 (Martens, N.R.G.¹, XX, 115), which forbade the restoration of certain watermills and ordered the demolition of others with the object of preventing the level of the water rising too high.

Lake of the Woods: Great Britain (for Canada)-United States, 24 February 1925 (*ibid.*, N.R.G.³, XXVIII, 460).

Lake Tana (an exclusively Ethiopian inland lake): Great Britain (for the Sudan)-Ethiopia, 15 May 1902 (*ibid.*, N.R.G.³, II, 826): prohibition of any work across the Blue Nile, Lake Tana or the Sobat which would arrest the flow of their waters into the Nile except in agreement with the Governments of Great Britain and the Sudan. Comp. Italy's recognition of the priority of the hydraulic rights of Egypt and the Sudan by Notes of 14/20 December 1925 (*ibid.*, N.R.G.³, XVIII, 257).

Lake Albert: Great Britain-Congo Free State, 9 May 1906 (*ibid.*, N.R.G.², XXXIV, 387), Article 3.

Lakes Tiberias and Hula: France-Great Britain as Mandatory Powers, exchange of Notes of 7 March 1923, cited above under (*b*): plans for the raising of the water level in the lakes by the building of a dam by the Government of Palestine under certain guarantees for the owners of lands.

Lake Raibl: Austrian Peace Treaty of St.Germain of 10 September 1919 (*ibid.*, N.R.G.³, XI, 691), Article 44 (2): admission of the right of Italy to divert the waters of this lake to the basin of the Korinitza.

Lake of Mont Cenis: Italian Peace Treaty of Paris of 10 February 1947 (*U.N.T.S.*, vol. 49, p. 3), Article 9 and Annex III, under A: guarantees given by France to Italy "in perpetuity" in respect of water supplies from this lake for hydroelectric purposes.

Lake Dojran: Yugoslav-Greek convention of 18 June 1959 (*U.N.T.S.*, vol. 363, p. 133), dealing in Article 1 with the level of the lake, the use of its waters for irrigation and various other hydro-economic questions.

On the many conventions relating to the construction of hydroelectric works see also section 7 below, p. 282.

The rules of international law which govern the diversion of water from a lake have been discussed with regard to *Lake Lanoux* in the Pyrenees by a five-man arbitral tribunal under the presidency of Sture Petrén in their award of 16 November 1957 (*A.A.*, XII, 281; *R.G.D.I.P.* 1958 (LXII), 79) in virtue of a Franco-Spanish special agreement of 19 November 1956.

This case was not decided exclusively on the basis of customary international law or of general principles because it depended also on the construction of the Franco-Spanish Boundary Treaty of Bayonne of 26 May 1856 and the additional Act of the same date. Nevertheless, general principles played an important part in the award of the five-member tribunal. The facts were as follows. The waters of Lake Lanoux, which is situated on the southern slope of the Pyrenees but within French territory, naturally flow through a single outlet (Font-Vive) to the river Carol, which up to a distance of 25 kilometres from the lake runs through French territory before crossing the Spanish frontier above the Canal of Puigcerda. France planned to divert the water towards the French river Ariège, a confluent of the Dordogne, and repeatedly since 1917 consulted the Spanish Government on the project. The latter urged for its examination in common and maintained that the existing treaty regime required previous agreement between the parties. The International Commission of the Pyrenees, created in 1875, was in fact consulted and a Mixed Commission of engineers was set up. However, the diplomatic exchanges and consultations dragged on for many years and were not resumed until after World War II, when the plans took further shape in more definite projects, according to which the waters of the lake would, after their derivation through the Ariège, be reconducted through a subterranean gallery to the river Carol at a place where it still runs in France and above Puigcerda. Under the first of these projects (1949) France would reconduct the water in such a quantity as corresponded with the real needs of the Spanish users, but under the second (1953), suggested by the French Electricity Company concerned, the quantity diverted would be completely restored. The negotiations, however, led to no result. Spain maintained her position, contending that the execution even of the last project without her consent would be an infringement of France's treaty obligations towards her because it would entail two basic changes in the "physionomie physique" of the existing hydrographic basin: not only would it replace the natural flow of the waters of the lake by a man-made hydraulic system, unilaterally constructed, but it would also cause them, instead of following their normal course via the river Ebro to the Mediterranean, to flow via the river Garonne to the Atlantic. France upheld her thesis that the proposed arrangement would in no way prejudice any Spanish interest and announced her intention to proceed with the carrying-out of the final plan, which implied the construction of a barrage in the lake for the generation of electricity—a feature of the project by which Spain would not profit.

The decision of the arbitral tribunal was to the effect that France was obliged under the treaty of Bayonne to negotiate with Spain in good faith before carrying out her project, but that she had complied with that obligation; that she was not bound, however, to delay the execution of the plan until agreement was reached about it; and that there was nothing in the project, as it had finally been worked out, that amounted to an illegal use by France of her sovereign rights over a national lake. In the course of its statement of reasons the tribunal made interesting observations concerning the reference by Spain to an asserted special Pyrenean customary law, manifested by the existence of "compascuités" or "faceries" which were themselves the residuum of a wider communitarian system that, in the Pyrenean valleys, was based on the rule that matters of common interest must be regulated by agreement, freely arrived at. The tribunal rejected this broad assertion as unwarranted. See for the text of the award with note by A.G.(ROS): *R.G.D.I.P.* 1958 (LXII), pp. 79 *et seq.* and pp. 119 *et seq.*; see further A. MIAJA DE LA MUELA, *Pacta de contrahendo en derecho internacional público* in *R.E.D.I.* 1968 (XXI), pp. 392 *et seq.*

Comp. on certain other frontier relations in Spain Chapter V, section 1 (Co-sovereignty), p. 431 and Chapter VI, section 1 (Mountain frontiers), p. 531.

(f) Lake regularization

On the regularization of the Lake of Lugano in order to protect its adjoining regions against damage by inundation, see the Italo-Swiss convention of 17 September 1955 (*U.N.T.S.*, vol. 291, p. 219), relative, *inter alia*, to a correction of the passage of Lavena.

(g) Prevention of water pollution

Lake of Konstanz (Bodensee): Baden-Württemberg-Bavaria-Switzerland-Austria, 27 October 1960 (*U.N. Legislative Series* ST/LEG/SER.B/12, p. 438): setting up of an international water preservation commission, charged (Article 4, *sub e*) with the drafting of regulations against further pollution of the lake. A convention to this effect was in fact drafted and concluded, but has proved to be of little avail owing to the fact that it only contains recommendations.

Lake of Geneva (Lac Léman): France-Switzerland, 16 November 1962 (*Recueil officiel des lois et ordonnances de la Confédération suisse* 1963, 961), setting up a mixed commission to study and prevent the pollution of the lake. See *R.G.D.I.P.* 1963 (67), p. 630 and 1969 (73), p. 500.

(h) Salt winning

Lake Assal: France-Ethiopia, 20 March 1897 (Martens, N.R.G.[3], II,

120) : "le lac Assal étant l'héritage de l'Empire d'Ethiopie, il est convenu qu'on ne défendra jamais de prendre dans le lac le sel destiné à l'Éthiopie et que l'arrangement qui a été fait avec une Compagnie au sujet du lac Assal reste intact."

(i) Common use for surrounding tribes
Lake Undur (Oumdour): French Equatorial Africa-Anglo-Egyptian Sudan, 10/21 January 1924, Martens, N.R.G.³, XVII, 406.

(j) Military clauses
(i) *use for vessels of war reserved for one of the riparian States*
This was for a long time the case of the *Caspian Sea* on which Russia, according to an old tradition, formulated in the Russo-Persian Treaty of Turkmanchai of 22 February 1828 (*ibid.*, N.R., VII, 564), had the exclusive right of maintaining a naval flotilla.[26] This unusual situation was, however, after World War I reversed on 26 February 1921 (*ibid.*, N.R.G.³, XIII, 173/179), Article 11.
(ii) *reduction of armaments or demilitarization*
An old example of the reduction of armaments on a border lake is given by the status of
the *Great American-Canadian Lakes* under the informal Rush-Bagot Agreement which dates back to April 1817 (*ibid.*, N.R., V, vol. suppl., 395): limitation on both sides of the naval force to be maintained on Lakes Ontario and Champlain to one, and on Lake Superior to two vessels, not exceeding 100 tons and armed with one 18 pound gun. There had still been made captures in prize on these lakes in the war of 1812 (comp. the data contained in the case of *Craft captured on Victoria Nyanza*, 25 November 1918 (*Br. and Col. Prize Cases*, III, 295; *Lloyd's Reports on Prize Cases*, VIII, 158).

Similar arrangements have been made with regard to
the *Great Lake of Cambodia* in 1870, when that lake still lay in the border area between Siam and Cambodia, comp. Siam's treaty with France (as Cambodia's protector State) of 14 July 1870 (Martens, N.R.G.², XII, 630),
and *Lake Ladoga* in 1920, when that lake was still a boundary lake (comp. below p. 580): Russo-Finnish Peace Treaty of Dorpat of 14 October 1920 (*ibid.*, N.R.G.³, XII, 37), Article 16: ban on military armaments.

---

26. The second paragraph of Article 8 runs as follows: "Quant aux bâtiments de guerre, ceux qui porteront le pavillon militaire russe, étant *ab antiquo* les seuls qui aient eu le droit de naviguer sur la mer Caspienne, ce même privilège exclusif leur est par cette raison également réservé et assuré aujourd'hui, de sorte qu'à l'exception de la Russie, aucune autre puissance ne pourra avoir des bâtimens de guerre sur la mer Caspienne".

(iii) *neutralization*

Lakes Peipus and Pskov: Russo-Esthonian Peace Treaty of Dorpat of 2 February 1920 (*ibid.*, N.R.G.[3], XI, 864),

and again *Lake Ladoga*, conditional upon the Baltic Sea being equally neutralized: Russo-Finnish Peace Treaty cited under (ii), same Article 16.

The would-be "neutralization" of the (at that time still Siamese-Cambodian boundary lake) Great Lake of Cambodia, agreed upon between France and Siam in 1870, was no neutralization at all, comp. *sub* (ii).

> No neutralization was agreed upon as regards *Lake Nyasa*, on which, in August 1914, the British Navy (one gunboat, H.M.S. *Guendolen*) gained Britain's first "naval victory" of World War I over the German Navy (also one gunboat, the Wissmann). Comp. the account in Dr. Oliver RAMSFORD's *Livingstone's Lake* (1966), and on the corresponding situation of *Victoria Nyanza* the data given in my *Le droit des prises de la Grande Guerre* (Leiden, 1924), 142.

(k) *Common research*

Recently, four African States—Cameroun, Chad, Niger and Nigeria —have begun, with the help of UNESCO, to undertake a thorough investigation of the sources of the basin of *Lake Chad*, in order to ameliorate the conditions in this huge swampy region and to combat the loss of water as a result of evaporation.

Section 2. INTERNATIONAL RIVERS

Introduction

In the introduction to Chapter II above I made the remark that international river law is so complicated that separate treatment of it is apposite. This complicated nature is apparent irrespective of whether the subject-matter is approached from an historical or from an analytical point of view.

Looked at historically, rivers have already played a rôle in international relations in early centuries. Apart from the fact that they often served as frontiers between large empires of the past and were an appropriate place for negotiations and the conclusion of treaties between sovereign rulers (comp. on the frontier function of rivers below, Chapter VI), there is evidence available from as early as the 12th century that international agreements were entered into with the object of ensuring freedom of navigation (river Po, 1177), and that States were held not to be allowed to interfere with the natural flow of the water of a river in their own interest, for example by damming it, and thus to cause flooding further upstream (river Rhine, 1165). Ever since then rivers have occasionally appeared in international enactments in connection primarily with navigation, but sometimes also with other uses or interests, such as the diversion of their water, or the prevention of flooding. The interests of navigation, however, have always remained paramount, and it was especially this aspect which has been the origin of a common law of international rivers at the beginning of the 19th century and has contributed to its further development. This process will be described below.

Looked at analytically, the subject is also somewhat difficult to master in view of the fact that there is a wide variety of possible uses of a river, a marked disparity in legal convictions in regard thereto in different parts of the world and in different periods, and an endless diversity of detailed regulations.

(a) Historical survey

I therefore propose to begin by giving a bird's-eye view of the development of international fluvial law. When we take the second half of the 18th century as the starting-point of our research, we find that a great number of territorial regulations, both in Europe and on the American continent, and even in Asia, by that time provided for the freedom of navigation on behalf of riparian States to which a specified river was common. Other, non-riparian States that might also be interested were still completely out of the picture and other interests than those of navigation did not as yet play an appreciable rôle. The occurrence of many of such provisions recognizing the principle of freedom of navigation did not, however, alter the fact that, especially in Western and Central Europe, navigation on many rivers was still seriously hampered by vexatious measures and ordinances of several kinds, such as the levying of river tolls, the exercise of the staple-right, officially granted by higher authority or simply usurped, the compulsory use of vessels under the flag of the territorial State for further inland water transport, or even, as was the case of the Scheldt since 1648, the entire closure of the river to foreign shipping. It was against such objectionable practices that the *Conseil Exécutif provisoire* of revolutionary France took its stand in its resolution of 16 November 1792 in which, referring to "the fundamental principles of natural law", it announced its intention of sweeping away all such obstacles to navigation. The text of the resolution is curious and deserves reproduction:

"Que les gênes et les entraves que jusqu'à présent la navigation et le commerce ont souffertes, tant sur l'Escaut que sur la Meuse, sont directement contraires aux principes fondamentaux du droit naturel que tous les Français ont juré de maintenir (!); que le cours des fleuves est la propriété commune et inaliénable de toutes les contrées arrosées par leurs eaux; qu'une Nation ne saurait sans injustice prétendre au droit d'occuper exclusivement le canal d'une rivière et d'empêcher que les peuples voisins qui bordent les rivages supérieurs, ne jouissent du même avantage".

This resolution was in fact carried out in regard first to the two rivers specifically mentioned, the Scheldt and the Meuse, and later also to other rivers running through countries occupied by the French armies.

In that period also (1804) began the legal history of the gradual liberation of the Rhine from a series of troublesome practices which had been in use on that river from of old, a development, however, which was fated to remain thwarted for some further decades by the vigorous resistance put up by those interested. Comp. on the Rhine below pp. 126 *et seq.*

The first attempt at formulation and codification of the liberal principles predicated by the French Revolution was made at the Congress of Vienna: the result was a series of nine basic Articles (108-116) embodied in the Final Act of 9 June 1815 as a replica of part (a) of Annex XVI to that same Act, two further parts of which already contained an elaboration of those basic Articles for the Rhine (b) and for its affluents—the Neckar, the Main and the Moselle—the Meuse and the Scheldt (c), respectively (Martens, N.R., II, 427, 434-449). This codification was designed to govern at least part of the international rivers of Europe in so far as they fell under the territorial sovereignty of the Contracting Parties (Austria, Spain, France, United Kingdom, Portugal, Prussia, Russia, and Sweden-Norway) and of those States which should still accede to the Final Act under Article 119. The Danube was not yet among the international rivers dealt with by the Congress of Vienna. See on the principles of Vienna below, p. 120.

On the basis of the general principles thus laid down, a certain number of special River Acts, *inter alia* for the Elbe, were successively drawn up, and a great many treaties in the course of the 19th century dealt in the same spirit with the freedom of navigation on other European rivers. The Danube was placed under the Vienna rules in 1856 by the Congress of Paris. Comp. on the main European rivers below, *sub* A, II, pp. 126 *et seq.*

Parallel with the development in Europe, but independently therefrom and with a distinctly less marked liberal "internationalizing" tendency, was the development on the American continent. On the other hand, the Congo Conference of Berlin of 1885 introduced a more liberal regime for the African rivers in the "Conventional Congo Basin", in particular the Congo and the Niger. Comp. below *sub* A—I (*b*), p. 121—. Occasional treaties between Asiatic States had in the meantime followed the same line.

But all those treaty regulations differed very considerably *inter se*, according to the special features of the rivers concerned, the political conditions under which their regime had to be determined, etc.

A new impetus was given to the development of fluvial law by the politically tainted provisions relative to it in the Peace Treaties after World War I (*e.g.*, Articles 327-362 of the Treaty of Versailles), designed to apply as a provisional regulation, and to be replaced within the term of five years by a world-wide new codification under the auspices of the League of Nations. On the same occasion specified rivers—the Rhine, the Elbe, the Oder, the Niemen and the Danube—were further "internationalized".

After a hard political struggle between the divergent continental and national currents of thought at the First Conference for Communications and Transit at Barcelona of March/April 1921, attended by 24 (or with the inclusion of Germany and Hungary 26) European, 12 South and Central American and 4 Asiatic States, a compromise solution for the regime of international rivers in general was arrived at in the Statute on Waterways of International Concern, annexed to the Convention of Barcelona of 20 April 1921 (Martens, N.R.G.³, XVIII, 709). Comp. on its contents below, p. 122.

The development, however, halted once again when in the thirties reactionary tendencies and the then ideological division of Europe affected the regime of the Danube and Nazi-Germany illegally denounced all the limitations on her territorial sovereignty in regard to the international waterways running through Germany. The chaotic political situation which at the moment still obtains in Central Europe as a legacy of World War II makes it impossible to foresee what the final outcome in this particular field of international regulation will be.

Side by side with the directed development, a development brought about by means of deliberate codification, of the law respecting navigation on international waterways, the law relating to various other uses of rivers continued to follow the traditional, more haphazard and undirected course of development, according as circumstances calling for regulation arose. Although this matter of international concern also gradually moves towards a deliberate formulation of general principles, it has not at present reached this stage in actual State practice. Comp. on this subject below, p. 208 *sub* B.

(b) *Analytical survey*

Let us now, after this cursory historical bird's-eye view of the evolution of international river law in the last two centuries, make a somewhat more systematic approach to the subject.

As I have remarked earlier, international law covers a wide field of fluvial activities and interests. Apart from a set of general rules on the freedom of navigation on international rivers, laid down in a number of multilateral conventions, and a few elementary principles sanctioned by custom in the field of neighbourly relations, the rules concerning international rivers are in the great majority of cases bilateral, and they present an endless variety of types of regulation of fluvial interests.

The main use made of international rivers is of course for navigation. In the principal collective treaties referred to above—the general Convention and Statute of Barcelona of 20 April 1921 and the treaties dealing with a number of specific rivers—the main concern is to safeguard the two paramount principles of freedom and equality or non-discrimination. Neither of these principles, however, is absolute, and the extent to which they are applicable differs from river to river. This remark relates to such subjects as: the extent of the group of nations entitled to free navigation, the reservation of cabotage and possible other navigation activities for the national flag, the limitation of the freedom of navigation to merchant ships, etc. A number of these subjects were already mentioned above. I therefore confine myself here to giving a brief supplementary summary of the manyfold topics which are dealt with usually in bilateral treaties in connection with navigation.

There is first the levying of taxes, either on shipping itself, or on the use of ports, locks, buoys and beacon-fires, piloting services, etc. In former centuries mere river tolls were numberless and formed a regular source of revenue for the equally innumerable local rulers whose domains happened to be favourably situated on the banks of a navigable river, and who were consequently in a position to dominate passing navigation from their castles on the Rhine, the Meuse, the Danube, etc. The Head of the Holy Roman Empire drew a substantial income from the grant of river tolls on its *stratae regiae* to commercial towns or its vassals, and this gradually also became the accepted practice of the latter towards their rear-vassals or vavasours or towards other towns. Of a great many purely riverine tolls—levied on fluvial navigation as such—history has handed down to us their origin, their gradual increase, the growing opposition or rivalry which they provoked, their curtailment and decline and their eventual abolition. It sometimes happened that two different tolls on shipping alone were levied by two local rulers on the same stretch of river or at the same place. A number of internationally notorious river tolls have persisted until late into the 19th century, but a general historical trend developed towards ending such impediments to international navigation. In one famous case, that of the "Rheinschiffahrt-Octroy" of 1804—Franco-German Convention of 15 August 1804, Martens, R², VIII, 261—, the levying of tolls on the Rhine was instituted with the specific object of paying out from the surplus of the revenues collected—after deduction of the costs of administration of the system—the compensation due to a great many small rulers on either side of the river who had fallen victim to the secularizations or mediatizations which were indispensable to a general territorial reorganization in the Napoleonic era. But on the whole, tolls levied merely for navigation on a river have long since vanished from the international scene, after having been in the first instance restricted by the fixing of (maximum) tariffs, by a limitation to well-defined objects, or by specific exemptions. Comp. on river tolls below, pp. 189 *et seq.*

History further records a number of other hindrances to free river shipping.

Among such other impediments to navigational freedom on international rivers mention must be made of:

(*a*) the closure of a river for the purpose of strangling foreign commercial competition, and

(*b*) the odious right—of medieval origin and more often than not based solely on gradual usurpation—exercised in particular by powerful river towns, to compel passing vessels either to stay for a short period in their harbours with the object of giving their citizens an opportunity of buying the merchandise they were carrying at preferential rates or before they continued their voyage, or to "break their cargo" by unloading and reloading it into vessels of the country concerned. This right in its different variants and under its various denominations of "staple-right" or "droit d'étape", "Umschlagerecht" (right to demand transshipment), or "recht van voorbijvaart" (right to stop passing vessels) was also exercised on many rivers in the interior. Hamburg, for example, very early usurped the right on the river Elbe and subsequently introduced it on the river Ems during its temporary occupation of the town of Emden (presumably as from 1431). Notorious "Umschlage-Häfen" (transhipment ports) along the course of the river Rhine were Cologne and Mainz. The right was even exerted much higher upon its course on or near the Lake of Konstanz. In the Low Countries it was exercised, *e.g.*, by the town of Dordrecht on the river Waal.

A more commendable object of regulation was, and still is, the care for the safety of fluvial traffic itself, to be secured by instructions for navigation, *e.g.*, with the object of preventing collissions; by the issuance of prescriptions for the floating of rafts down a river; by the requirement of the professional capability of masters, as evidenced by examinations and shipping licences or "patents"; by the setting-up of a piloting service, either compulsory or optional; by the building of jetties, or the instalment of a system of beaconing and lighting; by the prohibition of the transport of explosive, inflammable, corrosive and venomous materials, etc.

Police directions with a view to preventing illicit immigration or illegal imports or exports, or other customs infringements, or to avoiding the propagation of contagious human, animal or plant diseases over an international river are likewise necessary.

Sometimes special economic or social needs call for some form of international regulation, for example with the object of securing a just apportionment of freights among the different inland merchant fleets concerned or in order to secure decent labour conditions or to enforce other social provisions on river vessels. The pursuance of the former aim often plays a part in the fairly wide-spread tendency to reserve fluvial cabotage to the national flag.

The unity of a river system is occasionally symbolized by a special flag, or consolidated by the establishment of a fluvial jurisdiction entrusted with the task of adjudicating both in civil and in criminal matters concerning navigation (collisions, towing contracts, etc.), or reinforced by the organization of some form of collective administration of, or control over, *e.g.*, frontier waterways, or the introduction of a common legal regime thereof.

It need hardly be said that the pursuit of many of these aims requires suitable financial arrangements between the States concerned. The problem of cooperation in the field of common fluvial interests may be seriously complicated by a state of war even between one of the States concerned and a third party. There are also instances of the "demilitarization" or "neutralization" of a river.

Apart from navigation there are many other uses which are made of rivers, and many more interests which call for regulation. I will begin by grouping them summarily in the following pages in order to show the variety of treaty arrangements dealing with such fluvial uses and interests.

There are first those regulations which relate to the body of the river: its bed, its banks or its bridges, or which supply means of communication across it.

The main concern in this respect is, of course, the maintenance or improvement of the river bed and the river course by dredging, deepening, widening, straightening or the removal of rocks or reefs, shoals or sandbars, and many treaties have in fact been concluded with a view to ameliorating, normalizing or canalizing a river, or to constructing collateral canals, where unavoidable. Similar conventions deal with river banks: the upkeep or periodic inspection of river dykes or other protective devices, or of towing-paths, or with the construction of bridges across it. A river may need more or better ports. It may be desirable to install telegraph lines alongside it for the purpose of giving a timely warning of sudden dangerous rises of the water level, or to provide a ferry service across it. One-sided or common interests may require, or militate against, the construction of barrages to collect the water for hydroelectric schemes. Certain particularly unruly rivers urgently require provisions for the prevention or regularization of possible violent shifts of their bed.

Other international agreements deal with the prevention of abuses, such as: the discharge of sewage or industrial refuse into rivers; the diversion of their water for irrigation purposes, for the filling of connecting canals or for supplying other rivers with a deficiency of water with a supplementary quantity; the building of a dam in, or the diverting of redundant water from, a river with the result of overloading another, or of inundating adjacent territory. In former centuries watermills (*molendinariae naves*) and their possible abuse played an important part.

Prohibitions such as these are the counterpart of provisions providing for positive collaboration between States for the utilization of common rivers for purposes other than navigation, such as: fishing or the protection of the piscifauna, the building of hydroelectric installations, the development of irrigation systems, the feeding of canals of common interest, and in arid regions the watering of cattle.

From the above survey it is obvious that matters which come up for regulation by international conventions in respect of rivers are legion even apart from the main issue of navigation. An attempt to expose this chapter of international river law in more detail and systematically will be made below, *sub* A, III, pp. 183 *et seq.* and B, pp. 208 *et seq.*

As will become evident from the expositions which are to follow, it is not feasible to draw a legal picture of the regime of an "average" international river. Every such river is vested with its own status dependent upon what either the riparian States have freely agreed upon or an international gathering has been in a position to impose upon them. The only mandatory rules of a more general character are:

(*a*) those referred to above, laid down as a set of nine principles in the first of the three parts of Annex XVI to the Final Act of the Congress of Vienna of 9 June 1815 and reproduced in the Articles 108-116 of that Act itself (Martens, N.R., II, at p. 427 and pp. 434-449, respectively), designed to constitute a brief code of minimum standards of behaviour with regard to European rivers which separate, or successively flow through, different adjacent States; and

(*b*) those dating from more than a century later and formulated in the Statute annexed to the multilateral Convention of Barcelona of 20 April 1921 (*ibid., N.R.G.*[3], XVIII, 709), also referred to above, and intended to have a much wider scope, extending, as they do, to Contracting Parties from all parts of the world. The latter rules also constitute minimum standards, but they do not detract from the continued validity of possible stricter rules already in force respecting particular international rivers. Comp. for further particulars below, *sub* A, I (*c*), pp. 122 *et seq.*

There is still scope for a further attempt at systematization.

The international regime of rivers exhibits an extreme variety according to their nature (navigable or non-navigable), their course (through one single State, or between or successively through two or more different countries) and the various uses which can be made of them (navigation, irrigation, the generation of power, the building of dams for the formation of reservoirs, the diversion of superfluous water, the discharge of sewage or industrial waste, fishing, the feeding of lateral or other connecting canals, and in older times the operation of watermills,[27] and so forth).

Prominent among the criteria decisive of their legal regime is their status as national or "international".

National rivers—an unambiguous notion which indicates those rivers whose course is geographically confined to one State—fall, as a rule, from the point of view of international law under the exclusive jurisdiction of the territorial State. They may acquire a certain interest for the law of nations in so far as their use by the territorial State exceeds the legal limits set to it by the principles of neighbourly relations, for example, when the State concerned causes an excess of water carried by a national river to be abducted across the territory of an adjacent State to the latter's detriment. National rivers may sometimes, though rarely, retain their former status of international rivers if in the past they ran through different countries which later fell under the same territorial supremacy, such as is the case of the river Po, perhaps one of the most remarkable rivers from this point of view.

> Flowing past the now Italian cities of Turin, Piacenza, Cremona, Guastalla and Ferrara through a very wide delta with many arms and exclusively through Italian territory into the Adriatic, it ran for many centuries, from the Lombardian days until 1860, through a number of small countries, varying in different periods, and which successively fell a prey to foreign powers: the Holy Roman Empire, the kingdoms of France and Spain, Austria, Napoleon, who each in turn supplanted their predecessor. It has seen along its banks and in its basin the rise and fall of the margraviates, counties or duchies of Piedmont, Milan under the Visconti's and the Sforza's, Mantova, Guastalla and Montferrat under the Gonzaga's, Modena and Ferrara under the Este's, Parma and Piacenza under the Farnese's, and the prolonged hard fought struggle between the Empire and the powerful North-Italian cities.

27. "Molendinariae naves" are often mentioned in Austro-Turkish peace treaties, in particular of the 18th century. Comp. for example: Article 2 of the Treaty of Carlowitz of 26 January 1699 (Dumont, VII[2], 448): "Molendinariae autem naves in locis tantum quibus navigationi alterius nempe Caesarei Dominii nullatenus impedimento esse possint, communicatione Gubernatorum utriusque dominii et consensu ponantur; quinimo, ne diversione aquarum in Marusio cursus Caesarearum navium incommodum aliquod patiatur, nullatenus permittetur, ut, sive molendinorum, sive alia occasione ex Marusio aquae alio deriventur, seu deducantur", and Article 1 of the Treaty of Passarowitz of 21 July 1718 (Dumont, VIII[1], 524). Article 5 of the Navigation Regulations for the Danube section between the Iron Gate and Braila, annexed to the multilateral treaty of London of 10 March 1883 (Martens, N.R.G.[2], IX, 394), still mentions "les moulins fixes établis sur la voie fluviale" and "les moulins flottants". And there are many more relating to the same subject, comp. below *sub* A, (*g*) (3), p. 207.

Already in the 12th century the river Po was the object of the—unilateral—solemn "Pactum Ferrariae de tenenda aqua Padi omnibus aperta" of 8 June 1177 by which, in the presence of representatives of Milan, Bologna, Modena, Venice, Ravenna and Mantova and many others, "Consules Ferrariae iuraverunt aperire aquam Padi libere omnibus hominibus, et apertam omnibus hominibus eam tenere, nec ullo tempore eam claudere, et hoc observare bona fide et sine fraude ulla".[28] This old promise has been kept by the riparian States until the very end of the existence of the Po as a geographically international river. Even the Commanders-in-chief of the French and Austrian armies respected the freedom of navigation on the river in Article 3 of their military convention of 31 July 1800 (Martens, R², VII, 79) and the Po was expressly mentioned as falling under the newly formulated principles in Article 96 of the Final Act of the Congress of Vienna (*ibid.*, N.R., II, 379). The last confirmation of it was given by Austria, Modena and Parma in their treaty of 3 July 1849 (Martens, N.R.G.¹, XIV, 525).

The Po is, however, only one of the many rivers which have in the course of the centuries lost their international character in the geographical sense. I only refer to the Pruth, the Weser, the Newa, the Oxus and the Mississippi.

It is very doubtful if the river concerned in fact retains in such circumstances its original international status. Strong historical grounds must exist in order to admit this.

The notion of an *international* river, on the contrary, is not as unambiguous as that of a national river. The term can logically be applied to a river which geographically either separates two adjacent States or successively runs through different States. But in order to qualify for the legal status of an international river, at least as far as navigation is concerned, it must be moreover navigable and in open navigable communication with the high sea. This implies that such a river is only "international" from the point where it becomes navigable, and that, even if it is geographically international, it does not all the same deserve that qualification from the legal point of view when (*a*) it is entirely unnavigable, or (*b*) it flows into an inland lake or sea, or (*c*) its mouth is to such an extent barred by sandbanks, cays or reefs that regular navigation on it from and into the sea is impossible.

But that is not all: a river which is international in the legal sense can further enjoy different degrees of "internationality" or "internationalization", depending upon (1) the extent of the freedom of navigation thereon, (2) the mode of its administration by the riparian States, either individually *pro 'diviso* or jointly, and in the latter case: (3) the composition of the administrative body, and (4) its powers.

International rivers in the legal sense accordingly present an interesting scale of varying regimes. These have, however, one solid juridical minimum core in common, namely, that the right to navigate on them is not

28. Text reproduced by K. STRUPP in *Urkunden zur Geschichte des Völkerrechts* (Gotha, 1911), I, p. 4, from PASOLINI, *Documenti riguardanti antiche relazioni fra Venezia e Ravenna* (1881), doc. III, p. 13.

confined to the respective riparian States and their nationals in proportion only to the stretch of river over which the former exercise territorial sovereignty. Beyond this essential minimum, however, it is not possible to state any firm rule, the further elements of the specific fluvial regime depending upon the factors enumerated under (1)-(4).

ad (1). The extent of the freedom of navigation

Freedom of navigation on international rivers has only developed very slowly since about 1800. Up to that period not only was fluvial navigation subject to a great many burdens, exactions and limitations, but there were cases in which shipping on a river was totally denied by a lower to an upper State. The river Scheldt was notorious from this latter aspect: it was from 1648 (Article 14 of the Peace Treaty of Munster of 30 January 1648 between Spain and the United Netherlands, Dumont, VI^1, 429) to the end of the 18th century closed to shipping from and towards Antwerp, first to the Spaniards, later, as from the Austro-British-Netherlands treaty of Antwerp of 15 November 1715 (Dumont, VII^1, 458), j°. Article 7 of the Peace Treaty of Utrecht of 11 April 1713 between the Netherlands and France (Dumont, VIII^1, 366), to the Austrians, as was still confirmed by Article 7 of the Austro-Netherlands Treaty of Fontainebleau of 8 November 1785 (Martens, R^2, IV, 55). This did not alter until the principles of "natural law" professed by the French Revolution in regard to the freedom of navigation on international rivers, as formulated in 1792 (see above), were carried into effect.

But even if there was no official closing of the river, there were a great number of obstructions to fluvial shipping in force. To confine myself here to the Netherlands alone, I will mention in particular the rivers Meuse and Rhine. Although already in 1625 GROTIUS, in his famous treatise De jure belli ac pacis, theoretically defended, on the basis of his own "law of nature", in some well-known passages in lib. II, caput II, § XII, the freedom of navigation,[29] international practice—also in the territorial compass of the United Netherlands—entirely ignored this so-called jus naturae and inflexibly maintained and enforced its multitudinous restrictions upon shipping, among which were prominent the exaction of river tolls and the different Protean appearances of the right mentioned above, asserted by river towns, to interfere with passing cargo vessels, consisting, under various denominations—Umschlagerecht, recht van

---

29. Grotius argues there as follows: although "flumen, qua flumen dicitur, proprium est populi cuius intra fines fluit", "at idem flumen, qua aqua profluens vocatur, commune mansit, nimirum ut bibi hauririque possit"; reference being made, in his usual manner of arguing, to a line in Ovid's Metamorphoses (VI, 349): "Quid prohibetis aquas? Usus communis aquarum est", "ubi (Ovidius) et undas vocat munera publica, id est hominibus communia", and to Aeneid VII, 230, where Vergil "undam eodem sensu dicit cunctis patentem".

voorbijvaart, droit d'étape—, in the demand that their cargoes should be for a certain time held at the disposition of their citizens for preferential buying, or/and be transloaded into their own vessels for further transportation.

The river Meuse, in the middle section of its course, did not fall under the territorial sovereignty of the Netherlands until its constitution as a monarchy in 1813/1814, and the eventual delimitation of her territory in Article 66 of the Final Act of the Congress of Vienna of 9 June 1815 (Martens, N.R. II, 379). Up to that time the States General *(Generaliteit)* of the United Netherlands, their confederate central body, exercised sovereignty only over a few small patches of that part of the river, and even then not exclusively: the towns of Venlo and Stevensweert were entirely subject to their domination, but the town of Maastricht constituted for some centuries a condominium under the—unequally divided— joint authority of the States General and the bishopric of Liège.[30] For the far greater part of its course from the Maastricht region down-streams the Meuse was bordered by a curious multitude of minute, practically independent entities, some of which were even *reichsunmittelbar*, or by separate territories belonging to other large entities, such as the duchies of Brabant, Jülich and Cleves, or the Kingdom of Prussia. See on these entities the data in Chapter V, section 2, on Enclaves, p. 445.

Small wonder that under such conditions and even though there were no powerful merchant towns along its banks, navigation on the Meuse was subject to an incessant sequence of extortions, which are fully described in a contemporary report, handed down to us in the General State Archives (collection Bisdom), and which in the event led to the action taken by revolutionary France in 1792.

Though under different conditions of territorial sovereignty, the situation on the Rhine was not much more favourable to shipping. Two powerful merchant towns along its course, Mainz and Cologne, exercised their usurped right of "Umschlag", or lastbreaking, or staple; near Arnhem the ruler of the minute principality of Anholt was entitled to levy a toll on shipping, and so were other political units elsewhere. The special Navigation Act for the river Rhine, forming part b) of Annex XVI to the Final Act of 9 June 1815, still maintained a number of impediments to free navigation, although it abolished others. Only the subsequent Act of Mainz of 31 March 1831 (Martens, N.R., IX, 252) abrogated the remaining hindrances to free and unimpeded traffic at Mainz and Cologne. See for the legal history of the Rhine below, pp. 126 *et seq.* But even at the present time the freedom of Rhine navigation is not yet secured for good. On the contrary, the old guilds, abolished in 1815, have shown a curious tendency to reappear in an entirely novel

---

30. Comp. about this coïmperium below Chapter V, section 1, at p. 431.

shape, as a consequence of the trend of the modern socialist or quasi-socialist State to assume control of all the economic activity of its nationals, inclusive of the industry of fluvial navigation. The Netherlands Government thus got itself into difficulties as a consequence of its policy of subordinating trade navigation on the Rhine to a centralistic State control, for economic purposes.

The freedom of fluvial navigation may differ from a threefold aspect: (a) personal, (b) geographical, (c) substantive.

(a) From the *personal* point of view, fluvial navigation can be legally free for (i) shipping of the upper State(s) in respect of the lower State(s) exclusively, in order to enable the former to communicate with the sea, in which the legal situation bears resemblance to a State servitude; (ii) shipping of all riparian States mutually, so that ships of the lower State(s) also may inversely travel upstream, in which case the whole river enjoys a uniform regional regime to the benefit of (the nationals of) all the riparian States concerned; (iii) shipping of all States, whether riparian or not, in which case the legal situation exceeds that of a regional fluvial community and becomes really international by nature. In the cases under (ii) and (iii) the principle of freedom of navigation may be doubled by that of equality or non-discrimination.

(b) From the *geographical* point of view, the freedom of navigation may be confined to the international river proper. It may, however, also extend to its affluents even in the case where the latter (or sections of them) are themselves entirely national. This question of river law arose, from the aspect of the jurisdiction of the international river commission concerned, in respect of the Warta (Warthe) and the Noteć (Netze), both tributaries of the international river Oder, partly situated in Polish territory (comp. the Judgment of the Permanent Court of International Justice of 10 September 1929, *Publications P.C.I.J.*, series A, No. 23).—It may likewise cover any lateral canals constructed or to be constructed with the object of obviating the hindrances to shipping caused by local geological obstructions in a particular portion of the river bed. This was specifically stipulated, for example, in respect of the river Rhine.

(c) From the *substantive* point of view, there may be differences of various kinds.

(i) Freedom of navigation is as a rule only intended to cover economic needs or the interests of commerce; it does not, therefore, generally relate to the passage of public State vessels, let alone to that of men-of-war. The freedom of passage for such vessels will, consequently, be an exception, granted by a servitude-like treaty stipulation and in favour only of the upper State(s), although there may of course be special considerations that justify an extension of the freedom of such passage in both directions as a regional understanding.

(ii) The freedom of navigation, even of a commercial or other private nature, may further be subject to specific limitations, in particular owing to the policy of many riparian States of reserving for their own vessels the exclusive right of carrying persons and goods between two of their own fluvial ports, the so-called river cabotage. The claim relating to the asserted freedom of reservation of river cabotage to the national flag has played a conspicuous part in the history of the legal regime of the Rhine, on which a differentiation has even been made in the past between three types of cabotage:

great—*i.e.* purely fluvial navigation between ports in different Rhine States[31] *inter se*—,

small—*i.e.*, navigation between ports within the same Rhine State—, and

median—*i.e.*, navigation passing, even while remaining within the borders of one Rhine State, in either direction the ports of Cologne or Mainz, historically notorious for the right which those towns had usurped in the past to compel vessels to "break their cargo" there ("Umschlagerecht").[32]

(iii) It is for the rest still a matter for dispute what particular restrictions on shipping constitute genuine infringements of the freedom of navigation on a specific river. Certain restrictions on absolute freedom can hardly be held to be unlawful: social legislation for the protection of labour, for example, would seem to be harmless for the aspect of freedom of navigation. Well known lawsuits have in the course of time developed with respect to the rivers Congo and Rhine. As to the former, in the *Oscar Chinn* case (Judgment of the Permanent Court of International Justice of 12 December 1934, *Publications P.C.I.J.*, series A/B, No. 63) the permissibility of the establishment of a factual, as distinct from a

31. From 1815 to 1866: The Netherlands, Prussia, Nassau, Grand Ducal Hesse (-Darmstadt), Baden, Bavaria and France. In 1866 Nassau was engulfed by Prussia and consequently vanished from the Commission. In 1871 France ceased to be a Rhine State owing to her loss of Alsace-Lorraine to the German Reich, but those territories reappeared as a new Reichsland more or less independently as France's successor in the group of riparian States. In 1919 France emerged again in her old rôle of a riparian State and Switzerland was admitted as such. On that same occasion the system of weighted voting was introduced. The new grouping of West-German Länder after World War II in 1950 altered the picture once more: riparians are now The Netherlands, the West-German Länder Rhineland-Westphalia, Rhineland-Palatinate and Württemberg- Baden, France and Switzerland.

32. This treble aspect of Rhine cabotage underwent its first substantial change in 1866 when Prussia annexed Nassau, thus setting the nice legal problem of whether it was entitled juridically to transform the then "great" cabotage between Nassau and Prussia into a "small" cabotage, henceforth to be exercised inside the enlarged Prussian territory. A second substantial alteration took place in 1868 when the "Umschlagerechte" of Cologne and Mainz were abolished and there was no scope left for the concept of "median" cabotage.

legal, monopoly of shipping on the river—contrary to the principle of non-discrimination—was at stake. As to the latter, controversies have arisen in different variants: whereas the Netherlands Government maintained that they were legally free to interfere with purely inland shipping on the Netherlands part of the Rhine to the extent required by considerations of national economy, the German Government asserted, this time against protestations made by the Netherlands Government, that they were legally free to exclude Netherlands vessels from inner-German cabotage. See *infra*, pp. 142 *et seq.*

ad (2). The administrative regime

As a rule, each of the riparian States is entitled to exercise the fulness of its territorial sovereignty over the national section of the international river concerned, subject to the limitations exposed under (1). A special treaty arrangement is necessary in order to place such a river under the regime of a, more or less extensive, international administration by a River Commission set up by the riparian States collectively, or by an international Conference. This exceptional regime may be called that of "internationalization" of the international river in question; under it, the riparian States concurrently delegate certain public powers, which they would otherwise themselves exercise over their own section of the river, to an international body, for example in the field of the issuing of shipping regulations, the fixing of the level of remuneration for the use of the river, its amenities or piloting service, the approval of plans for the execution of technical works and its supervision, etc. This "internationalization" may again assume varying degrees of intensity, to be more precisely defined under (3) and (4).

ad (3). The composition of the international body

The most natural and indeed customary composition of an international river commission would seem to be that it consists of representatives of each of the riparian States, normally on a footing of equality, but under special circumstances, for example on account of an obvious difference between the weight of the interests at stake, on a "weighted" footing, proportionate to those interests. The original Rhine Navigation Commission of 1815 has for more than a century consisted of representatives of each of the riparian States on an equal footing.

Such was also the composition of the fluvial Commission, set up by Article 17 of the Peace Treaty of Paris of 30 March 1856 (Martens, N.R.G.[1], XV, 770) and intended to be permanent; that Commission, the "commission riveraine" (of the Danube), was to be composed of delegates of the riparian States: Württemberg, Bavaria, Austria, Turkey and the three Danubian Principalities.

Political considerations, however, sometimes cause an international river Commission to be further "internationalized" by the involvement in its composition of an outsider element, represented by non-riparian States. The first historical instance of such a composition was provided by the so-called European Danube Commission which, pursuant to Article 16 of the same Peace Treaty, consisted of representatives of Austria, France, Great Britain, Prussia, Russia, Sardinia and Turkey. It was (Articles 16 and 18 of the same Peace Treaty) originally especially entrusted with the temporary task of rendering better navigable the so-called Maritime Danube, at first from Isatcha, later (1878) from Galatz, and eventually (1883) from Braila to the Black Sea (comp. the Judgment of the Permanent Court of International Justice of 8 December 1927, *Publications P.C.I.J.*, series B, No. 14).—A similar composition was that introduced in 1919 for the Commissions of the Rhine, the Elbe and the Oder. Such an original internationalization of the administration of a river (as in the case of the Maritime Danube) or progressive internationalization of its administration when it is already endowed with an international (riparian) commission (as in the case of the Rhine) is, as experience teaches us, always the outcome of overwhelming political pressure by a combination of foreign victor States on the territorial State after a lost war. Where, as in the case of the Rhine, an outsider State was concerned which was unprepared to submit to the dictate of a group of victors, it proved much more difficult for the latter to impose their will: the Netherlands only acceded to the relative provisions of the Peace Treaty of Versailles (Articles 354 *et seq.*) after the acquiescence of the victors in two successive protocols, of 21 January 1921 and 29 March 1923, modifying certain details of the regime of the Rhine, imposed upon Germany (Martens, N.R.G.[3], XII, 603 and 605).

ad (4). The powers of the international body

An international river commission may be vested with advisory functions only, for example in respect of works to be undertaken, or the contents of regulations to be issued, by the riparian States themselves. They are, however, as a rule entrusted with independent pseudo-governmental powers either in the executive or in the legislative, or even in the judicial field. The powers of the first "internationalized" fluvial commission, as described under (3), namely the Maritime Danube Commission, set up in 1856, already chanced to be so wide that theorists have invented for the fluvial area under its control the peculiar qualification of a "Fluss-Staat", a fluvial State, endowed in their view with a territory, a government and a personal substratum of its own. Apart from the fact that none of the riparian States was in the least prepared to admit that the fluvial area concerned had an independent statal existence of its own and was, consequently, carved out of their respective national territories, the designation "Fluss-Staat" was wholly artificial and moreover theoretically incorrect for other reasons also. The frontier between the Danubian States concerned: Romania-Bulgaria and Romania-Ottoman Empire (in a later period Russia-Turkey) was invariably recognized as running along the thalweg of the river or of one or the other of its delta branches, so that the so-called "Fluss-Staat" really lacked a territory of its own. Neither had it a personal substratum, although the users of the river were in several aspects subject to its authority in virtue of a delegation of powers made by the riparian States. Finally, the Commission was entirely dependent upon the continuing will of its creators to maintain it in existence: no sooner should the latter agree upon its suppression than the Commission would cease to exist and its factitious "fluvial State" evaporate.

As far as the actual (pseudo-)governmental powers of commissions of this type are concerned, reference can be made to legislation in respect of navigation, sanitary control, Masters' qualifications, the use of ports, tariffs for piloting services, and so on; to executive functions such as river policing, the building of bridges, regularization of the course of the river or the removal of obstructions in the bed, etc.; to judicial authority, for example to adjudicate upon collisions, the infringement of fluvial ordinances, and so on. As every internationalized river has its own individuality, dependent upon its geographical features, its political importance, its economic rôle, etc., there are no general rules in existence relative to the extent of the powers of international river commissions. They can, consequently, only be stated with regard to a specific commission.

After this historical and systematic bird's-eye view of the vast field of international river law, let us now turn our attention to a more detailed inspection of its positive contents. I intend to describe the situation first in regard to navigation and directly connected subjects (A), then to other uses of international waterways (B), and finally to a few other subjects of treaty regulation (C).

A. *Navigational interests*

Under this heading I will introduce some further order by

I. dealing with the basic principles as formulated by the Congress of Vienna (1815), the Congo Conference of Berlin (1885) and the Conference of Barcelona (1921);

II. setting out or summarizing the legal regime that has successively attached to the rivers most famous from this aspect in international law, namely: the Rhine, the Danube, the Congo and the Niger, the Elbe and the Oder, and a few others;

III. concluding the survey by giving a brief systematic description of, mostly bilateral, treaty provisions and arbitration cases dealing with the most diversified interests of fluvial navigation, to begin with its freedom.

I. *The regimes established at Vienna (1815), Berlin (1885) and Barcelona (1921)*

(a) *The principles of Vienna* (1815)

The general regime of international rivers—*i.e.*, rivers which separate or traverse more than one State—as established by the *Congress of Vienna* (1815) amounted in essence to the following (Martens, N.R., II, 427-429; 434-436):

> The riparian States of each river shall regulate in common accord all matters relating to that river, on the basis of the principles, summarized below.
>
> Navigation on any such river shall be entirely free from the point where it becomes navigable to its mouth, shall not "sous le rapport du commerce" be prohibited to anybody, subject to their compliance with police regulations, which shall be the same for all and as favourable as possible to the commerce of all nations. The regime adopted for the collection of shipping dues and the policing of the river shall as far as possible be the same for the whole river and extend to those branches and tributaries which themselves separate or traverse different States. The navigation dues shall be fixed in a uniform and invariable manner, as far as possible independently of the nature of the cargo. Their scale shall not exceed that existing in 1815 and must be fixed according to local circumstances, but with a view to encouraging trade, in which respect the Rhine Octroy may serve as an approximate norm. The tariff once fixed may only be increased by common agreement and shipping may not be burdened with any other duties. There shall be as few collecting offices as possible, and changes shall only be allowed in common accord, barring the freedom of each State to reduce the number under its own control. Any riparian State shall see to the upkeep of the towing paths and also of that of the river bed within its territory, subject to joint action in the case of a boundary river. The establishment of "droits d'étape, d'échelle ou de relâche forcée" shall not be allowed any longer; those already existing shall only be retained if, to the exclusion of consideration of local interests, they are deemed by the riparian States to be necessary or useful for navigation and commerce in general. Customs control shall have nothing in common with shipping dues and must not hinder navigation. The river Statute once adopted may only be modified in common accord.

From the résumé above it follows that the fluvial regime created in Vienna was still only to a modest degree truly liberal. Indeed, no provision in it forbade either pure navigation dues, or the maintenance of existing staple and similar rights, or a reservation of fluvial cabotage to the national flag, their purport being rather mitigation than prohibition in those respects. The more detailed special River Acts annexed to the Final Act of Vienna under No. XVI, b) and c), respectively for the Rhine, and for its tributaries Neckar, Main and Moselle, the Meuse and the

Scheldt were in some respects more liberal (see below: under II, on the legal history of famous rivers, p. 126).

(b) The principles of Berlin (1885)

The much more liberal principles laid down for African rivers in the *General Act of the Congo Conference* of Berlin of 26 February 1885 (Martens, N.R.G.^{2}, X, 414) were intended to govern a wide range of waterways and to apply to them the more general principle of freedom of commerce in 1) the Congo basin, 2) a maritime zone along the Atlantic Ocean (from 2° 30' lat. south in the north to the mouth of the river Logé in the south), and 3) the zone adjoining the Congo basin eastward to the Indian Ocean (from 5° lat. north in the north to the mouth of the Zambesi in the south). The geographical basin of the Congo and its affluents under 1) was defined in Article 1 as being delimited: in the north, by the mountain ridges of the adjacent basins of the Nyari, the Ogowé, the Shari and the Nile; in the east, by the mountain chains east of the affluents of Lake Tanganyika; and in the south, by the mountain ranges of the basins of the Zambesi and the Logé, *i.e.*, all territories drained by the Congo and its tributaries, inclusive of Lake Tanganyika and its feeders. The principle of freedom with regard to the zone under 3) was subject to the consent of any sovereign State to which the territories concerned might actually belong. The freedom of navigation was not to be confined to rivers proper, but was to encompass also lakes, harbours, and future connecting canals. It was to imply freedom of taxes other than those of a compensatory nature, freedom of the carrying trade and even of fluvial cabotage, whilst any differential treatment was forbidden.

Chapters IV and V of the General Act contained more detailed Navigation Acts for the rivers Congo and Niger respectively. The Congo was to be more strictly "internationalized" than the Niger in that the Congo regime would be placed under the supervision of an International Commission—an expedient to which the two Powers exercising sovereignty or a protectorate over the territories bordering the Niger, Great Britain and France, objected in respect of that river. However, even the International Commission, planned for the Congo, was never established. Had it been in actual fact so established, it would have been vested with vast powers, legislative, executive, judicial: the issuing of regulations on navigation, river police, pilotage and quarantine, and the fixing of tariffs, all subject to the approval of the Powers represented on the Commission; the negotiating of loans; the undertaking of works in the interest of navigability of the rivers; penal or disciplinary repression of infractions. Comp. for further particulars on these two rivers *infra*, pp. 156 *et seq.*

(c) The principles of Barcelona (1921)

An epitome of the contents of the *Statute of Barcelona* of 1921 (Martens, N.R.G.³, XVIII, 709) gives the following picture of the present-day minimum standards of conduct of riparian States in respect of international rivers.

To begin with, the Vienna definition of the commonly so-called "international rivers" as "rivers which separate or traverse different States" was replaced by a new denomination and description. The Statute was to deal with "navigable waterways of international concern", a group of waterways obviously more comprehensive than the original group of Vienna. The Statute distinguishes, however, in this wider group two categories, respectively dealt with in the following exposition under A and B.

It follows from Article 1 j° Article 2 that the main group (A) consists of all those "navigable waterways of international concern" for which there is no international Commission upon which non-riparian States are represented (*i.e.*, an "internationalized" Commission), irrespective of whether there exists for the waterway concerned a merely "riparian" Commission or no Commission at all. This "normal" category again consists of two sub-groups, *viz.*, (i) those described in Article 1 under (1) in a complicated definition which I will reproduce below in a somewhat compressed form, and (ii) those described in Article 1 under (2): waterways, or parts of waterways, whether natural or artificial, expressly declared to be placed under the regime of the Statute either in a unilateral Act of, or in an *ad hoc* agreement made with the consent of, the territorial State.

The principal of these two sub-groups is defined in Article 1 (1) as encompassing:
all parts which are naturally navigable

> —*i.e.*, now used, or capable by their natural conditions of being used, for navigation which, in view of the economic condition of the riparian countries, is commercially and normally practicable—

to and from the sea

> (even though only with transhipment from one vessel to the other)

of a waterway which in its course, naturally navigable to and from the sea, separates or traverses different States,

> lateral canals constructed in order to remedy the defects of such a waterway being assimilated thereto, but tributaries to be considered as separate waterways—,

and also any part of any other waterway naturally navigable to and from the sea, which connects with the sea a waterway naturally navigable which separates or traverses different States.

Amongst the "navigable waterways of international concern" thus defined, mention is made in Article 2 of a special category (B) which, for specific purposes—fluvial cabotage; works for upkeep and improvement; administration of the river; navigation regulations, and public services of towage—stands out above the others, *viz.*, the, once again, twofold category of navigable waterways: (i) for which there is an international Commission upon which non-riparian States are represented, or (ii) which may in the future be placed in this category, either in pursuance of a unilateral Act of, or of an agreement made with the consent of, the territorial State.

I will now describe the status of these two categories *A* and *B separatim.*

A. The regime of the ordinary type of "navigable waterway of international concern" can be summarized as follows (Articles 3-12).

(Article 3) Free exercise of navigation to be accorded to vessels flying the flag of any other Contracting State (consequently not beyond this group as if the principle belonged to general international law), subject to reservations as to cabotage and to vessels of war or other State vessels. —(Article 4) Treatment of nationals, property and flags of all Contracting Parties in all respects on a footing of perfect equality, without distinction (*a*) between the riparian States *inter se*, or between the latter and non-riparian States, or (*b*) by reason of the point of departure or of destination, or of the direction of the traffic.—(Article 5) Freedom for any riparian State, barring specific obligation to the contrary, to reserve fluvial cabotage to its own flag, or to make it conditional upon reciprocity, with a further complicated rule contained in Article 5, *sub* 2. —(Article 6) Maintenance of the existing right of each Contracting State to police its territory and to enforce with as little impediment as possible of the freedom of navigation, on a footing of absolute equality, its laws relating to customs, public health, animal or plant diseases, emigration and immigration, and the import and export of prohibited goods.—(Article 7) A definite interdiction of shipping dues other than those in the nature of payment for services rendered and intended solely to cover the expenses of maintaining or improving the navigability of the waterway, or those incurred in the interest of navigation, such permissible dues to be levied with as little hindrance to international traffic as possible, both as regards their rates and the method of their application. —(Article 8) Transit of vessels and of passengers and goods to be governed by the Statute of Barcelona on Freedom of Transit (1921) with some additional facilities in the case of transit without transhipment.—(Article 9) Application of the above principles to the use of river ports (equality of treatment and facilities for all Contracting Parties *inter se* and with the territorial State, under certain reservations, and equality of customs duties, and of import and export facilities, in ports and elsewhere).—

(Article 10) Mutual obligation to refrain from prejudicing the navigability of the waterway or reducing the facilities for navigation, and to remove as rapidly as possible any obstacles and dangers; and to the regular upkeep of the waterway, with a reasonable contribution towards the cost by other riparians on valid reason being shown. In the absence of legitimate grounds for opposition, obligation of each riparian State not to refuse to carry out works necessary for the improvement of the navigability asked for by another riparian, if the latter offers to pay the cost of the works and a fair share of the additional cost of upkeep. Freedom for the territorial State to leave the carrying-out of works of upkeep or for the improvement of the navigability to a co-riparian. Freedom for riparian States jointly to close a waterway to navigation and, in exceptional cases, a qualified freedom even for one single riparian to do the same if it can justly allege an economic interest greater than that of more or less unimportant navigation. The duties of upkeep and improvement shall in the case of a delta, wholly situated in one and the same State, only apply to the principal branches deemed necessary for providing free access to the sea.—(Article 12) Separate exercise by each riparian State of the administration of its part of the river, and of the power and duty of publishing, and supervising the execution of navigation regulations, which, however, should preferably be as uniform throughout the whole course as the diversity of local circumstances permits.

B. The regime of the special type of navigable waterway of international concern, singled out in Article 2 and characterized by the existence of an international Commission upon which one or more non-riparian States are represented (or assimilated to that type *ad hoc*) is in certain respects different. Thus, the Act of Navigation concerned shall only allow to riparian States the right of reserving the local transport of passengers or of goods which are of national origin or are nationalized (Article 5 (1), second paragraph). In respect of such rivers, decisions in regard to works of upkeep and improvement will be made by the Commission, but they will be subject to testing by the Communications and Transit Machinery on the grounds that they are *ultra vires,* or that they infringe international conventions (Article 10 (5), second paragraph under (a) and (b)), whereas the closing of such rivers shall only be permissible if not only all the riparian States, but also the other States represented on the Commission agree (Article 10 (6), first paragraph). With regard to such rivers, the establishment of public services of towage or other means of haulage in the form of monopolies will only be permissible if the non-riparian States represented on the Commission also agree (Article 12, last paragraph). A special provision (Article 14) is devoted to the duties of an "internationalized" Commission: it shall have exclusive regard to the interests of navigation, and the Act of Navigation concerned shall define at least its four main powers and duties, listed under a)-d).[33]

The legal relation, in many respects somewhat difficult, between the new Statute, which is obviously meant to constitute a set of mandatory rules, and pre-existing or future treaties or Acts of Navigation is defined in Articles 13, 18 and 20:

(13) Treaties, conventions or agreements in force relating to navigable waterways, concluded by the Contracting States before the coming into force of this Statute, are not, as a consequence of its coming into force, abrogated so far as concerns the States signatories to those treaties.—Nevertheless, the Contracting States undertake not to apply among themselves any provisions of such treaties, conventions or agreements which may conflict with the rules of the present Statute.

(18) Each of the Contracting States undertakes not to grant either by agreement or in any other way, to a non-Contracting State treatment with regard to navigation over a navigable waterway of international concern, which as between Contracting States, would be contrary to the provisions of this Statute.

(20) This Statute does not entail in any way the withdrawal of existing greater facilities granted for the free exercise of navigation on any navigable waterway of international concern, under conditions consistent with the principle of equality laid down in this Statute, as regard the nationals, the goods and the flags of all the Contracting States; nor does it entail the prohibition of such a grant of greater facilities in the future.[34]

For the rest the Statute declares explicitly (Article 15) that it does not prescribe the rights and duties of belligerents and neutrals in time of war, but shall continue in force in time of war so far as such rights and duties permit.

The International Law Association has recently undertaken a private codification of certain principles of international river law which deals in six chapters respectively with (1) general aspects, (2) the equitable utilization of the waters of an international drainage basin, (3) pollution, (4) navigation, (5) timber floating, and (6) procedures for the prevention and settlement of disputes. See the Report of its 52nd Conference, Helsinki (1966), pp. 477-533, which also reviews the preparatory work in the preceding sessions of Edinburgh (1954), Dubrovnik (1956), New York (1958), Hamburg (1960), Brussels (1962) and Tokyo (1964). And see further for the separate subjects below.

33. To elaborate navigation regulations; to call attention to maintenance works useful to the riparian States; to receive all projects of riparian States for the improvement of the waterway; and to approve the collection of the dues permitted according to Article 7.
34. Comp. also Article 2 of the Convention (no infringement of the rights and obligations arising out of the provisions of the Peace Treaties after World War I) and Article 16 of the Statute (no imposing of any obligation conflicting with rights and duties under the League of Nations).

A. *The Rhine*

After what I have set out above on various aspects of fluvial treaty regulation in general, and subject to what I will be mentioning later in a systematic survey in their proper place about its particulars, I intend to sketch here the history of the legal regime of the Rhine along its main lines of development, and, for the rest, to deal in an Excursus (*infra* pp. 174-183) with the principal legal controversies to which that regime has given rise.

Legal history of the Rhine

Should one attempt to describe the history of the legal regime of the Rhine in the course of the centuries, that attempt would result in an elaborate dissertation which would exceed by far the limits of the present publication. I only cite from ancient sources a grant by Charlemagne, in 805, of freedom of navigation to a monastery; a series of cases in which freedom of shipping tolls was granted by different authorities to users of the river, e.g., by archbishop Arnold I of Cologne in 1147 to the Abbey of Egmond at Andernach, Neuss and Cologne (*Oorkondenboek van Holland en Zeeland*, ed. OBREEN (The Hague, 1937), p. 72), by the duke of Guelder in 1197 to the duke of Lorraine at Driel and by various local rulers in the beginning of the 13th century (1203, 1204, 1212) at Tiel, Strijen and other places; and a triple decision of the Emperor Frederick I of (November) 1165 between the bishop of Utrecht and the count of Holland, dealing respectively with—at different points—the digging of a drainage canal from the Rhine to the sea, the maintenance of a dam built in the Rhine for the purpose of diverting its water through another bed, and the removal of a second dam across the river in order to prevent further inundations (*Oorkondenboek*, p. 89).—Much later, in a letter of 16 January 1581, addressed to the Emperor Rudolph II (JAPIKSE, *Resolutiën der Staten Generaal*, III, 225), the States General of the United Netherlands invoked the *jus gentium* in support of their claim to freedom of trade on the Rhine.

Modern history of the river began at the end of the 18th century when France acquired its left bank:

> peace treaty of Basel of 5 April 1795 (Martens, R², VI, 45), Article 5; secret additional convention to the peace treaty of Campo Formio of 17 October 1797 (*ibid.*, R², VI, 426), Article 1; and peace treaty of Lunéville of 9 February 1801 (*ibid.*, R², VII, 296), Article 6.

Article 2 of the secret convention of 1797 already held out for France freedom of navigation on the Rhine between Hüningen (near Basel) and the frontier of the Batavian Republic, and freedom of exit for her ships from the river Moselle into the Rhine. These treaties formed the introduction to the modern regime of the Rhine.

126

The origin of a more detailed international regulation regarding this river and its affluents can be traced back to the settlement made in § 39 of the "Récès principal de la députation extraordinaire de l'Empire" (*Reichsdeputations-Hauptschluss*) of 25 February 1803 (Martens, R², VII, 443 *et seq.*, at p. 501), and the Franco-German Convention of 15 August 1804 on the Rhine Navigation Octroy (*ibid.*, R², VIII, 261), supplemented by a convention of 1 October 1804 (*ibid.*, VIII, 292).

The Resolution of 1803 had the dual object of (*a*) indemnifying, in accordance with the principles established at the Congress of Rastadt (comp. Article 7 of the treaty of Lunéville of 1801), from the bosom of the Empire, *inter alia* by means of the secularization of ecclesiastical principalities and the mediatization of other *reichsunmittelbare* territories east of the Rhine, the many hereditary secular princes who had lost their possessions on the left bank as a consequence of the cession thereof to revolutionary France by the above-mentioned peace treaties of Campo Formio and Lunéville, and (*b*) abolishing all pre-existing Rhine tolls with a view to their replacement by a uniform "Octroy" from which the maintenance of the navigability of the river and the indemnities for the dispossessed princes could be defrayed. The Octroy was to be regulated and collected jointly by France and the German Empire, which latter, however, delegated its rights to the Elector-Archchancellor Karl von Dalberg and empowered him to make all the necessary arrangements with France, subject to the approval of the College of Electors. The proceeds of the Octroy should not be higher than the total of the tolls just abolished: its tariff should be heavier for foreigners than for Frenchmen and Germans, for upstream than for downstream traffic; an easy system of perception by no less than five and no more than fifteen offices should be introduced under the general management of a Director-General of the Octroy, to be appointed by the French Government and the Elector-Archchancellor jointly. The gross proceeds were to be affected in the first place to the costs of common perception, administration and police; the surplus was to be divided into equal parts, each destined especially for the upkeep of towing paths and for works necessary for navigation; the remnant of the half assigned to the German side was mortgaged for the payment of the indemnities awarded to a number of princes and a possibly remaining balance would serve for the gradual amortization of the charges on the Octroy.

On the basis of this *Reichsdeputations-Hauptschluss* France and Germany, on 15 August 1804, concluded a further, very elaborate Convention in 132 Articles, on the Rhine Navigation Octroy by which, among other things, the *Stapelrecht* (*droit d'étape*) proper—that is, the "mise en vente forcée", practised by the "villes de station" Mainz and Cologne—was abolished (Article 8), but the old institutions of *relâche* and *échelle* (*Umschlag*) in the same ports were maintained, subject to certain minor alterations (Article 3). The levying of all river dues, other than the Rhine Octroy, retributions for the use of cranes, quays, etc. (Article 8) and a so-called *droit de reconnaissance*, owing by any vessel of a carrying capacity of 2500 kilograms or more which, loaded or unloaded, should pass any of the perception offices (Article 94),[35] was henceforth forbidden. Skippers' associations remained allowed (Article 14); their members in principle needed in proof of their nautical capability a formal "patent", but only for the "grande navigation" (passing from one Rhine State to another past either of the two key towns) and not for the "petite navigation", the exercise of which every territorial sovereign was entitled to authorize to the skipper concerned (Articles 19 *et seq.*).

The new regime thus established on the Rhine was revised by Annex XVI, *sub* b), of the Final Act of the Congress of Vienna of 9 June 1815 (*ibid.*, N.R., II, 447), which was an elaboration and further liberalization of the general rules concerning international rivers contained in Annex XVI, *sub* a), of 24 March 1815 (*ibid.*, N.R., II, 436) as inserted in Articles 108-116 of the Final Act itself (see for their main content above, p. 120). This Annex (which in its Article 28 expressly maintained the provisions of the *Reichsdeputations-Hauptschluss* of 1803) already contained in a set of 33 Articles the essential elements of the regime of the Rhine as it has survived until the present day. It proclaimed that navigation "dans tout le cours du Rhin, du point où il devient navigable jusqu'à la mer, soit en descendant soit en remontant" should be entirely free, and should not "sous le rapport du commerce, être interdite à personne" (Article 1). It required a uniform system, both for the levying of navigation duties and for river police, also extending, as far as possible, to those embranchments and confluents "qui, dans leur cours navigable séparent ou traversent différents Etats" (Article 2).[36] It laid down a moderate tariff of the navigation dues which remained allowed (Article 3) but which should never be farmed (Article 24), and made this tariff unalterable save by common consent (Article 4). It fixed the maximum number of admissible custom-houses, forbade their increase but allowed their reduction (Article 5).[37] It charged each riparian State with the mainte-

35. This "droit de reconnaissance", still maintained in Article 3 (2) of Annex XVI, *sub* b), of the Final Act of Vienna, was definitively abolished in 1868, see *sub* 5° C) of the *Protocole de Clôture* of the Revised Rhine Navigation Convention of Mannheim of 1868 (Martens, N.R.G.[1], XX, 371).
36. This provision has at a much later stage played a limited rôle in the dispute between Poland and certain Allied Powers before the Permanent Court of International Justice on the degree of internationalization of the affluents of the river Oder: the Warthe (Warta) and the Netze (Noteć). Comp. *Publications P.C.I.J.*, Series A, No. 23, and my paper in *The Jurisprudence of the World Court*, vol. I, pp. 192 *et seq.*
37. Comp. *e.g.*, the Franco-Baden agreement of 10 September 1820 (Martens, N.S., II, 385) by which the number of custom-houses between Basel and Strasbourg was reduced to two.

nance of its part of the towing paths and river bed (Article 7). It instituted a special Rhine navigation jurisdiction for the trial of disputes concerning the application of the river regulations, in two instances, the lower, local one connected with the perception offices, the other, in appeal, at the option of the appellant, to be lodged either with a superior national tribunal, to be designated by each riparian State, or with a new international body (Articles 8 and 9), the Central Commission of the Rhine, whose further tasks, constitution, chairmanship, procedure, personnel—an Inspector-in-chief, to be appointed by a complicated voting procedure (Article 13), and three sub-inspectors—, powers and general legal status were defined in detail (Articles 10-18). Article 17 expressly laid down that the Commission was to take its decisions by an absolute majority of votes, but that "ses membres devant être regardés comme des agents des Etats riverains, chargés de se concerter sur leurs intérêts communs, ses décisions ne seront obligatoires pour les Etats riverains que lorsqu'ils y auront consenti par leurs commissaires". A further important provision was that of Article 19 which, in addition to the abolition in 1804 of the *droits d'étape* proper, also abolished the still remaining special rights of *relâche (Halterecht), échelle (Stapelrecht)* and last-breaking *(rompre charge, Umschlag)* exercised by the towns of Mainz and Cologne, so that thenceforth no transshipment between the point where the river became navigable and "son embouchure dans la mer" would be required.[38] The existing skippers' associations, which were organised of old as guilds, lost their exclusive right of navigation on the river (Article 21). The vessels of the "Octroy" were to fly the flag of the riparian State to which they belonged, but with the addition of the word "Rhenus" (Article 23).—The Annex even foresaw the contingency of a future war between Rhine States: the perception of the right of octroy should then be continued freely, and the vessels and personnel of the Octroy service should enjoy "all the privileges of neutrality" (Article 26).

Corresponding provisions were laid down in Annex XVI, *sub* c), concerning the regime of various affluents of the Rhine, but they were less strict.

The preparation of final Regulations for the Rhine was entrusted to the Central Commission (Article 32). However, a long time has passed between the adoption of the principles of Vienna, summarized above, and their further—obligatory—elaboration in a definitive River Act, because the geographical extent of the regime proved an apple of discord from the outset. This Act was not in fact agreed upon by the riparian States until sixteen years later, when at long last a compromise solution was reached in the Convention of Mainz of 31 March 1831 (Martens,

38. These obsolete rights were likewise abolished, by Article 2 of Annex XVI, *sub* c), on the affluents of the Rhine: the Main and the Neckar.

N.R., IX, 252). As appears from the long preamble of that Convention the cause of this delay lay in a stubborn fight between the Government of the Netherlands and those of all the other riparian States jointly over two specific points, *viz.*:

(i) what exactly was the continuation of the river Rhine in the Netherlands downstream of its bifurcation west of Emmerich: only the northern branch, running from that bifurcation along Arnhem under the name of Rhine and further along Wijk bij Duurstede, where its name changes to Lek, or also the southern one, running past Nijmegen and Zaltbommel under the name of Waal (or, after its confluence with the river Maas or Meuse near Gorinchem, under that of Merwede)?

(ii) what was the precise meaning of the words "jusqu'à la mer", employed in Article 1 of Annex XVI B, which laid down the principle that navigation on the entire course of the Rhine should be free from the point where the river becomes navigable to the sea (Article 109 of the Final Act = Article 2 of Annex XVI A, just as, for that matter, Article 19 of Annex XVI B itself, employed another expression: "jusqu'à son embouchure dans la mer"), and what exactly was or were the geographical point(s) where the "river" ended and the "sea" began? The Netherlands Government upheld the thesis that only the northern Rhine-Lek branch was a continuation of the German Rhine, and that the Rhine ceased to be a river at the point to which the tide reaches, *i.e.*, Krimpen on the Lek (east of Rotterdam) or, in case the Waal should also have to be taken into account, at Gorinchem (or Gorcum) (east of Dordrecht), both river towns situated fairly far inland: the expression "jusqu'à la mer" was asserted to be something quite different from "jusque dans la mer". The practical reason for this second, to my mind legally untenable, thesis was that the Netherlands wished to reserve the right of levying a special due on seagoing vessels entering the tidal inlets towards Rotterdam and Dordrecht. The other Governments maintained that "unter der Benennung des Rheins habe (die Wiener Kongress-Akte) den ganzen Lauf, alle Arme und alle Ausmündungen dieses Stromes innerhalb der Niederlande ohne irgend einen Unterschied begriffen" (preamble of the Act of Mainz). A compromise solution[39] was in the event[40] adopted to the following effect.

39. "So haben die Uferstaaten für angemessen erachtet, alle die, über allgemeine Grundsätze der Wiener Kongressakte in Bezug auf die Rheinschifffahrt erhobenen Streitfragen, so wie die daraus abzuleitenden Folgerungen unberührt zu lassen und auf der Grundlage eines Gesammtinbegriffes gegenseitig gemachter und angenommener Vorschläge, jedoch unter dem ausdrücklichen Vorbehalte, dass diese Verständigung den beiderseits behaupteten Rechten und Grundsätzen in keiner Art Eintrag thun solle, eine Vereinbarung über diejenigen Massregeln und reglementarischen Bestimmungen zu treffen, deren die Rheinschifffahrt nich länger entbehren kann."

40. The failure of the delegates of the riparian States, represented on the Central

A water area—comprising, with the consent of the Netherlands, both the rivers Lek and Waal (Article 2)—was established on which the Rhine regime should apply to its full extent, the non-officially so-called "Conventional Rhine". This area, over which alone the Central Commission was to have jurisdiction, was, however, legally placed for navigation purposes in free communication with the open sea through the tidal waterways beyond Krimpen on the Lek and Gorcum (or Gorinchem).

The Convention, however, remained silent on the so-called "eaux intermédiaires" between the Rhine and the Scheldt, for the reason that at the time when its terms were finally agreed upon (1831), the insurrection of the population of the southern provinces of the Greater Netherlands had not yet found its final solution in the definitive separation of an independent new Belgian Kingdom from the Netherlands, and the Dutch Government therefore wished a postponement of the problem of the navigation on those intermediary waters, which either were already "international" in the sense of the Vienna rules, or would so become as the automatic consequence of the separation of the two countries (comp. the Bavarian Note of 5 August 1832 to the British Foreign Secretary Viscount Palmerston, upholding the right of the Rhine States to free navigation over these waters, in Martens, N.R. XII, 521).[41]

Under the Convention of Mainz navigation on both the "Conventional Rhine" and the connected tidal waterways should be free "jusque dans la mer" (Article 1). On these latter, however, foreign navigation should in either direction follow the (then) busiest waterways of the Rhine-Meuse delta (Article 3).[42] The Netherlands would be entitled to levy a

Commission, to agree upon a generally acceptable content of the definitive Act owing to the basic controversy had in the meantime in 1826 induced the Netherlands to unilaterally issue an interim Decree concerning Rhine Navigation. In this Decree, of 10 September 1826 (Martens, N.S., II, 472), the King of the Netherlands, referring to certain data borrowed from the *travaux préparatoires* of the International Rivers Commission of the Congress of Vienna, expressly limited the principle of the freedom of navigation to the northern of the two branches of the Netherlands Rhine, which runs past Arnhem, and its continuation westward, called the Lek. On that river stretch, extending only to Krimpen on the Lek, east of Rotterdam, the old shipping tolls were abolished and replaced by the navigation dues in conformity with Article 3 (1) of the Vienna Annex XVI, *sub* b), and the "droit de reconnaissance", maintained in Article 3 (2), was substituted for the old patent rights, owed by the masters. These provisions were, however, made subject to reciprocity on the side of the German Rhine States and France.

41. This question was only definitively solved by Article IX, § 5 of the Netherlands-Belgian Treaty of Separation of 19 April 1839 (Martens, N.R., XVI², 773) according to which navigation over these waterways from Antwerp to the Rhine and *vice versa* should remain free. On the same occasion the tariff of navigation dues fixed by the Act of Mainz for the Rhine was made applicable to the Easter Scheldt and the Maas (Meuse) (Article IX, §§ 4 and 7).

42. Namely, on the prolongation of the river Lek along Rotterdam and Brielle

special moderate "droit fixe" from vessels plying between Krimpen and Gorcum, on the one side, and the sea, on the other (Article 4). This compromise was reached under the German threat that otherwise Netherlands shipping would not be freely admitted on the German Rhine.

In spite of the general wording employed in Article 109 of the Final Act of Vienna and Article 1 of Annex XVI b): "La navigation ... ne pourra ... être interdite à *personne*", subject to the observance of uniform police regulations "aussi favorables que possible au commerce de *toutes les nations*", freedom of navigation was still only recognized by the Act for the benefit of vessels of the riparian States. One should not be misled by the generality of the text of Article 1, but rather be guided by the first and last paragraphs of Article 3, in connexion with Article 42 of the Act, from which it follows that the guaranteed freedom of navigation only concerned vessels which were the property of subjects of the riparian States and "belonged to Rhine navigation", that is, vessels whose masters possessed the necessary technical and geographical knowledge, testified to by a "patent", which could only be granted by the government of a Rhine State to its own citizens. Article 42, paragraph 3, 2nd sentence, expressly excluded any differentiation in this respect as between "great", "intermediary" and "small" navigation, *i.e.* respectively: 1) from one Rhine State to another, 2) within the same State but passing either of the old compulsory transhipment ports in Germany: Mainz and Cologne, and 3) within the same State without such passing.[43] The freedom of cabotage was part and parcel of the initial legal regime of the Rhine, and was in fact never in the following century encroached upon or doubted.

I will not go here into the details of the 10 Titles and 109 Articles of this elaborate Convention of 1831, but, with the object of orientation in the contents of early river law, confine myself to the following general survey. Title I defined the purport of the principle of freedom more closely. Title II fixed the tariffs and the method of perception of the only two permissible navigation duties to be levied on the river proper: one from the vessel (*Schiffsgebühr*) and one from her cargo (*Zoll von der Ladung*).

---

through the mouth of the river Meuse, or, in the event of the construction of a canal through the island of Voorne (which was in fact dug), along that canal towards the Haringvliet, against payment of a special tax on the same footing as Netherlands vessels; and on the prolongation of the river Waal, the Merwede along Dordrecht and Hellevoetsluis through the Hollands Diep and the Haringvliet.—Additional provisions were made for the eventuality that any of the designated channels should become unnavigable either through natural causes or as a result of hydraulic works: in that case the Netherlands would be obliged to designate another, equally good waterway.—The present big shipping canal, the "New Waterway" from Rotterdam to Hoek van Holland, was only constructed in 1864. Comp. the sketchmaps inserted at pp. 178-179.
43. This classification and terminology were not yet in use in 1804.

Title III dealt with the application of the national tax laws to Rhine shipping, Title IV with the capability of masters, which was to be certified by a patent, and the dissolution of the—since 1815 no longer monopolistic, but still existing—old skippers' guilds, Title V with freight prices, which were to be contracted in complete freedom,[44] and the right of commercial towns on the river to conclude "Rangfahrt" contracts with the object of organizing regular Rhine services at fixed hours and tariffs. Title VI contained police regulations on various subjects and Title VII provisions against the evasion of the navigation dues. Title VIII maintained the special tribunals for the cognizance of specific navigation cases, civil and criminal, while Title IX also continued the Central Commission in its existing composition and powers. A final Article (108) of this same Title again expressly provided for the maintenance, as far as possible, of freedom of navigation even in time of war and for the "neutrality" of the vessels employed, and the persons appointed in the service of administration of the Rhine navigation duties. The only Article (109) of Title X made any future alteration of the Act dependent upon the unanimous consent of all the riparian States.

The Act empowered the Central Commission to make proposals for its modification or completion, and the Commission often did so, with the result that many new Articles were in the course of years added to the original text. Comp. for those Articles (I-XIX), dating from 1834 to 1848: Martens, N.R.G.[1], II, 537-546; I, 386; VIII, 576; IX, 172, and XIII, 670.

The inner-German war of 1866 had no impact on the substance of the legal regime of the Rhine; it merely reduced, after its rapid conclusion, the original number of (seven) Rhine States by one, the duchy of Nassau being incorporated into Prussia, so that only six remained, namely, Baden, Bavaria, France, Hesse, the Netherlands and Prussia. This event might only have led to controversy if each riparian State had indeed possessed the monopoly of cabotage within its own territory, because it would then have been open to doubt whether the other riparian States, not directly involved in the annexation of Nassau by Prussia, were bound to acquiesce in an automatic "merger" of two, initially separate and limited, cabotage-stretches into one combined larger stretch.

A major, though not a basic, change in the legal regime only took place when the Rhine States, at the end of the 'sixties, concurred in the decision that it should be further liberalized and simplified. This common feeling led on Prussia's proposal to the replacement of the Act of Mainz by the Revised Convention of Mannheim of 17 October 1868 with *Protocole de Clôture* (Martens, N.R.G.[2], XX, 355, 371), which already showed the simplification in its outer form, containing, as it did, no more

44. The Rhine States still had agreed upon a regulation of freight prices on 27 August 1807 (Martens, R[2], VIII, 304).

than 48 Articles. The most important alterations concerned the following points.[45]

(a) The freedom of Rhine navigation on the footing of equality was extended to the flags of all nations, whether Rhine States or not (Article 1). As I remarked earlier (p. 132), this extension was in consonance with the clear text of the original principles of Vienna, but these had in 1831 been interpreted in a restrictive sense. Even in 1868, however, this extended freedom was not yet tantamount to absolute equality and non-discrimination between vessels of riparian and of non-riparian States. In two respects, indeed, inequality continued to exist in favour of ships "appartenant à la navigation du Rhin"—*i.e.*, those entitled to fly the flag of a riparian State—, namely, in that (pursuant to Article 2, para. 1, and Article 4) only the latter (i) were granted freedom of choice of the route which they wished to follow between Germany and the open sea or Belgium through Netherlands territory (see *ad d*), and (ii) could lay claim to treatment on the footing of national vessels (see *ad b*).

(b) Article 4 stipulated in express terms as a general principle national treatment on behalf of all foreign vessels belonging to Rhine navigation and their cargoes, in accordance with what had already been agreed upon between individual riparian States apart from the Act of Mainz.[46] The discrimination which was thus maintained between foreign vessels belonging to Rhine navigation and other foreign vessels was expressly emphasized in the *Protocole de Clôture, sub* 1°.

(c) The old "Schiffsgebühr" (ship toll) and "Zoll von der Ladung" (cargo duty), being mere navigation dues, were, together with the *droit de reconnaissance* (comp. *supra* p. 128), definitely abolished (Article 3 and *Protocole de Clôture sub* 5°, C). The Netherlands had already unilaterally suppressed all navigation dues on the Rhine (and the Ghelders IJssel) in 1850 (*Staatsblad* no. 48), and Prussia, which had ceased to levy the above dues on her stretches of the Rhine and the Main, moreover stipulated in her Peace Treaties with Baden of 17 August 1866 (Article 9), Bavaria of 22 August 1866 (Article 1°) and Hesse of 3 September 1866 (Martens

45. It is curious to note that even in 1868 the Contracting Parties still deemed it necessary expressly to rule out (Article 5) any compulsion on shippers to unload and tranship their cargo and any revival of the old abusive rights of *relâche* and *échelle*, as well as (Article 7) any transit dues.

46. H. VAN DER HOEVEN, *De Rijnvaartakten en de cabotage* (diss. Utrecht, 1956), pp. 70 *et seq.*, mentions the relevant provisions in the convention of 16 May 1865 between the States of the German Customs Union, Article 15 (*Rijndocumenten*, II, No. 330 at p. 70), the treaty of navigation between France and the *Zollverein* of 2 August 1862, Article 9 (Martens, N.R.G.[1], XIX, 286; *Rijndocumenten* II, No. 1313, at p. 19); treaty of commerce and navigation between The Netherlands and the *Zollverein* of 31 December 1851, Articles 1-10 (Martens N.R.G.[1], XVI[2], 216; *Rijndocumenten*, I, No. 258, at p. 521), and Franco-Netherlands treaty of commerce and navigation of 7 July 1865, Article 27 (*Rijndocumenten*, II, No. 331 at p. 70).

N.R.G.[1], XVIII, 333, 336 and 352) their co-operation in abolishing them.

(*d*) The old restriction on foreign Rhine skippers in the choice of their sailing route through the Netherlands to the sea or to Belgium (1831, Article 3) was lifted (Article 2), but only in favour of vessels belonging to Rhine navigation, and not of vessels of States outside the Rhine area (comp. *sub a*).

(*e*) The provisions concerning the freedom of contracting and on *Rangfahrten* (title V of 1831) were struck out because the former was held to be a matter of course and the latter were no longer practised.

(*f*) The old requirement of an examination for the obtaining of a skipper's patent was cancelled (pursuant to Article 15 and clause 4° A of the *Protocole de Clôture* only a certain minimum practice remained obligatory), and it became also possible to obtain a patent only for a specified portion of the Rhine.

(*g*) The formerly compulsory application for a concession to carry out steam navigation on the river was cancelled, as it was no longer an exceptional phenomenon.

A great parade has in addition been made of a further asserted change—and that for the worse—in respect of the freedom of cabotage on the Rhine. This so-called change has only been "discovered" much later: the freedom of cabotage on the Rhine had indeed been unwaveringly upheld and respected in the entire period between 1868 and World War II, and it is only since 1945 that this freedom has been encroached upon, first by the occupant Allied Powers on merely opportunistic economic grounds, and later by Germany from the same motive, but this time supported by a number of pseudo-legal arguments, invented *a posteriori*. This statement needs a brief substantiation.

As I have related earlier, the old abusive "staple right" (*droit d'étape*) proper on the Rhine was already abolished by Article 8 of the Franco-German Convention of 15 August 1804 and this abolition was followed in 1815 by that of the other still remaining rights of "relâche", "échelle" and "de rompre charge" (Article 19 of Annex XVI, *sub* b, to the Final Act of Vienna). This express cancellation of the obsolete rights, formerly levied in the ports of Cologne and Mainz, had deprived the special type of navigation, called "intermediary" (see p. 116), of the last remnant of its historical meaning. It ceased completely to have any further legal scope: there remained only "small" navigation (limited to one and the same riparian State) and "great" navigation (across inter-state borders). But this simplification did not in any way affect the existing situation with regard to cabotage: this remained as free as it had, in law and in fact, always been until that time. A contrary conclusion, it is true, has been drawn at a much later date from certain diplomatic exchanges during the preparation of the text of the new Convention of Mannheim (1868), but, as H. van der Hoeven has convincingly demonstrated in his academic thesis of 1956 at the University of Utrecht, *De Rijnvaartakten en de cabotage*, that conclusion, erroneously drawn therefrom by TELDERS in *Nederlandsch Juristenblad* 1937, p. 644, in connexion with a Judgment of the Supreme Court of 1934, is due to a simple misinterpretation of the *travaux préparatoires*, to which even the Netherlands Supreme Court fell a victim in 1954.[47]

Article 46 of the Act of Mainz (1831), inserted in Title IV and devoted to the right to exercise navigation on the Rhine, laid down in effect that the Act was intended to apply neither to (*a*) the transport of persons and goods from one bank to the other, nor to (*b*) cases where navigation by a master was limited to the territory of his own sovereign.[48] The provision under (*b*), according to which such a master was exclusively placed under the authority of the country where he carried on his trade, meant that the sovereign concerned was free to regulate Rhine navigation, exercised by his own subjects solely within his own territory, as he thought fit. Consequently, this particular group of masters did not automatically come under the general requirement of a patent for all fluvial navigation, as laid down in Article 42, para. 2. When an overall simplification of the Act of Mainz was considered and a provision was drafted pursuant to which the requirement of a patent was thenceforward expressly confined to "great" navigation, from one State to another or to the sea (see now Article 15 of the Revised Convention of Mannheim),[49] the old proviso in the second phrase of Article 46 of the Act of Mainz lost its meaning. Hence the—quite correct—remark made in a Prussian Memorandum

47. Judgment of 4 May 1954 (*Ned. Jur.* 1954, No. 382; *I.L.R.* 1954, p. 3). Comp. p. 137 below.
48. The French and German texts of Article 46 (1831) did not correspond in full. Whilst the German text ran as follows: "Das Uebersetzen von Personen, Pferden, Wagen, Gepäcke oder anderen Gegenständen von einem Ufer an das gegenüberliegende, und was sonst zum gemeinen Verkehr der beiden Ufer gehört, hat mit dieser Schifffahrtsordnung nichts gemein. Auch wird dieselbe überhaupt nicht angewendet, wo die Fahrt eines Schiffspatrons oder Führers auf das eigene Gebiet seines Landesherrn sich beschränkt.—Ein solcher steht allein unter der Obrigkeit des Landes, wo er sein Gewerbe treibt"; the parallel French text was couched in the following words: "Le transport de personnes, chevaux, voitures, effets et autres objets d'une rive à l'autre, et ce qui tient au commerce ordinaire des deux rives, n'a rien de commun avec le présent règlement, non plus que la navigation d'un patron ou conducteur restreint à l'exercer dans l'enceinte du territoire de son souverain, sans en dépasser les limites, un tel patron ou conducteur n'étant assujetti qu'aux autorités du pays où il exerce son métier".
49. "Le droit de conduire un bateau à voiles ou à vapeur sur le Rhin dans tout son parcours depuis Bâle jusqu'à la pleine mer ou sur une partie du fleuve appartenant à plusieurs Etats riverains n'est accordé qu'à ceux qui prouvent qu'ils ont pratiqué la navigation sur le Rhin pendant un temps déterminé et qu'ils ont reçu du Gouvernement de l'Etat riverain où ils ont pris domicile une patente les autorisant à l'exercice indépendant de la profession de batelier". Comp. for further details *sub* 4° of the *Protocole de Clôture*.

accompanying Prussia's proposals for the revision of the Act of Mainz, which explained the proposed substitution of a new Article 22 (now Article 24) for the old Article 46 as follows: "Der Art. 22 handelt von der Fährgerechtigkeit und entspricht dem ersten Satze des Art. 46 der Akte von 1831. Der übrige Inhalt dieses Artikels ist *als selbstverständlich weggelassen* [my italics, V.] worden". It was purely a mistake of TELDERS, in an article of 1937 (see below), to interpret that explanatory remark about the self-evident cancellation of the last part of Article 46 in the sense that it should be suppressed for quite a different reason, namely, that cabotage was in any case, as a matter of course, already reserved for vessels under the flag of the riparian State concerned. The provision was in fact never construed in that sense until after World War II.

The confusion which the italicized words "als selbstverständlich weggelassen" have in the 1930's caused in the Netherlands appears from the following survey.

In its judgments of 17 December 1934 (*Ned. Jur.* 1935, p. 5 and 11; *A.D.* 1933-1934, Case No. 4), by which the Supreme Court ruled that the Netherlands Law on the Proportionate Distribution of Freight of 5 May 1933 (*Staatsblad* no. 251) did not apply to Rhine shipping because of its inconsistency with the Convention of Mannheim, it based its decision, *inter alia*, on the historical argument that, as Article 46 (second sentence) of the Act of Mainz had not been transferred to the new Convention, it followed *a contrario* that the reservation of cabotage to the national flags was in 1868 deliberately abandoned.

FORTUIN, in an article in *Ned. Juristenblad* 1937, p. 565, was the first to suggest that the Supreme Court had made an historical mistake, that the argument *a contrario* was fallacious and that there had been no intention to change the existing situation under the Act of Mainz. He doubted, however, if the remark on the "Selbstverständlichkeit" of the cancellation, made by the Prussian Government in its commentary of 3 November 1868 concerning the Convention for the House of Representatives, had, as an *ex parte* statement *ex post*, any value for the interpretation of the Mannheim Convention of 17 October 1868.

TELDERS, in an article in the same periodical 1937, at p. 644, thereupon rightly dismissed this doubt by pointing out that exactly the same remark on the "Selbstverständlichkeit" of the deletion of Article 46 (second sentence) had already been made in the Prussian Government's commentary upon its proposals for a revision of the Act of Mainz of 17 September 1867, so that the Contracting Parties had accepted the new text with full knowledge of what its purpose was. And he argued further that the cancellation of the provision was intended to maintain a legal situation which in his view had already existed since 1831, namely, that cabotage was reserved for the riparian State concerned.

The Supreme Court was obviously so impressed by this argument derived from the three German words "als selbstverständlich weggelassen" that it later reversed its previous case law and held, in its judgment of 4 May 1954 (*Ned. Jur.* 1954, no. 382), that it followed from the genesis of Article 24 that the riparian States had preserved the right to restrict navigation "which was exercised by the State's own nationals inside its own frontiers".

Neither the Court nor the commentators on the controversy at the time made a distinction between masters of a river vessel with and one without a patent. What the commentators discussed was only whether the above passage in the judgment between quotes was aimed at exclusively inland voyages, or at inland voyages even as parts of an international voyage, or at voyages by exclusively inland businesses. These three possibilities of construction were on the basis of TELDERS's opinion of 1937 analysed by the Netherlands Rhine Navigation Commissioners in an advice to the Ministry of Foreign Affairs, inserted in *Verzamelde Geschriften van Prof. Mr. B. M. Telders* (The Hague, 1947), vol. IV, pp. 54 *et seq*. Their conclusion was that the third of the three interpretations was the only acceptable and that, therefore, the restriction of the freedom of Rhine navigation could as far as the Netherlands were concerned only apply to "purely Netherlands regular services run by a Netherlands national between Rhine ports situated in the Netherlands". The reservation of cabotage was thus confined within the strictest possible limits.

It was only in VAN DER HOEVEN's thesis of 1956 that the events of 1867/ 1868 and the meaning of the controversial three words were correctly construed, to the effect that, despite the restrictive appearance of the terms of the second sentence of Article 46 (1831), cabotage had always been free on the Rhine up to 1867/8 and that the cancellation of that sentence in 1868 did not produce any change in disfavour of this freedom.

It may further be stated that the new Article 24(1868) at the same time corrected an obvious mistake in the wording of Article 46 (1831): the text of the latter made the wrong impression as if a ferry service and "small cabotage" fell entirely outside the scope of the Act, but they did in fact come under the police regulations on navigation. Hence the new text of Article 24:

"Les dispositions de la présente Convention ne sont pas applicables aux transports d'une rive à l'autre, sauf la clause indiquée à l'article 32" (dealing with breaches of the rules on the policing of navigation).

Shortly after the conclusion of the Revised Act of 1868 the situation changed again owing to France's defeat in her war with Germany: France ceased to be a Rhine State and there only remained five, namely: Baden, Bavaria, Hesse, the Netherlands and Prussia.

The Act of Mannheim was in its turn complemented by a Protocol of 18 September 1895 (*Rijndocumenten*, II, no. 545, p. 379; *Tr. blad* 1955, no. 161, p. 44; *B.F.S.P.*, vol. 87, p. 788).

This treaty basis has subsisted until the Peace Treaty of Versailles (1919) after World War I which again produced a major change in the legal situation. Not only was France restored as a Rhine State, but Articles 354 *et seq*. of that Treaty also modified considerably the general regime of the Rhine. The modifications of the Revised Convention of Mannheim, which should for the rest continue to govern navigation on the Rhine, were to the following effect.

The Central Commission was to be "internationalized" by the admission of representatives of three non-riparian States and to comprise in future 19 members (2 for the Netherlands, Switzerland, Great Britain,

Italy, and Belgium each; 4 for the riparian German States together; and 4 for France, which in addition shall appoint the President); its headquarters shall henceforth be at Strasbourg (Article 355). The discrimination still in force between vessels belonging to Rhine navigation (*i.e.*, of the riparian States) and those of other nations was abolished for the benefit of the latter. None of the provisions of the Mannheim Convention on skipper's patents (Articles 15-20 and Final Protocol *sub* 4, A-B)[50] and pilots (Article 26) shall in future impede the free navigation of vessels and crews of all nations on the Rhine, and Article 22 (dealing with the necessity of a ship's patent) shall henceforth be applied only to vessels registered on the Rhine (Article 356). The relevant Articles 355 and 356, moreover, make a somewhat ambiguous mention of "decisions" of the Commission: did that imply a basic increase of the traditional powers of the Commission? Further detailed provisions were laid down in Articles 358-362, dealing successively with: (358) the right for France (*a*) to take water from the Rhine for navigation and irrigation canals and for any other purpose, and (*b*) subject to payment, to the power derived from works of regulation on the river, and to execute the necessary works even on the German bank,—with certain complementary obligations of Germany; (359) the requirement of previous approval by the Central Commission of the carrying out of further works in the bed or on either bank of the river; (360) the option for France to substitute herself as regards, or to denounce existing agreements between, Alsace Lorraine and Baden, and to have the necessary works for the upkeep or improvements of the navigability of the Rhine above Mannheim carried out; (361) the possible creation by Belgium of a deep-draught Rhine-Meuse waterway in the region of Ruhrort; (362) Germany's undertaking not to object to any proposals by the Central Commission for an extension of its jurisdiction to (i) the Luxemburg section of the Moselle; (ii) the Swiss section of the Rhine up to the Lake of Constance (both subject to the consent of the territorial State), and (iii) the lateral canals or channels which might be established to duplicate, improve or connect naturally navigable sections of the Rhine or the Moselle—no such extension having actually taken place.

Since, however, as the Allied and Associated Powers themselves recognized in Article 354 (5), the Treaty of Versailles could not legally alter the Convention of Mannheim without the consent of the Netherlands, the latter's opposition to a number of amendments led to the signature of two successive Protocols between the Netherlands and

50. Already earlier revised by a Convention of 4 June 1898 (Martens, N.R.G.[2], XXIX, 113; *Tr. blad* 1955, No. 161, p. 47). Protocol 43 of the Central Commission has subsequently, on 14 December 1922 (supplemented by Protocol 22 of 22 December 1923), recorded the conclusion of a new convention on Rhine skipper's patents (*ibid.*, at pp. 65 and 68).

Belgium, France, Great Britain and Italy, respectively on 21 January 1921 and 29 March 1923 (Martens, N.R.G³.,XII, 603, 605). By the first of these two protocols the provisions of the Treaty were modified, mainly to the effect that

(*ad* Article 355) the Central Commission was extended to 20 members by the increase of the number of Netherlands representatives from 2 to 3;

(*ad* Article 356) its provisions should not be interpreted as prejudging the territorial extent of the competence of the Central Commission nor the legal value of its regulations.

Further reservations made by the Netherlands related to the Articles 356-362 of the Treaty of Versailles, laying down, among other things, that

(*ad* Article 358²) the communication prescribed there shall be made prior to the execution of the works, which moreover may not be undertaken before having acquired the adhesion of the Central Commission, and that the "derivations" envisaged in that paragraph comprise lateral canals;

(*ad* Article 359) this does not prejudge the question as to whether the delegates of the Central Commission will be designated or not;

(*ad* Article 361) the Netherlands adhesion did not imply by itself the consent of the Netherlands to the creation of a deep-draught Rhine-Meuse navigable waterway in the region of Ruhrort, and that this Article only related to the German part of that waterway;

(*ad* Article 362³) this provision must be construed in the sense that, on the one hand, the new substituting lateral canals and channels envisaged there will be *ipso jure* subject to the jurisdiction of the Central Commission but that, on the other, such extension of its jurisdiction cannot be effected on Netherlands territory without the consent of the Netherlands.

The first Protocol of 1921, summarized above, did not yet, however, clarify sufficiently the legal value of the resolutions of the Central Commission. Therefor, a second Protocol was drawn up in 1923 which laid down that:

> "Les Résolutions de la Commission Centrale pour la Navigation du Rhin sont prises à la majorité des voix.
> Aucun Etat n'est tenu d'assurer l'exécution de celles de ces Résolutions auxquelles il refuserait son approbation".

As TELDERS has set out in his *Der Kampf um die neue Rheinschiffahrtsakte* (*Öffentlichrechtliche Vorträge und Schriften*, Heft 17, 1934, Königsberg; *Verzamelde Geschriften* vol. IV, p. 1), the development of the legal regime of the Rhine has ever since 1919 been dominated by specific demands of France relative to three points in which she was especially interested, *viz.* (*a*) France's hegemony in the Central Commission; (*b*) an extension of the latter's powers from the substantive point of view; (*c*) a territorial extension of its competence. Point (*a*) was in fact already achieved by the provisions of the Peace Treaty of Versailles, summarized above, but on points (*b*) and (*c*) France still strove after further gains. It was in the main[51] these French endeavours which in the 1930's made the ensuing negotiations for the adoption of a new Rhine Navigation Act, as prescribed in Article 354 of the Treaty of Versailles, difficult.

The first draft of a new Act was adopted by the enlarged Central Commission in its session of 18 November 1932 (see for its text the above-cited publication of TELDERS, *Der Kampf um die neue Rheinschiff-fahrtsakte*, pp. 17-51, with a draft *Protocole de Clôture* at pp. 53-55). Since, however, various delegations made reservations with regard to the draft of several articles or refused to endorse them, the politico-legal struggle continued and even on 4 May 1936, when a more definitive text of the new Convention was adopted, the delegations still differed to such an extent that the draft-Convention, the so-called Act of Strasbourg, could not yet be signed, but only initialled. The deadlock was then, on a combined Franco-German proposal, provisionally resolved by the adoption of a *modus vivendi*, but this again was rejected by the Netherlands. See for the text of the *modus vivendi*: Martens, N.R.G.[3], XXXVI, 769.

The new Act of May 1936 has never been definitively signed owing to the overthrow of the entire legal regime of the Rhine by Germany's decision, later in the same year, to denounce the Convention of Mannheim, entailing her withdrawal from the Central Commission, a withdrawal which was in 1937 followed by Italy.

Since this Act of Strasbourg, which was intended to effect a radical revision of the law relating to the Rhine, has thus remained a dead letter, I abstain from summarizing its contents.

Germany's denunciation of the Convention was, of course, illegal and null and void under international law, as I have at the time argued in a leading article "Acte van Mannheim vervallen?" (Has the Mannheim Act lapsed?) in the *Nieuwe Rotterdamsche Courant* of 23 November 1936, but it has caused much legal trouble as regards the normal operation of the traditional Rhine regime, as is evidenced by a number of cases which were brought before the Netherlands courts after 1936 (see *infra* pp. 181-182). It has not, however, prevented the adoption of revised regulations on navigation on the Rhine by the rump-Commission on 25 August 1938 (Martens, N.R.G.[3], XXXVI, 802) and has further induced three non-German States, namely, Belgium, France and the Netherlands, to agree upon an emergency arrangement of 3 April 1939 (*ibid.*, XXXVII, 398) of a very complicated character.

As from 1933, for the rest, the Netherlands legislature and Government had on their side also taken certain steps which tended to under-

51. An additional subject of controversy concerned the demand of the Netherlands Government to obtain for the port of Rotterdam the same facilities as had been granted to Antwerp in the form of the so-called "surtaxe d'entrepôt".

mine the foundations of the conventional Rhine regime by enacting laws or decrees on inland shipping which were at variance with the principles of the Mannheim Convention. However, these attempts were in 1934 fortunately thwarted in part by the Supreme Court (see below, p. 174).

The outbreak of World War II made all restoration or novel development of the traditional Rhine regime impossible. At the close of that war the situation was temporarily dominated by the Allied occupation of Germany which necessitated various emergency measures that made short shrift of the provisions of the Act of Mannheim. The Central Commission was reconstituted in the new composition of representatives of Belgium, France, Great Britain, the Netherlands, Switzerland and the United States,[52] and on the footing of one vote for each of the States represented. The gradually reconstituted federal State of West Germany, the German Federal Republic, was only readmitted to the Central Commission on 28 June 1950, following an exchange of notes between the Allied High Commission and the German Federal Chancellor (*Tr. blad* 1955, no. 161, p. 155), by which "Die Bundesregierung (sich verpflichtete), vom Zeitpunkt ihres Beitritts an, ebenso wie die jetzigen Mitglieder, alle sich aus dem Mannheimer Abkommen vom 17. Oktober 1868 und aus den seitdem daran vorgenommenen Abänderungen ergebenden Rechte und Pflichten auf sich zu nehmen".

It was only from this restoration of the traditional Rhine regime onwards that West Germany—to a certain extent following in the footsteps of the Netherlands since 1933—resolutely proceeded to sapping one of the foundations of that regime by claiming the right freely to legislate for her inland navigation contrary to the principle of freedom on the footing of complete equality which underlies the Mannheim Convention. Whereas the Netherlands Government had, with only partial success, attempted to restrict the liberty of their own inland navigation by forcing it into the strait waistcoat of a system of freight distribution contrary to the freedom principle (comp. on this complicated subject below, p. 174), Germany strove for a privileged position of her own inland navigation by shaking off one of the basic and never before disputed obligations under the Act, *viz.*, by denying to Netherlands Rhine vessels the traditional, more than secular, right of free cabotage on the river. This latter controversy has not yet found a solution, but the parties have by their general treaty of 8 April 1960 (*U.N.T.S.*, vol. 509, p. 246) agreed on the admissibility of an action on this and other accounts before the International Court of Justice by either side. See the article by B. Vitanyi in the *R.G.D.I.P.* 1969 (73), pp. 953-986.

52. The latter in virtue of an exchange of notes with France and Great Britain (*Annuaire européen*, 1956 (II), 278). The United States, however, withdrew again at the end of 1964 (*ibid.* 1964 (XII), 139 and *R.G.D.I.P.* 1965 (69), 151).

The protracted negotiations which have since then been resumed in Strasbourg for a revision of the Convention of Mannheim have in the event resulted in the conclusion, on 20 November 1963, of a new Convention (*Tr. blad* 1964, no. 83; *Les actes du Rhin et de la Moselle*, 1966, p. 54) with a much less ambitious content than that of 4 May 1936. It is indeed confined to a limited number of alterations of the old Convention of Mannheim, consisting of certain amendments to Articles 43 and 46 and the intercalation of five new Articles 34*bis*, 35*bis*, 35*ter*, 37*bis* and 45*bis*. Their purport was mainly to lay down generally acceptable rules concerning the system of voting on, and the legal force of, resolutions in the Central Commission, and to modify, or to fill certain gaps in, the existing special Rhine jurisdiction rules.

B. *The Danube*

The legal history of the Danube is, on the one hand, so complicated that to adequately describe it would need, and would deserve an elaborate monograph, but on the other, so important that it cannot be passed over in silence. I can only solve this dilemma by summarizing briefly here its general course.

The Danube, its tributaries and delta embranchments have been conspicuous of old for the political and legal rôle that they have played both in the delimitation of State frontiers between the Ottoman Empire, on the one side and Austria and Russia, on the other, and with regard to their use as navigable waterways.

In order not to go further back than the end of the 17th century, I only recall to mind here that large stretches of the lower Danube have for a long time, from the middle of the 15th to the end of the 17th century, been dominated exclusively or mainly by the Turks, until the second part of the 16th century as far up as to Belgrade, and since the ominous (first) battle of Mohács (1526) even extending to halfway between Ofen-Pest and Vienna. Its history in international law only began with the peace treaty—formally a twenty years' armistice—of Carlowitz of 26 January 1699 (Dumont, VII², 448), which marked the first serious decline of the power of the Turks after their second vain siege of Vienna (1683), as a result of their military defeats at Mohács (1687), Slankamen (1691) and Zenta (1697). This first treaty of a long series restored to Austria both Hungary and Transylvania with the exception of the Banate of Temesvár (enclosed between the rivers Maros, Theiss and Danube) which was to remain Turkish, and carried the new Austro-Turkish boundary from the confluent of the Theiss with the Danube further westward mainly along the river Save, again with the exception of an area opposite to Belgrade between the Danube and the Save, which was also left to the Ottoman Empire.[53]—At that juncture the

53. The new frontier was in fact to run from the Carpathian Mountains west-

Russians were still far from the Danube delta, being separated from it at their south-westernmost outpost on the Sea of Azow by the land of the Crimean Tartars, Yedisan and Bessarabia.

The following Austro-Turkish war and the ensuing peace treaty of Passarowitz (Požarevac) of 21 July 1718 (Dumont, VIII[1], 524) brought Austria new territorial gains, namely, the Banate of Temesvár, the adjoining Banate of Craïova (Little Wallachia) east of it up to the river Aluta (Oltŭ) and a large part of Serbia between the rivers Timok and Drina as far south as Novibasar, including Belgrade and the area opposite that town between the Danube and the Save mentioned above. The Danube thus became the boundary river between Austria and the Ottoman Empire from the mouth of the river Aluta to that of the river Timok, whereas its section between the Timok and Belgrade became an entirely Austrian river just as did the section of the Save between Belgrade and the mouth of the Drina.

However, fortune turned again in the following war, terminated by the peace treaty of Belgrade of 18 September 1739 (Wenck, I, 326) by which Turkey achieved the retrocession to her of Serbia, the Banate of Craïova and the Danube island of Orsova with a small plain facing it in the south-easternmost part of the Banate of Temesvár. As a result of this treaty the Save and the Danube finally became the Austro-Turkish boundary from the river Unna in the west to the river Timok in the east, whereas the entire further section of the Danube from the Timok to the delta remained under Turkish rule as the frontier between the Danubian vassal principalities of Wallachia and Moldavia (north) and Bulgaria and the Dobrudja (south). And so it remained for a long time until the legal situation changed again as a consequence of the emancipation of the Ottoman vassal States to the status of sovereignty in the period following the peace congress of Paris (1856).

As a counterpart to the Austrian advance on the Danube since the end of the 17th century, a similar Russian advance began, but only in the last quarter of the 18th century. After Azow had repeatedly become a bone of contention between Russia and the Ottoman Empire and had changed hands more than once, Russia's march towards the cupolae of the Aghia Sophia far away along the northern banks of the Sea of Azow and the Black Sea was initiated only by the Russo-Turkish war of 1768-1774, a war which proved disastrous for the Ottoman Empire and ended in the harsh peace treaty of Küçük Kaynarca of 21 July 1774 (Martens, R[2], II, 286), by the terms of which the nations of the Crimean Tartars

ward along the river Maros into the Theiss (Tisza), along this river southward to the Danube, over a short distance westward along the Danube itself, but then leaving it and winding through the countryside between the Danube and the Save towards the mouth of the river Bossuth, and finally along this river to the Unna,—all these rivers belonging to the Danube basin.

were freed from Turkish suzerainty and declared to be thenceforward independent nations "qui se gouvernent par elles-mêmes et ne dépendent que de Dieu seul",[54] under their own khans from the race of Djenghis Khan.

Although Russia gave up most of her conquests and returned the whole of Bessarabia, with the northern Kilia branch of the Danube in its delta, the vassal principalities of Moldavia and Wallachia and all the occupied islands of the Aegean archipelago to the Sublime Porte, the Crimea and the Kuban with the districts between the rivers Berda, Koushkaya-woda and Dniepr, and even all the land between the rivers Bug and Dniestr up to the Polish frontiers were ceded to the "independent" nation of the Tartars, but with some characteristic exceptions, namely, the fortresses of Kerch and Yenikalé (on the strait connecting the Sea of Azow with the Black Sea) and Kilboroun (Kinburn) at the mouth of the Dniepr, with some adjacent country on both sides of that mouth. The fortress of Ochakov east of Odessa, however, was left to the Ottoman Empire.—From the signing of that treaty onwards Russia's march on Constantinople went steadily on:

the Crimea and the island of Taman (at the eastern entrance of the Sea of Azow), the heritage of the Crimean Tartars, were incorporated into the Russian Empire on the strength of an Act of 8 January 1784 (Martens, R^2, III, 707), which proclaimed the river Kuban to be the frontier in the east and the Dniestr in the west;

in conformity with that development the Russo-Turkish boundary was, by the peace treaty of Jassy (Jaşi) of 9 January 1792 (*ibid.*, R^2, V, 291), expressly declared to be formed "pour toujours" by the Dniestr: it confirmed Russian rule over Yedisan;

by the treaty of Bucharest of 28 May 1812 (*ibid.*, N.R. III, 379) the boundary was again carried forward, to the river Pruth, and the left bank of the Danube was reached: the northern Kilia arm was to be the frontier, but the larger islands of the delta were to remain Turkish; thus Bessarabia was engulfed by the Russian Empire;

after a minor change in the boundary regulations by a protocol of 21 August 1817, confirmed by the treaty of Akkerman of 7 October 1826 (*ibid.*, N.R., VI, 1053), Russia pushed still further, across the Danube delta, in virtue of the peace treaty of Adrianople of 14 September 1829 (*ibid.*, N.R., VIII, 143), thus reaching her farthest territorial advance to the heart of the Ottoman Empire: the river Pruth remained the frontier, but the whole of the delta became Russian, inclusive of the southern, the St. Georges arm, the adjoining Turkish bank on the south to be left

54. In the official French translation of the treaty text (which was itself drawn up in Russian, Turkish and Italian), as given by Strupp, *Ausgewählte diplomatische Aktenstücke zur orientalischen Frage*, p. 18.

desert over a distance of two hours.[55] Comp. on these boundary regulations also Chapter VI, p. 514.

The advance of Russia was definitively halted by her defeat in the Crimean war (1853-1856), although even after the peace treaty of Paris of 30 March 1856 the Russian steam-roller has attempted to regain its impetus. Article 20 of that peace treaty (Martens, N.R.G.[1], XV, 770) forced the Russo-Turkish frontier back across the Danube delta and over the southern part of Bessarabia to a line running from the Black Sea near the lake of Bournu-Sola to the river Pruth via Trajan's wall and the river Yalpuck, allocating both those areas to the principality of Moldavia, then on its way to independence,[56] but Russia's return offensive of 1877 brought her back again to the Danube, though not further than the thalweg of the northern, Kilia branch, on the strength of Article 45 of the peace treaty of Berlin of 13 July 1878 (*ibid.*, N.R.G.[2], III, 449), the new independent Romania being pensioned off by the Great Powers and their "honest broker" Bismarck with the acquisition of the Dobrudja south of the Danube delta in exchange for Bessarabia to the north of it (Article 46). The result was that from 1878 onwards Russia and Romania became neighbours at the mouth of the Danube, divided by the thalweg of the northern, the Kilia arm, and its southernmost outlet to the Black Sea, the Vecchiŭ (or Stary) Stamboul.

This territorial situation changed again after the first World War, when the Principal Allied Powers were in a position, owing to the collapse of Russia, to reunite Bessarabia to Romania. This was done by their treaty of Paris with that country of 28 October 1920 (*ibid.*, N.R.G.[3], XII, 849), which once again made the Dniestr the frontier between Romania and Russia. The latter State would be invited to adhere to the treaty as soon as a Russian Government recognized by the High Contracting Parties should come into existence.

It is only against this background of a long series of territorial and political changes that the legal history of the Danube as an international river can be fully understood in its consecutive phases. After its tributaries had already, as they successively became Austro-Turkish boundary

55. The treaty does not specify what a distance of two hours is. It was probably intended to be measured by the step of a horse as was expressly stated in Article 7 of an earlier peace treaty between Russia and Turkey of 13 June 1700 (Strupp, *loco cit.*, p. 6) which delimited around the fortress of Azow "un périmètre de dix heures d'étendue, selon qu'elles se mesurent ordinairement au pas du cheval".
56. Article 21. This allocation was, however, in part repealed by a subsequent protocol of 9 January 1857 (*ibid.*, N.R.G.[1], XV, 793), confirmed by a treaty of 19 June 1857 (*ibid.*, XVI[2]. 11), which placed the Danube delta again under the "immediate sovereignty" of the Sublime Porte together with the Island of the Serpents off the coast, which had hitherto always been passed over in silence.

146

rivers in the period 1699-1739, been declared to be free for the various uses to which rivers could in those days be put—the watering of cattle, fishing, navigation by cargo-vessels; under certain conditions also the stationing of *molendinariae naves* for the purpose of diverting water from them,[57]—freedom of navigation on the Danube itself appeared in treaty law in 1774 (Article 11 of the peace treaty of Küçük Kaynarca), at a moment, that is, when Russia had not yet become a Danubian State. She was, however, at that time in a position to impose her will on the Sultan in order to acquire for herself the same rights which France and Great Britain in particular already possessed in virtue of the Capitulations, unilaterally bestowed upon them by the Sublime Porte:

> "... La Sublime Porte permet encore aux sujets de l'Empire russe de faire dans ses possessions le commerce par terre ainsi que par eau, en naviguant même sur le fleuve du Danube, ... avec tous les mêmes privilèges et avantages dont jouissent dans les susdites possessions les nations les plus amies de la Sublime Porte, et qu'Elle favorise le plus dans les privilèges de commerce, telles que les Français et les Anglais. Les Capitulations de ces deux nations et des autres doivent, dans toutes les occassions, comme si elles étaient insérées ici mot pour mot, servir de règle tant pour le commerce des Russes que pour les marchands russes ..."

When Russia became a riparian State of the Danube in 1812, it was stipulated in Article 4 *in fine* of the Russo-Turkish treaty of Bucharest that

> "Les bâtiments marchands des deux Puissances pourront entrer dans l'embouchure du Danube [*i.e.*, the Kilia arm], en sortir et naviguer sur toute l'étendue de ce fleuve",

with the special proviso, however, that

> "les vaisseaux de guerre russes ne pourront jamais remonter le Danube que jusqu'à son confluent avec le Pruth".

This freedom was extended in Article 3 of the Russo-Turkish treaty of Adrianople of 1829 to the effect that

> "Les bâtiments marchands des deux Puissances auront la faculté de naviguer sur le Danube dans tout son cours, et ceux qui portent le pavillon Ottoman pourront librement entrer dans les embouchures de Vili et de Souliné; celle de Saint-Georges demeurera commune aux pavillons de guerre et marchands des deux Puissances contractantes. Mais les vaisseaux de guerre russes ne

57. Comp. *e.g.*, Article 1, §§ 2 and 3 of the Austro-Russian treaty of Passarowitz of 21 July 1718: "... ut antehac (*viz.*, in Article 1, § 2 of the treaty of Carlowitz) circa fluvium Marusium observatum fuerat, Aluta, quoad potationem pecorum et piscationes, aliosque hujusmodi perquam necessarios usus, utriusque partis subditis communis sit.—Germanorum, eorundemque subditorum navibus onerariis e Transylvania in Danubium ultro citroque commeare liceat; subditis vero Valachis navicularum piscatoriarum, aliarumque cymbarum absque impedimento usus permittetur; naves tamen molendinariae in locis convenientibus, ubi navigationi mercatorum obesse non possunt, communi gubernatorum in confiniis existentium consensu collocentur".

pourront, en remontant le Danube, dépasser l'endroit de sa jonction avec le Pruth".

The first time that the Danube was expressly subjected to the Vienna regime of international rivers was, however, in a special Austro-Russian Convention of 25 July 1840 (Martens, N.R.G.[1], I, 208), in the preamble of which the two Emperors relate that

> "ils ne sauraient mieux atteindre (le) but (de faciliter, d'étendre et d'ac-croître de plus en plus les relations commerciales entre leurs Etats respectifs, en donnant le plus grand développement à la navigation du Danube) qu'en appliquant à ce fleuve les mêmes principes que le Congrès de Vienne a établis ..."

This bilateral decision, which implied freedom for vessels of all nations at peace with Russia and a prohibition of shipping tolls, was only made multilateral by Article 15 of the peace treaty of Paris of 30 March 1856 by which the Vienna principles were made applicable to the Danube and its mouths, and the importance of this stipulation was enhanced by the express declaration that it "fait désormais partie du droit public de l'Europe", and by placing it under a joint guarantee.

The Paris treaty (Articles 15-19) was at the same time the starting point of a very complicated development. It laid down the principles that the Danube should be free for all flags, that no impediments of navigation should be practised, and that no mere shipping tolls or dues on cargoes should be levied.

Two Commissions were set up:

(*a*) a temporary, the "European" Commission, consisting of repre-sentatives of seven States (Austria, France, Great Britain, Prussia, Russia, Sardinia and Turkey) with the specific task of clearing the mouths of the Danube and the adjacent sea area of sand and other obstructions. These works should be confined to the Danube downstream of Isaktcha; they should be terminated within two years. This Commission was empowered to defray the costs by the levying of dues, to be fixed by it by a majority decision and to be applied to all flags, on a footing of perfect equality. As soon as the clearing works should be completed, this Commission was to be dissolved and its powers to be transferred to the other Commission;

(*b*) a permanent, the "riparian" Commission, also consisting of representatives of seven States (of the riparians Austria, Bavaria, Turkey and Württemberg, and, subject to the approval of their delegates by the Sublime Porte, the three Danubian principalities of Serbia, Wallachia and Moldavia), entrusted with varied tasks: the elaboration of rules on navigation and fluvial police, the removal of all obstacles of whatever nature which still obstructed freedom of navigation, the carrying-out of necessary works anywhere else in the river, and, after the dissolution of the European Commission, the maintenance of the navigability of the mouths and the adjoining sea area. Each of the Contracting Parties

148

would be empowered to station two light vessels at the mouth of the river in order to assure the carrying-out of the rules on navigation etc., once they were fixed in common accord.

Later developments, however, have entirely upset the original scheme. The works on the mouth of the river took much longer than had been foreseen: after nine years, the Powers concerned, in the preamble of their Convention of 28 March 1866 for the approval of the *Règlement de navigation et de police* drawn up by the European Commission for the mouths of the Danube on 2 November 1865 (Martens, N.R.G.[1], XVIII, 143, 144), summed up a series of eight tasks which that Commission had in the meantime fulfilled to their entire satisfaction, but no resolution was taken even then to dissolve the European Commission. On the contrary, it remained in existence, was after fifteen years expressly maintained in its actual composition by Article 4 of the Pontus Treaty of London of 13 March 1871 (*ibid.*, N.R.G.[1], XVIII, 303) for a further period of twelve years, and finally made virtually permanent by reason of Article 2 of a new Danube Navigation Treaty entered into on 10 March 1883 at a Conference in London (protocols: Martens, N.R.G.[2], IX, 346; text of the treaty: *ibid.*, 392) which prolonged the powers of the Commission for a further period of twenty-one years, to be tacitly extended, each time for three years, from 1904, barring possible proposals of any of the Contracting Parties to alter its composition or powers, and it thus remained in office until the first World War.

The extension in terms of time was accompanied by an extension of the membership, Romania being also admitted to participate, and by an extension in geographical respect: whereas the power of the European Commission was initially, and was still under the *Règlement* of 1865 confined to the section between Isaktcha and the Black Sea, it was enlarged by Article 53 of the Peace Treaty of Berlin of 13 July 1878 (*ibid.*, N.R.G.[2], III, 449) to cover also the stretch between Galatz and Isaktcha, and once again by Article 1 of the Treaty of 10 March 1883, just mentioned, to extend as far upstream as Braila. Romania, which had in the meantime become fully independent, refused to join in the decisions of 1883 and it was this refusal which finally, after the lapse of a long period, led to advisory proceedings before the Permanent Court of International Justice (Advisory Opinion of 8 December 1927, *Publications P.C.I.J.*, series B, No. 14). The Court held, against the submission of Romania, "that under the law at present (1927) in force the European Commission of the Danube has the same powers on the maritime sector of the Danube from Galatz to Braila as on the sector below Galatz". The Court found at the same time that the dividing line between the respective competences of the European Commission and of the Romanian authorities, as far as the two main ports were concerned, was not territorial, but functional, namely to be fixed according to the criteria of navigation and of the obligation to ensure in that respect freedom and equal treatment of all flags.

For the rest, Romania's refusal in 1883 to accept the decision of the Great Powers was not the only instance of a lack of co-operation among the Powers involved in the maintenance and development of the legal regime of the Danube. The same unwillingness to allow the free exercise of national sovereignty to be fettered by "supra-national" decisions had already revealed itself on the occasion of the elaboration and enforcement of the first *Rules on navigation and river police*, drawn up by the Riparian Commission, pursuant to Article 17 under 1, of the Peace Treaty of Paris on 7 November 1857 (Martens, N.R.G.[1], XV, 788). Although the Great Powers refused to give their consent to this first Navigation Act on the ground that Austria had succeeded in reserving therein river cabotage for the riparian States, Austria nevertheless put it into force on her own territory, and so it remained until World War I.

There occurred, for that matter, other irregularities in the operation of the river regime. Thus, another *Règlement de navigation, de police fluviale et de surveillance*, which the European Commission, acting under a mandate conferred on it by Article 55 of the Peace Treaty of Berlin of 1878, drew up under the date of 2 June 1882 to regulate navigation on the Danube sector between the Iron Gates and Braila, has in spite of its formal adoption in Article 7 of the abovementioned Danube Navigation Treaty of 10 March 1883, never been carried into actual execution, owing to Romania's refusal to acquiesce in the permanent chairmanship of Austria-Hungary in the new "Mixed Commission of the Danube", set up for this particular sector of the river by Article 96 of the 1882 *Règlement* (texts in Martens, N.R.G.[2], IX, 392 and 394).

This third "Mixed" Commission, which was intended to be composed of representatives of four States: Austria-Hungary, Bulgaria, Romania and Serbia, would for the rest only have complicated still further the already involved regime of the Danube. Its establishment on paper was itself connected with the projected clearing operations directed to improving the navigation of the river on the dangerous stretch of the Iron Gates and the Cataracts near Turnu Severin. These hydraulic engineering works again have their own legal history. The removal of the obstacles was first agreed upon in Article 6 of the Pontus Treaty of 13 March 1871 (Martens, N.R.G.[1], XVIII, 303), and was entrusted to the riparian States concerned, acting in concert; they were empowered, in deviation from Article 15 of the Peace Treaty of Paris, to levy for that purpose from merchant vessels under all flags a temporary special tax. By Article 57 of the Peace Treaty of Berlin, however, the task of executing the hydraulic works was committed to the charge of Austria-Hungary alone, which would also be entitled to collect the tax. The mandate thus given to the Dual Monarchy was in its turn transferred by her to Hungary alone, but was in the event withdrawn by Article 350 of the Peace Treaty of Versailles (1919) and corresponding Articles in the other peace treaties, which opened a new phase in the legal history of the Danube.

The intricacy of this fluvial regime—three different commissions, partly sabotaged by the riparians Austria(-Hungary) and Romania; three different river sectors with shifting geographical limits; a variety of *Règlements de Navigation*, in part irregularly enforced, in part regularly enacted but not enforced—was paralleled by the complications at the mouths of the river, due to repeated territorial changes. As an example: when Russia had regained her foothold on the bank of the Danube at its delta in 1878 (Article 45 of the Peace Treaty of Berlin), she soon contrived, by Articles 3-6 of the Danube Navigation Treaty of London of 16 March 1883, to secure her liberation from certain burdens resting on riparian States. Article 3 eliminated any effective control by the European Commission of "those parts of the Kilia branch, the two banks of which belong to one of the riparians of that branch"; this somewhat cryptic formula withdrew from the supervision of the Commission the three northernmost outlets through which the Kilia branch empties itself into the Black Sea, leaving only the southernmost channel, the Stary (or Vecchiŭ) Stambul as a "mixed" branch.

This first long period of the fluvial law of the Danube, surveyed above from its inception in 1856, came to an end with the first World War. The peace treaties of 1919-1920 removed Germany, Austria, Hungary and Russia from the European Commission—had the Peace Treaty of Bucharest of 7 May 1918 between Germany and Austria-Hungary, on the one hand, and Romania, on the other (Martens, N.R.G.³, X, 856, Articles 24-26), not come to grief as a result of the final defeat of the Central Powers, the opposite development would have taken place: the States of the Entente would have been thrown out!—, and endowed the Danube with a modified regime, laid down in Articles 346-353 of the Peace Treaty of Versailles and the corresponding Articles of the other peace treaties. This amounted to the following:

Apart from its subjection to the temporary general fluvial regime established by the peace treaties pending the elaboration of a definitive Convention (which was to become the Statute of Barcelona of 1921), the Danube was by Article 331 declared "international" from Ulm to the Black Sea, inclusive of all navigable parts of its system which naturally provide more than one State with access to the sea, of all lateral canals and comparable artificial channels and a future Rhine-Danube navigable waterway should this be constructed. The European Commission reassumed the powers it possessed before the war, but as a provisional measure only representatives of Great Britain, France, Italy and Romania should constitute it. From the point where the competence of the

European Commission ceased (*i.e.*, Braila), the Danube system, as extended by Article 331, should be placed under the administration of a new "International Commission", which would no longer be merely "riparian", but was to be composed of two representatives of German riparian States, one representative of each of the other riparian States and one representative of each non-riparian State represented in the future on the European Commission. This new Commission was to undertake the administration provisionally, until such time as a definitive statute had been drawn up by the Powers nominated by the Allied and Associated Powers (to meet within one year). Germany agreed to accept their decisions as to the future regime of the Danube. As already remarked above, the mandate given in 1878 to Austria-Hungary to carry out works at the Iron Gates and her right to levy charges for that purpose were abolished.

The so-called Definitive Statute of the Danube was laid down in a Convention signed at Paris on 23 July 1921 (Martens, N.R.G.³, XII, 606) by the following eight States designated to that effect: Belgium, France, Great Britain, Greece, Italy, Romania, the Serb-Croat-Slovene State and Czecho-Slovakia, in the presence and with the participation of German, Austrian, Bulgarian and Hungarian representatives.

Navigation over the whole Danube system was declared to be unrestricted and open to all flags on a footing of complete equality, even between the subjects, goods and flags of the riparian State concerned and those of any other State, with only a limited reservation regarding cabotage (Article 22). Apart from the Danube itself and the lateral canals and other artificial channels alluded to above, the international river system was to include also the Austro-Czechoslovak frontier sections of the Morava and the Thaya, the Drave from Barcs, the Tisza (Theiss) from the mouth of the Szamos, and the Maros from Arad.

Of the two separate Commissions charged with assuring freedom and equal treatment, the European Commission (dealt with in Articles 4-7), was provisionally still composed of a representative each of France, Great Britain, Italy and Romania, but any European State which, in future, would be able to prove its possession of sufficient maritime commercial and European interests at the mouths of the Danube might, at its request, be accorded representation on the Commission by a unanimous decision of the governments already represented. The European Commission, whose statutory seat was to continue to be at Galatz, retained the powers which it possessed before the war and no alteration was made in its existing rights, prerogatives and privileges. Its authority was to extend under the same conditions as before, and without any modification of its existing limits, over the maritime Danube, that is to say, from the mouths of the river "to the point where the authority of the International Commission commence(d)" (this point being, pursuant to Article 9, Braila), and its powers could only come to an end as a result of an international agreement concluded by all the States represented on the Commission.

Romania's political sensitivity again prevented in 1921 any express and clear mention of a specific terminus of the powers of the European Commission. This ambiguity led to a new dispute between Romania and her partners in the Commission, which the Council of the League of Nations in 1925 brought before the Permanent Court of International Justice for an Advisory Opinion. As mentioned above, this Opinion was delivered on 8 December 1927: against the submissions of Romania which upheld her old thesis that the terminus had always remained Galatz, the Court held that it was Braila, and that the delimitation between the jurisdiction of the European and that of the International Commission in that port could only be of a functional and not of a geographical character. Comp. on this dispute my paper in *The Jurisprudence of the World Court*, vol. I, pp. 118 *et seq.*

For the rest, the Definitive Statute set out in much greater detail (Articles 8-38) the composition, functions, powers and duties of the new International Commission, whose statutory seat would for the first five years be at Bratislawa. This Commission was to be composed, in accordance with the Peace Treaties, of two representatives of the German riparian States, one representative of each of the other riparian States and one representative of each of the non-riparian States which were, or which might be in future, represented on the European Commission. Its authority was to extend over the Danube between Ulm and Braila and over the internationalized river system of tributaries; no other waterway should be placed under its authority without its unanimous consent. It was to be responsible for the unrestricted freedom of navigation and for the treatment of the subjects, goods and flags of all Powers on a footing of complete equality. It was charged with the drawing up of the general programme of important works of improvement, and with the control of the annual programmes of current works of maintenance and improvement drawn up by the individual riparian States. All the works were in principle to be undertaken by the latter, each within the limits of its own frontiers, the current works of maintenance in principle at their own cost, the more important works with the help of moderate navigation dues authorized by the Commission. Further provisions were intended to prevent any discrimination of flag, nationality, port of departure or destination, in the field of navigation dues, customs duties, the use of ports and quays, etc. The general freedom even of cabotage on a footing of perfect equality was only restricted (Article 22 and additional clauses in the Final Protocol) in respect of regular local services for passengers or for national or nationalized goods. Article 24 charged the Commission with the drawing up of uniform Regulations on navigation and river police, which each State should bring into force in its own territory by a legislative or administrative act.[58] Furthermore, special technical and administrative services with central headquarters at Orsova were to be set up in order to maintain and improve navigable conditions on the Danube section of the Iron Gates and the Cataracts (Article 32). A permanent technical commission for the regime of the waters of the Danube was later set up to act in accordance with a set of Rules relative to its attributions and functioning, approved by a Convention of 27 May 1923 (Martens, N.R.G.[3], XXIV, 672, 679), entered into by the riparian States.

Acting under Article 24 of the Statute of 1921, the International Commission has still drawn up on 1 January 1936 new Navigation and River Police Regulations (*ibid.*, XXXVI, 800).

The situation on the Danube changed, however, considerably a short time later as a consequence of the Agreement of Sinaia of 18 August 1938 (*ibid.*, XXXVII, 741). The so-called Definitive Statute of 1921 (Article 42) had foreseen the possibility of a revision of its terms at the expiration of five years if two-thirds of the (twelve) signatory States should so request, in which case the French Government was to summon a general Conference, and a note *ad* Article 42 in the Final Protocol had even foreshadowed the abolition of the European Commission prior to such expiration. It was not, however, this *modus procedendi* that was put into operation in 1938. Availing themselves of the sweeping discretionary powers which Article 7 of the Definitive Statute had conferred upon the States represented on the European Commission jointly, to terminate its powers by a unanimous agreement *inter se*, France and Great Britain, being in 1938, with Italy and Romania, the only States so represented, yielded, as far as they were concerned—Italy on that occasion still remaining aloof—, to Romania's incessant insistence that the "supranational" powers of the European Commission and its agencies on her national soil should be wiped out and transferred to an autonomous Romanian service. When Nazi-Germany was finally accorded representation on the Commission, in accordance with Article 4(2) of the Definitive Statute, by a decision of the then four Member States, including Fascist Italy, dated 1 March 1939 (*ibid.*, N.R.G.[3], XXXVII, 749), both Italy and Germany simultaneously adhered to the Sinaia Agreement, thus making it final and valid.

By this device an end was put to the time-honoured regime which had been established on the Danube in the interest of all seafaring nations by European Congresses, and lately by the Definitive Statute of 1921. Thus a long series of treaty provisions, dating from 1856, 1865, 1871, 1881 and

58. This mandate was first carried out by the promulgation of new Regulations on navigation and police, dated 6 November 1926 (Martens, N.R.G.[3], XXVIII, 171).

1882/3, expressly maintained without alteration by Article 5 of the latter Statute, by a single stroke lost their binding force with the connivance of France and Great Britain. This implied, among other things, the deletion of such offices, created in the common interest, as that of Inspector General of the Lower Danube and of Captain of the Port of Sulina, which were by the Sinaia Agreement replaced by the Directorate of the Maritime Danube, newly established as an autonomous service by the territorial State Romania.

However, the situation turned further to the worse as a result of World War II, which entailed the dissolution of both the European and the International Danube Commission in 1940.

At the Paris Peace Conference of 1946/1947, at which the Soviet Union was represented, the Western Powers attempted in vain to restore the non-riparian States in their position on a revived European Commission, but owing to Soviet opposition the only clause which emerged from the peace negotiations was the uniform clause in Part VII of the peace treaties with Romania (Article 36), Bulgaria (Article 34) and Hungary (Article 38), in the terms of which

> "Navigation on the Danube shall be free and open for the nationals, vessels of commerce, and goods of all States, on a footing of equality in regard to port and navigation charges, and conditions for merchant shipping. The foregoing shall not apply to traffic between ports of the same State",

thus also abolishing the freedom of cabotage.

The Conference on Danube affairs which followed, convoked to Belgrade by the Communist States and attended by the—then seven—riparian States (Bulgaria, Czechoslovakia, Hungary, Romania, Yugoslavia, Ukraina and the USSR), plus France, the United Kingdom and the United States (and Austria with only a consultative vote), failed to reach unanimity on the essentials of a new Danube regime and only succeeded in adopting on 18 August 1948 by a majority vote (7-3) a new Convention regarding the regime of navigation on the Danube (*U.N.T.S.*, vol. 33, p. 181), which was, however, rejected by the three Western Powers.

Looked at from the angle of general international law, this new Convention of Belgrade has come into being yet more irregularly than its earlier counterpart, the Sinaia Agreement, but it is for the time being actually in force. The new single Danube Commission, which has superseded the two old ones and is only composed of one representative of each of the Danube countries,[59] is more an instrument of consultation and co-ordination than a body vested with any real authority. The centre of gravity of the river administration is entirely shifted from the Com-

59. On 7 January 1960 Austria became a full member of the Danube Commission. See Whiteman, vol. 3, p. 900.

mission to the individual riparian States: each of them draws up its own navigation regulations where it is the only riparian State; where the banks are in different hands, the two States concerned act jointly; a special common river administration (by Romania and Yugoslavia) is only set up for the sector of the Iron Gates. Revenue and sanitary supervision, maintenance of the riverbed etc., are also left to the individual States. The new regime extends from Ulm to the Black Sea through the Sulina Channel and Canal. Navigation is nominally free for the national ships and goods of all States for merchant shipping, save for river cabotage which is reserved for each riparian State. Passage of warships from one State to another is restricted to the riparian States and then only in virtue of an agreement between them. Comp. *Völkerrecht* (Berlin-DDR, 1960), pp. 239/240.

On 30 November 1963 Yugoslavia and Romania signed a Final Act, Agreement and other Acts relating to the establishment and operation of the Iron Gates water power and navigation system (*U.N.T.S.*, vols. 512 and 513); among these acts were the Statute of the mixed Yugoslav-Romanian Commission for the Iron Gates and an exchange of letters concerning the adjustment of the frontier on the Danube.[60]

C. *The Congo and the Niger*

As I have set out above under I (*b*), p. 121, the regime of these two rivers forms part of a much wider regulation covering the whole of the "Conventional Congo Basin", as agreed upon in the General Act of the Congo Conference of Berlin of 26 February 1885 (Martens, N.R.G.[2], X, 414).

The general principles laid down in Chapter I of that Act were elaborated in two special Navigation Acts, forming Chapters IV and V, to the effect that on both the Congo and the Niger navigation would be entirely free for *all* nations, on a footing of complete equality, for the carrying of goods as well as passengers, in both directions from the sea to the ports of the interior and *vice versa*, also in the exercise of great and small cabotage. Any shipping monopoly, any transit dues, the establishment of any of the notorious "European" rights of *échelle, étape* (staple), *dépôt, rupture de charge* (last-breaking) or *relâche forcée*, and of any mere shipping toll, not being in the nature of a retribution for harbour, piloting, lighthouse, beacon lights or buoyage, and similar technical or administrative facilities or services, were forbidden. The regime thus detailed was to apply also to the affluents of the Congo and the Niger and, subject to the consent of the sovereign territorial Power concerned, to the streams, rivers, lakes and canals, situated in the zones described at p. 121 above, under 2) and 3). Roads, railways and lateral canals,

60. See S. Stojkovic, *L'importance de la construction du systéme hydro-électrique et de navigation dans le secteur des Portes de Fer pour la navigation internationale* in the *Yugoslav Review of International Law* 1968 (XV), pp. 120-135.

intended to supply the unnavigability or deficiencies of waterways would, as accessories thereof, share the same regime of freedom. There were even provisions dealing with the access of warships to the interior, with the neutralization of the rivers as part of the neutralization of the whole basin and with the continuing validity of the regime of freedom of navigation in time of war, for belligerent and neutral shipping alike, with the sole exception of the carriage of contraband of war.

This neutrality regime, however, completely collapsed in World War I, one of the reasons why the victor States at the Peace Conference of 1919 proceeded to the conclusion of an entirely new Congo Convention, that of Saint-Germain-en-Laye of 10 September 1919 (*ibid.*, N.R.G.[3], XIV, 12). A prospect of possible future modifications or ameliorations of the General Act of Berlin had already been held out in Article 36 thereof, but these were only to be made "d'un commun accord". Since the revision of 1919 was only agreed upon by the victorious Allied Powers[61] *inter se*[62] and an obligation to acquiesce in any such agreement could only be imposed by them upon the vanquished States (Peace Treaties: Articles 126 Versailles, 373 Saint-Germain, 290 Neuilly, 356 Trianon, 415 Sèvres and 100, no. 12 Lausanne), the fundamental question of the validity of such a procedure vis-à-vis other Parties to the General Act of 1885 was bound to arise when, in 1934, Great Britain and Belgium agreed to submit to the Permanent Court of International Justice a dispute which had arisen between them as to the construction of certain articles of the new Convention of Saint-Germain, just mentioned. (Comp. on these proceedings, known as the *Oscar Chinn* case, decided by a Judgment of 12 December 1934 (*Publications P.C.I.J.*, series A/B, No. 63), my *The Jurisprudence of the World Court*, vol. I, pp. 383 *et seq.*)

The Court has in its Judgment declined to enter into an examination of this question of principle, raised by the Netherlands Judge Van Eysinga, supported by the German Judge Schücking, and has decided the Anglo-Belgian controversy on the basis of the new Convention, almost exclusively on the ground, insufficient in my opinion, that the parties had submitted it to the Court as a dispute over the construction of that Convention.

Yet, there would have been ample reason to consider the question thoroughly, because the 1919 Convention has introduced basic changes

---

61. United States of America, Belgium, British Empire, France, Italy, Japan and Portugal.
62. Comp. Article 13 of the new Convention: "Except in so far as the stipulations contained in Article 1 of the present Convention are concerned, the General Act of Berlin of February 26th, 1885, and the General Act of Brussels of July 2nd, 1890, with the accompanying Declaration of equal date, shall be considered as abrogated, in so far as they are binding between the Powers which are Parties to the present Convention".

in the legal regime of the Congo. Not only was the principle of neutralization of the Congo basin abandoned and the abortive International Congo Commission definitively laid to rest, but basic alterations were also made in the essentials of the previous system of freedom and non-discrimination.

As Judge Van Eysinga has rightly argued in his dissenting opinion of 1934 (series A/B, No. 63, pp. 131 *et seq.*, at p. 138-139), the limitation, introduced by the 1919 Convention, of the category of persons who were to benefit by the stipulated equality of treatment, was clearly at variance with the provision of Article V (2) of the Congo Act of 1885 which guaranteed equal protection to all foreigners without distinction. For the rest, this Judge also gave a different construction of the treaty provisions in force—in that he strongly argued that the principle of equal freedom of navigation related not only to its nautical, but also to its commercial aspect, so that a preferential treatment of one user of the river as compared with another was also from the latter aspect an infringement of the Congo regime, even if such treatment was not inspired by the wish to discriminate between nationals and foreigners in favour of the former. Comp. for the rest, on this subject, my above-mentioned analysis of the *Oscar Chinn* case.

The outcome of World War II made already in itself certain alterations of the existing regime of the Congo Basin necessary, as was expressed *inter alia* in Article 42 of the Italian Peace Treaty of Paris of 10 February 1947 (*U.N.T.S.*, vol. 49, p. 3), by which Italy "accepted and recognized any arrangements which might be made by the Allied and Associated Powers concerned for the modification of the Congo Basin Treaties with a view to bringing them into accord with the Charter of the United Nations". However, the ensuing process of decolonization of Africa has placed the matter in an entirely new light and put the older essentially European regulations of 1885 and 1919 in jeopardy. Yet, the need for a liberal regime of the big African waterways has survived the basic revolutionary changes in the political situation on this Continent. This has been recognized by the Organization of African Unity in its conference of Addis Ababa of 1963. The recent development has indeed given birth to new African river communities:[63]

a union of the riparian States of the river Senegal (Mauretania, Mali, Senegal and Guinée), of an economic-technical nature, established in February 1965 at Saint Louis du Sénégal for the *aménagement* of that river, financed by the Member States and a special United Nations fund;

63. They have, for the rest, parallels in other communities, operating in different fields, such as the *Conférence sidérurgique d'Afrique occidentale* of October 1965 (Abidjan), attended by fourteen African States, which dealt with the production of iron and steel. See R. Yakemtchouk, *Le régime international des voies d'eau africaines* in the *Revue Belge de Droit International* 1969, p. 480.

a similar organization for the Chad Basin (Cameroun, Niger, Nigeria and Chad) under a Commission for that basin, June 1965,

and a Commission for the river Niger, assembled for the first time in April 1966, pursuant to a Convention of 1963 (Cameroun, Ivory Coast, Dahomey, Guinée, Upper Volta, Mali, Niger, Nigeria and Chad) and an Agreement of 1964 (*U.N.T.S.*, vol. 587, pp. 11 and 19 respectively). See *A.F.D.I.* 1963 (IX), pp. 866 *et seq.* and 1964 (X), pp. 813 *et seq.*; *R.G.D.I.P.* 1965 (69), pp. 276 *et seq.*

Further particulars concerning these river communities can be found, *inter alia*, in the article by J.-Cl. ANDRÉ, *L'évolution du statut des fleuves internationaux d'Afrique Noire* in *Revue juridique et politique* 1965 (19), pp. 284-310; *A.F.D.I.* 1966 (XII), pp. 782-783; L.A.TECLAFF, *The river basin in history and law* (The Hague, 1967), pp. 174 *et seq.* and *The law of international drainage basins* ed. by A.H.GARRETSON *et al.* (Dobbs Ferry, 1967), pp. 131-133; J.-Cl. GAUTRON in *A.F.D.I.* 1967 (XIII), p. 690.

D. *Weser, Elbe and Oder*

These three rivers are best known, from a legal-historical point of view, for the river tolls which have in the past burdened navigation on them. While referring for some further particulars concerning these three rivers to my systematic survey *infra sub* III, I will therefore pay special attention here in the first place to the history of those tolls.

1. *The Weser*

The *dominium Visurgis* had, from the beginning of the 13th century, formed the object of a dogged fight between three powers dominating parts of the river: the Archbishop of Bremen (in particular, Gerhard II), the city of Bremen, and the count of Oldenburg. In the usual manner of those days[64] a spurious international instrument, pretended to have been in fact issued by the Emperor Henry V and to date back to the year 1111,[65]

---

64. This applies *inter alia* to the counterfeiting of a privilege granted by the Emperor to a count in East-Friesland in 1464, comp. p. 4.

65. The pseudo-privilege of 14 May 1111 of the Emperor Heinrich V and the subsequent one of King Willem of 28 September 1252, in the text of which that of 1111 was transsumed, both equally false, have presumably been fabricated at the same time. The content of the asserted instrument of 1111, which contains a conferment of jurisdiction on the Weser, *inter alios* against pirates, upon Bremen, is historically impossible. I quote in support the interesting comment by the editors of the *Bremisches Urkundenbuch*, EHMCK und VON BIPPEN (1873) in vol. I, pp. 597 *et seq.*:

"Die Unechtheit des Heinrich'schen Privilegs ist seit langer Zeit allgemein anerkannt. Der einzige, der es je ernstlich zu vertheidigen unternahm, Goldast (*Vindiciae diplom. Bremenses b. de Westphalen*, Mon. ined., III, 1971 flg.), macht kaum diplomatische Gründe geltend, sondern wesentlich nur juristische. Ihm kam es bei der zwischen Bremen und Oldenburg im 17. Jahrhundert entbrannten Streit wegen der Hoheitsrechte auf dem Weserstrome lediglich darauf

had been concocted by the city authorities of Bremen as "proof" of their supreme authority over the Weser. It was not, however, this false document, but the actual display of its power over the lower course of the river that gradually established the City's supremacy, also against the Frisians and pirates who attempted to invade the area. About 1400 the City could be held to have in fact possessed itself of the *Stromhoheit*. A special navigation and fishing privilege, still granted to the City by Emperor Charles V on 20 July 1541, this time a genuine instrument, though cancelled shortly afterwards, but soon renewed,[66] was conducive to perpetuating this asserted, but essentially usurped supreme territorial power of the City.—The scales had, however, already begun to tip about 1500 in favour of the Duke of Oldenburg who, in the first quarter of the 16th century, conquered the left bank of the Weser, gradually strengthened his authority and was on 31 March 1623 by an Imperial diploma granted the right to levy a toll on the Weser, a right first exerted at Brake, later near Elsfleth in Oldenburg, near the place where the Hunte empties into the Weser. It is this toll which was mentioned in Article IX, § 2 of the Peace Treaty of Osnabrück of 24 October 1648 (Dumont, VI¹, 450). The resistance of the city of Bremen to that grant only served to bring down on its head a ban of the Empire. Since the 18th century the Dukes of Oldenburg claimed in their turn to have exclusive sovereignty over the lower Weser.

It was that Elsfleth toll which the Duke of Oldenburg has, at the beginning of the 19th century, put up a stubborn fight to retain against the main powers of Europe, a resistance which he has been able to sustain up to 1820. The course of this struggle can be followed from the following documents.

Reichsdeputations-Hauptschluss of 25 February 1803 (Martens, R², VII, 435 *et seq.*, at p. 488), § 27, para. 10: abolition of the toll against a territorial compensation (§ 3, para. 2). The text of the provision concerned still reflects the historical rivalry: "Pour mettre le commerce de Brême et la navigation du Bas-Weser à l'abri de toute entrave, le péage

an Bremens Rechtstitel auf dieselben zu erweisen, und angesichts dieses mit Leidenschaft verfolgten praktischen Zwecks war ihm die objective Würdigung des kläglichen Machwerks unmöglich". Comp. also the academic thesis (Göttingen, 1960) of J. G. SPIER, *Geschichte der bremischen Strom-, Schiffahrts- und Hafenpolizei.*

66. Bremen's "Stromhoheit" was in 1544 curtailed and reduced to the right of erecting beacons and of levying a toll. The continued disputes between the count of Oldenburg and the city of Bremen have first led to proceedings before the *Reichskammergericht* and subsequently (1576), thanks to the mediation of the Emperor, to a Convention between them in 22 Articles, dealing with the most varying subjects, *inter alia*, the right of conduct, the removal of rocks, fishing, beacons, freedom of toll in favour of citizens of Bremen, the attribution of sand islands in the river, action against pirates, dykes, and beer excise duty. This convention was in fact sanctioned by the Emperor in 1623.

d'Elsfleth est supprimé à perpétuité, sans pouvoir être rétabli sous aucun prétexte ou dénomination quelconque . . .". After protests of the Duke at Ratisbon (Regensburg),

Convention of 6 April 1803 with the mediating Powers France and Russia, Prussia also intervening (comp. *ibid.*, R², VII, 552-561): the Duke of Oldenburg acquiesces in the "suppression à perpétuité" of the toll and "se démet de l'investiture qu'(il) en avait reçu" (Article 1, § 2), but is granted the right, intended as a supplement to the territorial compensation already promised him a few weeks earlier, to retain the administration and the collection of the toll for ten further years, against his formal undertaking "à ne prolonger sous aucun prétexte par-delà le 1er janvier 1813 la perception temporaire qui lui est laissée" (Article 4), subject to the approval of the Emperor (Article 5), to the Duke's securing free navigation on the lower Weser (Article 6) and to an assurance that the tariff as established in accordance with the bill of enfeoffment, shall not be increased. And again an echo is heard, in Article 8, of the old struggle with Bremen: the Duke reserves to himself the right to conclude a direct amicable agreement with the City of Bremen to the effect of either terminating the collection of the toll within the ten years' period, or to confer it upon the city for the remaining years (Article 8), obviously against some form of additional compensation.—However, the ten years' period passed without a final solution being in sight, and the political events of the time were not conducive to promoting any either. Subsequently to the Congress of Vienna, the problem reappeared at the Conference of the five Powers of the Holy Alliance at Aachen of 1818, where they considered a proposal made by the Russian Cabinet to grant the Duke of Oldenburg a supplementary compensation on the consideration that he had in the mean time been bereft by the course of events of a considerable part of the benefit promised him in 1803, but came to the conclusion that, after the creation of the German Confederation in 1815, they lacked competence to deal with the matter. They therefore confined themselves in a protocol of 14 November 1818 (Martens, N.R. IV, 552-553) to a *démarche* addressed to the German Diet in support of a request of the Duke that he should still be left possessed of the toll for a few more years and of a final decision of the Diet itself, favourable to him in his dispute with the City of Bremen.—This intervention proved successful. As appears from a protocol of the German *Bundesversammlung* of 26 August 1819 (*ibid.*, IV, 645) a Commission of mediation, composed of the Commissioners for Prussia and Württemberg under the chairmanship of the Austrian President of the Diet (comp. on this method of solving disputes between member States of a confederation vol. II, p. 279 of this publication), had succeeded the previous day in achieving an agreement between the two member States to the effect that the levying of the Elsfleth toll was to come to an end on 7 May 1820, and that all claims and counterclaims of the parties on this account would thereby be set-off.

2. *The Elbe*

The river Elbe, which reaches the North Sea below Hamburg through a long estuary, has of old under the Constitution of the Holy Roman Empire formed a subject of contest between local rulers who disputed one another the exercise of various separate rights on or with regard to the river, especially the right of levying shipping tolls. There would seem to have been no less than thirty-five toll stations between Melnik and Hamburg.

Much older than the Weser toll *sub* 1 was that established on the Elbe at Stade, where the Schwinge empties itself into the river. It dated back to an ancient privilege granted by the Emperor to the City of Hamburg in the 13th century after that city had acquired the town of Stade in 1204. This Stade toll survived all the vicissitudes of the town where it was collected: its conquest by Hanover in 1626; its cession to Sweden by Article X, § 7, of the Peace Treaty of Osnabrück (1648), to be the capital of the new (Swedish) principality—the secularized former archbishopric —of Bremen; its temporary conquest by Denmark in 1712; its cession, together with the principality of Bremen, to Hanover by the Swedish-Hanoverian Convention of 9-20 November 1719 (Dumont, VIII², 15), which made His Britannic Majesty Duke of Bremen and Verden; its incorporation into the Kingdom of Westphalia in 1807; its occupation by the French in 1810, and its restitution to Hanover in 1813. This toll was not definitively given up by the latter State until 1861 (see below p. 192).

Controversy had also arisen about 1630 over another Elbe toll, levied by the King of Denmark, in virtue of an Imperial grant, at Glückstadt in Schleswig, halfway between Hamburg and the mouth of the river. Efforts by the Netherlands States General and different Baltic towns to achieve its cancellation met with a resolute refusal by King Christian IV in 1632 and again in 1639 (comp. AITZEMA, *Saken van Staet en Oorlogh* (folio edition, The Hague, 1669-1670), I, 1247).

Freedom of navigation on the river Elbe has moreover later become involved in, and intertwined with the struggle between the Dutch and the British, and their Chartered Companies, on the one hand, and the Emperor, on the other, over the Austrian Company of Ostende which continued to carry on trade with the East Indies contrary to the treaty provisions which prohibited such activities (comp. on this subject Part IV-A of this publication). In September 1731 a dispute arose between Great Britain and the United Netherlands jointly and the Senate of Hamburg over the fact that a vessel, the *Apollon*, flying the Prussian flag and coming from China and the Indies, had entered the Elbe, and over the refusal by the Senate to comply with a demand by the British and Dutch Governments to sequestrate and seize the vessel and her cargo on the ground of the illicit character of her trade. The city, of course, invoked the help of the Emperor against the joint demands which put the freedom of navigation on a river of the Empire and Hamburg's own essential trading interests in jeopardy. It provisionally maintained its refusal to accede to the British-Dutch requests by also denying that the vessel was an "interlope", engaged in illegal commerce, because she carried a Prussian passport. However, as appears from a Rescript of 1 October 1732 relative to a similar case (that of the *Marie-Armande*, sailing under the French flag), the Emperor felt unable to support the stand of the Hamburg Senate, so that the latter was in the event, on 15 January 1734, obliged to issue a decree prohibiting all commerce by "interlopes". The incident has been reported in detail by Rousset in his *Recueil*, vol. VIII, pp. 302-343 and 479-480. On that occasion the Senate of Hamburg relied upon the "Grand Privilege of the Elbe", granted by the Emperor Ferdinand II from Prague 3 June 1628 (Rousset, *Recueil*, VIII, 335). This instrument, *inter alia*, forbade the establishment of river dues on the stretch of the river between Hamburg and the sea.

Under modern conditions the Elbe first reappeared on the international scene at the beginning of the 19th century when by an exchange of Notes between the British envoy and Prince Charles of Hesse of 7 May 1801 its "neutrality" was restored (Martens, R^2, VII, 246-247), only to be impaired again by a naval blockade by North Germany in the Napoleonic era, on 8 April 1806 (*ibid.*, N.R., I, 436, 439). Soon afterwards, on the creation of the Kingdom of Westphalia by Napoleon, the river became the boundary between that Kingdom and Prussia. The Prusso-Westphalian treaty of 14 May 1811 (*ibid.*, N.R., I, 382) not only laid down an exact demarcation line in the river Elbe (comp. thereon Chapter VI *infra*, p. 555), but also provided for freedom of navigation on it for both the riparian States on a footing of equality.

In 1815 the Elbe came under the general rules of Vienna and was, more smoothly and quickly than the Rhine, endowed by an *Elbe-Schiffahrts-Kommission* (1819-1821) with a special River Act, dated 23 June 1821 (*ibid.*, N.R., V, 714). Though proclaiming in Article 1 the principle of the freedom of navigation, the Act obviously limited this freedom again, implicitly, to the riparian States and immediately excluded in the same Article the freedom of cabotage (comp. on this subject *infra* under III, pp. 196 *et seq.*). An additional Act of 13 April 1844 (*ibid.*, N.R.G.[1], VI, 386), however, laid down in more detail for whose ships Elbe navigation was to be free, *viz.*, pursuant to §§ 2 and 3: from the North Sea to any Elbe town, and *vice versa*, for the ships of all nations; between Elbe towns situated in different riparian States *inter se*, for the ships of all of them; and between Elbe towns situated in the same riparian State only to ships of that State, if so reserved.

The freedom of navigation did not imply prohibition of the levying of tolls. The existing dues were suppressed and replaced by two new specific, uniform taxes, the *Elbzoll* from the cargo and the so-called *Rekognitionsgebühr* from the vessel, the tariffs of which were fixed in the Act (Articles 7 *et seq.*). Moreover the old, historically famous *Stader* or *Brunshäuser Zoll* was in 1821 expressly left outside the operation of the Act (Article 15) and maintained, on the condition that Hanover should not increase it without previous agreement, in particular with the City of Hamburg. It was only finally abolished in 1861 by collective international action (see p. 191 below).

The new tolls, established in 1821, were in the course of time reduced, *e.g.*, discriminatorily in favour of Anhalt-Coethen, Anhalt-Dessau and Prussia, in virtue of a convention of 17 July 1828 (*ibid.*, N.R., VII, 653), to which Anhalt-Bernburg acceded by a convention of 17 May 1831 (*ibid.*, N.R., IX, 365). The Additional Act of 13 April 1844 (*ibid.*, N.R.G.[1], VI, 386) abolished the *Rekognitionsgebühr*, but increased the *Elbzoll* (§§ 20-23). Its final abolition as from 1 July 1870 only followed by a *Bundesgesetz* of the then North-German Federation of 11 June 1870, accepted also by Austria (*ibid.*, N.R.G.[1], XX, 345). Compensation was awarded to Mecklenburg-Schwerin and Anhalt from the Federal budget. Comp. *Die Elbzölle, Aktenstücke und Nachweise 1814 bis 1859* (Leipzig, 1860); WEISSENBORN, *Die Elbzölle und Elbstapelplätze im Mittelalter* (Halle, 1900).

After Germany's defeat in World War I, the Elbe, from its confluence with the Mltava (Moldau), and this latter river downstream of Prague, were with all navigable parts of these river systems internationalized ("declared international") by Articles 331 and 340 of the Peace Treaty of Versailles by the setting up of an International Commission on which, apart from the riparian German States and Czechoslovakia, the following States would be represented: Belgium, France, Great Britain and Italy. This regime, further detailed in a new River Act of 22 February 1922 (*ibid.*, N.R.G.[3], XII, 632) in replacement of that of more than a century ago, and later supplemented by an Additional Convention of 27 January 1923 (*ibid.*, XII, 889), was in turn unilaterally set aside in fact, though not in law, by Nazi-Germany on 14 November 1936 (*ibid.*, N.R.G.[3], XXXVI, 800). The division of Germany into two States with the Elbe as frontier after World War II has definitively put an end to the 1922 regime.

3. *The Oder*

The Oder, which flows into the Baltic through a haff past Stettin, has not, as far as I know, had in former centuries such a turbulent history as have the Rhine and the Elbe, although it is occasionally mentioned in international documents of older date.

Navigation on the Oder was burdened with a toll at Fürstenberg south of Frankfurt. This *Fürstenbergerzoll*, which had been levied by the Elector of Saxony, has become the subject of treaty regulation in the middle of the 18th century. Article 7 of the Peace Treaty of Dresden between Prussia and Saxony(-Poland) of 25 December 1745 at the close of the Second Silesian War (Rousset, *Recueil*, XIX, 423), in conformity with the pacification plan of Hanover of 26 August 1745 (*ibid.*, XIX, 441), provided for the exchange of certain Silesian enclaves in the Lausitz west of the Oder against the town of Fürstenberg on that same side of the Oder plus the toll which had been levied there by Saxony and the village of Schidlo on the eastern bank somewhat further to the south, to the effect that both banks of that stretch of the river would thenceforth appertain to Prussia. The treaty, moreover, forbade Saxony to establish a new toll on the Oder somewhere else. As the execution of the 1745 treaty had met with practical difficulties, the territorial arrangement was altered by Article 8 of the Prusso-Saxon Peace Treaty of Hubertsburg of 15 February 1763 which terminated the continental Seven Years' War (Martens, R², I, 146), to the effect that the town of Fürstenberg should remain under Saxony, but that the cession of the toll and Schidlo to Prussia should be increased with some further remaining Saxon possessions on the east bank of the Oder.

After World War I the Oder was endowed with an entirely new regime as a consequence of Germany's defeat, the rebirth of Poland and the emergence of an independent Czecho-Slovak State. These developments caused the Oder to be placed, just as the Elbe, under the administration of an International Commission from its confluence with the Oppa northward. This Commission was to comprise, pursuant to Article 341 of the Peace Treaty of Versailles, five representatives of the riparian States Prussia (3), Poland and Czechoslovakia (each 1), and one representative each of the non-riparian States France, Great Britain, Denmark and Sweden.

Just as the Maritime Danube, the Oder has in the inter-war period (in 1928) given rise to a (this time contentious) litigation between Germany, Great Britain, Denmark, France, Sweden and Czechoslovakia, on the one hand, and Poland on the other, brought before the Permanent Court of International Justice in virtue of a special agreement of 30 October 1928 (Martens, N.R.G.³, XX, 152), with the object of obtaining a judicial pronouncement on the territorial extent of the jurisdiction of the said Commission with regard to those parts of the tributaries of the Oder, the Warta and the Netze, which flow through Polish territory. On that dispute, decided by the Permanent Court on 10 September 1929 (*Publications P.C.I.J.*, series A/B, No. 23), comp. my paper in *The Jurisprudence of the World Court*, vol. I, pp. 192 *et seq.*

The "internationalization", thus more exactly defined by the Court, was in fact abolished by Nazi-Germany's resolve of 1936, unilaterally to denounce all the limitations placed upon her territorial fluvial sovereignty (Martens, N.R.G.³, XXXVI, 800), and it was further thoroughly affected by the ensuing outbreak of World War II in 1939.

The Oder, with its tributary the Neisse, has since then been in fact transformed into the new boundary river between East Germany and Poland, in accordance with paragraph IX^B of the Potsdam Agreement of 2 August 1945 (*Miscellaneous* No. 6 (1947), Cmd. 7087; *A.J.I.L.* 1945 (39), Suppl., p. 255), a provisional agreement which was subsequently confirmed by a bilateral treaty between the German Democratic Republic and Poland of 6 July 1950 (*U.N.T.S.*, vol. 319, p. 93), so that no trace remains of the type of "internationalization", as was established in Versailles. Comp. on the present status of Germany as a whole Part II of this publication pp. 109 *et seq.*

E. *Schelde (Scheldt) and Maas (Meuse)*

I combine these two rivers, which have also played a rôle in legal history, not because they present similar features—they are in fact different—but because they both discharge their water into the North Sea through the wide delta area of the Netherlands and are interconnected by the so-called "intermediary waters".

1. *The Schelde (Escaut)*

The Schelde is worth mentioning apart because it has been endowed with successive legal regimes which differ from the regime of most other rivers.

As set out above in my historical survey, p. 104, the Schelde—in its lower stretch more a broad estuary than an ordinary river—has been closed to all foreign shipping from the sea to the port of Antwerp (at first Spanish, since 1715 Austrian) and *vice versa*, for nearly a century and a half, from 1648 to 1795.

Pursuant to Article 14 of the Netherlands-Spanish Peace Treaty of Münster of 30 January 1648 (Dumont, VI¹, 429) no trading would be allowed from and towards the Southern Low Countries, in particular Antwerp, over the waters of the Schelde proper or through the Canal of Sas van Gent, the Zwin and other mouths of the river system,[67] in order to prevent Spanish Antwerp becoming a dangerous commercial rival of the Northern Netherlands ports. When at the close of the War of the Spanish Succession it was decided that, in accordance with the Grand Alliance of 1701, the formerly Spanish southern Low Countries should be transferred to the Emperor on behalf of the House of Austria, the Netherlands-Austrian-British Barrier Treaty of 15 November 1715

67. The text of this famous treaty provision runs as follows "Les Rivières de l'Escaut, comme aussi les Canaux de Sas, Zwyn, et autres bouches de Mer y aboutissans, seront tenuës closes du costé desdits Seigneurs Etats."

(Rousset, *Recueil*, I, 37) in its Article 26 expressly confirmed all the stipulations in the matter of commerce contained in the Netherlands-Spanish Peace Treaty of Münster. And so it has remained until in 1793-1795 the French successively "reunited" the Belgian provinces with France and the Netherlands were forced to cede Zeeland Flanders on the southern bank of the river to France (Article 12, *sub* 1° of their treaty of 16 May 1795, Martens, R², VI, 88). Even the Austro-Netherlands treaty of 8 November 1785 (*ibid.*, R², IV, 55) had still expressly maintained the existing situation in its Article 7:

> "Le reste du fleuve, depuis la ligne démarquée (*i.e.*, the boundary line between the two countries) jusqu'à la mer, dont la souveraineté continuera d'appartenir aux Etats-Généraux, sera tenu clos de leur côté, ainsi que les canaux du Sas, du Swin, et autres bouches de mer y aboutissans, conformément au Traité de Munster".

After the fall of Napoleon the situation changed again as a consequence of the union of all the Low Countries under a greater Kingdom of the Netherlands in virtue of the decisions of the Congress of Vienna (Article 65 of the Final Act), which made Antwerp a Netherlands port. On that occasion, the Schelde was subjected to the general regime of international rivers, as elaborated in a special Annex XIV c to the Final Act (comp. *sub* I, (*a*) above, at p. 120). There was at that juncture no longer ground for the Netherlands to attempt to restore the closure of the river to the detriment of Antwerp, which had meanwhile been made an exclusively commercial port by Article 13 of the (first) Peace Treaty of Paris of 30 May 1814 (Martens, N.R., II, 1, 13).

The situation changed again when the southern provinces rebelled against the Dutch rule in 1830 and seceded from the Netherlands proper. The draft conditions of the separation, as worked out by the Great Powers in London in their treaty of 15 November 1831 (*ibid.*, N.R., XI, 390), in Article 15 maintained the commercial status of Antwerp and in Article 9 embodied a number of provisions concerning in particular navigation on the Schelde (pilotage and beaconing, and maintenance of the channels to be submitted to common surveillance by a mixed commission; only moderate pilotage dues, equal for the ships of both countries; freedom of fishing also on a footing of equality) and on the "eaux intermédiaires" between the Schelde and the Rhine. The fixing of the tariffs of the *péages* was referred to other commissioners, pending which the tariffs of the Rhine Convention of Mainz of 1831 would apply. The definitive Treaty of Separation of 19 April 1839 (*ibid.*, N.R., XVI, 773) introduced some amendments or stated some of the points more precisely. Article 9, § 2 prescribed equality of pilotage dues in favour of all nations, and limited them provisionally to those levied according to a tariff of 1829 for the mouths of the river Maas. The choice of pilots from the two national piloting services would be completely free. Article 9, § 3, authorized the Netherlands Government to levy a fixed shipping due of 1,12, respectively 0,38 guilders per ton on vessels sailing up, respectively down the Western Schelde[68] between the sea and Antwerp. Independent Belgium immediately undertook, by a Law of 5 June 1839 (*ibid.*, N.R., XVI², 917), to assume the financial burden of this toll on foreign shipping to and from Antwerp by reimbursing it to the ships of all nations. On the redemption of this new toll of 1839 comp. below p. 192.

The river has since 1839 been the object of very detailed bilateral regulations with Belgium, in particular a series of five *Règlements* annexed to the Convention of 20 May 1843 (*ibid.*, N.R.G.¹, V, 294 *et seq.*), dealing with (I) navigation on the river and its mouths; (II) pilotage and surveillance in common; (III) lighthouses; (IV) fishing and fishing trade; (V) navigation on the intermediary waters between Schelde and Rhine, and further cited in my systematic survey under III, below, pp. 198 *et seq.*

Relations between the two countries have at a later stage, especially after World War I, become very strained in connection with annexionist tendencies in Belgium and with the latter's insistence upon the construction of a big shipping canal from Antwerp to the Rhine across Netherlands territory. A treaty to that effect was submitted to the Netherlands Parliament in 1925, but eventually rejected by the First Chamber. This dispute has only found a satisfactory solution in 1965 (see on this lingering conflict *infra* section 3 on International Canals, p. 222). Comp. C. SMIT, *De Scheldekwestie* (Rotterdam, 1966).

The Netherlands and Belgium have in their past and present political status for centuries also been divided by a dispute, still unresolved up to the present day, over their water boundary in the Wielingen mouth of the Schelde, which Belgium claims as her territory because it traverses her territorial sea, whereas the Netherlands maintain that the State frontier follows the midchannel of the passage. This controversy has on occasions become acute, especially in the period when Belgium was involved in World War I, in which the Netherlands remained neutral. Comp. on this boundary dispute *infra*, pp. 598 *et seq.*

2. *The Maas (Meuse)*

It would require entering into too many details to describe in full the legal history of the river Maas (Meuse). While referring to a number of elements in its regime mentioned elsewhere in this section, I will, instead of writing a more or less exhaustive monograph on this waterway, and only in order to give some idea of the complications which a river can cause, epitomize here some features of its history.

68. For the Eastern Schelde, only used for navigation between Antwerp and the Rhine, the tariff was to be that in force under the Rhine Convention of Mainz of 1831.

Owing, *inter alia*, to the fact that the banks of the river, especially in its middle course in what is now the Netherlands province of Limburg were bordered by a great many separate independent or quasi-independent political entities, some of them even *reichsunmittelbar* (comp. Chapter V, section 2 below, p. 445), the Meuse in the course of time became infected with a number of local shipping tolls. The Netherlands State Archives still contain a very interesting document in which all these tolls are listed. See on the tolls at Lith (1702) and Maastricht (1718) the Archives of the Council of State No. 2150.

This situation became still more complicated when after the Eighty Years' War between the Republic of the United Netherlands and Spain (1568-1648) the Lands of Overmaze (Trans-Meuse) were apportioned between the two States (Partition Treaty of 26 December 1661, Dumont, VI², 393), and when later, at the end of the War of the Spanish Succession (1702-1713), the areas which had remained Spanish in 1661 were re-distributed among Austria, the Netherlands and Prussia (Article 19 of the Peace Treaty of Baden of 7 September 1714, Dumont, VIII¹, 436; Rousset, *Recueil*, I, 1, and Article 18 of the Barrier Treaty of 15 November 1715, Dumont, VIII¹, 458; Rousset, *Recueil*, I, 37). Pursuant to these latter treaties the United Netherlands acquired the Maas towns of Venlo and Stevensweert and the largest part of the *ammanie (ambachts-heerlijkheid)* of Montfort, Austria kept the Maas town of Roermond further south, and Prussia remained in possession of the large rest of trans-Mosan Upper-Guelder.

One of the Maas tolls, originally levied at Gennep further downstream, had already much earlier formed an object of regulation, in connection, on the one hand, with the Brandenburg-Netherlands alliance during the War of the Jülich-Cleves Succession and, on the other, with a dispute between Friedrich Wilhelm of Brandenburg-Prussia and the princely house of Orange over the succession to the estate of the Stadhouder-King William III. The former had in the 1680's ceded the toll of Gennep to the latter and his heirs and descendents *(posteri)*. The toll had since then be levied further downstream at Grave, a possession of the house of Orange. After William III's death without *posteri* in 1702, however, the King of Prussia, in 1706, restored the toll on his own behalf at Gennep on the ground, which would seem to be a mere chicanery, that the cession and transfer had been in the nature of a concession, intended to lapse in case there should be no *haeredes posteri*. Although boatmen on the Maas protested against the new situation of two tolls on the river near each other, and the States General, in their capacity of executors of the will of William III, equally protested to the King of Prussia (DE LAMBERTY, *Mémoires pour servir à l'histoire du 18e siècle*, The Hague-Amsterdam, 1724 et seq., vol. 14 (Supplement), pp. 239, 240, 245), the toll at Gennep was maintained and in the event awarded to the King of Prussia in

Article 5 of his treaty of 14 May/16 June 1732 with the then Prince of Orange for the definitive partition of the Orange estate (Rousset, *Recueil*, VIII, 408) which moreover suppressed the toll at Grave. Comp. on this dynastic dispute Chapter III, section 1, § 2 *sub b*) *infra*, p. 306.

An increase—as, for that matter, a reduction—of existing shipping dues on the Maas was by Article 18, para. 6, of the above-mentioned Barrier Treaty of 15 November 1715 made inadmissible without previous agreement between the Netherlands and Austria.

The shipping dues on the then still Spanish part of the river had been pledged to King William III as a security for the payment of two "rentes" of 80.000 and 20.000 florins *per annum*, which the King of Spain had contracted by a transaction with the King-Stadhouder of 26 December 1687 (comp. Article 18 (7) of the same Barrier Treaty of 1715). By Article 12 of the above cited partition treaty of 1732 these two "rentes" were also apportioned, the first to the King of Prussia, the second to the Prince of Orange.

The States General often complained of the prejudice and embarrassment which Austria on her stretch of the Meuse caused to navigation and fluvial commerce.

In 1793 revolutionary France, in her own interest more than from idealistic motives, made a clean sweep of existing navigation dues in the countries under her domination, in particular also on the Meuse, an abrogation which was for the river stretch below Venlo confirmed by Article II, 3 of the secret Treaty of Campo Formio of 17 October 1797 (Martens, R^2, VI, 426). Just as the existing Rhine tolls, those levied on the Meuse were comprehended in the reparation settlement on behalf of the mediatized and secularized princes, laid down in the *Reichsdeputations-Hauptschluss* of 25 February 1803 (comp. § 3 of that instrument in Martens, R^2, VII, 443).

The international regime of the Meuse was, just as that of the Scheldt, specifically defined in Annex XVI c to the Final Act of the Congress of Vienna of 9 June 1815 (*ibid.*, N.R., II, 447).

The legal situation along the river became much less complicated as a consequence of the abolition of all the enclaves in what is now the Netherlands province of Limburg, pursuant to the territorial settlement laid down in Article 66 of the same Final Act of 1815.

Since the Southern Low Countries were on the same occasion incorporated into an enlarged Kingdom of the Netherlands, the middle and lower reaches of the Meuse fell for a time (1814-1831) entirely under one and the same sovereignty from the French border to the sea. This changed again, however, after the Belgian insurrection of 1830: in virtue of Article 4 of the Netherlands-Belgian Treaty of Separation of 19 April 1839 (*ibid.*, N.R., XVI, 773) the Meuse then became, as regards its stretch between Eysden and Maasbracht, a Netherlands-Belgian boundary river save for a semi-circular cis-Mosan bit of territory bulging out on its left bank, which was comprised within the town of Maastricht. But even in this new status the river preserved some peculiar features, in that (i) the boundary line in it was made subject to automatic changes in accordance with possible shifts of its bed or its thalweg (comp. on this particular feature *infra* Chapter VI, p. 567), and that (ii) this surface frontier was, moreover, coupled with an independent, possibly different subterranean boundary, following the extent of the mutual coal mining areas and consisting in an underground "wall" (comp. on this point, *supra*, p. 50).[69]

The other, foreign enclaves along the southern bank of the Meuse further downstream in the province of North Brabant had already been wiped out and awarded to the Batavian Republic by a treaty with France (5 January 1800, Martens, R², VII, 37).

All still existing shipping dues on the Netherlands Meuse (regulated after the separation from Belgium by *Règlement* No. VI of their treaty of 20 May 1843, *ibid.*, N.R.G.¹, V, 351) were, in connection with an earlier law relating to the abolition of those on the Rhine (8 August 1850, *Staatsblad* No. 48), also cancelled, by the law of 2 September 1851 (*Staatsblad* No. 131). At the same time the levying of shipping dues was terminated on the boundary Meuse by a treaty of 8 May 1851 (*Staatsblad* No. 133).

At a much later stage the Meuse once again reappeared on the international scene as a consequence of the use which both the Netherlands and Belgium made of its water by means of its diversion into new canals. Comp. on the dispute, caused thereby, my paper on the proceedings before the Permanent Court of International Justice, terminated by its Judgment of 28 June 1937 in the case of the *Diversion of water from the Meuse*, inserted in my *The Jurisprudence of the World Court*, vol. I, pp. 458 et seq.

Comp. on the legal regime of the Meuse: J. BARENTS, *Het internationaal statuut van de Maas* (academic thesis Leiden, 1940).

F. *The Moselle*

Other international features again, attach to the left tributary of the Rhine, the river Moselle (Mosel).

As appears from Article 17 (3) of a treaty between Austria (for the Low Countries) and France of 16 May 1769 (Martens, R², I, 661), the King of France had, in his capacity of Duke of Lorraine, levied in the past *droits de péage* at Nittel on the Moselle, but by that Article the

---

69. Comp. lately the article by E. VAN BOGAERT in the *Revue belge de droit international* 1965, p. 306, on *Het Belgisch verdragsrecht betreffende de uitbuitingsgrens der mijnen*.

Empress of Austria engaged to cease levying them there or elsewhere on the river.

Freedom of navigation from the Moselle into the Rhine formed the object of a stipulation in Article II, 2) of the secret articles of the Peace Treaty of Campo Formio of 17 October 1797 between France and the Emperor (*ibid.*, R², VI, 426) by which France extended her boundaries to the left bank of the Rhine.

The river subsequently came, together with the Main and the Neckar, under the provisions on international rivers in the Final Act of the Congress of Vienna of 1815 and, in particular, under its Annex XVI c, dealing with the future regime of the main tributaries of the Rhine, together with the rivers Meuse and Scheldt. As far as the Moselle was concerned, navigation on it was to enjoy the same freedom and equality of treatment as was established with regard to navigation on the Rhine itself. This special River Act was just as that concerning the Rhine susceptible of alteration only by common accord of all the parties to it. It did not, however, extend the jurisdiction of the Central Commission to the Moselle nor to any other of the rivers dealt with in Annex c. If the provisions of Article 4 of this Annex had been implemented, a more detailed River Act would have been laid down, which would have covered both the Meuse and the Moselle, as much as possible in conformity with the regime of the Rhine, and it would have been elaborated by those members of the Central Commission whose States were also riparians of both rivers. This, however, has never happened. The Netherlands and Belgium have, on the contrary, in 1842 agreed upon a special Statute for the Meuse alone. When the original Act of Mainz (1831) was superseded by the Revised Act of Mannheim (1868), the extension of the freedom and equality of navigation on the Rhine to all flags also applied to the Moselle.

By the Peace Treaty of Versailles (Article 362, *sub* 1°) Germany was forced to acquiesce in advance in a possible future proposal by the Central Commission of the Rhine to extend its jurisdiction to the Moselle below the Franco-Luxembourg frontier[70] down to the Rhine should Luxembourg consent thereto. This extension has not, however, in fact materialized.

Some years later France proceeded to canalise the river between Metz and Thionville on French soil (1932), and its further canalization from Thionville to Koblenz on the Rhine was prepared in collaboration between the three riparian States France, Luxembourg and Germany. This tripartite action foreshadowed already what was going to happen later. The further canalization of the Moselle was after World War II

---

70. Of course not upstream of that frontier, as the victor State France was quite prepared to impose burdens upon fellow States, but not to assume corresponding burdens itself.

by a Convention between the three riparian States (France, Luxembourg, and the German Federal Republic) of 27 October 1956 (*Les Actes du Rhin et de la Moselle*, Strasbourg, 1966, p. 25) entrusted to a government-owned limited liability company, the *Société internationale de la Moselle*, and an International Commission of the Moselle was set up. The parties to the 1956 Convention thereby established a preferential treatment in favour of themselves, which would seem to be an encroachment upon the legal principles of Vienna. And yet those principles are, in law, still undiminished in force as minimum requirements. Comp. on this subject the study of 1960 concerning *Le régime relatif à la navigation de la Moselle*, published by the foundation "Verkeerswetenschappelijk Centrum" (Centre for the Scientific Study of Traffic Problems) at Rotterdam, and the article by D. RUZIÉ, *Le régime juridique de la Moselle* in *A.F.D.I.* 1964 (X), pp. 764 *et seq.*

Excursus

NETHERLANDS CASE LAW CONCERNING THE RHINE

As I have limited my brief survey of Netherlands case law relative to Rhine navigation at pp. 180-181 of Part I of this publication to a few summary indications about its general trend, I return to this subject in more detail below. The treaty regime of the Rhine has indeed given rise to a flood of judicial decisions, especially in the Netherlands.

1) One of the most important subjects of dispute was the substantive extent of the freedom of navigation. This aspect of the Rhine regime has led in the Netherlands to a series of judgments, by which the Judiciary has hindered the Government from infringing essential provisions of the Convention of Mannheim. The first case concerned the controversy as to whether that Convention forbade the enactment of a Netherlands law which introduced a general system of compulsory freight distribution on Dutch waterways (prescribing for the conclusion of carrying contracts the approval of special chartering committees and threatening infringement of this provision with penalties) without making any exception or reservation as regards shipping on the Rhine. The intention of the Government in introducing the Bill in question undoubtedly was to extend the operation of the distribution system to that river, but during the parliamentary debates such a strong opposition from the point of view of the international engagements of the Netherlands arose against this implication of the proposed law that the Government, without amending the Bill to the effect of expressly excluding Rhine navigation from its operation, conceded that the question as to whether the Convention permitted the threatened curtailment of Rhine shipping would not be prejudiced by the adoption of the law, but was left for decision

to the Judiciary. After having piloted the Bill through Parliament by this unusual legislative procedure, the Government immediately caused Rhine skippers who ignored the Law to be prosecuted for trespassing it, but these prosecutions proved a complete failure for the Government.

Two lower Courts differed in their evaluation of the situation, as appears from their contradictory judgments of 21 and 29 June 1934, one rendered by the District Court of Rotterdam, the other by that of Arnhem. On appeal in cassation the Supreme Court found against the Government: it held, in effect, that the Law on Freight Distribution of 5 May 1933 could not be deemed to extend to the Rhine area because its application to it would be an illicit encroachment upon the freedom of navigation on the Rhine.[71] Curiously enough, the judgment of the Supreme Court almost coincided with the Judgment of the Permanent Court of Justice in the *Oscar Chinn* case relative to the freedom of navigation on the Congo. This was the reason why I have reported at the time on this Netherlands judgment in an Annex to my analysis of the Anglo-Belgian case in *The Jurisprudence of the World Court*, vol. I, at pp. 391 *et seq.* As I have set out the different legal questions involved in more detail there, I abstain here from going into a few other questions, *viz.*, whether the prohibition to encroach upon the freedom of navigation proper extends to a mere limitation of the freedom of loading, and what is the exact meaning of the prohibition of discrimination between different users of an international waterway.

A second case occurred after World War II, when the kindred question arose as to whether price control on freights instituted under a Law of 1939 to prevent the undue raising of prices could legally apply to Rhine transport in the light of the Mannheim Convention. This case related to the transport of a cargo of wood by a Netherlands vessel from one Netherlands Rhine port (Rotterdam) to another (Renkum, near Arnhem). The Courts again differed of opinion. The Disciplinary Court for Price Control found that the Law could so apply. The Court of Appeal held that it could not because its application to Rhine navigation

71. See the judgments in cassation of 17 December 1934 (*Weekblad v.h. Recht* 1935, No. 12849, *Ned. Jur.* 1935, pp. 5 *et seq.* and 11 *et seq*, briefly digested in *A.D.* 1933-1934, Case No. 4). Subsequent judgments of the Supreme Court of 30 March and 4 May 1936 and 28 December 1937 rightly held that the principle of freedom, thus recognized also in favour of purely inland navigation on the Rhine, did not give freedom to continue a water transport, which had begun on the Rhine, outside the area of that river: when venturing on other inland waterways without the required approval the skipper became punishable: *A.D.* 1935-1937, Case No. 55, at p. 166, *sub* (*a*).—Water transport on the *eaux intermédiaires* towards the river Scheldt south of the Haringvliet (*see infra* in the text *sub* 2) and *a fortiori* on the river Meuse (Maas) could also be legally brought under the operation of the Law on Freight Distribution: *A.D.* 1935-1937, Case No. 55, *sub* (*c*), at pp. 168-169, and in the text below *sub* 2).

would be contrary to the Convention. The Supreme Court, on 28 March 1950, maintained as a matter of principle its earlier judgments that the Convention was also applicable to purely inland navigation, but found that the Price Control Regulations did not violate its provisions because at the time when it was drafted the High Contracting Parties had in mind no conception of economic planning or any similar restrictions on freedom of contract or measures of "social legislation" (*A.D.* 1949, Case No. 29).[72]

The question acquired a more serious character when, in 1950, the Netherlands Government went to the extreme of stopping a Netherlands tugboat with a Belgian vessel in tow at the German frontier at Lobith from continuing their voyage from Dordrecht (Holland) to Duisburg-Ruhrort (Germany) because the owner of the tugboat was unable to produce a certain official declaration from one of the two private organizations entrusted by the Minister of Transport with the control of freight traffic on the Rhine. The refusal by the customs authorities and the Ministry of Transport to grant the necessary clearance was based on a Decree of 15 November 1940 enacted under the enemy German occupation ("provisionally" maintained in force after the liberation of the country) and two executive ordinances of 13 May 1948 and 28 March 1950. The Decree of 1940 had imposed upon the owners of Rhine vessels compulsory membership of one of those two shipping organizations, which faintly remembered of the old Rhine guilds. This notorious incident, called the "stop of Lobith" (*Boon and Chantiers Navals du Rupel v. State of the Netherlands*), resulted in another series of judgments, terminated by a new judgment of the Supreme Court of 22 March 1952 unfavourable to the Government (*Ned. Jur.* 1952, No. 125), reported in *I.L.R.* 1952, Case No. 34. The decision to stop Dutch vessels at the frontier was held to be contrary to the legal rules in force. The Supreme Court's statement of reasons shows, however, its desire to evade a straightforward pronouncement that already the Decree of 1940 (imposing compulsory membership of one of the two prescribed shipping organizations by the

---

72. Comp. with this pronouncement the following two foreign judgments. A German tribunal had in a decision of 25 September 1927 (*A.D.* 1927-1928, Case No. 84) held in the same sense as regards "social legislation", but that decision related to the application of the German Federal Insurance Code to the crews of foreign (*in casu* Swiss) ships employed in navigating German navigable waterways, including the Rhine.—On the other hand, the Swiss Federal Tribunal, in a judgment of 25 June 1948 (*A.D.* 1948, Case No. 25), held that, although the principle of free navigation on the Rhine did not prevent Switzerland from subjecting the crews of Swiss vessels to its compulsory accident insurance, "it may be argued that a riparian State cannot extend its legislation relating to accident insurance to the crews of foreign vessels passing through its territory or anchoring in its ports", because the obligations and formalities resulting from such legislation would interfere with the freedom of navigation.

shipowner) was contrary to the Convention of Mannheim: that Decree was indeed said not in itself to involve a real encroachment upon freedom of navigation—in my opinion a dubious assertion—, and the illegality was held to result, rather, from the way in which the conditions for, or the consequences of, membership were regulated. Now, the way in which the original Occupation Decree had been implemented by the post-war ministerial Ordinances of 1948 and 1950 was held to run counter to the freedom of Rhine traffic "since freedom of navigation can no longer be said to exist when the consent of an organization is required before permission is granted to make a journey on the Rhine". And the Court added that "even if the regulations concerned were indispensable for the Netherlands economy, they could still not be legally enacted as long as the Convention remains in force unaltered".—It must be stressed that the Decree and Ordinances concerned specifically related to, and covered all international inland navigation from Holland into Belgium or Germany.

When the Supreme Court was for the fourth time involved in a dispute on the legality of certain Government measures which infringed the traditional freedom of shipping on the Rhine, purely inland navigation was at issue. The District Court of Rotterdam had already in an earlier affair decided (4 December 1947, *A.D.* 1946, note *ad* Case no. 22) that the transport of a cargo from Nijmegen to Vlaardingen (both Dutch Rhine ports) in January 1947 and its unloading there without the permit required under another Occupation Decree, of 1941, on Inland Shipping (*Binnenscheepvaartreglement*)—equally issued on the orders of the enemy, equally "provisionally" maintained after the liberation of the country, and therefore odious to many Dutchmen—was not punishable because even purely inland navigation on the waters of the Rhine area was free under the Mannheim Convention, and because it did not appear that the Decree had been intended to infringe freedom of navigation on the Rhine—the latter again a very doubtful argument.

When the same question was brought before the Supreme Court a few years later and it might be expected that the Court would stick to its earlier opinion, it, on the contrary, made a complete *volte face* by reversing its earlier case law. What was at issue on that occasion was whether the Inland Navigation Rules 1947, based on the said Inland Shipping Decree of 1941, which had introduced a strict system of control on freight agreements on all Netherlands waterways, was, as far as navigation on the Netherlands Rhine by Netherlands skippers was concerned, at variance with the Convention of Mannheim. This time and unexpectedly, the Supreme Court, in direct contradiction to its earlier judgments, held that the Rules were compatible with the Convention on the ground, already discussed above, p. 137 and advanced by TELDERS, that the freedom principle sanctioned by the Convention of Mannheim did not apply to navigation pursued by the subjects of a riparian State within its own borders. This new argument did not, it is true, in this case serve to justify the reservation of cabotage on the Rhine to national vessels (as practised by Germany), but to empower the Government to fetter inland navigation on the Netherlands Rhine by Netherlands skippers by a restrictive system of freight control which it could not impose upon foreign skippers. However, the legal ground on which the Supreme Court based its findings on this occasion was exactly the same as that invoked by Germany, namely, the erroneous argument, rejected above, that, looked at in the light of the *travaux préparatoires*, the Mannheim Convention was not intended to interfere with purely inland navigation in each of the riparian States. See for further details *supra*, p. 135. It goes without saying that the Netherlands standpoint in the cabotage dispute with Germany was seriously impaired by this wrong interpretation of the Convention. Comp. for this judgment of 4 May 1954 (*Ned. Jur.* 1954, No. 382): *I.L.R.* 1954, pp. 3 *et seq.*, at p. 6.

2) Another series of questions arose with respect to the geographical extent of the water area of the Rhine. As it is hardly possible to appreciate the questions involved without the help of a map, I add a sketchmap to this exposition.

Whereas a German court held that a navigation incident occurring in the port of Kehl (opposite Strasbourg) did not come under the Convention (*A.D.* 1931/32, Case No. 56), Netherlands courts were generally of the opinion that the Convention could, according to local circumstances, very well apply also to harbours, river basins and suchlike (see my survey in *A.D.* 1935-1937, Case No. 55, *sub* (*b*)). For them the difficulty rather existed (*a*) in the drawing of a borderline between the Rhine area proper and the so-called *eaux intermédiaires* towards the south between that area and the river Scheldt, because the latter came only under the principle of the freedom of navigation but not, for example, under the jurisdiction of the special Rhine Navigation Courts and of the Central Commission; and (*b*) in the determination of which of the waterways that branch off in the Netherlands from the Rhine or the Lek to the north form part of the Rhine area. The borderline *sub* (*a*) was fixed in such a way that the Rhine area was held not to extend southward beyond the wide sea arm of the Haringvliet, and that the southernmore waterways to Zeeland province and Belgium came exclusively under the Netherlands-Belgian Treaty of Separation of 19 April 1839 (see my survey in *A.D.*, 1935-1937, Case No. 55, *sub* (*c*)). The partly contradictory decisions on the question *sub* (*b*) ruled that the natural river the Gelderse IJssel (branching off from the Rhine northward at Westervoort) does not, but that the artificial Merwede Canal (running from Wijk bij Duurstede, where the river changes its name to Lek, towards Amsterdam) does belong to the Rhine area. The latter judgment was clearly wrong. This legal uncertainty was caused by doubts about the question as to which

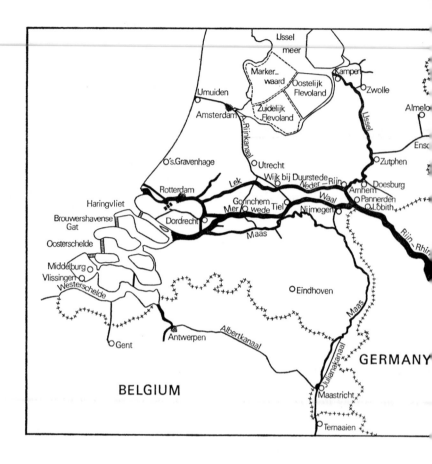

parts of the Rhine delta belong to the "embouchures" of the river. Comp. again on this somewhat complicated subject of the geographical extent of the Rhine area my above-mentioned survey in *A.D.* 1935-1937, Case No. 55, at pp. 166-169 and the sketchmap.

3) A further problem appeared to be whether Belgium was a party to the Convention of Mannheim and, therefore, bound by its provisions, especially with regard to the exclusive competence in Rhine shipping matters of the Rhine Navigation Tribunals as opposed to the ordinary courts. In a case arising from an accident of navigation between Belgian vessels in Netherlands territory, the Belgian court of the first instance held that Belgium was not a party to the Convention in spite of her representation on the Central Commission for Navigation on the Rhine pursuant to Articles 354 and 355 of the Peace Treaty of Versailles, and that, therefore, the Convention was not applicable in Belgian courts; in

178

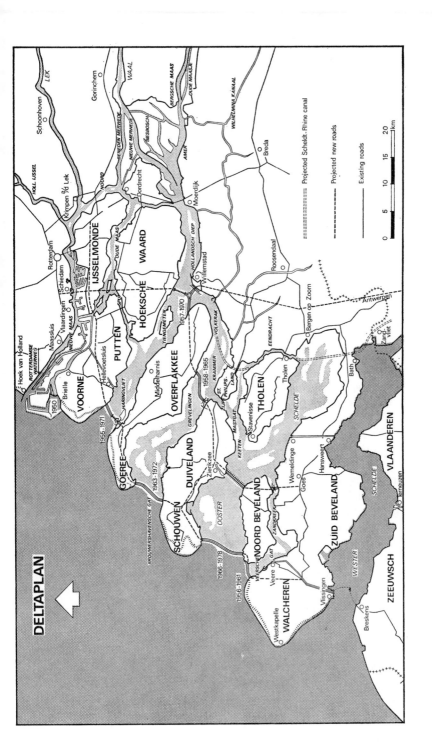

DELTAPLAN

Hoek van Holland
ROTTERDAMSE WATERWEG
Maassluis
Vlaardingen Schiedam
Rotterdam
Krimpen a/d Lek
KILL IJSSEL
Schoonhoven
LEK
Gorinchem
WAAL
BENEDEN MERWEDE
NIEUWE MERWEDE
BERGSCHE MAAS
OUDE MAASJE
WILHELMINA KANAAL
NOORD
Dordrecht
Moerdijk
AMER
BIESBOSCH
Breda
NIEUWE MAAS
OUDE MAAS
Maasland
1950
Brielle
VOORNE
Heenvliet
PUTTEN
IJSSELMONDE
HOEKSCHE WAARD
HOLLANDSCH DIEP
Willemstad
Roosendaal
1955-1971
HARINGVLIET
Middelharnis
OVERFLAKKEE
TIENGEMETEN
1957-1970
VOLKERAK
1958-1965
KRAMMER
ST. PHILIPS LAND
ZIJPE
MASTGAT
KEETEN
EENDRACHT
Bergen op Zoom
Antwerpen
Bath
Zandvliet
1963-1972
GREVELINGEN
DUIVELAND
Zierikzee
OOSTER
Stavenisse
THOLEN
Tholen
SCHELDE
BROUWERSHAVENSCHE GAT
1966-1978
SCHOUWEN
VEERSCHE GAT
ZANDKREEK
Veere
NOORD BEVELAND
Wemeldinge
Goes
Hansweert
ZUID BEVELAND
VLAANDEREN
SCHELDE
Terneuzen
1956-1961
Westkapelle
WALCHEREN
Vlissingen
WESTER
ZEEUWSCH
Breskens

.... Projected Scheldt-Rhine canal

------- Projected new roads

———— Existing roads

0   5   10   15   20 Km

any case it had not been duly published in Belgium so that it was not binding on Belgian nationals. The Court of Appeal added that, even assuming the applicability of the Convention to Belgian boatmen navigating the Rhine, the ordinary Belgian courts would nevertheless have jurisdiction to deal with the case on the ground that its Article 34 did not prevent Belgian citizens from seising them of a private dispute, not involving any alien. The Court of Cassation limited itself to stating that the Convention was not binding upon Belgian nationals for lack of publication in the *Moniteur belge*. See *I.L.R.* 1952, Case No. 107 and 1953, p. 409.

Netherlands Courts had to deal with the same problem: whereas the District Court of the Hague on 29 November 1950 doubted if Belgium had ever become a party to the Mannheim Convention, but left this point undecided, the Court of Appeal of the Hague on 27 June 1951 held that she had; the judgments are reported in *A.D.* 1952, Case No. 34, at pp. 150 and 152.

4) The question of jurisdiction has on the whole played a prominent part in the national case law. It had several aspects, one of substance (or "absolute" competence), one of "relative" competence from the international angle, one of "relative" competence from the national angle, and one connected with the illegal denunciation of the Convention of Mannheim by Nazi-Germany in 1936.

(*a*) The substantive question—jurisdiction *ratione materiae*—was whether in the case of a collision on the Rhine the masters or shipowners involved could escape adjudication by the Rhine Navigation Tribunals on the pretext that the collision was not governed by the legal rules regarding tort, but by those relating to the improper performance of a towing contract, and that the provisions of the Mannheim Convention concerning this Rhine jurisdiction were not intended to cover such contractual cases. The ordinary Dutch District Courts which were seised on this account on more than one occasion rejected this argument as unfounded, and considered themselves as having no jurisdiction. Comp. the cases of *the Vredeburg v. the Sarina Dorina* (a collision on the German Rhine near Xanthen in the British Zone, 1948) of 17 December 1952 (*I.L.R.* 1952, Case No. 108) and of *Den Breejen v. Lloyd Schlepp-schiffahrt A.G.* (a collision in the French occupation Zone) of 2 January 1957 (*ibid.* 1957, p. 97).

(*b*) The international aspect of the question of "relative" competence —jurisdiction *ratione loci*—concerned the question of whether a particular case of collision which occurred between Netherlands vessels on the Rhine in Germany, France or Switzerland could legally be tried by the Netherlands Rhine Courts when seised by those involved. The Netherlands Rhine Navigation Tribunals denied this and held that their foreign counterparts alone had jurisdiction: *The Vredeburg v. the Sarina Dorina,*

17 December 1952 (*I.L.R.* 1952, Case No. 35); the *Tanutra* case of 17 April 1953 (*ibid.*, 1953, p. 164).

(*c*) The national aspect of the same question of "relative" competence —jurisdiction *ratione loci*—was whether the parties to a Rhine navigation case in respect of which a specific Dutch Rhine Navigation Tribunal was normally competent according to the place on the Rhine where the collision had occurred, were allowed to seise another such Dutch Tribunal. The District Court of Rotterdam, acting as a Rhine Navigation Tribunal, affirmed this in cases where both parties agreed, as was often done, but denied it in regard of possible cases where the defendant would object to a deviation from the normal distribution of jurisdiction. Comp. the judgment of the District Court of Rotterdam, acting as a Rhine Navigation Court, in a case relating to a collision on the river Waal in the normal jurisdiction of the District Court of Arnhem (*I.L.R.* 1954, p. 300), but in which the Court of Rotterdam affirmed its own jurisdiction.

This judicial practice is, however, contrary to the opinion held on this jurisdictional issue by the Central Commission adjudicating in appeal from judgments rendered by national Rhine Navigation Tribunals, as appears from its judgment of 13 November 1929 in the matter of the *barge Antoinette v. Dredging Comp. X* (*A.D.* 1929/1930, Case No. 57): the parties had agreed to bring the case not before the normally competent Rhine Navigation Tribunal of Germersheim, but before that of Ludwigshafen; the latter had adjudicated on the claim, but was held by the Central Commission to have been incompetent. This judgment was, however, in its turn contrary to the earlier case law of the German *Reichsgericht*: judgment of 27 October 1915 (*Fontes Juris Gentium*, series A, sec. 2, vol. I, p. 492). As is evident from note II added to the abovementioned case of 13 November 1929 (Case No. 57), the national German appellate tribunal in Rhine Navigation matters in its turn vacillated in its case law: after having first espoused the opinion of the Central Commission, it later took sides with the *Reichsgericht*.

(*d*) The fourth aspect could only give rise to controversy after Germany had denounced her international obligations under the Convention of Mannheim by a diplomatic Note of 14 November 1936 (Martens, N.R.G.[3], XXXVI, 800) and abolished the Rhine Shipping Tribunals, whose jurisdiction had just been newly regulated by a law of 5 September 1935 (*RGBL.* I, p. 1152), by a new Law of 30 January 1937. The Netherlands courts, of course, held this denunciation to be illegal, but they had to draw their legal conclusions from the illegal factual situation thus created. Seeing that there was no longer any factual reciprocity in the observance of the traditional Rhine regime, the Netherlands Rhine Navigation Tribunals—especially the Rotterdam District Court, being the court most frequently seised in that capacity—found that they had ceased to operate as such and that, consequently, the ordinary rules of the Codes of Commerce and of Civil Procedure must temporarily be applied again to Rhine navigation cases, implying the reassumption of jurisdiction by the normal courts, the substitution of the normal to the summary procedure, the cessation of the treaty exemption from judicial dues, and possible other consequences. See, *e.g.*, the judgments of the District Court of Rotterdam of 6 April 1938, confirmed by the Court of Appeal at The Hague on 9 June 1941 (*A.D.* Suppl. vol. 1919-1942, Case No. 124), 9 June 1944 (*ibid.*, 1946, Case No. 22) and 27 September 1957 (*I.L.R.* 1957, p. 99).

This temporary judicial practice was only reversed after the Occupant Powers of Western Germany had established special courts of justice which were intended to act as Rhine Navigation Courts, and had invested them with the necessary jurisdiction. See for some historical data the judgments of the District Court of Rotterdam of 17 April 1953 and 14 January 1954 (*ibid.*, 1953, pp. 164-165, respectively 1954, pp. 276-277). Uncertainty as to what exactly the Occupant Powers had decreed on this subject at first caused some confusion in the Netherlands courts. What had actually happened in Western Germany was that in each of the three occupation zones the traditional Rhine Navigation jurisdiction was re-established as from 1 January 1946, subject however during a number of years to specific restrictions. These restrictions as laid down, for instance, in Article III of the British Military Government Ordinance No. 65, excluded from the jurisdiction, *inter alia*, "contentious civil cases in which any national of the United Nations is a defendant, or being a plaintiff is made defendant to a counterclaim". Some of the restrictions were removed by Law No. 13 of the Council of Allied High Commissioners of 25 November 1949, in force as from 1 January 1950, providing, *inter alia* (Article 10), that the time during which German courts had no jurisdiction as a result of enactments of the Occupying Powers, should not count in the computation of time for periods of limitation. The Dutch Courts held, however, that this safeguarding provision did not operate in proceedings which had been commenced prior to 1 January 1947, the date of the reconstitution of the Rhine Navigation Tribunals (in the French zone by Ordinance No. 73 of 6 December 1946). See the *Clemence* case (relative to a collision between a Belgian and a Dutch vessel on 13 September 1946 on the Rhine in the French zone of occupation), in which the summons had been issued on 5 June 1948; it was decided against the plaintiff by a judgment of the District Court of Rotterdam of 21 November 1950 (*Ned. Jur.* 1952, No. 185), digested in *I.L.R.* 1950, p. 125. A corresponding case (*re the Maas*) had been adjudicated on 19 April 1950 by the District Court of Dordrecht (*Ned. Jur.* 1951, No. 144, digested in *I.L.R.* 1950, Case No. 31), which left undecided (i) whether the Convention of Mannheim had not been suspended by the war between Germany and the Netherlands; (ii) whether the Allied occupation authorities were competent to enact the above mentioned ordinances; and (iii) if so, whether the Netherlands courts must take notice of them. This latter judgment gave also some further details on the legal development since 1936 with regard to the German stretch of the river.

5) The ordinary District Court of The Hague was once seised by a shipowner, victim of an accident on the river Waal near Nijmegen whereby his ship, the *Sint-Theresia*, struck a solid object below the surface of the water which later appeared to be a caisson that had been used in 1944 by British troops as an anchor for one of their pontoon bridges, and sustained damage. The owner and his insurers sued the State of the Netherlands for damages on the grounds that it was liable for the consequences of a failure to perform its duty under Article 28 of the Convention of Mannheim to keep the channel in a good state of maintenance. The Court affirmed that the State was in principle under the legal obligation invoked by the claimants, but found, after a further enquiry had been ordered and made, that the State had in fact done all that it reasonably could do to prevent damage (*I.L.R.* 1951, Case No. 35).

6) Sometimes also, the execution of judgments, rendered in Rhine navigation cases by a Tribunal of a Rhine State, in another has come up before the municipal courts. Comp. *e.g.*, the judgment of the Tribunal of Strasbourg of 20 February 1927, digested in *A.D.* 1927-1928, Case No. 83: a judgment of the Rhine Navigation Court of Rüdesheim must be executed on French territory pursuant to Article 40 of the Mannheim Convention.

To conclude this exposition, I wish to state that the Central Commission has also developed a body of case law of its own in appeal cases.[73] On the discrepancy between this case law and certain judgments of municipal courts, on the one hand, and the German *Reichsgericht*, on the other, comp. note II *ad* Case No. 57 in *A.D.* 1929-1930. Netherlands courts designated for the trial of Rhine navigation cases in appeal under the Law of 16 July 1869 (*Staatsblad* No. 139), amended by that of 19 March 1913 (*ibid.*, No. 103), would seem never to have been seised by the parties, or very seldom.

III. *Systematic survey of matters of fluvial law, regulated mainly by treaties*

Apart from the major rivers which rank first in the history of international fluvial law and on which I have given some details under II above, a large number of other boundary or boundary-crossing rivers, less famous in this respect, have also played a—varying—rôle in treaty law. I will

73. See Henri WALTHER, *La jurisprudence de la Commission Centrale pour la navigation du Rhin* (Strasbourg, 1948).

now draw those other rivers also into an overall systematic survey of subjects of bilateral, or by exception multilateral treaty regulation.

Such treaty regulations have, already a long time ago and prior to the first attempt at codification in Vienna (1815), first and foremost laid down freedom of navigation for the riparian States and their subjects.

This principle of freedom of navigation is in the usual construction closely accompanied by that of non-discrimination, in all respects, between the different users of the river. This was expressed, with regard to wharfage, cranage, weighage, storage and similar dues, in Article 3, 2nd para. of the Shipping Regulations for the Danube of 2 June 1882, endorsed by Article 7 of the Treaty of London of 10 March 1883 (Martens, N.R.G.[2], IX, 392), as follows:

> "Toutefois, ces droits devront être prélevés indistinctement, suivant des tarifs fixes et publics, sans égard à la provenance des bâtiments et de leurs cargaisons, et pour autant seulement que les bâtiments assujettis à ces droits auraient profité desdits établissements",

and with regard to the levying of special temporary taxes to defray the costs of expensive works for the improvement of the river, in Article 18 (3) of the Definitive Statute of 23 July 1921 (ibid., N.R.G.[3], XII, 606) as follows:

> "The incidence of navigation dues may in no case involve differential treatment in respect of the flag of the vessels or the nationality of persons and goods or in respect of ports of departure or destination or control of the vessels; ...".

This principle of equality or non-discrimination has, however, in actual practice given rise to serious controversy about its purport. When discussing the legal situation on the Rhine (supra, p. 142), I have already expatiated on certain forms of discrimination between nationals of a riparian State and foreigners which have been, or are still, practised on the river, either in favour of the former (cabotage), or in their disfavour (fettering of purely inland navigation by a system of compulsory economic ordering).

The dispute on the purport of the principle of non-discrimination in river law has come to a head in the Oscar Chinn case between Great Britain and Belgium of 1931-1934, adjudicated by the Permanent Court of International Justice by its Judgment of 12 December 1934 (Publications P.C.I.J., series A/B, No. 63), discussed in my The Jurisprudence of the World Court, Vol. I, pp. 383 et seq. I will not return to that case here save for stating that the Judgment was to the effect that discrimination cannot be held to be present if an, even indisputable, difference in treatment between nationals and foreigners is the consequence of factual circumstances and does not depend on any intention to injure especially the foreigners.

Over and above the operation of the principles of freedom of navigation and of non-discrimination there is, however, a variety of other matters which have in the course of time come up for regulation by treaty. I will endeavour to systematize them under this heading for the sake of orientation in the contents of international fluvial law, as it has developed historically before and after the Congress of Vienna.

Navigation proper

1. *Freedom of navigation*

On obvious historical grounds attention must first be focussed on *Europe*. One of the oldest instruments relating to freedom of fluvial navigation is that of 8 June 1177 concerning the river Po, unilateral Ferrarian in form, but conventional in substance, owing to the participation of representatives of neighbouring States. This specific charter of freedom was confirmed for the last time by a treaty between Austria, Modena and Parma of 3 July 1849 (Martens, N.R.G.[1], XIV, 525). Comp. for particulars above, pp. 111-112.

Old regulations on the freedom of navigation prior to the Final Act of Vienna (1815) can be cited, *e.g.*, with regard to many rivers belonging to the Danube basin. (Comp. on the Danube itself, which was already declared free in 1774 and 1829, *supra*, under II B, pp. 143 *et seq*).

> Maros, Theiss and Save: Articles 2, § 2, and 5, § 2 of the Austro-Turkish peace treaty—or, more correctly (see Article 20), armistice treaty—of Carlowitz of 26 January 1699 (Dumont, VII[2], 448).
> Aluta (Oltŭ) and Timok: Articles 1, § 2 and 2, § 2 of the Austro-Turkish peace treaty of Passarowitz (Požarewac) of 21 July 1718 (Dumont, VIII[1], 524).
> Dniestr: Article 3 of the Austro-Russian Treaty of Leopol of 19 March 1810 (Martens, N.R., I, 252), freedom "comme par le passé".
> Pruth: Article 4 of the Russo-Turkish peace treaty of Bucharest of 28 May 1812 (Martens, N.R., III, 397).

The same applies to certain rivers flowing through parts of Poland affected by the partitions of that country by Austria, Prussia and Russia (1773-1795).

> Dwina: Article 4 of the Russo-Polish treaty of 15 March 1775 (*ibid.*, R[2], II, 145).
> Bug and Vistula: Articles 1 and 4 of the Austro-Polish treaty of 9 February 1776 (*ibid.*, II, 124).
> Pilića and two other rivers: Article 2 of the treaty between Prussia and Poland of 25 September 1793 (*ibid.*, V, 544).

In northern Italy the river Adige was declared to be free by Article 11 of the peace treaty of Campo Formio of 17 October 1797 (*ibid.*, R[2], VI, 420), confirmed by Article 14 of that of Lunéville of 9 February 1801 (*ibid.*, VII, 296). Freedom of navigation was likewise expressly laid down for the Lower Weser, despite the temporary maintenance of the Elsfleth toll (comp. below), in Article 6 of the Convention of Regensburg of 6 April 1803 (*ibid.*, R², VII, 552), and for the Elbe in the Prussian-Westphalian treaty of 14 May 1811 (*ibid.*, N.R., I, 382).

On the *American* continent, too, a few conventions were concluded between European colonial Powers already in the second half of the 18th century to the effect that a specific river was declared free for navigation in favour of the nationals of the riparian States.

> Mississippi: Article 7 of the peace treaty of Paris of 10 February 1763 (Martens, R², I, 104) between France, Great Britain and Spain and Article 8 of the Anglo-American peace treaty of Versailles of 3 September 1783 (*ibid.*, III, 553).
> Ríos Belice and Hondo: Article 6 of the Anglo-Spanish peace treaty of Versailles of 3 September 1783 (*ibid.*, III, 541).
> Arawari between French and Portuguese Guyana: Article 7 of the peace treaty of Amiens of 25/27 March 1802 (*ibid.*, R², VII, 404).

Spain and Portugal, however, were not so liberally-minded in their mutual relations in South America in this respect. This is evidenced by the contents of their boundary treaty of San Ildefonso of 1 October 1777 (*ibid.*, II, 545) by which either party reserved for itself the exclusive authority over, and use of, specific rivers—*inter alia* the Río de la Plata and the Uruguay as to Spain, the Jauru as to Portugal (Articles 3 and 10) —and for the rest laid down the following principle (Article 11):

> "La navigation des fleuves que traverse la ligne de division, sera commune aux deux nations jusqu'à l'endroit où les deux rives n'appartiendront qu'à une seule des deux Couronnes, et depuis le point que commencera son droit de propriété sur les deux rives, elle sera maîtresse de la navigation, à l'exclusion de l'autre, de sorte que ladite navigation sera commune, ou appartiendra exclusivement à une seule, selon que les rives dépendront des deux Puissances ou d'une seulement . . .".

This general attitude occasionally took a more liberal turn after the emancipation of the Spanish colonies in the first part of the 19th century, but even then the development lagged far behind the freer trend in Europe as heralded by the French Revolution. There the Congress of Vienna not only undertook a general codification of the basic rules of European fluvial law, but also applied the freedom principle to a number of specific rivers, namely, the Rhine and its tributaries, the Meuse and the Scheldt (in Annexes XVI, b and c to the Final Act), the rivers in the whole expanse of old Poland (Article 14), the Ems (Article 30) and the Po (Article 96). This general trend did not necessarily imply the immediate liberation of shipping from the traditional shipping dues and other burdens. Comp. on that subject *infra*, under 2(*a*), p. 189.

Since 1815 several specific River Acts have continued the general line of liberalization, as appears from conventions dealing with the following European rivers:

the Elbe, *Elbschiffahrts-Akte* of 23 June 1821 between ten riparian States (*ibid.*, N.R., V, 714): freedom subject to important reservations, see below. A new Navigation Act was established after World War I: 22 February 1922 (*ibid.*, N.R.G.[3], XII, 632);

the Weser, Convention of 10 September 1823 between Prussia, Hanover, Electoral Hesse, Brunswick, Oldenburg, Lippe and Bremen (*ibid.*, N.R., VI, 301), with similar reservations;

the Douro, Conventions between Spain and Portugal of 31 August 1835 (*ibid.*, N.R., XIV, 97) and 23 May 1840 (*ibid.*, N.R.G.[1], I, 98);

the Neckar, *Neckarschiffahrtsordnung* of 1 July 1842 (*ibid.*, N.R.G.[1], IV, 630);

the Ems, Convention between Prussia and Hanover of 13 March 1843 (*ibid.*, N.R.G.[1], V, 125);

the Pruth, Convention of 15 December 1866 between Austria, Russia and the United Principalities of Moldavia and Wallachia (*ibid.*, N.R.G.[1], XX, 296), confirming a much older tradition, dating from 1812, and modified by a Convention of 2 March 1895 (*ibid.*, N.R.G.[2], XXXIV, 350);

the Boyana: Article 29 of the Peace Treaty of Berlin of 13 July 1878 (*ibid.*, N.R.G.[2], III, 449).

On the *American* continent, too, the principle of freedom of navigation, at least as far as shipping belonging to nationals of the riparian States was concerned, penetrated into State practice, but it did so only at a much slower rate and, as it were, more reluctantly.

As to South, Central and Spanish North America:

Colorado, Gila and part of the Río Bravo del Norte: Articles 6 and 7 of the peace treaty of Guadelupe Hidalgo of 2 February 1848 between the United States and Mexico (*ibid.*, N.R.G.[1], XI, 387 = XIV, 7);

Paraná and Uruguay: Article 1 of the treaties entered into on 10 July 1853 by Argentina, on the one hand, and France, Great Britain and the United States, respectively, on the other (*ibid.*, N.R.G.[2], X, 294);

Sarstoon: Article 6 of the Convention between Great Britain (for British Honduras) and Guatemala of 30 April 1859 (*ibid.*, N.R.G.[1], XVI[2], 366);

Putumayo and Amazon: modus vivendi between Brazil and Colombia of 24 April 1907 (*ibid.*, N.R.G.[3], I, 789);

Río de la Plata: restatement of the principle by a joint declaration of Argentina and Uruguay of 5 January 1910 (*ibid.*, N.R.G.[3], VI, 876), *sub* 3;

Paraguay, Paraná and Río de la Plata: treaty of navigation between Argentina and Paraguay of 24 January 1967 (*R.G.D.I.P.* 1967 (71), p. 294); see J. C. PUIG, *El conflicto fluvial con el Paraguay y el tratado de navegación de* 1967 in the *Revista de Derecho Internacional y Ciencias Diplomáticas* 1966/67 (XV, XVI), p. 119;

riverain areas of the boundary between Brazil and British Guyana: exchange of notes of October/November 1932 (*L.N.T.S.*, vol. 177, p. 128), *sub* 1(vi).

The general attitude in Latin America was perhaps best reflected in Article 7 of the boundary treaty between Bolivia and Brazil of 27 March 1867 (*ibid.*, N.R.G.[1], XX, 613) pursuant to which

> "Sa Majesté l'Empereur du Brésil accorde, *comme concession spéciale* (italics applied), la liberté pour le commerce et la navigation marchande de la République de Bolivie des cours d'eau navigables qui traversant le territoire du Brésil vont se jeter dans l'Océan",

and *vice versa*,—with special provisions in Articles 8 and 9 relating to navigation on the river Madeira.

In North America the dispute between the United States and Canada (Great Britain) concerning their exact water boundary from the mouth of the Saint Lawrence to the Lake of the Woods could only be finally resolved by a compromise solution which linked that problem with the freedom of navigation on the waterways concerned. Comp. on this subject Chapter VI, at pp. 555 *et seq.*

As to *Asia* it is scarcely possible to state any general trend, but there were instances of liberalization of fluvial navigation even there, in particular under European influence. I cite the following examples:

the Amur, Sungari and Ussuri, Article 1 of the Russo-Chinese boundary treaty of Aighoun of 28 May 1858 (*ibid.*, N.R.G.[1], XVII[1], 1): freedom of navigation for Chinese and Russian vessels; express interdiction for vessels of any other State;

the Bokhara section of the Amu-Daria (Oxus), Article 3 of the treaty of 10 October 1873 between Russia and Bokhara (*ibid.*, N.R.G.[1], XX, 92): freedom of navigation for Russian State and merchant vessels. On the contrary: Article 5 of the treaty of 24 August 1873 between Russia and Khiva (*ibid.*, XX, 97): navigation by Khivian and Bokharan vessels only in virtue of a special permission of the higher Russian authorities in Central Asia;

the Mekong: Anglo-Siamese Convention of 17 July 1927/21 August 1928 (*ibid.*, N.R.G.[3], XXIII, 212); comp. also Article 4 of the Franco-Siamese treaty of 12 February 1904 (*ibid.*, N.R.G.[2], XXXII, 130);

the Indus: declared "free for all nations" by a decree of the Governor-General of India, 13 March 1843 (*ibid.*, N.R.G.[1], V, 125);

Soviet-Chinese rivers, Article 8 of the Treaty on Principles of 31 May 1924 (*L.N.T.S.*, vol. 37, p. 180): reciprocal freedom of navigation on rivers and lakes.

Occasionally, the opening of purely national rivers for international traffic was unilaterally imposed upon Far Eastern countries by Western

European powers; comp. *e.g.*, Article 11 of the treaty of Saïgon between France and Annam of 15 March 1874 (Martens, N.R.G.², II, 206): freedom of passage on the river of Nhi-Hâ from the sea to Yunnan; or Article 5 of the Anglo-Chinese treaty of 5 September 1902 (*ibid.*, XXXIII, 284), providing for the removal of artificial obstructions to navigation in the Canton River. Japan has followed the same practice vis-à-vis China, comp. Article 6 of their Peace Treaty of Shimonoseki of 17 April 1895 (*ibid.*, XXI, 642).

In *Africa* the trend has generally been very favourable to freedom of navigation thanks to the Congo Conference of Berlin of 1885, which adopted a very liberal regime indeed. Comp. on the freedom of navigation in the Congo basin above *sub* I *b*, p. 121, and for further liberalizations the following instances:

Zambesi, Shiré and Pungwé: after a Convention between Great Britain and Portugal of 20 August 1890 (*ibid.*, N.R.G.², XVI, 929 = XVIII, 154) had declared (in Article 11) navigation on all lakes, rivers and canals in their respective spheres of influence in Central Africa free to both flags, and in addition (in Article 12) navigation of the Zambesi and the Shiré free for the ships of all nations, a further Agreement of 14 November 1890 (*ibid.*, XVI, 942 = XVIII, 160) stressed the somewhat unilateral character of that liberalization by laying down a number of engagements undertaken by Portugal vis-à-vis Great Britain in that respect for the same two rivers plus the Pungwé.

Cross River: Anglo-German Agreement of 11 March 1913 under (2) (*ibid.*, N.R.G.³, IX, 190): navigation on its course within British Southern Nigeria open to German merchant vessels.

Manoh River: Agreement between Great Britain (for Sierra Leone) and Liberia of 10 April 1913 (*ibid.*, IX, 200), customs regulations.

Sometimes the outbreak of war leads to a temporary suspension of the freedom of navigation. Comp. *e.g.*, the Turkish instructions of 29 April 1877 (Martens, N.R.G.², III, 199, 200) with regard to the Danube, being at that time a defence line of the Ottoman Empire.

As a rule, Navigation Acts now contain a provision to the effect that freedom of navigation shall be upheld as far as possible even in time of war. See Article 15 of the Statute of Barcelona of 20 April 1921 (*ibid.* N.R.G.³, XVIII, 730).

2. *Other matters directly connected with navigation*

In more or less direct connexion with (freedom of) navigation proper mention can be made of the subjects of regulation, listed below under (*a*) to (*e*).

(*a*) *River tolls and their redemption*

As I remarked earlier, the freedom of navigation on international rivers does not imply by itself the abolition of all shipping dues. From the outset a clear distinction must be made between duties levied for the simple fact of navigating on a river and those which are intended as a remuneration for specific services rendered, such as piloting, harbour facilities, the working of locks or bascule bridges, etc. Whereas the latter have always been, and still are, considered lawful, the former have since the first quarter of the 19th century met with increasing disapproval, although those interested have put up a tenacious resistance to their abolition.

The difference between the two groups of dues has repeatedly been expressed in more or less detail in a number of treaties relating to river navigation. See for example the elaborate Articles 2 and 3 of the Shipping Regulations worked out by the European Danube Commission on 2 June 1882, endorsed by Article 7 of the Treaty of London of 10 March 1883 concerning navigation on the Danube (rejected by Romania) (Martens, N.R.G.[2], IX, 392):

> (Article 2) "Il ne sera perçu sur le Danube aucun péage basé uniquement sur le fait de la navigation du fleuve, ni aucun droit sur les marchandises, tant qu'elles se trouveront à bord des bâtiments transports ou radeaux".
> (Article 3) "Les Etats riverains ont le droit de percevoir dans leurs ports respectifs les droits de quai, grue, balance, magasinage, débarquement pour les établissements existants ou à établir.
> . . .
> Il est bien entendu que [les] tarifs ne pourront être une source de revenus financiers, mais qu'ils produiront seulement la quotité nécessaire au payement de l'intérêt et à l'amortissement du capital de premier établissement et d'entretien . . .".

This had already been expressed much more briefly in Article 1 of the Austro-Russian Convention of 25 July 1840 (Martens, N.R.G.[1], I, 208) and in Article 15 (2) of the Peace Treaty of Paris of 30 March 1856 (*ibid.*, XV, 770). It was even deemed necessary to stipulate an express exception to the latter Article in Article 6 of the Pontus Treaty of London of 13 March 1871 (*ibid.*, XVIII, 303) in order to make permissible the levying of a "taxe provisoire" for so long as would be indispensable to reimburse the heavy expenses which would be incurred by clearing the obstacles to navigation in the Danube sector of the Cataracts and the Iron Gates.—A corresponding provision was inserted in Article 6 of the 1883 Convention, authorizing Russia, subject to prior consultation with the European Commission, to levy certain tolls (*péages*) in order to cover the costs which she would incur for the execution of works on behalf of the amelioration of navigation in the Kilia branch of the Danube (Article 5).—See also Articles 16 and 18 of the so-called Definitive Statute of the Danube of 23 July 1921 (*ibid.*, N.R.G.[3], XII, 606).

The development of this subject has shown a marked, but slow tendency towards liberalization in the sense that less considerable navigation dues have first been gradually lightened and later abolished altogether either by convention or unilaterally by the State concerned, and that a few important historical river tolls have been redeemed in concert between interested States by international agreements of major importance, one, the Elsfleth toll on the Weser, in the first quarter of the 19th century, the others, the Elbe toll of Stade and the Scheldt toll, only in the third quarter of that century.

One of the first deliberate instances of the abolition of pure river tolls was that of the shipping dues levied on the river Meuse downstream of Venlo by Article II, 3 of the Franco-Austrian peace treaty of Campo Formio of 17 October 1797 (*ibid.*, R^2, VI, 426).

The many pre-existing river tolls on the *Rhine* were formally "suppressed" by Article 39 of the *Reichsdeputations-Hauptschluss* of 25 February 1803 (*ibid.*, R^2, VII, 435), but at the same time replaced by what was then called a "navigation octroy", a uniform levy, *inter alia* for the specific purpose of providing the necessary money for the indemnification of former secular or ecclesiastical rulers, hit by the successive mediatizations and secularizations in the Napoleonic era. This "octroy" was expressly limited to a maximum, viz., the combined amount of the tolls just suppressed. Its tariff was, as far as goods were concerned, discriminatory in character in the special sense that it was heavier not only for ascending than for descending vessels, but also for foreign shipping than for French and German vessels. Comp. also Article 99 of the subsequent Franco-German Convention of 15 August 1804 (Martens, R^2, VIII, 261) on the Rhine Navigation Octroy, and for the further development *supra*, pp. 127 *et seq.*

A further river toll, notorious for the part it played in the past, and which was in the event abolished soon after the Congress of Vienna, was the Elsfleth toll on the river *Weser*, mentioned above under II, pp. 160 *et seq.*

Another historical river toll was levied on the river *Elbe* at Stade, also called the Brunshäuser toll. As I have remarked above (p. 162), this toll was much older than that of Elsfleth on the Weser, being established by an ancient privilege granted by the Emperor to the City of Hamburg in the 13th century after that city had acquired the town of Stade in 1204, and it has survived until 1861. At an international conference at Hanover, held in June 1861 (protocols: Martens, N.R.G.^{1}, XVII^1, 406-418) sixteen Powers, assembled there with the kingdom of Hanover, by their Convention of 22 June 1861 (*ibid.*, XVII^1, 419) agreed upon the suppression of the Stade toll against a compensation to Hanover of 2.857.338 2/3 German Thaler, to be apportioned among the Contracting Parties in conformity with a fixed scale.

This redemption of the Stade toll did not, however, mean the total abolition of all tolls on the river Elbe. As I have set out above (p. 164), the original Navigation Act of 23 June 1821 (*ibid.*, N.R., V, 714) had indeed established two new different shipping tolls on the river, the Elbe toll (on cargo) and the so-called *Rekognitionszoll* (on vessels). The latter was abolished in 1844, the former only in 1870 (see p. 164).

A redemption similar to that of the Stade toll on the Elbe followed two years later in respect of the much more important *Scheldt* toll. The history of that toll is again entirely different. As I have set out above (pp. 166-167), the river Scheldt was, as a means of preventing Spanish Antwerp becoming a dangerous commercial rival of the United Netherlands, by Article 14 of the Peace Treaty of Münster of 30 January 1648 (Dumont, VI[1], 429) closed to traffic altogether, and it has remained so closed ever since for about a century and a half (1648-1795).

However, the situation changed basically after revolutionary France, the champion of the freedom of fluvial navigation, at least when it was in her favour, in her turn took over the Belgian provinces from Austria by Article 3 of her peace treaty with that country of Campo Formio of 17 October 1797 (*ibid.*, R[2], VI, 420) and began to penetrate into the northern provinces, starting with her acquisition, by Article 12, *sub* 1[0] of her treaty with the Republic of the United Netherlands of 16 May 1795 (*ibid.*, R[2], VI, 88), of that part of the province of Zeeland situated on the southern bank of the Scheldt.

It was under these conditions that Belgium, after an agreement with the Netherlands of 12 May 1863 (*ibid.*, N.R.G.[1], XVII[2], 230), took the initiative of freeing the river from the dues by redeeming them through the payment to the Netherlands of a sum, representing the capitalized value of the toll (17,141,640 florins), with the financial assistance of all interested sea-faring nations. At a Conference, assembled for that purpose in Brussels on 15/16 July 1863 (protocols: *ibid.*, XVII[2], 235), a solution was reached in the multilateral treaty of Brussels of 16 July 1863 (*ibid.*, XVII[2], 223), concluded between Belgium and twenty maritime nations, to the following effect.

The Netherlands consented to the cancellation of the toll for the benefit of all flags, and engaged never to establish it again (*ibid.*, XVII[2], 232). Belgium assumed a corresponding obligation and undertook vis-à-vis the Netherlands to indemnify the latter by paying out to her the capitalized amount of 17,141,640 guilders, payable in instalments; after payment of the first instalment (one third) the toll would cease to be collected. The seafaring nations obliged themselves to reimburse to Belgium two thirds of the total indemnity,—one third to remain as her own share—according to a scale of assessment proportionate to their varying navigational interests. Belgium in turn engaged vis-à-vis those Powers to completely cancel the tonnage dues, until then levied in Belgian ports, to reduce the piloting dues both in those ports and on the river to an agreed scale, and, with the concurrence of the municipality of Antwerp (*ibid.*, XVII², 233), also to lessen certain local dues.

This complicated solution having thus been adopted, a number of other maritime nations, which initially remained precluded from the benefit of the cancellation or reduction of the Belgian duties (Article 7 of the multilateral treaty), still joined the scheme in later years, *e.g.*, Greece, 20 September 1864 (*ibid.*, N.R.G.², I, 113, 114), Argentina, 2 October 1868 (*ibid.*, N.R.G.¹, XX, 354), Mecklenburg-Schwerin, 18 March 1870 (*ibid.*, N.R.G.², I, 115, 116), Spain, 14 June 1870 (*ibid.*, I, 116). As between Belgium and Hanover the solution had already been found in 1861, as it were in an "exchange" of the redemption of the Elbe toll *inter partes* for that of the Scheldt toll (Convention of 18 February 1861, *ibid.*, N.R.G.¹, XVII¹, 306). See for certain ancillary agreements: Great Britain-Belgium, 3 August 1863 (*ibid.*, I, 111): details on the payment of the British share,—and 11 August 1863 (*ibid.*, I, 128): Belgian declaration of intention vis-à-vis the Netherlands.

(b) Staple and similar rights

The practice of compelling passing seagoing or river vessels to break their cargo in specified ports, either with the object of securing a right of preemption of the goods in favour of the inhabitants of such ports, or of enforcing their transhipment into other vessels, is very old and has survived for a very long time.

> That this institution is indeed of great age, is evidenced, *e.g.*, by documents handed down to us from the 14th century, relating to a grant made by the then Count of Holland to the town of Dordrecht. After some initial friction between Count Willem III and the town (1326, 1330), his successor Willem IV, on 11 September 1344, decreed that all merchant vessels ascending the river Maas from the sea were to unload their cargo at Dordrecht and there to load it again. This grant was confirmed in 1350 by Countess Margaretha and in 1355 by the Regent for Willem V, Duke Albrecht of Bavaria who, however, in 1379 declared two other towns, in the separate county of Zeeland, Zierikzee and Middelburg, to be exempt from this staple right. The curious confirmation of the ancient privileges of Dordrecht by the Church Council of Basel on 29 December 1435 would seem to have comprised also the staple grant. Comp. B. VAN RIJSWIJK, *Geschiedenis van het Dordtsche stapelrecht* (diss. Leyden, 1900).

As I have already had an opportunity to mention in my analytical survey at p. 108, the staple right and comparable rights were especially exercised on German rivers, such as the Elbe and the Rhine. These rights were more often than not usurped by the commercial towns rather than regularly granted to them by a higher authority. A striking example of this old abuse is that practised by Hamburg in the 15th century on the river Ems in the port of Emden. After its occupation of the town of Emden in 1431 (comp. *infra*, p. 392) Hamburg soon proceeded to apply its staple claims in respect of navigation on the river Elbe also to navigation on the Ems in the port of Emden; comp. also *infra* p. 221.

The historical importance of the rights in question has obviously been so great that they have left their traces far into the 19th century and that it has still been deemed necessary at that late stage to expressly forbid their future establishment on international waterways, as though they could have been legally revived in the absence of such an express prohibition. Examples of the reminiscence of these old abuses are a convention of 1867 between Baden and Switzerland relative to the *Untersee* in the Rhine (comp. p. 95 *supra*) and chapters IV and V of the General Act of the Congo Conference of 1885 relative to the rivers Congo and Niger (comp. p. 156 *supra*).

It was occasionally mentioned in treaties—comp. *e.g.*, Article 2 of the separate Act, signed by Prussia and Poland on 18 March 1775 (Martens, R², II, 164), reserving the "droit d'étape" to the Prussian town of Königsberg on the river Pregel—and it still remained conditionally tolerated on international rivers in general, as far as previously established rights of that nature were concerned, by Article 114 of the Final Act of the Congress of Vienna (= Article 7 of *Règlement* XVI a), which, however, prohibited the establishment of new staple and similar rights for the future:

> "On n'établira nulle part des droits d'étape, d'échelle ou de relâche forcée. Quant à ceux qui existent déjà, ils ne seront conservés qu'en tant que les états riverains, sans avoir égard à l'intérêt local de l'endroit ou du Pays où ils sont établis, les trouveraient nécessaires ou utiles à la navigation et au commerce en général".

As far as concerns the Rhine, the old staple right proper, defined as "la mise en vente forcée, de quelqu'espèce de marchandises ou denrées que ce soit, lors de leur station dans les ports des villes de Mayence et de la Cologne", was already definitively abolished by Article 8 of the Franco-German Convention of 15 August 1804 (*ibid.*, R², VIII, 261), whereas pursuant to that same Article all duties which had so far been levied in those towns on account either of that staple, or of "la relâche forcée, l'échelle etc. sous les noms de droits d'étape, de transit, d'accis et sous quelqu'autre dénomination ou prétexte que ce puisse être" would cease to be due from the day when the levy of the new "right of octroy" would commence. On the other hand, the old institutions of *relâche* and *échelle (Umschlag)* themselves, as they were practised in Mainz and Cologne, were expressly maintained by Articles 3-7 of the Convention. This was motivated by the need "que la navigation sur la partie supérieure, moyenne et inférieure du Rhin soit exercée par les embarcations dont la construction et la capacité sont le mieux appropriées à chacune de ces parties du fleuve, et par les bateliers qui sont le plus à portée d'en avoir la connaissance et la pratique", and implied that the town of Cologne would remain "la station de la navigation" between Holland and Mainz and the town of Mainz that between Cologne and Strasbourg, to the effect that vessels passing one of these towns in either direction would be obliged "de s'arrêter au port de cette ville, d'y rompre charge et de verser leur chargement dans d'autres embarcations".—This obstacle to navigation was, however, on the proposal of the Rivers Commission of the Congress of Vienna, definitively swept away by an express provision (Article 19) in the special River Act for the Rhine (Annex XVI b) which, contrary to the general rule of Article 114 of the Final Act, laid down that the abolition of the staple right proper on the Rhine, as agreed upon in 1804, was extended as yet to the other old institutions of *relâche*, *échelle* or *Umschlag* (last breaking) to the effect "qu'il sera libre de naviguer sur tout le cours du Rhin..., soit en remontant, soit en descendant, sans qu'on soit obligé de rompre charge, et de verser les chargemens dans d'autres embarcations dans quelque port, ville ou endroit que cela puisse être".—However even half a century later it was evidently still deemed desirable to repeat the interdiction of these obsolete rights in express terms in Article 5 of the Revised Convention of Mannheim of 17 October 1868 (Martens, N.R.G.[1], XX, 355):

"Les bateliers ne pourront nulle part ... être contraints à décharger, soit en tout, soit en partie, ou à transborder leurs chargements.—Tout droit de relâche et d'échelle est et demeure supprimé".

On certain inner-German rivers the "Stapel- und Umschlagsrechte" still existing there were cancelled on the occasion of the creation of a Customs Union between Prussia, Bavaria, Saxony, Württemberg, the two Hessen's and the Thuringian Customs Union: Article 16 of the Treaty of Accession of Baden to that Union, of 12 May 1835 (*ibid.*, N.R., XIII, 228).

Even as late as 1867 it was obviously still held necessary, in Article I (4) of a Convention between Switzerland and Baden of 28 September of that year (*ibid.*, N.R.G.[1], XX, 139) to state in so many words that "Stapel- und Umschlagerechte" "were and remained abolished" on the Untersee, inclusive of the stretches of the Rhine between Konstanz and Schaffhausen.

An express provision in Articles 14 and 27 of the General Act of the Congo Conference of 26 February 1885 (*ibid.*, N.R.G.[2], X, 414) forbade the establishment of staple and similar rights on the rivers Congo and Niger (comp. above p. 121) and this prohibition was renewed in express terms in Article 6 of the new Convention of Saint-Germain-en-Laye of 10 September 1919 (*ibid.*, N.R.G.[3], XIV, 12): "[La navigation] ne subira aucune obligation d'échelle, d'étape, de dépôt, de rupture de charge ou de relâche forcée".

(c) *River cabotage*

The term "cabotage" is borrowed from maritime navigation, a context in which, however, it can be understood not only in the ordinary sense of navigation along the coast ("entre cabo y cabo") between two or more seaports of the same State, but also in the wider special sense of navigation between a mother country and its colonies overseas, which was also often reserved in the past to the national flag (comp. the "rule of the war of 1756" in the law of prize, comp. my *Le droit des prises de la Grande Guerre* (Leyden 1924) p. 996). When applied to fluvial navigation the term has equally appeared to be susceptible of two different interpretations. Whereas it is usually understood as meaning navigation between two or more ports, situated on the same national stretch of a multinational river, the term was employed during the elaboration of the Elbe régime in the 1820's in the sense of exclusively fluvial navigation, even between ports of successive national river stretches, as contradistinguished to navigation from the river into the sea, and *vice versa*.

Reservation of fluvial cabotage in the normal sense to the national flag was, and still is, the rule, freedom for other flags to participate in it a rare exception. Comp. for Europe:

the Elbe: Article 1 of the Navigation Act of 23 June 1821 (Martens, N.R., V, 714) and Article 13 of the new Statute of 22 February 1922 (*ibid.*, N.R.G.[3], XII, 632);

the Weser: Article 1 of the Act of 10 September 1823 (*ibid.*, N.R., VI, 301);

the Douro: Article 1, § 1, of the Convention between Portugal and Spain of 23 May 1840 (*ibid.*, N.R.G.[1], I, 98);

the Neckar: Article 45 of the Act of 1 July 1842 (*ibid.*, N.R.G.[1], IV, 630);

the Danube: under Article 22 (1) of the Navigation Act of 23 July 1921 (*ibid.*, N.R.G.[3], XII, 606) "the transport of goods and passengers between the ports of the same State" was, in principle, as free as between the ports of separate riparian States, but Article 22 (2) made a reservation for "a regular local service for passengers and for national or nationalized goods between the ports of one and the same State". Under the peace treaties of Paris of 10 February 1947 (*U.N.T.S.* vol. 42, p. 3; vol. 41, p. 21 and p. 135): "traffic between ports of the same State" was expressly excluded from the freedom of navigation (Article 36 of the treaty with Romania, 34 of that with Bulgaria, and 38 of that with Hungary). This rule has been since then maintained under the Communist domination.

On the Rhine the freedom of cabotage has never been impaired for more than a century; it has only become controversial in recent times. The correct legal solution of that controversy, until now officially unresolved, is that cabotage has always been, and still is, in law free along the whole course of the river. Comp. on this complicated subject my separate section on the history of the Rhine, *supra*, pp. 135 *et seq.*

As to the American continent:

on the waterways common to Bolivia and Brazil cabotage was reserved to the national flags by Article 7 (3) of their boundary treaty of 27 March 1867 (Martens, N.R.G.[1], XX, 613);

on those common to Brazil and Colombia fluvial cabotage was also excepted from the freedom of navigation: Article IV *in fine* of their treaty of 24 April 1907 (*ibid.*, N.R.G.[3], I, 786): "Fica entendido e declarado que não se comprehende nessa navegação a de porto a porto do mesmo paiz, ou de cabotagem fluvial, que continuará sujeita em cada um dos dois Estados ás suas respectivas leis";

on the waterways common to Argentina and Paraguay cabotage is excepted from the freedom of navigation: Article 3 of the treaty of 24 January 1967 (*R.G.D.I.P.* 1967 (71), p. 294).

The opposite principle, in favour of the freedom of cabotage, was adopted for the African rivers:

Article 13 of the General Act of the Congo Conference of Berlin of 26 February 1885 (Martens, N.R.G.[2], X, 414) granted to all Contracting Parties on a footing of complete equality freedom "pour le grand et le petit cabotage" on the river Congo and its branches; the same applied to the Niger on the strength of Article 26 of the same Act. This liberal principle was reaffirmed in Articles 1 and 2 of the Convention of Saint-Germain-en-Laye of 10 September 1919 (*ibid.*, N.R.G.[3], XIV, 12).

Further bilateral Conventions between colonial Powers have also applied the principle of freedom of cabotage. See, for example, Article 11 of the Convention of 20 August 1890 between Great Britain and Portugal (*ibid.*, N.R.G.[2], XVI, 929 = XVIII, 154): "no differential treatment shall be permitted as regards transport or coasting trade".

See for a survey of treaty regulation of fluvial cabotage the *Annuaire de l'Institut de droit international* 1929, pp. 356 *et seq.*

(d) Regulation of river traffic

A great many conventions have been concluded in the past and there are still many in force, which laid or lay down rules for traffic on international rivers, dealing with such subjects as:

the technical aspects of navigation proper in general:

Rhine, Title VI of the Act of Mainz of 31 March 1831 (Martens, N. R., IX, 252); *Règlement de police pour la navigation du Rhin et le flottage*, of 17 October 1868 (*ibid.*, N.R.G.[2], IV, 599, with Protocol at p. 617), repeatedly amended; new *Règlement* of 14 September 1912 (*ibid.*, N.R.G.[3], XX, 154), also repeatedly amended (1921, 1923, 1925, 1926, 1928, 1929 (*ibid.*, N.R.G.[3], XXII, 85); revised edition 25 August 1939 (*ibid.*, XXXVII, 398).

Danube, a series of Regulations for different stretches of the river; comp.

e.g., chapters 1-10 of section II (Articles 11 *et seq.*) of the *Règlement* of 2 June 1882 (*ibid.*, N.R.G.², IX, 394), dealing with such matters as: passing or overhauling on the river or on towing-paths, sailing by night or in fog, anchoring, shipwreck or grounding, the throwing-out of ballast, lightening of vessels, towing, and harbour police, and for further details my account of the history of the legal regime of the Danube, pp. 143 *et seq.*

Pruth, regulations of 8/9 February 1871 (*ibid.*, N.R.G.², I, 485), drafted by the Mixed Austro-Russo-Romanian Commission.

Scheldt, *Règlement* No. I, annexed to the Convention of 20 May 1843 (*ibid.*, N.R.G.¹, V, 295-306).

Intermediary waters between the Rhine and the Scheldt, *Règlement* No. V, annexed to the same Convention (*ibid.*, V, 339-350).

Meuse, Titre IV of the *Règlement* No. VI, annexed to the same Convention (*ibid.*, V, 351-366, 382), amended 31 October 1885 (*ibid.*, N.R.G.², XI, 663).

customs control:

Meuse, on customs control: Articles 16-31 of the above-mentioned *Règlement* no. VI of 1843.

Rhine, on customs control: *Titre* III of the Act of Mainz of 31 March 1831 (*ibid.*, N.R., IX, 252); Articles 9 *et seq.* of the Revised Act of Mannheim of 17 October 1868 (*ibid.*, N.R.G.¹, XX, 355); on the establishment of joint customs control on the Netherlands-German border by successive agreements of 1928, 1957 and 1961 (see *Tr. blad* 1958, Nos. 6 and 93; 1962, Nos. 72 and 75).

Danube, on customs control: Articles 6 and 7 of the above-mentioned Regulations of 2 June 1882:

"Les lignes douanières suivront partout les rives du fleuve sans jamais le traverser. Il s'ensuit que les bâtiments, transports, radeaux etc., tant qu'ils sont en voie de navigation ou à l'ancre dans le lit du fleuve, sans faire aucune opération de commerce avec la rive, sont entièrement en dehors de toute action des douanes".

Scheldt, on customs control: Articles 19 *et seq.*, of *Règlement* No. I of 1843, cited above.

Bolivian-Brazilian common rivers, on customs control: Articles 15 *et seq.* of the Convention of 27 March 1867 (*ibid.*, N.R., XX, 613).

sanitary control: elaborate provisions on this control, to be exercised by the *Conseil supérieur de santé* at Constantinople, on which foreign missions would be represented, in section II, § 3 (Articles 18-20) of the Public Act concerning navigation on the mouths of the Danube of 2 November 1865 (Martens, N.R.G.¹, XVIII, 144); Article 6 of the Act of 28 May 1881 additional to that Public Act (*ibid.*, N.R.G.², VIII, 207); and on quarantine precautions to be taken in the case of the outbreak of epidemics in maritime Danube ports or higher up along the banks of the river, Article 10 of the above-mentioned *Règlement* of 2 June 1882.

the prevention of dangers arising from the transport of inflammable, corrosive, explosive or venemous cargoes:

Rhine, Regulations dating as far back as 17 October 1868 (*ibid.*, N.R.G.², IV, 613, comp. however 617), replaced by those of 2 September 1879 (*ibid.*, VIII, 202) and subsequent ones.

Danube, Articles 60 and 61 of the above-mentioned *Règlement* of 1882.
Meuse, Article 43 of the above-mentioned *Règlement* No. VI of 1843.
Scheldt, Article 29 of the above-mentioned *Règlement* No. I of 1843.

guarantees for the capability of masters:

Rhine, requirement of a shipper's patent: Title IV of the Act of Mainz of 1831; Articles 15 *et seq.* of the Revised Act of Mannheim of 1868 and *Protocole de Clôture*, sub 4°, A and B (*ibid.*, N.R.G.[1], XX, 355), amended 4 June 1898 (*ibid.*, N.R.G.[2], XXIX, 113); Convention of 14 December 1922, supplemented 22 December 1923 (*ibid.*, N.R.G.[3], XV, 219, 223).
Elbe, Convention of 19 June 1925 (*ibid.*, N.R.G.[3], XXIX, 483, 487).
Meuse, Articles 32 *et seq.* of the above-mentioned *Règlement* No. VI of 1843.

shipwreck or grounding of vessels:

Meuse, Article 40 of the same *Réglement.*

social provisions for the benefit of the crews:

Elbe, conditions of labour and social assurance in favour of the crews of Czech vessels on the river in Germany: Convention of 15 December 1924 (*ibid.*, N.R.G.[3], XXII, 458);
Oder, identical convention of the same date (*ibid.*, 455); Rhine, social security for all members of crews: convention of 13 February 1961 (*Les Actes du Rhin et de la Moselle*, Strasbourg, 1966, p. 56; *Tr. blad* 1962, No. 13).

The imposition of legal obligations in this field upon owners of vessels on the Rhine was held by the Netherlands Supreme Court not to be at variance with the freedom of navigation. Comp. on this subject § 2 *sub* b of Annex A to Chapter II, section 1, at p. 176 and footnote 72.

(e) Beaconing and lighting—Pilotage

Comp. on *beaconing* and *lighting:*

on the Scheldt: Article 9, § 2 of the Treaty of Separation of 19 April 1839 (Martens, N.R., XVI[2], 773); *Règlement provisoire* II of 23 October 1839 (*ibid.*, XVI[2], 1008)—common surveillance—; Article 18 of the treaty of The Hague of 5 November 1842 (*ibid.*, N.R.G.[1], III, 613); *Règlement* No. III, annexed to the Convention of Antwerp of 20 May 1843 (*ibid.*, N.R.G.[1], V, 294 *et seq.*, at p. 332). New beacons or other lights: Conventions of 26 December 1865/31 March 1866 (*ibid.*, N.R.G.[2], I, 130/131), 8 May/2 August 1873 (*ibid.*, I, 134/135), 11 June 1880/ 9 February 1881 (*ibid.*, VIII, 156/157 and 160/161), 27 October 1904/ 5 April 1905 (*ibid.*, N.R.G.[2], XXXIV, 579/580), 30 April/8 October 1907 (*ibid.*, N.R.G.[3], I, 893/894);

on the Meuse: Article 41 of *Règlement* No. VI of 1843;

on the Rhine: Article 28, (2) (3) of the Revised Convention of Mannheim;

in the Ems estuary (and the adjacent territorial sea): Netherlands-German Convention of 16 October 1896 (*ibid.*, N.R.G.[2], XXV, 56);

on the Weser: upkeep of the buoys *(amarques)* on the lower part of the river, Convention between Bremen, Oldenburg and Prussia of March 1876 (*ibid.*, N.R.G.², II, 290), extended to the section between Bremen and Wegesack 20 March 1886 (*ibid.*, XII, 358).

On the system of lighthouses at the mouths of the Danube: Article 17 of the Public Act of 2 November 1865 (*ibid.*, N.R.G.¹, XVIII, 144) and Article 5 of the Act of Galatz of 28 May 1881 additional to that Public Act (*ibid.*, N.R.G.², VIII, 207). Lighthouses have played a prominent rôle in the Ottoman Empire as a whole. Comp. the judicial and arbitral proceedings relating to Turkish lighthouse concessions in *Publications P.C.I.J.*, series A/B, Nos. 62 and 71 and *A.A.*, vol. XII, pp. 161 *et seq.*

Comp. on *pilotage*:

on the Scheldt: Article 9, § 2 of the Netherlands-Belgian Treaty of Separation of 19 April 1839 (*ibid.*, N.R., XVI², 773); *Règlement provisoire* I of 23 October 1839 (*ibid.*, XVI², 1006); Article 19 of the Treaty of The Hague of 5 November 1842 (*ibid.*, N.R.G.¹, III, 613); *Règlement* No. II, annexed to the Convention of Antwerp of 20 May 1843 (*ibid.*, V, 294, at p. 307-332); Convention of 12 May 1863 (*ibid.*, N.R.G.¹, XVII², 230): reduction of the pilotage dues, which, moreover, shall not be higher than those levied on the mouths of the river Meuse; Convention of 15 July/19 September 1863 (*ibid.*, N.R.G.², I, 126, 127): harmonization of the existing regulations on the piloting service with the treaty of 12 May 1863; Convention of 10 April/2 August 1873 (*ibid.*, I, 129, 130): partial exemptions of the compulsory employment of pilots; Convention of 29 June/29 September 1875 (*ibid.*, I, 223, 224): abolition of certain pilotage dues in favour of ships which take a pilot in the Channel or the Pas-de-Calais; Convention of 7 April/17 July 1876 (*ibid.*, II, 4, 5): modification of the system of signals for the calling of pilots, originally laid down in Article 16 of *Règlement* II of 1843 (above), followed in 1900/1901 by the introduction of the Code international des signaux (*ibid.*, N.R.G.², XXXIII, 266; N.R.G.³, XLI, 353);

on the Danube: Title II, chapter 11 (Articles 66-71) of the Navigation Regulations, adopted by the European Danube Commission on 2 June 1882 and confirmed by the London Convention of 10 March 1883 (*ibid.*, N.R.G.², IX, 392, 394);

on Spanish and Portuguese rivers: reciprocal exemption of small boats from the obligatory use of pilots, and from payment for such use, exchange of Notes of 4 May 1906 (*ibid.*, N.R.G.³, V, 879);

on the Río de la Plata: 14 August 1888 (*ibid.*, N.R.G.², XXVII, 58 = N.R.G.³, II, 795): organization of the piloting service by a Convention between Argentina and Uruguay;

on the river of Canton: 17 August 1843 (*ibid.*, N.R.G.¹, V, 511).

3. *The river bed and ancillary works*

Other matters for international regulation are those connected with the upkeep and improvement of the river bed, with embankments, towing paths and bridges, with the establishment of ferries across the river, or with the construction of telegraph or telephone lines along it. See below under (f) to (h).

(f) Regularization, widening, deepening.—Upkeep and inspection
Among the hundreds of treaties dealing with the improvement of rivers in the interest of international navigation, there are a number of major importance.

(1) *Regularization, etc.*
Famous projects for the regularization or amelioration of international waterways have been made and carried out in accordance with inter-state agreements *e.g.*, in respect of the following rivers:

the Danube: (*a*) section below Isaktcha, inclusive of the Sulina and St. George branches and mouths: Article 16 of the Peace Treaty of Paris of 30 March 1856 (*ibid.*, N.R.G.¹, XV, 770)—comp. the preamble and Articles 2 and 3 of the Danube Navigation Act of 2 November 1865 (*ibid.*, N.R.G.¹, XVIII, 144); (*b*) section of the Iron Gates and the Cataracts downstream of Orsova (between Turnu-Severin and Moldova): Article 6 of the Pontus Treaty of 13 March 1871 (*ibid.*, N.R.G.¹, XVIII, 303), Convention between Austria-Hungary and Serbia of 8 July 1878 (*ibid.*, N.R.G.², VIII, 319 = XIV, 277), Article 57 of the Peace Treaty of Berlin of 13 July 1878 (*ibid.*, N.R.G.², III, 449), Article 350 of the Peace Treaty of Versailles of 1919 (*ibid.*, N.R.G.³, XI, 323); Articles 32 and 33 of the Definitive Statute of 23 July 1921 (*ibid.*, N.R.G.³, XII, 606); (*c*) the Kilia branch (which was at the time in part a Russo-Romanian boundary river and in part a river under the exclusive sovereignty of either Romania or Russia): Articles 3-6 of the London Treaty on Danube Navigation of 10 March 1883 (*ibid.*, N.R.G.², IX, 392). And on works of improvement in general under the supervision of the International Commission: Articles 11-14 of the Definitive Statute of 1921.
See for further particulars on these hydraulic works my seperate section on the Danube regime, at pp. 148-150;

the Whang-Poo. By Articles 6, last paragraph, and 11 of the Final Protocol of Peking of 7 September 1901 concerning the re-establishment of friendly relations between China and eleven Powers, represented in the Far East (Martens, N.R.G.², XXXII, 94) China undertook to contribute financially to the improvement of the navigability of the course of the river Pei-Ho (already started in 1898) and to the rectification and amelioration of the course of the river Whang-Poo. The latter works were to be directed and controlled by a River Conservancy Board of mixed (Chinese and foreign) composition, and to be carried out at the joint expense of China herself and of the interests involved, in accordance with an annexed *Règlement* No. 17 (*ibid.*, N.R.G.³, VI, 688). In 1905 the eleven foreign Powers concerned, at the request of China, consented to alter the arrangement in the sense that China should carry out the work herself and at her own expense without levying any taxes for that purpose and under the security of the sum total of certain opium duties, but under the supervision of the Consular Corps and on the understanding that the original *Règlement* should resume its force if China did not fulfil her engagements under the new Arrangement of 27 September 1905 (*ibid.*, N.R.G.³, VI, 685). A provisional supplementary Arrangement followed on 4 April 1912 (*Treaties and Agreements with and concerning China* 1894-1919, ed. by J.V.A. MacMurray, New York, 1921, vol. II, p. 954). After World War I Article 129 of the Peace Treaty of Versailles laid down *sub* 2 that the Arrangements of 1905 and 1912 should again apply, subject, however, to China's release from the advantages or privileges which she had allowed Germany under those Arrangements. Comp. the corresponding provisions in Article 114 of the Austrian and Article 98 of the Hungarian Peace Treaty;

the Saint Lawrence. The work of constructing a navigable waterway, a very great enterprise between the Great Lakes and the St. Lawrence, was preceded by an American-Canadian Agreement during World War II of 14/31 October/7 November 1940 (Martens, N.R.G.³, XLI, 113; *L.N.T.S.*, vol. 203, p. 268) regarding the early development of certain portions of the Great Lakes-St. Lawrence Basin project for the purpose of providing an adequate supply of power. The construction of the seaway was only undertaken in virtue of a later exchange of notes of 30 June 1952 (*U.N.T.S.*, vol. 234, p. 200):

> "When all arrangements have been made to ensure the completion of the power phase of the St. Lawrence project, the Canadian Government will construct locks and canals on the Canadian side of the International Boundary to provide for deep-water navigation to the standard specified in the proposed agreement between Canada and the United States for the development of navigation and power in the Great Lakes-St. Lawrence Basin, signed March 19, 1941 . . ."

This waterway presents the features of a canal rather than of a river. See for the Gut Dam arbitration L. Erades in *N.T.I.R.* 1969 (XVI), p. 161.

Many other hydraulic operations of a similar nature have been projected and carried out in all parts of the world, for example with regard to the following rivers:

the Ems, deepened and regularized in virtue of a Prussian-Hanoverian Convention of 9 July 1827 (Martens, N.R.G.¹, IV, 207);

the Lahn, made navigable pursuant to an agreement between the riparian States of 16 October 1844 (*ibid.*, N.R.G.¹, VII, 420);

the Inn, object of an Austro-Bavarian agreement of 19/31 August 1858 (L. Neumann and A. de Plason, *Recueil des traités et conventions conclus par l'Autriche*, Nouvelle suite, Vienna, 1877-1912, vol. II, p. 157; *U.N. Legislative Series ST/LEG/SER.B/12*, p. 464);

the Mincio, to be rectified and endiked under Article 20 of the Austro-Franco-Sardinian Peace Treaty of Zürich of 10 November 1859 (Martens, N.R.G.[1], XVI[2], 531);

the San and the Vistula, regularized on the strength of an Austro-Russian Convention of 20 August 1864 (*ibid.*, XX, 288);

the Rhine, whose bed has again and again been corrected or deepened in various sectors, in virtue of treaties between Baden and Bavaria, 14 November 1825 and 27 May 1832 (*ibid.*, N.R., XI, 454);—between Austria and Switzerland, 19 September 1871 (*ibid.*, N.R.G.[1], XX, 171), 30 December 1892 (*ibid.*, N.R.G.[2], XXI, 50),[74] 19 November 1924 (*ibid.*, N.R.G.[3], XVII, 844) and 10 April 1954 (*U.N. Legislative Series ST/LEG/SER.B/12*, p. 501);—between Prussia and Hesse, 30 January 1884 (*ibid.*, N.R.G.[2], XII, 345);—between Austria and Liechtenstein from their frontier to the mouth of the Ill, 23 June 1931 (*ibid.*, N.R.G.[3], XXV, 791);—between the Netherlands and Germany, the so-called old mouth of the Rhine 1918-1921 (*ibid.*, N.R.G.[3], XIV, 472, 475);—between Switzerland and Germany, section Kehl-Istein, 28 March 1929 (*ibid.*, XXIV, 633, 636);—between France and Germany (Basel-Strasbourg), 27 October 1956 (*U.N. Legislative Series ST/LEG/SER.B/12*, p. 660);

the Old IJssel, regularized by the building of a barrage under a Netherlands-German Convention of 10 March 1894 (Martens, N.R.G.[2], XXII, 549);

the Niers, Netherlands-German Convention of 16 May 1895 (*ibid.*, XXIII, 44);

the Dinkel and Vecht rivers, Netherlands-Prussian Convention of 17 October 1905 (*ibid.*, N.R.G.[3], III, 203);

the Lower Weser, deepened pursuant to a treaty between Prussia and Bremen, 29 March 1906 (*ibid.*, N.R.G.[3], I, 331);

the Main, canalized in virtue of a Convention between Baden, Bavaria and Hesse, 21 April 1906 (*ibid.*, I, 349);

the Elbe, ameliorated by Prussia and Hamburg, 1908-1910 (*ibid.*, IV, 844, 873/874);

the Olsa and the Petrudka, regularized in accordance with a treaty between Poland and Czechoslovakia, 18 February 1928 (*ibid.*, XXX, 555);

the Reggia Molinara, between Chiasso and Como, canalized by

---

74. The latter operation has been accompanied by a new frontier delimitation in the old bed of the Rhine between Brugg and the Bodensee: protocols of 19 May 1903, 14/17 May 1909, 25 February 1913, 28 April 1914 and 20 April 1915 (Martens, N.R.G.[3], IX, 754-762).

Italy and Switzerland, 5 April 1951 (*U.N. Legislative Series ST/LEG/ SER.B/12*, p. 850);

the Moselle, canalized in virtue of a Convention entered into by France, Luxembourg and the Federal Republic of Germany on 27 October 1956 (*ibid.*, p. 424); comp. *supra* p. 174;

the Mekong, huge improvement scheme, now in process of execution, on the basis of preparatory studies, directed by the United Nations Economic Commission for Asia and the Far East (ECAFE); comp. the Statute of the Committee for Co-ordination of Investigations of the Lower Mekong Basin, established by the four Governments directly concerned—Cambodia, Laos, Thailand and the Republic of (South-)-Vietnam—of 31 October 1957 (ECAFE, E/CN. 11/475, annexes I and II; see Whiteman, vol. 3, p. 905).

On the canalization of rivers see also section 1, § 3 of this Chapter and the corresponding section 3 of this Annex, and on further major hydraulic works section 1, § 7 and the corresponding section 7 of this Annex *infra*, pp. 282 *et seq.*

(2) *Upkeep and inspection*

In many conventions, provisions have been laid down for the maintenance of the navigation channels.

International commitments to keep them in good order are to be found, *inter alia*, concerning:

the Meuse, in Article 38 (2) of the *Règlement* VI of 1843 (Martens, N.R.G.^{1}, V, 351);

the Rhine, in Article 28 of the Mannheim Convention of 1868 (*ibid.*, XX, 355);

the Scheldt, in Article 69 of *Règlement* No. II of theBelgo-Netherlands Treaty of 20 May 1843 (*B.F.S.P.*, vol. 37, p. 1248);

German-Lithuanian boundary rivers, in an agreement of 29 January 1928 (*ibid.*, N.R.G.^{3}, XXI, 410).

In respect of the Río Grande del Norte and the Río Gila, Article 3, *in fine*, of the Convention between the United States and Mexico of 12 November 1884 (*ibid.*, N.R.G.^{2}, XIII, 673 = XIII, 675) lays down that the protection of the banks on either side against erosion by facing of stone or other material not unduly projecting into the current of the river shall not be deemed an (otherwise forbidden) artificial change.

See on dredging operations in the African river Tanoe the Franco-British exchange of notes of 16/25 June 1907 (*B.F.S.P.*, vol. 100, p. 498).

See on the repair and maintenance of non-navigable watercourses, "mitoyens" (divided along the median line) between Belgium and France: 22 June 1882 (*ibid.*, N.R.G.^{2}, IX, 55), and between Belgium and Luxembourg: 27 November 1886 (*ibid.*, XII, 534).

(g) *Ancillary works*
  (1) *Dykes, embankments, towing paths*
—On dykes, see the provisions relating to the rivers—
  Mincio, dealing with constructions on either bank of this tributary of
the Po or on its bed for the purpose of rectification and endiking:
Article 20 of the Peace Treaty of Zürich of 10 November 1859 (*ibid.*,
N.R.G.¹, XVI², 531) and the items *sub* 10) at p. 9 and *sub* 14) at p. 16
of the Act of Delimitation of the Austro-Sardinian frontier of 16 June
1860, as inserted *ibid.*, XVII², 5;
  Danube, referring to the endiking of the mouth of the Sulina branch:
preamble and Article 2 of the Public Act of 2 November 1865 (*ibid.*,
N.R.G.¹, XVIII, 144).
—On embankments, see the provisions relating to
  the Austro-Polish boundary rivers, Article 5 of the treaty of 9 February
1776 (*ibid.*, R², II, 124): only useful and harmless constructions on the
banks allowed;
  Dajabón (or Massacre), boundary river between the then Spanish,
respectively French possessions on the island of Santo Domingo, Article 4
of the treaty of 3 June 1777 (*ibid.*, R², II, 519): forbidding the execution
of works on either bank which might obstruct the free flow of the water,
reinforced by an authorization of either commandant to inspect the
opposite bank, to complain of contraventions to his opposite number and,
if need be, to destroy such works himself;
  Lauter, then boundary river between France and Bavaria, Article 4
of their treaty of 5 July 1825 (*ibid.*, N.S., II, 439): prohibition or limitation of the construction of new buildings on its banks.
—On towing paths, see the provisions relating to the rivers—
  Rhine, Peace Treaty of 22 August 1796 between France and Bavaria
(*ibid.*, N.S., II, 91): undertaking by the Margrave to clear a strip of
36 feet wide on Baden soil to serve as towing path; prerogative of France
to prosecute shipping offences committed on that path; Article 68 of the
Act of Mainz of 1831 (*ibid.*, N.R., IX, 252) prohibiting the use of more
than three horses on one tow-rope, in order to spare the towing paths;
Article 28 of the Revised Convention of Mannheim of 1868: undertaking
to maintain the existing towing paths in a good condition;
  Meuse, *Règlement* VI of 1843 (*ibid.*, N.R.G.¹, V, 361), Article 38:
obligatory upkeep of towing paths;
  Danube, Article 9 of the Shipping Regulations of 2 June 1882 (*ibid.*,
N.R.G.², IX, 394): no interruption of circulation on existing or new
towing paths and undertaking to maintain them in good order;
—On the inspection of dykes, embankments and towing paths in the
Netherlands-German frontier area: Conventions of January/February
1865 and 8 November 1905 (*ibid.*, N.R.G.², XXXV, 721).

(2) *Locks*

A ban on the construction of locks in a stretch of the river Scheldt near Mortagne, where France would become the neighbour of the Austrian Low Countries, inserted in Articles 20 of the Treaties of Rastadt of 6 March 1714 and of Baden (Switzerland) of 7 September 1714 (Dumont VIII[1], 415, 436) between France and the Emperor and Empire, was expressly maintained in force by Article 8 of the Franco-Austrian treaty of 16 May 1769 (Martens, R[2], I, 661).

(3) *Bridges, ferries, mills*

—On bridges

Vistula: right for the Free City of Cracow to let its bridges be based on Austrian territory on the right bank of the river, and its obligation to keep them in repair, Article 4 of the Austro-Russo-Prussian Treaty of 3 May 1815 (*ibid.*, N.R., II, 251);

Mincio: rules on ownership, upkeep, construction, etc. of bridges across its boundary stretch, Article 19 of the Peace Treaty of Zürich between Austria, France and Sardinia of 10 November 1859 (*ibid.*, N.R.G.[1], XVI[2], 531);

Rhine: no obstruction of navigation by bridges; passage across them without undue delays; no dues for opening or closing, Article 30 of the Revised Convention of Mannheim of 1868 (*ibid.*, N.R.G.[1], XX, 355). See for an example of a consent, given by the Central Commission for Rhine Navigation to a riparian State to build bridges across the Rhine, its Protocol of 12 October 1874, authorizing the construction of two bridges near Nijmegen and Arnhem by the Netherlands (Netherlands *Staatsblad* 1875, No. 98); bridge near Kehl opposite Strasbourg, between Alsace and Baden, 1 March and 1 July 1920 (*ibid.*, N.R.G.[3], XIII, 556 and 612); suppression of the railway bridge near Hüningen, 6 November 1934 (*ibid.*, N.R.G.[3], XLI, 344);

Danube: choice of the best place for a bridge near Silistria, October/November 1879 (*ibid.*, N.R.G.[2], VI, 255);

Main: bridge at Offenbach between Prussia and Hesse, 2 July 1885 (*ibid.*, N.R.G.[2], XII, 352);

Meuse: conditions for the building of bridges across it: 7 April 1886 (*ibid.*, XII, 532).

Comp. on State boundaries on bridges *infra*, Chapter VI, section 2, pp. 574 *et seq.*

—Ferries were the object of regulation, *e.g.*, in the following treaties:

Military Convention between the Governor of the fortress of Ehrenbreitstein and a brigadier commanding the French troops there, of 10 June 1797, to re-establish a flying-bridge across the Rhine near Koblenz (*ibid.*, R[2], VI, 384);

France-Sardinia, 2 August 1835 (*ibid.*, N.R., XIII, 406), regulating the establishment of "bacs et bateaux de passage" on boundary rivers;

206

Rhine Navigation Acts of 31 March 1831 (*ibid.*, N.R., IX, 252), Article 46, and 17 October 1868 (*ibid.*, N.R.G.[1], XX, 355), Article 24: the provisions of the Conventions do not in general apply to transports from one bank to the other; Article 67[2] of the 1831 Act: no obstruction to navigation;

Netherlands-Belgian *Règlement* VI relative to the Meuse, of 20 May 1843 (*ibid.*, N.R.G.[1], V, 351), Article 44: mutual consideration by ordinary shippers and ferry farmers of their respective "crossing" interests;

France-Baden, 30 September 1860 (*ibid.*, N.R.G.[1], XVII[1], 275) on ferry services ("service des bacs") across the Rhine.

—Mills on a river with the object of withdrawing water from it for irrigation purposes have formed the object of treaty regulation for centuries. Comp. besides the data in my historical survey (p. 109) the following provisions of later dates, partly still obtaining at present:

on the Bug: Article 1 of the Austro-Polish boundary treaty of 9 February 1776 (*ibid.*, R[2], II, 124): authorization to continue to use them, conditional upon their causing no harm to either navigation or the opposite bank;

on Polish boundary rivers, Article 23 of the Russo-Austrian treaty of 3 May 1815 (*ibid.*, N.R., II, 225) and Article 21 of the Russo-Prussian treaty of the same date (*ibid.*, II, 236): "sovereignty" over the existing mills to be exercised by the State in whose territory the village of which they depend is located; no new mills to be established without the consent of both riparian governments;

on the Rhine, Article 67(2) of the Convention of Mainz of 31 March 1831 (*ibid.*, N.R., IX, 252) and Article 30 of the Revised Convention of Mannheim of 17 October 1868 (*ibid.*, N.R.G.[1], XX, 355): no obstruction to navigation shall be caused;

on the Meuse, Article 38 (2) of the Netherlands-Belgian *Règlement* VI of 1843, cited *sub* (2): measures against their obstructing navigation;

on the Pruth, Article 16 of the Convention between Austria, Russia and the United Principalities of Moldavia and Wallachia of 15 December 1866 (*ibid.*, N.R.G.[1], XX, 296): prohibition to establish them;

on the Danube, Article 5 of the Shipping Regulations of 2 June 1882 (*ibid.*, N.R.G.[2], IX, 394), which made a distinction between *moulins fixes* and *moulins flottants*—probably the *molendinariae naves*, mentioned in Article 2 of the Peace Treaty of Carlowitz of 26 January 1699 (Dumont VII[2], 448)—and further dealt with *roues d'irrigation*.

(4) *Telegraph or telephone lines along rivers*

See on this subject: section 6 of this Annex, *infra* p. 279.

Under this heading also I intend to describe the legal situation follow-ing the main categories of interests involved.

Side by side with the navigational interests described under A (pp. 119 *et seq.*), mention must be made of the various—permissible or for-bidden—uses of rivers, or of interests other than navigation, regulated by positive treaty texts, and dealt with below under 1 to 4.

1. *Fishing in common rivers*

Many treaties deal with fishing, either in boundary rivers or in rivers which run through different States successively. Most of them have the object of guaranteeing freedom and equality of fishing to the respective subjects or of regulating the exercise of the trade, but some are specifically intended to protect the fish fauna.

Comp. already the old regulations laid down for the rivers:

Maros and Tisza (Theiss), in Article 2 of the Austro-Turkish peace treaty of Carlowitz of 26 January 1699 (Dumont, VII², 448);

Aluta (Oltŭ), in Article I (2) of the Austro-Turkish peace treaty of Passarowitz of 21 July 1718 (*ibid.*, VIII¹, 524),—both declaring "usum communem" *(inter alia)* "ad piscationem".

From a much later period:

Scheldt, *Règlement* No. IV, annexed to the Belgo-Netherlands Con-vention of Antwerp, 20 May 1843 (Martens, N.R.G.¹, V, 294 *et seq.*, at p. 334-339, 381);

Franco-Swiss boundary rivers: 28 December 1880 (*ibid.*, N.R.G.², IX, 111), repeatedly amended, in 1888 (XIV, 410), 1891 (XVIII, 238 and 848), 1904 (XXXIII, 501);

Lake of Geneva and boundary rivers: 20 January 1909 (*ibid.*, N.R.G.³, V, 318);

Italo-Swiss boundary rivers: 8 November 1882 (*ibid.*, N.R.G.², IX, 564), repeatedly modified, in 1898 (*ibid.*, XXIX, 133), 1906 (*ibid.*, XXXV, 471), 1907 (*ibid.*, XXXV, 485), 1911 (*ibid.*, N.R.G.³, VII, 867);

Swiss-Baden boundary rivers: Rhine between Konstanz and Basel: 9 December 1869 (*ibid.*, N.R.G.¹, XX, 166), 25 March 1875 (*ibid.*, N.R.G.², II, 60-63), 3 July 1897 (*ibid.*, XXV, 396), amended 17 No-vember 1908 (*ibid.*, N.R.G.³, IV, 875), 14 November 1911 (*ibid.*, VIII, 898);

Limburg-Prussian boundary rivers: 5 November 1892 (*ibid.*, N.R.G.², XXIV, 153; comp. also 557);

German-Polish boundary rivers: 10 December 1927 (*ibid.*, N.R.G.³, XXX, 291);

German-Lithuanian boundary waters (Kurisches Haff, Skirwieth, Russ, Memel and others): 29 January 1928 (*ibid.*, N.R.G.³, XXI, 421);

Canadian-American boundary rivers: 11 January 1909 (N.R.G.³, IV, 208, 216) on their use in general; 11 April 1908 (*ibid.*, IV, 188) on the protection of edible fish in the rivers concerned;

Finnish (Russian)-Swedish boundary rivers (Torneå and Muonio): 6 April 1872 (Martens, N.R.G.², I, 596), 23 February 1897 (*ibid.*, XXIX, 48), 10 May 1927 (*ibid.*, N.R.G.³, XXVIII, 791) on salmon fishing;

Tana: Finno-Norwegian treaty of 29 June/14 July 1920 (*ibid.*, N.R.G.³, XIV, 635);

Bidassoa: Franco-Spanish Conventions of 18 February 1886 (*ibid.*, N.R.G.², XII, 687), 19 January 1888 (*ibid.*, N.R.G.³, III, 253), 4 October 1894 (*ibid.*, VII, 421), 9 June 1906 (*ibid.*, VII, 422), 6 April 1908 (*ibid.*, III, 256);

Pruth: Russo-Romanian treaties of 22 February 1901 (*ibid.*, N.R.G.², XXX, 487) and 29 October 1907 (*ibid.*, N.R.G.³, I, 907), relating also to the Danube;

Danube: Bulgaro-Romanian treaty of 29 November 1901 (*ibid.*, XXXIII, 277); Serbo-Romanian treaty of 15 January 1902 (*ibid.*, XXX, 642).

Among multilateral treaties on fishing in rivers mention must be made of the conventions concluded by certain riparian Rhine States, respectively on salmon fishing, 30 June 1885 (*ibid.*, N.R.G.², XI, 561) and on uniform rules concerning fishing in general, 18 May 1887 (*ibid.*, XIV, 350).

I will follow up this list with a few details of the contents of such conventions.

Scheldt, 20 May 1843 (Netherlands-Belgium; *ibid.*, N.R.G.¹, V, 294).

(1) Freedom of fishing for respective subjects on the river proper and on connected waters.

(2) Absolute equality.

(3 *et seq.*) Requirement of a certificate; fixed remuneration; delivery of a permit for all kinds of fish; number to be painted on the vessel; surveillance by the States.

(8 *et seq.*) Special concessions for artificial mussel-banks and the use of "gords" (fixed palings on the river-bed with fish-traps); protection of such banks and "gords" against destruction, etc.

(11) Each State issues its own fishing regulations; notification to the other party.

(15) Each State prosecutes trespasses by the other's subjects committed on its own territory; notification of the prosecution and the sentence to the national State.

(16) Free importation of catches, reciprocally.

(17 *et seq.*) Customs regulations.

Rhine

Salmon Convention 30 June 1885 (Germany-the Netherlands-Switzerland; accession of Luxembourg for the Moselle) (*ibid.*, N.R.G.², XI, 56).

(1) No obstructions in the river between Schaffhausen and Lobith (Nether-

lands), across more than half of its bed, by fixed installations, to bar the passage of salmon. Applies also to confluents.

(2) Limitation of the use of drift-nets near accesses to spawning grounds.

(3) Two months' prohibition of the use of drag-nets.

(4) Suspension of any salmon and shad fishing weekly during twenty-four hours.

(5) Special permits required for salmon fishing on Upper Rhine (between Mannheim and Schaffhausen falls) during at least six weeks between 15 October and 31 December annually, and only if special conditions for propagation are fulfilled.

(7) Measures for the furthering of the increase of the salmon stock.

(8) Individual State regulations for minimum sizes of the salmon to be caught and sold.

(9) Each State shall issue regulations for the implementation of the treaty; penal provisions; control personnel.

(10) Occasional meetings of delegates to discuss salmon fishery interests.

A sad thing is that the progressing pollution of the Rhine has destroyed the entire stock of salmon.

Fishery Convention 18 May 1887 (Switzerland-Baden-Alsace) (Martens, N.R.G.², XIV, 350). Uniform rules on fishing on the Rhine.

(1) As to migratory fish: no fixed installations to bar more than half of the river.

(2) As to all fish: prohibition of width of net-meshes under a certain minimum.

(3) Provisions concerning drift-nets etc.

(4) Interdiction of the use of explosives, poisonous or stunning substances, fire-arms, etc.

(5) Fixing of minimum length of fish for selling.

(6) Compulsory periods of prohibition of fishing of a series of fish categories, etc.

Danube and Pruth 22 February 1901 (Russia-Romania) (*ibid.*, N.R.G.², XXX, 487).

(2) Minimum mesh-width.

(3) Minimum space between trellies between fixed barrages.

(4) No explosives, poisoning, narcotics.

(5) No fixed installation across more than half the river-bed against fish migration.

(6) Prohibition of fishing from 1 April to 1 June, in aid of propagation.

(7) Minimum size of catchable fish.

(11) In certain territorial sea areas (mouths of the Danube) absolute prohibition of fishing throughout the year.

Frontier waters Colombia-Venezuela: 5 August 1942 (*B.F.S.P.*, vol. 144, p. 1127), Articles 22 and 23.

(22) Fishing rights may not be exercised beyond the centre-line of rivers and non-navigable streams.

(23) It shall be forbidden to divide the frontier waters by means of fixed nets or by any other device which shall impede the free passage of fish from one bank to the other.

It shall equally be forbidden to fish by means of explosive, poisonous or noxious substances, or to use any other methods of catching fish, except by fish-hooks.

Franco-German Sarre (Saar) boundary, 27 October 1956 (*J. Off. Rep. Franc.* 1957, p. 460).

> Art. 6 (1). La pêche dans la partie de la Sarre formant cours d'eau frontière appartient à la France en amont du kilomètre 70,270 (kilométrage rive gauche) et à la République Fédérale d'Allemagne en aval de ce point.
> (2) Separate regulations on fishing and protection of the fish-fauna, but as much as possible in line with one another.

2. *Diversion of water*

Diversion of water from a common river can be planned or carried out for irrigation, canal-feeding, hydro-electric, or similar purposes. Sometimes such a diversion is prohibited, sometimes it is made subject to conditions, sometimes it is planned in common.

An old prohibition to divert water from the upper reaches of a common river can already be found, *inter alia*, in Article 2 of the Austro-Turkish Peace Treaty of Carlowitz of 26 January 1699 (Dumont, VII[2], 448) with regard to the river Maros:

> "... quinimo, ne diversione aquarum in Marusio cursus Caesarearum navium incommodum aliquod patiatur, nullatenus permittetur, ut, sive molendinorum, sive alia occasione ex Marusio aquae alio deriventur, seu deducantur".

At a later period the very detailed Austro-Venetian treaty of 25 June 1764 (Martens, R[2], I, 240), with a supplement of 19 June 1765 (*ibid.*, I, 254), regulated in detail the use of the waters of the river Tartaro for the benefit of the inhabitants of Mantova and Verona, in particular for the irrigation of rice-fields.

As regards the Meuse (Maas), the diversion has been quantitatively determined: Belgo-Netherlands treaty of 12 May 1863, amended 11 January 1873 (Martens, N.R.G.[2], I, 117 and 123), which gave rise to the proceedings of 1937 before the Permanent Court of International Justice (*Publications P.C.I.J.*, series A/B, No. 70); comp. my *The Jurisprudence of the World Court*, vol. I. pp. 458 *et seq.*

Further instances of treaty regulation concerning water diversion are those relative to:

boundary rivers between Bohemia and Silesia: Article 6 of the Austro-Prussian treaty of 9 February 1869 (*ibid.*, N.R.G.[1], XX, 310);

the Atbara (an affluent of the Nile): no irrigation-works allowed on that river: Anglo-Italian additional protocol of 15 April 1891 (*ibid.*, N.R.G.[2], XVIII, 178);

Río Grande: convention between the United States and Mexico of 21 May 1906 (*ibid.*, N.R.G.[2], XXXV, 461): diversion of its water for the irrigation of Mexico;

Tigris and Euphrates: Article 3 of the Franco-British Convention of 23 December 1920 on certain points connected with the Mandates for Syria and the Lebanon, Palestine and Mesopotamia (*ibid.*, N.R.G.[3], XII, 582): preliminary examination of any plan of irrigation, formed by the Government of the French-mandated territory, the execution of which would be of a nature to diminish in any considerable degree the waters of those two rivers;

Upper Jordan, Yarmuk and other affluents: Article 8 of the same Convention: setting-up of a mixed commission of experts to examine irrigation plans from those rivers for the benefit of French-mandated territory;

Lake Raibl and its derivative watercourse, Article 44 (2) of the Peace Treaty of Saint-Germain-en-Laye of 10 September 1919 (*ibid.*, N.R.G.[3], XI, 691): Austria concedes to Italy the right to divert the water to the basin of the Korinitza;

Vistula, regulations for the access to, and use of this river by the population of Eastern Prussia, in accordance with Article 97 (5) of the Peace Treaty of Versailles, 21 November 1924 (*ibid.*, N.R.G.[3], XXII, 435);

Gash, agreement between Eritrea and Sudan of 12/15 June 1925 (*ibid.*, N.R.G.[3], XVIII, 111) concerning the use of its water by the Government of Eritrea for works at Tessenei;

Isar, agreement between Austria and Bavaria of 16 October 1950 in order to ensure the maintenance of a sufficient volume of water in its bed (*U.N. Legislative Series ST/LEG/SER. B/12*, p. 469).

Comp. for the regulations laid down by Yugoslavia and Italy in the Italian Peace Treaty of Paris of 10 February 1947 (*U.N.T.S.*, vol. 49, p. 3) concerning the water supply

for Gorizia and vicinity: Article 13 j.° Annex V;

to Northwestern Istria: Article 21 (5) j.° Annex IX, *sub* A;

and on a co-ordinated plan for the exploitation of the water resources of the river Roya: Annex III, *sub* B, 4(b).

See for further details especially on hydraulic works: section 7 of the Annex to Chapter II, section 1 *infra*, pp. 282 *et seq.*

The diversion of water from an international river or the threat of an arbitrary or excessive withdrawal therefrom has repeatedly given rise to inter-state disputes, sometimes of a very dangerous nature.

3. *Measures to prevent or remedy floods*

Precautionary measures against floods have played a major rôle in Netherlands-Belgian relations, owing to the repeated inundations by natural causes of the border region between the Zeeland part of Flanders (south of the river Scheldt) and the adjoining part of (at the time Austrian) Flanders.

The first treaty provisions concerning inundations were inserted in Articles 16 and 17 of the Austro-Netherlands-British Barrier Treaty of 15 November 1715 (Dumont, VII[1], 458), but they were still intended to authorize the States General to cause inundations for the defence of the Demer line between the Scheldt and the Meuse and of their frontier area between the sea and the Scheldt. When the political tension between the Austrian Emperor Joseph II and the United Netherlands reached a peak in the 1780's and the commanders of the Dutch towns of Sas van Gent and Philippine in Zeeland Flanders had, as a measure of military defence, inundated the surroundings of those towns with salt water, they concluded an agreement with the Commissioner of the Emperor on 1 April 1785 to the effect that the inundation with salt water would be replaced by fresh water flooding through an aggregate of existing sluices (Martens, R[2], IV, 9).—The subject of flooding was regulated later in the same year in Article 6 of the Austro-Netherlands Treaty of Fontainebleau of 8 November 1785 (*ibid.*, R[2], IV, 55), providing, *inter alia*, for the construction of sluices and the setting up of a Netherlands-Austrian Commission.—Subsequent treaties have built further on the juridical basis thus laid, in order to prevent, or remedy the consequences of, future flooding. See Article 8 of the Treaty of Separation between the Netherlands and Belgium of 19 April 1839 (*ibid.*, N.R., XVI, 773) and Article 20 of their treaty of The Hague of 5 November 1842 (*ibid.*, N.R.G.[1], III, 613).

Hungary and Romania have also agreed on measures to combat inundations by boundary rivers: Bucharest, 16 April 1924 (*ibid.*, N.R.G.[3], XXII, 250 = XXIV, 839) and conventions of 9 June 1950 and 2 July 1962. See further: USSR-Hungary, treaty of 9 June 1950 relative to the river Tisza; USSR-Romania, treaty of 25 December 1952 relative to the river Pruth; Hungary-Czechoslovakia, 16 April 1954; Hungary-Yugoslavia, 8 August 1955 and Hungary-Austria, 9 April 1956. The texts of most of these conventions can be found in *U.N. Legislative Series ST/LEG/SER. B/12*; many other conventions are also mentioned there. Comp. on this subject G. HERCZEGH, *Some legal questions of the utilization of the waters of international rivers* in *Questions of International Law* (Budapest, 1968), p. 107.

4. *River pollution*

The need for international co-operation against the draining of sewage into common rivers, or the pollution of their water by other, especially industrial, substances, waste of an obnoxious nature, or run-off from agricultural pesticides involving sheep dips, is becoming more and more urgent. The need is already very obvious, *e.g.*, for the Bodensee (Lake of Konstanz) and the Rhine.

As it is, general principles in the field of decent neighbourly relations require that riparian States abstain from polluting the water of their common rivers, but their actual practice does not, regrettably, live up to those principles.

In this respect also, as in several others, relations between individual States of the United States of America have set an example of reasonable conduct after a dispute had arisen between them. When the State of Missouri was threatened by pollution of the Mississippi as a consequence of the digging of a drainage canal from Lake Michigan to the river on the orders of the Sanitary District of Chicago (Ill.), the resulting dispute was in 1906 resolved by a judgment of the Supreme Court to the effect that the deleterious effects of the construction of the drainage canal had not been proved, but that Missouri was free to bring a new action against Illinois should such proof become possible in the future. See for the successive stages of these proceedings *re Missouri v. Illinois*: 180 U.S. 208 (1901), 200 U.S. 496 (1906) and 202 U.S. 598 (1906); J.B.SCOTT, *Judicial settlement of controversies between States of the American Union*, vol. II, pp. 1286 *et seq.*, 1464 *et seq.*, and 1517 *et seq.*

The pollution of international rivers has since then to an increasing degree become a public nuisance owing, in particular, to progressive industrialization and a devastating lack of care in obviating its actual results in producing river pollution. Treaty regulations on this subject have as a consequence become more and more urgently necessary.

Comp. the following treaty provisions:

Franco-Belgo-Luxembourg Protocol of 8 April 1950 (*U.N.T.S.*, vol. 66, p. 286) establishing a "Commission Tripartite Permanente des Eaux Polluées".

Franco-West German treaty of 27 October 1956 for the regulation of the Saar question (*U.N. Legislative Series ST/LEG/SER. B/12*, p. 659), Article 8:

> "Les deux Gouvernements prennent, chacun dans le domaine de sa compétence, les mesures nécessaires en vue d'assurer la pureté et la salubrité des eaux de la Sarre. Ils prennent les mêmes engagements en ce qui concerne les affluents de la Sarre. Ils encourageront la constitution de groupements ou d'associations ayant pour objet de maintenir la salubrité des eaux."

Euratom treaty of 25 March 1957 (*U.N.T.S.*, vol. 298, p. 267), Articles 35-39 in Chapter III on "La protection sanitaire" against excessive radio-activity of the atmosphere, waters and soil.

Netherland-West German treaty of 8 April 1960 (*U.N.T.S.*, vol. 508, p. 14), Article 58(2)(e) : measures required to prevent such excessive pollution of the boundary waters as may substantially impair the customary use of the waters by the neighbouring State.

How little effective the existing international regulations against water pollution at the present moment still are, was recently demonstrated by the very serious poisoning of the Rhine—"Europe's biggest sewer"—by the insecticide endosulphan (June 1969) in spite of the multilateral Convention of 29 April 1963 aimed at preventing further pollution (Netherlands *Tr.blad* 1963, No. 104) and of the "Charte européenne de l'Eau" proclaimed at Strasbourg on 6 May 1968 (*Ici l'Europe*, June/July 1968). Regulations such as these are indeed more often than not insufficiently stringent to achieve their aim. See A. BERNARDINI, *La Carta europea dell'acqua* in *La Comunità Internazionale* 1968 (23), pp. 51 *et seq.*

The International Law Association in its session of 1966 in Helsinki adopted a Resolution—the "Helsinki Rules on the Use of Waters of International Rivers"—, Chapter 3 of which (Articles IX-XI) deals especially with pollution. These Rules run as follows (*Report of the 52nd Conference*, 1966, pp. 494 *et seq.*):

Ch. 3 POLLUTION

Article IX

As used in this Chapter, the term "water pollution" refers to any detrimental change resulting from human conduct in the natural composition, content, or quality of the waters of an international drainage basin.

Article X

1. Consistent with the principle of equitable utilization of the waters of an international drainage basin, a State
   (a) must prevent any new form of water pollution or any increase in the degree of existing water pollution in an international drainage basin which would cause substantial injury in the territory of a co-basin State, and
   (b) should take all reasonable measures to abate existing water pollution in an international drainage basin to such an extent that no substantial damage is caused in the territory of a co-basin State.
2. The rule stated in paragraph 1 of this Article applies to water pollution originating:
   (a) within a territory of the State, or
   (b) outside the territory of the State, if it is caused by the State's conduct.

Article XI

1. In the case of a violation of the rule stated in paragraph 1(a) of Article X of this Chapter, the State responsible shall be required to cease the wrongful conduct and compensate the injured co-basin State for the injury that has been caused to it.
2. In a case falling under the rule stated in paragraph 1(b) of Article X, if a State fails to take reasonable measures, it shall be required promptly to enter into negotiations with the injured State with a view toward reaching a settlement equitable under the circumstances.

Comp. on the subject the article by A. P. LESTER, *River pollution in international law* in *A.J.I.L.* 1963 (57), pp. 828 *et seq.*; P. STAINOV, *Les aspects juridiques de la lutte internationale contre la pollution du Danube* in *R.G.D.I.P.* 1968 (72), pp. 97 *et seq.*, and Whiteman, vol. 3, p. 1040.

5. Timber floating

Timber floating has recently been made the subject of a private codification by the International Law Association. See Chapter 5 (Articles XXI-XXV) of its Helsinki Rules on the Use of the Waters of International Rivers (*Report of the 52nd Conference*, Helsinki, 1966) to the following effect (pp. 511-516):

Article XXI

The floating of timber on a watercourse which flows through or between the territories of two or more States is governed by the following Articles except in cases in which floating is governed by rules of navigation according to applicable law or custom binding upon the riparians.

Article XXII

The States riparian to an international watercourse utilized for navigation may determine by common consent whether and under what conditions timber floating may be permitted upon the watercourse.

Article XXIII

1. It is recommended that each State riparian to an international watercourse not used for navigation should, with due regard to other uses of the watercourse, authorise the co-riparian States to use the watercourse and its banks within the territory of each riparian State for the floating of timber.
2. This authorization should extend to all necessary work along the banks by the floating crew and to the installation of such facilities as may be required for the timber floating.

Article XXIV

If a riparian State requires permanent installation for floating inside a territory of a co-riparian State or if it is necessary to regulate the flow of the watercourse, all questions connected with these installations and measures should be determined by agreement between the States concerned.

Article XXV

Co-riparian States of a watercourse which is, or is to be used for floating timber should negotiate in order to come to an agreement governing the administrative regime of floating, and if necessary to establish a joint agency or commission in order to facilitate the regulation of floating in all aspects.

Timber floating had already been the subject of treaty regulation. Comp. *e.g.*

Finland-Soviet Union, 28 October 1922 (*L.N.T.S.*, vol. 19, p. 170), modified 15 October 1933 (*ibid.*, vol. 149, p. 267);

Finland-Sweden, 17 February 1949 (*U.N.T.S.*, vol. 197, p. 148), relative to the Torneå and Muonio frontier rivers.

6. Reed cutting

See the agreement between Denmark and Germany regarding *inter alia* reed cutting in de Vidaa river, annexed to their treaty of 10 April 1922 (*L.N.T.S.*, vol. 10, pp. 187, 243).

C. *Further subjects of treaty regulation*

1. *Military or defence interests*

In different historical periods and in different areas of the world rivers have been placed under a regime of demilitarization to the effect that a ban was put either on their navigation by warships, or on the construction or maintenance of fortifications along their banks. A few examples may suffice:

the Scheldt: a ban on fortification of a certain boundary point on the river (Mortagne), convention between France and Austria (for the southern Low Countries) of 16 May 1769 (Martens, R², I, 661), Article 8, referring to older provisions of 1713 and 1714;

all boundary rivers between the possessions of the Empire and the Cisalpine Republic: no armed vessels to be kept on them, Article 11 of the Peace Treaty of Campo Formio of 17 October 1797 (*ibid.*, R², VI, 420);

the Adige: prohibition of armed vessels, Article 14 of the Franco-Austrian Peace Treaty of Lunéville of 9 February 1801 (*ibid.*, R², VII, 296);

the Danube and its tributaries: demolition of fortifications along the Danube and the Save in virtue of the Austro-Turkish Peace Treaty of Belgrade of 18 September 1739 (Wenck, I, 326); Article 12 of the preliminary Russo-Turkish Peace Treaty of San Stefano of 3 March 1878 (Martens, N.R.G.², III, 246), and Article 52 of the Peace Treaty of Berlin of 13 July 1878 (*ibid.*, III, 449): demolition of all fortifications between the Iron Gates and the mouth—not put into effect; prohibition of warships downstream of the Iron Gates—subsequently ignored by a flotilla of Romanian torpedo-boats;

the Boyana: Article 29 of the same Peace Treaty of Berlin of 1878: no fortifications along its course, except for a zone of 6 kilometres from Skutari;

the Mekong: Articles 2 and 3 of the Franco-Siamese treaty of 3 October 1893 (*ibid.*, N.R.G.², XX, 172 = 752): no Siamese armed vessels on the river and its confluents and demilitarization of its right bank for a breadth of 25 kilometres;

certain rivers in the Sino-Annamite border region: Article 6 of the Franco-Chinese commercial convention of 27 June 1887 (*ibid.*, N.R.G.², XV, 849): no admission of warships, troop carriers, etc.;

the rivers in Central Africa, common to France and Germany pursuant to the Kiderlen Wächter-Cambon Agreement of 4 November 1911 concerning their possessions in Equatorial Africa (*ibid.*, N.R.G.³, VI, 323), Article 9: no fortifications along the course of common waterways.

On the other hand, the right of transit on international rivers for warships has occasionally been expressly granted by one riparian State to another. Comp. for

the Danube between its mouth and its confluence with the river Pruth in the period between 1812 and 1856, first on the northern Kilia branch (Article 4 of the Russo-Turkish Peace Treaty of Bucharest of 28 May 1812, *ibid.*, N.R., III, 397) and later, since 1829 (Article 3 of the Peace Treaty of Adrianople of 14 September 1829, *ibid.*, N.R. VIII, 143), on the southern Saint Georges branch: above p. 147;

the rivers common to Bolivia and Brazil: Article 22(1) of their boundary treaty of 27 March 1867 (Martens, N.R.G.[1], XX, 613), subject to a reservation in Article 22(2), limiting the number of warships on the tributaries of the Amazonas.

Side by side with the demilitarization of rivers, their neutralization has also formed the object of treaty regulation (see for the difference between these two institutions Chapter V, section 10 *infra*, p. 500).

2. *River Commissions*

A river community can become so intimate as to call for the creation of common organs for the promotion of common interests.

As I have set out earlier in my historic-analytical introduction (pp. 117 *et seq.*), the management and control of a waterway of international concern can show very different degrees of "internationalization", the simplest variant being that of regular consultation between the governments concerned about matters of common fluvial interest, sometimes in the form of a permanent Commission of delegates of the riparian States for this purpose, the most "integrated" variant being the establishment of an international Commission on which non-riparian States are also represented, which is vested with legislative, judicial and executive powers, and which has an administrative apparatus of its own, personified, *e.g.*, in such officers as the harbour-master of Sulina in the Danube delta (Convention of 29 November 1880, *ibid.*, N.R.G.[2], IX, 717), abolished in 1938. The community idea is sometimes symbolized by a common flag, insignia or uniform:

Rhine, Article 107 of the Rhine Navigation Convention of Mainz of 1831 (*ibid.*, N.R., IX, 252) (flag);

Danube, Article 26 of the Definitive Statute of 23 July 1921 (*ibid.*, N.R.G.[3], XII, 620) (insignia and uniform) and Article 18 of the Convention of 18 August 1948 (*U.N.T.S.*, vol. 33, p. 181) (seal and flag).

See on this type of internationalization the paragraphs on the Danube, the Rhine, the Elbe and the Oder, *supra* pp. 126 *et seq.*

The competence of such Commissions has sometimes been the object of judicial proceedings, in particular as regards the Oder Commission and the European Danube Commission, mentioned *supra*, pp. 165 and 149.

218

See on the simpler, less integrated forms of joint administration the regulations which are or were embodied in

Article 26 of the Convention between Austria, the Danube Principalities and Russia of 15 December 1866 (*ibid.*, N.R.G.[1], XX, 296), with *Règlement* of 8/9 February 1871 (*ibid.*, N.R.G.[2], I, 485), relative to the setting-up of a mixed commission for the river Pruth, and in the conventions between

Sweden and Norway of 26 October 1905 (*ibid.*, N.R.G.[2], XXXIV, 710) concerning the regime of their common waterways;

Germany and Poland of 14 March 1925 (*ibid.*, N.R.G.[3], XXII, 527), 19 August 1926 (*ibid.*, XXVII, 506) and 16 February 1927 (*ibid.*, XXVIII, 828) relative to the administration of the boundary sections of the rivers Netze and Küddow, Oder, and Warthe, respectively;

Austria and Czechoslovakia of 12 December 1928 (*ibid.*, N.R.G.[3], XXV, 163) concerning the frontier sections of the rivers Danube, Morava and Thaya.

3. *Financial agreements between riparian States*

Financial agreements are often called for because specific hydraulic works, though of common importance, (*a*) must or may by mutual arrangement be carried out by one of the riparian States, subject to its right of redress against its co-riparians for a pro-rata contribution, (*b*) may be of paramount importance for one of them, so that the others are only responsible for a minor part of the expenses, or (*c*) may be profitable for all seafaring nations so that it is reasonable that their cost is accordingly partially defrayed by non-riparian States, or covered by the establishment of a special shipping toll.

Comp. on the clearing-away of the obstacles to navigation in the Iron Gates my paragraph on the Danube *supra*, p. 150; on the works to make the Whang-Poo navigable *supra*, p. 201; on the carrying out of hydraulic works in the Rhine *supra*, p. 203. The recent Netherlands-Belgian treaty of 13 May 1964 for the realization of an improved connection between the Rhine and the Scheldt, partly by a new canal, partly by the improvement of existing waterways, contains an apportionment of the costs between the parties (see p. 223 *infra*) on the consideration that the works are chiefly in the interest of Belgium (*U.N.T.S.*, vol. 540, p. 3).

Comp. further the general clause obtaining in Article 10(2), 2nd sentence, of the Statute of Barcelona of 20 April 1921 (Martens, N.R.G.[3], XVIII, 717):

"In the absence of an agreement to the contrary, any riparian State will have the right, on valid reason being shown, to demand from the other riparians a reasonable contribution towards the cost of upkeep".

4. *Adjudication of disputes. Arbitral awards or judgments in this field*

Apart from the many arbitral decisions on the *tracé* of river boundaries, sometimes even on the choice between two different systems, as in the case of Argentina *v.* Brazil (comp. *infra* in the Chapter on State boundaries, pp. 537 *et seq.*, at p. 548), and from judicial pronouncements on the extent of the jurisdiction of international river commissions, mentioned in the paragraphs on the Danube and the Oder (*supra*, pp. 149 and 165), arbitrators or tribunals have often, already centuries ago, been called upon to decide other fluvial disputes. I only refer, by way of example, to the following subjects:

—the damming of a river, causing its overflow: award of the Emperor Frederick Barbarossa of November 1165 against the Count of Holland who had constructed a dam in the river Rhine and thus inundated the bishopric of Utrecht (*Oorkondenboek van Holland en Zeeland etc.*, ed. OBREEN, 1937, p. 90);

—the pollution of rivers by sewage or factory effluents: judgments of the United States Supreme Court in Missouri *v.* Illinois, 180 U.S. 208 (1901) and 200 U.S. 496 (1906), relative to the discharge of sewer-sludge of Chicago into the upper reaches of the Mississippi (comp. above *sub* B, 4, p. 214);

—the diversion of water from a river for irrigation or canal feeding purposes: judgment of the United States Supreme Court in a dispute of 1907 between Arkansas and Colorado regarding the diversion of water from the river Arkansas (206 U.S. 46 (1907));

Judgment of the Permanent Court of International Justice of 28 June 1937 (series A/B, No. 70) concerning the reciprocal claims of the Netherlands and Belgium with regard to the diversion of water from the Meuse (comp. my *The Jurisprudence of the World Court*, vol. I, pp. 458 *et seq.*);

—shifts of the bed of a river:

repeated clashes between the United States and Mexico over the Río Grande del Norte, resulting in an arbitral award of 15 June 1911 (Martens, N.R.G.[3], VI, 66), repudiated by the United States (see *infra* p. 613);

—financial controversies:

arbitral award of 26 March 1816 by an Imperial-Royal Commission relative to the payment of rents of the Rhine Navigation Octroy (*ibid.*, N.R., IV, 225), commented upon in DE LAPRADELLE-POLITIS, *Recueil des arbitrages internationaux*, vol. I, pp. 218-255.

Sometimes River Acts contain compromissory clauses providing for the arbitral settlement of future disputes. See, *e.g.*, *Réglement* No. I of 20 May 1843 (Martens, N.R.G.[1], V, 295), Articles 32 *et seq.*, with regard to the Scheldt.

Very old plans for the construction of "international" canals which have either never or only partially been materialized have been handed down to us historically.

When in 1165 Emperor Frederick I Barbarossa sat in judgment at Utrecht over certain disputes which had arisen between the Count of Holland, the Bishop of Utrecht and the Count of Guelder, one of the orders he gave was that a canal should be dug from the river Rhine near the southeastern tip of the bishopric and the boundary of Guelder towards the sea in order to protect the region against recurrent flooding.[76]

When the city of Emden in the second half of the 15th century actually enforced a—usurped—staple-right on shipping passing up and down the river Ems to the prejudice of the bishop of Münster and the city of Groningen, the two latter conceived a plan to dig a canal from the territory of the bishopric to the Dollard in order thus to avoid navigation past Emden. The plan was in fact partly carried out (1480-1484), but was eventually abandoned; hence the name Kostverlorenvaart (canal of wasted expenses).

In the period of his governorship of the Spanish part of the Low Countries at the beginning of the 18th century, Prince Eugene of Savoy projected the construction of a canal from there to the Rhine. This canal also, the *fossa Eugeniana*, never materialized, just as, for that matter, have the two modern successors to that project also failed to do, *viz.*, those for the construction of an Antwerp-Gladbach canal (or a road) across the Netherlands province of Limburg (comp. below in section 5 on Roads and Railways), and of a canal from the river Maas (Meuse) to the Rhine off Ruhrort, as contemplated in Article 361 of the Peace Treaty of Versailles (1919).

The latter Treaty was on the whole particularly elaborate on the subject of canals thus proving their international economic and political importance.

> Article 361, just mentioned, gave Belgium the right, within a period of 25 years to decide to create a deep-draught Rhine-Meuse navigable waterway in the region of Ruhrort. Germany would in that case be bound to construct the portion thereof, situated within her territory, in accordance with Belgian plans, agreed to by the Central Rhine Navigation Commission,

---

75. Purely national canals, such as the canal recently constructed between the Baltic and the Caspian Sea, seldom have any importance for international law.
76. Judgment of 25 November 1165 (*Oorkondenboek van Holland en Zeeland tot het einde van het Hollandsche Huis (1299)*, edition OBREEN, p. 89): ". . . ut terra illa, quę vulgo Noda dicitur, ad faciendum aquęductum ab incolis provincię, qui tanto dampno et periculo aquarum subiacebant, ita perfodiatur, quod aqua Rhen[i, per eundem meat]um effluens, in mare, quod ibi vicinum est, sine lęsione in perpetuum fluat et decurrat . . .".

failing which that Commission would be empowered to carry out the construction works instead. The Commission would then choose and occupy the necessary ground, subject to the payment by Germany of indemnities fixed by the Commission, and moreover would divide the cost of initial construction among the States crossed by the waterway, which would itself be placed under the same administrative regime as the Rhine.

Article 358, paragraphs 1 and 2, granted to France the right, subject to guarantees for a continued undiminished navigability of the Rhine under the control of the Central Rhine Navigation Commission, to feed her navigation and irrigation canals, constructed or to be constructed, with water taken from the Rhine on the whole of its course between the two extreme points of the French frontiers, and to Belgium the corresponding right to feed her future Rhine-Meuse waterway, should it be in fact constructed under Article 361.—Article 358, paragraph 3, sub (1), on the other hand, forbade Germany to undertake or to allow on her side the construction of any lateral canal or any derivation on the right bank of the river opposite the French frontiers.

Germany was also forced, by Article 362, sub 3°, to agree to offer no objection to any proposals of the Central Rhine Navigation Commission for extending its jurisdiction to lateral canals and channels which might be established in the future either to duplicate or improve naturally navigable sections of the Rhine or the Moselle, or to connect two naturally navigable sections thereof.

Finally, Article 353 foresaw the possible construction of a deep-draught Rhine-Danube navigable waterway which in case of its realization would be subject to the general navigational regime laid down in Articles 332-338.

Corresponding provisions are to be found in Articles 291 et seq. of the Peace Treaty of St.-Germain (1919).

Very strong national sentiments were aroused in the Netherlands in the twenties of this century by the conclusion by the Netherlands Government of a treaty with Belgium, dated 3 April 1925, providing, *inter alia*, for the construction of a Scheldt-Rhine Canal, aimed at providing Belgium with a better waterway between Antwerp and the Rhine than that offered by the existing natural communications between the two big rivers through the so-called "intermediary waters", mentioned in Article 2 of the Revised Convention of Mannheim (1868) and, already at an earlier stage, in Article IX, § 5, of the Belgo-Netherlands Treaty of Separation of 19 April 1839, in Articles 38-49 of the subsequent Treaty of The Hague of 5 November 1842 and in *Règlement* No. 5, inserted in the Convention of 20 May 1843 (Martens, N.R., XVI, 773; N.R.G.[1], III, 613, and N.R.G.[1], V, 339, respectively), and which had already undergone a change in the original shipping route in 1867.[77] The 1925 Treaty

77. This change also concerned a canal: when the Kreekrak and the Sloe, being the natural channels between the eastern and the western branches of the river Scheldt and themselves constituting part of the "intermediary waters", were dammed in 1867 for the construction of a railway connecting the provinces of Northern Brabant and Zeeland, The Netherlands, in compliance with Article IX, § 8 of the Treaty of Separation of 19 April 1839 (Martens, N.R., XIV, 773, 778), gave Belgium compensation by digging a canal through the Zeeland island of South-Beveland. See the map on p. 179.

was only forced through the Second Chamber of the Netherlands Parliament in the face of strong opposition, but was in the event torpedoed by a majority against it in the First Chamber. The controversy lingered on for a long time, but has recently found a final solution, satisfactory to both parties, in a new treaty, signed on 13 May 1963. According to that treaty (*U.N.T.S.*, vol. 540, p. 3) (Articles 2-4) a better trade route was to be made between the seaport of Antwerp near Zandvliet and the Rhine by means of the construction of a canal towards and across the Eastern Scheldt and through the Eendracht northwards to the Krammer. The expenses of the works were to be defrayed mainly by Belgium on whose behalf they were undertaken, those on Belgium soil entirely, and most of the others, on Dutch soil, up to 85 % (Article 19). The statute of the new canal was regulated in detail in Articles 32 *et seq.*: freedom of navigation and at least national treatment in regard to transports. Shipping should continue to dispose of a convenient connection between the terminus of the new canal in the Krammer and the river Waal, however, at the choice of the Netherlands (Articles 34 and 37). Moreover the existing waterway across the island of Zuid-Beveland was not to be disused or basically altered without Belgium's consent (Article 33^2). The construction of lateral canals branching off from the main canal was reserved on both sides (Article 39). An Arbitral Commission was set up, vested with exclusive jurisdiction over possible disputes (Articles 42 *et seq.* and Annex III).

Two other canals in the border region of the two countries have likewise aroused strong political feelings and even led to litigation before the Permanent Court of International Justice. This was the case of the *Diversion of water from the river Meuse* of 1937 (*Publications P.C.I.J.*, series A/B, No. 70). It proceeded from a dispute over the correct construction of a Belgo-Netherlands Treaty of 12 May 1863 (Martens, N.R.G.^{2}, I, 117), as amended by a treaty of 11 January 1873 (*ibid.*, I, 123), dealing with the permissible quantities of water to be diverted from the river Meuse into the Belgian Albert Canal, and over the construction by The Netherlands without previous agreement with Belgium of the lateral Juliana Canal below Maastricht (1934). Comp. on these proceedings my *The Jurisprudence of the World Court*, vol. I, pp. 458 *et seq.*

The main purpose for which canals are constructed and the main use which is made of them is of course for navigation, but they may occasionally also be dug, or at least used, to other ends, for example drainage or irrigation.

When one surveys the aggregate of the inter-state agreements, old and new, on canals of international concern in order to form a general idea of the various types of interests involved, they can be classed in a number of categories. VAN EYSINGA has undertaken such a classification and analysis in particular for the Netherlands frontier-crossing canals in his study *Ontwikkeling en inhoud der Nederlandsche tractaten sedert 1813* (The Hague, 1916), pp. 136 *et seq.* The Netherlands are indeed very rich in frontier-crossing canals, partially in consequence of the separation of Belgium in 1839: four with Belgium—apart from the above-mentioned big Scheldt-Rhine canal projected in 1925 and its successor on which agreement was reached in May 1963: Bruges-Sluis, Ghent-Terneuzen, the Zuid-Willemsvaart Maastricht-'s-Hertogenbosch, and Liège-Maastricht—and four with Germany, summed up in the Netherlands-German protocol of 17 May 1876, confirmed by a Convention of 12 October 1876 (Martens, N.R.G.[2], II, 11 and 12). Without therefore going more deeply into the special conditions of Dutch frontier-crossing canals, I will confine myself to giving here a summary, but somewhat wider survey of the various matters which come up for regulation, in respect of canals in general, illustrated by a few examples. They concern:

(*a*) construction in common of a new canal and apportionment of the costs, proportionate to the interests involved on either side:

> Prussia and France, 4 April 1861 (Martens, N.R.G.[1], XVII[1], 309), concerning the construction of a canal between the Rhine-Marne Canal and the collieries of the Saar basin;
> Prussia and Schaumburg-Lippe, 19/30 October 1906, concerning the construction of a canal between the Rhine and the Weser (*ibid.*, N.R.G.[3], I, 339), modified by treaties of 1/3 March 1911 (*ibid.*, VII, 889) and 13 December 1920 (*ibid.*, XV, 827),

or (*a*[1]) widening or improvement of an existing canal, and the costs involved:

> Belgium and The Netherlands, four times in succession (1879, 1896, 1902 and 1961) for the improvement of the Ghent-Terneuzen canal in the exclusive interest of Belgium (Martens, N.R.G.[2], VIII, 152; *Staatsblad*, 1897, No. 70; *ibid.*, 1903, No. 258; 20 June 1960, *U.N.T.S.*, vol. 423, p. 19).

(*b*) maintenance of a canal, protection of its banks, or embankment:

> Belgium and The Netherlands, Articles 32-40 of *Règlement* No. 7, annexed to the Convention of 20 May 1843 (Martens, N.R.G.[1], V, 294 *et seq.*, at p. 375), concerning the protection of the banks of the Ghent-Terneuzen canal;
> Belgium and The Netherlands, 5 September 1850, concerning the upkeep of the Liège-Maastricht canal (*Staatsblad* No. 64);
> Germany and The Netherlands, 16 May 1895, concerning the upkeep of the Niers canal (Martens, N.R.G.[2], XXIII, 44).

(*c*) assurance, requested and granted, that should either of the parties desire in future to connect its canal system with that of the other, the necessary permission will be granted, without however any guarantee of active collaboration or of an adequate financial contribution being given:

> The Netherlands and Prussia, 17 May and 12 October 1876 (*ibid.*, N.R.G.[2], II, 12, 11) with regard to four frontier-crossing canals from the provinces of Groningen, Drente and Overijssel into Germany.

(d) lateral canals:

(i) ban upon the construction along a river by one State of one or more lateral canals which may be prejudicial to the fluvial interests of the other:

> Comp. the provision in Article 358, para. 3(1) of the Peace Treaty of Versailles, mentioned above.

or (ii) inversely, express concession of the right to construct such canals:

> Comp. the provisions in Article 358, para. 1, *sub* (a) and *in fine* of the same treaty.

or (iii) construction of a lateral canal in common:

> Hanover and Prussia: lateral Ems canal past Lingen towards Meppen, constructed in accordance with § 2-*c* of an Agreement reached at Berlin between expert commissioners of the two States on 26 April 1820 (Hanoverian *Actenstücke*, Zweite Diät, Heft IV, Litt. B., Anlage No. 23) for the implementation of Article 5 of the Prusso-Hanoverian treaty of 28 May 1815 (Martens, N.R., II, 316), annexed under No. 6 to the Final Act of the Congress of Vienna (Martens, N.R., II, 379 *et seq.*, at p. 429, Article 118);
>
> Belgium and The Netherlands: lateral Meuse canal between Liège and Maastricht, constructed in the exclusive interest of Belgium, treaty of 12 July 1845 (*ibid.*, N.R.G.¹, VIII, 383).—Another lateral canal, the Juliana canal along the Netherlands Maas between Maastricht and Maasbracht was, on the contrary, at a much later stage (1934) built by The Netherlands on its own authority without previous agreement with Belgium and was one of the elements in the proceedings before the Permanent Court, mentioned above. The whole system of canals, thus established, was subsequently further improved by the construction of a better connection between the Juliana canal and the (Belgian) Albert canal: Convention of 24 February 1961 (*U.N.T.S.*, vol. 474, p. 167);
>
> Germany, France and Switzerland, agreement on the construction of a lateral Rhine canal near Kembs, the project for which was adopted in their agreement of 10 May 1922 (Martens, N.R.G.³, XX, 194), with a subsequent Convention of 27 August 1926 (*ibid.*, XX, 202) for the regulation of Franco-Swiss relations in respect of certain clauses of the legal regime of this future diversion of the Rhine.
>
> Comp. also on possible future lateral canals Article 358 of the Peace Treaty of Versailles.

or (iv) freedom of navigation on any lateral canals which might be constructed as a substitute for unnavigable stretches of the Congo and the Niger, in general, stipulated by Articles 16 and 29 of the General Act of the Congo Conference of Berlin of 1885 (*ibid.*, N.R.G.², X, 414).

(e) grant by one State to another of a concession for the construction of a canal through its territory:

> Comp. on the Panama and the projected Nicaragua canal below, p. 232; and concerning the—optionally road or—canal-servitude on Netherlands Limburg, established by Article XII of the Belgo-Netherlands Treaty of Separation of 19 April 1839 (*ibid.*, N. R., XVI, 773), below section 5, under A, p. 250.

(*f*) feeding of a frontier-crossing canal:

> France and Germany, 23 April 1873, in respect of the Marne-Rhine canal (*ibid.*, N.R.G.², X, 449), amended 8 November 1883 (*ibid.*, X, 452);
> Belgium and France, 14 May 1884, aimed at facilitating the alimentation of the canal de l'Espierre (*ibid.*, XII, 621).
> The feeding of canals was also at stake in the case of 1937 concerning the "prises d'eau de la Meuse" before the Permanent Court, mentioned above.

(*g*) freedom of shipping:

> The Netherlands and Belgium, Article X of the Treaty of Separation of 19 April 1839 (*ibid.*, N.R., XVI, 773), containing a general clause on the free use of all frontier-crossing canals by the inhabitants of both countries;
> Article 284 of the Peace Treaty of St.-Germain with Austria (1919): duty-free canal transit on the footing of national treatment for Allied vessels in Austria;

(*h*) levying, reduction, or abolition of navigation dues:

> Prussia and France, 4 April 1861 (Martens, N.R.G.¹, XVII¹, 309): duties proportionate to the distance covered (Saar);
> Franco-Russian Peace Treaty of Tilsit of 9 July 1807 (*ibid.*, R², VIII, 637), Article 4: freedom from tolls on the Bromberg canal.

(*i*) rules on navigation, the organization of a piloting service, policing, the prevention of collisions, the removal of wrecks, the capacity of masters, the tonnage of vessels allowed to pass, safeguards against the transport of dangerous materials:

> The Netherlands-Belgium: *Règlement* No. 7 of 20 May 1843, concerning navigation on the Ghent-Terneuzen canal (*ibid.*, N.R.G.¹, V, 367).

(*j*) draining of canal sections, situated on the territory of one State, which may cause inconvenience to another; temporary suspension of shipping for the carrying-out of necessary repair or maintenance work:

> Belgium and France, 2/10 December 1841 (*ibid.*, N.R.G.¹, II, 323), for the "concordance du chômage annuel" on rivers and canals of common interest;
> Belgium and France, 31 May 1882 (*ibid.*, N.R.G.², VIII, 446), regulating the emptying of a "bief de partage" on Belgian territory which causes the water to flow into French territory through three different floodgates (*déversoirs*);
> Belgium and The Netherlands, 2 August 1884 (*ibid.*, XI, 636); mutual consultation in order to cause as little inconvenience as possible;
> Belgium, France and Germany, 8 October 1887 (*ibid.*, XV, 747), providing for the synchronization of necessary temporary interruptions of canal traffic for the preparation and execution of repair and other works in the Rhine-Rhône canal, with corresponding "chômages" of the canals from Liège to Maastricht and Antwerp;
> similar agreements for the four Belgo-Netherlands frontier-crossing canals: 2 August 1884 (*ibid.*, XI, 636).

(*k*) construction of subsidiary works such as telegraph or telephone lines for the better operation of the canal service:

France and Germany, 20 March 1883 along the Marne-Rhine canal (*ibid.*, X, 451);

The Netherlands and Belgium, 10 August 1882 (*ibid.*, VIII, 440) and 10 April 1886 (*ibid.*, XI, 668) along the canals connecting Liège, Maastricht and 's-Hertogenbosch.

(*l*) use of a ship-canal for the draining-away of redundant water from the surrounding countryside or, inversely, a ban on such use; draining of a canal for irrigation purposes:

An old example of a drainage canal, apart from that ordered by Barbarossa in 1165 to be built in The Netherlands, mentioned above, was that around the former French settlement of Chandernagore in British India: when this establishment was given back to France by Article 13 of her Peace Treaty with Great Britain of Versailles of 3 September 1783 (Martens, R², III, 519), this restitution expressly included "la liberté d'entourer Chandernagore d'un fossé pour l'écoulement des eaux".

The drainage of the Flanders countryside was always a matter of considerable concern for the Government. It was regulated in Article 6 of the treaty between Austria and the States General of the United Netherlands of 8 November 1785 (*ibid.*, IV, 55), confirmed by Article 8 of the Belgo-Netherlands Treaty of Separation of 19 April 1839 (*ibid.*, N.R., XVI, 773). The matter was resumed in Article 20 of the executive treaty of 5 November 1842 (*ibid.*, N.R.G.¹, III, 613) and in a further, more detailed Convention especially on the drainage of Flanders, of 20 May 1843 (*Staatsblad* 1844, No. 11; *U.N. Legislative Series ST/LEG/SER.B/12*, p. 541), by which the parties agreed that the Ghent-Terneuzen canal, at least in its lower part, should after a term of two years no longer serve for draining purposes. Comp. now Articles 33-35 of the treaty of 20 June 1960 (*U.N.T.S.*, vol. 423, p. 19).

The Netherlands-Belgian boundary treaty of 8 August 1843 (*B.F.S.P.*, vol. 35, p. 1202), Article 36, maintained in general the *status quo* as to the draining of all boundary waters and forbade further draining.

Comp. on draining canals also: the Netherlands-Prussia, 17 October 1905 (Martens, N.R.G.³, III, 203).

(*m*) measures against pollution of the canal water:

the Netherlands and Belgium, 13 May 1963 (*U.N.T.S.*, vol., 540, p. 3), Article 17, relating to the Rhine-Scheldt canal; *idem*, 20 June 1960 (*ibid.*, vol. 423, p. 19), Articles 27-31, relating to the Ghent-Terneuzen canal;

or (*m*¹) measures against salting of the canal water from the sea:

same treaties, Articles 15/16 and 32 respectively.

(*n*) organization of the common administration of a canal (a very rare occurrence):

the St. Lawrence canal is administered by two (a Canadian and a USA) national agencies, whose activities have been coordinated by a series of international and less formal agreements (R. R. BAXTER, *The law of international waterways*, Cambridge Mass., 1964, p. 93).

(*o*) organization of a system for the settlement of possible disputes:

Article 42 of the above-mentioned Rhine-Scheldt canal treaty, 1963.

Comp. on the intersection of canals by a new boundary the historical case of the Rhine-Rhône and the Marne-Rhine canal as a consequence of the cession of Alsace-Lorraine to Germany in 1871. The former was at that time entirely French, the second was already intersected by a Franco-German boundary. See Article 14 of the treaty of 11 December 1871 (Martens, N.R.G.[1], XX, 847), additional to the Peace Treaty of Frankfurt.

The southern provinces of The Netherlands present similar intersections as a consequence of the separation of Belgium in 1830/1839.

More recent cases are those of the Einser canal in the now only partly Hungarian Burgenland (protocol of 13 October 1921, *ibid.*, N.R.G.[3], XIX, 763) and of a number of canals in the former German Reich, now intersected by the frontiers between the German Federal Republic and the German Democratic Republic.

On the canalization of rivers (such as the Saint Lawrence waterway and the Moselle) see section 2 *supra*.

When a canal is very exceptionally a boundary canal, the State frontier will as a rule run along its middle and along the middle of the bridges, if any.

I now come to the three sea-connecting canals which have become famous in diplomatic history and in international law.

The Suez Canal

The legal history of the Suez Canal began by the enactment by the Viceroy of Egypt on 30 November 1854[78] of a provisional firman authorizing the formation of a company for the carrying-out of a plan for the construction of a fresh water and a maritime canal through the isthmus of Suez. That firman was followed up by a second act of concession of 5 January 1856, containing in an annex the Statutes of the company to be created and authorizing the execution of the project as soon as the firman would have been approved by the Sublime Porte. An Egyptian Decree of 20 July 1856 laid down regulations on the use of indigenous labour, and after further preparations the *Compagnie universelle du Canal maritime de Suez* was founded and the work on the fresh water canal started in 1859. The first section of the latter canal between Cairo and Ouady was, after its completion, retroceded, under safeguards in favour of the Company, to the Viceroy by a Convention of 18 March 1863, followed up by a further Convention of 20 March 1863, stipulating the financial participation of Egypt in the enterprise. It was only by a Note of 6 April 1863 that the Sultan made known his conditional consent to the Egyptian firman of 5 January 1856. The fresh water canal was com-

78. See for the documents concerning the Suez Canal *The Suez Canal, A selection of documents . . . 1854—1956*, London, 1956.

228

pleted in December 1863. Meanwhile, disputes had arisen between the Company and the Viceroy, concerning, *inter alia*, the admissibility and legal consequences of the unilateral cancellation by the Khedive of the Regulations of 20 July 1856 (provoked by the excessively high number of casualties amongst the *fellahin*), and the retrocession of the second section of the fresh water canal Ouady-Ismailia-Suez to Egypt. Emperor Napoleon III of France, appointed as arbitrator in this pseudo-international controversy by a *compromis* of 21 April 1864, gave his award on 6 July 1864 (Martens, N.R.G.[1], XVIII, 243). This award was implemented by a new Convention between the Khedive and the Company of 30 January 1866. The final contract between Egypt and the Company, in which regard was had to the Note of the Sultan of 6 April 1863, was only concluded on 22 February 1866 (*ibid.*, XVIII, 260), confirmed by the Sultan on 19 March 1866 (*ibid.*, 267). In this contract the regime of the maritime canal was provisionally described and the legal status of the *Compagnie universelle* defined in more detail. The maritime canal was officially opened with great splendour on 19 November 1869. The maximum gauge of vessels to be admitted to the canal was fixed by a Khedival Decree of 12 July 1873 (*ibid.*, N.R.G.[2], III, 562). On 25 November 1875 the British Government bought the Viceroy's shares in the Company's capital for £ 4.000.000 (*ibid.*, III, 528). After Britain's occupation of military keypoints in Egypt in the summer of 1882, the further fate of the Suez canal became more than before a matter of international concern. As a consequence, lengthy discussions and negotiations, in particular between Great Britain and France and with the Ottoman Empire, followed. After a Turkish declaration of 30 March/ 2 April 1885 (*ibid.*, XI, 96) and a first international Conference at Paris, from 30 March to 12 June 1885 (*procès-verbaux* in Martens, N.R.G.[2], XI, 307) had failed to produce a definite result, a second Conference at Constantinople succeeded, after a long-drawn out diplomatic correspondence between France and Britain (*ibid.*, XV, 213-331), in reaching agreement on the future legal regime of the canal by the Convention of 29 October 1888 (*ibid.*, XV, 557), the main provisions of which are summarized below.

(1) The maritime canal shall always be free and open, in time of war as in time of peace, for any merchant vessel or man-of-war, without distinction of flag. No blockade of the canal shall be allowed.—(2) The safeguards for the fresh water canal, laid down in a declaration inserted in the Convention of 18 March 1863, are maintained, and (3) all the accessories to both canals shall be respected.—(4) The freedom of passage extending even to men-of-war of belligerent States, no act of hostility or act intended to obstruct that freedom shall be permissible in the canal, its ports of access and a three-miles maritime area around them, even when the Ottoman Empire itself is a belligerent; but restrictions are imposed on the provisioning and victualling of belligerent vessels of war and on the duration of their stay in the canal.

—(5) Barring accidental obstruction in the canal, debarcation and embarcation of troops, ammunition and war material will be forbidden.—(6) The regime of prizes shall be equated to that of men-of-war.—(7) Nowhere in the canal shall the Powers maintain vessels of war, except for their right, if they are not at war, to station each two such vessels at most in the ports of Port Said and Suez.—(8) A certain type of international control of the true observance of the treaty, to be exercised by the foreign diplomatic agents, is organized, in particular to counter the erection of works or the gathering of forces prejudicial to the freedom and safety of navigation.—Moreover, (9) the Egyptian and, if need be, the Ottoman Government shall see to its execution and (10) be empowered to take the necessary measures for the defence of Egypt and the maintenance of public order, even if contrary to the provisions *sub* (4), (5), (7) and (8), provided that (11) those measures do not obstruct the freedom of passage and that no permanent fortifications be erected.—(12) No discrimination of any kind in respect of the use of the canal shall be allowed, but the rights of Turkey as the territorial Power are reserved.

Great Britain did not, however, formally accept these stipulations. Prior to the signing of the Convention, her delegates indeed expressed the important reservation that "en présentant ce texte de traité comme le régime définitif destiné à garantir le libre usage du canal de Suez, (ils) pensent qu'il est de leur devoir de formuler une réserve générale quant à l'application de ces dispositions en tant qu'elles ne seraient pas compatibles avec l'état transitoire et exceptionnel où se trouve actuellement l'Egypte et qu'elles pourraient entraver la liberté d'action de leur Gouvernement pendant la période de l'occupation de l'Egypte" (Martens, N.R.G.², XV, 288).

The further legal history of the Canal was to a great extent dominated by the political development, first of Franco-British and later of Anglo-Egyptian relations. The culminating-points of this development were the following.

By Article 6 of her great political *entente* with France of 8 April 1904 (Martens, N.R.G.², XXXII, 3), Great Britain adhered to the stipulations of the Convention of 1888, subject to the suspension of the carrying-out of the last sentence of § 1 and of § 2 of Article 8 thereof (dealing with the setting-up of an international supervision of the freedom of navigation).

After Turkey's entry into the war against the Allied Powers on 5 November 1914 Great Britain, by an Order in Council of 18 December 1914 (*B.F.S.P.*, vol. 109, p. 436), proclaimed her protectorate over Egypt, which was recognized by her Allies and later formalized by the Peace Conference of 1919/1920 (comp. Article 147 of the Treaty of Versailles and corresponding Articles of the other peace treaties, including the abortive Sèvres Treaty with Turkey (Article 101). Already prior to the Peace Treaty of Lausanne of 24 July 1923, by which Turkey finally acquiesced in her loss of Egypt, Great Britain had, under the mounting pressure of Egyptian nationalism dissatisfied with the outcome of the negotiations, by a telegraphic diplomatic circular to foreign Powers of 15 March 1922 (Martens, N.R.G.[3], XIII, 489), accompanied by a proclamation of the new King of Egypt of the same date (*ibid.*, XIII, 490), announced her decision to recognize Egypt's independence, subject to four reservations, the first of which was that "the security of the communications of the British Empire in Egypt" was "absolutely reserved to the discretion of His Majesty's Government until such time as it (might) be possible by free discussion and friendly accomodation on both sides to conclude agreements in regard thereto" with the Government of Egypt. See for details: *Egypt no. 1 (1922). Correspondence respecting affairs in Egypt*, Cmd. 1592. On 3 August 1929, the foundation of an Anglo-Egyptian *entente* was laid in an exchange of Notes between the two countries (*ibid.*, XXI, 128), in which the Suez canal was again mentioned.

On the further development of the Anglo-Egyptian relations by the Convention of 26 August 1936 (*ibid.*, N.R.G.[3], XXXIII, 325), which also covered the Suez Canal, comp. my Excursus in Part II of this publication ("The Anglo-Egyptian compromise of 1936"), pp. 428-434. After World War II with its fierce fighting in North Africa had blown over and a relatively quiet period had set in, the situation suddenly changed as a result of the decision of the Egyptian Government, for reasons foreign to the Canal itself, to nationalize the Suez Canal Company by a Law of 26 July 1956 (*Archiv des Völkerrechts* 1958-59 (7), p. 146). The Company was thereby dissolved; its inland and foreign assets were transferred to the Egyptian State, while a prospect of compensation was held out for its shareholders on the basis of the stock exchange quotations at Paris of the day before; the administration of the Canal was handed over to an Egyptian management. This decision did not in itself affect the international legal status of the Canal, nor did it establish new sovereign rights of Egypt with regard to it, but it encroached upon the rights and financial interests of the Company and its shareholders.

Hence the protests by the French and British Governments, supported by the United States Government, and the demand, made by an international conference in London, 16-23 August 1956 (Cmd. 9853), but rejected by Egypt (Cmd. 9865), for the transfer of the management to an international body. A further conference in London, 19-21 September 1956, set up a Suez Canal Users' Association with the task of regulating the traffic through the Canal and collecting the Canal dues, but that Association was also still-born. Intervention by the Security Council led to a Resolution of 13 October 1956 (S/3671) adopting the following principles: respect of Egyptian sovereignty; free passage for all ships; shipping dues to be fixed in common accord between Egypt and the users of the Canal, part of their proceeds to be destined for improvements; pending questions between the Company and Egypt to be settled by arbitration. A recommendation to Egypt to accept the London plan and to co-operate with the Suez Canal Users' Association was, however, wrecked on a veto of the Soviet Union.

There was much theoretical discussion concerning the legal issues raised by the nationalization. Egypt asserted that she was not obliged under international law to maintain the management of the Canal by the Company or by an international body, because the concession and further contracts with the Company were not governed by international law, because such management was not prescribed in any international treaty, not even in that of 1888, and because the case did not come, either, under any general rule of customary law; the Company derived its legal status inside and outside Egypt exclusively from an authorization by the Egyptian Vice-Roy of 1856. Since, however, on the other hand, the Company was governed by French company law, a shareholders meeting, held in Paris in June 1957, transferred its seat to Paris and transformed it into a company with legal personality under French commercial law. This course of events gave rise to nice legal questions relative to the identity of the Canal Company after its dissolution in Egypt and its rebirth in France.

The whole situation had in the meantime become legally inextricable as a consequence of the warlike action, undertaken in October and November 1956 by Israel, Great Britain and France, followed by a new armistice, and at a later stage as a result of a new *Blitzkrieg*, the Six Days' War of June 1967, which advanced the Israeli armistice line to the Canal. Traffic through it has since remained completely paralysed.

See Y. VAN DER MENSBRUGGHE, *Les garanties de la liberté de navigation dans le canal de Suez* (Paris, 1964) and *The Suez Canal settlement, a selection of documents...October 1956-March 1959* (London, 1960).

The Panama Canal

The first traces to be found in treaty law of international concern with a future trans-isthmian canal to connect the Atlantic and Pacific Oceans date back to the middle of the 19th century, when New Granada (the predecessor of Colombia) and the United States agreed in their treaty of friendship and commerce of 12 December 1846 (Martens, N.R.G.[1], XIII, 653) that, should certain plans, then under consideration, materialize, the neutrality of the isthmus of Panama and of any canal across it should be secured and navigation through it should be free. At that juncture special interest in such an inter-oceanic canal was also shown by Great Britain, which had already established possessions or zones of influence on the east coast of Central America in Belize and on the Mosquito Coast. With a view to Great Britain's interests there and to those of her world-wide maritime commerce in general the British Government of the day staked out fairly widely Great Britain's claim to achieve a position of equality with the United States in all matters of essential importance in connection with the future inter-oceanic canal. England provisionally attained her object by concluding with the United States the Clayton-Bulwer Treaty of 19 April 1850 (*ibid.*, N.R.G.[1], XV, 187), with accompanying interpretative notes of 29 June/4 July 1850 (*ibid.*, 192-195).[79]

> Neither of the Contracting Parties should have exclusive control over the canal, nor erect any fortifications commanding it, make use of any political ascendancy in the areas concerned or strive for commercial or navigational privileges. In case of war between the Parties their vessels should be exempted from the exercise of the right of prize in the canal and in an adjoining maritime zone; the canal itself was to be protected against interruption, seizure or confiscation, and its neutrality guaranteed. Accession of third States was to be furthered, and treaty stipulations to be entered into with such of the Central American States as were qualified for co-operation in carrying out the "great design" of the Convention, namely, "that of constructing and maintaining the canal as a ship-communication between the two oceans, for the benefit of mankind, on equal terms to all, and of protecting the same."

Even the *tracé* of the future canal was at that time still far from finally fixed: as late as in the middle seventies, eight different *tracés*, not merely across the isthmus of Panama proper, but also through Nicaragua, still contended for priority,[80] and it was only in 1879 that the definitive *tracé* (from the town of Panamá to that of Colón) was chosen and the Frenchman de Lesseps founded his *Compagnie universelle du Canal interocéanique de Panama*. This company soon began its work on the strength of a concession already granted to it in 1878 by Colombia. The execution of the plan met, however, with the greatest obstacles and finally the Company became bankrupt in 1888. Meanwhile the Nicaraguan *tracé* had remained on the map as a possible rival *tracé* (comp. a treaty of 15 November 1883 between Nicaragua and El Salvador, *ibid.*, N.R.G.[2], XIV, 228), but after the formation of a new French company, the *Compagnie nouvelle du Canal de Panama*, in 1894 and further setbacks the United States took the matter in hand by the end of the 19th century, finally decided in favour of the Panama *tracé* between the cities of Panamá

79. On the exchange of the instruments of ratification the British plenipotentiary declared "that Her Majesty does not understand the engagements of that Convention to apply to Her Majesty's Settlement at Honduras, or to its dependencies."
80. From the gulf of Uraba to the bay of Chirichiri; from the same gulf to the gulf of San Miguel; from the Acanti bay to the latter gulf; from the gulf of San Blas to the roadstead of Chepillo in the bay of Panamá; from Greytown (Nicaragua) through Lake Nicaragua to Brito; and three different *tracés* from Limón bay along the Panamá railroad to Panamá town.

and Colón, and went through with the plans by first rebutting excessive British claims to equality in respect of the building and future control of the canal and by then breaking the resistance of Colombia to the acceptance of the American terms and supporting the claim of the, already discontented, Panamanian area of Colombia to an independent national existence. Hence the wellknown series of international events which mark the diplomatic history of the Panama Canal in the first years of the 20th century, *viz.*,

5 February 1900, the first Hay-Pauncefote Treaty (Martens, N.R.G.², XXIX, 498), still conceived as additional to the Clayton-Bulwer Treaty of 1850, and laying down in substance the following:

> (1) the canal may be constructed under the auspices of the Government of the United States which shall also have and enjoy the exclusive right of providing for the regulation and management of the canal; (2) the "general principle" of neutralization, established in Article 8 of the 1850 Treaty, is specified in seven rules, substantially as embodied in the Suez Canal Convention of 29 October 1888, still including (*sub* 1°) the express provision that the principle of the freedom of navigation shall apply "in time of war as in time of peace", and the clause (*sub* 7°) that "no fortifications shall be erected commanding the canal or the waters adjacent"; (3) other Powers shall be invited to adhere.

This treaty was, however, rejected by the United States Senate and replaced, on

18 November 1901, by the second Hay-Pauncefote Treaty (*ibid.*, N.R.G.², XXX, 631) which altered the 1900 treaty considerably

> by (*a*) superseding entirely the Clayton-Bulwer Treaty of 1850;
> by (*b*) striking out the express qualifying provision *sub* 1° as well as the prohibition *sub* 7°, and
> by (*c*) dropping the adhesion clause,—while at the same time providing (*d*) that no change of territorial sovereignty or of the international relations of the country or countries traversed by the canal—"by whatever route may be considered expedient"—shall affect the general principle of neutralization or the obligations of the High Contracting Parties under the present Treaty.

4 November 1903, declaration of independence of the Republic of Panamá (as formally repeated in its Constitution of 16 February 1904, *ibid.*, N.R.G.², XXXI, 641), followed by her *de jure* recognition by the United States;

18 November 1903, Hay-Varilla Treaty between the United States and Panamá (*ibid.*, N.R.G.², XXXI, 599) governing the future relations between the two States in respect of the Panama Canal Zone. After a preamble, reciting that an Act of Congress of 28 June 1902 had "authorized the President to acquire within a reasonable time the control of the necessary territory of the Republic of Colombia", and that "the sovereignty of such territory (was) actually vested in the Republic of Panama", Article 1 began by stating that the United States guarantees and will

234

maintain the independence of the Republic. The other 25 articles dealt with the various grants agreed upon, the mutual rights of the parties in respect of the Canal Zone, the pecuniary compensation, the neutrality of the canal and the entrances thereto, its defence and a few matters concerned with certain successory effects and with possible future constitutional changes.

The grant comprised: (Article 2) the use, occupation and control in perpetuity of a zone of land and land under water for the construction, maintenance, operation, sanitation and protection of the canal of the width of ten miles extending to the distance of five miles on each side of the center line of the route of the canal to be constructed,—beginning in the Caribbean Sea and ending in the Pacific Ocean, on both sides at a distance of three marine miles from mean low water mark, but to the exclusion from the grant of the cities of Panamá and Colón, although these also were included in the zone; (Article 3) all the rights, power and authority within the zone which the United States would possess and exercise if it were the sovereign of the territory concerned, to the entire exclusion of their exercise by Panamá; (Article 4) the right to use, so far as necessary, the rivers, streams, lakes and other bodies of water within the limits of Panama for navigation, the supply of water or water power or other purposes; (Article 5) in perpetuity a monopoly for the construction, maintenance and operation of any system of communication by means of canal or railroad between the Caribbean Sea and the Pacific Ocean; (Article 7) the right to acquire by purchase or by the right of eminent domain all necessary properties in the cities of Panamá and Colón; (Article 8) all rights to property of the New Panamá Canal Company and the Panamá Railroad Company within the Zone; (Article 17) the use of all Panamanian ports open to commerce as places of refuge for vessels connected with the canal; and (Article 22) Panamá's rights under the concessionary contract to participate in the future earnings of the canal, to canal property at the expiration of the 99 years term of the contract, and to other related assets.—In addition to the grants listed above, Panamá shall (Article 25) sell or lease to the United States lands adequate and necessary for naval or coaling stations on both coasts, for the efficient protection of the canal and preservation of its neutrality.

The compensation due for the rights thus granted shall be $ 10.000.000, at once, and after nine years an annual payment of $ 250.000, both in gold coin (Article 14).

As to the neutrality of the canal and the entrances thereto, and to the conditions of its public use the Convention simply refers to the (second) Hay-Pauncefote Treaty of 1901.

Certain questions of State succession are solved in Articles 20 and 21: Panamá shall, within the limits set by international law, take the necessary steps for the annulment or modification of any anterior treaty inconsistent with the Hay-Varilla Treaty, in which she might have succeeded as the successor of Colombia, and will be sole liable on account of possible anterior debts etc., or concessions or privileges to other governments, etc.

Continuity in Panamá's treaty obligations is insured by Article 24 which lays down, on the one hand, that "no change either in the government or in the laws and treaties of the Republic of Panamá shall, without the consent of the United States, affect any right of the United States under the present Convention" and, on the other, that "if Panamá shall hereafter enter as a constituent into any other Government or into any union or confederation of states, so as to merge her sovereignty or independence in such Government, union or confederation, the rights of the United States under this Convention shall not be in any respect lessened or impaired."

With a view to the opening of the canal in 1914 the Congress of the United States on 24 August 1912 passed an *Act to Provide for the Opening, Maintenance, Protection, and Operation of the Panamá Canal and the Sanitation and Government of the Canal Zone (ibid., N.R.G.³, VII, 22)*, in which a provision was inserted to the effect that "no tolls shall be levied upon vessels engaged in the coastwise trade of the United States." This discriminatory provision in favour of United States vessels met with severe criticism from other countries and was repealed by a further Act of 15 June 1914 (*ibid.*, IX, 3).

The Panamá Canal toll rates were prescribed by a Proclamation of the President of 13 November 1912 (*ibid.*, VIII, 671).

A precise delimitation of the Canal Zone was agreed upon in a treaty with Panamá of 2 September 1914 (*ibid.*, IX, 4).

The dispute between the United States and Colombia about the secession of Panamá was only finally settled by their Convention of 6 April 1914 (*ibid.*, XII, 131) and a subsequent protocol of 1 March 1922 (*ibid.*, XII, 135).

On 5 August 1914 the United States, moreover, entered into a further treaty with Nicaragua on a possible future canal through Nicaragua with a terminal in the Gulf of Fonseca (*ibid.*, IX, 350). This treaty has in its turn led to a dispute between Nicaragua and its fellow riparian States of that Gulf, El Salvador and Honduras. Comp. on this dispute the section on State frontiers in bays (*infra* pp. 606 *et seq.*), and on the validity or nullity of international juridical acts Part VI of this publication.

After the Second World War the mounting discontent of Panamá over the considerable restrictions upon her territorial sovereignty in the Canal Zone has led to lengthy negotiations with the United States concerning a change in the existing treaty relations, and moreover for the conclusion of a further treaty under which a new sea level canal might be constructed across Panamá. On 24 September 1965 the President of the United States made a statement on these subjects, part of which is quoted in *A.J.I.L.* 1966 (60), pp. 397-398. According to that statement, the main areas of agreement reached were the following: The 1903 Treaty will be abrogated. The new treaty will effectively recognize Panamá's sovereignty over the present Canal Zone. The new treaty will terminate after a specified number of years, or on or about the date of the opening of the sea level canal, whichever occurs first. A primary objective of the new treaty will be to provide for an appropriate political, economic and social integration, by orderly transition, of the area used in the canal operation with the rest of Panamá. The new treaties will provide for the defense—including the neutralization—of the existing canal and any sea level canal which may be constructed (this subject to be regulated in a separate third treaty). United States forces and military facilities will be maintained under a base rights and status of forces agreement. The United States will make studies and site surveys of possible routes in Panamá with respect to the sea level canal, including an investigation into the feasibility of nuclear excavation of such a canal. Both canals shall be open at all times to the vessels of all nations on a non-discriminatory basis. On the further developments comp. *The Department of State Bulletin* 1967 (57), pp. 65, 165, 302, 474; 1968 (59), p. 369.

The Kiel Canal

When the construction of a canal connecting the North Sea with the Baltic from the Elbe estuary to Kiel was still at the planning stage, that canal would have by virtue of the local conditions been built as a truly international waterway since its *tracé* was to run partly through Prussian territory and partly through territory of the duchy of Holstein which, united in a real union with Schleswig, was linked by a personal union with the Crown of Denmark, though at the same time forming part of the German Confederation of 1815. When Denmark lost the Elbe duchies after her short war of 1864 with that Confederation, the Holstein area, earmarked for the construction of the future canal, changed its legal status as it was placed under the co-sovereignty of Austria and Prussia in virtue of the Peace Treaty of Vienna of 30 October 1864 (Martens, N.R.G.[1], XVII[2], 474). This again changed when, by their Convention of Gastein of 14 August 1865 (*ibid.*, XVIII, 2), the two co-sovereigns, while formally maintaining their co-imperium over the duchies *de jure*, agreed upon a factual division of the exercise of their powers in such a way that Schleswig was henceforth to be administered by Prussia and Holstein by Austria. Hence the provision inserted in Article 7 of the Gastein Convention pursuant to which Prussia should remain entitled to construct the projected canal across Holstein territory. The whole area only finally became exclusively Prussian as a consequence of the liquidation of the relationship of co-sovereignty by the

237

Austro-Prussian Peace Treaty of Prague of 23 August 1866 (*ibid.*, XVIII, 344) following their short war of 1866, in the course of which the Prussian general Manteuffel had occupied Holstein (*ibid.*, XVIII, 16). From that year onwards the Kiel Canal was to become, and was indeed opened in 1895 as, an entirely Prussian canal, not subject to any international interference. This underwent a change again when Germany, after her defeat in World War I, was compelled to accept the internationalization of the canal by Articles 380-386 of the Peace Treaty of Versailles (1919).

Controversies over the true construction of the relevant treaty provisions arose during the Russo-Polish war of 1920, when Poland objected to Germany putting a ban from considerations of neutrality on the transport of contraband of war towards Poland through the canal. Proceedings followed before the Permanent Court of International Justice, which in its first Judgment of 28 June 1923 (*Publications P.C.I.J.*, series A, No. 1) found against Germany. Article 380 of the Peace Treaty of Versailles laid down indeed that "the Kiel Canal and its approaches shall be maintained free and open to the vessels of commerce and of war of all nations at peace with Germany on terms of entire equality." The Court rightly held that this clear and unequivocal provision made illegal any attempt by Germany, on considerations of neutrality during the Russo-Polish war, to close the canal for ships carrying contraband to Poland (comp. on this Judgment my *The Jurisprudence of the World Court*, vol. I, pp. 41 *et seq.*).

Under the Hitler regime Germany freed herself from the burdens laid upon her in 1919 with respect to the internationalization of her waterways, including the Kiel Canal, by a diplomatic Note on German waterways of 14 November 1936 (Martens, N.R.G.³, XXXVI, 800). In a judgment of 1 June 1950 (*I.L.R.* 1950, Case No. 34) in a collision case a German Supreme Court for the British occupation zone still considered it doubtful if the canal had remained an international waterway because Germany's step of 1936 had not met with any serious resistance on the part of the signatory Powers of the Treaty of Versailles, but it could discard that question because a collision even in an internationalized canal could in no case be treated like a collision on the high seas. The final outcome of the diplomatic struggle over the legal status of the Canal would still seem to hang in the balance.

Comp. on this subject the *Wörterbuch des Völkerrechts*, vol. I, p. 85 (I. von Münch, *Ari-Fall*) and vol. II, p. 220 (V. Böhmert, *Kieler Kanal*), and Whiteman, vol. 3, p. 1256.

Section 4. MARITIME PORTS

As some details on river ports have been given above, p. 123 (*ad* Article 9), this section will be limited to maritime ports.

In former centuries there was no international obligation to open maritime ports to foreign trading vessels. In his doctrinal note to the arbitral award of 30 November 1843 in the *Portendick* affair (De Lapradelle-Politis, *Recueil des arbitrages internationaux*, I (Paris, 1957, 2nd ed.), pp. 512 *et seq.*, at p. 532), Paul FAUCHILLE stated correctly that

"à l'époque où s'éleva le conflit ..., il était admis sans difficulté qu'un Etat pouvait arbitrairement fermer ses ports aux navires étrangers. C'est que le commerce mutuel des Etats était alors considéré, non comme un droit véritable, accompagné d'un devoir corrélatif, mais comme une simple faculté".

The United States Court of Appeal, Second Circuit, still held on 4 May 1960 (278 F. 2nd 49 [1960] A.M.C. 795; *I.L.R.*, vol. 31, p. 137), in the case of *Khedivial Line, S.A.E. v. Seafarers' International Union et al.*, that it was not demonstrated that international law granted an unrestricted right of access to harbours by ships of foreign States and that such access was merely a matter of comity (the famous Anglo-American concept, discussed in Part I of this publication, pp. 45 *et seq.*).

Great Britain only accorded the privilege of trading with her colonies to Prussian vessels by an Order in Council of 3 May 1826 (Martens, N.R., II, 469).

As appears from Martens, N.R.G.[1], X, 610 (footnote) the Portuguese colonies—the Sunda islands of Solor and Timor, Goa *c.a.*, Damão, the island of Díu, Mozambique, Angola and Benguela, the establishments and islands São Tomé and Principe on the coast of Guinea, and the Cabo Verde islands—were still in 1847 closed to foreign trade.

This subject of the freedom of trade with foreign countries has played an important rôle in the famous controversy concerning the freedom of the seas. Comp. Part IV-A of this publication, Chapter I.

Overseas colonial ports, in particular, were often closed to foreign commerce as a matter of policy. Their opening to such commerce by way of exception in time of war has even given rise to fierce international disputes. One of the forms in which this happened in the past connects this subject with the international law of prize, where the opening of colonial ports which were normally closed to foreign shipping to neutral commerce in time of war gave birth to a new rule called the "rule of the war of 1756". Under this rule a belligerent power usurped the right to seize and confiscate neutral vessels which availed themselves of a permission granted to them as an exception by the other belligerent to establish commercial intercourse with its colonies. This old rule on "reserved navigation", as it was also called in French, was still echoed in Article

57 (2) of the London Declaration on maritime warfare of 26 February 1909 (*ibid.*, N.R.G.[3], VII, 39), where it appears in the following formula:

"Le cas où le navire neutre se livre à une navigation réservée en temps de paix reste hors de cause et n'est nullement visé par cette règle (*i.e.*, the rule according to which the neutral or enemy character of a vessel is generally determined by the flag which she is entitled to fly)."

On its application in World War I see my *Le droit des prises de la Grande Guerre* (Leiden, 1924), § 562, pp. 996-998.

Apart from this special case States were free, as a matter of "domestic jurisdiction" and at their own discretion, to close or open specific ports to foreign trade. When they opened them, they sometimes even found occasion in their own interest to make the ports which they opened "free ports".

This legal situation of the past has even, to a certain extent, in principle remained the same. Not all maritime ports are indeed *ipso jure* open to foreign commerce and every State has in principle preserved the freedom to decide which of its ports it will open to this end. This freedom must, however, at present be held to be subject to the limitation that a State shall not close all its ports to foreign shipping. Another restriction upon the freedom of closing national ports is that the territorial State may be held liable for any damage which foreign ships suffer from a closure decreed without timely previous notification (comp. the *Portendick* affair, cited above).

The opening of a sea port to foreign trade was in most cases an autonomous decision of the State concerned, but it could also be stipulated by treaty. Conventions of this type were sometimes entirely voluntary, sometimes imposed upon a State.

Examples of the autonomous unilateral opening of one or more sea ports or of their voluntary opening by treaty are legion.

I only cite a letter addressed in the name of the Emperor of Morocco to the States General of the United Netherlands in May 1786, opening the port of Larrash to Dutch merchants, and similar orders of the same Emperor in favour of other foreigners with regard to the ports of Tangier, Mogador and Rabat (Martens, R[2], IV, 111, 112).

Instances of an (at least initially) enforced opening are provided by what happened especially in China and Japan.

In the period following the Opium War of 1840 many Chinese ports were in succession opened to international trade by treaty.

Comp. *e.g.*, Articles 2 and 10 of the Anglo-Chinese Peace Treaty of Nanking of 29 August 1842 (*ibid.*, N.R.G.[1], III, 484) concerning the ports of Canton, Amoy, Fu-chao, Ningpo and Shanghai (comp. also the Regulations of July 1843, *ibid.*, III, 490 = V, 424); the exchange of letters between France and China of September 1843 relating to the same five ports (*ibid.*, III, 574); the treaties of China with the United States of 3 July 1844 (summary: *ibid.*,

VII, 134), Article 3; with Sweden-Norway of 20 March 1847 (*ibid.*, XVII², 193), Article 3; with the States of the German Zollverein of 2 September 1861 (*ibid.*, XIX, 168), Article 6.

The same procedure was followed in the case of Japan subsequent upon her breaking-open by the United States Navy, under Commodore Perry in 1853-1854:

> *e.g.*, treaties of Japan with the United States of 31 March 1854 (*ibid.*, N.R.G.¹, XVI¹, 563), Article 2, relating to the ports of Simoda and Hakodade; with Great Britain of 13 October 1854 (*ibid.*, XVI¹, 566), Article 1, relating to the ports of Nagasaki and Hakodade; with Russia of 26 January 1855 (*ibid.*, XVI², 454), Article 3, relating to all three.

As no Moroccan ports in sufficient number were in the beginning of this century opened to foreign trade, France by Article 11 of her Cambon-Kiderlen Wächter convention with Germany of 4 November 1911 (*ibid.*, N.R.G.³, V, 643) undertook to bring pressure to bear upon the Moroccan Government to induce it to open new ports for that purpose in addition to those already opened in 1786, as the need should arise. An additional exchange of notes (Martens, N.R.G.³, VI, 323) stipulated that this should be done in particular with regard to the port of Agadir.

When surveying the many historical documents relating to the opening of seaports one must distinguish between those which were intended to do only that and those which, over and above, made the port(s) concerned "free ports". The text of the documents is not always perfectly clear.

Free ports were as a rule established by national decrees with a general scope, issued by the Governments concerned. The creation of others was, however, stipulated by treaty and was then often limited to ships under the flag of the other contracting party either unilaterally or reciprocally. To give some idea of the frequency, variety and location of free port regimes I choose from the ample source material available the following examples.

Livorno: comp. section 1 of Chapter II *supra*, p. 24;

Marstrand: edict of the King of Sweden of 15 August 1775 (*ibid.*, R², II, 400);

ports of France in Europe and her American insular possessions; Article 30 of the Treaty of Commerce between France and the United States of 6 February 1778 (*ibid.*, R² II, 587 *et seq.*, at p. 601) in the terms of which

> "Pour d'autant plus favoriser et faciliter le commerce, que les sujets des Etats-Unis feront avec la France, le Roi T.C. leur accordera en Europe un ou plusieurs ports-francs, dans lesquels ils pourront amener et débiter toutes les denrées et marchandises provenant des treize Etats-Unis; S.M. conservera, d'un autre côté, aux sujets des dits Etats, les ports francs, qui ont été et sont ouverts dans les isles Françoises de l'Amérique; de tous lesquels

ports-francs les dits sujets des Etats Unis jouiront conformément aux règlements, qui en déterminent l'usage".

In the last period of the old kingdom of France, an Arrêt du Conseil d'Etat of 14 May 1784 (*ibid.*, R², III, 742) decreed that the harbour and the upper town of Dunkerk and the port, town and territory of Marseille would continue to enjoy the "franchises" of which they were possessed, and that new free ports were established at L'Orient, Bayonne and Saint-Jean-de-Luz; all of these were however abolished again in 1790 and 1794, respectively, by the new revolutionary government (*ibid.*, 742, note);

Göteborg: Ordinance of the King of Sweden of 22 May 1794 (*ibid.*, R², V, 617);

Lisbon: proclamation of the Queen of Portugal of 13 May 1796 (*ibid.*, R², VI, 206); comp. also the Royal Ordinance of 6 August 1806 directed against certain abuses (*ibid.*, R², VIII, 467);

Odessa: ukas of Tsar Alexander I of 29 April 1817 (*ibid.*, N.R., III, 101);

Sicilian ports: decree of King Ferdinand I of the Two Sicilies of 23 March 1819 (*ibid.*, N.R., V, 350), abolition of the so-called system of the *luogo di bastimento*, and its replacement by a *scala franca* in the customs-area of Palermo; confirmation of the *porto franco* of Messina;

a great number of "free warehousing ports", established by an *Act to Regulate the Trade of the British Possessions Abroad* of 1826 or, in virtue of that Act, by a series of Orders in Council of 1831 and 1832 in Nova Scotia, Canada, New Brunswick and in the islands of Grenada, Jamaica, Tortola, St. Vincent, St. Christopher, Mauritius, Anguilla and Nevis (*ibid.*, N.R., X, 322, 372, 389, 396, 403; XI, 432, 475, 483, 488); comp. also the subsequent instruments of 16 February 1842 relative to the establishment of free ports in Hongkong and Tinghai (Chusan) (*ibid.*, N.R.G.¹, III, 86) and in New Zealand of 27 August 1842 (*ibid.*, III, 481);

Macao: decree of the Queen of Portugal declaring its ports free ports, 20 November 1845 (*ibid.*, N.R.G.¹, VIII, 613);

Punto Arenas: decree of the Government of Costa Rica of 5 March 1847 (*ibid.*, N.R.G.¹, X, 485);

Geestemünde (Weser): Hanoverian law of 19 June 1847 (*ibid.*, N.R.G.¹, X, 599);

Bremen and Hamburg: Article 34 of the German *Reichsverfassung* of 1871 (*ibid.*, N.R.G.¹, XVIII, 582/592);

Batum: Article 59 of the Peace Treaty of Berlin of 13 July 1878 (*ibid.*, N.R.G.², III, 449). This provision which ran as follows:

"S. M. l'Empereur de Russie déclare que son intention est d'ériger Batoum en port franc, essentiellement commercial", has later given rise to the famous controversy as to whether the high-handed closure of this port by Russia in 1886 was at variance or, on the contrary, compatible with the provision quoted, which, in the Russian view, was according to the text itself "une déclaration libre et spontanée de S.M. l'Empereur Alexandre II". Great Britain protested against this unilateral action, comp. *Staatsarchiv* XLVIII, 38-45. In my view it is hardly possible to read into the text a strict obligation undertaken by Russia to maintain Batum in the status of a free port: though it may be assumed that Russia's co-contractants have constructed it in the sense of a lasting undertaking, Russia certainly has not; the conclusion would seem to be that in the absence of consensus no real obligation was created in 1878.

Comp. on the legal situation in free ports the detailed regulation concerning the Porti Franchi Vecchio and Nuovo in Trieste in Annex VIII to the Italian Peace Treaty of Paris of 10 January 1947 (*U.N.T.S.*, vol. 49, p. 3).

Free ports are particularly useful as transit ports to and from land-locked States, and various peace treaties, especially those concluded after World War I, have guaranteed to the latter such outlets on behalf of their foreign trade. Comp. *e.g.*, the free port regime of:

the German ports of Hamburg and Stettin for the benefit of Czecho-slovakia (in the legal form of a lease for 99 years): Articles 363 and 364 of the Peace Treaty of Versailles of 28 June 1919 (Martens, N.R.G.³, XI, 323);

Italian and Serb-Croat-Slovene ports on the Adriatic, which formerly belonged to Austria, for the latter's benefit: Article 311 of the Peace Treaty of St. Germain of 10 September 1919 (*ibid.*, XI, 691);

Trieste for the benefit of Yugoslavia, Italy and the States of Central Europe: Article 85 and Annex VIII of the Italian Peace Treaty of Paris of 10 February 1947 (*U.N.T.S.*, vol. 49, p. 3), maintained in substance by the American-British-Yugoslav-Italian Memorandum of Understanding of 5 October 1954 (*U.N.T.S.*, vol. 235, p. 99);

the Greek port of Saloniki for the benefit of the Serb-Croat-Slovene State: Conventions of 10/20 May 1923 (Martens, N.R.G.³, XXI, 691, 695), 11 October 1928 (*ibid.*, XXI, 708) and 17 March 1929 (*ibid.*, XXI, 710).

In Article 335 of the (abortive) Peace Treaty of Sèvres with Turkey of 10 August 1920 (*ibid.*, XII, 664) a number of Eastern ports were declared "ports of international concern", including the establishment of free zones in them. This declaration extended to the ports of Constantinople, from St. Stefano to Dolma Bagtchi, Haydar Paşa, Smyrna, Alexandretta, Haifa, Basra, Trebizond and Batum. As to Trebizond (Article 352), free access to the Black Sea by its port was accorded to the then planned sovereign State of Armenia, which would be granted a lease in perpetuity of an area in that port, to be placed under the general regime of free zones. As to Batum (Article 351), free access to the Black Sea was accorded to Georgia, Azerbaijan, Persia and Armenia. As to Smyrna (Article 350), Turkey herself would be accorded a lease in perpetuity of an area under the general regime of free zones. The regime laid down for those ports should not prejudice the territorial sovereignty of the State concerned and was defined in detail in Articles 336-345 under the headings Navigation, Dues and charges, Works, Free Zones (Articles 341-344) and Disputes. The Peace Treaty of Sèvres was, however, in 1923 replaced by that of Lausanne of 24 July 1923 (*ibid.*, XIII, 338), which no longer contained any corresponding provisions.

In another treaty of Sèvres of the same date relative to Thrace (*ibid.*, XII, 779) Bulgaria was ensured free access to the Ægean Sea and accorded a lease in perpetuity of a free zone in the port of Dedeagăç, which was to become Greek. This port was also declared a port of international concern. Comp. on this Articles 4-16 of the treaty. The latter Article provided for the forming of an International Commission charged with ensuring the execution of the regime of the port. This treaty of Sèvres was, subject to certain amendment, put into force by Protocol no. XVI of the Peace Treaty of Lausanne (*ibid.*, XIII, 448).

Specific ports situated at political nerve-centres have sometimes been endowed with an elaborate special regime. I cite as examples the ports of

Danzig: Article 104 of the Peace Treaty of Versailles, Article 18 and chapter III of the Convention of Paris between Poland and the Free City of 9 November 1920 (*ibid.*, XIV, 45), the Warsaw agreement of 24 October 1921 (*ibid.*, XVI, 135), and a further Convention of 3 May 1923 (*ibid.*, XVII, 236),

and of Tangier: Articles 40-43 of the Convention of Paris of 18 December 1923 (*ibid.*, XIII, 246), instituting a Port Commission. Comp. on the Tangier Zone Chapter V, section 7 *infra*, p. 488.

Mention must also be made of the Conference concerning Land-locked States of 1958 which preceded the first Conference on the Law of the Sea, and parts of whose conclusions were inserted in the Conventions adopted at this Conference. They were further worked out in a new Conference at New York which resulted in another Convention of 8 July 1965 on Transit Trade of Landlocked Countries (*U.N.T.S.*, vol. 597, p. 3). This long-winded Convention, preceded by a preamble reaffirming eight principles adopted by the U.N. Conference on Trade and Development, lays down on behalf of land-locked countries freedom of transit from and towards the sea, exempt from customs duties and special transit dues, and guarantees them further facilities (means of transport, tariffs, storage, free zones, etc.). See on this subject Cl. PALAZZOLI, *De quelques développements récents du droit des gens en matière d'accès à la mer des pays dépourvus de littoral* in *R.G.D.I.P.* 1966 (70), pp. 667-735.

The special case of free zones in ports was dealt with in Articles 8-11 of the Recommendations of the League of Nations Barcelona Conference of 20 April 1921 relative to ports placed under an international regime (comp. *League of Nations Barcelona Conference. Introduction and complete text of conventions and recommendations adopted*, Lausanne-Genève, 1921, pp. 68-72).

Even ports can serve political aims, as is apparent from the clause obtaining in Article 10 of the Soviet-Persian treaty of 26 February 1921 (Martens, N.R.G.³, XIII, 173) by which (*sub e*) the then R.S.F.S.R., "repudiating the tendencies of world imperialism", as practised by the Tsarist Government in the past, renounced all its rights to the port constructions of Enzeli on the Caspian Sea.

Maritime ports or their revenues have occasionally been given in pledge for the regular payment of State debts. Comp. on the port of Alexandria Part II of this publication, p. 396 and A. N. SACK, *Les effets des transformations des états sur leurs dettes publiques* . . . (Paris, 1927), p. 195.

The legal regime of maritime ports, with respect to which the Barcelona Conference of 1921 had already adopted a number of Recommendations, is since the Geneva Conference of 1923 defined on a multilateral basis in the Statute annexed to the Convention of 9 December 1923 (*ibid.*, XIX, 250).

The main provisions of this Statute on the International Regime of Maritime Ports, defined (Article 1) as "all ports which are normally frequented by seagoing vessels and used for foreign trade", are to the following effect.

Subject to reciprocity (8) there shall be equality of treatment between the State's own vessels, their cargoes and passengers, and those of any other State, in regard of freedom of access to, and use of, the port and full enjoyment of its benefits as regards navigation and commercial operation, including the allocation of berths, loading and unloading faculties, dues and charges (2). The latter must be published, just as must bye-laws (4). No discrimination as to custom duties on imports or exports may be made according to the flag flown, nor any other discrimination (reference is made to Articles 4, 20, 21 and 22 of the Railway Statute of Geneva) (5, 6). The Statute does not apply to the maritime coasting trade (9). Any State is free to arrange its towing and piloting services as it thinks fit; where the assistance of pilots is compulsory, the principle of equality again applies, save for a possibility of exemption in favour of technically expert subjects of the State of the port (10, 11). Certain restitutions apply to ships engaged in the transport of emigrants (12). The Statute applies to all ships, whether publicly or privately owned or controlled, with the exception of foreign warships and other foreign vessels exercising any kind of public authority (13), and of fishing vessels and their catch (14). The principle of equality can not be invoked in cases where a State has been granted special transit facilities by treaty (15). No transit need be allowed as regards passengers and goods whose entrance is prohibited (17). In emergency cases in which national safety or vital interests are involved deviation from the main Articles 2-7 is permitted for a period as short as possible (16). The Statute is not intended to deal with belligerents and neutrals in time of war, but even then it remains in force as far as possible (18). The contracting parties are under a general obligation to amend earlier treaties and to modify earlier concessions for the exploitation of maritime ports which are at variance with the Statute (19). Where greater facilities have been granted in the past these are not withdrawn by the Statute, nor will their grant be excluded in the future (20). Final provisions deal with the somewhat complicated modalities of a procedure for the solution of disputes (21, 22).

Free access to seaports does not extend to warships. Their access has always been and still is generally subject to specific conditions or restrictions as to previous notification, number and duration of stay. This subject is one that still typically belongs to the matters of domestic jurisdiction, since no binding general rule of treaty or customary law exists and every State is free to deal with it in the manner which it thinks fit. I will therefore confine myself to giving some examples of treaty provisions or of regulations adopted in this field by a few coastal States chosen at random.

Early peace treaties often laid down rules concerning the access of warships to the ports of the other party. Comp. for example: Article 26 of the Anglo-Netherlands treaty of Westminster of 5 April 1654 (Dumont, VI², 74) pursuant to which the maximum number of warships that would have free access was eight, and they were not allowed to remain in port longer than was necessary. A greater number would not be admitted without previous consent, unless it was a case of necessity.

When Spain by Article 22 of the treaty with Portugal of San Ildefonso of 1 October 1777 (Martens, R², II, 245) restored the island of Santa Catarina and the adjacent part of the South American continent to Portugal, the latter undertook in return not to admit foreign squadrons or warships—as, for that matter, foreign trading vessels—to the port of the island either in time of peace or of war; the undertaking was later mitigated by Article 5 of their Pardo Treaty of 1 March 1778 (*ibid.*, II, 612).

The rules on the admittance of foreign warships to Dutch ports have been issued by successive Royal Decrees. That of 2 February 1893 (*Staatsblad* no. 46) disposed that save in special circumstances no more than three warships of the same power should at the same time be within Netherlands territory; previous consent of the Minister of the Navy was required for the entry into specific inlets from the sea; warships were not allowed to stay in a port for more than a fortnight nor to return within thirty hours after their departure; special categories of warships were exempted from the restrictions (*e.g.*, those with a foreign sovereign on board); specific activities by foreign warships in the territorial waters were forbidden; they were liable to expulsion in the case of contravention to the rules; the Government reserved the right to enact further restrictions in case of war or danger of war, or for the maintenance of neutrality. —The rules of 1893 were replaced by those of 30 October 1909 (*ibid.*, no. 351), which were in their turn supplanted in the inter-war period by more up to date rules, of 2 June 1931 (*ibid.*, no. 237).

The legal scene changes completely in time of war. Apart from the antiquated "rule of the war of 1756" cited above p. 239, and the law of blockade, which both make navigation towards ports of a belligerent State risky for neutral trading vessels—rules belonging to the law of prize—, there is the law of neutrality proper which restricts the freedom of both belligerents and neutrals in respect of the entry, stay and departure of belligerent warships in neutral ports. This subject is regulated by Convention XII of the Second Hague Peace Conference of 18 October 1907 (Martens, N.R.G.³, III, 713).

The legal rules, it is often asserted, also change in the case of what is habitually called a pacific blockade, that is, an action undertaken by a State in time of peace against another State as a means of compulsion short of war, for the purpose of bringing pressure to bear upon the latter to comply with its obligations, or to stop illegal behaviour. It consists in an attempt to cut off one or more foreign ports by the stationing of one or more warships off the coast of the other party. It may be that the action is only directed against vessels of that party; in that case it is generally unopposed by third States. However, when it is also aimed at intercepting ships of third States, it is doubtful whether and to what extent such a pacific blockade is legally permitted. If it can be held to be to a certain extent allowable, then third States have in any case a claim that the blockade be notified in sufficient time in advance in order that their vessels can avoid sailing to the port(s) concerned, and that possible damage resulting from the blockade be compensated. Comp. on this type of blockade Part IX of this publication.

Section 5. ROADS AND RAILWAYS

As I have indicated in a short § 5 on Roads and Railways in Chapter II, I will now enter into a more detailed separate exposition of this subject in international law.

A. *Roads*

The construction of international roads has sometimes been preceded by elaborate inter-state conventions. A rather complicated case of international negotiation and regulation was, *e.g.*, that of the mountain roads dealt with in the Austro-Sardinian Convention of 20 May 1824 (Martens, N.R., VI, 446).

The parties to that convention undertook to repair and improve the roads over the San Bernardino and Splügen passes—the first task to be performed by Sardinia, the second by Austria with the consent of the Swiss Canton of Grisons to be applied for by Sardinia—and jointly to seek permission from the Canton of Ticino for Sardinia to repair and improve the road to Lumino, a permission which was granted by the latter Canton by a further convention of 7 September 1824 (*ibid.*, VI, 573) in the form of an undertaking by Ticino to build a new road itself, conditional upon Sardinia making a financial contribution.

Trade routes through Switzerland have, for that matter, already played an important rôle in early centuries when rival Cantons or towns strove for a monopoly and disputes were occasionally referred to arbitration.[81]

Very recent examples of international co-operation with the object of facilitating modern road traffic are the Italo-Swiss Convention of 23 May 1958 on the construction and operation of a road tunnel under the Grand-Saint-Bernard (*U.N.T.S.*, vol. 363, p. 81) and the Franco-Italian convention of 14 March 1953 for that of a combined autostrada and railway tunnel through the Mont Blanc (*U.N.T.S.*, vol. 284, p. 221).

The autostrada along the west coast of North America from Alaska through Canada to California is also famous. The project of the Great Pan American Highway to connect the Latin American countries on the eastward side from north to south across the Central American isthmus has not yet been fully realized (there is still a gap of 240 miles, called the Darién Gap, between Panamá and Colombia to be bridged); see, *e.g.*, Annex LXXIX to the Final Act of the 10th Inter-American Conference at Caracas, March 1954, charging the 6th Pan American Highway Congress with a study of how to finance the enterprise (*Compilation officielle*, Caracas, 1957, p. 101) and the O.A.S. study of 21 March 1969.

In the imperialist-colonialist era the construction of roads (just as of railways) has often played a part in the building-up of colonial empires or in facilitating the exploitation of their natural resources.

Thus, Great Britain, for the then Anglo-Egyptian Sudan, and Italy, in an exchange of notes of 14/20 December 1925 (Martens, N.R.G.[3], XVIII, 257), agreed upon a joint approach to Ethiopia with a view to bringing pressure to bear upon the latter to consent to the construction of a motor road from the frontier of the Sudan to Lake Tana with the object of facilitating the building and exploitation of a barrage there.

Ethiopia, in its turn, in an agreement with Italy of 2 August 1928 (Martens, N.R.G.[3], XXX, 334), allowed the latter to build an autostrada between Dessé and Assab, combined with the establishment of a free zone in the port of the latter town on the Red Sea, already annexed by Italy in 1882 (*ibid.*, N.R.G.[2], VIII, 511).

The political rôle of roads and other means of communication (such

---

81. Comp. E. Usteri, *Das öffentlich-rechtliche Schiedsgericht in der schweizerischen Eidgenossenschaft des 13.-15. Jahrhunderts* (Zürich, 1925).

as railways and telegraph and telephone lines) in the past was stressed and strongly denounced by the then Federal Socialist Republic of the Soviets of Russia in Article 10 of her treaty with Persia of 26 February 1921[82] in the following wording which is worth recalling in the light of later tendencies in Soviet policy vis-à-vis weaker countries in her usurped sphere of influence:

> "The Russian Federal Government, having abandoned the colonial policy, which consisted in the construction of roads and telegraph lines more in order to obtain military influence in other countries than for the purpose of developing their civilisations, and being desirous of providing the Persian people with those means of communication indispensable for the independence and development of any nation . . ."

The R.S.F.S.R. gratuitously renounced her rights, *inter alia*, to two main roads, constructed by Tsarist Russia, from Enzeli to Teheran and from Kazvin to Hamadan.

The main rôle which international roads have played in international law, at least in the past, is perhaps that of their use as march- and supply-routes for foreign troops.

> A well known example of such a military route servitude is that which was imposed upon Prussia by Article 16 of the Franco-Prussian Peace Treaty of Tilsit of 9 July 1807 (*ibid.*, R², VIII, 661) for the benefit of the kingdom of Saxony with the object of enabling the latter to establish and maintain unhampered communication for military transports between Saxony proper and her new acquisition, the duchy of Varsovia, created by Article 15, j.° 13 of the same treaty. As appears from the detailed elaboration of this servitude by the additional Franco-Prussian Convention of Elbing of 13 October 1807 (*ibid.*, VIII, 682, also—but in a different French version and under a wrong date—inserted *ibid.*, VIII, 646), it was fairly onerous for Prussia.

The establishment of military routes through foreign territory remained widespread and indeed necessary in a Germany politically organized in the German Bund from its inception in 1815 until well beyond the middle of the 19th century, owing to the fact that this confederation constituted a patchwork of often minute separate political entities. Hence a long series of "Durchmarsch- und Etappen-Konventionen" entered into in particular by Prussia with a large number of other member States, such as Saxe-Weimar (1816, 1830, 1837, 1847, *ibid.*, N.R., IV, 334; IX, 150; XIV, 604; X, 632), Lippe, Hesse-Darmstadt, Oldenburg and Hanover. Those *conventions d'étape* were as a rule very detailed.

> I refer, among many others, to the Convention between Prussia and Brunswick of 8 September 1835 (*ibid.*, N.R., XVI, 60), in which the parties laid

---

82. French translation from the Persian and Russian texts in Amedeo GIANNINI's *I documenti diplomatici della pace orientale* (Rome, 1922), series II, pp. 13 *et seq*. See also *L.N.T.S.*, vol. 9, p. 383.

down not only a specification of the main and secondary roads to be used, the contracts between the governments and with the local authorities concerned, the setting-up of special Brunswick "Etappenbehörden", the difference in treatment of smaller and bigger detachments, the conditions of the quartering of troops on the inhabitants for the night, the tariffs of payments for services rendered and their liquidation, the particulars of the requisitioning of means of conveyance and of forage, but also such further details as the menu for meals of officers and men, with coffee, but without beer, the stabling of horses, provision for cases of illness, the supply of (voluntary) guides, the manner of settlement of possible disputes, and many more.

Even as late as 1865 Prussia still expressly maintained, in Article 4 of her treaty of Gastein with Austria of 14 August 1865 (Martens, N.R.G.[1], XVIII, 2) concerning a provisional division of the Elbe duchies of Schleswig and Holstein, held by the two States in common pursuant to their Peace Treaty with Denmark (Berlin, 1864), her right to two military routes *(Militär-Heerstrassen)* through the duchy of Holstein from Lübeck to Kiel and from Hamburg to Rendsburg.

> Similar arrangements were made in other parts of the world. See, for example, Article 4 of the secret treaty of 28 November 1844 between Austria, Lucca, Modena, Sardinia and Tuscany (comp. *ibid.*, N.R.G.[1], XII, 425 and XV, 5), providing for the construction by Tuscany of a road to be open not only for travellers and the transport of merchandise, but also for the marching of troops between Massa and the territory of Garfagnana.

When the enlarged Kingdom of The Netherlands of 1814/1815 was finally dismembered by the treaties of 19 April 1839 (*ibid.*, N.R., XVI, 770, 773 and 788), Belgium was, by Article 12, granted the right to demand from The Netherlands that, should she in the future construct a road or a canal through her own territory to the river Meuse opposite the Netherlands canton of Sittard (Limburg), such a road or canal be carried on across that canton to reach the German frontier. This potential road or canal burden on Netherlands territory was, however, expressly abrogated by a joint declaration made on the occasion of the exchange of the ratifications, on 18 June 1873, of a new Netherlands-Belgian treaty of 13 January 1873 (*ibid.*, N.R.G.[2], II, 1 and 3) whereby Belgium was granted the right to build instead of a road or canal a railway through the same province, but at another point (Roermond), to connect Antwerp with Gladbach. Comp. *sub* B (Railways) below, at p. 255.

Another road, in Central America, is famous for its political and legal importance, namely, that once planned between the capital of Guatemala and the Atlantic coast near Belize. It has never been in fact built, but it was projected in Article 7 of the "boundary treaty", *alias* treaty of cession, between Guatemala and Great Britain of 30 April 1859 (*ibid.*, N.R.G.[3], XXVI, 45). Its construction was intended to serve as a compensation to Guatemala for the abandonment of her territorial rights to British Honduras or Belize; the failure of Great Britain to fulfil her

obligation in respect of the construction of the road, jointly with Guatemala, is the main argument of the latter State for denying the continued
binding force of the 1859 treaty.

On the rôle of roads in the delimitation of State frontiers see the
particulars given in Chapter VI below, pp. 515-516 and 535-536.

B. *Railways*

Although the history of railways in international law has only commenced
in the late thirties of the 19th century when this new means of conveyance,
inaugurated in England in the 'twenties, began to cross State frontiers,
first within the German Confederation of 1815 and soon afterwards on
the international level proper, the number of bilateral and multilateral
treaties concerning railways is much greater than that concerning international roads.

> The first conventions of the confederal type dated from 10 January 1838 and
> related to the construction of railways between the rivers Main and Neckar
> (Baden-Frankfurt-Hesse Darmstadt, Martens, N.R., XV, 351) and between
> Frankfurt and Offenbach (Frankfurt-Hesse Darmstadt, *ibid.*, XV, 354). They
> were soon followed by a number of others in the 1840's (*ibid.*, N.R.G.[1], II,
> 31, 385; IV, 660—an, at that time still confederal, railway from Vienna via
> Prague to Dresden—; V, 467; VI, 530; VIII, 619, 626; XI, 407).
>
> Meanwhile, they had begun to cross the frontiers of the German Bund, with
> Belgium (a special type of Convention between the Belgian Government and
> the German *Société rhénane de chemins de fer* of Cologne of 18 October 1839,
> *ibid.*, N.R., XVI, 1003, supplemented 28 April 1840, *ibid.*, N.R.G.[1], I, 56,
> for the purchase of 4,000 shares in an enterprise to connect Belgium with the
> Rhine via Aachen); towards Denmark (two conventions of 8 November
> 1841, *ibid.*, N.R.G.[1], IX, 511 and 513: connection Berlin-Hamburg on the
> right bank of the Elbe via Danish Lauenburg), and so on.
>
> A few years later France, Belgium and Germany already deemed it neces-
> sary to issue common rules in the field of customs control on their frontier-
> crossing railways (Règlement of 8 October 1848, *ibid.*, N.R.G.[1], XI, 474).

More and more railway connections between neighbouring countries
called for an increasing number of bilateral treaties, first in Europe,
later also in America, Asia and Africa, either for the construction of
railway lines in common, or for unilateral concessions to build them, or
for simple junctions *(raccordements)*.

The most common type of international railway convention is that
providing for the junction of two existing national railroads or networks
across the boundary, or for the construction of a new frontier-crossing
line, sometimes through a boundary tunnel. Agreements of this kind are
so numerous that only a few of them will be cited here in order to facilitate consultation of their usual contents.

Europe.
Austria Hungary-Serbia, 9 April 1880 (Martens, N.R.G.[2], VI, 366), in
execution of an obligation assumed at the Congress of Berlin, 1878 (Buda-

pest-Belgrade-Niš, with further connections with Turkey and Bulgaria);
Germany-Luxembourg, 21 July 1883 (*ibid.*, X, 446) between St. Vith and
Ulflingen;
Serbia-Turkey, 4 June 1887 (*ibid.*, XVI, 572);
Austria Hungary-Russia via the Bucovina, 14 January 1893 (*ibid.*, XX,
416);
Russia-Germany, 6 December 1904 (*ibid.*, XXXII, 374 = XXXV, 486);
France-Spain through the Pyrenees, 18 August 1904 (*ibid.*, N.R.G.³, I,
209), with additional protocols of 8 March 1905 (*ibid.*, I, 213) and 15 April
1908 (*ibid.*, IV, 249);
Switzerland-Italy, 12 November 1908 (*ibid.*, XIV, 479), the Centovalli
line from Locarno to Domodossola;
France-Switzerland, two conventions of 16 December 1908 (*ibid.*, V, 302
and 305), the first relating to the Martigny-Chamonix railway, the second to
that between Nyon and Divonne-les-Bains;
Sweden-Finland, 28 June 1924 (*ibid.*, XXIV, 872);
Italy-San Marino, 26 March 1927 (*ibid.*, XXX, 426);
Norway-Sweden, 19 November 1927 (*ibid.*, XXIX, 887).

Comp. for other continents:

America.
Argentina-Bolivia, 30 June 1894 (*ibid.*, N.R.G.³, VI, 293) and 11 December 1902 (*ibid.*, VI, 296); 18 May 1907 (*ibid.*, VI, 774); 17 June 1913 (*ibid.*,
X, 272);
Bolivia-Brazil, Article 7 of a treaty of delimitation of 17 November 1903
(*ibid.*, N.R.G.³, III, 62); protocol of 28 December 1912 (*ibid.*, IX, 511);
Bolivia-Chile, Article 3 of the peace treaty of 20 October 1904 (*ibid.*,
N.R.G.³, II, 174); 27 June 1905 (*ibid.*, VI, 603); 26 May 1908 (*ibid.*, VI,
609). Comp. on the particulars of the latter two railways below, p. 254.
See also the plans for the construction of:
an inter-oceanic railroad across the isthmus, contemplated by Guatemala
and Honduras in Article 24 of their treaty of 12 September 1885 (*ibid.*,
N.R.G.², XIV, 268);
a Pan American Railroad, discussed at the 4th Conference of July-August
1910 at Buenos Aires (*A.J.I.L.* 1910 (IV), pp. 777-793 and referred to by
STRUPP, *Urkunden zur Geschichte des Völkerrechts* (Gotha, 1911), II, pp. 114
et seq., *sub* II and XIX).
Asia.
Russia-China, the Manchurian or Chinese Eastern Railway, linking the
Russian Transbaikal line with the Ussuri railway (1896). See for further
particulars concerning this railway below, p. 269.
Railways radiating inland from the various European colonies or lease
areas on the coast of China. See for further data below, p. 271.
See for the Baghdad railway (1899) below, p. 266.
Caucasus railroads, Soviet Russia-Armenia-Azerbaijan-Georgia-Turkey,
convention of 9 July 1922 (Martens, N.R.G.³, XXII, 91).
Africa.
United Kingdom (for the Sudan)-Ethiopia, Article 5 of the boundary
treaty of 15 May 1902 (*ibid.*, N.R.G.³, II, 826) for the construction of a
railway through Abyssinian territory to connect the Sudan with Uganda;
Portugal (for Mozambique)-Great Britain (for Transvaal), 1 April 1909
(*ibid.*, IV, 885) concerning, *inter alia*, their railways, renewed 31 March 1923
(*ibid.*, XVII, 228);

France (for Morocco)-Spain, 27 November 1912, Article 9 and annexed Protocol, concerning the construction of a railroad between Fez and Tangier (*ibid.*, VII, 323, 333).

However, the need for multilateral regulation of matters of common concern grew and led to the conclusion of a series of collective conventions,[83] dealing with such subjects as
the sealing of railway trucks subject to customs inspection:

Final Protocol of 15 May 1886 (*ibid.*, N.R.G.[2], XXII, 42), amended 18 May 1907 (*Unité technique*) (*ibid.*, N.R.G.[3], II, 878);

the conditions of the transportation of goods, passengers and luggage by rail:

Conferences of May/June 1878, September/October 1881 and July 1886 (*ibid.*, N.R.G.[2], XIII, 3, 139 and 380 *et seq.*), followed by the multilateral Convention of 14 October 1890 (*ibid.*, XIX, 289), setting up a common Bureau at Berne, and a number of additional agreements: 20 September 1893 (*ibid.*, XXII, 517), 16 July 1895 (*ibid.*, XXIV, 562), 16 June 1898 (*ibid.*, XXX, 184) and 19 September 1906 (*ibid.*, N.R.G.[3], III, 920). The Convention of 1890 was replaced, pursuant to the intentions made known by Article 366 of the Peace Treaty of Versailles (1919), by two parallel Conventions of 23 October 1924, respectively for goods and for travellers and their luggage (*ibid.*, XIX, 476 and 558); Annex I to the first of these two Conventions was later replaced by a Convention of October 1932 (*ibid.*, XXX, 783);

the technical standardization of railways (gauge, construction of the rolling-stock, state of upkeep, conditions of loading):

Agreement of 15 May 1886 (comp. Article 282, *sub* 4°, of the Peace Treaty of Versailles);

the use of railway carriages in common:

an intra-German affair, Convention of 21 November 1908 (*ibid.*, N.R.G.[3], II, 925).

More recently the international regime of railways has been made the object of multilateral treaty regulation. The first steps were taken at the first General Conference on Communications and Transit assembled at Barcelona under the auspices of the League of Nations in March/April 1921, and resulted in the adoption by the participating States of a set of seven recommendations for the facilitation of the international transport of goods and of passengers and luggage over the railways under their

83. With regard to one of those conventions, *viz.*, that concerning the Eurofima (20 October 1955; *U.N.T.S.*, vol. 378, p. 159), it must be remarked that this is an association of a type quite different from that created in 1890 with its Permanent Bureau at Berne. This Eurofima is in fact an association of a private law nature, set up by a great number of railway administrations with the object of financing under favourable conditions the common purchase and resale to its members of rolling-stock. It has its statutory seat at Geneva.

253

sovereignty or authority without discrimination, *inter alia*, with regard to the tariffs, according to the nationality of the passengers, or the owner- ship or commercial origin or destination of the goods, and for the recip- rocal utilization and exchange of their rolling-stock (see for their text the League of Nations publication *Official Instruments approved by the Conference*, under no. 7). The subject was later discussed in more detail at the second General Conference at Geneva in November/December 1923, which adopted a Statute on the International Regime of Railways annexed to a Convention of 9 December 1923 (text: Martens, N.R.G.[3], XIX, 214).

This Statute on the International Regime of Railways can be char- acterized as a codification of the minimum requirements for a well- regulated system of international railway traffic, as had already been laid down earlier in a large number of mostly bilateral conventions. It deals in six Parts successively with the interchange of international traffic by rail (junction of international lines; working arrangements for international traffic); reciprocity in the use of rolling stock and technical uniformity; relations between the railway and its users; tariffs; financial arrangements between railway administrations in the interest of inter- national traffic, and ends with a number of general subjects (cases of emergency and other extraordinary circumstances; the settlement of disputes, etc.).

In the course of that arrangement of subject matters of inter-state regulation, concerning both passengers and goods transport, attention is further paid to the construction of new lines, common frontier stations, time tables, through trains or carriages, standardization, through con- tracts, etc.

The construction of railways

The circumstances under which the construction of a railway was decided upon sometimes presented unusual features. Thus it happened by way of exception that a State undertook, as a *quid pro quo*, to construct a railway for the benefit of another State, for example in the cases, already mentioned above, of Brazil vis-à-vis Bolivia—Article 7 of their boundary treaty of 17 November 1903 (Martens, N.R.G.[3], III, 62)— and of Chile vis-à-vis Bolivia—Article III of their Peace Treaty of 20 October 1904 (*ibid.*, II, 174), with an executive Convention of 27 June 1905 (*ibid.*, VI, 603) and an additional Protocol of 26 May 1908 (*ibid.*, VI, 609).

The engagement entered into by Brazil to construct a railway on her territory between the port of San Antonio on the river Madeira and Guajaramerín on the river Mamoré, with an embranchment to the confluence of the rivers Beni and Mamoré, is explained by the fact that a new boundary delimitation to which Bolivia consented was so favourable to Brazil that the latter was prepared to construct that railway in return.

The final loss by Bolivia of her coastal provinces, occupied since 1884 by Chile, in 1904 was in part compensated by an undertaking by Chile to build at her cost a railway to connect her new Pacific port of Arica with el Alto de la Paz, and moreover, to assume a limited guarantee of the financial obligations which Bolivia might assume within the next thirty years for the construction of five more railways. The ownership of the section of the Arica-La Paz railway to be constructed on Bolivian territory was to be transferred to Bolivia at the expiry of fifteen years.

Another undertaking of the same type is that of Portugal vis-à-vis the United Kingdom for the construction of a railway between Pungwe and the British sphere of influence, Article 14 of their convention of 11 June 1891 (*ibid.*, N.R.G.², XVIII, 185).

Third States have occasionally facilitated the building of new railways by making a financial contribution.

A recent example of such an arrangement is that between the Chinese People's Republic, Zambia and Tanzania of 5 September 1967 (*The Times* of 6 September 1967) by which the former undertakes to pay £ 100.000.000 for the construction of a railway between the latter two countries in order to avoid transit via Rhodesia to Mozambique.

On other occasions a State granted to another the right to construct a railway across its territory inland or to a third State: the case, already mentioned earlier under Canals and Roads, at p. 250, of a railway for the benefit of Belgium across the Netherlands province (then "duchy") of Limburg, with the object of connecting Antwerp with Gladbach in Germany, treaty of 13 January 1873 (*ibid.*, N.R.G.², II, 1).—Comp. also the Treaty between France and the principality of Monaco of 2 February 1861 (*ibid.*, N.R.G.¹, XVII², 55), Article 5 (2): construction of a railway from Nice to Genova across the principality, and the Convention of 26 March 1927 (*ibid.*, N.R.G.³, XXX, 224) for the facilitation of railway traffic between Germany and Poland across the territory of the Free City of Danzig.

Similar concessions have also been granted, *e.g.*, in the following colonial cases:

between the Sudan and Uganda through Ethiopia, convention between Great Britain and Ethiopia of 15 May 1902 (*ibid.*, N.R.G.³, II, 826), Article 5;

reciprocally between two separated French zones of influence *inter se* across a German zone, and *vice versa*: Franco-German Convention of 4 November 1911 concerning Equatorial Africa (*ibid.*, N.R.G.³, V, 651), Article 7: Germany will not object to the building of a railway through the Congo Zipfel and the Ubanghi Zipfel between Gabon and Central

Congo and between the latter and the river Ubanghi-Shari, nor will France object to the continuation of the Cameroon railway from the coast to Brazzaville via the French zone (comp. Article 13); Article 8 (3): corresponding provision relative to a (road or) railway between Benoué and Logone north or south of the Mayo-Kebi.

The projected construction of a railway between Uganda and Tanganyika has led to an alteration of the boundary between the Belgian and British zones in the Mandated Territory of Ruanda: correspondence of April-September 1923 (*ibid.*, N.R.G.³, XV, 232 *et seq.*).

Again another variant is the right granted by State A to State B to build a particular stretch of a projected railway line over A's territory for the technical reason that geographic conditions prevent its construction entirely over B's own territory.

> A complicated example of such a situation was contemplated in Article 5 of the Franco-British Convention of 23 December 1920 on certain points connected with the Mandates for Syria and the Lebanon, Palestine and Mesopotamia (*ibid.*, N.R.G.³, XII, 582). The frontier was to run from Nasib on the Hedjaz Railway to Semakh on the southern shore of Lake Tiberias through the valley of the Yarmuk—which was in principe to remain in the territory under the French Mandate to the North—as closely as possible to the south of that railway in such a manner as to allow the construction in the same valley of another railway, entirely situated in the territory under the British Mandate to the South (Article 1). Should even a readjustment of the frontier thus drawn (as foreseen in Article 5(3) of the Convention) fail to make it possible to construct a parallel British railway in the valley entirely within the limits of the areas under the British Mandate, then that second railway would be allowed in certain places to enter the territory under French Mandate, in which case the French Government should recognize the full and complete extraterritoriality of the British section which had thus come to be located in the territory under the French Mandate (Article 5(4) of the Convention).

Uncommon form of exploitation or use of a railway

A State may grant to another State, or to the public railway administration of another State, the right to exploit a railway line within its territory.

> Thus Luxembourg, by a Convention of 11 November 1902 (*ibid.*, N.R.G.², XXXI, 436), consented to the exploitation of the Luxembourg section of the Guillaume-Luxembourg railway by the Imperial General Directorate of the Railways of Alsace-Lorraine. An express provision in Article 2 of this Convention prohibited the transport of troops, arms, war material and ammunition on this section of the line, a clause which was, of course, violated by Germany in 1914, together with the neutrality of Luxembourg herself. Germany was later, by Article 40 of the Peace Treaty of Versailles of 28 June 1919, deprived of the benefit of the provisions inserted in her favour in the 1902 Convention.

A convention may provide for the joint use of railway tracks, or for the common administration of regional railways.

256

In Article 5, § 1 of her agreement of 23 December 1920 with Great Britain (*ibid.*, XII, 582), France agreed to facilitate by a liberal arrangement the joint use of the section of the existing railway between the Lake of Tiberias and Nasib.

Germany and Poland set up a common administration of the Upper-Silesian railway system, in order to remedy the unfortunate consequences of the partition of Upper Silesia, 23 February 1924 (*ibid.*, XXII, 163).

By a Soviet-Chinese Convention of 14 August 1945 (*U.N.T.S.*, vol. 10, p. 300) agreement was reached on the joint use of the Tchang-Tchun railway for a period of thirty years.

As was sometimes the case of roads, it also occasionally happened that a State allowed another to use a railway for the transportation of troops and of war material across its territory.

Because of her status of permanent neutrality a very cautious attitude was taken by Switzerland in her agreement with the Grand-Duchy of Baden of 29 August/4 September 1899, in connection with earlier provisions (of 1852, 1867 and 1898) on military transports over the Baden-Rhine Valley railway Basel-Schaffhausen-Konstanz across Swiss territory: the passage of armed men was to remain limited to the number of thirty (*ibid.*, N.R.G.², XXX, 269).

By Article 13 of their above-mentioned Convention of 4 November 1911 concerning Equatorial Africa (*ibid.*, N.R.G.³, V, 651) France and Germany promised each other in advance freedom to transport troops over the railways which they authorized each other to build across their own zone of influence.

In the Middle East stipulations on the subject of military transports were made in Article 5(2) and (4) of the Franco-British Convention of 23 December 1920, just mentioned, and subsequently confirmed by a new Anglo-French agreement on Palestine and Syria/Lebanon of 7 March 1923 (*ibid.*, N.R.G.³, XVII, 208, 209), in respect of both the old Hedjaz railway through the Yarmuk valley in Syria and the possible frontier-crossing stretches of the new railway line which Great Britain might build in that same valley.

A similar right, *in casu* to use sections of the Baghdad Railway for the carriage of troops and war material, was reciprocally granted to their opposite number by France (for Syria) and Turkey in their agreement of Ankara of 20 October 1921 (*ibid.*, N.R.G.³, XII, 826), confirmed by Article 3, 1° of the Peace Treaty of Lausanne of 24 July 1923 (*ibid.*, N.R.G.³, XIII, 342).

Pursuant to Article 10(2) of that agreement of 1921

"La Turquie aura le droit de faire ses transports militaires par chemin de fer de Meidan-Ekbes à Tchoban-Bey dans la région syrienne, et la Syrie aura le droit de faire ses transports militaires par chemin de fer de Tchoban-Bey jusqu'à Nousseibine dans le territoire turc".

The British Government objected to the contents of the Franco-Turkish agreement, *inter alia*, on the ground of this freedom for Turkey to transport troops over the French section of the Baghdad railway from Konia to Nusaybin (comp. *Correspondence* between the two Governments in a British White Paper *Turkey, No. 1 (1922)* [Cmd. 1570]), but its objections were unsuccessful.

Minor or more *technical interests*, which likewise require regulation, are for example:

the designation of two, or at a later stage one "international station" on a frontier-crossing line—

> separate stations of Modane and Ventimiglia on the Franco-Italian Riviera railway, Convention of 20 January 1879 (*ibid.*, N.R.G.², VI, 470); joint internatial frontier stations, *inter alia*, of Predeal, on certain railroads connecting Hungary and Romania, Convention of 14 March 1891, with a provisional declaration of the same date (*ibid.*, XVIII, 823 and 832);

the establishment of a custom office or a sanitary control service on neighbouring territory—

> Germany on Swiss soil in the Badener Bahnhof in Basel, Conventions of 7 August 1873 and 3 June 1886 (*ibid.*, N.R.G.², I, 243 and XIV, 329);

the exemption of rolling-stock from any act of seizure—

> Austro-German agreement of 17 March 1887 (*ibid.*, N.R.G.², XII, 303);

the fixation of tariffs—

> Article 10 of the new Swiss-German-Italian Gothard Convention of 13 October 1909 (*ibid.*, N.R.G.³, VIII, 195), amended by a series of subsequent conventions between 1 July 1918 (*ibid.*, XII, 310) and 26 July 1930 (*ibid.*, XXVIII, 477);

the recruitment of railway staff on each other's territory—

> Franco-British Convention of 23 December 1920, mentioned above, Article 7, by which the parties undertook to put no obstacle in their respective mandatory areas in the way of the recruitment of railway staff for any section of the Hedjaz railway.

Equality of treatment

The principle of equality of treatment in railway matters was sanctioned in the Franco-German Conventions of 4 November 1911 (*ibid.*, N.R.G.³, V, 643 and 651): Article 6 of the Convention concerning Morocco, prescribing a system of public tender for the construction of new railway lines, and Article 14 of that concerning Equatorial Africa as to the conditions of transport of persons and goods on the railways.

Railways given in pledge

Railways have sometimes been given in pledge for international loans and subsequently been run by a creditors organization. This has been the case of the railroads of Egypt in 1877 and of Bulgaria in 1892.[84]

---

84. Comp. Part II of this publication, at p. 396 and A.-N. SACK, *Les effets des transformations des états sur leurs dettes publiques etc.*, Paris, 1927, vol. I, p. 195.

After Peru's bankruptcy in 1884 as a consequence of the War of the Pacific a creditors organization was set up in 1890 in the shape of the (mainly British) Peruvian Corporation which, in return for their consent to the cancellation of Peru's public debt, obtained control over the national railways for a period of sixty years.

Nationalization or (re)purchase of railways

Other international agreements contain provisions concerning the right of the territorial sovereign to nationalize a railway, to (re)purchase or rescind a concession, or to regulate the procedure and/or the legal consequences of such operations.

Austria's right of "devolution" respecting the railways existing in her Lombardo-Venetian Kingdom which was transferred to Sardinia by Articles 10(2,3) and 11 of their Peace Treaty of Zürich of 10 November 1859 (Martens, N.R.G.,[1] XVI[2], 531).

Netherlands-Belgian conventions of 31 October 1879 dealing, *inter alia*, with the transfer to the Netherlands of the Dutch section of the railway line from Antwerp to the Hollands Diep, with a branch line from Roosendaal to Breda, thus far run and owned by a private Belgian company (*ibid.*, N.R.G.[2], VIII, 152) and of 23 April 1897 concerning the repurchase of the railway from Tilburg to Turnhout, mentioned in a dissenting opinion joined to the Judgment of the International Court of Justice of 20 June 1959 in the *case of Certain Plots of Land* (*I.C.J. Reports* 1959, at p. 247).

In 1883 the South African Republic and Portugal concluded a treaty giving Portugal the right to build a railway from Lourenço Marques to the Transvaal. Portugal subsequently gave a concession to an international company including American and British shareholders, to construct the said railway. In 1889 she rescinded the concession and nationalized the railway. This gave rise to an arbitration between her and the United States and Great Britain, acting in virtue of their right of diplomatic protection of the shareholders of the concessionary company, before the "Arbitral Tribunal of the Delagoa", composed of three Swiss lawyers, at Bern. The amount of compensation due was fixed at more than 15 millions Swiss francs: final award of 29 March/30 May 1900 in Martens, N.R.G.[2], XXX, 329-421.

Belgo-German Convention of 15 April 1897 (Martens, N.R.G.[2], XXV, 337) concerning the contemplated nationalization by Belgium of certain railways until then run by the Grand Central Belge, in particular the Aachen-Maastricht line, situated mainly on Netherlands territory.

Treaty between Austria-Hungary and Saxony of 26 April 1904 for the taking-over of a private railway by the latter (*ibid.*, N.R.G.[3], I, 202).

Russo-Turkish and Russo-Bulgarian protocols of 3 March/20 April and 19 April 1909 for the settlement of the financial obligations of Bulgaria arising from her seizure of the *Chemins de Fer Orientaux* after her declaration of independence (*ibid.*, N.R.G.[3], IV, 54 and 56).

The nationalization (*rachat*, *Verstaatlichung*) of the St. Gothard railway by Switzerland on 1 May 1909 made the conclusion of a new Convention between Germany, Italy and Switzerland necessary: see their Convention of 13 October 1909, with note of 22 March 1913, in Martens, N.R.G.[3], VIII,

259

195, 206, replacing their earlier treaties of 15 October 1869 (*ibid.*, N.R.G.[1], XIX, 90), 28 October 1871 (*ibid.*, 103), 12 March 1878 (*ibid.*, N.R.G.[2], IV, 676) and 16 June 1879 (*ibid.*, 680).

On the repurchase of the Chinese Eastern railway by China from the Soviet Union by their Convention of 31 May 1924, see below *sub* (*c*), (ii), p. 273.

A further financial problem arose from the nationalization in 1957 of the railway, with accessories, of the Antofagasta (Chile-Bolivia) Railway Company. As this railway failed to prosper under Bolivian management and in 1961 was on the brink of total collapse, the old British management of the said Company was again called in to straighten out its affairs. They accepted the invitation subject to a promise of £ 2,5 million compensation to the Company's shareholders, a promise which, however, was not fulfilled. When, in 1967, the railway was again on the verge of collapse, the World Bank announced that it was prepared to lend Bolivia the sum of at least three millions which was needed for the urgent replacement of rolling-stock and track, but on the condition that the Bolivian Government "can show good title to the railway", *i.e.* only after an arrangement to pay the compensation promised (*The Sunday Times*, 9 April 1967).

Other financial adjustments

Financial matters relating to railways also often called for international adjustment:

Franco-Tunisian Convention of 15 March 1910 (Martens, N.R.G.[3], VI, 908) for the distribution of the burden of a financial guarantee in aid of a private railway network in Tunisia over the Contracting Parties;
   Protocol between Greece and the Serb-Croat-Slovene Kingdom of 17 March 1929 (*ibid.*, XXI, 740) concerning the settlement of financial claims pertinent to the Saloniki-Gevgelia railway;
   Greco-Spanish agreement of 11 July 1932 (*ibid.*, XXX, 357) giving the Spanish bondholders the benefit of a convention for the reorganization of the service of the debentures of the Saloniki-Monastir railway, concluded on 10 March 1932 between the Hellenic Government and the National Association of French Bondholders.

The legal status of railways in time of war

The fate of railway material in time of war is governed, as between belligerents, by Article 53 of the Regulations concerning the laws and customs of land warfare, annexed to Convention IV of The Hague of 10 October 1907, and as between belligerents and neutral powers by Article 19 of Convention V of the same date concerning the rights and duties of neutral powers and persons in the case of land warfare, according to which:

"Le matériel des chemins de fer provenant du territoire de Puissances neutres, qu'il appartienne à ces Puissances ou à des sociétés ou personnes privées, et reconnaissable comme tel, ne pourra être réquisitionné et utilisé par un belligérant que dans le cas et la mesure où l'exige une impérieuse nécessité. Il sera renvoyé aussitôt que possible dans le pays d'origine.

Le Puissance neutre pourra de même, en cas de nécessité, retenir et utiliser, jusqu'à due concurrence, le matériel provenant du territoire de la Puissance belligérante.

Une indemnité sera payée de part et d'autre, en proportion du matériel utilisé et de la durée de l'utilisation''.

Railways have on a few occasions formed the object of Advisory Opinions or Judgments of the Permanent Court of International Justice, namely, those of

3 March 1928 (*Publications P.C.I.J.*, series B, No. 15), relating to pecuniary claims of Danzig railway officials against the Polish Railways administration (see my *The Jurisprudence of the World Court*, vol. I, pp. 136 *et seq.*);

15 October 1931 (series A/B, No. 42), concerning railway traffic between Lithuania and Poland (*loco cit.*, vol. I, pp. 270 *et seq.*); and

30 June 1938 and 28 February 1939, regarding the Panevezys-Saldutiskis railway, mentioned below.

Many of these matters are too technical or of too little importance to be dealt with here in detail, and the conventions concerned are only mentioned to serve as examples of the different types of international regulation required and as a means of orientation in the subject. I will therefore confine myself in the further text mainly to expatiating a little on three subjects of major interest, viz. (*a*) the effect of territorial changes on the regime of railways, (*b*) the legal history and regime of one of the main international railway lines (through the Saint-Gothard), and (*c*) the role of railways in imperialist politics in general and, in particular, the legal-diplomatic history of a couple of famous "political" railway systems.

(a) *Railways in case of cession or the dismemberment of a State*

Railways may be seriously affected by the dismemberment of States. One of the most complicated examples is the case of the West-Russian railway system which was disrupted after World War I and the Bolshevik revolution by the emergence of three new independent Baltic States. A dispute between Estonia and Lithuania, caused by this disruption, was brought before the Permanent Court of International Justice in 1937, but was shipwrecked there in 1939 (Judgment of 28 February 1939, *Publications P.C.I.J.*, series A/B, No. 76) on certain preliminary objections, set out elsewhere (comp. on this Judgment my *The Jurisprudence of the World Court*, vol. I, pp. 554 *et seq.*).

Many other examples of railway communications, intersected by new State frontiers in earlier or more recent years, can be cited from other parts of the world.

Article 10 of the Peace Treaty of Zürich of 10 November 1859 between Austria, France and Sardinia (Martens, N.R.G.[1], XVI[2], 531) confirmed

261

the existing concessions for railways in Lombardy after its cession to Sardinia.

Article 12 of the Austro-Italian Peace Treaty of Vienna of 3 October 1866 (*ibid.*, N.R.G.[1], XVIII, 405), by which Austria acquiesced in the reunion (via a transitional cession of Venice to France by a Convention of 24 August 1866, *ibid.*, XVIII, 414) of the Lombardo-Venetian Kingdom with the Kingdom of Italy, provided for a corresponding administrative and economic separation of the Venetian and Austrian railway networks. This provision was not, however, finally implemented until ten years later, by a treaty of 29 February 1876, with two supplementary declarations, of the same date and of 13 August 1876 (*ibid.*, N.R.G.[2], II, 357).

By Article 16 of the Franco-German treaty of Frankfurt of 11 December 1871, additional to the Peace Treaty (*ibid.*, N.R.G.[1], XX, 847), Germany was substituted for France in the rights and obligations resulting from a number of railway concessions, *inter alia*, concerning the railways from Colmar to Munster and to the Rhine, subject as to some others to negotiations concerning the concession clauses.

The emancipation of Bulgaria[85] and Serbia since the Congress of Berlin of 1878 made it necessary to provide for their substitution in the rights and obligations of the Sublime Porte *vis-à-vis* certain railway companies and Austria-Hungary, and for the construction of a number of new railway junctions. See Articles 10 (Bulgaria) and 38 (Serbia) of the main treaty of 13 July 1878 (*ibid.*, N.R.G.[2], III, 449) and the quadrupartite Convention of 9 May 1883 (*ibid.*, IX, 720) which contained detailed provisions on various subjects connected with the change in the situation (*tracés* of the new junction railways, their technical uniformity, non-discrimination, tariffs, direct and indirect connections with other States of Europe, sanitary and customs regulations, etc.).

New corresponding arrangements were necessary at the close of the Balkan Wars. Comp. Article 16 and Annex IV, Protocol No. 1 (relating to the Oriental railways) of the Bulgaro-Turkish Peace Treaty of Constantinople of 29 September 1913 (*ibid.*, N.R.G.[3], VIII, 78); Article 14 of the Greco-Turkish Peace Treaty of Athens of 14 November 1913 concerning the same railways and those between Saloniki-Monastir and Saloniki-Dedeağç (*ibid.*, VIII, 93); and Article 11 of the Serbo-Turkish

85. The rights and obligations of the Porte with regard to the railways in Eastern Roumelia were still entirely maintained (Article 21). The whole of the outstanding railway debts of Bulgaria on account of the Ruschuk-Varna line and her part of the network of the *Compagnie des Chemins de fer Orientaux* were after her declaration of independence in 1908 finally settled, after intervention of Russia, by a Turco-Bulgarian Protocol of 19 April 1909 (Articles 1 and 7) (Martens, N.R.G.[3], IV, 57), a direct Arrangement with the *Compagnie des Chemins de fer Orientaux* of 26 June 1909 (*ibid.*, IV, 61) and a Russo-Turkish declaration of 21 December 1909 (Articles 3 and 4) (*ibid.*, IV, 54).

Peace Treaty of Constantinople of 14 March 1914 (*ibid.*, VIII, 643) relative to the Oriental and Saloniki-Monastir railways.

The dismemberment of the Austro-Hungarian Monarchy in 1918 entailed the disruption of a vast railway system which necessitated special regulations, comprising the laying down of new working conditions, the establishment of new frontier stations, the operation of the line between those stations and, in particular, the reorganization, with the object of ensuring their continued regular utilization, of the railroads of the former Dual Monarchy, owned by private companies, which came to be situated in the territory of more than one State.

> Comp. on this matter Articles 319 and 320 of the Peace Treaty of St.-Germain (1919) and Articles 302-304 of the Peace Treaty of Trianon (1920), Articles 2(*sub* 4) and 3 (*sub* 2) of the Treaty of Sèvres of 10 August 1920 relative to certain frontiers of Czechoslovakia and Romania (*ibid.*, N.R.G.³, XII, 815), the executive agreement of Rome between Austria, Hungary, Italy and the Serb-Croat-Slovene State of 29 March 1923 for the administrative and technical reorganization of the railway system of the South Austrian Railway Company (*ibid.*, N.R.G.³, XVIII, 820), and the arbitral awards of 7 October 1933-29 June 1938 (*A.A.*, vol. III, no. 51, pp. 1795 *et seq.*)[86]
> An additional Convention concluded in Rome at the same date (Martens, N.R.G.³, XVIII, 871) for the implementation of Article 311 (3) of the Peace Treaty of St.-Germain, dealt with the regulation of transit and communications on the network of the Danube-Save-Adria Railway Company.—Comp. also the Italo-Hungarian agreement of 27 March 1924 concerning the Adriatic traffic and the South Austrian Railway Company.
> See further Articles 372 Versailles (1919), 243 Neuilly (1919) and 106 Lausanne (1923).

Provisions on the facilitation of railway traffic in transit through their territory were inserted in the peace treaties of Paris of 10 February 1947, with Bulgaria (Article 30) and Hungary (Article 34).

(b) The St. Gothard line

This line may serve as one of the most famous examples of international regulation. On 13 October 1869 an international conference held in Berne between Baden, the North-German Federation, Italy, Switzerland and Württemberg resulted in a final protocol (*ibid.*, N.R.G.¹, XIX, 82) providing for the construction of a railway through the St. Gothard: there was to be created for this purpose a company, the *Société du chemin de fer du St.-Gothard*, in whose general assembly, pursuant to a special protocol (*ibid.*, 89), the Swiss cantons should be represented. Immediately following the adoption of that protocol, a convention was concluded between Italy and Switzerland for the construction and subsidization of

86. Other similar arbitral awards relate to the Austro-Hungarian railways Sopron-Közseg (18 June 1929, *A.A.*, vol. II, no. 25, p. 961) and Barcs-Pakrac (5 October 1934, *A.A.*, vol. III, no. 41, p. 1569), and to a German-Romanian dispute about the railway Bužau-Nehoiaşi (7 July 1939, *A.A.*, vol. III, no. 53, p. 1827).

the planned railway (15 October 1869, *ibid.*, 90), with a number of additional articles of 26 April 1870 (*ibid.*, 98). This was followed, on 28 October 1871, by a tripartite convention—replacing an earlier convention of 20 June 1870 with the North-German Federation which had meanwhile ceased to exist—between the new German Reich, Italy and Switzerland concerning the accession of the Reich to the 1869 convention and its participation in the subsidies (*ibid.*, 103).—After the financial basis of the undertaking had thus been laid, the two States directly involved in the technical execution of the plan agreed upon the junction of the Gothard railway with the Italian railway net and the construction of international railway stations by their convention of 23 December 1873 (*ibid.*, N.R.G.[2], II, 74) with an additional protocol of 12 February 1874 (*ibid.*, II, 81), later followed by a further protocol of 5 February 1880 (*ibid.*, IX, 568).—In the mean time a new financial basis was laid for the construction of the tunnel between Göschenen and Airolo and of the railway at German-Italian-Swiss conferences at Luzern (June 1877, *ibid.*, N.R.G.[2], IV, 625) and Göschenen (September 1877, *ibid.*, 675) which resulted in a new convention of 12 March 1878 (*ibid.*, 676), additional to that of 15 October 1869.—Finally the policing service, for several purposes, was to be organized on the international stations of Chiasso and Luino (16 February 1881, *ibid.*, VIII, 584, with supplementary agreements, *ibid.*, VIII, 586 and IX, 569), dealing with such matters as customs, police, sanitary police, postal, telegraph and telephone communications.—The exploitation of the Gothard line began in May 1882; a second track was only added to the original single line pursuant to a new convention of 4/22 October 1887 (*ibid.*, XVIII, 673).

The relations between Germany, Switzerland and Italy with regard to the Gothard railway were placed on a new footing by their tripartite Convention of 13 October 1909 with final protocol (Martens, N.R.G.[3], VIII, 195, 202), complemented by an Italo-Swiss agreement of the same date (*ibid.*, VIII, 210). This new regulation was occasioned by the nationalization of the Gothard line by the Swiss Confederation and it replaced the Conventions of 1869, 1871, 1878 and 1879, but maintained in force those of 1873, 1881 and 1882. It deals, among other things, with Switzerland's obligation to secure an uninterrupted exploitation of the railway as "une grande ligne internationale", the treatment of traffic and transport on the footing of the "most favoured railway" (Articles 7-9), the admissible maximum tariffs, and arbitration.

In Article 374 of the Peace Treaty of Versailles (1919), Germany undertook to accept, within ten years, on request being made by the Swiss Government after agreement with the Italian Government, the denunciation of the 1909 Convention, and, in the absence of agreement as to the conditions of such denunciation, the decision of an arbitrator designated by the United States.

264

Corresponding arrangements were later made for the construction of he *Simplon line* through a tunnel between Brig and Domodossola—convention between Switzerland and Italy of 25 November 1895 concerning the construction and the exploitation of a railway through the Simplon by a concessionary *Compagnie des chemins de fer Jura-Simplon (ibid.*, N.R.G.[2], XXVII, 406 = XXVIII, 34), followed by those of 2 December 1899 respecting the future junction of their respective railway systems at the station of Iselle (*ibid.*, XXIX, 446), 16 May 1903 sanctioning the construction and exploitation of the line by the Swiss Confederation itself (*ibid.*, XXXI, 552) and 18 January/7 April 1906 relating to the customs, police, sanitary control, postal, telegraph and telephone services on the line Brig-Domodossola and in the international station of Domodossola (*ibid.*, XXXV, 184)—, and the recent combined railway and road tunnel through Mont Blanc between Chamonix and Entrèves—convention between Italy and France of 14 March 1953 (*U.N.T.S.*, Vol. 284, p. 221).

(c) *Railways in imperialist politics in general*

The most interesting aspect of railways in international law is the fact that they have often served imperialist designs. As is well known from diplomatic history, railways have often played a prominent and even a baleful part in international relations, in their capacity of instruments for the expansion of political power. Notorious examples of this motive for the construction of railways are the cases of the Baghdad railway line, the Manchurian (Chinese Eastern) railway, various railroads by which the States possessing colonies or leased territories on the coasts of China have penetrated into her inland territory, and a number of railways constructed in Africa.

How important this aspect of the construction of railways has been, can be inferred from the frank confession made not long ago by the Government of a State which has once been involved in one of the most ambitious imperialist railway projects, namely Russia. Tsarist Russia had indeed made ample use of railways with a view to establishing a foothold in the heart of Asia, especially in Manchuria, and to gradually strengthening it. Comp. *e.g.*, her treaty with China of 14 August 1911 (Martens, N.R.G.[3], VII, 651) and my exposition below on the Manchurian or Chinese Eastern railway. Soviet Russia has never denounced this typical imperialist thrust towards the eastern shores of China and has on the contrary readily endorsed the effects of that Tsarist expansion, in spite of her condemnation, as a matter of principle or at least of lip-service, of a similar, but much less spectacular penetration by Tsarist Russia into Persia. In respect of this latter country, Soviet Russia has indeed, by Article 10 of her Convention of 26 February 1921 (*L.N.T.S.*, vol. 9, p. 383; Amedeo GIANNINI, *I documenti diplomatici della pace orientale* (Roma, 1922), series II, pp. 13 *et seq.*) expressly "repudiated the tendencies of world imperialism which strives to construct in foreign countries roads and telegraph lines not so much with a view to the cultural development of the peoples as to ensure for itself the means of military penetration", and renounced all her rights to two Russian-built railways, *viz.*, from Djulfa (on the Araxes) to Tabriz, and from Sufyan (on that railway) to Lake Urmia, together with a number of roads, telegraph and telephone lines, lake navigation services and port installations.

In order to prevent international rivalry States have occasionally agreed upon a mutual limitation upon their pursuit of new railway concessions in a third country:

> Anglo-Russian notes of 16/28 April 1899 (Martens, N.R.G.², XXXI, 9; XXXII, 118) by which the two States committed themselves not to seek, nor to allow their subjects to seek, any new railway concessions from China, as to Great Britain north of the Great Wall, as to Russia in the Yangtse Basin, and not to obstruct each other's applications in respect of the areas thus reserved for either of them.

I will further deal in some detail with

The Baghdad and Manchurian Railways

This is not the place to record in detail the political development promoted or achieved by these two famous railway projects. I will therefore confine myself to giving a few particulars concerning their legal and especially their international law aspect.

(i) The Baghdad railway project (see Part II of this publication, pp. 565-566, with map) was an ambitious undertaking planned by the German Empire, in close collaboration with German financial circles, in the last decade of the 19th century. It was intended to greatly enhance Germany's power and influence in the Middle East by the construction of a railway line between Konya and Baghdad and beyond. The first part of a railroad into Anatolia, form Haydar-Paşa to Ismit, had already been built in the seventies of the 19th century. It had in 1888 been transferred to the *Deutsche Bank* and in 1889 and following years prolonged to Ankara and Konya via Eski-Şehir by the *Société du Chemin de fer Ottoman d'Anatolie*, founded for that purpose in 1889 pursuant to a first concessionary contract with the Bank of 4 October 1888, with the participation of French financiers. The Council of Administration of the company, on 23 December 1899, entered into a studies contract with the Ottoman Minister of Commerce with a view to preparing a plan for the extension of the railway from Konya to Baghdad. This line was to run across the Tarsus through the Cilician Gate, via Adana across the Euphrates, via Mosul, along the Tigris and via Baghdad to Basra at the mouth of the Shatt-al-Arab, or—what promised to be a much more suitable terminus—Kuwait at the head of the Persian Gulf. The railway was in fact for the greater part constructed as planned, but failed to reach its most promising terminus on the Persian Gulf owing to a politically unsurmountable bar placed in its path by the British Government in the form of an agreement with the Sultan of Kuwait, obliging the latter not to allow the completion of the railway line towards his capital. The different stages of this chapter of diplomatic history are only partly reflected in inter-state conventions.

The basic instrument of the enterprise which endorsed the line of the introductory research was not an international treaty at all. It was a concessionary contract entered into by the Ottoman Government and the *Société du Chemin de fer Ottoman d'Anatolie* on 5 March 1903, confirmed by an Imperial firman of 21 March 1903 (translation of its text in STRUPP's *Urkunden zur Geschichte des Völkerrechts* (Gotha, 1911), vol. II, pp. 257-271), granting a concession to the said company for the construction of a railroad from Konya via Adana, Mosul and Baghdad to Basra, with four branch-lines, *inter alia*, to Aleppo and the Persian Gulf. The concession for the railway, to be built under governmental control in sections of about 200 kilometres each, was to have a duration of 99 years. The Anatolian Railway Company was to found a subsidiary company under Ottoman law—the *Société Impériale Ottomane du Chemin de fer de Bagdad*—for this purpose. Elaborate financial arrangements, including a security to be deposited by the Company, the promise of a State guarantee to the Company of a fixed annuity for every kilometre built and run, and a 4% loan to be issued on behalf of the Ottoman Government by a group of financiers, represented by the *Deutsche Bank*, with the collaboration of the Council of Administration of the Public Ottoman Debt, and on the security of tithes owed to the State by certain vilayets, and of the railway itself, its rolling-stock and the Company's share in its receipts. The Baghdad Railway Company was empowered to avail itself of electric energy produced by natural hydraulic forces, and to build a telegraph line and defences along the railway, to construct ports at Baghdad and Basra, and warehouses, etc.—Supplementary concessionary contracts followed in 1908 (text: *loco cit.*, vol. II, pp. 272-278) and 1911. The projected *Société Impériale Ottomane du Chemin de fer de Bagdad*, subject to Ottoman law, was duly founded (text of the statutes: *loco cit.*, vol. II, note 2 *ad* pp. 276 *et seq.*), and a loan floated by the *Deutsche Bank* in three series, two in 1903 and one in 1908 respectively (see for the 1903 loan contracts: *loco cit.*, vol. II, note *ad* pp. 264 *et seq.*). The construction from Adana on the Gulf of Alexandretta towards the East was so far advanced in 1911 that in that year Germany found that the time was ripe to convene a conference with Russia at Potsdam and to act directly on the international level by concluding an agreement with Russia on 19 August 1911 at St.Petersburg (Martens, N.R.G.³,

V, 673) in which she disavowed any intention to seek railway and other concessions for herself in the area north of a line running through Persia. Russia on her part undertook to apply for a Persian concession to build a railway from Teheran to the Turco-Persian frontier with the object of connecting it with a branch of the Konya-Baghdad line, the general importance of which she expressly recognized with the accompanying promise not to counteract its completion in any way.

The planned branch-line to the Persian Gulf was, as remarked, made impossible in 1911 by another international agreement, entered into between Great Britain and the sheikdom of Kuwait (see for the history of the railway: U. GEHRKE and G. KUHN, *Die Grenzen des Irak*, Stuttgart, 1963, pp. 77-80; see also the supplementary volume with many documents).

The ambitious scheme, described above, in the event foundered on the common defeat of the German Reich and Turkey in World War I. This total failure was sealed by the loss by Germany and her nationals of all their property, rights and interests abroad, and the loss by Turkey of long sections of the Konya-Baghdad line together with the territories through which they ran: in North Syria as a result of the new frontier *tracé*, agreed upon in Article 8 of the Franco-Turkish Agreement of Ankara of 20 October 1921 (*ibid.*, XII, 826) and upheld by Article 3, *sub* 1° of the Peace Treaty of Lausanne of 24 July 1923 (*ibid.*, XIII, 338) —a *tracé* which was substituted for the original one fixed in Article 27, *sub* II (2) of the (abortive) Peace Treaty of Sèvres of 10 August 1920 (*ibid.*, XII, 664)—, and in Mesopotamia as a consequence of its severance from Turkey under Article 3, *sub* 2° of the Peace Treaty of Lausanne. Three different sections of this famous railway were still mentioned by name in Article 4 of the Tripartite Agreement of Sèvres between the British Empire, France and Italy respecting Anatolia of 10 August 1920 (*ibid.*, XII, 785): the Anatolian railway, the Mersin-Tarsus-Adana railway and part of the Baghdad line which was to remain in Turkish territory, were thenceforth to be worked by a company whose capital would be subscribed by British, French and Italian financial groups.— The final outcome of the complicated developments after World War I was that the concessionary contracts regarding those three sections would, according to an official letter of the President of the Turkish delegation at the Lausanne Peace Conference to the President of the Third Committee of 24 July 1923, be maintained in conformity with Protocol XII of that date concerning certain concessions duly granted by the Ottoman Government prior to 29 October 1914, and that the service of the three loans of 1903 and 1908 would be apportioned among the successor States (comp. about this arrangement Articles 47-51 and the Tableau (part A) annexed to section I of Part II of the Peace Treaty of Lausanne, with the letters exchanged under 5-c appended to

268

the Treaty, in Martens N.R.G.³, XIII, 437 and 453).—The Grand National Assembly of Turkey had already consented in Article 10 of the above-mentioned Franco-Turkish Agreement of Ankara of 20 October 1921 to the transfer of the concession of the section of the Baghdad line between Bozanti and Nusaybin and of a number of embranchments constructed in the Adana Vilayet, to a French group. The Ankara Agreement was in express terms maintained in force by a correspondence between the French and Turkish delegations of 24 July 1923, annexed to the Peace Treaty of Lausanne (*ibid.*, XIII, 450).

(ii) The North Manchuria or Chinese Eastern railway, a continuation of the Transbaikal line of the Siberian railway, was in fact built by Imperial Russia between the Sino-Siberian frontier and the Ussuri line, running to Vladivostok ("Ruler of the East"), and was also planned in the last decade of the 19th century. Apart from its strategic importance for Russia, this line was also expected to open vast areas with great mineral wealth for exploitation. It was in particular this latter feature which gradually resulted in this Chinese Eastern railway becoming a Russian instrument for the expansion of Russia's political power in the Far East by means of a rapid extension of her economic activities, spreading like an oilstain from the railway proper into its surrounding mining and trade districts. It has ever since maintained a prominent position in diplomacy in the Far East, in particular as a consequence of the increasing rivalry in China between Russia and the "rising sun" of Japan. Diplomatic history reflects its importance, for international law also, *inter alia*, in the following instruments.

Just as in the case of the Baghdad railway, the construction of the Manchurian railroad has from the outset rested on an agreement—of 8 September 1896—between the territorial Power concerned (China) and an ostensibly private company, the Russo-Chinese Bank, which, however, was in actual fact a Russian State enterprise. On the strength of that agreement a further company was to be formed, under the name of "Chinese Eastern Railway Company", for the construction and working of a railway within the confines of China, from the Western border of the province of Wei-Lun-Tsian to the Eastern border of that of Ghirin, and for the connection of that railway with those branch-lines which the Imperial Russian Government was going to construct to the Chinese frontier from Transbaikalia and the southern Ussuri lines. As appears from its Statutes, confirmed by the Emperor of China on 16 December 1896 (see for their text: *ibid.*, N.R.G.², XXXII, 122), this new railway company was to be bound hand and foot to the Imperial Russian Government (§ 3), which also gave a comprehensive financial guarantee (§§ 11 *et seq.*). The concluding paragraphs of the Statutes (§§ 29 and 30) provided for the gratuitous entry into possession of the railway by the Chinese Government at the expiry of 80 years and for their right to acquire it, on refunding all the outlays, on the expiration of 36 years.[87]

The first foreign Power to interfere with the railway expansion of Russia towards the East was Great Britain which, in an exchange of notes with Russia of 16/28 April 1899 (Martens N.R.G.², XXXI, 9 = XXXII, 118), delimited their respective spheres of action by agreeing that, in their search for further railway concessions, Britain would not go beyond the Great Chinese Wall and Russia would not proceed in the basin of the Yangtsze, on the understanding that certain agreements already reached in respect of a couple of branch-lines (from the South to Newchwang and Sinminting, respectively) would remain unimpaired.

It was not long, however, before another Power, Japan, likewise betrayed misgivings about Russia's intentions and took a vigorous stand against the latter's factual occupation of Manchuria. Great Britain at first attempted to forestall a further disintegration of China by an Agreement with Germany of 16 October 1900 (*ibid.*, N.R.G.², XXXII, 92), adhered to by Japan on 29 October (*ibid.*, N.R.G.³, II, 3), and by a further Agreement with Japan of 30 January 1902 to secure the independence and territorial integrity of China and Korea (*ibid.*, N.R.G.², XXX, 650 = XXXI, 258). But Japan and Russia came into headlong collision over their competing interests in the Far East owing to the latter's tardiness in evacuating Manchuria (comp. their correspondence from 28 July 1903 to 6 February 1904 in Martens, N.R.G.², XXXI, 613 *et seq.*), and finally fought their rivalry out in a war which put an end to Russia's further thrust eastward.

The shift of power in the Far East between Japan and Russia as a result of Russia's defeat in their 1904 war and the Peace Treaty of Portsmouth of 5 September 1905 (*ibid.*, N.R.G.², XXXIII, 3) had its consequences also for the Far Eastern railways system. On that occasion Russia transferred to Japan, together with the lease of the Liao-tung peninsula (Port Arthur and Talien), the Port Arthur-Changchun railway with all its appurtenances, including all coal mines in the said region belonging to, or worked for the benefit of, the railway.

> These transfers needed the consent of China; this was in fact granted in the Sino-Japanese treaty of 22 December 1905 (*ibid.*, N.R.G.², XXXIV, 748), by which Japan undertook to conform as far as it was possible to the original Sino-Russian agreements concerning the construction and exploitation of the railways.

87. By an exchange of notes between Japanese and Chinese representatives of 25 May 1915 following a set of exorbitant Japanese claims, known as the "twenty-one demands" (Martens, N.R.G.³, IX, 334 *et seq.*, at p. 340/341) it was agreed that the date for restoring the South Manchuria Railway to China should fall due in the year 2002 and that the redemption clause was cancelled. See *infra* in the text, p. 273.

The Contracting Parties of Portsmouth further agreed to exploit their respective railways in Manchuria exclusively for commercial and industrial, to the exclusion of strategic, purposes, and to conclude a separate convention for the regulation of their connecting railway services in Manchuria (Articles 6-8). This separate technical Convention, entered into on 13 June 1907 (*ibid.*, N.R.G.³, I, 809), provided for the connection of the Russian and Japanese railways in Manchuria at Kwantchentsy, and for the necessary measures to be taken in order to ensure the punctual observance of the treaty by the Chinese Eastern and South Manchuria railway companies. It was followed by a Convention between the same two Powers of 4 July 1910 (Martens, N.R.G.³, III, 753) which provided for friendly cooperation with a view to the amelioration of their respective railway lines in Manchuria and the improvement of the connecting service of the said railways and to abstain from all competition prejudicial to the realization of this object, and by a further convention of 14 August 1911 (*ibid.*, VII, 651), dealing with the direct transport of goods over the Manchurian railways.

As remarked above, the construction of the Chinese Eastern railway was not exclusively a railway enterprise, as it was accompanied by further expansionist activities, such as the exploitation of coal mines along its track for the supply of fuel, the building of houses for the miners, the organization of municipalities on their behalf on the real state belonging to the railway, etc.

> How far this "oilstain" had successively spread can best be gathered from Article 3, *sub* B of a convention between Manchukwo and the USSR of 23 March 1935 (see below, p. 274), in which the following "auxiliary enterprises of the railway" are enumerated: forest concessions and lumbering, coalmines, power stations, a printing plant, a nursery and greenhouses in Harbin, workshops of the Ways Department, wool-washing and hydraulic works, water works in Harbin, a soft drinks factory, a sawmill, gradations of beans, waste clearing works, an hotel, health resorts and sanatoria, hospitals and clinics, a library and an economic bureau.

Comp. further on this latter expansion of Russian influence the Russo-Chinese arrangement of Peking of 10 May 1909 (*ibid.*, N.R.G.³, IV, 706), which stressed the "fundamental principle" that the establishment of the municipalities could in no way prejudice the sovereign rights of China. Other powers have later secured for themselves the application to their own subjects of the municipal administrative and financial regime, established in the zone of the Chinese Eastern Railway, *e.g.*,

> Russia-Great Britain, 30 April 1914 (*ibid.*, XII, 157);
> Russia-The Netherlands, 25 September 1915 (*ibid.*, XII, 160).

Side by side with the (Russian) Chinese Eastern railway approaching from the west, other railways had indeed meanwhile begun to spread their web over China from the treaty ports on her coast, for example

271

that constructed by Russia from her leased territory of Port Arthur and Talien to Changchun. Sometimes the railways thus constructed by foreign powers were afterwards purchased by China. This was, for example, the case of the Hsinmintun-Mukden railway which was bought by her from Japan with the financial help, for its reconstruction, of the South Manchurian Railway Company, which also lent to the Chinese Government half of the necessary funds for the continuation of the Changchun line to Kirin (Agreements of 15 April 1907 and 12 November 1908 (*ibid.*, N.R.G.[3], VI, 770 and 772). Further Sino-Japanese agreements followed on 19 August and 4 September 1909 (*ibid.*, N.R.G.[3], II, 671 and 672), dealing respectively with the reconstruction of the Antung-Mukden Railway (implying a change in the existing gauge and necessary rectifications of the line), and with the "five Manchurian questions", including a further extension by China of the Kirin-Changchun railway to the southern boundary of Yenchi and its connection with a Korean railway.

On the eve of World War I the situation underwent a new change as a result of the expulsion of the Chinese Army and the Mandarins from Mongolia across the frontier and the emergence of a, to all intents and purposes independent State (Outer) Mongolia, separated from China. Russia forthwith concluded with this State a treaty of friendship and commerce, with Protocol, at Urga on 3 November 1912 (Martens, N.R.G.[3], VII, 11, 15 = VIII, 693) and a further convention of 30 September 1914 (*ibid.*, X, 373) dealing with the right of the Mongolian Government to build railways within the boundaries of its own territory subject, however, to previous consultation with Russia, and to certain restrictions should Mongolia plan to concede their construction to third countries and accept their financial help. By a tripartite arrangement of 7 June 1915 to which China was also a party (*ibid.*, X, 374), the relations between China, Russia and "His Holiness the Great Venerable Sacred Reincarnated Khan of Outer Mongolia"—a title which was declared in Article 4 to have been conferred upon the ruler by the President of the Republic of China—were regularized. Mongolia recognized (*a*) the Sino-Russian Declaration and Notes of 23 October (5 November) 1913 (*ibid.*, VIII, 145), by the terms of which Russia recognized that Outer Mongolia was under the suzerainty of China and China recognized its autonomy, and (*b*) also directly China's suzerainty. On the other hand China and Russia together recognized "the autonomy of Outer Mongolia forming part of Chinese territory"; within the limits of that autonomy Outer Mongolia would be entitled to conclude agreements with foreign powers of a commercial and an industrial nature (Articles 1, 2 and 5).

This convention closely followed another development which had meanwhile taken place, namely, Japan's sudden assault on China, in

272

January 1915, with her notorious "twenty-one demands" which, apart from various other matters, also related to Chinese railways. Comp. on these demands and their final, in a reduced form, incorporation into the Sino-Japanese agreements of 25 May 1915 (*ibid.*, IX, 334): Part I of this publication, p. 246. The agreements related, *inter alia*, to the financing of the Chefoo-Weihsien railway by Japanese bankers, should Germany waive her financing privilege (Article *sub* (*a*), 2); the prolongation of the 80 years' term of the South Manchurian and Antung-Mukden railways to 2002, respectively 2007 (Article *sub* (*b*), 1); a basic revision of the Kirin-Changchun Railway Loan Agreement (Article *sub* (*b*), 7), and a preference for Japanese capitalists to finance possible new railways in Southern Manchuria and (Chinese) Eastern Inner Mongolia.

The Peace Treaty of Versailles of 1919 deprived Germany of all her privileges and possessions in China, including her rights in the Tsingtao-Tsinanfu Railway, in favour of Japan (Article 156^2). This was the motive behind China's refusal to sign it. Japan later retroceded these possessions to China by the treaty of Washington of 4 February 1922 (*ibid.*, XIII, 186), Article 1, with an accompanying series of Notes exchanged between China, Japan and the United States.

It was not until 1924-1925 that the Soviet Union concluded two conventions intended to base her relations with China, on the one hand, and with Japan, on the other, on new foundations.

> By the first of the two, dated 14 March 1924, the Soviet Union annulled all Tsarist treaties and, as far as she herself was concerned, all international acts relating to China (Articles 3 and 4);
> consented to the repurchase by China of the Chinese Eastern railway and to the transfer to her of all shares in the Company (§ 2);
> took over the sum total of the shareholders', bondholders' and creditors' claims against the Company, dating from prior to the revolution of 9 March 1917 (§ 4);
> and waived all the concessions acquired by the Tsarist Government in China (Article 10) and Russia's share in the Boxer Indemnity of 1901 (Article 11).

However, this convention was not ratified in this form because of the pro-tests raised by the other powers involved, and was replaced by a slightly altered new treaty of 31 May 1924. Comp. A. N. SACK, *Les effets des transformations des Etats sur leurs dettes publiques etc.*, vol. I (Paris, 1927), p. 246 and notes 2-5, who refers: for the text of the repurchase to the *L.N.T.S.*, vol. XXXVII, p. 177; for a Sino-Soviet agreement for the provisional management of the railway of the same date to *ibid.*, vol. XXXVII, p. 195; and for a subsequent treaty of Mukden with Tchang Tso Lin of 20 September 1924 to *China Year Book* 1925/1926, p. 797.

The 1924 treaty between the USSR and China was later cited in Article 4^2 of the Convention between the USSR and Manchukwo of 1935, dealt with below.

The second convention, dated 20 January 1925 (Martens, N.R.G.³, XV, 323), the first which the Soviet Union concluded with Japan after her collapse in World War I and the Bolshevist revolution, laid down new foundations for their future relations. Article 2 stipulated that, save for the Peace Treaty of Portsmouth of 5 September 1905 (*ibid.*, N.R.G.², XXXIII, 3), all treaties concluded between Japan and Russia prior to 7 November 1917 should be re-examined at a later conference and be liable to revision or annulment as altered circumstances might require. Nothing special was stipulated concerning railways either in the Convention or in two annexed Protocols.

When in 1935, after her invasion of Manchuria, Japan transformed that country into the puppet State of Manchukwo, the Soviet Union ceded to the latter all rights she possessed relative to the Manchurian (or Chinese Eastern) Railway with all the "auxiliary enterprises" enumerated above p. 271, in consideration of which Manchukwo undertook to pay to the Soviet Union 140 million yen. This arrangement was made by their treaty of 23 March 1935 (*ibid.*, XXX, 649), complemented by a tripartite treaty of the same date to which Japan was also a party (*ibid.*, 663) and by a special guarantee by Japan for the payment "in view of the close and special relations between herself and Manchukwo" (*ibid.*, 666).

Finally, in 1951, Japan was forced to renounce all special rights and interests in China: Article 10 of the Peace Treaty of San Francisco of 8 September 1951 (*U.N.T.S.*, vol. 136, p. 45).

Section 6. TELEGRAPH AND TELEPHONE LINES,
CABLES AND PIPE LINES

Telegraph lines have not made their appearance in international law until just on the eve of the second half of the 19th century,[88] when a Conference of plenipotentiaries of Austria and Prussia in Berlin resolved by a protocol of 3 October 1849 (Martens, N.R.G.¹, XIV, 591) to establish an electro-magnetic telegraph connection Trieste-Vienna-Oderberg (frontier)-Berlin-Hamburg. Shortly afterwards, the way was paved to a world-wide telegraphic union by the foundation (25 July 1850) of a German-Austrian and (29 December 1855) of a West-European Telegraph Association of national State telegraph administrations of Belgium, France, Sardinia, Spain and Switzerland. These later merged and expanded over the whole of Europe at the first International Telegraph Conference of Paris (Convention of 17 May 1865, *B.F.S.P.*,

88. The first telegraph line which has been used in actual practice was that of 1844 along the Taunus railway.

vol. 56, p. 295). The Union thus created later set up an International Bureau at Bern and spread its tentacles over Asiatic Russia and British India at the second conference at Vienna (Convention of 21 July 1868, *loco cit.*, 59, 322). At the third Conference at Rome (Convention of 14 January 1872, *loco cit.*, 66, 975) it also admitted private telegraph enterprises, but without the right to vote. In the event, at the fourth Conference at St. Petersburg it agreed upon the text of two intentionally separate collective Conventions of 22 July 1875 (Martens, N.R.G.[2], III, 614). The first of these two was signed by Government delegates of diplomatic rank and laid down the permanent basic principles regarding international telegraphic communications, both as between States and vis-à-vis the public; the second, the so-called *Règlement de service international*, laid down an elaborate set of far more detailed technical rules agreed upon between the telegraph administrations, which would be susceptible of alteration by them jointly.[89] Since then many more such technical Conferences have been held: in London (28 July 1879, *ibid.*, VIII, 51), Berlin (17 September 1885, *ibid.*, XII, 205)—where the telephone was also introduced as an international means of communication—, Paris (21 June 1890, *ibid.*, XVII, 294), Budapest (22 July 1896, *B.F.S.P.*, vol. 88, p. 1120), London (10 July 1903, *ibid.*, vol. 97, p. 737) —where new apparatuses were introduced and the *Règlement de service international* was thoroughly revised—, Lisbon (11 June 1908, Martens, N.R.G.[3], V, 208), St. Petersburg (29 October 1925, *ibid.*, XXV, 303), Brussels (22 September 1928, *L.N.T.S.*, vol. 88, p. 347), Cairo (4 April 1938).

The Bureau of the International Telegraph Union, founded in 1865 (see also Part I of this publication, p. 351), was charged with the work of the International Radio Telegraph Union, created at the conference of Berlin on 3 November 1906 (Martens, N.R.G.[3], I, 147). The rules of the latter Union were modified in London (5 July 1912) and Washington (25 November 1927). Both Unions fused at the congress of Madrid, 9 December 1932 (*L.N.T.S.*, vol. 151, p. 5) into the International Telecommunication Union; this convention and the radio regulations of Cairo, 1938, were revised at Atlantic City (2 October 1947, *U.N.T.S.*, vols. 193, 194 and 195), Buenos Aires (22 December 1952), Geneva (21 December 1959) and Montreux (12 November 1965, *Tr. blad* 1966, No. 201); on 3 November 1967 a partial revision of the radio regulations of Geneva, 1959, was signed (*Tr. blad* 1968, No. 135). The telegraph and telephone regulations of Cairo, 1938, were revised at the congress of Paris (5 August 1949) and Geneva (29 November 1959, *Tr. blad* 1959, Nos. 190 and 191).

89. Great Britain only acceded to the Union on 7 January 1876 (Martens, N.R.G.[2], III, 689).

The principles underlying the provisions of the basic Convention of 1875, which has remained in force for many decades, are as follows.

The use of international telegraphs shall be open for everyone and the secrecy of the messages shall be respected, but without the Contracting Parties assuming any liability on this account. A sufficient number of special wires shall be allocated to the international service. State telegrams shall have priority. Reasons of State may justify a temporary suspension of the service. Certain bases for the formation of international tariffs are agreed upon. Provision is made for the holding of periodic administrative conferences of the International Telegraphic Union. The Parties reserve the right to enter into special agreements.[90]

The technical *Règlement de service international* consisted of 84 Articles— dealing with such matters as the establishment of an international network, the language of the telegrams, the tariffs, the symbols to be used, the order and direction of the transmission, possible interruptions thereof, the delivery of the messages, special and urgent telegrams, replies prepaid, multiple and service telegrams, reimbursements, accountability, the costs of the International Bureau. It has been repeatedly reconsidered and revised at subsequent technical conferences. At Lisbon, in 1908, a *Tableau des Taxes* was annexed to the Convention proper.

Against this general legal background of guiding principles, hundreds of special telegraph conventions, mostly bilateral, often essentially tripartite, have in the course of the last century been concluded. States have already at a relatively early date proceeded to conclude bilateral agreements, such as the Anglo-Persian Conventions of 23 November 1865, 2 April 1868 and 2 December 1872 (Martens, N.R.G.[2], II, 516, 520 and 522) concerning the establishment of telegraphic communications with India across Persia; the Russo-Turkish Convention of 2 November 1871 (*ibid.*, N.R.G.[2], I, 628) relative to the laying of a submarine cable between Odessa and Constantinople; the Anglo-Spanish declaration of 25 December 1875 (*ibid.*, II, 470) on the telegraphic service between Spain and Gibraltar. A very special case was that of the telegraph line built between Bucharest and Varna during the Crimean War in virtue of a Franco-British convention of 1 February 1855 (*ibid.*, N.R.G.[1], XV, 616).

The great majority of telegraph and/or telephone conventions are aimed at regulating in detail the junction of national trunk-lines or, at a later stage, cables, or the construction of new international lines as a joint enterprise, or at furthering the efficiency of the international telegraphic or telephonic service. I will only give below by way of orienta-

90. The German Reich, *e.g.*, had in fact entered into separate agreements with all its neighbours. Bavaria and Württemberg had an independent right of treaty making in this field.

276

tion a brief survey of the different kinds of international agreements in this field.

The usual bilateral type of telegraph or telephone convention is represented, *e.g.*, by the Agreement of 5 February 1912 regulating the telephone service between Great Britain and France (*ibid.*, N.R.G.[3], IX, 536), superseding an earlier one of 29 July 1902 (*B.F.S.P.*, vol. 95, p. 59). It provides for the diameter, conductivity and insulation of the submarine cables and land wires by means of which telephonic correspondence between the two countries shall be maintained, and for the possibly necessary increase of the number of lines. It deals with their protection against disturbing influences, the cost of erection and maintenance of the lines (each State on its own territory) and the reservation of the circuits specially allocated to the Franco-British telephone service exclusively for that service. It further adopts a conversation of three minutes as the usual unit, both for the collection of charges and for the duration of communications, regulates in detail the charges and their apportionment to the Parties, provides for a system of subscription for calls at fixed times during the night and for the organization of a telephone advice service, lays down that, after agreement, either of the two administrations shall be at liberty to establish telephone relations with another country through the telephonic system of the other administration, and finally repeats, or refers to, the basic principles of the Convention of St. Petersburg (1875).

A few other examples of this very frequent type of agreement are the post and telegraph convention between Prussia and Russia of 11 October 1866 (Martens, N.R.G.[1], XVIII, 364); the telephone conventions between France and Italy of 16 July 1899 and 18 July 1907 (*ibid.*, N.R.G.[3], IV, 681, 684); the telegraph conventions between Colombia and Ecuador of 5 May 1906 (*ibid.*, VI, 628) and between Great Britain (for Belize, British Honduras) and Mexico of 27 May 1910 (*ibid.*, VII, 288); the British-Norwegian telegraph convention of 30 December 1910 (*ibid.*, N.R.G.[3], VII, 847), dealing with communications through the submarine cable [91] between Northumberland and Arendal, which is expressly declared to be joint property; the telephone conventions between Italy and San Marino of 11 December 1910 (*ibid.*, VII, 827) and between France and Luxembourg of 7 April 1912 (*ibid.*, IX, 572); the convention between the Hedjaz and the Sudan (together with Great Britain) of 18 December 1926 (*ibid.*, XXIII, 211) relative to the cable between Jeddah and Port Sudan, also declared to be joint property of the parties.

An interstate telegraph line was projected on a multilateral basis in Article 19 of the treaty of 14 January 1872, setting up a Provisional Central American Union (*ibid.*, N.R.G.[2], V, 476).

The usual type of essentially tripartite Convention is that which pro-

91. Submarine cables are the object of special international protection. Comp. on this protection Part IV-A of this publication relative to the High Seas.

vides for the establishment and exploitation of a telegraph or telephone line connecting States A and B across the territory of State C.

Many such conventions have in the course of time been concluded, *e.g.*:
The Netherlands-France via Belgium, 15 September 1911 (*ibid.*, N.R.G.³, VIII, 886);
Germany-Italy via Switzerland, January/February 1912 (*ibid.*, IX, 528);
The Netherlands-Russia via Germany, May/June 1912 (*ibid.*, IX, 611);
Switzerland-England via France, 8 September/26 November 1923 (*ibid.*, XIV, 455) and 28 December 1922/5 February 1923 (*ibid.*, XIV, 458);
Norway-USSR via Finland, 19 September 1921 (*ibid.*, XVI, 253);
Switzerland-Czechoslovakia via Germany, 14/27 February/24 March 1923 (*ibid.*, XVII, 201);
Switzerland-Luxembourg via France, 31 January/7 March 1924 (*ibid.*, XVII, 438);
The Netherlands-Austria via Germany, 17 December 1926/12/22 January 1927 (*ibid.*, XXVIII, 567);
The Netherlands-Czechoslovakia via Germany, 18 December 1926/11/22 February 1927 (*ibid.*, XXVIII, 570).

I will take as an example the above-mentioned Convention concluded in January/February 1912 by the competent Departments of Switzerland, Germany and Italy, and completed by an Italo-German Convention of 23 April/18 July 1912 (*ibid.*, N.R.G.³, IX, 528 and 532). With a view to facilitating direct telephonic communications between Italy and Germany, the Swiss administration shall, at its own expense, establish and maintain from one frontier of Switzerland to the other a telephonic circuit by a double wire—remaining its property—which shall not comprise any intermediary station on Swiss territory and remain exclusively allocated to such transit communications. The German and Italian administrations, inversely, undertake to establish a direct telephonic connection across their national territory on the same conditions on behalf of Switzerland, should the latter demand this in the future. The connections shall be made from Milan via Chiasso—Zürich and via Iselle (Simplon)—Basel, and fulfil certain detailed technical requirements. Switzerland shall receive a fixed charge for any unit of conversation up to a fixed total annual minimum amount. For the rest, reference is again made to the Convention of St. Petersburg of 1875 and the Service Regulations of Lisbon of 1908, and further to a special agreement between the German and Italian administrations, mentioned above. The latter proceeds on the usual lines of bilateral conventions.

The establishment of international telegraph and telephone lines was facilitated for the new States which emerged from World War I by the undertaking imposed by the Peace Conference on the vanquished States (comp. *e.g.*, Article 283, last paragraph, of the Peace Treaty of Versailles; Article 235, *in fine*, St. Germain; Article 218, *in fine*, Trianon) not to refuse their assent to the conclusion by the new States of the special agreements referred to in the conventions relating to the International Telegraphic Union, whilst special additional stipulations were imposed upon Austria and Hungary in favour of the Allied Powers generally and of the Czecho-Slovak State in particular, by Articles 326-327 St. Germain and Articles 309-310 Trianon.

For the sake of completeness only, I will still refer here to other international conventions concerning far-distance communications which do not, however, properly belong to this chapter on State Territory, *viz.*, those of 14 March 1884, 1 December 1886 and 23 March 1887, with Final Protocol of 7 July 1887, regarding the protection of submarine cables (Martens, N.R.G.[2], XI, 281; XV, 69) and the International Radio-Telegraphic Convention of 5 July 1912 (*ibid.*, XI, 270).

Sometimes, the conventions had other, technical or administrative, ends in view, such as those intended to better regulate or to protect ordinary traffic through international rivers, canals or tunnels or over international railways by the construction of a telephone or telegraph line alongside them.

Comp. *e.g.*, Article 14 of the Italo-Swiss conventions of 23 December 1873 concerning the construction of the Gothard railway (*ibid.*, N.R.G.[2], II, 74), the agreements between Belgium and France of 9 August 1881 (*ibid.*, VIII, 444) for facilitating the servicing and manoeuvring of the barrages of the canalized river Meuse, and between Belgium and the Netherlands of 10 August 1882 (*ibid.*, VIII, 440, 444, supplemented by a declaration of 10 April 1886, *ibid.*, XI, 668) for warning shipping against a rise of the level of the water of that same river and the connected canals; and the Franco-German convention of 20 March 1883 (*ibid.*, X, 451) for the servicing of the Marne-Rhine canal.

But even such conventions as ostensibly merely provide for the construction or junction of telegraph and/or telephone lines as an ordinary means of far distance communication may have a more or less pronounced political undertone. Thus, the importance of the Russo-Chinese Convention of 25 August 1892 (Martens, N.R.G.[2], XXVII, 176) for the junction of the Imperial Russian and Chinese telegraph lines cannot be assessed without due regard being paid to the imperialistic trend of Russia's policy in respect of the Far East in the nineties of the 19th century; the Statutes of the Chinese Eastern Railway Company indeed authorized Russia to build a telegraph line of her own along the future Manchurian railway.

The same applies to conventions on telegraphic or telephonic connections in other regions affected by imperialistic or colonialistic tendencies, especially in Asia and Africa.

In Article 10 of the Soviet-Persian Convention of 26 February 1921 (*ibid.*, N.R.G.[3], XIII, 173) it was openly recognized that telegraph lines have in the past often served the purpose of military penetration. In connexion therewith the RSFSR renounced gratuitously in favour of

279

Persia all telegraph and telephone lines built by the Tsarist Government inside the Persian borders.

The construction of telegraph and telephone lines has sometimes been drawn into the system of the "open door" by a provision intended to ensure that there should be an equal opportunity for all to compete: Article 6 of the Franco-German Convention of 4 November 1911 concerning Morocco (*ibid.*, N.R.G.³, V, 643) indeed prescribed that concessions to construct them should be granted by the Moroccan Government on the basis of a public tender.

Asia

> France-Siam, 15 November 1882 (*ibid.*, N.R.G.², IX, 708), construction of a telegraph line between the frontier of the, at that time still Siamese, province of Battambang and Bangkok; France-China, 1 December 1888 (*ibid.*, XXXIII, 557), linking-up of the telegraph lines of the French protectorate of Tongkin with those of China; the Netherlands-Germany, 24 July 1901 (*ibid.*, N.R.G.³, VII, 272) for the establishment of cable communications between their respective colonial possession; Great Britain-China, 23 May 1905 (*ibid.*, N.R.G.², XXXV, 382) concerning telegraph communications in Burma.

Africa

Telegraph and telephone lines have also played an important rôle in Africa as instruments of colonial expansion or consolidation. Examples:

> Great-Britain-Portugal, 11 June 1891 (*ibid.*, N.R.G.², XVIII, 185), Article 15; French Congo-Portuguese Congo, 11 July 1908 (*ibid.*, N.R.G.³, IV, 830); Belgian Congo-Portuguese Angola, 18 January 1912 (*ibid.*, IX, 525); Belgian Congo-Uganda, 29 July 1924 (*ibid.*, XVII, 597).
>
> The important Franco-German Convention on Equatorial Africa of 4 November 1911 (*ibid.*, V, 651) made a special provision necessary with respect to the French telegraph line along the Ubanghi river which would be cut off as a consequence of the cession of the so-called *Ubanghi Zipfel* to Germany. Article 6 of the Convention laid down that the line across the *Zipfel* would remain French and that France would remain in charge of the exploitation, maintenance, repair and refitment, but that it would also be available for use by the German authorities.

Heated diplomatic discussions have even developed, in 1894, around a telegraph line (as also, for that matter, around a railway), planned by Great Britain with the object of connecting her territories in South Africa with her sphere of influence on the Nile across a strip of territory, 25 kilometres wide, of the then Independent Congo State, extending from the most northerly port on Lake Tanganyika to the most southerly point of Lake Albert Edward, to be leased for that purpose to Britain (Articles 3 and 5 of the Agreement of 12 May 1894, Martens, N.R.G.², XX, 805). The whole project met with strong opposition, and not solely for that reason, from Germany and was in the event abandoned through the cancellation of the said Article 3 (comp. *ibid.*, XXI, 531, 676 and XX, 809, and below p. 586.)

Telegraph and telephone communications are adversely affected by war. Comp. on this point Article 53 (2) in section III of the Regulations concerning Warfare on Land, annexed to Convention IV of the second Hague Peace Conference of 18 October 1907, pursuant to which, *inter alia*, "all means affected on land, at sea or in the air to the transmission of news" in occupied territory may be seized even if they belong to private persons, subject to subsequent restitution or indemnification.

Pipelines

Very strong political undertones can be detected in conventions concerning the construction, exploitation and legal status of oil or gas pipelines. Well-known incidents in the Middle East and in North-Africa have proved how precarious the existence of such pipelines can be, since they can be and are in fact sometimes cut off by the territorial State even contrary to valid undertakings.

Frontier-crossing pipelines need not necessarily be constructed on the strength of international conventions; their construction can also be authorized by parallel national concessions. Thus, while a few oil pipelines in the Middle East, such as those from Iraq to the Mediterranean, and from the Sahara (Ouan Taredert in Algeria) to Cekhira (Tunisia) have formed the object of inter-State agreements, the European pipelines from Rotterdam to the Ruhr, from Marseille northward and from Trieste northward have been laid in virtue of separate concessions, unilaterally granted by the territorial States concerned under their municipal mining laws.

After the Franco-British Agreement of San Remo regarding Petroleum of 24 April 1920 (Martens, N.R.G.[3], XII, 579), Great Britain was empowered by France to carry a pipeline along the existing Hedjaz railway track in the valley of the Yarmuk under the British Mandate (Article 5, § 2 of the Franco-British Convention of 23 December 1920 concerning the Mandates for Syria and the Lebanon, Palestine and Mesopotamia, *ibid.*, XII, 582).

So long as France and Great Britain practically dominated the oilfields in the Middle East, as divided among them by the said Agreement of San Remo, they were at liberty to agree *inter se* on the construction of pipelines and could be reasonably sure of their safety once they had been constructed. The Petroleum Agreement (Article 10) provided for the construction of two separate pipelines (and of railways necessary for that purpose and their maintenance) from Mesopotamia and Persia through French spheres of interest to a port or ports on the Eastern Mediterranean, and (Article 13) for one to the Persian Gulf. Details concerning the tracé of a pipeline to the Mediterranean through the valley of the Yarmuk river were inserted in Article 5 (2) *j.*° 6 of the

Convention of 23 December 1920. Although arrangements regarding permanent earth-bound installations must be considered as constituting State servitudes and the new Arab States would be the first to blame Israel or, for that matter, any fellow Arab State, should the occasion arise, for violating the law of nations if the latter States should seize the opportunity of cutting-off a foreign pipeline laid across their territory, the safety of these modern means of transportation in the Middle East became increasingly aleatory as the Mandated Territories of Iraq, Jordan, Syria and the Lebanon emerged to independence. And the same must be feared with regard to the Sahara pipelines.

See the publication of the O.E.C.D. special committee for oil: *Pipelines in the U.S. and Europe and their legal and regulatory aspects* (1969).

Section 7. HYDROGRAPHIC SYSTEMS

In Chapter II, section 1, *supra* p. 26, I have devoted a short separate § 7 to coherent hydraulic systems as parts of State territory, and that for three reasons: their extreme economic importance; the difficulty from a systematic point of view that they would otherwise have needed treatment in both the paragraph on lakes (§ 1) and that on rivers (§ 2); and the element of man-made origin which distinguishes them, just as canals, from rivers.

Hydrographic systems are among the most important, and in certain cases very controversial, issues in modern international fluvial law. The economically vital use that can be made of rivers is either for the irrigation of arid regions—such as Northern Mexico from the Río Grande—, or for the generation of electric power, especially by means of the construction of weirs and artificial lakes—such as the Kariba dam between Zambia and Rhodesia. Very often both these uses are combined. When, for example, the French and British Governments concluded their Convention of 23 December 1920 on certain points connected with the Mandates for Syria and the Lebanon, Palestine and Mesopotamia (Martens, N.R.G.[3], XII, 582), they contemplated in Article 8 the use that could be made of the Upper Jordan and the Yarmuk for irrigation as well as for hydroelectric purposes. In other cases either the need for irrigation or that for the generation of hydroelectric power will be paramount. But there is no ground for dealing with them separately.

Modern international economic planning has lately extended the establishment of hydraulic systems to rivers or lakes which are not international in any sense, from the consideration that financial help from international sources is needed for their construction. Hence the many national hydraulic systems "internationalized" as a result of loans granted by organizations such as I.D.A. (International Development

Association). Comp. for example the loan contracts between the Bank for Development and Reconstruction and Ceylon (*U.N.T.S.*, vol. 198, p. 313; 323, p. 51; 414, p. 349), Costa Rica (vol. 414, p. 313), Portugal (vol. 492, p. 89), etc.

What exactly the juridical position with regard to the use of rivers or lakes of international importance for purposes such as irrigation or the generation of electric power is in cases where no international agreement has been reached and where, as a consequence, that position can only be assessed by the application of either customary international law or its "general principles", is extremely controversial. It would seem to be fairly certain that there are in this field a few elementary principles in force which are inspired by the need for good neighbourly relations (comp. Part VI of this publication), but it must be conceded that their substantive content is scanty, vague, unsettled and precarious.

The Organization for Communications and Transit of the League of Nations has in its second general conference at Geneva of 1923 attempted to lay down a certain codification of the rules obtaining in this field, but the result was not very significant. The Convention of 9 December 1923 (Martens, N.R.G.[3], **XIX**, 290) formulated them as follows (summary):

(1) Any State is free "dans le cadre du droit international" to carry out on its own territory all hydraulic works which it deems desirable.

(2) The Contracting States shall make studies in common to seek the most favourable solution and to draw up, if possible, a common programme. This will, however, only be obligatory for a State after its formal acceptance.

(3) A State must enter into negotiations with any other State concerned if it wishes to execute hydraulic works which either need carrying-out partly on its own territory and partly on that of another State.

(4) Negotiations are also obligatory if the execution of the works might result in serious prejudice to another State.

(6) sums up the topics which might usefully be dealt with in the agreements envisaged under (3) and (4).

The unsettled state of the law in this field is also evidenced by the discussions which have later taken place both in the Institut de droit international (1961) and in the International Law Association (in its biennial sessions ever since 1956), where a strong antithesis revealed itself between the protagonists of State sovereignty in this domain as the paramount principle and the champions of the idea that river basins must be considered as constituting coherent legal systems subject to a common body of rules.

On the report of its Yugoslav member Andrassy, the Institute, in its Salzburg session of 1961 (*Annuaire*, vol. 49-II, pp. 84-192), could not go any further than enumerating in a preamble a few very broad general considerations and formulating certain rules deemed mandatory and certain additional recommendations. These rules employ the unfortunate, but fairly common method of "codifying" a doubtful subject matter by

283

referring to other rules or principles which remain uncodified, a method not conducive to a clear insight into what international law dictates or forbids. Thus we read in Article 2 of the resolution of 11 September 1961:

> "Every State has the right to utilize waters which traverse or border its territory, subject to the limits imposed by international law (?) and, in particular, those resulting from the provisions which follow.
> This right is limited by the right of utilization of other States interested in the same watercourse or hydrographic basin."

Other "recognized rules" are in proportion, *e.g.*, Article 3:

> "If the States are in disagreement over the scope of their rights of utilization settlement will take place on the basis of equity, taking particular account of their respective needs, as well as of other pertinent circumstances (?)"

A sad thing is that no agreement could be reached on the overt recognition of the legal unity of an international river basin and that the statement of the law rather got stuck in the dogma of State sovereignty.

The resolution of the Institute had been preceded by the award by a five-member arbitral tribunal created for the settlement of a Franco-Spanish dispute relative to the diversion of water from the Lake of Lanoux in the Pyrenees by France for hydroelectric purposes (*A.A.*, vol. XII, p. 281), summarized *supra*, section 1, pp. 100 *et seq.*

The results reached by the International Law Association in its consecutive sessions of 1956 and following years were on the whole much more satisfactory than those of the Institute.

A resolution of that Association, called the Helsinki Rules on the Uses of the Waters of International Rivers of 1966 (*Report of the 52nd Conference, Helsinki*, 1966, pp. 477 *et seq.*), in its Chapters 1 and 2 indeed laid down the following principles:

Ch. I. GENERAL

Article I

The general rules of international law as set forth in these chapters are applicable to the use of the waters of an international drainage basin except as may be provided otherwise by convention, agreement or binding custom among the basin States.

Article II

An international drainage basin is a geographical area extending over two or more States determined by the watershed limits of the system of waters, including surface and underground waters, flowing into a common terminus.

Article III

A "basin State" is a state the territory of which includes a portion of an international drainage basin.

Article IV

Each basin State is entitled, within its territory, to a reasonable and equitable share in the beneficial uses of the waters of an international drainage basin.

Article V

(1) What is a reasonable and equitable share within the meaning of Article IV is to be determined in the light of all the relevant factors in each particular case.

(2) Relevant factors which are to be considered include, but are not limited to:

- (a) the geography of the basin, including in particular the extent of the drainage area in the territory of each basin State;
- (b) the hydrology of the basin, including in particular the contribution of water by each basin State;
- (c) the climate affecting the basin;
- (d) the past utilization of the waters of the basin, including in particular existing utilization;
- (e) the economic and social needs of each basin State;
- (f) the population dependent on the waters of the basin in each basin State;
- (g) the comparative costs of alternative means of satisfying the economic and social needs of each basin State;
- (h) the availability of other resources;
- (i) the avoidance of unnecessary waste in the utilization of waters of the basin;
- (j) the practicability of compensation to one or more of the co-basin States as a means of adjusting conflicts among uses; and
- (k) the degree to which the needs of a basin State may be satisfied, without causing substantial injury to a co-basin State.

(3) The weight to be given to each factor is to be determined by its importance in comparison with that of other relevant factors. In determining what is a reasonable and equitable share, all relevant factors are to be considered together and a conclusion reached on the basis of the whole.

Article VI

A use or category of uses is not entitled to any inherent preference over any other use or category of uses.

Article VII

A basin State may not be denied the present reasonable use of the waters of an international drainage basin to reserve for a co-basin State a future use of such waters.

Article VIII

1. An existing reasonable use may continue in operation unless the factors justifying its continuance are outweighed by other factors leading to the conclusion that it be modified or terminated so as to accommodate a competing incompatible use.

2. (a) A use that is in fact operational is deemed to have been an existing

use from the time of the initiation of construction directly related to the use or, where such construction is not required, the undertaking of comparable acts of actual implementation.

(b) Such a use continues to be an existing use until such time as it is discontinued with the intention that it be abandoned.

3. A use will not be deemed an existing use if at the time of becoming operational it is incompatible with an already existing reasonable use.

As far as positive treaty regulations are concerned, remarkable results have been achieved in different parts of the world. I can only enter, in some deatil, into a limited number of such regulations, some of them made in direct connection with the disruption of a river basin caused by changes in territorial sovereignty, others without any such connection.

A valuable collection of legislative texts and treaty provisions concerning the utilization of international rivers for other purposes than navigation has under that title recently been published in the *United Nations Legislative Series* (ST/LEG/SER. B/12). The latest instrument inserted in that collection dates from January 1961. The total number of international agreements listed amounts to 253. They are arranged in four sections geographically according to Continents (Africa, America, Asia and Europe) and in each section alphabetically, according to the names of the States involved. They exhibit a great variety of purposes and regulations.

Other collections are confined to certain areas, such as that entitled *A compendium of major international rivers in the ECAFE region*, published in the United Nations *Water Resources Series* under No. 29, dealing, *inter alia*, with the Mekong, Red, Brahmaputra, Ganges and Indus rivers.

International arrangements of this type may simply be intended to fix an equitable apportionment of the available volume of water among the adjacent States and to make the requisite agreements with this end in view, but their object is often farther-reaching, namely, to agree upon the construction or joint construction of a barrage to store the water of the upper reaches of a river in an artificial lake—or, as the case may be, to regulate the legal consequences of a territorial disruption of an already existing hydrographic system.

Instances of the first type are the following.

In *America*:

Rio Grande, Gila, Colorado, Tijuana.

The often tense relations between the United States and Mexico in the field of boundary rivers have formed the object of a series of conventions. The Peace Treaty of Guadelupe Hidalgo of 2 February 1848 (Martens, N.R.G.[1], XIV, 7) and the Gadsden Treaty of 30 December 1853 (*ibid.*, N.R.G.[2], I, 1) still only dealt with navigation, but subsequent conventions have extended the scope of the regulation to irrigation, flood control, prevention of drastic changes in, and regularization of the river bed, and the generation of hydroelectric power.

Convention of 21 May 1906 (*ibid.*, N.R.G.[2], XXXV, 461), providing for the delivery to Mexico, after the completion of a storage dam near

Eagle (New Mexico) and the distributing system auxiliary thereto, of 60.000 acre-feet of water annually from the river under a number of express reservations, formulated in Articles 4 and 5: the delivery of water shall not be construed as a recognition by the United States of any claim on the part of Mexico to the said waters, or as the establishment of any general principle or precedent; the arrangement extends only to the portion of the Río Grande which forms the international boundary from the head of the Old Mexican Canal down to Fort Quitman, Texas.

Convention of 3 February 1944 (*U.N.T.S.*, vol. 3, p. 314) relating to the utilization of the waters of the Colorado and Tijuana rivers, and of the Río Grande (Río Bravo del Norte) from Fort Quitman (Texas) to the Gulf of Mexico, with supplementary Protocol of 14 November 1944. This Convention deals with the diversion of water for storage, or to utilize it for domestic and municipal uses, agriculture and stockraising; electric power; and other industrial uses, in that order of preference, whether this be done by means of dams across the channel, partition weirs, lateral intakes, pumps or any other method. The use of the rivers for navigation, fishing and hunting, and any other possible beneficial uses only come lowest in the order of preferences. The very elaborate convention further deals with the voluntary or involuntary discharge of water for flood control, return flow, border sanitation problems, the distribution of the available water between the two countries, the joint construction of storage dams, flood control works, plants for generating hydroelectric energy, etc.

Agreement of 24 October 1960 (*U.N.T.S.*, vol. 401, p. 137) for the construction of a new, the Amistad Dam on the Río Grande to complement the Falcón Dam.

St. Lawrence basin, Great Lakes, Niagara Falls.

Another long series of agreements has laid down rules to govern Canadian-American relations with respect to the use of the waters of these rivers and lakes for various purposes, especially navigation and the generation of electric power. All later agreements were concluded on the basis of the original Treaty between Great Britain and the United States relating to boundary waters of 11 January 1909 (Martens, N.R.G.[3], IV, 208; *B.F.S.P.*, vol. 102, p. 137) which still gave clear priority to navigation over power. This treaty assigned to the parties exclusive jurisdiction and control over the use and diversion of all waters on their own side of the boundary line, provided against obstructions in boundary waters, limited the diversion of waters from the Niagara River, made provision for the maintenance of the level of the lakes etc., and set up an International Joint Commission. Subsequent agreements have dealt with the level of the Lake of the Woods (1925), Lake Memphremagog (1935), Rainy Lake (1938) and Lake St. Francis (1941) (*L.N.T.S.*, vol. 43, p. 252; *For. Rel. U.S.*, 1935, vol. II, p. 53; *L.N.T.S.*, vol. 203, p. 208;

U.N.T.S., vol. 23, p. 276, 280), the development of certain portions of the Great Lakes St. Lawrence Basin project (1940) (*L.N.T.S.*, vol. 203, p. 268), the uses of the waters of the Niagara River (1950) (*U.N.T.S.*, vol. 132, p. 224), the construction of remedial works at Niagara Falls (1954) (*U.N.T.S.*, vol. 236, p. 382), etc., more and more also for hydro-electrical purposes.

Columbia. Other agreements between Canada and the United States have prepared the development of the Upper Columbia River basin for various purposes: domestic water supply and sanitation; navigation; efficient development of water power; control of floods; irrigation; reclamation of wet lands; conservation of fish and wildlife: February-March 1944—study to be made by a joint commission from the points of view of navigation, power development, irrigation, flood control and other beneficial public uses (*U.N.T.S.*, vol. 109, p. 192); treaty relating to co-operative development of the water resources of the Columbia River basin, 17 January 1961 (*U.N.T.S.*, vol. 542, p. 244).

A marshland section of the *Pilcomayo* River: Argentina-Paraguay, 1 June 1945 (*U.N. Legislative Series ST/LEG/SER.B/ 12*, p. 149)—construction of works for the purpose of ensuring the stability of a boundary line and the utilization of the flow of the waters, prepared by a joint technical commission; preceded by another treaty of 5 July 1939 (*B.F.S.P.*, vol. 143, p. 340), setting up a technical commission to draw up a plan of works necessary to regulate the proportional distribution of the flow of the river into two branches on the north and on the south of the frontier. Comp. p. 21.

Rapids of the *Uruguay* River in the area of Salto Grande: Argentina-Uruguay, 30 December 1946 (*U.N. Legislative Series ST/LEG/SER.B/12*, p. 160)—creation of a joint technical commission, responsible for dealing with all matters concerned with the utilization, damming and diversion of the waters, for the production of energy.

Waterfalls in the Acaray and Monday rivers, tributaries of the *Paraná* river: Brazil-Paraguay, 20 Januari 1956 (*ibid.*, p. 169)—hydrological surveys to be made by Brazil; determination in advance of the percentage (20) up to which Brazil shall have the right to consume the electric power to be produced by future generators.

Rapids of the River *Paraná* (Apipé Falls): Argentine-Paraguay, 23 January 1958—creation of a joint commission for the utilization of their water-power and the improvement of the navigability of the river.

Lake Titicaca: exchange of notes of 20 April 1955, preliminary convention of 30 July 1955 and the agreement of 19 February 1957 between Bolivia and Peru concerning the use of the Lake for hydroelectric and other purposes (see *U.N. Legislative Series ST/LEG/SER.B/12*, p. 165).

In *Africa*:

Nile: exchange of notes of 26 January 1925 (Martens, N.R.G.[3], XXI,

125) between Egypt and Great Britain concerning the appointment of a Commission for the purpose of examining the basis on which irrigation of the Sudan can be carried out.

Nile Waters Agreement of 7 May 1929 regarding the use of Nile water for irrigation purposes (*ibid.*, N.R.G.³, XXI, 97; *L.N.T.S.*, vol. 93, p. 44), concluded between Great Britain and Egypt pending agreement on the status of the Sudan, providing for "such an increase of the quantity of the Nile water thus far utilised by the Sudan as does not infringe Egypt's natural and historical rights in the waters of the Nile and its requirements of agricultural extension". The Agreement was based on the findings of the 1925 Nile Commission (Sennar Dam on the Blue Nile with the Gezira Irrigation Canal; Gebel Aulia Dam on the White Nile) and specified the periods and volumes of the allowed discharges.

Full utilization of the Nile waters for the common benefit of Egypt and the Sudan was only ensured by their Agreement of 8 November 1959 (*U.N.T.S.*, vol. 453, p. 51), providing for the construction by Egypt of the Sudd el Aali Reservoir at Aswan and by the Sudan Republic of the Roseires Reservoir on the Blue Nile, for the sharing of their benefits and for further projects to be carried out for increasing the water supply by the prevention of excess losses in the swamps of the Upper Nile basin.

Kunene River: Agreement between Portugal (for Angola) and the Union of South Africa (for its then Mandated Territory of South West Africa) of 1 July 1926 (N.R.G.³, XXIII, 302; *L.N.T.S.*, vol. 70, p. 316) concerning the utilization of the water of that river for the purposes of generating hydraulic power and of inundation and irrigation in the Mandated Territory, creating a servitude-like right of the latter to use the Kunene Falls in Angola for those purposes.

Owen Falls in Uganda: Great Britain-Egypt, 30-31 May 1949—construction of a dam for the production of hydro-electric power and for the control of the waters of the Nile (*U.N.T.S.*, vol. 226, p. 274).

Shiré Valley and Lake Nyasa project, Portugal-United Kingdom 21 January 1953 (*U.N.T.S.*, vol. 175, p. 14): construction of a dam, stabilization of the lake and production of hydroelectric energy.

Kariba Dam, an undertaking by the Federation of Rhodesia and Nyasaland, which obtained an international character after Northern Rhodesia's (Zambia's) separation from the federation in 1962.

Europe.

Douro. Spanish-Portuguese Convention of Lisbon of 11 August 1927 to regulate the hydroelectric development of the international section of the river (*L.N.T.S.*, vol. 82, p. 131) in accordance with an earlier Agreement of 29 August/2 September 1912 on the exploitation of border rivers for industrial purposes (*U.N. Legislative Series ST/LEG/SER.B/12*, p. 908). The Convention regulates the distribution of the expected power in two zones; provides for the mutual establishment of the necessary servitudes "on a private footing" in favour of reservoirs, dam-supports, off-lets or other installations of the other Party; forbids the transfer, lease or cession of the power belonging to each country to another country, and foresees the appointment of a Spanish-Portuguese International Commission.

A large number of other hydraulic, most hydroelectric systems, *inter alia* on the following rivers or lakes:

Meuse: Belgium-the Netherlands, 12 May 1863 (Martens, N.R.G.², I, 117), 11 January 1873 (*ibid.*, I, 123)—derivation of water from the river for the feeding of navigation canals and for irrigation; subject of proceedings before the Permanent Court of International Justice (*Publ. P.C.I.J.*, series A/B, No. 70).

Rhône: France-Switzerland, 4 October 1913 (Martens, N.R.G.³, X, 290)—partition of the hydraulic power created by a new "usine de la Plaine" between France and the Canton of Geneva.

Doubs: France-Switzerland, 19 November 1930 (*ibid.*, N.R.G.³, XXVI, 312; *B.F.S.P.*, vol. 133, p. 487)—barrage on the river at la Grande Beuge (Canton of Neuchatel).

Maritza-Evros: Greece-Turkey, 20 June 1934 (*U.N. Legislative Series ST/LEG/SER.B/12*, p. 803)—elaborate convention concerning a number of hydraulic works to be carried out on both banks of the river.

Sauer (Sûre): Luxembourg-Rhineland-Palatinate, 25 April 1950 (*Mémorial du Grand-Duché de Luxembourg*, No. 46, 24 July 1953; *U.N. Legislative Series ST/LEG/SER. B/12*, p. 721)—construction of a hydroelectric power-plant.

Inn, respectively Danube: Austria-Bavaria, agreements of 16 October 1950, respectively 13 February 1952 (E. HARTIG, *Internationale Wasserwirtschaft und internationales Recht*, 1955, Annexes 7 and 9; *U.N. Legislative Series ST/LEG/SER. B/12*, pp. 470 and 476)—joint development and utilization of water power on frontier sections by two joint-stock companies.

Drava, respectively Mura: Austria-Yugoslavia, 25 May 1954, respectively 16 December 1954 (*U.N.T.S.*, vol. 227, p. 128 and vol. 396, p. 100) concerning different water economy questions; setting-up of two Permanent Austro-Yugoslav Commissions and provision for arbitration.

Lake Dojran: Greece-Yugoslavia, 31 March 1956, 1 September 1957, 18 June 1959 (*U.N. Legislative Series ST/LEG/SER. B/12*, pp. 811, 813 and 818, and *U.N.T.S.*, vol. 363, p. 34), dealing with the level and the flowing-out of the waters of the lake, their utilization, hydroeconomic studies to be undertaken, the setting-up of a Permanent Mixed Commission, etc.

Lake Ohrid, Crni Drim, Beli Drim, Lake Skadar (Skutari) and Boyana River, Albania-Yugoslavia 5 December 1956 (*U.N. Legislative*

Series ST/LEG/SER. B/12, p. 441)—different water economy questions; statute of a mixed Commission.

Pasvik (Paatso): Norway-USSR, 18 December 1957 (*U.N.T.S.*, vol. 312, p. 274)—utilization of water-power and construction of water-lifting dams and power-stations by the parties. Because of the construction of a certain dam, a lake formed and in June 1969 an agreement was signed defining part of the common boundary, the old line having become partly obsolete as a result of the lake (*Bulletin of Legal Developments* 1969, p. 130).

Our: Luxembourg-Rhineland Palatinate, 10 July 1958 (*U.N. Legislative Series ST/LEG/SER. B/12*, p. 726)—construction of hydroelectric power-installations near Vianden.

Lake Inarî: Finland-Norway-USSR, with additional protocol, 29 April 1959 (*U.N.T.S.*, vol. 346, p. 212)—regulation of the lake by means of the Kaitakoski hydroelectric power-station and dam.

Less important instances are that of different provisions in the Italian Peace Treaty of Paris of 10 February 1947 (*U.N.T.S.*, vol. 49, p. 3), embodying a guarantee given

by France to Italy, in connexion with Italy's cession of the Mont Cenis plateau and the Tenda-Brigue district to France, for a sufficient supply of water from the Lake of Mont Cenis, and of electricity produced at different hydroelectrical plants, *inter alia*, on the river Roya: Article 9, *j.*° Annex III, *sub* A I-IV and B, 1 and 4 (a);

by Italy and Yugoslavia jointly to the newly projected Free Territory of Trieste for the maintenance of the existing supply of electricity to that territory: Article 21 (5), *j.*° Annex IX, *sub* B.

Asia.

Upper Jordan and Yarmuk: Article 8 of the Anglo-French Convention relating to their employment for the purposes of irrigation and the production of hydroelectric power in the period of the League of Nations Mandates (23 December 1920, *L.N.T.S.*, vol. 22, p. 355); Agreement between Jordan and Syria for the same purposes, 4 June 1953 (*U.N.T.S.*, vol. 184, p. 25).

Araxes: barrage of Sardarabad, Russo-Turkish protocol of 8 January 1927 (*B.F.S.P.*, vol. 127, p. 926).

Tigris and Euphrates: construction of barrages and other works on Turkish territory at the expense of Iraq for the purposes of irrigation and the production of hydroelectric power, protocol of 29 March 1946 (*U.N.T.S.*, vol. 37, p. 286).

Helmand River: treaty of 7 September 1950: plan for the apportionment of its waters for use in Iran and Afghanistan, to be prepared by a Commission of three foreign engineers (*U.N. Legislative Series ST/LEG/SER. B/12*, p. 270).

Argun and Upper Amur Rivers: joint scientific research by China and the Soviet Union to prepare a scheme for the multi-purpose exploitation of these rivers, agreement of 18 August 1956 (*U.N. Legislative Series ST/LEG/SER. B/12*, p. 280).

The following two cases are typical instances of a territorial disruption of existing hydrographical systems:

Mekong: establishment of a Committee for Co-ordination of investigations of the Lower-Mekong Basin by Cambodia, Laos, Thailand and the Republic of Viet-Nam in response to an ECAFE decision of 1957 in favour of studies relating to the development of the area of the drainage basin of the Mekong river. See its statute of 31 October 1957 in *U.N. Legislative Series ST/LEG/SER. B/12*, p. 267. These studies have led to the carrying-out of plans for different sections of the Mekong, comprising, *inter alia*, the construction of a dam in the Tonle Sap, a tributary in Cambodia.

Indus: a very detailed Indus Waters Treaty India-Pakistan, signed at Karachi on 19 September 1960 between the Presidents Nehru and Ayub Khan (*U.N.T.S.*, vol. 419, p. 125). Attribution of all the waters of the Eastern Rivers (Sutlej, Beas and Ravi) for unrestricted use to India (Article 2), and of all those waters of the Western Rivers (Indus, Jhelum and Chenab) which India is under obligation to let flow under Article 3 (2) for unrestricted use to Pakistan. Construction by the latter of a system of works, the replacement from the Western Rivers of water supplies for irrigation canals in Pakistan which were hitherto dependent on water supplies from the Eastern Rivers (Article 4), conditional upon a fixed financial contribution of India (Article 5). Future cooperation for the optimum development of the rivers in their common interest (Article 7). Setting-up of a Permanent Indus Commission (Article 8). Scheme for the settlement of disputes (Article 9), worked out in Annexures F and G. A very elaborate Annexure D deals with the generation of hydroelectric power, an equally elaborate Annexure E with the storage of waters by India on the Western Rivers. See H. R. Külz, *Further water disputes between India and Pakistan* in *I.C.L.Q.* 1969 (18), pp. 718 *et seq.*

As can be gathered from my brief indications relative to the various international agreements listed above, they are very different in scope and elaborateness. Some of them are merely preparatory. Some are intended to regularize existing waterways, others to apportion the water available, others again to carry out huge construction works, either for irrigation purposes or for the generation of hydroelectric power. Many establish joint commissions to secure their correct implementation; a number of them provide for the arbitral settlement of possible disputes. I cannot go here into further details.

As I have stated above in Chapter II, section 1, § 8, p. 27, the Conference on the Law of the Sea (Geneva, 1958) has only dealt with bays surrounded by territory of one and the same State (Article 7, para. 1), and has left the regime of pluristatal bays completely without regulation. It has, moreover, been unable to draw a distinction between a bay and an estuary, which it could not define. The International Law Commission had made an attempt to say at least something about an estuary; its proposal, laid down in Article 13 of its 1956 draft, was to the effect that

> "1. If a river flows directly into the sea, the territorial sea shall be measured from a line drawn *inter fauces terrarum* across the mouth of the river.
> 2. If the river flows into an estuary the coasts of which belong to a single State, article 7 (relating to bays) shall apply."

As the I.L.C. could not make it clear what was the difference between the cases envisaged in paragraphs 1 and 2, and what is an estuary (a concept which was during the discussions wrongly identified with a delta—in fact quite a different configuration), the proposed Article was "pruned" and de-latinized so as to be left saying nothing more than that, if a river flows directly into the sea, the baseline shall be a straight line across the mouth of the river between points on the low-tide line of its banks.

What finally emerged from the discussions was a fairly complicated set of definitions and demarcations of a bay in Article 7, paras. 2-5, of Convention I (*U.N.T.S.*, vol. 516, p. 205). These paragraphs serve to define the characteristics of a bay and to indicate where is the dividing line in an indentation between the internal waters of the coastal State and its territorial sea:

> "(2) ... a bay is a well-marked indentation whose penetration is in such proportion to the width of its mouth as to contain landlocked waters and constitute more than a mere curvature of the coast. An indentation shall not, however, be regarded as a bay unless its area is as large as, or larger than, that of the semi-circle whose diameter is a line drawn across the mouth of that indentation.
> (3) For the purpose of measurement, the area of an indentation is that lying between the low-water mark around the shore of the indentation and a line joining the low-water marks of its natural entrance points. Where, because of the presence of islands, an indentation has more than one mouth, the semi-circle shall be drawn on a line as long as the sum total of the lengths of the lines across the different mouths. Islands within an indentation shall be included as if they were part of the water area of the indentation.
> (4) If the distance between the low-water marks of the natural entrance points of a bay does not exceed twenty-four miles, a closing line may be

293

drawn between these two low-water marks, and the waters enclosed thereby shall be considered as internal waters.

(5) Where the distance between the low-water marks of the natural entrance points of a bay exceeds twenty-four miles, a straight baseline of twenty-four miles shall be drawn within the bay in such a manner as to enclose the maximum area of water that is possible with a line of that length."

The last paragraph of Article 7 lays down that the foregoing provisions shall not apply to so-called "historic" bays, or in any case where the straight baseline system is applied.

The twenty-four miles rule in my opinion must not be considered mandatory: this breadth is not meant to be a fixum, but a maximum, that is, nothing prevents a coastal state to reduce that breadth to the effect that a larger part of the bay area changes from internal waters to territorial sea.

Inlets from the sea present an author with difficulties from a systematical point of view. They are only certain to form inland State territory or internal waters, and they consequently only belong to the present section 8 in so far as they are situated on the land side of the said closing line and are bordered by only one State. If they are bordered by two or more States, their legal status is extremely uncertain. It is possible that such bays or other inlets also constitute inland State territory, either *pro diviso* or *pro indiviso* (as an area under co-sovereignty), but they may equally well be either territorial sea or even part of the open sea. There is no general imperative rule in existence and the coastal States are, at least to a certain extent, free to regulate the status of such inlets in common accord as they deem fit. They are, in particular, under no international obligation vis-à-vis third States to treat a common bay with a closing line of less than twenty-four miles and a wider pocket of water inside as open sea for the only reason that it is surrounded by more than one State. Although this has sometimes been asserted in legal literature to be the case, the assertion is unsupported by actual State practice. On the other hand, the coastal States may, as between themselves, become involved in an international dispute, when they are not in agreement about the legal status of the bay, as has been the case of the Gulf of Fonseca (*A.J.I.L.* 1917 (11), p. 674). In so far as such a disagreement concerns the exact *tracé* of the frontier between their respective internal waters or territorial seas inside a bay, I refer to Chapter VI below.

The exception in regard to "historic bays", made in Article 7, para. 6, of Convention I of Geneva confronts us with the uncertainty of that concept. It has from time to time been invoked by coastal States in international disputes and proceedings, both with respect to unistatal and to pluristatal bays. Comp. Part IV-A of this publication. Several bays of Great Britain and on the east coast of the United States have been claimed as internal waters by the States concerned (see Whiteman, vol. 4, p. 233). The characterization of certain bays as "historic" has played an important rôle in the North Atlantic Fisheries case of 1910 between the United Kingdom and the United States (*A.A.*, vol. XI, p. 167).

Among the main instances of bays which are, rightly in my opinion, claimed by the adjacent State to be "historical" I place on record the following:

in Great Britain, parts of the Moray Firth and the Firth of Clyde and part of the Bristol Channel;

in Canada, the Bay of Chaleurs and Conception Bay;

in the United States, Chesapeake and Delaware Bays and the Bay of Fundy;

in Central America, the Gulf of Fonseca;

in France, the Bay of Granville (Cancale);

in Norway, the Vestfjord and the Varangerfjord;

in the Soviet Union, the sea of Azov;

between Ceylon and India, Palk's Bay and the Gulf of Manaar;

in Tunisia, the Gulfs of Gabès and Tunis.

The character of an historical bay has been claimed for many more inlets from the sea, for example, in Aequatorial Africa, but in a number of cases without much foundation. The claim must in particular be rejected with respect to the Bay of Hudson (comp. on this water area Part IV-A of this publication).

I will not go further into this subject, on which a wealth of details can be found in GIDEL's *Le droit international public de la mer* (Paris, 1934, vol. III, pp. 652-663) and in BOUCHEZ's *The regime of bays in international law* (Leyden, 1963).

The Soviet Union also has claimed one of her bays, that of Peter the Great, as internal water by a Decree of 21 July 1957 (see Whiteman, vol. 4, pp. 250-257), which delimited it by a line connecting the mouth of the Tyumen-Oula river with Cape Povorotnyi. Protests against this decree by Japan, the United States and the United Kingdom were refuted by the Soviet Government on various grounds, *viz.*, the particular geographical configuration and economic and military importance of the bay; the historical rights which Tsarist Russia already attributed to herself in the Regulations for Sea Fisheries in the Territorial Waters of the Government General of the Amur of 1901; recognition of the bay as internal waters by neighbour States such as the Chinese People's Republic, and Japan's tacit acceptance of the claim in her fishery conventions with the Soviet Union of 1907, 1928 and 1944, which granted Japanese fishermen the right to fish in the bay. The Soviet Union has not altered her attitude since.

As to the other exception—cases where the straight baseline system is applied—the following may be recalled. It is the Anglo-Norwegian *Fisheries* case of 1951 (*I.C.J. Reports* 1951, p. 116) which has paved the way for further legal development in this field through the endowment of a specific type of "inlets from the sea" with a new hitherto unknown international regime. This was subsequently worked out and codified by the first Conference on the Law of the Sea of 1958. I refer to those maritime areas which were legally separated from the high seas by a system of "straight base lines", as had been applied by Norway for the delimitation of her territorial sea and sanctioned by the International Court of Justice as constituting a permissible method of such delimitation. As large parts of these maritime areas, which as a consequence became, or were recognized by the Court's ruling as internal waters of Norway, had until then belonged to either her territorial sea or even to the high seas, some mitigation of their legal transformation into internal waters was deemed necessary by the International Law Commission. It felt that this could be done by restricting the characterization of the maritime areas concerned as internal waters by the qualification that the right of free passage through that particular category of internal waters should not be impeded. The Conference of 1958 endorsed this proposal in a generalized form, thus making it thenceforth applicable to all identical geographical situations, by laying down in Article 4(5) of Convention I that

> "The system of straight baselines may not be applied by a State in such a manner as to cut off from the high seas the territorial sea of another State,"

and in Article 5(2) that

> "Where the establishment of a straight baseline in accordance with article 4 has the effect of enclosing as internal waters areas which previously had been considered as part of the territorial sea or of the high seas, a right of innocent passage, as provided in articles 14 to 23, shall exist in those waters."

In this geographical constellation of a *skjærgaard* or in comparable situations, the content of the right of a State respecting such constructive "internal" coastal waters, in so far as their designation as such is permissible at all, is, consequently, considerably restricted so as to assimilate that right rather to that respecting its territorial sea.

Comp. on this subject also my remarks in Part IV-A of this publication relating to Maritime Straits and the provision embodied in Article 16(4) of Convention I, in the terms of which

> "There shall be no suspension of the innocent passage of foreign ships through straits which are used for international navigation between ... part of the high seas and ... the territorial sea of a foreign State."

CHAPTER III

ACQUISITION AND LOSS OF TERRITORY

Introduction

When attempting, starting from the sources, to form a general idea of the history of territorial acquisitions and losses from the point of view of an international lawyer, one can approach by different ways, each of them offering interesting perspectives.

Thus, one can take the various "titles" or causes of acquisition or loss, old and new, as one's starting point and then, with the object of giving an overall survey, systematize the data in accordance with that multiplicity of titles in their individual historical development.

One can also choose one or more specific States as one's point of departure and then, reaching back into the past, reconstruct the formation of the State(s) concerned, thus uncovering the various titles which have played a rôle in that formation.

A third approach is to analyse more concretely the many territorial disputes, new and old, which have left their traces in history, with a view, in particular, to assessing the validity of the contradictory claims.

I intend in principle to take the first line.

As I have remarked earlier in the introductory Chapter I, old conceptions of the nature of territorial supremacy—feudal, dynastic, patrimonial—had their corollary in old modes of acquisition and loss of the same. A number of these are now entirely obsolete. Others have survived in name but are now adapted to modern conceptions of territorial sovereignty. A few novel methods have emerged.

Among the obsolete modes of acquisition or loss[1] may be cited: marriage, inheritance *ab intestato*, succession in virtue of a will, division of dynastic estates, a family pact or pact of confraternity, an Imperial "expectative", a Papal grant, a clause of "reversibility", feudal forfeiture, a pseudo-judicial decision of a "chambre de réunion", the lapse of a mortgage, discovery or symbolic occupation, and the creeping effect of a personal union.

---

1. A number of them are *expressis verbis* listed in treaties of the past: see *e.g.*, Article 2 of the Austro-Netherlands-British Barrier Treaty of 15 November 1715 (Dumont, VIII[1], 458).

Among those modes which existed in the past and still exist, though partially in a new notional guise, I cite: cession without *quid pro quo* (donation), cession against some monetary return (sale), exchange, effective occupation, conquest and adjudication by some recognized international authority.

Novel or still doubtful modes of acquisition are: acquisitive prescription and "novation" by the conversion of a *jus in territorio alieno* into full sovereignty.

I will first deal, in section 1, with the antiquated modes of acquisition and loss. They may at first sight appear to be of merely historical interest but, as actual experience proves, their impact on inter-state relations must still at the present time occasionally be taken into account in order to arrive at a correct evaluation of unsolved international territorial disputes. Reference may be made to the feudal origin of certain legal relationships which the International Court of Justice was called upon in 1953 to appraise in respect of the small Channel Islands groups of the Minquiers and the Ecrehos off the French coast[2] and to early conceptions of the law of nations with regard to the acquisition of territorial sovereignty by means of discovery or symbolic occupation in the Netherlands-American case of 1925/1928 concerning the island of Palmas or Miangas, decided by an award of Max Huber of 4 April 1928.[3] And these are certainly not the only cases, for there are many more in which obsolete institutions may still make their influence felt on the evaluation of present-day unsolved territorial problems.

Section 1. OBSOLETE MODES OF ACQUISITION AND LOSS

(A) *Acquisition*

§ 1. *Marriage*

Many States owe their present territorial shape and extent in part to marriages contracted in former centuries between rulers of smaller political units or between such a ruler and the heiress or heir of another political entity. Looked at from the legal point of view, a difference must be made between (*a*) cases in which a territory was given directly as a dowry and (*b*) those in which the respective domains initially continued to be governed as separate units, but were ultimately merged. In the latter case developments indeed often tended to gradually weld the territories of the spouses together under a common dynasty, because

2. Judgment of 17 November 1953 (*I.C.J. Reports* 1953, p. 47); Comp. my *The Jurisprudence of the World Court*, II, pp. 169-177.
3. *A.A.*, vol. II, pp. 829 *et seq.*

the personal element in the relationship by far outweighed the legal element of their constitutional diversity. Thus, the countries, originally only linked by the marriage bond between members of two different dynasties, became in fact united by the joint effect of their actually being governed by the husband, the operation of the laws on succession, the adoption of a common constitution, or at least the mutual adaptation of their systems of constitutional law. This particular mode of territorial acquisition partly overlaps that discussed in § 3 below, the creeping effect of a personal union.

There have also been cases in which the treaty that underlay the merger provided for both the union of the two countries and the marriage of their rulers. This was, for example, the case of the treaty of Volkovysk of 1385 between Poland and Lithuania sealing, for the purposes of the union, the marriage between Grand Duke Jagiello of Lithuania (baptized under the name Vladislav) and Queen Jadviga (Hedwig) of Poland, which indeed followed in 1386. The two countries, which had continued their existence under separate governments—Lithuania under a relative of King Vladislav II, Grand Duke Vitold—, were further united by the Treaty of Horodlo of 1413. Comp. *The Cambridge Medieval History*, vol. VII (1932), p. 259.

When perusing the famous treaty collections of the past, one comes across an infinity of marriage agreements of both types which, however, are not always clearly distinguishable. They often also included diverse clauses of an entirely different nature.

Comp. for example, in a first contract concerning the intended marriage of Charles of Austria (the later King Carlos I of Spain, Charles V as Emperor) with Renée of France, daughter of Louis XII, of 24 March 1515 (Dumont, IV¹, 199), two special clauses, one providing for a solution of all controversies pending between the two countries, the other forging a "ligue offensive et défensive" between them.

Such contracts, however, repeatedly miscarried and left no trace in legal history, or they failed in the first instance to produce the desired effect and only succeeded at a later stage. A peculiar type of marriage agreement was that of an arrangement laid down in an arbitral award in which the arbitrator acted as a marriage-broker. On the other hand, there also occurred various cases in which the effect of a princely marriage upon the territorial *status quo* was expressly excluded.

(*a*) Among the cases in which the princely bride directly brought her bridegroom territory in marriage as a dowry, I will cite that of Bombay ("la bonne baie", Portuguese since 1530) and Tangier (Portuguese since 1471), which both served as dowries of Catharine of Portugal to King Charles II of England on the occasion of their marriage (contract of 29 May 1662; J. Ferreira Borges de Castro, *Collecção dos tratados, convenções, contratos e actos publicos ... desde 1610 até o presente*,

Lisboa, 1856-1858, vol. I, p. 234). The first was, however, transferred in 1668 to the British East India Company against a perpetual ground-rent, the second abandoned again to the Moors in 1684 because of the costliness of its retention for the British Crown.—Much earlier, in the same way, King Alfonso X *el Sabio* of Castile, who claimed the right of suzerainty over the "Kingdom of the Algarves" which had been wrested from the Moors by Alfonso III *o Restaurador* in 1251, abandoned his claim in favour of the latter on the occasion of his marriage to a natural daughter of the Spanish King in 1253.[4]—Under the same token Anna of Brittanny's successive marriages with the kings of France Charles VIII (6 December 1491, Dumont, III², 271/273) and Louis XII (7 January 1499, *ibid.*, III², 405) caused Brittanny definitively to devolve upon France at her death in 1514. The first of these two marriage contracts even expressly defined the establishment of the dowry as a *donatio inter vivos.*—The history of Navarra offers another, again much older example. This country fell first to France in 1284 as a consequence of Queen Juana's marriage with the French king Philippe (IV) le Bel,[5] but it recovered its independent existence after Philippe's death in 1314. It was, however, later, in 1458, united with Aragón on the accession to the throne of Aragón of King Juan II, husband of Queen Blanca of Navarra.

(*b*) More important and interesting are the cases in which the effect of the marriage was only indirect and yet ended in fusing the actual or future possessions of the spouses into one single political community.

The house of Austria was particularly famous for its talent for expanding its empire by wedlock: the marriages of the Austrian prince who later became Emperor Maximilian I with the rich heiress Mary of Burgundy in 1477 and of their son Philippe le Bel of Burgundy with Juana (later surnamed la Loca) of Aragón-Castile in 1495 are a striking evidence of the truth of the famous distich "Bella gerant alii, tu, felix Austria, nube; Nam quae Mars aliis, dat tibi regna Venus".

Peculiar marriage schemes were often laid down in peace or other political treaties, or occasionally even in arbitral awards.

Thus, in the Franco-Spanish Peace Treaty of Noyon of 13 August 1516 (Dumont, IV¹, 224) it was stipulated that, should the daughter of King François I of France marry the new King Carlos I of Spain, then sixteen years old, the latter would in that capacity cede to her all rights

---

4. Hence the fossilized title: "Rey de Portugal y de los Algarves".
5. That is why already the kings of France Philippe IV and Louis X carried the additional title of "roi de Navarre" from 1284 to 1316. It later fell into desuetude and was only revived in the 16th century, when, in 1589, the then ruler of Lower Navarre (north of the Pyrenees) Henry III succeeded as Henry IV to the throne of France. Upper-Navarra (south of the Pyrenees) had meanwhile been conquered by Ferdinand of Castile in 1512.

to Naples, the whole of which his grandfather Ferdinand of Aragón "el Católico" had conquered in 1504 after a short period of occupation in common with France. In that treaty of 1516 provision was even made for indemnification in the case of non-compliance, but the whole stipulation proved abortive. As abortive, for that matter, as had already proved to be his above-mentioned earlier marriage contract of 1515 with Renée of France: the Spanish king, having become Emperor Charles V in 1519, in 1526 finally married Isabel of Portugal.

A case of a double marriage contract was that concluded on 22 July 1515 (Dumont, IV¹, 211) between King Vladislav of Bohemia and Hungary and Maximilian I of Austria for a future marriage between Vladislav's son (the later King Lewis II) and Maximilian's grand-daughter Maria (sister of Carlos I of Spain, the later Emperor Charles V), on the one hand, and between Maximilian's grandson (the later Emperor Frederick I) and Vladislav's daughter Anna, on the other, under the liberal proviso, for the rest, that the agreement should be null and void in case the princes and princesses concerned should be disinclined to contract the contemplated marriages. They were, however, concluded in fact in 1521/22 and have, in combination with an *Erbverbrüderung*[6] between the two sovereigns, contributed to the subsequent subordination of Hungary to Austria.

The marriage contract between Philip II of Spain and Queen Mary I of England of 1 January 1554 (Rymer, *Foedera*, XV, pp. 393-4, 400 (2nd ed., 1728)) disposed that future children were to succeed to the maternal possessions, whereas the paternal possessions (Spain, Naples, Sicily, Milan and further Italian cities) were to devolve upon Charles (Don Carlos), the son of Philip's first marriage to Maria of Portugal. Only on the demise of Don Carlos without heirs should the paternal possessions devolve upon the first-born son of the two royal spouses, who was in any case to acquire Burgundy and the Low Countries. However, the childless royal marriage already ended in 1558 by Mary's death.

A Franco-Scottish treaty of April 1558 (Dumont, IV¹, 21) arranged the marriage between the fifteen years old Queen of Scotland Mary Stuart and the fourteen years old son of King Henri II of France, François, and stipulated that in the case of the Queen's decease without children her Kingdom would fall to France. François succeeded his father on his death on 10 July 1559 as King of France, thus establishing a personal union between France and Scotland, but this was of very short duration since he died on 5 December 1560, leaving his widow to engage in her fatal career which ended in her execution in London on 8 February 1587. This was another of the many abortive marriage treaties between princes in the past.

6. Comp. on this type of agreement § 2 below, *sub* (*c*), p. 307.

A noteworthy example of a royal marriage arranged by an arbitral award is that suggested in 1299 by Benedetto Gaetano (Pope Boniface VIII) "as a private person" adjudicating between King Philippe IV of France and King Edward I of England, according to which the latter's son Edward (II) was to marry the former's daughter Isabelle. This marriage was indeed contracted on the strength of the Anglo-French Treaty of Montreuil of 19 June 1299 (Dumont, I[1], 317), but proved disastrous for the British King whose wife—the "she-wolf of France"—later, in 1325, rebelled against him and caused his death in 1326.

On the equally ominous marriage arranged by the Anglo-French Peace Treaty of Troyes of 21 May 1420, comp. § 2 below, *sub* (g), p. 323.

The unification of Spain and that of the Low Countries were also to a large extent due to marriages. Comp. on the growth of the latter into a powerful State by means of various titles of acquisition of territory my Excursus below, pp. 341 *et seq.*

The very frequent marriage contracts of later periods are commonly purely dynastical without territorial consequences for the States concerned. Comp. among many others the treaties between Austria and Portugal, 24 June 1708 (Martens, S. I, 422); Spain and Portugal, 3 September and 1 October 1727 (*ibid.*, S. I, 454, 468); Great Britain and Prussia, 18 December 1857 (Princess Victoria and Prince Frederick William of Prussia) (*ibid.*, N.R.G.[1], XX, 436) and 26 February 1879 (Arthur, Duke of Connaught and Princess Louise of Prussia) (*ibid.*, N.R.G.[2], IV, 434); Great Britain and Russia, 22 January 1874 (Alfred, second son of Queen Victoria, and Grand Duchess Maria Alexandrovna, the daughter of the Tsar) (*ibid.*, N.R.G.[1], XX, 450); Great Britain and Spain, 7 May 1906 (Princess Ena of Battenberg and King Alfonso XIII) (*ibid.*, N.R.G.[2], XXXV, 453).

On the other hand, as remarked above, there also occurred on different occasions stipulations in a marriage contract between members of different dynasties which in so many words provided for the renunciation by the bride of possible future claims to succession to the throne in her own House. Comp. *e.g.*, the separate marriage contract additional to, and implementing Article 33 of the Peace Treaty of the Pyrenees of 7 November 1659 (Dumont, VI[2], 264), which was entered into by Louis XIV and Maria Teresa, Infante of Spain (*ibid.*, VI[2], 293), by which the latter, prior to her marriage in her own name and for the subsequent period jointly with her bridegroom, renounced against a dowry of 500,000 gold crowns any right of succession to the throne of Spain. Comp. also Article 2 of the marriage contract (*Eheberedung*) between Karl Theodor, Elector of Bavaria and the Palatinate, and Maria Leopoldina, princess of Austria, of 1795 (*ibid.*, N.S. I, 275).

On other occasions marriages of this type were completely prohibited.

General

The acquisition of territorial possessions by *inheritance*, as frequently occurred in former centuries, is equally hardly any longer imaginable under modern conditions, although it might still, conceivably, happen between communities living under an absolutist monarchical régime, *e.g.*, in the Arab world. But on the whole, it is a thing of the past, however strongly it has made its influence—a still lasting influence—felt in the course of history.

This mode of acquisition of territorial supremacy was closely linked with the patrimonial conceptions of the Middle Ages when the Prince was entitled to a sort of public ownership of his domains. In those conditions there was nothing strange in the current idea that a prince could divide his country amongst his sons or other heirs, nor in the fact that on the death of another prince he inherited the latter's possessions and thus joined them to his own, albeit under the condition that he should maintain his new subjects in the rightful enjoyment of the privileges which had accrued to them under their former ruler. Such inheritance could (*a*) be the outcome of the normal functioning of an accepted traditional law of succession *ab intestato*, often of feudal origin. It could (*b*) result from a will or a *donatio mortis causa*, made by the late ruler. It could (*c*) be based on a dynastic "family pact" (*pactum gentilicium*), *Erbverbrüderung* or "*pactum confraternitatis*". It could (*d*) spring from an "expectative" (expectancy) or an "Eventual-Investitur", granted by the Emperor to a particular prince or princely house. It could (*e*) be the automatic consequence of a clause of "reversion" attached to a feudal grant. It could (*f*) be effected by a division of the princely domains among different heirs pretenders in common accord. There are finally also cases in which (*g*) the succession to the throne by a foreign ruler was stipulated by an international treaty. A few historical examples may serve to illustrate this legal phenomenon of the past.

(*a*) *Succession ab intestato*
The most striking example of the fatal rôle which disputes about the order of dynastic succession have played in feudal times is the origin of the Hundred Years' War between England and France (1337-1453), which was caused by competition between five rival hereditary systems. Comp. on this subject note 52 at pp. 431-432 of Chapter XVIII on the history of the law of nations in Part I of this publication.

This war was only one of the many wars of succession which have disturbed interstate relations, especially in the 17th and 18th centuries. Since, however, such wars have been caused not only by controversies over succession *ab intestato*, but also by disputes over wills, family pacts, and other titles of territorial acquisition, discussed in this section 1, I will return to this type of war in a separate Postscript below, p. 331.

Inheritance has, on the other hand, contributed in no small measure to the upbuilding of kingdoms and empires, which were thus welded together in the course of time by successive hereditary acquisitions of territorial supremacy. The Low Countries of the middle of the 16th century were a curious historical product of the gradual fusion of seventeen different entities by the operation of a number of different legal titles of acquisition of territory under the Houses of Holland, Brabant, Hainault, Bavaria and Austria, among which not the least important was that of hereditary succession. This variety of titles may justify my adding another separate exposition in the Excursus below, pp. 341 *et seq.*

As a few examples of the many conflicts arising from contradictory hereditary claims, I refer to

the succession in Mecklenburg in the period 1728-1730. Comp. for the details—a genealogical table of the house of Mecklenburg, the protest of its duke to the German Diet, the exchange of notes between the duke and Sweden, the relevant decrees of the Emperor, and the duke's appeal to England for help—the deduction in Rousset, *Recueil*, VII, pp. 20 *et seq.* and 253 *et seq.*;

the claims of the Elector of Hesse to the succession of the duchy of Brabant, advanced in an elaborate memorandum inserted in the same *Recueil*, XX, pp. 360 *et seq.*

(b) Wills

Wills have also frequently and of old played a part, and often a baleful part, in political history.

As old examples of testamentary dispositions I cite

from the 13th century the will executed by the Emperor Frederick II in 1250 to the effect that his eldest son Conrad (already elected as King of the Romans) would become his main heir, and that his further domains would devolve on his bastard son (*nothus*) Heinrich (the Kingdom of Jerusalem or the Arelatic Kingdom), his second son Manfred (the principality of Tarente and the *baliatus* of Sicily) and his grandson (*nepos*) Frederick (the duchies of Austria and Styria);

from the 14th century the will of duke Thibaut II of Lorraine of 24 April 1312 (Dumont, I[1], 427), with an additional codicil.

Most notorious is the will made on 2 October 1700 by king Charles II of Spain (Martens, N.R.G.[1], X, 327), which led to the War of the Spanish Succession. The projected succession to the throne of Spain after the impending death of Carlos II, initially regulated by a treaty of partition, entered into by the so-called Maritime Powers (England and the Netherlands) and France on 11 October 1698 (Dumont, VII[2], 442) and allocating Spain itself with the Low Countries and the Spanish colonies to young Joseph Ferdinand of Bavaria; Naples and Sicily to the Dauphin of France, and the duchy of Milan to Archduke Charles of Austria, came to nought owing to the sudden death of the Bavarian prince on 6 February 1699. A second treaty of partition, concluded between the same Powers on 13 March 1700 in London and 25 March 1700 at The Hague (*ibid.*, 477), which in its turn allotted the crown of Spain with the Low Countries and the Indies to Archduke Charles of Habsburg; Naples, Sicily, the duchy of Lorraine and that of Bar to the Dauphin of France, and the duchy of Milan to the duke of Lorraine, was stranded on the refusal of Emperor Leopold I to accept the conditions attached to the deal. Under French pressure the Spanish King, who had already made successively two other wills in conformity with the treaties of partition, thereupon, a few weeks prior to his death on 1 November 1700, made his above-mentioned third will in favour of Louis XIV's grandson Philip of Anjou, second son of the Dauphin of France, subsidiarily of his younger brother the Duke of Berry, Archduke Charles, the duke of Savoy and his sons, all descendants of the sister of Philip II of Spain (Martens, N.R.G.[1], X, 327). When neither the Emperor nor the Maritime Powers were prepared to acquiesce in the main testamentary disposition, this opposition in 1702 resulted in a long war of succession, which after a number of separate peace treaties in 1713, 1714 and 1715 at Utrecht, Rastadt and Baden, was only finally liquidated as between Spain and the Emperor at Vienna in 1725. Comp. on other aspects of this case *infra*, p. 316.

Comparable developments in Austria have plunged Europe into war as a consequence of the Pragmatic Sanction, issued as a *Hausgesetz* by the Emperor Karl VI in 1735 (Wenck, I, 1-8).

Since opposition to wills or similar dispositions of ruling princes has often in the past operated as a cause of war, just as have uncertainty or controversies relative to succession *ab intestato* (above *sub* (*a*) or other titles of territorial acquisition listed in this section 1, I refer again for a further discussion of this type of international conflict to my Postscript below, p. 331.

Many successive wills executed by members of the Netherlands House of Orange have also overstepped the limits of purely dynastic effects and produced international repercussions.

See on the various wills, and other instruments, disposing of the possessions of the House of Orange, whose members were related to foreign royal houses:

27 June 1609, division of the estate of Prince William the Silent (d. in 1584) among his three sons Philips Willem, Maurits and Frederik Hendrik (Dumont, V[2], 113);

20 February 1618, will of Prince Philips Willem (d. in 1618) on behalf of his brother Prince Maurits (*ibid.*, V[2], 305);

13 April 1624, will of Prince Maurits (d. in 1625) on behalf of his brother Prince Frederik Hendrik (*ibid.*, V², 472);

30 January 1640, will of Prince Frederik Hendrik (d. in 1647) on behalf of his son Willem II, married to Harriet Mary Stuart (d. in 1650), and subsidiarily of his four daughters successively (Rousset, *Suppl.*, III¹, 295);

7 December 1646, marriage contract between Frederik Hendrik's eldest daughter Louise Henriette (d. in 1667) and the Elector Friedrich Wilhelm I of Brandenburg (d. in 1688) (Dumont, VI¹, 353);

18 October 1695, will of Willem II's son William III, King of England (d. in 1702) on behalf of his cousin Johan Willem Friso of Nassau-Dietz (d. in 1711) (Rousset, *Recueil*, VIII, 404);

14 May/16 June 1732, following a long controversy, final division of the estate of the House of Orange between Johan Willem Friso's son Willem IV and Louise Henriette of Orange's son King Friedrich I of Prussia (Rousset, *Suppl.*, II², 335; *Recueil*, VIII, 408). This latter contract was of direct international importance for different reasons. The discrepancy between the wills of Frederik Hendrik and William III caused a conflict between Prussia and the Republic of the United Netherlands, whose States General were the appointed excecutors of King William III's will. The estate, moreover, comprised a number of dynastic possessions outside the Netherlands, such as the principality of Orange in France, the counties of Mörs and Lingen in Germany, the seigniory of Montfoort in Limburg and certain possessions in the southern Low Countries. The final division of the estate in 1732 expressly maintained the competitors in the enjoyment of certain titles and arms attached to the countries lost, in particular those of Orange. As the latter had already been ceded by the King of Prussia to France by their Peace Treaty of Utrecht of 11 April 1713, the Prince of Orange in 1732 declared himself as acquiescing in that cession and committed himself not to disturb the King of France in the peaceful possession and enjoyment of the principality. The stipulation of Article 4 of the contract of 1732 is curious:

"Le Seigneur Prince aura la liberté d'imposer le nom de la Principauté d'Orange à tel autre de ses domaines qu'il trouvera convenable, et d'en retenir le titre et les armoiries tant pour lui que pour ses héritiers et descendants mâles et femelles, de même qu'il a été stipulé par le traité [d'Utrecht] en faveur du Seigneur Roi [de Prusse], et promet et s'engage Sa Majesté d'employer ses bons offices pour que le Roi Très Chrétien y donne son consentement, afin d'ôter et abolir toute matière de nouvelle discorde. Bien entendu que cela ne portera aucun préjudice à S.M. le Roi de Prusse, par rapport aux titres et armoiries d'Orange qui seront toujours continuez dans sa Famille Royale aux Princes et Princesses de Prusse".

A case in which in quite a different part of the world a sovereign assertedly divided his estates between his sons in virtue of a will or a similar document still occurred in 1844 when Sultan Sayid-Sa'id, the ruler of Muscat (Oman) and Zanzibar, in a letter addressed to the British Foreign Secretary Lord Aberdeen, conferred upon one of his sons, already installed as vice-roy of his Asian domains, and upon another, vice-roy of his African possessions, the title of heir presumptive of the respective territories under their rule. A dispute between the rulers concerned after their father's death over the validity and scope of this paternal ruling led to an arbitral award by the Governor General of

India, Lord Canning, of 2 April 1861 which in fact endorsed that ruling. Comp. the detailed discussion of that case in DE LAPRADELLE-POLITIS, *Recueil des arbitrages internationaux*, vol. II, pp. 55-77.

Another example of a testamentary disposition by an absolute monarch in Africa was the will of King Leopold II of the Belgians, in his capacity of Sovereign of the Congo Free State, of 2 August 1889 (CALVO, *Droit international théorique et pratique*, 1887-1896, VI, 58) in the following terms:

> "Déclarons par les présentes, léguer et transmettre, après notre mort, à la Belgique, tous nos droits souverains sur l'Etat indépendant du Congo".

The transfer to Belgium did not, however, in the event take place on the strength of that will, but of a formal treaty of cession of 28 November 1907 (Martens, N.R.G.³, II, 101). Comp. on these events Chapter III, section 3, § 5 of Part II of this publication, p. 129.

(c) Dynastic or family pacts[7] and pacta confraternitatis

I can only quote a few of the many examples of this obsolete mode of acquisition of territory which was once in frequent use, especially within the compass of the Holy Roman Empire and in Italy.

This type of compact between dynasties occurred (i) in time of peace, in view of a possible future extinction of one of them, or of a kindred dynasty.

A very old instance of such an *Erbeinigungsvertrag* is that of Pavia of 4 August 1329 (HERZBERG, Recueil, II, 142), which has always remained the basis of the relationship between the Electors of Bavaria and the Palatinate.[8]

> This dynastic compact, entered into following an earlier partition pact of 1313 between Rudolph I of Bavaria and his brother Ludwig (Emperor since 1314), was to the effect that the former's sons Rudolph and Ruprecht were to acquire the Palatinate with part of the Nordgau (Oberpfalz); that the electoral dignity was to alternate between the two lines of Bavaria proper and the Palatinate; that in the case of extinction of one of the two lines the other would come into its inheritance, and that none of the rulers should ever alienate any of the dynastic possessions.—The Palatinate was, however, granted a permanent electoral seat of its own by the Golden Bull of the Emperor Karl IV of January/December 1356 (ZEUMER, *Quellensammlung*, 2nd ed., I, No. 148, p. 192). Comp. on this subject also Article IV,

7. Pacts under this name sometimes served other, less important purposes, witness the so-called Family Pact of 15 August 1761 between France and Spain (Martens, R², I, 16) which was intended to lay down detailed rules of a diplomatic *protocolaire* character (complemented later by an additional agreement for the interpretation of Article 24: 2 January 1768, *ibid.*, R², I, 479).
8. Comp. already the Convention between the palsgraves and dukes of Bavaria Ludwig and Heinrich of 30 June 1281, confirmed by the Emperor Rudolph I (Lünig, *Teutsches Reichs Archiv, Part. Spec., Cont.* II, *Abs.* I, 130; Dumont, I¹, 247).

§ 10 of the Peace Treaty of Osnabrück and the parallel Article 18 of that of Münster of 24 October 1648 which expressly mention the existence and validity of certain *pacta gentilicia* concerning the *Electoralis successio*, entered into by the Heidelberg and the Neuburg branches of the house of the Palatinate, and ratified by earlier Emperors (ZEUMER, *ibid.*, II, nos. 197 and 198, pp. 395 and 434).

It was to this old treaty and three subsequent *Haus-Unions-Erneuerungen* of 1568, 1578 and 1673, and to comparable juristic elements in the at that time burning question of the succession of the Orleans dynasty to the Spanish throne alleged in support, that Pope Clement XI in his "Super-Arbitral-Spruch" of 17 February 1702 (Martens, R.², II, 7) referred when deciding a dispute between the Electors of Bavaria and the Palatinate. Many later conventions have perpetuated this interdynastic relationship: further *Haus-Unions-Erneuerungen* of 1728 and 1734, an *Unions-Tractat* of 5 October 1761, an *Erbeinigungsrecess* of 5/22 September 1766 (Martens, R.², I, 408), a *wechselseitige Erbverbrüderung* of 26 February 1771 (*ibid.*, R.², II, 5), and the curious *Constitutum mutui possessorii* of 19 June 1774 (*ibid.*, R.², II, 284)—whereupon comp. Chapter V, section 1 on co-sovereignty below, p. 435—to which the duke of Pfalz-Zweibrücken acceded on 8 March 1778 (*ibid.*, R.², II, 582, 585), and which was finally guaranteed by the contracting and mediating powers of the peace settlement of Teschen of 13 May 1779. Comp. Article 16 of the main treaty and the additional instruments (*ibid.*, R.², II, 661 and 668 *et seq.*)

Other instances are:

the convention of Naumburg of 30 March 1614 between the Electors of Saxony and Brandenburg and the Landgraves of Hesse (Dumont, V², 242) for their mutual succession;

the conventions of 26 June 1744, 6 February 1745 and 16 December 1748 between the ducal houses of Saxe-Gotha and Saxe-Hildburghausen (*ibid.*, N.S., I, 734, 737, 740), embodying, on the basis of older agreements of 1679, 1680 and 1683 and Imperial decisions of 1714 and 1725, an *Eventual-Sukzession* by way of an agreed partition, first of the lands of Saxe-Coburg-Meinungen, and later of those of Saxe-Weimar. Comp. also the further agreements of January 1787, April 1789 and 28 July 1791 between the different branches (*ibid.*, N.S., I, 238, 242, 254, 263-273).

Article 16 of the Final Act of Vienna of 9 June 1815 (*ibid.*, N.R., II, 379) still confirmed the king of Saxony's old right of "succession éventuelle" in the possessions of the Ernestine branch of his house.

Such pacts were also concluded between members of the same dynasty, as occurred on 11 February 1780 between the reigning duke Charles of Württemberg and his two brothers (Martens, R.², III, 1).

The same type of compact between dynasties was further practised (ii) in connection with the termination of a war which had broken out as a consequence of the actual extinction of a dynasty. This happened in the case of the War of the Bavarian succession of 1778, whereupon comp. the Postscript below, at p. 340.

This well-known type of covenant between ruling houses for the mutual passing of territorial sovereignty from one house to another should either of the two become extinct, was also called a "confraternity part".

Examples of such *pacta confraternitatis*, which were fairly frequent, were those concluded

> in 1516 between Maximilian I of Austria and Vladislav II of Bohemia and Hungary, strengthened by the mutual marriage contract cited above in § 1. Marriage;
> in 1537 between the duke of Silesia and the Elector of Brandenburg in respect of Lower Silesia;
> in 1691 by the last ruling prince of East-Friesland and the duke of Brunsvick-Lüneburg (Hanover) (Rousset, *Receuil*, XIX, 5, 7), discussed below under (*d*) Expectancy.
> Comp. further below under (*e*) Reversion.

Another form was that of inter-dynastic conventions for the partition of family estates. They all fit into the patrimonial conceptions of public law in past centuries, but they have unmistakably left deep furrows even in the present-day community of European States.

Hereditary pacts between German princes needed confirmation by the Emperor. See for example:

> 25 September 1279 (Dumont, I¹, 245): confirmation by the Emperor Rudolph of an *Erbvertrag* concluded between duke Heinrich of Silesia and King Ottocar of Bohemia.

This requirement of Imperial confirmation as a condition of the validity of hereditary pacts within the Empire was expressly laid down in a rescript of the Emperor Rudolph I of Habsburg of 1290. At a later stage such a confirmation was in its turn made subject to the consent of the Electors. Comp. on 15th century *Erbverträge*: those between the princes of Thuringia (1403, 1410), between Karl IV and the counts of Austria (1404), between the princes of Anhalt (1413), between Saxony, Hesse and Brandenburg (1457) and between the Elector and the dukes of Saxe-Weimar and Meissen (1485). Comp. for the text of one of these, that between the members of the House of Anhalt of 23 April 1413: Rousset, *Suppl.*, I¹, 332.

Other hereditary pacts of later dates were:

the *Erbverbrüderung* of 1671 relative to Lauenburg, one of the elements in a complicated hereditary fight in 1689;

the partition treaty of 18 May 1745 between Austria and Saxony concerning Silesia (Martens, S., I, 270), which was rather an agreement for the partition of Prussian territory;

the *Nassauische Erbverein* of June 1783 (*ibid.*, R.², III, 648), ratified by the Emperor (*ibid.*, 647, 683) and transferred to the Grand Duchy of

(d) *Expectancy*

The grant of an "expectative" (*Anwartschaft, Expektanz*) was a well-known device, of feudal origin, used by the Head of the Holy Roman Empire to assure in advance to a specific Prince his succession to another princedom in the case of its future vacancy. Originally it was within the powers of the Emperor alone to grant such "expectatives". This was changed by Article 8 of the permanent *Wahlkapitulation* of the Emperor Ferdinand II of 1711 (Article 11 of the draft published in Zeumer, *Quellensammlung*, 2nd ed., II, No. 205, pp. 474 *et seq.*) whereby it was laid down for the first time that the Emperor would only be empowered to grant them with the consent of the Princes Electors (comp. Rousset, *Recueil*, VII, p. 346, *sub* 2).

Examples of this type of territorial grant are the following.

"Lettres d'investiture", accorded on 4 November 1570 (Dumont, VI[1], 183) by the Emperor Maximilian II to King Frederick II of Denmark and the two brothers Adolph and Johann, dukes of Schlesvig-Holstein, for the "expectative féodale" of the counties of Oldenburg and Delmenhorst.

In accordance with Article 3 of a treaty, entered into by the Emperor Ferdinand III and the Elector of Bavaria Maximilian I on 28 June 1638 (Martens, N.S., II, 556), the former granted to the latter, by an Imperial Diploma of 22 September 1638 (*ibid.*, II, 561), "gratiam expectativam ad successionem in Ducatu Mirandulae et Marchionatu Concordiae".

Article XI, § 6 of the Peace Treaty of Osnabrück of 24 October 1648 (Zeumer, *Quellensammlung*, 2nd ed., II, No. 197, pp. 395 *et seq.*) gave the Elector of Brandenburg the expectancy of the archbishopric of Magdeburg as an eternal fief, should it become vacant.

Such "expectatives" quite often collided with family pacts or *pacta confraternitatis* and then gave rise to inter-state disputes or even to wars of succession.

In 1694 the Emperor Leopold I granted to the then Elector of Brandenburg Frederick III the expectancy with regard to the principality of East-Friesland should the male line of the latter house become extinct. In so doing the Emperor disposed of the principality contrary to a preceding *Erbverbrüderung* (*traité de confraternité et d'union héréditaire*), which had been concluded on 20 March 1691 between Prince Christian Eberhard and Duke Ernst August of Brünswick-Lüneburg (Rousset, *Recueil*, XIX, 45-52) and the normal operation of which would have entailed Brunswick-Lüneburg's succession to the principality. When the male line of the East-Frisian house became in fact extinct on 26 May

1744, the King of Prussia, heedless of the confraternity pact, lost no time in possessing himself of the principality, and he remained in possession despite the protests of the King of Great Britain in his then capacity of Duke of Brunswick-Lüneburg and a *Conclusum*, unfavourable to the King of Prussia, of the Electoral College of 23 September 1745 which annulled the investiture granted to the King of Prussia by the Vicar of the Empire. Comp. on the paper battle joined by the two pretenders and on their respective legal arguments the "Instruction solide du droit de succession" of the Elector of Brunswick-Lüneburg and the "Défense de la déduction fondamentale concernant le droit de succession" of the Prussian Court in Rousset, *Recueil*, XIX, 3-45, respectively 53-121, and for the text of the *Conclusum*: *ibid.*, 121-122. As appears from the Elector's Instruction (*ibid.*, 5, 7), the last Prince of East-Friesland had vainly invoked in 1725 and 1732 the help of the Elector of Brunswick-Lüneburg, suggesting to him that the *pactum successorium* should be renewed; Great Britain in the event acquiesced in Prussia's claim. Special attention was paid in Article II (2) of the Peace Treaty of Dresden between Maria Theresia and the King of Prussia of 25 December 1745 (Wenck, II, 191; Rousset, *Recueil*, XIX, 432) to other "expectances et survivances" granted by a former Emperor, which the Empress renounced, but these only related to Silesia, ceded by her to the King of Prussia by their Peace Treaty of Breslau of 11 June 1742. However, the fact that the King of Great Britain, in his capacity as such, by Article 9 of the treaty of 1745, guaranteed that treaty "dans toute son étendue", thus covering all the States of the Prussian King without exception, and moreover, in his other capacity of Elector of Brunswick-Lüneburg, by Article 11 of the same treaty, was comprised in it, would seem to have been sufficient ground for Prussia to argue that the King of Great Britain, Elector of Brunswick-Lüneburg, no longer invoked his claim to East-Friesland on the basis of his confraternity pact of 1691 with Prince Christian Eberhard (comp. Rousset, *Recueil*, XIX, p. 107).

Another conflict had arisen in 1689 in respect of the duchy of Lauenburg to which different pretenders laid claim after the extinction of the Askanian branch of the house of Saxony-Lauenburg. But in that case the Elector of Saxony took possession of the duchy on the double ground of an *Expectanzverschreibung* of the Emperor Maximilian I of 1507 and an *Erbverbrüderung* of 1671. The duchy was later sold by Brunswick-Lüneburg (1702).

The grant of an *Anwartschaft* or *expectative* as described above was often accompanied by another ceremony of feudal origin, namely an *Eventual-Investitur*. This was a conditional enfeoffment with stronger legal effect than the grant of a simple expectancy in that (*a*) it gave the person enfeoffed and his descendants a more definite, hereditary right to the fief, albeit under the condition precedent *(condition suspensive)* of the extinction of the dynasty of the present vassal, and that *(b)* it also legally bound the descendants of the liege lord who granted it.

An early instance of such a conditional enfeoffment was the *Eventual-Investitur* with the duchy of Jülich that was conferred upon duke Albrecht of Saxony by the Emperor Frederick III at Graz by a Diploma of 26 June 1483 and later confirmed by the Emperor Maximilian I in 1495, in the eventuality of the extinction of the ducal house of Jülich in the male line (Dumont, III², 121). This investiture was, however, already ignored when duke William VIII of Jülich died in 1511, leaving behind only a daughter, married to a son of the duke of Cleves. The Emperor found a way out by formally investing William's son-in-law with the duchy, while reserving Saxony's rights of expectancy. When the ducal house of Jülich became finally extinct in 1609, a bitter dispute over the succession arose between three pretenders in the female line (which had meanwhile, in 1546, been declared entitled to succession by another Emperor, Charles V), both *inter se* and between them and the duke of Saxony. The latter based his right to succession on the text of the instrument of investiture:

> "Donnons, concédons de présent, & en vertu de ces Lettres, sur l'heure & immédiatement ... dès à présent comme pour lors, & pour lors comme dès à présent",

whereas the Elector of Brandenburg, married to one of the female pretenders, contested their character as an *Eventual-Investitur* and maintained that both grants, of 1483 and of 1495, were "de simples expectatives" and no genuine investitures. Comp. on this controversy Rousset, *Recueil*, VII, pp. 300-456, at p. 356, and on the further development of this dispute below, Chapter V, section 1, at pp. 434 *et seq.*

One of the most renowned *investitures éventuelles* is that which the Emperor Charles VI, with the consent of the Imperial Diet of Regensburg of 7 December 1722, on 9 December 1723 issued from Vienna in favour of the Spanish Infante Don Carlos, son of the new Anjou King Philip V of Spain and his consort, born duchess of Parma, with regard to his future succession in the Grand Duchy of Tuscany and the duchies of Parma and Piacenza as a *feudum Imperii*. The letters which documented this *Eventual-Investitur* and which were referred to as "Lettres d'Expectative contenant l'Eventuelle investiture" in Article 6 (1) of the Peace Treaty of Vienna between the Emperor and the King of Spain of 30 April 1725 (Dumont, VIII², 106; Rousset, *Recueil*, II, 110; IV, 110), were followed by a series of further instruments in the style of those days, *viz.*, guarantees for their execution given by the Kings of Great Britain on 23 January 1724 (Rousset, *Recueil*, V², p. LIV) and of France on 28 January 1724 *(ibid.*, V², p. LVIII); *Reversales* for the fulfilment of their conditions by the then King of Spain Luís I of 28 February 1724 (*ibid.*, V², p. L), and on 13 April 1728, various instruments emanating from the Emperor in Vienna, namely his full powers for the seizing possession of Tuscany, a rescript to the dowager princess of Tuscany, a *mandement* to the subjects of Tuscany to recognize Don Carlos as their sovereign, and a decree addressed to the Senate of Florence enjoining them to put Don Carlos in possession of Tuscany (*ibid.*, V², pp. LXII-LXXIV). All these complicated instruments served for the implementation of the Quadruple Alliance Treaty of 2 August 1718, adhered to by the Emperor and the King of Spain in 1719 and 1720 and confirmed by their final Peace Treaty of Vienna of 1725 for the liquidation of the War of the Spanish Succession.

Pope Innocent XIII, who claimed territorial rights concerning the duchies for the Holy See, formally and strongly protested against this "Eventualis Investitura Ducatus Parmae et Placentiae" in March/April 1723 (*ibid.*, I, 309, 316) on the ground that the said duchy "nulla ratione ad jura Imperii pertinet", but on the contrary "non alterius quam S.Sedis ac Romani Pontificis directo, alto et supremo Dominio subest". Comp. on this papal claim Part (Vol.) II of this publication, Excursus to Chapter V, section 1, p. 329, and on further particulars regarding the political fate of the duchies below under (*e*) *Reversibility*, pp. 317 *et seq.*

The Act of 24 January 1737 by which duke François of Lorraine, the husband of Maria Theresia, the later Emperor Franz II, was on the expected death of the last Medici of Tuscany without male descendants enfeoffed with that Grand Duchy, in exchange for Lorraine which was given to the ex-king of Poland, Stanislas Leszczynski, was also in the nature of an "investiture éventuelle" (Martens, S., I, 234). He succeeded in fact in 1737 on the death of Grand Duke Giovanni Gasto from the house of Medici, as a result of which the Grand Duchy fell to the house of Austria as a secundogeniture. This implied that when a Grand Duke himself succeeded to the throne of Austria, he had to renounce the investiture of Tuscany in favour of a younger brother or a son. This happened on the death of the Emperor Joseph II in 1790, when his brother Leopold II, at the time Grand Duke of Tuscany, succeeded him as Emperor: the latter on 21 July 1790 renounced the grandducal dignity in favour of his second son Ferdinand (*ibid.*, R.², IV, 478), who in his turn on 22 February 1791 confirmed the laws and statutes of Tuscany (*ibid.*, 482) and received the homage of his new subjects (*ibid.*, 483).

Another instance of this special type of investiture of still later date related to the Imperial fiefs granted to the ducal house of Modena. It was, by a *Kaiserliches Commissions-Decret* of Joseph II of 13 December 1770 (*ibid.*, R.², I, 715-720; Wenck, III, 810-815) conferred upon Archduke Ferdinand of Austria, in the eventuality of the extinction of the male line of descendants of the house of Este, which had kept its old possessions on

313

the strength of Article 5 of the preliminary Peace Treaty of Aachen of 30 April 1748 (Wenck, II, 310; Rousset, *Recueil*, XX, 158). This house, however, only became extinct on the death of Hercules III Rinaldo in 1803, when the then Archduke became in fact the successor to those fiefs.

A modern instance of the old "succession éventuelle" in the form of a protectorate, completely outside the traditional compass of the Holy Roman Empire, was that established as late as 1918 by a treaty of 17 July of that year (Martens, N.R.G.³, XI, 313) in favour of France with regard to the principality of Monaco, should the reigning house of Grimaldi become extinct. Prince Rainier's marriage to Grace Kelly has, however, provisionally banged the door on France's ambitions. Comp. on Monaco Part II of this publication, Chapter VI, section 2A, *sub* (*b*), p. 459.

(e) *Reversibility*

Clauses of reversion of feudal tenures and territorial supremacy have played a major role in international relations of the past and continued to do so until as late as the middle of the 19th century. The purpose of the clause was to lay down in advance that in the case, in particular, of the extinction of the male line of succession to the throne in State A, its territory would return to State B. This institution of reversibility has been familiar to different parts of Europe, especially Italy, where it has existed, *inter alia*, in respect of Sardinia and Sicily, of Parma, Piacenza and Guastalla, of Modena and of Lucca, and has been the cause of continual complications.

Sardinia and Sicily.

When the death of King Carlos II of Spain and the succession of a French prince, King Louis XIV's grandson Philippe, to the Spanish throne in 1700 had plunged the main Powers of Europe into the War of the Spanish Succession, a number of important political decisions became necessary (comp. on this war the Postscript *infra*, p. 334). Among them was a redistribution of the possessions of the Spanish Monarchy outside peninsular Spain and her colonies amongst different pretenders, in particular the Emperor Karl VI. This redistribution only took place by successive stages.

The Grand Alliance of 7 September 1701 between Great Britain, the Netherlands and the Emperor (Dumont, VIII¹, 89)—later acceded to by Brandenburg-Prussia, Denmark, the Empire, Portugal, Savoy and Sweden—provided for an allocation of the Spanish Low Countries, the duchy of Milan, the Kingdom of the Two Sicilies (Naples and the island of Sicily) and the ports of the Grand Duchy of Tuscany to the Emperor. When, however, in 1713 the war was terminated by a series of separate peace treaties in Utrecht, that between Spain and Savoy of 13 August 1713 (*ibid.*, VIII¹, 401), confirming an earlier treaty of cession of 10 June 1713 (*ibid.*, 389), allotted the island of Sicily to the duke of Savoy who was to be thenceforth styled King of Sicily and was in actual fact crowned as such at Palermo. This aroused the fury of the Emperor who refused to recognize Victor Amedeus II as the ruler of Sicily and refused to conclude a peace treaty with Spain. The allotment of Sicily to the duke of Savoy was made conditional upon the reversion of the island to Spain in case the male line of succession in the house of Savoy should become extinct. At the further peace congresses of Rastadt and Baden between the Emperor and Empire and France—treaties of 6 March and 7 September 1714 (*ibid.*, 415 and 436; Rousset, *Recueil*, I, 1)[9]—France undertook (Baden, Article 30) not to disturb the Emperor in the peaceful enjoyment of the countries which he then possessed, *viz.*, the Kingdom of Naples, the duchy of Milan, the island and Kingdom of Sardinia, and the ports and towns on the coast of Tuscany. As the Emperor remained unwilling to conclude a definitive peace treaty with Spain and the latter's leading statesman, Cardinal Alberoni, endeavoured to regain for Spain the Italian territories lost in Utrecht, by in 1717/1718 invading first Sardinia and then Sicily, the other Powers, in particular France, Great Britain and the Netherlands, formed a common front to uphold the solutions embodied in the peace treaties of 1713 and 1714, if necessary by joint military and naval action. This was first done by their Triple Alliance Treaty of The Hague of 4 January 1717 (Dumont, VIII[1], 531; Rousset, *Recueil*, I, 89), and later, on 2 August 1718, by a very elaborate set of solutions hammered out at London in the so-called Quadruple Alliance Treaty (Dumont, VIII[1], 531; Rousset, *Recueil*, I, 180) for the final pacification of Italy, implying *inter alia*, an exchange of Sicily for Sardinia in favour of the Emperor (Dumont, VIII[1], 531; Rousset, *Recueil*, I, 191). The suggestions made in this treaty were intended to be imposed upon the reluctant States, the Empire, Spain and Savoy, and secret additional Articles provided for concerted action against them, should they refuse to make peace on that basis (Dumont, VIII[1], 539; Rousset, *Recueil*, I, 211). This new alliance was originally only a bilateral one, forged between France and Great Britain, but intended to achieve also the accession of the Emperor and the Netherlands. The Emperor indeed accepted its terms on 14 September 1718 (Rousset, *Recueil*, I, 209); the Netherlands only followed, against strong Spanish opposition, on 16 February 1719.[10] As the duke of Savoy had meanwhile also accepted the conditions in November 1718 (Rousset, *Recueil*, I, 230), the Emperor and the duke, thenceforward to be styled

9. As the preamble of the Peace Treaty of Baden relates, the agreements reached at Rastadt had not been finalized there for lack of the "solemnitez requises", or had been adjourned and referred to a new congress "plus solemnel et plus général qui se tiendrait en Suisse, en observant les usages accoutumez".
10. See on the accession of the Netherlands: Rousset, *Recueil*, I, 292 *et seq.*

King of Sardinia instead of King of Sicily, finalized their deal by a treaty of exchange of 8 August 1720 (Rousset, *Suppl.*, II², 156).

The enterprise of Spain against the two islands in the Mediterranean[11] had in the mean time broken down under a naval action by Great Britain near Sicily and a joint military invasion by Great Britain and France[12] against Cataluña, which caused Alberoni's fall in December 1719 and Spain's belated acceptance of the suggestions of the Quadruple Alliance on 17 February 1720 (Rousset, *Recueil*, I, 299).

The ultimate conclusion of a peace treaty between Spain and the Emperor still dragged on for a further five years after mediation efforts by France and Great Britain at a Congress at Cambrai in 1724 had failed to smooth out the remaining minor differences between the two. The treaty of Vienna of 30 April 1725 (Dumont, VIII², 106; Rousset, *Recueil*, II, 110)—this time negotiated on the Spanish side by the diplomat-adventurer Ripperda of Dutch extraction—endorsed the main solutions reached at Utrecht, subject to the exchange of Sicily for Sardinia, and provided, in accordance with Articles IV and VI of the Quadruple Alliance Treaty, for the renunciation by Spain of her right of reversion with regard to the Kingdom of Sicily in exchange for the corresponding right of reversion in respect of the island and Kingdom of Sardinia. The customary formalities appear from the following text of Article VII of the Peace Treaty:

> "Sa Majesté Catholique d'Espagne pour Elle, ses Successeurs & Héritiers au Royaume d'Espagne, pour les Descendants de l'un & de l'autre sexe, renonce pour jamais aux Droits de Reversion du Royaume de Sicile, réservé à la Couronne d'Espagne par l'Acte de Cession, fait par le Roi de Sardaigne en Juin 1713, & promet de faire remettre entre les mains de Sa Majesté Impériale les Lettres de Reversion dressées à ce sujet, en même temps que la ratification du présent Traité, sauf le Droit de Reversion sur l'Isle & Royaume de Sardaigne apartenant à Sa Majesté Catholique, suivant le second Article des Conventions entre l'Empereur & le Roi de Sardaigne".

The Pope had in the mean time protested against these transactions on the ground that Sicily belonged from of old to the Holy See. See his protest to the Congress of Cambrai of 16 February 1723 (Rousset, *Recueil*, I, 309); comp. Part II of this publication, p. 329.

The whole arrangement was for the rest shortly afterwards upset as a consequence of the War of the Polish Succession (1733-1738), comp. below, pp. 318 and 338.

---

11. See for an attempt of the Court of Spain to justify its naval action against Sardinia and Sicily in 1717-1718 its letters and manifestos, inserted in Rousset, *Recueil*, I, 161 et seq., 170 et seq., 234 et seq.
12. Comp. on the rupture between France and Spain the French Manifesto, inserted in Rousset, *Recueil*, I, 267 et seq.

Parma, Piacenza and Tuscany.

Another of the essential suggestions laid down in the Quadruple Alliance Treaty of 1718 (Article V) related to the duchies of Parma and Piacenza and the Grand Duchy of Tuscany. This suggestion was inspired by fear lest the impending extinction in the male line of the house of Farnese in the duchies and that of Medici in the Grand Duchy should provoke a new war in Italy owing, on the one hand, to possible claims of Queen Elisabeth of Spain, in her own right a duchess of Parma (granddaughter of duke Ranuccio II Farnese), and on the other, to rival claims of right advanced with regard to all three by the Emperor and Empire. It provided for the following arrangement (Article V). The duchies and Grand Duchy were to be recognized in future and *in perpetuum* by all the contracting parties as male fiefs of the Holy Roman Empire. Once the extinction of the houses of Farnese, respectively Medici, in the male line should in fact take place, the Emperor would on his own behalf consent that the eldest son of the Queen of Spain and his legitimate male descendants, or subsidiarily, her younger sons, should succeed in those States, and would employ his good offices also to obtain the necessary consent of the Empire. Following that, the Emperor was to issue, without prejudice to the rights of the present rulers of Farnese and Medici, the required "lettres d'expectative, contenant (on behalf of the Infante Don Carlos) l'investiture éventuelle" (comp. *sub* (*d*) *supra*) and to hand them over to the King of Spain—a procedure by which "la féodalité (était) établie sur lesdits Etats, en faveur de l'Empereur et de l'Empire".

The conditions laid down in the Quadruple Alliance Treaty of 1718 were also as far as these clauses were concerned in the event incorporated into Article VI of the Peace Treaty between the Emperor and Spain of 30 April 1725 (Dumont, VIII², 106; Rousset, *Recueil*, II, 110). This also provided against a union of the crown of Spain with that of the duchies and against the exercise of a guardianship of the Spanish Monarch over their ruler(s). It endorsed moreover the mutual promise of the parties "en bonne foi et saintement" to abstain from sending their soldiers into the duchies and Grand Duchy during the lifetime of their rulers. Livorno and the main towns of the duchies should be garrisoned by neutral, preferably Swiss troops. The latter engagement was, however, soon broken. Spain, ostensibly to secure the future succession of Don Carlos, sent troops into the Grand Duchy and duchies and saw her illegal action condoned by France and Great Britain in their tripartite treaty of Sevilla of 9 November 1729 (Dumont, VIII², 158; Rousset, *Recueil*, V², i), acceded to by the United Netherlands on 21 November 1729 (Dumont, VIII², 160; Rousset, *Recueil*, V², XXXIV). The new situation was subsequently confirmed by Article 3 (with annexed declaration) of another treaty of Vienna between the Emperor and Great Britain of 16 March

1731 (Dumont, VIII², 213; Rousset, *Recueil*, VI, 13), acceded to by the States General by an "Acte de concurrence" of 20 February 1732 (Rousset, *Recueil*, VI, 442), and a further treaty of 22 July 1731 between the Emperor, Great Britain and Spain (*ibid.*, VI, 193).

The last male Farnese, duke Antonio of Parma and Piancenza had just died in 1731. This caused the crown of the two duchies to devolve upon Don Carlos, Infante of Spain. As to Tuscany, Spain thought fit at the same time to regulate the succession in the Grand Duchy in a family pact with the house of Medici of 25 July 1731 (*ibid.*, VI, 233) and the conditions under which the Spanish troops could provisionally stay there in a *Règlement* of October 1731 (*ibid.*, VI, 259).

The scene changed again as a consequence of the involvement of Spain in the War of the Polish Succession of 1733 on the side of France. This war ended by another Peace Treaty of Vienna (preliminary: 3 October 1735; definitive: 18 November 1738—Wenck, I, 1 and 88; Rousset, *Recueil*, X, 519 and XIII, 421), in virtue of which the Emperor got the two duchies back in full sovereignty (Article 5 of 1735) in exchange for Naples and Sicily which he left on that occasion to the Spanish dynasty as a secundogeniture of the Spanish Bourbons under Don Carlos and his male descendants (Article 3), and for the recognition of his Pragmatic Sanction by Sardinia and France (Rousset, *Recueil*, XIII, 504 and XVIII, 93).

In the same period the Grand Ducal house of Tuscany also became extinct as a consequence of the death of the last Medici, Giovanni Gasto, in 1737. In view of this impending demise the same Peace Treaty of Vienna of October 1735 had already provided for the *Eventual-Sukzession* in that Grand Duchy, not of Carlos of Spain, but of duke Franz Stephan of Lorraine, Maria Theresia's husband, the later Emperor Franz II, who had to be endowed with another duchy in order to make room in Lorraine for the ex-king of Poland, Louis XV's father-in-law (Articles 1 and 2 of the Treaty of 1735). But whereas Lorraine was only ceded to Stanislas as a temporary abode for his lifetime and was to fall after his death to France in virtue of another right of reversion (which became in fact operative in 1766), the cession of Tuscany to Franz Stephan was meant to be a hereditary enfeoffment: the house of Habsburg-Lorraine has indeed, after an interval in the Napoleonic era, continued to rule in Tuscany until 1859, when the Grand Duchy was engulfed by the kingdom of Sardinia-Italy.

By this course of events the two duchies and the Grand Duchy were definitively separated, the former under Austria, the latter as a secundogeniture under a Spanish prince.

All these changes in the period 1718-1738 were only incidents in an endless train of events which has stretched far into the 19th century, and bears a striking witness to the political and legal international complications caused by the obsolete institutions and formalities of the feudal system. That is why I will give below some further details concerning this case of reversibility.

The fate of Parma and Piacenza was after their severance from Savoy-Sardinia, their liberation from all bonds of reversion to the Spanish Crown, and their abandonment to Austria as male fiefs of the Empire in 1735 again put in jeopardy as a consequence of the following War of the Austrian Succession of 1740-1748. In the course of that war Maria Theresia, by Article 9 of her treaty of alliance with Sardinia and Great Britain of Worms of 13 September 1743 (Wenck, I, 677), more or less under duress ceded a number of her Italian possessions to Sardinia in return for the help of her allies, among them the town of Piacenza and part of that duchy between Pavia and the river Nura (= Nure). Although the duchies were again conquered by Spain in 1745 and reconquered by Austria in 1746, they ended at the Peace Congress of Aachen (Aix-la-Chapelle)—Article 4 of the preliminary Treaty of 30 April 1748; Article 7, with inserted Acts of Cession (at pp. 190 and 193), of the definitive treaty of 18 October 1748 (Wenck, II, 310 and 337; Rousset, *Recueil*, XX, 158 and 179) by being retroceded to the Spanish Infante Don Felipe:

> "Les Duchez de Parma, de Plaisance & de Guastalla seront cédés au Sérénissime Infant Don Philippe pour lui tenir lieu d'établissement avec le Droit de Réversion aux présents Possesseurs[13] après que Sa Majesté le Roi des Deux Siciles [14] aura passé à la Couronne d'Espagne, ainsi que dans le cas où ledit Sérénissime Infant Don Philippe viendrait à mourir sans Enfans".

The negotiations at Aachen were held up at first by the reluctance of Maria Theresia to submit to the conditions (see her protest of 4 May 1748 in Wenck, II, 321 and her initially only conditional acceptance on 23 May, *ibid.*, 323, followed on 25 May by an unconditional acceptance, *ibid.*, note at p. 325).

The transaction was still further complicated by a traditional protest by the Pope: just as he had done on earlier occasions (1723), would do again in 1815 and would even continue to do until 1847 (Martens, N.R.G.[1], XV, 40), he objected to the deal on the ground that Piacenza was of old a fief of the Holy See (Rousset, *Recueil*, XX, 232, in connexion with *ibid.*, I, 309, 316). Comp. on this papal claim Part II of this publication, Excursus to Chapter V, section 1, at p. 329. On the other hand, the member States of the Alliance of Worms of September 1743, Austria, Great Britain and Sardinia, had been in agreement that the King of Sardinia should hold Piacenza in fief from the Emperor. Hence the ces-

13. *Viz.*, the Emperor of Austria in respect of Parma and Guastalla, respectively the King of Sardinia in respect of Piacenza.
14. At that moment Don Carlos, the elder brother of Don Felipe.

sion of this duchy to the Infante of Spain at Aachen by these two rulers jointly.

The renewed right of reversion has since then formed the subject of many subsequent treaty provisions.

During the Seven Years' War of 1756-1763 the King of France, by a letter of 5 February 1759, promised the King of Sardinia that in case he should not at the time of the conclusion of peace be in possession of Piacenza with its territory up to the river Nura, as foreseen in the Treaty of Aachen, he would obtain a satisfactory equivalent. This promise was communicated to and endorsed by the King of Spain. As Sardinia had not yet in fact obtained such an equivalent in 1763, the three Contracting Parties to the Convention of 10 June 1763 (Martens, R.^{2}, I, 197), France, Spain and Sardinia, recognized afresh in favour of the King of Sardinia his right of reversion with respect to Piacenza and its territory, under the accompanying engagement of France and Spain meanwhile to pay out to him an amount of annual revenues equal to that which he would receive if he were really possessed of Piacenza *cum annexis*.

Complementary conventions of the same date (10 June 1763; *ibid.*, R.^{2}, I, 107, 201) confirmed the right of reversion in respect of the duchy of Piacenza in favour of Sardinia, and that in respect of the duchies of Parma and Guastalla in favour of Austria in the eventuality that the Spanish Infante Don Felipe, successor designate to the throne of the three duchies, would decease without male descendants. This right of reversion was once again recognized and maintained by Article 99 (2) of the Final Act of Vienna of 9 June 1815 (*ibid.*, R.^{2}, II, 379), but on that occasion qualified by the stipulation that it was not to take effect until after the demise of the ex-Empress of France, Marie Louise, because she was endowed with the duchies of Parma, Piacenza and Guastalla. It was further confirmed by Article 7 of the treaty of Paris of 10 June 1817 between the six Great Powers *inter se* (*ibid.*, N.R., IV, 416) and that of Florence of 28 November 1844 between the Grand Duke of Tuscany, the duke of Parma and Lucca, and the duke of Modena, acceded to by Austria and Sardinia (*ibid.*, N.R.G.^{1}, XV, 4, 5; comp. also XIII, 425). However, already by a separate article adopted by Austria and Sardinia, additional to the treaty between the Great Powers and Sardinia of 20 May 1815—kept secret until 1836 and inserted only in 1857 in Martens's *Recueil* (N.R.G.^{1}, XV, 41)—the two Powers, beneficiaries of the stipulation, had agreed that in the case of the foreseen reversion of the duchies to them the town-fortress of Piacenza should remain "en toute souveraineté et propriété" with the Emperor of Austria against a certain territorial compensation for Sardinia. However, it proved impossible to reach agreement on any such further territorial adjustment in Northern Italy because the duke of Modena was only prepared to collaborate on the condition that he acquired the duchy of Guastalla, then combined

320

with that of Parma—a transaction to which the Emperor of Austria had to give his consent in his capacity of beneficiary of the right of reversion in respect of Guastalla. The difficulties were in the event, in 1844, solved by a "transfer" of the existing "reversibility" of Guastalla in favour of Austria to certain other territories which the duke of Parma was going to obtain in exchange for Guastalla in Lunigiana. The new right of reversion with respect to these estates in Lunigiana to Austria was, however, on that same occasion (1844) further ceded by Austria to Sardinia in exchange for the future abandonment of the town of Piacenza to Austria, already stipulated on her behalf in the secret additional Article of 20 May 1815. This entire system of "reversibilities" finally crumbled in 1847, on Marie Louise's death in December. A few months prior to that event the duke of Lucca had already renounced his right of reversion in favour of the Grand Duke of Tuscany: 5 October 1847 (Martens, N.R.G.[1], XV, 36).

This piece of political history (comp. also the introduction to *I. Traités relatifs aux relations territoriales de l'Italie* in Martens, N.R.G.[1], XV, pp. 1 *et seq.*) is only one example which shows the extreme complexity of relationships in feudal and post-feudal times.

The duchy of Lucca, which had for a long time remained an independent republic, but was in 1805, together with Piombino (see Part II, p. 53), granted by Napoleon as a hereditary principality to his sister Elisa and her husband Bacciocchi, was in 1815 temporarily given to the then Queen-Regent of Etruria, Maria Louise and her descendants, *viz.*, until the moment when she or they should be restored in the possession of the duchy of Parma, which was in the same year provisionally granted to another Maria Louise, Napoleon's spouse. On the latter's death (which only occurred in December 1847) the ruler of Lucca would succeed to the ducal throne of Parma, and Lucca would by way of reversion fall to the Grand Duke of Tuscany. See Articles 101 (3) and 102 (1) of the Final Act of the Congress of Vienna of 9 June 1815 (Martens, N.R., II, 379). The then duke of Lucca did not, however, wait for the demise of the ex-Empress to renounce his duchy in favour of the Grand Duke of Tuscany (Act of abdication of 5 October 1847, *ibid.*, N.R.G.[1], XV, 36) and only succeeded in Parma in December of the same year.

When Prussia and France in Article 5 of their secret treaty of Berlin of 5 August 1796 (*ibid.*, R.[2], VI, 59) agreed that the Prince of Orange should receive compensation for the loss of his dignity of *Stadhouder* in Holland and his real estate on the left bank of the Rhine, *inter alia*, by the secularization on his behalf of the bishoprics of Würzburg and Bamberg, an additional clause stipulated their reversion in favour of the house of Brandenburg should the house of Orange become extinct in the male line.

Complicated stipulations concerning future reversion were still laid down in Article 18 (2) of the Final Act of Vienna of 9 June 1815: whereas the Emperor transferred to the ruling house of Prussia his right of reversion in respect of that part of the two Lausitz which had passed to Prussia, he reserved for himself the power to reassume that right in the case of extinction of the house of Brandenburg.

The abolition of obsolete feudal rights in the last part of the 18th and the first part of the 19th century was sometimes accompanied by an express cancellation of the connected right of reversion of the territory concerned. Thus, by the treaty between Poland and Prussia of 18 September 1773, one of the treaties finalizing her first partition (Martens, R^2, II, 149), Poland *expressis verbis* waived in favour of Prussia two old rights of reversion which had accrued to her in the middle of the 17th century, *viz.*:

(Article 3) that of the Kingdom and fief of Prussia which had been stipulated in favour of the Crown of Poland by Article 6 of the Treaty of Velan of 19 September 1654 (Dumont, VI^2, 192) in case the male line of succession of the elector Friedrich Wilhelm of Brandenburg should become extinct;

(Article 4) that of the districts of Lauenburg and Butow which Poland could claim in virtue of the Convention of Bydgošć (= Bromberg) of 6 November 1657 (Lünig, *Pars Spec., Cont.* II, *Forts.* I, p. 114, 116; *Pars Spec., Th.* III, p. 171).

A third Article (5) in addition abolished a further old Polish right based on the same treaty of Bydgošć, *viz.*, of repurchasing the territory of Draheim. Comp. on this right, possibly also accompanied by a right of reversion, Chapter V, section 6, p. 479 below.

A new right of reversion was still created by Napoleon in Article 3 of a treaty with the Grand Duchy of Frankfurt of 16 February 1810 (*ibid.*, N.R., I, 241), by which it was stipulated that in case Napoleon's adopted son prince Eugene, the heir designate to the throne of the Grand Duchy after the death of the Prince Primate, should himself die, the Grand Duchy was to revert to France. (Comp. also Article 3 of the *procés-verbal de remise* of 15 May 1810, *ibid.*, N.R., III, 185).

(f) Partition inter vivos

It was not only by a testamentary disposition or will that a prince could give a binding ruling on the future fate of his possessions: he was also held entitled to do it during his lifetime, in particular by dividing them between or among his sons or other relatives. Such a partition of princely domains by the present ruler was in old days also a valid title of acquisition of territory in favour of the persons thus assigned. Since this mode of acquisition partly overlaps with other modes, listed in this § 2, and partitions of territory equally occurred without any connection with hereditary succession, I only mention this title of acquisition here, for the sake of completeness, while intending to return to it later, p. 384.

It goes without saying that a dynastic partition as envisaged here is entirely a matter of the past and has become obsolete, save for a few very rare exceptions in cases where the absolute ruler still adheres to Louis XIV's constitutional principle that "l'Etat c'est moi".

(g) *International treaties concerning succession to the throne*

One of the historically most ominous treaties concluded between sovereign States with the object of ensuring the succession of the head of one of them to the throne of the other was that of Troyes of 21 May 1420 (Dumont, II², 142). It was, under the influence of Queen Isabeau, wife of the lunatic King Charles VI of France, arranged by the Bourguignons; it provided for the acceptance of Henry V, King of England, as regent and heir designate to the French throne following his marriage to Charles VI's daughter Catherine, to the detriment of his legitimate successor, the Dauphin. This treaty entailed the latter's exclusion from the French throne by the *Parlement de Paris* (1421) and the subsequent recognition of Henry V's infant son as King of France after the death of both Charles VI and Henry V (1422). This treaty was the prelude to the dramatic developments which culminated in the appearance of the Maid of Orleans and the Dauphin's reinstatement on the French throne as Charles VII (1429).

Treaties of this type could in the era of patrimonial dynastic State conceptions easily lead to the actual acquisition of territory by the strongest of the partners.

It is, however, also possible that a treaty on succession to the throne does not relate to a one-sided, or possibly mutual, designation of a future bearer of the crown as between the parties, but to succession to the throne in a third State. This is a sort of intervention in the affairs of a foreign State which in former times of dynastic and patrimonial conceptions could also result in the acquisition of territory by the successor thus designated. Comp. the example of the Conferences of London of April-June 1852 concerning the succession to the throne in the Danish monarchy (Martens, N.R.G.¹, XVII², 311 *et seq.*). See Part II of this publication, p. 147.

§ 3. *The creeping effect of a personal union*

It was a scarcely avoidable consequence of political relations and constitutional conditions of former centuries that personal unions of a more intimate kind should result in the final amalgamation of the countries concerned in one single State. This is obvious in the case of a marriage

323

between heads or members of monarchical dynasties, mentioned in § 1 above, but it could likewise occur without such an occasion.

Thus, in 1397, the three Scandinavian countries were temporarily united by the energetic action of Margareta, daughter of King Waldemar IV of Denmark and (since 1363) wife of King Haakon VI of Norway, Denmark being a free electoral, Norway a hereditary kingdom.

After the death of her minor son Olav V in 1387, for whom she had reigned as Queen-Regent, in Denmark since the death of her father in 1375 and in Norway since the death of her husband in 1380, she first united Denmark and Norway under her crown. After her victory over Sweden's King Albrecht of Mecklenburg in 1389, she was also recognized as ruler in Sweden, achieved the election of her second cousin Erik as her successor, and finally, in 1397, united the three countries by the Union of Kalmar. Comp. on this development Part II of this publication, Chapter IV, section 1, § 2, *sub (b)*, p. 149.

Another well-known example of the creeping effect of a personal union can be drawn from another development in Northern Europe, namely, the history of the duchy of Schleswig in its relation to the kingdom of Denmark. Comp. on this development the same Chapter, section and § of Part II, *sub (a)*, pp. 143 *et seq.*

The amalgamation was, in these cases also, often delayed or prevented by the fact that the personally united countries were placed under separate rulers, one the monarchical head of the union, the other his vice-roy or lieutenant, just as was occasionally the case of two countries united by the marriage of their rulers. Comp. *e.g.*, the cases of Aragón, Sardinia and Sicily.

§ 4. *Actes de pariage*

A curious medieval institution which also brought about territorial changes was that of *pariage*. This juridical act consisted in a ruler's surrender of part of his domains to a more powerful ruler on the understanding that the latter undertook to protect the former's remaining possessions. It was frequently practised in the relation between an ecclesiastical and a secular ruler, and it sometimes resulted in a, somewhat limping, condominium or co-imperium. Many of such *lettres de pariage* dating from the 12th and the 13th centuries can be found in vol. XI of the *Ordonnances de France*.

The undertaking by the more powerful ruler was, *e.g.*, to the effect that he should build a castle in the possessions which his opposite number retained (see, *e.g.*, the *lettres de pariage* of 1179 relative to the land of Lorrets in *Ordonnances de France*, XI, 213). The stronger party was generally prohibited from alienating his portion, for the obvious reason that the object of the deal might thereby be easily frustrated. A corresponding prohibition did not as a rule hamper the freedom of the party who sought protection.

The oldest example of a *pariage* which J. J. RAEPSAET (*Oeuvres complètes*, IV, pp. 375 *et seq.*) has been able to discover dates back to 1155, when such a transaction was made between King Louis VII of France and the abbot of St.-Jean de Sens (*Ordonnances de France*, XI, 203). Other *pariages* cited by RAEPSAET are those of 1282 by which a certain seignior Thierry returned half of the woods and mines in his indefensible fief of Hayangs near Metz to Count Henry of Luxembourg "à charge de défendre et protéger le dit Thierry et hoirs dans la jouissance de l'autre moitié", and of 1288 by which an abbot in Hainault presented the count of Hainault with half of his fishing rights on the rivers Sambre and Eppre, plus half of his goods in mortmain on the condition that the count should guarantee him the further possession of the other half.

A *pariage* was not always based on a convention between the rulers concerned: it could also be, and in actual fact occasionally was, the outcome of an arbitral award. A famous instance of a *pariage* created in the latter manner is that of Andorra, a curious remnant of the feudal ages, which rests upon an arbitral award of 8 September 1278 that established an unusual type of co-sovereignty, originally between the bishop of Urgel, on the one hand, and the count of Foix, later the King of Navarre and the King of France, and now the President of the French Republic, on the other. Comp. also *infra*, Chapter V, section 1, on Co-sovereignty, p. 431.

§ 5. *Discovery or symbolic occupation*

An old title for the acquisition of territorial rights was discovery. Discovery did not need, but generally used to be accompanied by some form of symbolic action, such as the planting of the national flag, or the erection of a primitive monument enclosing a formal document stating that possession had been taken of the territory. This mode of acquisition was commonly acknowledged as such by writers on the law of nations of the 15th and 16th centuries, such as Vitoria, Freitas and Suárez.

In the first half of our century these old doctrinal discussions were revived in certain arbitration cases, especially that between the Netherlands and the United States concerning sovereignty over the Palmas or Miangas island, located between Celebes and the Philippines, adjudicated by Professor Max HUBER in an award of 4 April 1928 (*A.A.*, II, 829). The Arbitrator discussed in detail what were the legal effects of discovery as such, *i.e.*, the mere fact of seeing unknown land, without any act, even symbolical, of taking possession. He stated that there were two interpretations: the first, that discovery as such involved *ipso jure* territorial sovereignty and, consequently, a definitive title; the other, that it merely created an "inchoate title", a *jus ad rem*.

In the first interpretation, account must be taken of a problem of intertemporal law. The effect of discovery is to be determined by the rules of international law in force at the time, but a distinction must be made between the creation of rights and their continued existence:

> "The same principle which subjects the act creative of a right to the law in force at the time the right arises, demands that the existence of the right, in other words its continued manifestation, shall follow the conditions required by the evolution of law" (*loco cit.*, p. 845).

In the second interpretation the inchoate title of discovery existed, it is true, without external manifestation, but it had, at any rate since the 19th century, to be completed within a reasonable period by the effective occupation of the land claimed to have been discovered. This theoretical approach to the problem of discovery in the light of accepted principles of inter-temporal law is certainly correct: the successive stages through which a territorial claim passes in the course of the centuries must each be judged in conformity with the law prevailing at the time. Thus it may occur that a territorial claim which could initially be rightly founded on mere discovery or symbolic occupation—or, for that matter, on papal adjudication (comp. below § 6)—can no longer be so founded at a later stage of legal history.

Comp. for the rest section 2, § 2 *infra*, pp. 349 *et seq.*

§ 6. *Papal grant or adjudication*

Taking possession of territory in virtue of a papal grant was once a famous and widely recognized procedure. The Popes have for a very long time professed and vindicated their right to proceed by way of such grants. Since I have dealt with this form of the exercise of worldly power by the Pope in some detail in my Excursus to Chapter V, section 1 of Part II of this publication, pp. 308 *et seq.*, at pp. 330 and 331, I will not go any further into this special mode of acquisition of territory here. The theoretical basis and validity of this asserted pontifical right has already been disputed at an early stage even by Catholic writers, such as DE VITO-RIA, but the claim itself has undoubtedly left its traces in the political history of the world. Papal grants were not, however, so sacrosanct as to prevent the beneficiaries entering into agreements *inter se* for the alteration of boundaries determined by the Pope, as is evidenced, *e.g.*, by the Spanish-Portuguese Treaty of Tordesillas of 7 June 1494 (Dumont, S., I, 372, 389; Navarrete, II, 147), which shifted the demarcation line, drawn by the Bull *Inter caetera* of Pope Alexander VI of 4 May 1493 westward, in favour of Portugal. This shift was, however, still formally confirmed in 1506 by Pope Julius II. These 15th and 16th century territorial arrangements were later in express terms set aside by Spain and Portugal in Article 21 of their boundary treaty of 1 October 1777 (Martens, R², II, 545).

Papal grants of a territorial nature have since long fallen into desuetude.

Comp. for further particulars concerning these and other papal grants, apart from my abovementioned Excursus in Part II of this publication, the relevant historical data in Part IV-A thereof, in the context of the struggle for the freedom of the sea.

§ 7. *"Reunions" by special pseudo-judicial bodies*

Most notorious as examples of the application of this method of annexing foreign territory under a false juridical guise is the series of "reunions", practised by the Government of France subsequent to the Peace Congress of Nijmegen of 1678-1679. This method consisted in submitting certain historical claims of France relating to non-French borderlands in the north and north-east to pseudo-judicial bodies, the so-called *chambres de réunion*, established at Metz, Besançon and Breisach, in order to camouflage their (re-)annexation pure and simple in virtue of a "judgment" to the effect that they belonged to France, mostly on the ground of old feudal titles. Comp. on this practice of the French kingdom RANKE, *Französische Geschichte*, III, pp. 336 *et seq.*

This curious device is mentioned in this section 1 as a separate (spurious) title of acquisition because it belongs entirely to the past. France has, it is true, followed a somewhat similar course of action by her numerous "reunions" in the Napoleonic era, but I relegate those actions to section 2, § 3 *infra*, p. 358, dealing with annexation or incorporation, because she did not in that period feign to adopt a pseudo-judicial method to disguise pure and simple acts of aggression.

As to the action of the *chambres de réunion*, France was later forced to retrocede most of the territories thus acquired at the Peace Congress of Rijswijk of 1697. Comp. on the restitution of the countries, thus arbitrarily "(re)united" with France to their rightful sovereign Article 4 of the Peace Treaty of Rijswijk between the Empire and France of 20 October 1697 (Dumont, VII², 422):

> "Restituentur in primis Sacrae Caesareae Majestati et Imperio, ejusque Statibus et Membris, a Sacra Regia Majestate Christianissima quaevis tam durante bello et via facti, quam Unionum nomine occupata Loca et Jura, quae extra Alsatiam sita, aut in indice Reunionum a legatione Gallica exhibito expressa sunt, cassatis, quae ea de causa a Cameris Metensi (Metz) et Vesontina (Besançon), ut et Consilio Brisacensi (Breisach) edita sunt, Decretis, Arrestis, et declarationibus, omniaque in eum statum reponentur quo ante illas occupationes, Uniones, seu Reuniones, fuerunt, nullo deinceps tempore amplius turbanda seu inquietanda ..."

327

It is curious to state that in the course of the 18th century the King of Denmark also resorted to the same type of pseudo-judicial "reunion" with his kingdom of territory, situated in the border region between Danes and Germans, *viz.*, the duchy of Schleswig. Comp. for further details HATSCHEK-STRUPP's *Wörterbuch des Völkerrechts und der Diplomatie* (Berlin, 1925), II, 486 *sub voce* Schleswig-Holstein.

Comp. for the rest below, section 2, § 3, under Annexation, pp. 356 *et seq.*

§ 8. *Secularization*

Secularization was the operation by which an ecclesiastical State—archbishopric, bishopric, abbey or *Probstei* (provostship)—was deleted as such and sovereignty over its territory transferred to a secular power. This operation has already been mentioned in another context, namely, in Part II of this publication on the Subjects of international law, where it has been considered in § 2 of Chapter I, section 2, dealing with international persons of the past, pp. 23-28. But from a systematical point of view and because an ecclesiastical State was sometimes only partially effaced, it deserves mention also in this Part III on Territory, where I will, however, limit myself to making a few summarizing observations.

The method of augmenting the territory of a State by adding to it that of an ecclesiastical unit hitherto vested with secular power, was practised in successive historical waves of secularization.

It began, as one of the means of terminating the Thirty Years' War of Religion in the first half of the 17th century, at the Peace Congress of Westphalia with the wiping out of a number of ecclesiastical States in Protestant parts of the Holy Roman Empire as such and their subsequent transfer as secular territories to Protestant rulers. The Peace Treaty of Osnabrück of 24 October 1648 (Dumont, VI^1, 450; Zeumer, *Quellensammlung*, 2nd ed., vol. II, No. 197) indeed deleted the archbishopric of Bremen and the bishopric of Verden (*cum annexis*) as ecclesiastical states and granted their territory in fief to Sweden under the title of a duchy (Article X, § 7). In the same way the margraves of Brandenburg acquired in fief the bishoprics of Halberstadt, Minden and Cammin, and the expectancy in case of its vacancy of the archbishopric of Magdeburg (Article XI, §§ 1, 4, 5 and 6). On the bishopric of Osnabrück comp. further Article XIII of the same Treaty and on the bishoprics of Metz, Toul and Verdun Articles 70 and 71 of the Treaty of Münster of the same date (Dumont, VI^1, 469; Zeumer, *ibid.*, II, No. 198).

After revolutionary France had already annexed a number of ecclesiastical entities within her own boundaries or on the left bank of the Rhine by her policy of "reunions"—Avignon (1790-1791), the rural part of the bishopric of Basel (1792), the abbey of Stavelot (1793), the bishopric of Liège (1793)—(comp. on this subject *infra*, § 3 of section 2 on Annexation or Incorporation, p. 358), a second wave of systematic secularizations followed as a consequence of the definitive acquisition of the left bank of the Rhine by France in virtue of the Peace Treaty of Lunéville of 7 February 1801 (Martens, R², VII, 296): the ensuing *Reichsdeputations-Hauptschluss* of 25 February 1803 (*ibid.*, R², VII, 436) indeed wiped out twenty-three more ecclesiastical territorial units, not only on the left bank but also on the right bank, as to the latter with the object of carving them up as compensation for secular Powers and even for two special ecclesiastical units, the Knights of Malta and of the Teutonic Order, for their losses on the left bank. I gave a list of the former *reichsunmittelbare* ecclesiastical territories, thus engulfed by temporal States, at p. 28 of Part II of this publication.

The last ecclesiastical units were abolished on the creation of Napoleon's Confederation of the Rhine of 12 July 1806 (*ibid.*, R², VIII, 480)—various commanderies of the Teutonic Order and abbeys—, whereas the Final Act of the Congress of Vienna of 9 June 1815 (*ibid.*, N.R., II, 379) still mentions them but only as things of the past, see Article 23, referring to the secularized Chapters of Elten and Herford and the secularized *Probstei* of Cappenberg, and Article 45, *sub* 1.

Comp. further on this subject Part II of this publication Chapter I, section 2, § 2, pp. 23-28.

§ 9. *Mediatization*

Much of what has been said in § 8 on secularization also applies to mediatization. This operation consisted in the depriving of smaller independent secular principalities and cities of their status of immediate individual members of the Holy Roman Empire and the incorporation of their territory into that of bigger fellow member States. In this respect also, the French conquests on the left bank of the Rhine, and the increase of Napoleon's influence on its right bank have been the main agents of territorial changes of this type, which have—via the *Reichsdeputations-Hauptschluss* of 1803 and the establishment of the Confederation of the Rhine in 1806[15]—in the event been confirmed on the occasion of the political reshuffle of Europe at the Peace Congress of Vienna. This included the establishment of the new German *Bund*, whose Constitution of 8 June 1815 (*ibid.*, N.R., II, 353; French translation: 369) embodied

---

15. Among the territories, mediatized in virtue of the Constitution of the Confederation of the Rhine, I mention the (or various) possessions of the Prince of Thurn and Taxis, the well-known Postmaster-General of the Empire; and of the prince and counts of Löwenstein-Wertheim and Solms; the counts of Bentheim, Steinfurt, Siegen and Dillenburg; the duke of Looz; and the Imperial city of Frankfurt.

in Article 14 detailed provisions concerning the future status of the mediatized princes in the compass of the *Bund*. Comp. on these mediatizations *e.g.*, Article 43 of the Final Act of the Congress.

See on a curious epilogue of these mediatizations in the middle of the 20th century the prolonged lawsuit instituted by a member of the princely house of Salm-Salm in Netherlands Courts after World War II, mentioned below in this publication, p. 448.

(B) *Loss*

After what I have set out under (A), *supra*, pp. 298 *et seq.* there is scarcely any need to expatiate on the various modes of the loss of territory, which is usually only the reverse, the reflected image of its acquisition. Feudal tenures could in the past and did in actual fact often get lost either by the extinction of the male line of succession in the dynasty of the vassal, or by his neglect or refusal to fulfil specific obligations imposed by feudal law, or still worse by forfeiture on the ground of his felony.

Famous examples of this have been handed down to us from early centuries. Such an automatic lapse, or such a forfeiture pronounced by the liege lord and his feudal court, as a consequence of which the feudal tenures reverted to the liege lord for free disposal—in later time often subject to approval by some other authority, such as *e.g.*, the college of Electors in Germany—in favour of other tenants, or for disposal in conformity with some prior arrangement, frequently occurred in the Holy Roman Empire, in Italy, in France and elsewhere. It is only possible to cite here a few instances of the lapse or forfeiture of feudal tenures.

The reversion of a territory to the liege lord as a vacant fief (*eröffnetes Mannslehen, heimgefallenes Lehn*) on the death of the last male descendant of the house of the vassal was a very frequent occurrence.[16]

Examples:

return of the duchy of Burgundy (between Chalons, Saône and Chatillon, Seine) to France by a decree of King Jean of 1361 for its enfeoffment as a French fief to his son Philippe of Valois, who had

---

16. I eliminate here the cases in which it was even doubtful whether the fief was hereditary at all. This was often a controversial point, as appears, *inter alia*, from a legal dispute concerning the fief of East Friesland, see Rousset, *Recueil*, XIX, 58 *et seq.*

There were also many cases in which the fief could legally devolve upon descendants in the female line, but it was sometimes doubtful whether this was indeed the case, and also whether a ruler could legally change a normal male fief into a *feudum femininum (Weibslehn, Kunkellehn, Spindellehn)*. The Emperor as the *Oberlehnsherr* certainly had the power to do it. Thus, the Emperor Charles V in 1546 declared the sisters of the last duke of Jülich to be entitled to succession in the duchy.

already received the Franche-Comté (Hochburgund) as a German fief from the Emperor Karl IV;

return of the duchy of Burgundy and the Burgundian towns in Picardy to France under the reign of Louis XI on the death of duke Charles the Bold at Nancy in 1477;

similar return of the counties of Provence, Anjou and Maine on the demise of René II of Anjou in 1480,—

reversions which finally broke the power of the great vassals of the French Crown and effected the rise of an absolute French monarchy;

investiture of Felipe, Prince of Spain, with the duchy of Milan by his father, the Emperor Charles V, on 11 October 1540 (Dumont, IV², 200) "post reversionem ad Imperium per obitum ducis Francisci Sforzae".

Failure or refusal by a vassal to request the renewal of his fief, either on his own succession to it, or on the succession of a new liege lord to the throne was also a legal cause for withdrawal of the fief from the liege man. A hard struggle of this type occurred at the end of the 13th century, when (in 1294) King Edward I of England at first refused to obey the summons by his liege lord for his fiefs on French soil, King Philip IV, to come to France in order to do homage and deliver the oath of allegiance for them. The dispute was in the event resolved by their treaty of Paris of 20 May 1303 (Dumont, I², 334) (Part II of this publication, p. 347).

The gravest case of feudal conflict was, of course, that of felony, when the liege man rebelled against his lord, as happened on many occasions. Such felony led, for example, to the cancellation by a feudal court of the fiefs of Anjou, Normandy and other possessions of the English King on French soil in 1202 (comp. on these events the judicial assessment by the International Court in its Judgment in the *Minquiers and Ecrehos* case of 17 November 1953, *I.C.J. Reports* 1953, pp. 47 *et seq.*, at p. 56).

Another example is the forfeiture of the fief of the duke of Mirandola, marquis of Concordia, in 1711 and its grant as an "eingezogenes Reichslehn" (forfeited Imperial fief) by the Emperor to the duke of Modena.

Loss of territory could in former centuries also be the consequence of a debtor's failure to redeem a debt for the security of which he had given it in pledge to his creditor. Comp. Chapter IV, section 1 *infra*, p. 387.

Postscript ad section 1, (A), § 2 (Hereditary succession)

All the variants of dynastic arrangements surveyed in section 1, (A), § 2, above, may now be considered to have had their day. What remains of them in the present century are the usual constitutional provisions in monarchical States governing the order of succession to the throne and, very rarely, the belated operation of a dynastic pact, kept in force by an international treaty. A fairly recent instance of the latter contingency is the disruption of the succession of the House of Orange-Nassau in the Grand Duchy of Luxembourg in 1890. Unlike the subsidiarily cognatic character of the order of succession in that House the order of succession in the House of Nassau-Weilburg was strictly agnatic. It was based on a family pact, concluded between the two branches of the House of Nassau in June 1783, the so-called *Nassauische Erbverein*, confirmed by Emperor Joseph II on 29 September 1786 (Martens, R.², III, 647). It was transferred in 1815 from the four principalities of Orange-Nassau to the Grand Duchy of Luxembourg by Article 71 of the Final Act of the Congress of Vienna (*ibid.*, N.R., II, 379, at p. 414). This divergence between the two orders of succession caused the replacement of the house of Orange-Nassau by that of Nassau-Weilburg, when Queen Wilhelmina succeeded in the Netherlands in 1890. This cause of a change of dynasty in Luxembourg has not prevented the Grand Duchy from altering its Constitution in 1907 by itself adopting a cognatic order of succession,[17] as soon as it had become obvious that the male Nassau-Weilburg line was equally running out with Grand Duke Wilhelm (deceased in 1908).

For the rest, the inconvenience of such hereditary acquisitions of territorial sovereignty had already become obvious long ago, owing to the danger of the accumulation of power and the consequent disturbance of the existing political equilibrium. This has led to the express prohibition of concentrating two specific crowns on one head, as occurred, *e.g.*, in the following instances (comp. on this subject Part II of this publication, the Excursus to Chapter VI, pp. 471 *et seq.*).

One of the most famous historical examples of such a prohibition is that laid down in a Basic Law enacted by the Spanish Cortes on 9 November 1712 and later transformed into an international undertaking and further confirmed by the Peace Treaties of Utrecht of 1713/1714: Article 6 of the Franco-British and Article 31 of the Franco-Netherlands treaty of 11 April 1713 (Dumont, VIII¹, 339 and 366, respectively), Article 37 of the treaty between Spain and the Netherlands of 26 June 1714 (*ibid.*, VIII¹, 427), Article 4 of that between Spain and England of 13 July 1713 (*ibid.*, VIII¹, 393), Article 2 of the Quadruple Alliance Treaty of 22 July/2 August 1718 (Rousset, *Recueil*, I, 180) and Article 3 of the Peace Treaty of Vienna between the Emperor and Spain of 30 April 1725 (Rousset, *Recueil*, II, 110). In some of these treaties the mutual renunciation of the French crown by the new Anjou King of Spain, Philip V, and of the Spanish crown by the Dukes of Berry and Orléans were textually inserted, and a clause was added embodying the principle that the two crowns should remain by law inviolably separated as "le fondement du salut public", or, as it was expressed

---

17. Even at that time protests were still, but vainly, raised on the basis of the "Erbverein" by the nearest agnatic relative, the Count of Merenberg, born from a morganatic marriage of Prince Nicolas of Nassau with Natalia, daughter of the Russian author Pushkin.

in the Anglo-Spanish treaty "justo potentiae equilibrio". The engagement of France vis-à-vis Great Britain has had a late epilogue in the middle of the 19th century in a protracted Anglo-French dispute on the international legality of a planned marriage of the Spanish Infante Luisa Fernanda with the duke of Montpensier, son of King Charles VIII of France from the house of Bourbon. The very complicated elements of that dispute (1842-1847) can be extracted from the lengthy diplomatic correspondence in Martens, N.R.G.[1], X, 149-413.

Comp. also the renunciation clause, inserted in Article 33 of the Peace Treaty of the Pyrenees of 7 November 1659 (Dumont, VI[2], 264) and already alluded to above in § 1 (Marriage) and the "Eheberedung" (marriage contract) between the Elector of Bavaria and Princess Maria Leopoldina of Austria of 1795 (Martens, N.S., I, 275) by which the bride, "wie auch bei dem durchleuchtigsten Erzhaus Oestreich von alters her Herkommens ist", renounced all hereditary claims to the Austrian crown *ab intestato*.

The prohibition, obtaining in the Netherlands Constitution of 1815 (Article 29[1]), of the union of the crown of the Netherlands with any foreign crown had its origin in the corresponding prohibition included in Article 6 (1) of the Peace Treaty of Paris of 30 May 1814 (*ibid.*, N.R. II, 1), in connection with a then contemplated betrothal of the Crown Prince Willem (II) to an English princess, prior to his final marriage with the Russian princess Anna Pavlovna. The prohibition was in later constitutions (1848, 1887) reduced in scope in order to legalize the already existing personal union with Luxembourg.

A combination of the crowns of Bavaria and Greece was expressly forbidden in Article 8 of the treaty of 7 May 1832 between France, Great Britain and Russia, on the one hand, and Bavaria, on the other (*ibid.*, N.R., X, 550), and a similar interdiction was stipulated in respect of the crowns of Denmark and Greece in Article 6 of a similar Convention of 13 July 1863 (*ibid.*, N.R.G.[1], VII[2], 79): "En aucun cas ne seront réunies sur la même tête la couronne de Grèce et celle du Danemark".

Corresponding provisions were inserted in a number of documents regarding the historical dynastic relations between Denmark on the one hand, and the (Danish) duchy of Schleswig and (German) county of Holstein, on the other.

Wars of Succession

Rival and contrasting titles of succession or diputes over testamentary dispositions have time and again caused tension in international relations or even wars. Considering the immense impact which those disputes and wars have had on the shaping of Europe, I will, in addition to the data already given in § 2 of this section, summarize below the main instances with a short survey of their causes and ultimate solutions.

(a) *War of the Jülich-Cleves Succession* (1609 *et seq.*), with an epilogue in the middle of the 18th century.

Referring for further details to section 1 of Chapter V (on Co-sovereignty) below, pp. 434 *et seq.*, I confine myself here to stating that the War of the Jülich-Cleves Succession of 1609 and following years resulted from rival claims, partly advanced by three female descendants of the last duke and partly by the Duke of Saxony as holder of an Imperial expectancy with respect to the same succession. Comp. on the conflicting claims, *inter alia*, Rousset's *Recueil*, VIII, 1-54 (Palatinate), 64-82 (Brandenburg) and 437-479 (Sulzbach, Pfalz-Neuburg), Rousset's own exposition in VIII, 54-64, and the genealogical table in VII, 300. The dispute[18] developed in various stages, via condominia, first *pro indiviso*, later *pro diviso*, ultimately resulting in a final partition of the estate between Brandenburg and the Palatinate (1666).

The dispute had an epilogue in the 1730's, when different pretenders again opposed one another (Pfalz-Neuburg, Pfalz-Zweibrücken, Sultzbach, Prussia, Saxony), see Rousset, *Recueil*, III, 192; VII, 294; XII, 1 and XIII, 1. Comp. also the *Observations sur une pièce publiée par la Maison Electorale Palatine de Neuburg et par celle de Sulzbach sous le titre de Vraye Exposition du Fait dans l'affaire de Juliers &c contre la Maison Electorale et Ducale de Saxe*, with 54 Annexes, published in 1739, but without further indication of the place of publication.

(b) *War of the Spanish Succession*

After what I have set out above in this Chapter, section 1, § 2 (in particular, pp. 304 *et seq.*), a summary of the causes, development and termination of the War of the Spanish Succession can be very succinct.

It was caused by the danger that on the death of King Carlos II of Spain either the French or the Austrian dynasty would succeed to the throne of Spain and that thus an overwhelmingly strong power would be created, a development that other main European powers were unprepared to tolerate.

> The three main pretenders on the ground of dynastic relationship were: Archduke Karl of Austria, second son of the Emperor Leopold I, himself a grandson of King Felipe III of Spain and married to a younger daughter of Felipe IV; Philippe of Anjou, grandson of King Louis XIV of France, himself married to the eldest daughter of Felipe IV; and Prince Joseph Ferdinand of Bavaria, grandson via his mother of the same Emperor Leopold I and his Spanish consort.

Hence the conclusion of a treaty, aimed at preventing both these eventualities, between the so-called Maritime Powers (England and the

18. It had already in an early stage given rise to a treaty between the Republic of the United Netherlands and Brandenburg and Neuburg relative to the traffic of goods on the rivers Rhine and Maas: 21 September 1611 (Dumont, V², 174).

United Netherlands) and France on 11 October 1698 (Dumont, VII², 442). According to it the crown of Spain was to devolve upon the young Electoral Prince of Bavaria Joseph Ferdinand. The plan was adopted by Carlos II in a will of 14 November 1698, but it was soon afterwards wrecked on the death of the Bavarian Prince on 6 February 1699. This fact led to the conclusion of a second treaty by England, the United Netherlands and France on 25 March 1700 (Dumont, VII², 477), by which it was stipulated that the crown of Spain would devolve upon the Austrian Archduke Karl, but that France would acquire Spain's outer possessions in Italy (Milan, Naples, Sicily) and Lorraine. This treaty, again incorporated in a will of Carlos II, however, also miscarried, this time owing to the Emperor's refusal to consent to the latter clauses. A third will of Carlos II of 2/5 October 1700 (Dumont, VII², 485) finally disposed that the Spanish crown would devolve upon Louis XIV's grandson Philippe of Anjou,—a disposition which the other main powers, after the death of Carlos II on 1 November 1700, were unwilling to accept. This opposition led to a war which was initiated by the Emperor in July 1701 and subsequently involved for many years, on the one hand, France, Spain and their allies Bavaria and Cologne, and on the other, England, the United Netherlands, the Emperor, and (since 1703) Prussia, Savoy and Portugal.

Comp. on the complicated history of the succession to the Spanish throne about 1700 the exposition by David J. Hill in *A history of European diplomacy* (London, 1914), vol. III, pp. 250-276, and Table VI at pp. 690-691.

This war was waged in northern Italy, the region of the Lower Rhine, southern Germany, Austria, the southern Low Countries, Spain (capture of Gibraltar in 1704) and the colonies in America.

The conditions of the peace to be concluded were laid down in great detail by the Maritime Powers and the Emperor in the Triple or Grand Alliance Treaty of 7 September 1701 (Dumont, VIII¹, 89). Should France and Spain be unwilling to accept them, then the Contracting Parties would take the necessary steps to enforce them. The peace was in fact, after many changes of fortunes—the death of William III of Orange on 19 March 1702; the battles of Blenheim (1704), Ramillies (1706), Turin (1706), Oudenaarde (1708) and Malplaquet (1709); fruitless peace conferences in The Hague (1709) and Geertruidenberg (1710); the succession of Archduke Karl to the Imperial throne in April 1711; change of front of the new Tory Ministry in 1711—concluded on the basis of the conditions embodied in the Triple Allience Treaty of 1701. The Peace Congress was opened in Utrecht in January 1712 and led, after formal declarations of renunciation of all hereditary claims to the throne of France by the new Anjou King of Spain, Felipe V (5 November 1712; Dumont, VIII¹, 310) and to the throne of Spain by the French dukes of Berry and Orleans (19 and 24 November 1712; Dumont, VIII¹,

339 in Article VI) to the conclusion of a series of peace treaties, first and mainly in that town and subsequently in Rastadt, Baden (Switzerland) and Vienna.

These various treaties are incorporated in Dumont's *Corps Universel*, vol. VIII[1]:

> 11 April 1713, France-Great Britain, p. 339;
> „ „ „ France-Portugal, p. 353;
> „ „ „ France-Prussia, p. 356;
> „ „ „ France-Savoy, p. 362;
> „ „ „ France-United Netherlands, p. 366;
> 13 July 1713, Spain-Great Britain, p. 393;
> 13 August 1713, Spain-Savoy, p. 401;
> 6 March 1714 (Rastadt), France-Emperor and Empire, p. 415;
> 26 June 1714, Spain-The Netherlands, p. 427;
> 7 September 1714 (Baden), France-Emperor and Empire, p. 436 (also Rousset, *Recueil*, I, 1);
> 6 February 1715, Spain-Portugal, p. 444;
> and further in the same collection, vol. VIII[2]:
> 30 April 1725 (Vienna), Emperor-Spain, p. 106 (also *Recueil*, II, 110);
> „ „ „ (Vienna), Empire-Spain, p. 113 (also *Recueil*, II, 123).

See for the Peace Congress of Utrecht, *inter alia*: *Actes et Mémoires et autres pièces authentiques* (Utrecht, 1714-1715), vols. I-VI. *Histoire du congrès de la paix d'Utrecht comme aussi de celle de Rastadt et de Bade* (Utrecht, 1716).

The main contents of these peace treaties were, in accordance with the Grand Treaty of Alliance, as follows.

Recognition of Philippe of Anjou as King Felipe V of Spain, subject to reciprocal renunciation by this King of the crown of France, and by the dukes of Berry and Orleans of that of Spain.

Cession to the House of Austria, *via* the detour of a transfer by France to the United Netherlands, of (i) the Spanish Low Countries as they were according to the Peace Treaty of Rijswijk of 1697—except (*a*) part of Upper Guelder, which France ceded to Prussia on the strength of full powers granted to her by Spain, and (*b*) an undefined territory in either Luxemburg or Limburg, which was destined to become a principality for the princess Orsini, but was never ceded to her—, and (ii) the then French part of the Low Countries (Tournay, Fournes, Ypres), both subject to the arrangements made by the Barrier Treaty (comp. *infra*, Chapter IV, pp. 420 *et seq.*). Temporary provisions in favour of the Elector of Bavaria—his maintenance in the sovereignty over Luxembourg, Namur and Charleroi, ceded to him in 1702 and 1712, until he should be reintegrated in his old possessions and social position in Germany.

Various arrangements concerning the former Spanish territories in Italy: maintenance of the duke of Savoy in the possession of Sicily—subsequently exchanged for Sardinia[19], subject to a system of reversion (comp. above, pp. 315 *et seq.*) of the country to Spain in the case of extinction of his house in the male line and to the possible succession of his own house to the throne of Spain in the case of extinction of the latter's monarchy; maintenance of the Emperor in the possession of Naples, Milan, the ports of Tuscany, Mantova, Mirandola and Comacchio; maintenance of the duke of Savoy in certain territories in Upper Italy, ceded to him in 1703 (part of Monferrato, provinces of Alessandria and Valenza, area between the rivers Po and Tanaro, Lomellina); the duchies of Tuscany, Parma and Piacenza to become *feudi masculini* of the Empire, which in the case of extinction of the houses of Medici and Farnese would be granted by investiture to Don Carlos of Spain; Livorno to remain for ever a free port; fixation of the Franco-Savoy boundary along the summits of the Alps.

Certain arrangements in respect of Germany: cession of Alt-Breisach, Freiburg and Kehl by France to the Empire; restoration of the duke of Bavaria and the archbishop of Cologne in their pre-war possessions.

The King of Prussia, apart from achieving the cession of Upper Guelder *(supra)*, is recognized as sovereign of Neuchâtel and Valengin in Switzerland, but renounces his claim to the principality of Orange *c.a.* in France, whose title and armours he is, however, authorized to maintain.

Guarantee given by France of the succession of the house of Hanover in Great Britain. France acquiesces in the demilitarization of Dunkerk. Spain cedes Gibraltar and Minorca with Port Mahon to Great Britain.

Various colonial arrangements: ban on the transfer by Spain of any of her American colonies to France or any other power; prohibition by Spain to all nations, except the Netherlands, to trade with the Spanish East Indies; cession by France to Portugal of the territory between the Vincent-Pinçon (or Yapoc) and the Amazon, both of whose banks were to belong to Portugal; cession by Spain to Portugal of the territory of Sacramento on the north bank of the Rio de la Plata; restitution by France to Great Britain of the Hudson Bay, Nova Scotia and Newfoundland (except Cap Breton), subject to the reservation by France of the right of fishing and the drying of fish on the coasts of Newfoundland (comp. on this subject *infra*, Chapter IV, p. 423); Anglo-Spanish Assiento Treaty for the term of thirty years (comp. Part V of this publication).

(c) War of the Polish Succession (1733-1738)

This war was caused by the rivalry between two parties in the Polish Diet on the occasion of the election of a successor to the throne after

19. The duke of Savoy was crowned in Palermo in 1713, but was not recognized as King of Sicily either by the Emperor, or by the Pope.

August II's demise in 1733, each party supported by foreign Powers. Whereas France favoured Louis XV's father-in-law Stanislas Leszczynski, who had already been elected earlier under Swedish pressure in 1704, but was eliminated again in 1709, Russia supported August II's son August (III). The armed conflict spread far beyond its area of origin to other countries: Saxony, Russia and the Emperor Charles VI on the one side and France, Sardinia and Spain on the other. As a result the war was waged in different parts of Europe: on the Baltic coast, on the Rhine, in Lorraine, in Northern Italy and in the two Sicilies.

It was ended by the preliminary Peace Treaty of Vienna of 3 October 1735 between the Emperor and France (Wenck, I, 1 et seq.) and the final Peace Treaty of Vienna of 18 November 1738 between the Emperor and the other belligerent Powers (ibid., I, 88 et seq.), to the effect that

August III of Saxony was recognized as King of Poland;

Stanislas Leszczynski received for his life-time compensation for his loss of Poland in the cession of the duchies of Bar and Lorraine;

Lorraine was entirely severed from the Holy Roman Empire and was to devolve upon France after Stanislas's death (in fact in 1766);

the duke of Lorraine was to succeed in Tuscany after the extinction of the House of Medici there (in 1737);

the Emperor abandoned Naples and Sicily to the Spanish Infante Don Carlos as a secundogeniture, in exchange for the duchies of Parma and Piacenza; and

the Powers concerned recognized Charles VI's Pragmatic Sanction of 1713.

(d) War of the Austrian Succession (1740 et seq.)

The Pragmatic Sanction of the Emperor Charles VI which provoked so much political unrest in Europe dates originally from 19 April 1713. According to this document—an Austrian *Hausgesetz*, enacted by the Emperor—all the Austrian *Erblande* (hereditary lands) were to remain always undivided ("in forma perpetui indivisibilis ac inseparabilis Fideicommissi primogeniturae affecti pro universis Suae Maiestatis, utriusque sexus haeredibus"), *viz.*, in the absence of male descendants, first under the reign of his oldest daughter Maria Theresia and her descendants and only after the extinction of her line of succession, under that of the two daughters of Charles VI's older brother, the late Emperor Joseph I (deceased 1711), married to the Electors of Saxony and Bavaria, and their descendants. It took a long time for this *Hausgesetz* to be adopted as a *Staatsgesetz* by the *Stände* (Estates) of the individual *Erblande* (1720-1723) and it finally became a constitutional law of the State in 1724. This Pragmatic Sanction (text in Wenck, I, 123) was successively guaranteed by a number of European Powers, *viz.*:

Spain in Article 12 of her Peace Treaty of Vienna with the Emperor of 30 April 1725 (Rousset, *Recueil*, II, 110);

the Elector of Cologne in 1726 (*ibid.*, XVI, 425);

Great Britain in Article 2 of her Treaty of Alliance of Vienna with the Emperor of 16 March 1731 (*ibid.*, VI, 13, 34), acceded to by the United Netherlands by an *Actus Concurrentiae* of 20 February 1732 (*ibid.*, VI, 442, 453) subject to a separate Article (*ibid.*, 451, 462);

the Imperial Diet on 11 January 1732 (*ibid.*, VI, 347-350) against the hostile votes of Bavaria, Saxony and the Palatinate (*ibid.*, VI, 315-347);

Denmark and Russia in 1732 (*ibid.*, VII, 446, 466);

Poland in August 1733 (*ibid.*, IX, 137 *et seq.*);

France in Article VI of her Peace Treaty of Vienna with the Emperor of 3 October 1735 after the War of the Polish Succession, made definitive on 18 November 1738 (Rousset, *Suppl.*, II², 546; Wenck, I, 1-88);

the King of Sardinia in 1743 (*ibid.*, XVIII, 93).

However, it soon appeared after the death of Charles VI in 1740 how little value could be attached to such international guarantees, especially when their observance is obstructed by a number of quite different disturbing political factors.

Thus King Frederick II of Prussia, although prepared in principle not to take sides against Maria Theresia in the impending imbroglio of the Austrian succession (1741-1748), made an exception for certain duchies of Lower Silesia, hereditary fiefs of the Crown of Bohemia, on the ground that they had, on the death of the last, childless duke in 1547, devolved upon the house of Brandenburg on the strength of an *Erbverbrüderung* of 1537, authorized in 1498 and 1511 by the then King of Bohemia Vladislav. King Ferdinand I, King of Bohemia since 1526, refused, however, in 1546 to recognize that *Erbverbrüderung* on the ground that the fiefs, though hereditary, were inalienable, and would therefore on the death of the reigning duke return to the Crown of Bohemia. Two centuries later King Frederick II of Prussia saw his chance to wrest the duchies from Maria Theresia, who was forced to cede the greater part of Silesia (except the principalities of Teschen, Troppau and Jägerndorf) to Prussia by the preliminary and final Peace Treaties of Breslau of 11 June and of Berlin of 28 July 1742 after the first Silesian war of 1740 (Wenck, I, 734-784), and subsequently to confirm that cession by the Peace Treaty of Dresden of 25 December 1745 after the second Silesian war of 1744 (Wenck, II, 191-206).

France proved disloyal to her undertakings vis-à-vis the Empress and took the side of the Elector of Bavaria by declaring war on her on 26 April 1744.[20]

20. The alleged Franco-Bavarian Treaty of Nymphenburg of 22 May 1741 has been proved to be a forgery; what was entered into on that occasion was a

The Netherlands hesitated for a long time, since a number of the confederated Provinces—Groningen, Zeeland, Friesland, and Utrecht—were reluctant to honour the Republic's engagements without the concurrence of France, and the constitutional structure of the United Netherlands, based on the principle of unanimity, paralysed any common action. They were only directly involved in the war as a consequence of France's invasion of the Low Countries in 1747 (Rousset, *Recueil* XVII, 177, 486; XX, 82). See also: A.BEER, *Holland und der österreichische Erbfolgekrieg* (Vienna, 1871).

The War of the Austrian Succession, which had thus been ended in 1742/1745 between Austria and Prussia, and was further terminated between Maria Theresia and the Bavarian pretender, the Elector Maximilian III Joseph, at Füssen and Munich on 22 April 1745 and 21 July 1746 (Wenck, II, 180, 229), ultimately came to a general end by the preliminary and final Peace Treaties of Aachen of 30 April and 18 October 1748 (Wenck, II, 310-431; Rousset, *Recueil*, XX, 158 and 179).

(e) *War of the Bavarian Succession* (1778-1779)

The war of the Bavarian Succession of 1778 was caused by the death of the childless Elector Maximilian Joseph from the Wittelsbach line at the end of 1777. According to an existing *Hausvertrag* his successor would be Karl Theodor of the Palatinate from the Sulzbach line of the house of Bavaria. When, however, this successor consented to the occupation by the Emperor Joseph II of large parts of the inheritance as assertedly Austrian, Bohemian or Imperial fiefs, as a compensation for the Emperor's loss of Silesia, this solution, which entailed a dismemberment of Bavaria, was objected to by the nearest agnatic relative, the duke of Zweibrücken. This pretender was supported by King Frederick II of Prussia who was unprepared to acquiesce in this increase of Austrian power. The short war which thus broke out, fought mainly between Austria and Prussia, was ended by the Peace Treaty of Teschen of 13 May 1779 (Martens, R.², II, 661), which divided the allodial estates of the Bavarian succession in a different way.

Other disputes of the same type have not led to war, but have had nternational repercussions, such as that concerning the principality of Orange in the south of France. This principality, enclaved in Southern France, had already been coveted earlier by Louis XIV. France occupied it during her war with the United Netherlands of 1672. It was, however, expressly recognized as a sovereign possession of the House of Nassau by Article 13 of the Anglo-French Peace Treaty of Rijswijk

treaty between Bavaria and Spain of 28 May 1741, also relating to the Austrian succession. Comp. annex to *Allgemeine Zeitung*, 3/5 January 1903.

of 20 September 1697 (Dumont, VII², 399). Its fate after Willem III's death hung in the balance for many years and gave rise to a bloodless war of succession between France, acting through a pretender to the principality from the house of Longueville, the Prince of Conti; the King of Prussia Frederick I in his capacity as son of the eldest daughter of the stadhouder Frederik Hendrik of Orange, on the ground of the latter's will; and the hereditary Stadhouder of Friesland Johan Willem Friso, grandson of Frederik Hendrik's second daughter in virtue of Willem III's will. The French Parliament adjudicated the principality to the Prince of Conti as *dominium utile* under the suzerainty of France and this decision was confirmed by Article 10 of the Franco-Prussian Peace Treaty of Utrecht of 11 April 1713 in exchange for certain concessions to the King of Prussia. Comp. for some further details: this Chapter III, above p. 306.

On the Spanish-Portuguese conflict of 1580 comp. Part II of this publication, p. 134.

Excursus

GROWTH OF THE NETHERLANDS

As a typical example of the formation of States in earlier centuries I will briefly set out below the course of the process by which the separate Low Countries have gradually developed into a coherent group of States.

The Northern provinces of *Holland* and *Zeeland*,[21] the nucleus of the later Republic of the United Netherlands, which had already become closely related much earlier and had together, in 1299, on the death of Count Jan I of Holland, passed by hereditary succession from the house of Holland to that of Hainault, were male fiefs of the Empire. When the last Count from the latter house, Willem IV, was slain in 1345 in a war with the Frisians, he left only a sister, Margareta, who could by right only succeed to the County of *Hainault* (Henegouwen), which was a female fief. She was nevertheless also enfeoffed by her husband Emperor Ludwig of Bavaria with Holland (inclusive of *Friesland*) and Zeeland, and this resulted in war between Margareta and her son Willem of Bavaria (the initial stage of a long drawn-out civil war, known as the "Hoekse en Kabeljauwse twisten"). This war between mother and son was terminated by their peace treaty of 7 December 1354 (Dumont, I², 292) by the terms

21. The southern part of Zeeland, *i.e.*, that to the southwest of the then main branch of the Scheldt, the Eastern Scheldt, was for a long time disputed between the Counts of Holland and those of Flanders: it was made a sort of condominium by their treaty of Bruges of 7 March 1167 (*Oorkondenboek van Holland en Zeeland, ed.* Obreen, p. 94) and was only ceded to Holland by that of Paris of 6 March 1323.

of which Margareta was to keep Hainault, but to abandon Holland and Zeeland to her son, who thus became, as Willem V, the first Count of these provinces from the house of Bavaria.

In the southern part of the Low Countries the Duchy of *Brabant* and the County of *Flanders* (Vlaanderen) were paramount. The Ducal dynasty of Lower Lorraine or Brabant had already acquired the Duchy of *Limburg* at the end of the 13th century. This was ceded to Jan van Brabant by Count Adolph of Mons in 1282 (Dumont, I¹, 250), but a period of rivalling claims to it after the death of Duchess Irmgard (1283) was only brought to a close by the battle of Woeringen (1288). Baldwin IV and V of Flanders had in the first half of the 11th century extended their domains across the borders of Western Francia (under the partition treaty of 843) to areas subject to the Emperor. Hence the distinction between the old Crown Flanders and the new Imperial Flanders which legally remained a fief of the Holy Roman Empire. This complex was in 1384, together with *Artois, Antwerp* and *Malines* (Mechelen), acquired by Philip II the Bold, Duke of Burgundy, as a consequence of his marriage to Margareta of Flanders.

Antwerp and Mechelen had already been the object of a forced cession to Flanders in 1356/1357.

Antwerp was known as the marquisate of the Holy Roman Empire, a separate entity, whose fate was later closely connected with that of Brabant.

The legal status of Mechelen became very problematic since, in the second half of the 13th and the first quarter of the 14th century, it had been the object of incompatible pledges, first to the Duke of Brabant by a self-styled "seignior" from the Berthout family, and later to the Count of Hainault by the Bishop of Liège, who probably had the strongest claim to it, a complication which of course made the seigniory an apple of discord between Brabant and Hainault. At a later stage, however, after the redemption of his debt to the Count of Hainault, the Bishop, in 1333, pledged Mechelen afresh, this time to Louis de Nevers, Count of Flanders, which in turn antagonized Brabant and Flanders. After an intervention by the King of France and a tentative solution of the difficulties by the establishment of a temporary condominium, the Bishop of Liège finally sold the property of the seigniory to Count Lodewijk van Male of Flanders. The controversies over Mechelen have since then subsided.

Artois had passed through a series of equally complicated developments owing to its donation as a dowry by Count Philip of Flanders (in whose family it had been since Baldwin Iron-Arm's marriage to Judith, daughter of Charles the Bald, in 863) to a niece of his on the occasion of her marriage to King Philippe II Auguste of France as early as 1180. The ties, thus established between France and Artois (which King Louis IX subsequently raised to the rank of a county in 1237 on its cession to his brother Robert, Dumont, I, 174), have exerted a lasting influence on its fate. Long after the county had passed to the house of Burgundy in 1384 on Philip II the Bold's marriage to Countess Margaret of Flanders, Louis XI of France renewed his country's claim to Artois, subsequently to the death of Charles the Bold in 1477. Comp. however further in the text.

The very complicated further developments in the period 1417-1433 in the reign of Jacoba, the last ruler of the house of Bavaria as Countess of Holland, Zeeland, Friesland and Hainault, who was during her short life successively married to Crown Prince Jean de Touraine of France, Duke Jan IV of Brabant, King Henry IV of England's brother Earl Humphrey of Gloucester, and a Netherlands nobleman Frank van Borselen, Stadhouder of Zeeland, in the event resulted in a solid union of the two main groups of provinces. This union was brought about by the energetic interference in Jacoba's affairs of her cousin Philippe le Bon (III) of Burgundy, who forced her by their treaty of Delft of 3 July 1428 (Dumont, II², 218) to accept him as the regent of, and the future successor to, her four dynastic dominions. This Burgundian Duke, who had in the mean time, in 1421, also added *Namur* (Namen) to his possessions by a treaty of sale subject to the right of usufruct for the vendor during his lifetime (he died in 1429), and on the death of the then (childless) Duke in 1430 acquired, by hereditary succession, the Duchies of Brabant and Limburg, with Antwerp, finally, in 1433, supplanted Jacoba (who died in 1436), thus uniting under his rule, together with his ancestral Duchy of *Burgundy*, all the other eleven provinces, successively mentioned above, of which Friesland alone was very reluctant element. The Duchy of *Luxembourg* was further added to Philip's possessions by a treaty of sale of 1441 by which Elisabeth of Görlitz, the widow of Antoine of Brabant (who died in 1415), under pressure of rival claims of Saxony and Thüringia sold to him all her rights to that Duchy. Those rights were held by her rivals only to consist in a right of pledge, subject to redemption. See DE NÉNY, *Mémoires historiques et politiques des Pays-Bas autrichiens* (2nd ed., Brussels, 1785), p. 5.

Under his son and successor Charles the Bold (1467-1477) the Duchy of *Guelder* (Gelderland, Gelre), then under the rule of dukes from the Holland house of Egmond, also fell temporarily to the house of Burgundy, but, pursuant to a treaty with Duke Arnout of Guelder of 20 June 1473 (Dumont, III¹, 607), only as a pledge for a loan granted to him by the wealthy Burgundian Prince. This relation lasted until 1492, when there were a series of military clashes and the Duchy was redeemed.

The influence and power of the house of Burgundy was still considerably enhanced by the marriage of Charles the Bold's daughter Maria to Maximilian, the son of Emperor Frederick III (see the marriage-contract of 18 August 1477 in Dumont, III², 9), a bond which entailed, on Maria's death in 1482, the transition of the rule over the united Low Countries from the house of Burgundy to that of Austria, Maria's son Philip the Fair succeeding under the guardianship of his father Maximilian. The latter became engaged in a fierce struggle with the King of France over, among other things, the County of Artois, the Duchy of Burgundy and the *Franche-Comté* (Freigrafschaft of Burgundy, or Hochburgund), the first of the two Burgundy's being part of France, the second a fief of the German Empire. After France's old claims to Artois had been satisfied by an arrangement embodied in the peace and marriage treaty with Louis XI of Arras (Atrecht) of 23 December 1482 (Dumont, III², 100), Maximilian (who later became Emperor in 1493) after its failure terminated the war with France by entering into the peace treaty, with Charles VIII, of Senlis of 23 May 1493 (Dumont, III², 303) by which he left the Duchy of Burgundy to France, but his house was restored in the possession of the Franche-Comté and Artois. In the subsequent peace treaty of Cambrai (Kamerijk)—the famous "Paix des Dames", negotiated between the mother of King François of France and the aunt of Emperor Charles V—of 5 August 1529 (Dumont, IV², 7) France waived her former suzerain rights to Crown Flanders and Artois.[22] This was confirmed by the subsequent peace treaty of Crespi of 18 September 1544 (*ibid.*, IV², 350; IV³, 30).

Friesland (Frisia), that had never really submitted to the Burgundian dynasty and had, pursuant to an enfeoffment by Emperor Maximilian I in 1498 (G. F. SCHWARTZENBERG's *Charter-Boek van Vriesland*, Leeuwarden, 1773, vol. II, p. 209), passed under the authority of the Dukes of Saxony in the capacity of heriditary "potestates", first Albrecht and later George, was on 19 May 1515 (*ibid.*, p. 305) sold by the latter Duke to Emperor Charles V, who could, however, only gradually conquer the province in 1524 against the fierce resistance of the freedom-loving Frisians, assisted by the Duke of Guelder (comp. the definitive treaty of 20 December 1525).

The only provinces of the Low Countries which at that juncture still remained outside the reach of the house of Austria were—apart from the episcopal principality of Liège and the abbey of Stavelot (Stablo)—the Bishopric of *Utrecht* with its trans-IJssel appendix (*Overijssel*), the northeastern province of *Groningen* (Stad en Ommelanden, *i.e.*, town and surrounding areas), the so-called "Landschap" *Drenthe*, and the Duchy of Guelder, linked with the County of *Zutphen*, which had already been acquired in 1179 by the then Count of Guelder by way of inheritance and which had since been inseparably united with Guelder. The latter became a duchy in 1338.

The secular powers ("temporaliteit") over Overijssel and Utrecht were bought by Charles V from the Bishop-Elect Heinrich of Bavaria by a series of treaties, in particular those of 12 February 1528 (regarding Overijssel) (J. J. DODT VAN FLENSBURG, *Archief voor kerkelijke en wereldsche*

---

22. This was not, however, the end of the dispute over Artois: the county was in fact recaptured by France in 1640 and finally retroceded to her by the peace treaty of the Pyrenees of 7 November 1659 (Dumont, VI², 164), confirmed on this point by the subsequent Peace Congresses of Nijmegen (1678), Rijswijk (1697) and Utrecht (1713).

geschiedenissen, inzonderheid van Utrecht, I, 3, p. 93) and 20/21 October 1528 (regarding Utrecht) (VAN DE WATER, *Groot Placaatboek der Staten's Lands van Utrecht mitsgaders van de stad Utrecht*) with the subsequent consent of Pope Clemens VII by a Bull of 20 August 1529 (comp. Part II of this publication, pp. 25-26).

The acquisition of the Bishopric of Utrecht-Overijssel (Over- and Nedersticht) was on 10/15 December 1536 followed by a treaty of sale concerning Groningen, Drenthe and Coevorden[23] after a series of political and military developments which brought Groningen successively under the—at least nominal—authority of the Saxon Dukes of neighbouring Friesland (1499-1506), of Count Edzard I of adjacent East Friesland (1506-1514), and even of Duke Karel of Guelder (1514-1536). But in this case also, Emperor Charles V's superior forces prevailed and Groningen with Drenthe were in the event incorporated into his possessions by the treaty of Grave of 10 December 1536 (SCHWARTZEN-BERG, *Charterboek*, II, 690).

The last of the Low Countries to come under Charles V's authority was the Duchy of Guelder with the County of Zutphen. This Duchy-County had in 1492 legally emerged from its status since 1473 as a pledged territory under the Burgundian and Austrian princes, but had only been in fact reconquered from Maximilian many years later, in 1513, by Arnout of Guelder's grandson Karel. The latter was, however, subsequently forced to yield to superior power by agreeing to accept his Duchy and County as a fief from the hands of the Emperor Charles V by their treaty of Gorcum (Gorinchem) of 3 October 1528 (Dumont, IV[1], 514). In order to escape from this extorted submission, Duke Karel of Guelder even took the unusual course of conferring his dominion in fief upon King François I of France (at whose court he had passed his youth) by a treaty of 14 October 1534 (I. A. NIJHOFF, *Gedenkwaardigheden uit de geschiedenis van Gelderland*, VI-3, no. 1772, p. 1067). However, on his death in 1538 his subjects refused to recognize that transaction and paid allegiance to Willem, Duke of Jülich, Cleves and Bergh, despite the fact that the latter had waived all his claims to Guelder by a treaty with Charles the Bold of Burgundy of 20 June 1473 (Dumont, III[1], 607). It was only this Duke Willem of Jülich who was in his turn, and this time irretrievably, forced to cede his duchy and county to Charles V by their treaty of Venlo of 7 September 1543 (Dumont, IV[2], 264/266), a cession which was completed by a provision of the Peace Treaty of Crespi of

23. The "landschap" Drenthe, then a province of the second rank, has never figured separately among the titles of Charles V, but it did not for that reason become a part of either Groningen or Overijssel. A promise of the Emperor to join Drenthe after its purchase to Overijssel was indeed subsequently redeemed. —The express mention of (the Drenth town of) Coevorden in the treaty of cession is explained by the very special status which that town had formerly enjoyed under ancient documents.

18 September 1544 between François I of France and the Emperor (Dumont, IV², 350 = IV³, 30), by which the former waived all his claims to Guelder based on the treaty of 14 October 1534, mentioned above.

This latter cession completed the union under one dynasty of the seventeen Low Countries, namely: four duchies (Brabant, Limburg, Luxemburg and Guelder), seven counties (Flanders, Artois, Hainault, Holland, Zeeland, Namur, and Zutphen), one margraviate (Antwerp), five seigniories (Friesland, Mechelen, Utrecht, Overijssel with Drenthe, and Groningen). All these provinces, together with *Franche-Comté*, were in the event united with the 10th, Burgundian *Kreis* of the Holy Roman Empire (created in 1512) by the treaty of Augsburg of 26 June 1548 (Dumont, IV², 340/342), inclusive of Utrecht and Guelder which had formerly—lately under the reorganization of the Empire in 1521—belonged to the 5th, Lower Rhine-Westphalian *Kreis*. The treaty of Augsburg, however, left only a faint residu of authority over the Low Countries to the Emperor and Empire. The manner in which the last formal bonds between the Low Countries of 1548 and the United Netherlands of 1579, on the one hand, and the Emperor and Empire, on the other, were gradually loosened and ultimately evaporated entirely form an interesting chapter of diplomatic history of its own.

Comp. Srbik, *Die österreichischen Staatsverträge* (introduction to volume III concerning the Netherlands); *Weensche gezantschapsarchieven 1670-1720 (Rijks Geschiedkundige Public.*, Nos. 67 and 79); Joh. de Meerman, *Specimen juris publici de solutione vinculi quod olim fuit inter S. R. Imperium et Federati Belgii Respublicas* (Leyden, 1774).

Even after 1543 the Prince-Bishopric of Liège and the Abbey of Stavelot remained quasi-independent and so they continued until their "réunion" with France in 1793, as to the Abbey on 2 March (Martens, R.², V, 188), and as to the Bishopric on 8 May (*ibid.*, 190), comp. p. 359 *infra*.

Section 2. PRESENT DAY MODES

Introduction

In a great many cases the acquisition of territorial sovereignty by one State is accompanied by the loss thereof by another, but this is not necessarily so. Although there would, therefore, be some ground for dealing with the two subjects separately, they are as a rule so closely interrelated and are, on the whole, so parallel that I will refrain from analysing them apart, in order to avoid the necessity of recurring to cross-references, and will rather treat them jointly.

When a land territory—the basic element of the domain of a State—is acquired or lost, all other additional elements are necessarily included:

346

the subsoil, the air column and, in the case of a coastal State, its territorial sea and its sovereign rights to the continental shelf. The separate transfer and acquisition of such additional elements of territorial sovereignty, divorced from the basic land territory, is only possible to a very limited extent. Comp. on this subject the observations made in Chapter II, section 3 *supra* on the Territorial Sea, at p. 55.

The following juridical acts or further legally relevant facts can operate as titles by which territorial sovereignty can be

(a) acquired:	(b) lost:
1. facts of nature;	1. facts of nature;
2. occupation of *terra nullius*;	2. dereliction;
3. annexation or incorporation;	3. merger;
4. cession or exchange;	4. cession or exchange;
5. adjudication; and possibly	5. abjudication; and possibly
6. acquisitive prescription;	6. extinctive prescription;
7. novation.	7. novation.

Most of these modes of acquisition are "original" in the sense that the new sovereign does not derive his title from his predecessor; only that *sub* 4 and possibly that *sub* 7 can be correctly qualified as "derivative". This theoretical distinction has little importance.

Territorial contiguity is no title of acquisition, although it has sometimes been advanced as such. I agree entirely with Max Huber's pronouncement in his arbitral award of 4 April 1928 relating to the *Island of Palmas* (*A.A.*, vol. II, p. 829) and confine myself therefore to quoting below a few passages thereof (at p. 854), without further investigating this spurious title:

> "Although States have in certain circumstances maintained that islands relatively close to their shores belonged to them in virtue of their geographical situation, it is impossible to show the existence of a rule of positive international law to the effect that islands situated outside territorial waters should belong to a State from the mere fact that its territory forms the *terra firma* (nearest continent or island of considerable size). Not only would it seem that there are no precedents sufficiently frequent and sufficiently precise in their bearing to establish such a rule of international law, but the alleged principle itself is by its very nature so uncertain and contested that even Governments of the same State have on different occasions maintained contradictory opinions as to its soundness ... Nor is this principle of contiguity admissible as a legal method of deciding questions of territorial sovereignty, for it is wholly lacking in precision and would in its application lead to arbitrary results ...".

This is also why I reject as completely unfounded the argument of contiguity or propinquity, alleged by the Netherlands Government in 1964 in support of their political action against the so-called REM island, an unauthorized television station on the Netherlands part of the continental shelf at a considerable distance from the coast in the North Sea (comp. on this action Part IV-A of this publication on the High Seas).

There is first the automatic acquisition of territorial sovereignty as a result of accretion to the sea-coast, and its image, the loss of territorial sovereignty by avulsion. Comp. on this contingency Part VI of this publication on Juridical facts as source of international rights and obligations, Chapter I.

Then there is the equally automatic acquisition of territory by the emergence of an island or shoal in the territorial sea of a State, and its image, the loss of territory by the submersion of an island either in the territorial sea of a State or in the high seas.

The legal effect of the emergence of an island in the high seas is different: this comes to the surface as *terra nullius* and requires occupation by a State *animo et corpore* in order to create territorial sovereignty; there is no scope here for the automatic operation of the so-called principle of contiguity. In November 1968 a volcanic island about 32 ft. high and 650 ft. long appeared in the sea off the south coast of Iceland about ten miles southwest of the Vestmann Islands.

The emergence of an island in the territorial sea operates an extension of territorial sovereignty only indirectly, that is to say, the area over which that new sovereignty extends is not the island itself, for this emerged in a zone which was already State territory, but an adjoining part of the open sea which becomes included within the range of the territorial sea by the effect of its outer boundary bulging at the normal distance around this new island. (See the commentary of the International Law Commission *ad* Article 10 of its draft Articles on the Law of the Sea of 1956 *sub* 1). On the other hand, the possible submersion of an island in the territorial sea will reduce the maritime territory.

The possible submersion of an island in the open sea causes the loss of both land territory and the surrounding sea area. This phenomenon would seem to have taken place with the Clipperton Island in the eastern part of the Pacific Ocean at 10,5° lat. North and 109° long. West after its adjudication to France by the then King of Italy in a Franco-Mexican arbitration of 1909-1931 (special agreement of 2 March 1909, Martens, N.R.G.[3], V, 8; followed after World War I by an arbitral award of 28 January 1931, *A.A.*, vol. II, p. 1105). It is doubtful whether, if the island rose again, it would *ipso facto* return to France; it would in my opinion rather re-emerge as an *insula nullius*.

I will have to return to facts of the types mentioned above as a source of international rights and obligations, also, in Part VI of this publication.

§ 2. *Effective occupation of terra nullius, or its counterpart: dereliction of State territory*

(a) *Occupation animo et corpore*

As is since long generally recognized, *terra nullius* can on the whole no longer be acquired by simple discovery or mere symbolical occupation, but only be brought under State sovereignty by effective occupation *animo et corzore*, once one of the most important unilateral juridical acts.

This basic principle of modern international law is authoritatively set out by Professor Max Huber in his arbitral award of 4 April 1928 concerning the *Palmas (Miangas) Island* cited above, section 1, § 5, in which he also discussed the related principle of inter-temporal law pursuant to which the validity of an act or a legal situation must be judged in accordance with the law in force at the time (see pp. 325-326).

Requirements for the acquisition of territorial sovereignty over *terra nullius*—to all intents and purposes nowadays a thing of the past—are already since long twofold, *viz.*,—(i) that the acting person proceeds in the name of his State with the intention of acquiring the territory on its behalf, and (ii) that the action is accompanied or followed by a certain measure of actual exercise of State authority, dependent, for the rest, upon the nature and location of the territory concerned.

ad (i). A private person cannot without the express authorization or subsequent confirmation of his State acquire for the latter territorial sovereignty by the occupation of *terra nullius*. What he can do—a nowadays equally hypothetical case—is to create a sovereignty of his own and to establish a new State under his rule, after the fashion of King Leopold II of the Belgians in the Congo or of Sir James Brooke in Sarawak. If the private person concerned acts on behalf of a government, the latter must have the intention of bringing the territory under the sovereignty of its State. This may sometimes be doubtful and may in that case afterwards lead to international controversy. Such a controversy may also arise, theoretically, over the validity of an occupation effected by a government in disregard of possible constitutional requirements or limitations. Uncertainty is, however, more likely to spring from the other requirement

ad (ii). The measure of the required actual display of State authority necessarily is the function of the natural or geographical conditions of the territory concerned. The less habitable, the farther distant from civilization it is, the less intensive may be the establishment of actual State supervision. There cannot be a hard and fast rule in this respect. Most international disputes have in later periods turned upon the efficiency, and the maintenance of the efficiency, of State authority over the

349

territory in question.[24] A fair number of inter-state controversies have arisen precisely over this second requirement of occupation *corpore* and various arbitrators and arbitral or judicial tribunals have racked their brains over this ticklish *quaestio facti* which lends itself only in small measure to the formulation and application of general principles as it is essentially relative by nature. Comp. among others, the above-mentioned arbitral award of 1928 in the *Island of Palmas* case, the Dano-Norwegian case concerning the *Legal Status of Eastern Greenland* of 1933 before the Permanent Court of International Justice, and the Franco-British *Minquiers and Ecrehos* case of 1953.[25] Comp. on these latter two cases my *The Jurisprudence of the World Court*, vol. I, pp. 323-337 and vol. II, pp. 169-177.

The modern requirements of occupation of *terra nullius* were formulated in 1904 by King Vittore Emanuele III of Italy in his award of 6 June of that year as arbitrator between Great Britain (for British Guyana) and Brazil (Martens, N.R.G.[2], XXXII, 485, 487) in the following passages:

"That the discovery of new channels of trade in regions not belonging to any State cannot by itself be held to confer an effective right to the acquisition of the sovereignty of the said regions by the State, whose subjects the persons who in their private capacity make the discovery may happen to be;

That to acquire the sovereignty of regions which are not in the dominion of any State, it is indispensable that the occupation be effected in the name of the State which intends to acquire the sovereignty of those regions;

That the occupation cannot be held to be carried out except by effective, uninterrupted, and permanent possession being taken in the name of the State, and that a simple affirmation of rights of sovereignty or a manifest intention to render the occupation effective cannot suffice;

That the effective possession of a part of a region, although it may be held to confer a right to the acquisition of the sovereignty of the whole of a region which constitutes a single organic whole, cannot confer a right to the acquisition of the whole of a region which, either owing to its size or to its physical configuration, cannot be deemed to be a single organic whole *de facto*."

Occupation of *terra nullius* as a title of acquisition of State territory, once a frequent international juridical act, has become extremely rare, but it can still take place occasionally.

As recorded examples of such occupation of *terra nullius*, certified by an official declaration to that effect, I will cite one old and one very recent such event.

The old instance is that of Netherlands mariners who in 1616 under

24. On the Canadian Indian tribes see the judgment of the Supreme Court of New Brunswick of 20 May 1958 in *I.L.R.*, vol. 27, pp. 1 *et seq.*
25. Comp also the Anglo-Portuguese dispute over territory and islands of the Delagoa Bay, decided by the French President Mac Mahon in favour of Portugal in 1875 (Martens, N.R.G.[2], III, 517); the Anglo-Spanish dispute over the Caroline islands in 1885 (*ibid.*, XII, 283, 287 *et seq.*).

their Master Schouten sailed south of Tierra del Fuego and called one of the larger islands found there Staten Island after the States General —an other Staten Island than that of New York. The document which was drafted by the Master on that occasion as evidence of the occupation of the islands on behalf of the Republic of the United Netherlands can be found in Rousset, *Suppl.*, II[1], 282. This intended juridical act has not, however, produced any legal effect since the States General have not actually endorsed the action taken.

The recent instance, which has produced legal effect, dates only from 18 September 1955 when four men were as a landing party transported by helicopter from the British survey ship H.M.S. *Vidal* to the uninhabited Atlantic islet of Rockall, 250 miles west of the Outer Hebrides, and formally annexed it to the United Kingdom on the authority of the Queen. The Admiralty announcement of 21 September 1955 stated that the occupation of this tiny rocky islet was necessary because it was "within the sector of the sea which is likely to be within the orbit of the projected guided missile range in the Hebrides", and a spokesman of the Ministry of Defence explained that the annexation of this *insula nullius* was required in order to avoid the possibility of embarrassing counter-claims by some other Power, once the Hebridean guided missile project was under way. The landing party spent three hours on Rockall, erected a flagstaff, hoisted the Union Jack, and cemented a pre-fabricated brass plaque into the rock recording the occupation, while a 21-gun salute was fired by H.M.S. *Vidal*. This occupation was not formally promulgated in any public State paper, but was published, *inter alia*, in *The Times* of 22 and 24 September 1955.

Occupation of *terra nullius* has taken place in particular in the field of colonial expansion and has then taken various forms.

The legal process of the acquisition of sovereignty by means of occupation of *terra nullius* by a chartered company was described by the same arbitrator, King Vittore Emanuele III of Italy, in the same award of 6 June 1904 (Martens, N.R.G.[2], XXXII, 485; English translation *ibid.*, 487) relative to the frontier between Brazil and British (formerly Netherlands) Guyana in the following passages:

"That ... the right of the British State as the successor to Holland, to whom the Colony belonged, is based on the exercise of rights of jurisdiction by the Dutch West India Company, which, furnished with sovereign powers by the Dutch Government, performed acts of sovereign authority over certain places in the zone under discussion, regulating the commerce carried on for a long time there by the Dutch, submitting it to discipline, subjecting it to the orders of the Governor of the Colony, and obtaining from the natives a partial recognition of the power of that official;

That like acts of authority and jurisdiction over traders and native tribes were afterwards continued in the name of British sovereignty when Great Britain came into possession of the Colony belonging to the Dutch;

That such effective assertion of rights of sovereign jurisdiction was gradually developed and not contradicted, and, by degrees, became accepted even by the independent native tribes who inhabited these regions ...".

It was often accomplished in the form of the conclusion of a convention with an indigenous prince or chieftain which contained a formal cession of the territory concerned by its ruler to the colonizing power or chartered company. In other cases the convention provisionally only granted to the latter limited territorial rights. In his recent study *An introduction to the history of the law of nations in the East Indies* (Oxford, 1967) C. H. ALEXANDROWICZ has analysed a large number of conventions in Asia from this particular point of view.[26]

Colonizing powers have also often proceeded by the way of establishing a "protectorate" over the local ruler or of placing his territory under their "protection", sooner or later followed by its degradation to, or annexation as a colony.

As Professor Huber has set out in his above-mentioned arbitral award of 1928, such territorial acquisitions were often couched in obsolete feudal forms as a curious anachronism, to which I have already drawn attention in Part II of this publication, Chapter VI, section 1, pp. 354-355.

Other occupations were performed by the colonizing power unilaterally, without any previous convention and following on a forcible conquest, by the enactment of a national law or decree, which either established a "protectorate" or simply incorporated the country concerned into that power's dominions, or created on its own behalf a so-called "zone of influence" or "sphere of interest".

On other occasions again, the operation was carried out by bilateral conventions between colonizing powers, intended to mutually delimit the respective zones of influence which they planned to bring under their territorial sovereignty.

Whichever of these formal methods was employed, the operation always resulted in the acquisition of colonial territory by means of the, once generally recognized, title of occupation of *terra nullius*. However unpalatable this may sound to the newly emergent sovereign States of Africa and other parts of the world, this old mode of acquisition is still up to the present time producing its traditional effects, as even their governments must necessarily recognize: their States would not even

---

26. The Netherlands-Belgian case of 1959 regarding certain enclaved plots of land in the Netherlands province of North Brabant (*I.C.J. Reports* 1959, p. 209; comp. my *The Jurisprudence of the World Court*, vol. II, pp. 353 *et seq.*) and the Thai-Cambodian case of 1961-1962 concerning the temple of Preah-Vihear (*I.C.J. Reports* 1962, p. 6; comp. my *Jurisprudence*, vol. II, pp. 425 *et seq.*), though not relating to controversies over occupation of *terra nullius*, gave also rise to very similar problems of the effectiveness of the display of State sovereignty.

exist in their present form if their country had not been colonized by western powers in the past. It would moreover only have given rise to widespread legal and political chaos if they had been tempted by their anti-colonialist feelings into making a *tabula rasa* of all these under-standings between their former "masters" in the imperialist era. And the world witnesses how jealously the new States defend as their "nation-al frontiers" the demarcation lines drawn up in the past. Territorial adjustments had, for the rest, continued to take place even under the Mandates system of the League of Nations.

This applies to the boundary agreements between the Mandated Territories of Ruanda-Urundi (Belgium) and Tanganyika (Great Britain), 1923 and between Angola (Portugal) and South West Africa (Union of South Africa), 1926. Comp. Part II of this publication, pp. 100-101.

Instances of the varying forms of occupation of *terra nullius* distin-guished above are the following.

a. Formal cession of the colonial territory by its ruler.

Ceylon, treaty of 14 February 1766 of the Netherlands States General and the Dutch East India Company with the king of Candy (Martens, R², I, 317); cession of all the coastal areas;
New Zealand, treaty of Waitangi with the Maori chiefs, 5-6 February 1840 (Hertslet, VI, p. 579);
Land in the Punj Mahals, treaty with the Scindias of Gwalior, 12 December 1860 (Aitchison, vol. 5, p. 422);
Lagos, treaty with the king of that country, 6 August 1861 (*B.F.S.P.*, vol. 52, p. 181).

b. Establishment of a colonial protectorate.

Comores, Anjouan and other islands between North Madagascar and Mozambique, which France first attached to herself by protectorate treaties of 1882 (Martens, N.R.G.², IX, 241) and 1886, but subsequently annexed as colonies by a law of 25 July 1912; the Comores are mentioned in Martens's *Recueil* as from 1843;
a series of tribal lands in Africa, subjected by Germany to her "protec-torate" in 1884/5 by formal treaties with their chiefs, under such colourful titles as the "sovereign captain" Josef Fredericks of Bethania; Manasse, the "sovereign of the Red Nation"; Hermannus van Wijk, the "independent chief of the Bastards", and the tribal chief of the Herreros (*ibid.*, N.R.G.², XI, 464, 479, 480 and 482).
"Letters Patent of Protection" were granted by the German Emperor to the *Gesellschaft für deutsche Kolonisation* and the *New Guinea Company* on 27 February and 17 May 1885 (*ibid.*, N.R.G.², XI, 468 and 476). A catalogue of all the territories successively placed under the "protection" of Germany was laid before the *Reichstag* by the Chancellor Bismarck in a Memorandum of 2 December 1885 (*ibid.*, XI, 485).

c. Acceptance of an overseas ruler as a vassal.

See the arguments discussed by Max HUBER in his award in the *Palmas* case of 1928 *sub* IV (*loco cit.*, pp. 855 *et seq.*). The Netherlands had argued that the many conventions concluded by the Dutch East India Company with native principalities were all based on the conception that the prince received his principality as a fief of the Company or the Dutch State, which was suzerain. The Arbiter endorsed this view, stating that the form of the legal relations created by such contracts was most generally that of suzerain and vassal (or of the so-called colonial protectorate) and that such suzerainty over the native State became the basis of territorial sovereignty as towards other members of the community of nations.

d. Delimitation of zones of influence.

Notification by a German declaration of 6 April 1886 (*ibid.*, N.R.G.², XI, 505) of a German-British demarcation of *Machtsphären* in the Western Pacific;

Franco-British Agreement of 16 November 1887 concerning the New Hebrides and the Society Islands leeward of Tahiti (*ibid.*, N.R.G.², XVI, 820).

The former declaration, which is further dealt with in Part IV-A of this publication on the High Seas, contained a mutual undertaking not to make acquisitions of territory, accept protectorates, or interfere with the extension of the other's influence, and to give up any acquisition of territory or protectorates already established in that part of the Western Pacific lying on the other side of the conventional line.—The genesis of the latter agreement is explained in section 1 of Chapter V on Co-Sovereignty below, at p. 437.

I will have to return to the legal nature of such zones of influence, which do not yet constitute territorial sovereignty, in Chapter V on Exceptional territorial situations, section 9, pp. 494 *et seq.*

The competition between the European Powers in Africa in the 1880's led to the convocation of the Congo Conference at Berlin, which in Chapter VI (Articles 34 and 35) of its General Act of 26 February 1885 (*ibid.*, N.R.G.², X, 414) laid down two basic rules which were thenceforward to govern the validity of new occupations on the African mainland:

"(34) La Puissance qui dorénavant prendra possession d'un territoire sur les côtes du Continent Africain situé en dehors de ses possessions actuelles, ou qui, n'en ayant pas eu jusque-là, viendrait à en acquérir, et de même, la Puissance qui y assumera un protectorat, accompagnera l'acte respectif d'une notification adressée aux autres Puissances signataires du présent Acte, afin de les mettre à même de faire valoir, s'il y a lieu, leurs réclamations.

(35) Les Puissances signataires du présent Acte reconnaissent l'obligation d'assurer, dans les territoires occupés par elles, sur les côtes du Continent Africain, l'existence d'une autorité suffisante pour faire respecter les droits acquis et, le cas échéant, la liberté du commerce et du transit dans les conditions où elle serait stipulée".

These articles related exclusively to the African mainland, to the exclusion of the surrounding islands, especially Madagascar which France was unprepared to have comprised within the strict rules. Neither had they any direct relevance for other Continents, but they have in fact developed into a new customary international law.

Many conventions have been concluded since the Conference of Berlin for the African mainland between the colonizing Powers with the purpose of delimiting their spheres of influence as between themselves. A survey of these will be given in Chapter V, section 9 below, pp. 497 *et seq.*

(b) Dereliction animo et corpore

Just as a State can acquire territorial sovereignty by effective occupation, so it can also lose it by dereliction of a territory *animo et corpore.*

Such a dereliction took place, *e.g.*, in 1684 by England with regard to Tangier, which had in 1662 been given to king Charles II of England as a dowry on the occasion of his marriage to Catharina of Portugal, but was given up because the cost of keeping it was too high (comp. *supra,* p. 299); in 1767 with regard to the then Danish ports of Saffy and Salé in Morocco, owing to the fact that the Danish Company had been dissolved and had ceased to make the required payments. Denmark undertook to pay off the Company's debt and authorized the Emperor of Morocco to dispose of the two ports as he thought fit: treaty of 25 July 1767 (Martens, R^2, I, 461).

The reality of such an intentional dereliction can at a later stage become controversial between States. This has in fact been the case and has always played first fiddle in the acrimonious dispute between the United Kingdom and Argentina over the Falkland Islands (or Islas Malvinas). This controversy indeed mainly centres around the question as to whether the British Government, which had occupied the islands about 1770, had derelinquished them in fact and with the intention of doing so, in 1774. Comp. on the origins of this dispute the following data:

After a Spanish force had on 10 June 1770 dislodged the English occupants from Port Egmont, the Spanish Government disavowed this action by a declaration of 22 January 1771, accepted by Great Britain (*ibid.*, R^2, II, 1-4). Three years later however, on 22 May 1774, the British Commander left the islands while taking the precaution of fixing on the fortress a leaden plaque to the effect that the islands appertained in law to King George III (text *ibid.*, R^2, II, 4) and leaving the British flag flying. After independent Argentina had emerged from the dismemberment of the Spanish colonial empire in 1810 and following years, the islands were again occupied in fact by Great Britain in January 1833, thus antagonizing the Argentinian Government which has ever since maintained its claim to the Islas Malvinas (*e.g.*, message of President Rosas of 1 January 1848, concerning the British reoccupation (*ibid.*, N.R.G.[1], XI, 381). See on this controversy, which also raised the question of the effect of the Monroe doctrin: H. KRAUS, *Die Monroedoktrin in ihren Beziehungen zur amerikanischen Diplomatie und zum Völkerrecht* (Berlin, 1913), pp. 168-170, with further references.

Annexation (incorporation), in certain periods also called by the decep-
tive name of "reunion", can be partial or total. If it is partial, it certainly belongs to the present Part III on State Territory. If it is total, it
operates, in so far as its intended legal effect is recognized, as the extinction of an existing State. From that aspect annexation has already
been dealt with in Part II of this publication on The Subjects of International Law, Chapter III, section 3, pp. 127 *et seq.*, but it must also
be mentioned here.

Annexation in either sense has in common with occupation that it is
a unilateral international act, but it is distinguished from occupation by
the fact that it concerns not no man's land, but a territory which is
placed under the sovereignty of another State. In former times the right
of conquest was repeatedly and openly recognized. See for example
the Austro-Sardinian treaty against France of 23 May 1794 (Martens,
N.S., II, 87), which also provided in advance for a repartition of possible future spoils, and Napoleon's Decree of 30 March 1806 (*ibid.*, R²,
VIII, 424). Indian princes also occasionally acquiesced in the operation
of this "right" in their dealings with colonizing Powers or Chartered
Companies, comp. *e.g.*, the Convention between the Netherlands East-
Indian Company and the King of Johore of 10 November 1784 (*ibid.*, R²,
V, 82), cited in Part II of this publication, pp. 41-42 ("in virtue of the
right of warlike conquest"). Under modern international law annexation
is gradually assuming the character of an unlawful act, under the influence of such political dogma's as the Stimson doctrine (1932) or of
such treaty provisions as Article 10 of the League of Nations Covenant.[27]
Although it is, as a consequence, increasingly considered as an international delinquency, it may under conditions unfavourable to the
maintenance of the rule of law in the international community, still
produce the normal effects of a juridical act (comp. about the coincidence
of these two qualifications: Part VI of this publication and about the
erroneously so-called "principle" of effectiveness: Part I of this publication, Chapter VII, pp. 293 *et seq.*).

A. *Partial annexation*

Annexation of part of the territory of another State can occur during a
war or in time of peace.

(i) When it takes place in the course of a war, annexation is no longer
recognized as a valid title of acquisition of territorial sovereignty, as it

27. "The Members of the League undertake to respect and preserve as against
external aggression the territorial integrity and existing political independence
of all Members of the League . . ."

was in former centuries. Nevertheless such annexations have still unlawfully occurred in our century.

Italy annexed Tripolitania and Cyrenaica during her war with Turkey by a Royal Decree of 5 November 1911, confirmed by a Law of 25 February 1912 (*ibid.*, N.R.G.[3], VI, 3, 4), which she was not prepared to revoke, but the international validity of which Turkey on her side was unwilling to recognize formally, so that a peculiar face-saving device had to be invented at their Peace Conference of Ouchy-Lausanne in order to produce a legal formula which could legitimate the *fait accompli*.

> Comp. the preamble of the Italo-Turkish modus procedendi of 15 October 1912 (*ibid.*, N.R.G.[3], VII, 3), in which the Parties stated the difficulty of achieving a termination of the war owing to "l'impossibilité pour l'Italie de déroger à la loi du 25 février 1912, qui a proclamé sa souveraineté sur la Tripolitaine et sur la Cyrénaïque, et pour l'Empire Ottoman de formellement reconnaître cette souveraineté", and Articles I and III, with the Annexes nos. 1 and 3 of the said modus vivendi, by which the "difficulty" was solved in this manner that the Imperial Government would issue a firman addressed to the populations of Tripolitania and Cyrenaica, granting them complete autonomy, and appointing certain Ottoman representatives in their countries, and that the Royal Government would thereupon enact a Decree, granting them freedom of worship and allowing the further pronouncement of the name of the Sultan as Khalif in public prayers.

Great Britain, on the outbreak of war with Turkey in 1914, took similar action with regard to Cyprus, which had since 1878 only been under her "administration and occupation" (comp. Chapter IV, section 3 *infra*, p. 409), by an Order in Council of 5 November 1914.

The return of Alsace-Lorraine to France at the end of World War I as from the date of the armistice of Compiègne of 11 November 1918 (comp. Article 51 of the Peace Treaty of Versailles) was artificially clothed in the special juridical form of a "réintégration dans la souveraineté française", so far as possible with retroactive effect (see in particular the Annex to section V of Part III of the Treaty), motivated by the fact that in 1871 the representatives of this Franco-German borderland had solemnly protested against its separation from France. See the preamble to the said Article 51:

> "Les Hautes Parties Contractantes, ayant reconnu l'obligation morale de réparer le tort fait par l'Allemagne en 1871, tant au droit de la France qu'à la volonté des populations d'Alsace et de Lorraine, séparées de leur Patrie malgré la protestation solennelle de leurs représentants à l'Assemblée de Bordeaux".

The, eventually abortive, attempts of Hitler Germany in World War II to annex, with final effect, large territories around her borders: the Free City of Danzig, the Polish Corridor, Polish Upper-Silesia and other parts of Western Poland, Bohemia-Moravia (in addition to the Sudeten-German area, already "ceded" to her earlier) under the disguise of a

357

"protectorate", Alsace-Lorraine, Moresnet, Luxembourg, Schleswig, are too well-known to be expatiated upon here, just as are the comparable actions of the Soviet Union with regard to large areas on her western border.

(ii) Even in peace time annexation of parts of foreign State territory still occurs occasionally in our own age. Apart from the so-called "cession" of the Sudeten-German area to Germany by Czechoslovakia, just referred to, by the "agreement" of Munich of 29 September 1938 (comp. on the collaboration of Great Britain and France with Hitler the correspondence in Martens, N.R.G.³, XXXVI, 3, 24) prior to the outbreak of World War II, there is the unlawful annexation by India of the Portuguese enclaves in 1960, connived at by the United Nations.

In former centuries such annexations of parts of foreign State territory in time of peace were much in use. I need only recall the long series of "réunions" which King Louis XIV of France carried out in the 17th century after the Peace Congress of Nijmegen of 1678, under the pretext of a formal adjudication of the territories concerned by mock tribunals, the so-called "chambres de réunion", already mentioned *supra* under a special heading *sub* A, § 7, p. 327. The later series of "réunions", proclaimed by the successive highest State organs of revolutionary France in the period between 1789 and 1806, on the contrary, betrayed no special desire of their authors to offer some sort of judicial justification of their infringements of the established order. Collections of such partial (or even total) "réunions" of foreign State territory with France are inserted in Martens' *Recueil*², V, 145-190 (1789-1795) and VI, 656-700 (1798-1806).

These forcible "réunions", often without any formal war intervening, which succeeded each other in a long series and practically without interruption in the Napoleonic era, added large areas in Europe either to France herself, or to her factitious satellite States, such as the Cisalpine Republic, the Kingdom of Westphalia or the Kingdom of Holland.

They were at first effected (*a*) in the form of unilateral decrees issued by the French Government in power at the time, although they were usually represented in their preamble as being acts of compliance with requests addressed to France—assertedly in response to the Decrees of the French National Convention of 19 November and 15 December 1792 expressing France's "résolution d'aider et secourir tous les peuples qui voudront conquérir leur liberté" (Martens, R², V, 170)—by the "sovereign people" concerned, represented, for example, by the National Assembly of Porrentruy (the seat of the new so-called Rauracian Republic in the bishopric of Basel) or that of the Allobroges (the new name for the people of Savoy).[28]

28. Comp., *e.g.*, the following formula: "sur le vœu libre et formel qui lui a été

At a later stage, however, such "réunions", though not less forcible nor more solidly based than their unilateral counterparts, were often moulded (*b*) in the juridical form of bilateral treaties.

(*a*) Instances of the former type—by French decrees—were the "réunions" with France (all cited below from Martens's *Recueil*, 2nd ed. or—where indicated—his *Nouveau Recueil*) :[29]

in 1789, of Corsica (V, 145), declared to be part of France; comp. on the legal history of this island Chapter IV, § 1 *infra*, p. 389;

in 1791, of the Papal town of Avignon and the County of Venaissin (V, 149); see for the protest by Pope Pius VI: V, 151;

in 1792, of Savoy (V, 164);

in 1793, of the newly constituted Rauracian Republic (V, 180); the town and county of Nice (V, 168)—comp. on its later history the treaties of 24 March and 23 August 1860 (N.R.G.[1], XVI[2], 539 and XVII[2], 22) by which Sardinia ceded Nice to France—; the principality of Monaco (V, 170)—comp. on the legal history of this principality Part II of this publication, pp. 459 *et seq.*—; a series of areas and towns in the then Austrian Low Countries (now Belgium): Brussels, Hainault, Ghent, Tournay and the Tournaisis, Leuven (Louvain), Namur, Ostende, Bruges, consolidated and completed with the rest of those countries in Flanders, Brabant and Austrian Guelder by a general decree of 1 October 1795 (V, 186); the *reichsunmittelbare* abbey of Stavelot and the bishopric of Liège (V, 188 and 190); the bishopric of Basel (V, 180); the principality of Salm (V, 174), and the Rhine town of Mainz (V, 175);

in 1795, of the duchy of Bouillon by a decree of the Convention nationale (V, 190)—comp. on the legal dispute to which this duchy gave rise in 1815: Article 69 of the Final Act of the Congress of Vienna (N.R., II, 379) and p. 10 *supra;*

in 1797, of the Valtellina, Chiavenna and Bormio districts in the border zone between the duchy of Milan and the Grisons, incorporated into the shortlived Cisalpine Republic by a proclamation of Bonaparte (VI, 403);

in 1798, of the republic of Mulhouse (VII, 656, by a decree disguised as a treaty); comp. on this Napoleonic structure Part II of this publication, p. 48;

in 1800, of the Navarese part of Piedmont, joined to the Cisalpine Republic (VII, 667);

in 1802, of the island of Elba (VII, 677)—on whose curious rôle in different respects in international law comp., *e.g.*, Part II of this publication, p. 509;

adressé par plusieurs communes étrangères, circonvoisines ou enclavées, réunies en assemblées primaires, faisant usage de leur droit inaliénable de souveraineté, à l'effet d'être réunies à la France comme parties intégrantes de la République" (Decree of the National Convention of 14 February 1793, Martens, R[2], V, 170), —a formulation with which the present day Communist appeal to requests made by "liberation movements" in various countries has a remarkable amount in common.

29. In order not to interrupt the actual sequence of the long series of annexations of this type I insert among them also a number of total "reunions" which belong strictly speaking to the category under B(ii), pp. 363 *et seq.*

of the rest of Piedmont (VII, 676);[30] of the duchies of Parma, Piacenza and Guastalla (VII, 678 *et seq.*)—comp. also 1808 (N.R., I, 324);

in 1805, of the Ligurian Republic (the old Republic of Genova; VII, 685-688; 697), asserted by Napoleon no longer to have a real chance of independent existence after Piedmont's annexation by France and England's refusal to recognize Genova in any other than its former constitutional form;

in 1806, of the principality of Neuchâtel, the county of Valengin and the principality of Anspach (VIII, 411), and of Massa and Carrara and the Garfagnana, joined to the newly created hereditary principality of Lucca (VIII, 311, 432); of the former Venetian States, incorporated by a proclamation of Prince Eugène, viceroy of Italy, of 31 December 1805 and a decree of 30 March 1806 (VIII, 427) into the Napoleonic Kingdom of Italy, into which the Italian Republic had been converted by the Constitutional Statute of 17 March 1805 (VIII, 308);

in 1807, of East Friesland and Jever, joined to the Napoleonic Kingdom of Holland (VIII, 718), Article 1;

in 1808, of the German Rhine towns of Kehl and Wesel (N.R., I, 322); and of the State of Tuscany (N.R., I, 324);

in 1809/1810, of the Papal States (N.R., I, 341, 342);

on 9 July 1810, of the last remaining, northern part of the then Kingdom of Holland (N.R., I, 338 and 346) after its successive territorial mutilations by the treaties of cession of 16 May 1795, 11 November 1807 and 16 March 1810, cited below;

also in 1810, the three large Hansa towns and the duchy of Lauenburg (N.R., I, 346); of Valais—the later Swiss canton which had been declared "independent" in 1802 (VII, 564)—(N.R., I, 344).

(*b*) A number of other States, districts or towns were annexed in virtue of formal treaties, imposed by France upon her opposite numbers, usually followed up or implemented by unilateral *Sénatusconsultes*, Imperial decrees, etc. Treaties of this type have deleted or mutilated the following States:

the Netherlands as far as its south-westernmost part (the island of Walcheren except the port of Vlissingen (Flushing), which was provisionally left under the regime of Franco-Netherlands co-sovereignty, Article 14) was concerned, 16 May 1795 (R², VI, 88);

the Republic of Geneva, entirely wiped out, 26 April 1798 (R², VII, 659);

the counties of Nassau-Üsingen and Nassau-Weilburg, forced to cede to France the towns of Kassel and Kostheim and the Rhine island of Sankt Peter, 12 March 1806 (R², VIII, 407);

the then (since the Franco-Batavian treaty of 24 May 1806, VIII, 449) Kingdom of Holland, as regards its still existing co-sovereign rights to the port of Vlissingen, 11 November 1807, Article 6 (R², VIII, 718), followed by a *Sénatusconsulte* of 21 January 1808 (N.R., I, 322), and subsequently its

30. The history of this latter reunion witnesses to the forcible character of these operations, comp. R², VII, 663 *et seq*: initial protests of the ruling prince; a declaration by the military administrator General Jourdan of 1801 pursuant to which the country had not yet been incorporated into France; a popular request for such incorporation; cession by the ruling prince of the government of the country to his brother; a declaration by France that this cession was null and void, eventually followed by a formal reunion.

360

remaining territory on the left bank of the Rhine, 16 March 1810 (N.R., I, 327), followed by another *Sénatusconsulte* of 24 April implementing this latter reunion (I, 330) and, only a few months later, on 9 July 1810, by an Imperial decree proclaiming unilaterally the reunion of the entire Kingdom with France (*supra*);

the Kingdom of Hanover, united with the Napoleonic Kingdom of Westphalia, 14 January 1810 (N.R., I, 235).

A certain number of political operations of a similar type and effect were performed by Napoleon in a different form, *viz.*, by cutting more or less extensive bits of territory out of one or more existing States and then elevating them to the rank of independent satellite States. This method was, *e.g.*, employed for the creation of a duchy of Berg from parts of Prussian and part of Bavarian-Palatine territory on 15 March 1806 (R², VIII, 418), and of a duchy of Cleves from Prussian territory on 16 March 1806 (VIII, 413, 414). Since I have given a survey of these new formations in Part II of this publication (p. 47) I merely recall this device in passing.

B. *Total annexation*

The annexation of an entire State is quite a different juridical act, because it terminates the existence of the international person, victim of the operation. This type of annexation can also take place (i) in time of war, and (ii) in time of peace.

(i) *In time of war*

The rule. The complete collapse of a State in a war entails, as a rule, its annexation by the victor State, but there are two exceptions, *viz.*, when (*a*) the vanquished State is a member of a coalition which continues the fight; (*b*) the victor State lacks the will to annex the vanquished State. Moreover, the international community sometimes refuses to recognize the annexation and its legal effects with ultimate success.

Examples of a normal *debellatio* through war, which automatically implies the disappearance of the vanquished State as a subject of international law, are legion and far from being a thing of the past. More often than not the accomplished fact of subjugation is sufficient to cause the territory of the victim State to fall under the sovereignty of its opponent. A peace treaty is not needed nor customary nor even very easy to conceive juristically, although the *debellatio* and the resulting effects are often laid down in a written document of some kind, such as a capitulation or an undenounceable armistice. Thus, the conquest by Great Britain of the two Boer Republics in 1900 was so documented in two capitulations, of the Orange Free State on 24 May 1900 (Martens, N.R.G.², XXXII, 141) and of the South African Republic (Transvaal) on 1 September 1900 (*ibid.*, XXXII, 154), followed by two annexation proclamations of 24 May and 1 September 1900 respectively (*ibid.*,

XXXII, 141 and 154).—The defeat of the then member States of the old German Bund (1815-1867): the kingdom of Hanover, the electorate of Hesse, the county of Nassau and the free city of Frankfurt in their short war with Prussia was sealed by the capitulation of the Hanoverian forces at Langensalza, 29 June 1866 (*ibid.*, N.R.G.[1], XVIII, 315) and a Prussian law for the reunion of the territories of those member States with Prussia of 20 September 1866 (*ibid.*, XVIII, 378), followed by an *Inkorporations-Patent* of 3 October 1866 (*ibid.*, 386).[31] The landgrave of Electoral Hesse only finally acquiesced in the situation, thus created by Prussia, by Article 1 of his treaty with that State of 26 March 1873 (*ibid.*, N.R.G.[2], X, 504) in the following formula:

> "Seine Hoheit der Landgraf Friedrich erkennt die Einverleibung des vor-
> maligen Kurfürstentums Hessen in die Preussische Monarchie als einen
> unabänderlichen staatsrechtlichen Akt an und entsagt für sich und seine
> Descendenz zu Gunsten der Krone Preussen allen Ansprüchen auf die
> Regierung des früheren Kurstaates . . .".

Such a *debellatio* is in the great majority of cases final, but it may, under exceptional circumstances, be reversed by a revival of the victim, as the resurrection of Ethiopia after the defeat of Italy in World War II has shown.

Exception (*a*). So long as the outcome of a war fought by a coalition is not definitely decided against it, the *debellatio* of one of the allies has no final legal effect and even a formal annexation, such as that of Luxembourg by Hitler Germany in 1940, is null and void.

Exception (*b*). For a *debellatio* to produce the normal double effect of the disappearance of the international person concerned and the passing of its territory under the sovereignty of the victor State, it is essential that the fact of the conquest be accompanied by the *animus* of the victor State(s) to destroy the victim and to incorporate its territory into its (their) own. Although the fact of Germany's utter defeat in May 1945 was undeniable, the other necessary element, the *animus debellandi* (in the usual sense) was lacking in the victor States. As a result, Germany's unconditional surrender did not imply her incorporation *pro indiviso* into the territory of the four Great Allied Powers, although the war was at that time to all intents and purposes terminated. Comp. in particular paragraph 5 of the preamble of the Declaration of 5 June 1945 regarding the defeat of Germany and the assumption of supreme authority with respect to Germany (*U.N.T.S.*, vol. 68, p. 189), and for a general discussion of the German problem Part II of this publication, Chapter III, section 1, Annex (A), pp. 109 *et seq.*

---

31. Accomodations respecting their possessions were made by Prussia with the electoral family of Hesse, the ducal family of Nassau and the royal family of Hanover in conventions of 17 September 1866 (Martens, N.R.G.[1], XVIII, 388), 18 September 1867 (*ibid.*, 392) and 29 September 1867 (*ibid.*, 396).

(ii) *In time of peace*

The annexation of a whole State by another in time of peace, or at least without a formal war being in progress between the annexing and the annexed State, can have very different causes and take different forms. It can be (*a*) a resigned surrender with the object of avoiding otherwise inevitable increasing political pressure or a military conquest, or simply a unilateral action by a militarily overwhelmingly strong Power. It can be (*b*) a voluntary merger, in particular into a racially or religiously kindred State, or (*c*) the voluntary accession of a State to an existing federation. It can be (*d*) a specimen of "colonialist" expansion. Finally it can be (*e*) the outcome of an authoritative political decision of Great Powers or of an international conference, *e.g.*, for the purpose of reorganizing the general political structure or of liquidating a previous artificial temporary political solution. In all these cases new territory is acquired by the annexing State, even in case (*c*) when the annexed State becomes a member State of a federation and retains part of its rights of government.

ad (*a*). Instances of the first variant of annexation under compulsion are the incorporations of

the khanate of the Crimea and Kuban Tartars by Russia by a Manifesto of 8 April 1783 (Martens, R², III, 581);

Georgia by Russia by a Decree of 24 July 1783 (*ibid.*, R², III, 686);

the duchy of Curlandia by Russia in 1795 (comp. the diplomatic instruments of 28 March of that year *ibid.*, R², VI, 24, 30, 40, 42, 43);

the remnants of the Polish State by its third partition in 1795 (comp. the Austro-Russian declaration of 3 January 1795, *ibid.*, R²., VI, 168, and the tripartite Convention of St. Petersburg of 24 October 1795 (*ibid.*, VI, 171);

the Empire of Korea by Japan by a formal treaty of 22 August 1910 (*ibid.*, N.R.G.³, IV, 24).

ad (*b*). Instances of the second occurrence of a voluntary merger into a racially or religiously kindred State are provided by the national history of Italy and Greece.

Thus a number of independent States of long standing in the Appennine peninsula were in the period between 1859 and 1870 successively incorporated into the Kingdom of Sardinia, in 1861 renamed Kingdom of Italy.

An earlier national movement of the same type in 1848 had miscarried: the reunions with the Kingdom of Sardinia, proclaimed by the people of Piacenza (27 May), Lombardy (13 June), Modena and Parma (16 August), Menton and Roccabruna (18 September), were soon reversed. The unification movement in Italy did not succeed until ten years later (1859-1860)—Lombardy, Marches and Umbria, Naples and Sicily (*ibid.*, N.R.G.¹, XVII², 50 *et seq.*)—and was only completed in September

1870 by the annexation of the remnant of the former Papal States. I confine myself to only briefly recalling these events in this context of the acquisition of territorial sovereignty, while referring for their other aspect (extinction of States) to Chapter III, section 3, § 5, of Part II of this publication, pp. 127 *et seq.* Their mention in the present Chapter and section also, is justified by the consideration that the political events really constituted the acquisition of territory by the Kingdom of Sardinia. The Italian Courts have indeed in later years, in fact still fairly recently, had to deal with the legal side of the development, in particular in connexion with the problem of State succession, and on that occasion ruled that all the other former political units on Italian soil have in 1859-1860 merged in the Kingdom of Sardinia, later Italy, which alone survived the unification movement as an international person. The territory of all those other States has consequently, looked at from a juridical point of view, been added to that of Sardinia. Comp. for further particulars on this subject Part II of this publication, pp. 94 *et seq.*

The history of modern Greece shows similar mergers, *viz.*, those of the Republic of the Ionian Islands, a British protectorate since 1815, by a treaty of 29 March 1864 (Martens, N.R.G.[1], XVIII, 63) (comp. on this subject Part II of this publication, p. 129), and of the two small insular Turkish vassal States of Samos and Crete, whose existence as such dated from 1832 and 1899 respectively, after the Balkan wars in 1913 (comp. the same Part II, pp. 386). The *enosis* movement in Cyprus might easily have led to a corresponding result.

The incorporation of the former kingdom of Montenegro into the new Serb-Croat-Slovene Kingdom of 1918 would seem to fall into the same category of cases.

A very special case of voluntary merger, though not on ethnical grounds, which is indeed unique in diplomatic history, was the incorporation of the whole Congo Free State as a colony into Belgium in 1908 (treaty of 28 November 1907 (*ibid.*, N.R.G.[3], II, 101) with Additional Act of 5 March 1908 (*ibid.*, II, 106), after an earlier treaty of cession of 9 January 1895 (*ibid.*, N.R.G.[2], XXI, 693), preceded by the famous "testament of the King of the Belgians" Leopold II of 2 August 1889 (Strupp, *Urkunden*, II, p. 91), had been rejected by the Belgian Parliament. Comp. on this case also Part II of this publication, p. 129.

ad (c). The best known example of territorial expansion by means of the admission of one or more independent States to an existing federation is that of Texas to the United States. The territory of this federation was indeed increased by the admission to it of Texas, an independent State since 3 November 1835 (*ibid.*, N.R., XIII, 429), in virtue of a treaty of 12 April 1844 (*ibid.*, VI, 378) and an ensuing vote of the North-American Convention of 4 July 1845 (*ibid.*, VIII, 119).

ad (d). Annexation of primitive States or State-like communities by

364

highly developed western States as colonies or colonial protectorates has played a prominent rôle in the history of colonialist expansion. Here also, the annexation was sometimes performed by means of delusive formalities, having the outer appearance of a cession. Reference can be made, for example, to the incorporation of the cannibal "king" Thakombau's Fiji archipelago into the British Empire in 1874, introduced by a resolution of that king and other high chiefs of the islands of 30 September 1874, by which they "give their country, Fiji, unreservedly to Her British Majesty, Queen of Great Britain and Ireland", followed by a deed of cession of the islands to Queen Victoria "in full sovereignty and dominion", dated 10 October 1874, countersigned by Sir Hercules Robinson, a "gentlemen's agreement" in which no terms were struck, and a proclamation by the latter of the same date declaring the islands "to be from that time forth a possession and dependency of the British Crown" (*ibid.*, N.R.G.[2], II, 529, 530, 532). The "king"'s favourite war club—a lump of black ironwood, embellished for the occasion with silver olive leaves and silver doves—sent to the Queen on the cession of the kingdom, remains to the present day the mace in the Parliament of the Crown Colony of Fiji.[32]—A comparable, though less romantic, event was the incorporation of Tahiti and the Society Islands into the colonial empire of France by a treaty of 29 June 1880 (*ibid.*, N.R.G.[2], IX, 221).

Differing from the case of Texas mentioned *sub (c)*, the incorporation of the Hawaiian (formerly Sandwich) Islands by the United States in 1898 still took place in the colonial sphere. After an earlier treaty between the United States and the Hawaiian Islands of 14 February 1893 had been withdrawn by President Cleveland on 9 March 1893 (*Foreign Relations of the U.S.A.* 1894, App. II, in particular pp. 20 *et seq.*, 196 *et seq.* and 1190 *et seq.*; J. B. MOORE, *A Digest of International Law*, Washington, 1906, vol. I, p. 498), the annexation of Hawaii took place a few years later under the following circumstances.

After the reigning indigenous monarchy had been deposed by a revolution, supported by American troops (see Part II, p. 183), and the Republic of Hawaii had been established by an Act of 3 July 1894 (*For. Rel. of the U.S.A. 1894*, p. 1372), the islands were annexed by the United States in virtue of a Congress Resolution of 7 July 1898 (30 *Stat.* 750; Martens, N.R.G.[2], XXXII, 72) referring to the formal consent of the Government of Hawaii to the cession of all rights of sovereignty, declared in conformity with the provisions of the Hawaiian Constitution. Hawaii was only admitted as a member State of the Union in 1959.

ad (e). Examples of the incorporation of one or more existing States by a resolution of certain Great Powers or of an international Congress are

32. Comp. *Fiji* in *The British Survey, Popular Series*, No. 144, pp. 1 and 2.

well-known from the beginning of the 19th century, but they can be cited from more recent periods as well.

The systematic secularizations and mediatizations from 1800 onward are most conspicuous in this respect. Comp. on these types of territorial arrangement §§ 8 and 9 of section 1 *supra*, pp. 328 and 329.

More isolated instances are those of the winding-up of Free Cities, *e.g.*, that of Cracow by its incorporation into Austria in 1846 in virtue of a joint decision of Austria, Russia and Prussia (see Part II of this publication, p. 503), and that of the Free City of Trieste in 1954 by the States directly interested (see the same Part II, p. 505).

§ 4. *Cession*

Cession of territory has taken place for centuries, but in former ages it presented different features and took different juridical forms. When, for instance, certain North-German towns and districts were surrendered to Sweden at the Congress of Westphalia—Peace Treaty of Osnabrück of 24 October 1648 between the Emperor and Sweden (Dumont, VI[1], 469)—this took place, pursuant to Article X in the form of a cession as a "hereditary fief" of the western part of Pomerania (Vorpommern), Rügen, Stettin, Wollin, the mouth of the Oder and the Frische Haff, and as an "everlasting and immediate fief of the Empire" of the town and port of Wismar and the bishopric of Verden.

General

This mode of acquisition, through the transfer of territorial sovereignty by one State to another[33] can take different forms, in particular those of (*a*) a gratuitous transfer, either under factual compulsion, or by way of a donation or a voluntary cession; (*b*) a transfer against some countervalue in money by way of "sale"; or (*c*) a mutual transfer by way of exchange.[34] In the ages of patrimonial conceptions these different modes of transfer were much more akin to the corresponding modes of transfer of private property than they are nowadays. There are plenty of instances of such transfers in any of the three categories mentioned. I will only enumerate

33. This type of juridical act is essentially international in character, unlike other juridical acts, also called "cession" which are recorded in legal history, but belonged to the domain of national public law, such as the cession which Yolanda marchioness and countess of Namur, made of that county to her son Philip on her departure with her husband Peter to mount the Imperial throne of Constantinople in 1216 (Dumont, I[1], 156).

34. The Franco-Belgian agreements of 6 February 1895 (Martens, N.R.G.[2], XX, 698 = XXI, 672) and 23 December 1908 (*ibid.*, N.R.G.[3], VI, 336) concerning the *droit de préférence* of France to the Congolese possessions expressly contradistinguished in their Articles 1 and 2 the cases of "aliénation à titre onéreux", "échange" and "cession à titre gratuit".

a few of them below, with the sources where the relevant documents can be found, in order to facilitate consultation and comparison of their contents both in former centuries and in modern times. Consultation of such a series of treaties alone can show what were the topical subject matters which in a given historical period came up for regulation on the occasion of a cession of territory, and what were the changes in their general content which have gradually developed in the course of time. Many of those rules and changes can, from a systematical point of view, best be described in the wider context of a chapter on State succession because they are common to all instances of a shift of territorial sovereignty, by cession or otherwise. Others are, on the contrary, peculiar to the particular case of cession. I intend to give a brief historical survey of subjects regulated in treaties of cession in Part VI of this publication.

At the beginning of the 19th century the extent of the territories to be exchanged or ceded was repeatedly determined by the number of the inhabitants. This was, for example, the measure applied in Article III, *sub* 5 of the Franco-Austrian Peace Treaty of Vienna of 14 October 1809 (Martens, N.R., I, 210): an area of 400.000 people.

One of the somewhat absurd problems which faced Prussia and Hanover as late as 1837 was that the latter had a twenty-years old claim, with regard to the Lower County of Lingen ceded by her to Prussia under their exchange treaties of 29 May 1815 (*ibid.*, N.R., II, 316) and 13 September 1815, that 1654 "Seelen" (souls) should still be transferred to her by Prussia, in order to restore the demographic balance. This claim was offset by a Prussian counter-claim to the transfer to her of (146—100) subjects in connection with an additional exchange of certain hamlets. There thus remained (1654—46=) 1608 "fehlende Seelen", still to be "überwiesen" to Hanover. This human drama in Gogol'an style[35] ended, however, in an "opéra bouffe":

> "Statt Ueberweisung der hiernach fehlenden 1608 Seelen macht sich die Krone Preussen verbindlich, jeden Kopf mit einer jährlichen Rente von 3½ Reichsthaler Preussische Courant zu reluiren" (Article 3 of the Prussian-Hanoverian treaty of 25 November 1837, Martens, N.R., XIV, 468).

It is curious to note, for that matter, that even the famous political instrument, the Final Act of the Congress of Vienna of 9 June 1815 (*ibid.*, N.R., II, 379), still contained a number of such transfers of territory measured by "souls". Comp. Articles 33, 39, 47 and 49. The latter Article, in particular, is typical for this method of procuring an "Equivalent an Land und Leuten" (the expression used in Article 8 of the Peace Treaty of Hubertsburg between Poland/Saxony and Prussia of 15 February 1763, *ibid.*, R², I, 146): Prussia reserved for herself a territory in the former Department of the Sarre, comprising 69.000 souls, Saxe-

---

35. The allusion is to his Мёртвые Души (Dead Souls) of 1842.

Coburg and Oldenburg each of 20.000, Mecklenburg-Strelitz and Hesse-Homburg each of 10.000, and the Count of Pappenheim (thenceforth placed under the sovereignty of the King of Prussia) of 9.000 souls.

Another method of determining the extent of lands to be ceded, differing from a geographical description, was adopted in Article III(3) of the treaty of 24 January 1776 between France and Nassau-Weilburg (*ibid.*, R², II, 432), *viz.*, by delimiting their surface in such a way that they would yield a fixed annual rent. Whereas this clause would still seem to relate to the transfer of property, an engagement by the King of France towards the King of Sardinia of 5 February 1759 obviously concerned a transfer of sovereignty: "à proportion du revenu réel" of the territory comprised in the transaction. The same proportion was fixed in the above-mentioned Article 8 of the Peace Treaty of Hubertsburg of 1763, amending that of Dresden of 25 December 1745 (Wenck, II, 194).

A well-known controversy relates to the juridical effect, merely "personal" or "real", of a treaty of cession, *i.e.*, to the question as to whether such a treaty only creates a "contractual" obligation for the ceding State to transfer the territorial sovereignty over the *cessum* to the cessionary State by a further act-in-law and accordingly still needs for its full operation the supplementary actual transfer of power by what could be called by a private law analogy a "conveyance", or whether, on the contrary, it operates immediately and of itself the transfer of territorial sovereignty without any further "real" transaction being necessary. Again there is no hard and fast mandatory rule in force. The parties are completely free to stipulate as they choose, and no asserted legal principle of "effectiveness" or otherwise, sometimes wrongly represented as logically imperative, can ever hinder them from validly stipulating that territorial sovereignty shall pass to the cessionary State as from the moment of the coming into force of the treaty of cession, even though the actual exercise of that sovereignty is only assumed by that State at a later date. In such a case the theoretical construction of the juridical operation must be that the parties, in common accord, wish the administrative organs which are in function at the time of the entry of the treaty into force to provisionally remain in office under the international responsibility of the new sovereign pending the actual transfer of power over the territory concerned.

There are instances of either variant. Thus, the immediate passing of territorial sovereignty was expressly stipulated in the Dano-American treaty of cession of 4 August 1916 concerning the Danish Virgin Islands of St. Thomas, St. John and St. Croix; see Article 4 of that treaty (Martens, N.R.G.³, X, 357), according to which agents for the formal delivery would be delegated immediately after the payment of the stipulated sum, but "the cession with the right of immediate posession (was) nevertheless to be deemed complete on the exchange of the ratifications of the Convention without such formal delivery". On the other hand, Article 6 of the Austro-Polish convention of 9 February 1776 (*ibid.*, R², II, 124), among many others, provided for an actual transfer of power by the assumption of the administration as a precondition of the final passing of territorial sovereignty.

Pursuant to an Edict of the Grand Duke of Baden of 13 August 1806 (*ibid.*, R², VIII, 501) the newly acquired territories would remain under their former rulers until they would be delivered. "Conveyance" was also foreseen in the Anglo-Netherlands Colonial Treaty of 17 March 1824 (*ibid.*, N.S., I, 628, 638, 641)—actual transfer on 1 March 1825— and in the Franco-Bavarian treaty of cession of 5 July 1825 (*ibid.*, N.S., II, 439).

Article 3 of the Russo-Japanese treaty of exchange of 7 May 1875 (*ibid.*, N.R.G.², II, 582) relative to southern Sakhalin and the Kurile islands disposed, not very clearly, as follows:

> "La remise réciproque des territoires désignés . . . aura lieu immédiatement après l'échange des ratifications du présent traité et lesdits territoires passeront à leurs nouveaux possesseurs, avec les revenus, à dater du jour de la prise de possession; mais la cession réciproque avec le droit de possession immédiate doit, toutefois, être considérée complète et absolue à dater du jour de l'échange des ratifications".

Difficulty can only arise in cases where the treaty is silent and where no common intention of the parties can be inferred from the *travaux préparatoires*. Although there is no compelling intrinsic reason for holding that in such a case the cession on paper, in order to produce its full legal effects, must be supplemented by the actual transfer of the administration to a representative of the cessionary State, practical grounds would seem to recommend a solution to that effect. The method of transfer of the Danish Virgin Islands would in that light appear as a somewhat unusual procedure, attributable to the special circumstances of that transfer during World War I, but not contrary to the *jus latum*.

The controversy regarding this problem has sometimes caused trouble between a contracting party and a third State. It has, *e.g.*, played a major role in a case of 1804 before the British High Court of Admiralty (5 *C. Rob. Adm.* 106)—the *Fama* case—, discussed in J.B. Scott, *Cases on International Law* (St.Paul, 1922), pp. 181-185. The dispute related to the legal effect of the Franco-Spanish Treaty of San Ildefonso of 19 August 1796 (Martens, R², VI, 255), providing *inter alia* for the cession of Louisiana by Spain to France: was this territory at the time of its warlike occupation by Great Britain in 1803 still to be considered as Spanish, or had it already come under French sovereignty despite the fact that the treaty was entered into secretly during the Franco-British War and was not to take effect until after the termination of that war—in which, however, Spain had meanwhile joined in on the

French side in 1796. Sir W. Scott held the "general law of property" applicable that "there should be both the *jus in rem* and the *jus in re*", so that "until possession was actually taken, the inhabitants of New Orleans continued under the former sovereignty of Spain". I agree with Strupp's criticism of this judgment in *Wörterbuch des Völkerrechts und der Diplomatie* (Berlin, 1924), vol. I, pp. 300-301 that, apart from the contractual derogation in this particular case from the general rule, the theory of the British Prize Court which started from an unwarrantable application of principles of private law to inter-State relations was wrong and that sovereignty must on the contrary be held as a rule to pass to the cessionary on the coming into force of a treaty of cession.

Acknowledgement of the truth that a cession of territory is not simply the transfer of a *res*, but rather the placing of the population of a defined area under another domination than it was subject to before is sometimes expressed by the formula that the cession includes "all the subjects, vassals, etc..." living in that area: convention of 24 May 1772 between France and the bishopric of Liège (Martens, R², II, 46, 48). Moreover, the treaty of cession often contained an express provision releasing the inhabitants from their oath of allegiance, or was followed by an express proclamation to that effect by their former sovereign. Comp. *e.g.*, the "Acte de renonciation" of the King of Saxony of 22 May 1815 (*ibid.*, N.R. II, 286). The treaty of cession was in many cases also followed by an express Decree for the formal incorporation of the *cessum* into the cessionary state. See the Prussian *Patent* of 22 May 1815 following the treaty of 18 May 1815: *ibid.*, N.R. II, 287.

On very rare occasions a cession was only temporary. The cession of Halland by Denmark to Sweden by their treaty of Brömsebro of 13 August 1645 (Dumont, VI¹, 314) was only for thirty years, but it became final in virtue of the treaty of Röskilde of 8 March 1658 (Dumont, VI², 205). The island of Tigre in the Gulf of Fonseca was ceded by Honduras to the United States for the period of eighteen months, with the aim of preventing its occupation by an enemy power during the discussions over a Canal Treaty: convention of 28 September 1849 (Martens, N.R.G.¹, XV, 186).

Political events or considerations sometimes led to the complicated procedure of the cession of territory by State A to State C via an intermediary State B. Examples:

cession of the Southern Netherlands to Austria after the War of the Spanish Succession by the detour of a transfer to the Republic of the United Netherlands, followed by their further cession by the latter to Austria, as arranged by Article 9 of the Peace Treaty of Baden of 7 September 1714 (Dumont, VIII¹, 436; Rousset, *Recueil*, I, 1) and Article 1 of the Barrier Treaty of 15 November 1715 (Dumont, VIII¹, 458; Rousset, *Recueil*, I, 37);

370

transfer of Lombardy by Austria to the Kingdom of Sardinia via a formal cession to France: Peace Treaties of Zürich of 10 November 1859 between Austria and France (Articles 4 and 5) and between France and Sardinia (Article 1) (Martens, N.R.G.[1], XVI[2], 516 and 525);

a parallel transfer of Austrian Venice to Italy via France; Article 1 of the Peace Treaty of Vienna between Austria and France of 24 August 1866 (*ibid.*, XVIII, 414) and Article 3 of that between France and Italy of 3 October 1866 (*ibid.*, 405).

The simple relinquishment by a State of territorial sovereignty in virtue of a treaty, without its cession to another State, must be distinguished from the traditional operation of a cession. Examples thereof are Cuba in 1898 and certain Japanese possessions in 1951.

Whereas by Articles 2 and 3 of the Peace Treaty of 10 December 1898 (*ibid.*, N.R.G.[3], XXXII, 74) Spain ceded to the United States the island of Puerto Rico and other Spanish islands in the West Indies, the island of Guam in the Marianas and the archipelago of the Philippine Islands, she only "relinquished" (in Article 1) "all claim of sovereignty over and title to Cuba...". This relinquishment was followed by the adoption on 21 February 1901 of the Constitution of the sovereign Republic of Cuba by her Constitutional Convention, the approval by the United States Congress on 2 March 1901 of eight articles concerning the future relations between the United States and that Republic (the so-called Platt Amendment), their addition to the latter's Constitution on 12 June 1901, and the conclusion of an American-Cuban treaty on 22 May 1903 (*ibid.*, N.R.G.[2], XXXII, 79).

By Article 2 of the Peace Treaty of San Francisco of 8 September 1951 (*U.N.T.S.*, vol. 136, p. 45) Japan simply renounced—in addition to all right, title and claim to the Pacific Islands formerly under her Mandate and all claim to any right or title to or interest in connection with any part of the Antarctic area—all right, title and claim to a number of continental and insular territories without a corresponding cession to any other State, *viz.*, Korea (whose further independence she recognized), Formosa and the Pescadores, the Kurile islands, her (southern) portion of Sakhalin and the islands adjacent to it, the Spratly and the Paracel Islands.

On the other hand, a formal "renunciation" of certain territory was sometimes a camouflage for what was in actual fact a cession: Article 22 of the Prusso-Saxon treaty of 18 May 1815 relative to the duchy of Warsaw (*ibid.*, N.R., II, 272).

A few details follow below with regard to the three variants of cession distinguished at the beginning of this paragraph.

(a) *Cession without quid pro quo.—Donation*

This is by far the largest group because it includes, besides the nowadays rare event of a genuine donation *liberalitatis causa*, most cessions imposed upon a vanquished State by its victor(s) or upon an unwilling State by an international Congress. A great many peace treaties contain provisions for such cessions.

As I intend to give a brief survey of the great historic peace treaties up to the 20th century, together with some documentary data concerning the peace conferences at which they were negotiated and concluded, in Part VI of this publication, I will not go into this matter here.

The 20th century presents territorial cessions in virtue of the peace treaties of

Portsmouth, 5 September 1905 (Martens, N.R.G.^{2}, XXXIII, 3): Russia cedes to Japan the southern portion of Sakhalin and all islands adjacent thereto, and the lease of Port Arthur, Talien and adjacent territory and territorial waters (comp. below Chapter IV, section 2, p. 402).

Ouchy-Lausanne, 18 October 1912 (*ibid.*, N.R.G.^{3}, VII, 7), cession of Tripolitania and Cyrenaica by Turkey to Italy in the disguise of two unilateral declarations, for reasons of prestige, see above p. 357.

London, 30 May 1913 (*ibid.*, VIII, 16) after the first War of the Balkans, embodying the cession by Turkey to the Allied Balkan States jointly of all her territories on the European continent west of the line Enos (Aegean Sea)-Midia (Black Sea), except Albania, and of the island of Crete (Articles 2 and 4), and leaving it to the Great Powers to delimit and organize a new Albanian State (Article 3) and to decide upon the fate of all Ottoman islands in the Aegean Sea other than Crete, and of the Mount Athos peninsula (Article 5).

Versailles, 28 June 1919 (*ibid.*, XI, 323): cession by Germany, partly subject to the result of a plebiscite and a final decision of the Principal Allied and Associated Powers, of various parts of her territory, respectively—apart from all her colonies—to Belgium (Prussian Moresnet), France (Alsace-Lorraine), Czechoslovakia (frontier area of Silesia), Poland (parts of Prussia and Upper Silesia), Denmark (Northern Schleswig) and Lithuania (Memel Territory).

Neuilly, 27 November 1919 (*ibid.*, XII, 323): cession by Bulgaria of certain frontier regions to the Serb-Croat-Slovene State and Greece, and of her territories in Thrace to the Principal Allied Powers for transfer to Greece.

Trianon, 4 June 1920 (*ibid.*, XII, 423): cession by Hungary of the Burgenland to Austria, Transylvania to Romania, and certain frontier areas to the Serb-Croat-Slovene State and Czechoslovakia.

Dorpat, 14 October 1920 (*L.N.T.S.*, vol. 3, p. 5), confirmed 12 March 1940 (*B.F.S.P.*, vol. 144, p. 383): cession of the province of Petsamo

(Petchenga) by the Soviet State to Finland. This province returned, however, to Russia by the armistice agreement of 19 September 1944 (*B.F.S.P.*, vol. 145, p. 513), confirmed by Article 2 of the Peace Treaty of 10 February 1947 (*U.N.T.S.*, vol. 48, p. 203).

Lausanne, 24 July 1923 (Martens, N.R.G.³, XIII, 338): apart from Turkey's loss of all her Arab outer possessions, cession to Italy of the Dodecanese.

Paris, 10 February 1947 (*U.N.T.S.*, vol. 49, p. 3): cession by Italy to France of the Mont Cenis Plateau and the Tenda-Briga district; to Yugoslavia of some territory at the eastern boundary of Italy (Articles 5, 11 and 22), Zara and various islands in the Adriatic, including Pelagosa; and to Greece of the Dodecanese.

Paris, 10 February 1947 (*ibid.*, vol. 42, p. 3): (confirmation of the) retrocession of Bessarabia by Romania to the Soviet Union, in accordance with their earlier Agreement of 28 June 1940 (see *A.J.I.L.* 1944 (38), p. 667).

Paris, 10 February 1947 (*U.N.T.S.*, vol. 41, p. 135): retrocession by Hungary to Romania of Transylvania, respectively to Czechoslovakia of a frontier area, in the form of two corresponding declarations that the Vienna Awards by Hitler and Mussolini in favour of Hungary of 30 August 1940 (Martens, N.R.G.³, XXXIX, 348), respectively 2 November 1938 (*ibid.*, XXXVI, 662) were null and void.

Paris, 10 February 1947 (*U.N.T.S.*, vol. 48, p. 203): retrocession by Finland to the Soviet Union of the province of Petsamo (Pechenga).

San Francisco, 8 September 1951 (*ibid.*, vol. 136, p. 45): cession by Japan, in the prevailing political situation couched in the form of a "renunciation of all right, title and claim", of a number of islands, among others, Formosa, the Pescadores, the Kurile Islands and the southern half of Sakhalin.

(b) *Cession against a pecuniary counterpart*

If a cession of this type is still called a sale, one must bear in mind that what is "sold" here is nowadays an aggregate of sovereign competences, or rather overall territorial supremacy, regarding a defined portion of the earth without any relation to, or effect upon, the ownership of the ground and other immovables—except the public property of the "selling" State—, and that, moreover, the "purchase price" has often little to do with any "proprietary" value of the real object of the "sale", as it is often only intended to give compensation for the State property transferred as an accessory to the cession of territorial sovereignty. Comp. as examples the treaties relating to the sale of

the duchies of Bremen and Verden, 20 November 1719, by Sweden to Hanover (Dumont, VIII², 15), 1.000.000 Reichsthaler;

Stettin and Vorpommern (Pomerania Citerior) between the rivers

Oder and Pehne, 1 February 1720, by Sweden to Prussia (Dumont, VIII², 21), 2.000 000 Reichsthaler;

Ingermanland, Esthonia, Livonia and parts of Finland, 10 September 1721 (Nystad), by Sweden to Russia (Dumont, VII¹, 36), 2.000.000 Reichsthaler;

Louisiana, 30 April 1803 (first of the two conventions additional to the main treaty of cession), by France to the United States (Martens, R², VII, 714): 60.000.000 francs;

Florida, 22 February 1819, by Spain to the United States (*ibid.*, N.R., V, 328): a maximum of $ 5.000.000, to exonerate Spain from demands on account of claims of its citizens;

Texas, New Mexico and Northern California, 2 February 1848, by Mexico to the United States (peace treaty of Guadelupe Hidalgo, *ibid.*, N.R.G.¹, XI, 387 = XIV, 7): $ 15.000.000;

a further northern strip of territory, 30 December 1853, by Mexico to the United States (the so-called Gadsden Treaty, *ibid.*, N.R.G.², I, 1): $ 10.000.000;

Alaska, 30 March 1867, by Russia to the United States (*ibid.*, N.R.G.², I, 39): $ 7.200.000 in gold;

the Netherlands possessions on the coast of African Guinea, 25 February 1871, to Great Britain (*ibid.*, N.R.G.¹, XX, 553): a fair price to be paid only for the stores and movable articles transferred, still to be fixed, but not exceeding £ 24.000;

the island Saint Barthelémy, 10 August 1877 with protocol of 31 October 1877, by Sweden to France (*ibid.*, N.R.G.², IV, 366): 80.000 francs for domanial possessions and 320.000 francs to cover the costs of repatriation of officials and their pensioning off;

the Philippines, 10 December 1898, by Spain to the United States (Peace Treaty of Paris, *ibid.*, N.R.G.², XXXII, 74): $ 20.000.000;

the Carolines, 30 June 1899, by Spain to Germany (*ibid.*, N.R.G.², XXXII, 66): 25.000.000 pesetas;

the Danish Antilles or Virgin Islands of Saint Thomas, Saint John and Saint Croix, 4 August 1916, by Denmark to the United States (*ibid.*, N.R.G.³, X, 357): 25.000.000 gold-dollars.

(*c*) *Mutual cession or exchange*

This type of cession will often occur in the simple variant of (α) a frontier rectification or in that of (β) a mutual transfer of enclaves, but it is sometimes of much greater moment, when, for instance, (γ) it relates to vast territories which form the object of an exchange for the purpose of rounding off the respective areas of political or colonial power.

(α) Frontier rectifications have been in the past and still are at present legion and they do not, as a rule, present any special interesting features.

374

They are prompted for example, by the wish to bring the course of a river or other waterway, a road or a railway within the (exclusive) territorial compass of the same State, to correct the effect of a shift of the bed of a boundary river, to remove the inconvenience of a town or village being intersected by the State boundary, to secure or maintain intact the integrity of real estates on either side of the border, to obtain a better defensible frontier, or to achieve control over areas inhabited by co-racial or co-religious groups. When, for example, the Austrian and Saxon delegates agreed upon the exact *tracé* of the Bohemian frontier by their treaty of 5 March 1848 (Martens, N.R.G.[1], XIV, 64), they drew it in places in such a way that it would henceforth follow the boundaries of the respective private estates.

A recent example of a major and systematic frontier rectification is that of the Netherlands-German treaty of 8 April 1960 (*U.N.T.S.*, vol. 508, p. 14).

(β) Exchanges of mutual enclaves have become increasingly rare as the number of enclaves progressively decreased. Many parts of Europe in earlier centuries abounded in enclaves and exclaves as a result of the operation of the feudal system. The once numerous enclaves in what is now Belgium were in the course of the 18th century gradually liquidated by the conclusion of a number of treaties of exchange between Austria and France, Austria and the bishopric of Liège, and Austria and the Republic of the United Netherlands. The territorial patchwork of what is now Netherlands Limburg, which lasted for many centuries, was ultimately eliminated by Article 66 of the Final Act of the Congress of Vienna of 9 June 1815 (*ibid.*, N.R., II, 379).—Occasionally North-Italian enclaves were rounded up through agreements between the various dukedoms and principalities concerned.—And the immense mosaic of dispersed patches of territory of one and the same State all over the Holy Roman Empire and its successors since 1806 gradually decreased through the combined effect of the operation of family pacts, the secularization of ecclesiastical circumscriptions, the mediatization of small *reichsunmittelbare* territorial units, conquest and also voluntary exchanges. Comp. on this particular subject Chapter V, section 2 below, pp. 443 *et seq.*, 449.

(γ) Wide political compacts have also played a major rôle in the reshuffling of territorial sovereignty in Europe and elsewhere by way of exchange, just as, for that matter, in overseas possessions, but there in a typically colonial variant.

Important territorial exchanges in Europe have been those of

Sardinia for Sicily in 1720, when the duke of Savoy gave up the latter island to the Emperor, who in his turn renounced his claims to the former;

Sicily and Naples for Parma and Piacenza in 1735, when the Emperor

375

accepted the two duchies in exchange for his abandonment of the Kingdom of the Two Sicilies to the Spanish monarchy as a secundogeniture;

Tuscany for Lorraine in 1738, when the then duke of Lorraine gave up his duchy in favour of the ex-King of Poland Stanislas Leszczynski and became himself the hereditary Grand Duke of Tuscany,—all three exchanges dealt with *supra* in the context of the right of reversion, section 1, § 2, *sub (e)*, pp. 318 *et seq.*;

various territories in Germany between Hanover and Prussia in 1815, Articles 27-29 of the Final Act of the Congress of Vienna of 9 June (Martens, N.R., II, 379), in conformity with the preceding bilateral treaty of 29 May 1815 (*ibid.*, N.R., II, 316): Prussia cedes to Hanover, *inter alia*, the principalities of Hildesheim and East Friesland and the Lower County of Lingen in exchange for that part of the duchy of Lauenburg situated on the right bank of the Elbe;

the Dobrudja for Bessarabia in 1856, when Russia achieved her aim of reaching the northern branch of the Danube via Bessarabia, and Romania was bought off with the Dobrudja and an area to the south: Articles 45 and 46 of the Peace Treaty of Paris of 13 July 1878 (*ibid.*, N.R.G.², III, 449).

In Asia Japan exchanged her southern half of the island of Sakhalin for the Kurile islands, treaty with Russia of 7 May 1875 (Martens, N.R.G.², II, 582).

In colonial areas such important exchanges have sometimes taken the form of mutual acquiescence in conquests made by the adversary during a preceding war and acceptance of the *uti possidetis* at its conclusion as the new territorial situation.

This was the solution adopted, *inter alia*, by the Netherlands and Portugal in their peace treaty of 6 August 1661 (Dumont, VI², 366)—involving the abandonment by the Netherlands of their Brazilian colonies and by Portugal of her East Indian colonies —and by the Netherlands and England in their peace treaty of Breda of 21/31 July 1667 (*ibid.*, VII¹, 44)—sanctioning the actual loss of New York by the Netherlands and that of Surinam by England.

Other colonial exchanges have taken place between:

Great Britain and France in virtue of their peace treaty of Versailles of 3 September 1783 (*ibid.*, R², III, 519): cession of the islands of St. Pierre and Miquelon, Tobago and certain possessions in Senegal by Great Britain to France, in exchange for the restitution of other islands by France to Great Britain and for a change in the fishing rights of France in Newfoundland;

Great Britain and Spain pursuant to their treaty of 3 September 1783 (*ibid.*, R², III, 541), providing for the cession of the island of Minorca and the two Florida's by Great Britain in exchange for Spain's restitution

376

of the Providence and Bahama islands and an extension of Great Britain's existing wood-cutting rights in Belize (Honduras);

France and Spain in virtue of their treaty of San Ildefonso of 1 October 1800 (De Clercq, I, 411), whereby the latter retroceded West-Louisiana to France;

the enlarged Kingdom of the Netherlands and Great Britain in virtue of their colonial treaty of 17 March 1824 (*ibid.*, N.R., VI, 415 = N.S., I, 628)—involving the mutual surrender of certain territorial rights or claims to the island of Sumatra by Great Britain in exchange for certain possessions or claims on the Asian main land by the Netherlands (comp. *infra* Chapter V, section 6, p. 480);

Great Britain and the Netherlands by two connected Conventions of 25 February and 2 November 1871 (*ibid.*, N.R.G.[1], XX, 553 and 556, respectively XX, 564) relating to Guinea and Sumatra.

Such colonial exchanges frequently related to the respective island possessions of the contracting parties on which further comp. the Excursus *supra*, pp. 29 *et seq.*

Unusual exchanges were those of an European possession, namely Heligoland, by Great Britain to Germany against the latter's claims to the protectorate of Zanzibar by their treaty of 1 July 1890 (*ibid.*, N.R.G.[2], XVI[2], 902).

Reference must also be made in this context to the politically momentous, but unexpectedly shortlived Convention between Germany and France, the so-called Kiderlen Wächter-Cambon Agreement of Berlin of 4 November 1911, concerning their possessions in Equatorial Africa (*ibid.*, N.R.G.[3], V, 651), by which large areas, then under the colonial rule of France, south and east of the German Cameroons, including a strip of territory along the southern boundary of Spanish Río Muni and the "Kongo"- and "Ubanghi-zipfel", were exchanged against the so-called "Entenschnabel" south-east of Lake Chad between the rivers Logone and Shari, then under the colonial rule of Germany (now part of the Republic of Chad).

A territorial exchange sometimes took the form of a mutual renunciation of claims to territory which the contracting parties declared were thereby reciprocally "compensated". Comp. the convention between Xavier, the Administrator of Saxony on behalf of the Prince Elector Stanislas August, and the latter in his capacity of King of Poland, during the period of the personal union between the two States: 6/20 October 1765 (*ibid.*, R[2], I, 302, 304).

On other occasions the cession of a territory was indirect, *viz.*, by State A to State B as a compensation for another territory which the latter was forced to cede to a third State C. This was the case of Louisiana and Florida at the end of the Seven Years' War: by a secret treaty of 3 November 1762 France ceded Louisiana and New Orleans to Spain

377

to make good the loss which Spain would have to suffer as a consequence of her compulsory cession of Florida to Great Britain. Comp. Article 20 of the Peace Treaty of Paris of 10 February 1763 (*ibid.*, R², I, 104). In actual fact, Spain only got possession of Louisiana in 1769 and kept it until 1800, when she retroceded it to France by their treaty of San Ildefonso of 1 October 1800 (referred to in Article 1 of their subsequent treaty of 30 April 1803, *ibid.*, R², VII, 706). In the meantime she had also regained Florida from Great Britain by their Peace Treaty of 3 September 1783 (*ibid.*, R², II, 541). Both Louisiana and Florida were in the event sold to the United States: Louisiana by France on 30 April 1803 (*ibid.*, R², VII, 706), Florida by Spain on 22 February 1819 (*ibid.*, N.R., V, 328).

§ 5. (*a*) *Adjudication*—(*b*) *Abjudication*

(*a*) *Adjudication* is an independent mode of acquisition of territory only when its allocation to a specific State is constitutive by nature, that is, when the task of the adjudicating authority is not "simply" to decide judicially by a declaratory pronouncement to whom the territory belongs in law,[36] but when it is entitled or especially empowered to allocate it to a State to which it does not appertain.

It is not always easy to distinguish between these two sets of cases, since there are often disputes which linger in the crepuscular middle zone between adjudication proper and a declaration of law. Thus an arbiter can be obliged to give a judgment on the basis of the law: if he cannot find satisfactory grounds in favour of one of the parties and wishes to avoid, or is prevented from giving, an award of *non liquet*, he will be forced into a position in which he cannot but simulate that his award is a declaration of the law. In such a case he can camouflage this fact by the legal argument, sometimes advanced, that if a territorial situation is not absolutely clear, an arbiter is empowered to weigh the relative strength of the contradictory claims and so to decide the dispute on that legal basis. This was the situation which Max HUBER in his award of 1928 in the *Palmas Island* case envisaged "for argument's sake". After having held that "the conditions of acquisition of sovereignty by the Netherlands (were) to be considered as fulfilled" and thereupon stated that the United States as successors of Spain (were not) in a position "to bring forward an equivalent or stronger title" because neither the title of discovery, nor that of contiguity, nor that of recognition by treaty held good, the Arbiter went on as follows:

36. The percentage of arbitral awards and judicial pronouncements dealing with territorial disputes is very large. I have tried in an Annex (*infra*, p. 610) to collect and systematize the most important of them with the necessary references to parties, date, main subjects and collections where they can be found.

"The same conclusion would be reached, if . . . it were admitted that the evidence . . . did not . . . suffice to establish continuous and peaceful display of sovereignty over the island . . . In this case no Party would have established its claims to sovereignty over the island and the decision of the Arbitrator would have to be founded on the relative strength of the titles invoked by each Party. . . .—A solution on this ground would be necessary under the Special Agreement . . . For since, according to the terms of its Preamble, the Agreement . . . has for object to "terminate" the dispute, it is the evident will of the Parties that the arbitral award shall not conclude by a "non liquet",[37] but shall in any event decide that the island forms a part of the territory of one or the other of two litigant Parties . . ." (*A.A.*, vol. II, at p. 869).

There are also cases in which the two variants coincide in the sense that the arbiter is bound in the first place to give a strictly legal verdict, but is empowered subsidiarily to adjudicate the disputed territory to one of the parties or to divide it between them. And in such a case again, he may easily be tempted, because of his conviction as to what the solution ought to be, into simulating that his award, though it is in fact a free adjudication, is a statement on the legal validity of the respective claims.

This was not the attitude taken by the President of Argentina as Arbitrator in the boundary dispute between Bolivia and Peru, in his award of 9 July 1909 (Martens, N.R.G.³, III, 53; *A.A.*, vol. XI, p. 133), who stated a *non liquet* as regards the true legal position and thereupon proceeded to determine the frontier *ex aequo et bono* (comp. Chapter VI *infra*, p. 518).

When an arbiter or tribunal is formally authorized to adjudicate territorial sovereignty to one of the contestant parties, this authorization can be to the effect of either giving them a discretionary power of decision, or instructing them to decide the issue by applying certain binding norms, specifically laid down for that purpose in the international instrument concerned. The occasions for such a constitutive adjudication may vary. The two main cases are the following: (*i*) an insufficiently coherent State is dismembered and the parts into which it disintegrates must be allocated to one or more existing or new States; (*ii*) a State is forced, usually as a consequence of a lost war, to renounce its sovereignty over part of its territory, with the object of its allocation to one or more other States. The decision on such territorial issues will in the majority of cases be taken by a political body rather than by a more impartial judge or tribunal.

(*i*) In the absence of positive rules of general international law for the solution of cases of dismemberment, there will always be a certain element of arbitrariness in the adjudication of the disintegrated parts, in

37. This reasoning would seem to prove that the Arbitrator, in my opinion rightly, admits the legal possibility of a *non liquet* in other circumstances. To construe this award as a precedent against the admissibility of a *non liquet* would be a clear fallacy.

particular in the choice between the various criteria which may present themselves for application: the ethnical composition of the population, economic coherence, religious factors, the need of defence, social or tribal structures, and so on. The principal criterion will probably be the ethnical factor, but other criteria may equally be taken into consideration. Examples of adjudication of territory of this category are, apart from the reshuffle of the Balkan States in 1913 and the decisions of the Conference of Ambassadors after World War I concerning Teschen, Eastern Galicia, Thrace, etc.:

the arbitral award of the British Commissioner Major S. G. Tallents determining the frontier between the new States of Estonia and Latvia after the dismemberment of western Russia in 1918: decision of 1/3 July 1920, rendered in virtue of a special agreement of 22 March 1920 (Martens, N.R.G.³, XIV, 93), printed in a Memorandum of the Secretary-General of the League of Nations, dated 24 November 1920 (Document of the Assembly 20/48/70, Annex VII, at p. 21), and followed up by further bilateral agreements of 10 October 1920 and 1 November 1923 (Martens, N.R.G.³, XV, 686 and XVII, 829);

the (abortive) arbitral award of President Woodrow Wilson of 22 November 1920, fixing in pursuance of Article 89 of the (equally abortive) Peace Treaty of Sèvres of 10 August 1920 (Martens, N.R.G.³, XII, 664) the future territory of the projected new Armenian State towards the south and the southwest (*Bulletin de l'Institut Intermédiaire International* 1934 (XXXI), p. 329);

the Resolution of the Council of the League of Nations of 16 December 1925 (Martens, N.R.G.³, XXI, 689) adjudicating the Mosul vilayet to Iraq on the strength of Article 3 of the Peace Treaty of Lausanne of 24 July 1923 (*ibid.*, N.R.G.³, XIII, 342), as construed by the Permanent Court of International Justice in an Advisory Opinion of 21 November 1925 (*Publications P.C.I.J.*, series B, No. 12). The very thorough enquiry instituted with regard to the various aspects which that vilayet presented, by a Commission of experts set up for that purpose by the Council of the League of Nations, is extremely interesting: it is to be found in a special publication elucidated by a wealth of illustrative map material, which at the time appeared as a League of Nations Document C. 400. M. 147. 1925. VII (30 September 1924).

(*ii*) Adjudication of territory severed from a vanquished State and left to the victors for final disposal has occurred very frequently, especially in this century, after the Balkan Wars and the First and the Second World War. The ultimate decision was often, but very far from always, prepared by a plebiscite and thereupon finalized by a political decision of the Great Powers. I will go into this procedure in more detail in Part V of this publication, dealing with the personal substratum of the State. The validity and construction of such adjudications have sometimes been disputed, even before the Permanent Court of International Justice, comp. its Advisory Opinions of 6 December 1923 (Jaworzina, series B, No. 8) and 4 September 1924 (Monastery of Saint-Naoum, series B, No. 9), analysed in my *The Jurisprudence of the World Court*, vol. I, pp. 36-39.

(*b*) *Abjudication* is seldom used in international instruments as a term to denote the act of a judicial or quasi-judicial body depriving a Sovereign or State of his (its) territory, a procedure which has in itself become very rare under modern conditions.[38] A very old (feudal) example can be found in the preamble of the treaty of Bruges of 7 March 1167 between Philip of Alsace, count of Flanders, and Floris III, count of Holland (*Oorkondenboek van Holland en Zeeland*, ed. OBREEN, p. 94), in which mention is made of a dispute between the two counts through the latter's fault

> "quę in tantum excrevit, quod omnis terra, quam de me (count Philip) in feodo tenebat, iudicio baronum meorum, videlicet parium ipsius comitis Hollandię, ei abiudicata fuit . . .".

§ 6. (*a*) *Acquisitive or* (*b*) *Extinctive Prescription*

(*a*) *Acquisitive prescription*

It is still a matter of considerable controversy whether public international law indeed recognizes prescription as a means of the acquisition of foreign territory and, if so, under what conditions as to the requirements of good faith on the side of the acquiring State and of a specified lapse of time.[39]

I stress the word "foreign" because there is little sense in introducing the private law concept of acquisitive prescription (*usucapio*) into the doctrine of public international law in cases where the only question at issue is whether a State can rightfully claim that it has acquired a valid title of sovereignty by continuous and peaceful display of State authority over *terra nullius*, or where two, or for that matter more, States advance arguments, supported by evidence, in favour of their claim that they, and not their rival(s), have first occupied such *terra nullius*. And yet, in such cases the principle of "prescription" is sometimes wrongly invoked. What is at stake there is, rather, the necessity of weighing the validity of the respective arguments and proofs on the balance of the effectiveness of the display of State authority by each of the contestants. I cannot,

---

38. What was in fact an abjudication was the United Nations Resolution of 1966, No. 2145 (XXI) to deprive the Republic of South Africa of its Mandate over South West Africa, which the Republic wrongly considered as having become its national territory.
39. See H. LAUTERPACHT, *Private law sources and analogies of international law* (London, 1927), pp. 116-117 and 275-277.

therefore, approve of the use in such circumstances of reasonings based on "prescription".

An analogy in the law of nations with the concept of acquisitive prescription in private law is only justified when the territory concerned has in the past appertained to State A, but is at a later stage claimed by State B to have passed into its sovereignty by peaceful overt possession during a prolonged period of time. In cases of that type the appurtenance of the territory to State A in the past may in itself be controversial and must then first be decided. Or it may be undisputed but later have lapsed as a consequence of subsequent dereliction of the territory concerned, alleged by State B, but disputed by State A (see the Falklands Islands case). If the dereliction has in actual fact occurred, then there is again no scope for invoking the principle of prescription.

I will therefore deal further exclusively with the standard case in which a reference to acquisitive prescription might supposedly not be out of place: namely, where State A was once in fact the rightful possessor of the territory, but where State B has later gradually possessed itself of it by extending its own sovereign authority over it, thus ousting State A. This is the only contingency in which the analogous transfer of *usucapio* into the law of nations might be logically apposite, but in that variant I, for one, consider it to be a juridical myth and an erroneous incorporation of "general principles of (private) law" into the law of nations.[40]

The problem of acquisitive prescription proper must, moreover, be sharply distinguished from that of immemorial possession or *unvordenklichen Besitzstand*. The latter title of territorial sovereignty is generally recognized and indeed cannot be dispensed with. It has been generally acknowledged as an essential and undeniable legal foundation of the territorial *status quo*. Comp., *inter alia*, the following statements of the principle:

reply of king Stanislas-August of Poland to the declaration of the three powers concerning their intended dismemberment of his country in September 1772 (Martens, R², II, 106 *et seq.*, at p. 108):

> "Mais comme on ne peut nier que des transactions ensevelies dans l'oubli de plusieurs siècles, anéanties par des stipulations postérieures, ne soient contraires au démembrement actuel; les titres ne peuvent être admis, sans infirmer la sûreté des possessions de toutes les souverainetés du monde, sans ébranler la base de tous les Trônes";

preamble of the Convention between France and the bishopric of Liège concerning a disputed terrain "entre deux eaux" of 11 June 1778 (*ibid.*, R², II, 81):

> "le travail des commissaires fait sur les lieux ..., ayant convaincu Sa Majesté et le prince-évêque de Liège de l'inutilité des tentatives qu'on

---

40. I may be allowed to refer to my observations on this topic in Part I of this publication, pp. 59 *et seq.*

feroit pour décider aujourd'hui une contestation qui, faute de preuves suffisantes, n'a déjà pu l'être il y a plus de deux siècles; le Roi et ledit prince-évêque et son église ont pris le parti de trancher sur ces difficultés, au moyen d'un accommodement équitable et amiable";

arbitral award of 13 September 1902 between Austria and Hungary relative to the frontier between Galicia and Hungary near the Meerauge lake (*ibid.*, N.R.G.[3], III, 71 *et seq.*, at p. 80):

"Unter unvordenklichem Besitzstande wird ein solcher Besitzstand verstanden, wo der Beweis, dass es jemals anders war, nicht geführt werden kann und wo keine lebende Person von einem anderen Stande der Dinge jemals gehört hatte. Dieser Besitz muss ferner ununterbrochen und unangefochten sein . . .".

As to acquisitive prescription proper, it is well known that State practice has shown great vacillation in this field, particularly in the nineties of the 19th century in Latin America where three different attitudes were taken in respect of the idea of prescription.

Whereas the treaty of 7 October 1894 between Honduras and Nicaragua (LA FONTAINE, *Pasicrisie*, p. 478) disposed that "La Comisión mixta, para fijar los límites, atenderá al dominio del territorio plenamente probado, y no le reconocerá valor jurídico a la posesión de hecho que por una u otra parte se alegare" (Article 4) and that between Honduras and El Salvador of 19 January 1895 (*ibid.*, p. 505) mitigated this absolute prohibition by laying down that "A la posesión solamente deberá darse valor en lo que tenga de justo, legítimo y fundado, conforme a los principios generales del derecho y a las reglas de justicia que sobre el particular tiene sancionadas el Derecho de Gentes" (Article 4), the special agreement between Great Britain and Venezuela relative to their boundary dispute of 2 February 1897 (Martens, N.R.G.[2], XXVIII, 328), on the contrary, provided for arbitral proceedings on the following basis: "Adverse holding or prescription during a period of fifty years shall make a good title; the arbitrators may deem exclusive political control of a district, as well as actual settlement thereof, sufficient to constitute adverse holding or to make title by prescription".

I personally attribute no validity to these latter provisions as evidence of the recognition of the principle of acquisitive prescription in the law of nations, and therefore, refrain from expressing any opinion on the period of the "adverse holding" required for its alleged operation, but which it is impossible to define. Moreover, the classic absolute requirement of *bona fides* of the occupant at the commencement of his "adverse holding" would in international relations more often than not either have to be dropped altogether or at least be tampered with.

(b) *Extinctive prescription?*

For the reasons adduced *sub* (*a*) I do not see what use there would be for the idea of extinctive prescription as regards the loss of State territory by means of *usucapio* by another State.

Quite a different matter is its possible usefulness for the subject of the extinction of State debts as a consequence of a prolonged lapse of time. Comp. on this subject Part VI of this publication dealing with international juridical facts as sources of rights and obligations between States.

Again quite different is the question of the validity of a reference by State A to the "general principle of (private) law" relative to both *usucapio* and extinctive prescription, with the aim of supporting a claim by one of its nationals against State B on the ground that the latter refused him the benefit of that "general principle" in his private law dealings.

§ 7. *Partition of territorial domains*

Acquisition or loss of territorial sovereignty can also be the effect of a partition of the country concerned between or among two or more States, but there is little scope for digression on that variant in a separate paragraph because the cases here envisaged are very dissimilar and have already been, or will still be mentioned in other appropriate contexts.

See on partition:

of a country in virtue of one or the other hereditary title: section 1, § 2 above, pp. 303 *et seq.*;

with the object of winding up an existing co-imperium (*e.g.*, of the Elbe duchies of Schleswig-Holstein in 1865): Chapter V section 1, below pp. 429 *et seq.*; an analogous procedure is the dissolution of a joint (colonial) protectorate (Samoa): Chapter VI, section 2, of Part II of this publication, p. 417;

of a free city or territory (Trieste): Chapter VI, section 4 of Part II of this publication, pp. 504 *et seq.*;

of part of the territory of a State by other States *inter se*: this Chapter, section 2, § 3 on annexation or incorporation, *supra* pp. 356 *et seq.* Notorious instances are the actual partitions of Poland, the first by Austria, Prussia and Russia in 1772 and the second by Prussia and Russia in 1793, and the potential partition of Prussian Silesia between Austria and Saxony by their secret treaty of alliance of Leipzig of 18 May 1745 (Martens, S, I, 270);

of an entire State by other States *inter se*: Chapter III, section 3, § 5 of Part II of this publication on the extinction of States, at pp. 127 *et seq.* Again the most notorious instance of this procedure is the actual third partition of Poland in 1795, which extinguished the whole State.

§ 8. *Novation*

This title of acquisition is very rare. It consists in the gradual transformation of a right *in territorio alieno*, for example a lease, or a pledge, or certain concessions of a territorial nature, into full sovereignty without any formal and unequivocal instrument to that effect intervening. The Orkney and Shetland Islands, Corsica, Nijmegen, originally only given in pledge, may serve as historical examples (comp. Chapter IV, section 1, *infra* pp. 387 *et seq.*). I will confine myself here to the two cases which until recently have given rise to considerable political controversy, namely those of (1) British Honduras (Belice) and (2) certain Portuguese enclaves in India.

(1) It is beyond all doubt that the British claims in respect of Spanish, later Guatemalan, Belice were in origin nothing other than the right, guaranteed by Spain to Great Britain on behalf of her nationals by Article 17 of their Peace Treaty of Paris of 10 February 1763 (Martens, R², I, 104), not to be molested in their trade of cutting Campeachy wood in the Spanish territories bordering the Bay of Honduras:

> "Et Sa Majesté Catholique ne permettra point que les sujets de Sa Majesté Britannique, ou leurs ouvriers, soient inquiétés, ou molestés, sous aucun prétexte que ce soit, dans les dits lieux, dans leur occupation de couper, charger, et transporter le bois de teinture ou de Campêche . . . Et Sa Majesté Catholique leur assure, par cet article, l'entière jouissance de ces avantages et facultés sur les côtes et territoires espagnols . . .".

There was no mention in this Article of any territorial limits of this concession. Nor was there yet, in the preliminary Articles of peace, agreed upon at Versailles on 20 January 1783 (*ibid.*, R², III, 510), any other mention of limits of the concession than that these were still to be fixed (Article 4), but an express reservation was added to this Article to the effect that "bien entendu que ces stipulations ne seront censées déroger en rien aux droits de (la) souveraineté (de Sa Majesté Catholique)". The territorial extent of the concession was, however, under the same reservation, by Article 6 of the definitive peace treaty between Great Britain and Spain of 3 September 1783 (*ibid.*, R², III 541), expressly confined to that portion of eastern Central America which is situated between the rivers Hondo in the North and Belice in the South. This concession was, by Article 2 of the subsequent treaty of 14 July 1786 (*ibid.*, R², IV, 133), without any basic change of its legal nature extended, locally, beyond the river Belice southwards to the river Jabón (or Sibun) and, substantively, by an additional concession to cut other wood as well, inclusive of mahogany, and to gather all kinds of fruits or other products of the earth which grow by nature and without cultivation, to the express exclusion of the establishment of sugar and coffee plantations and of factories of any kind, "tous les pays en question étant reconnus pour appartenir incontestablement et de droit à la Couronne d'Espagne". In the following half-century, however, not only did the woodcutters concerned gradually extend their trade still further southward to the river Sarstoon, but in addition a British territorial administration, which had in the mean time been established in this region, increasingly tightened its initially totally unauthorized governmental grip on the country as if it were a British colony. The question became acute on the occasion of the conclusion of the Clayton-Bulwer treaty of 19 April 1850 (*ibid.*, N.R.G.[1], XV, 187), when Great Britain took exception to a possible construction by the United States of Article 1 of that treaty to the effect that this would prevent her from henceforth claiming Belice as her territory. In the following years there was an intense diplomatic struggle between England and Guatemala, *inter alia*, on the nature of the British territorial rights in connection with the necessity of delimiting the boundaries of the Belice settlement: whilst the British Government refused to agree to anything other than a simple delimitation of the boundaries of the respective State territories, the Guatemalan Government initially held to the theory that the British territorial demands should be satisfied in the juridical form of a cession of territory. However, the British view, in the given circumstances of power relations, prevailed.

This course of events exhibits a case of novation of a concessionary right into complete sovereignty.

(2) In the case of the *Right of passage over Indian territory* between certain Portuguese enclaves the International Court of Justice has, in its Judgment of 12 April 1960 on the merits (*I.C.J. Reports* 1960, p. 6), theoretically constructed, in my opinion in fact invented, a similar process of tacit novation of a simple grant, made in the past by the Mahrattas to Portuguese authorities, into sovereignty by the later action of the British successors to the Mahratta State. Comp. my *The Jurisprudence of the World Court*, vol. II, at pp. 389 *et seq.*

CHAPTER IV

INTERNATIONAL RIGHTS IN TERRITORIO ALIENO

In the present Chapter, I intend to deal successively with four characteristic types of a right *in territorio alieno*, namely, international pledges, international leases, transfer into foreign "occupation and administration", and State servitudes. When attempting to classify the many historical instances of such rights, one meets with the difficulty of assigning the right place to a number of them, as they can often be reasonably classed under two different headings. I could only remove this obstacle by a perhaps somewhat arbitrary choice, remedied by cross-references.

Section 1. INTERNATIONAL PLEDGES

The pledging of territory as a security for the repayment of public debts, or in lieu of a dowry stipulated on the occasion of a princely marriage was very customary in earlier centuries. As HALLECK, in his *International Law* (4th ed., London, 1908), I, 166, recalls to mind, already about the year 1200 princes gave their country in pledge: in order to raise money to engage in the First Crusade Robert Duke of Normandy mortgaged his duchy to his brother William for a certain weight of silver and transferred its possession to him before leaving for the Holy Land. Such pledges, however, often ended in complete annexation of the territory concerned by the creditor prince, just as was, for that matter, the case of territorial leases, to be dealt with in section 2, *infra*. There are many famous instances of such a transformation, especially of the first variant. More often than not the tenuous ties which remained between the former ruler and the territory thus given in pledge or mortgage to another ruler dissolved gradually and almost imperceptibly without any explicit document to that effect having been handed down to posterity. Sometimes, however, the ties were severed in express terms and the rights *in territorio alieno* thus formally transmuted into what we now call full territorial sovereignty. Very occasionally also, the territory given in security for a debt was subsequently redeemed by the debtor and thus returned to him in complete sovereignty.

An example of the first development is that of the originally Imperial town of Nijmegen which was in 1248 given in pledge to the then Count of Guelder by the Emperor of the Holy Roman Empire William of Holland, who was in urgent need of financial assistance.[1] The town, which has never been officially ceded to the duchy of Guelder or to the Republic of the United Netherlands, has thus in the course of time gradually changed from its original status of a pledge into that of an integral part of Gelderland and the Netherlands. There is a curious proof of the fact that this transformation was already acknowledged at an early date, when the municipal authorities of Nijmegen were cited before the *Reichskammergericht* for having usurped the right of minting, and in support of their claim to freedom from Imperial control in that respect sollicited a legal opinion from the Law Faculty of the University of Louvain. The Faculty argued that, although the town had originally been an Imperial town, it had since in fact been detached from the Empire as a consequence of the pledge and the Emperor's failure to reimburse the loan. Comp. *Bijdragen voor vaderlandsche geschiedenis en oudheidkunde*, 1st series, vol. 7 (1850), pp. 118-139.

An entirely different instance of an international mortgage that occurred in the United Netherlands at a much later date, but which on the contrary bore a temporary character, was that of the pledging of the so-called "pandsteden" or mortgage towns Brielle and Vlissingen (Flushing) to England in the early period of the emergence of the United Provinces to independence as a sovereign confederation. In the treaty of 10 August 1585 (Dumont, V[1], 454), by which Queen Elizabeth I undertook to protect the young confederacy against its former sovereign the King of Spain, it was stipulated that—in addition to the acceptance by the Netherlands of an English Lieutenant-General, the Earl of Leicester, as a supreme authority, and to the admission of English members to the Netherlands Council of State with the right to vote—two towns in the provinces of Holland and Zeeland, respectively, should be given in pledge for the due reimbursement of the expenditures that England would have to make for the fulfilment of the promise of protection. All of those three fetters on Netherlands sovereignty under the treaty of protection were successively, first loosened and then abandoned: the Earl of Leicester left the country in 1588 without being replaced by a successor; the English members of the Council of State left that body in 1625; and the pledge of the two "pandsteden" came to an end in 1616 after a final financial settlement (see the article of J.A. VAN ARKEL, *De inlossing der Engelse pandsteden in 1616*, in *Tijdschrift voor Geschiedenis* 1968 (81), p. 59).

1. In the same year the Emperor gave the town of Duisburg in pledge.

388

Another famous case, of again much later date, was that of the pledging of Corsica to France by Genoa. Since the Genoese were unable to successfully oppose the insurgents of Corsica (who formally complained of their treatment by Genoa at the Peace Congress of Aachen (Aix-la-Chapelle) of 1748, Rousset, *Recueil*, XX, 215) with their own forces, and since earlier aid agreements with France of 1737, 1752, 1755, 1756 and lately 6 August 1764 (Martens, R², I, 265) had not been sufficiently successful, Genoa by a treaty of 15 May 1768 (*ibid.*, I, 591) agreed with France upon a firmer occupation of a number of Corsican towns and ports by French troops with the object of restoring order on the island. The occupied areas, in which France would thenceforth exercise all rights of military sovereignty, without however thereby acquiring territorial sovereignty proper in the civil sphere, were to serve as a pledge for the costs of this military aid. France would not be empowered to dispose of the occupied areas in favour of a third Power without the consent of Genoa, and the latter would be entitled to demand reinstatement in its sovereignty against payment of the expenses incurred by France. This pledge, which France soon treated as a disguised cession—witness Article 2 of her treaty of 25 August 1770 with the Bey of Tunis (*ibid.*, R², I, 700) in which the latter "reconnaît pleinement et pour toujours la réunion de l'île de Corse aux états de l'empire de France"—, was thus tacitly in fact converted into full French sovereignty, a change which was formally effected by a Decree of the National Assembly of 30 November 1789 (*ibid.*, V, 145), by which the island was "déclarée partie de l'Empire français". After the Constitution of Genoa had been transformed by a Convention with France of 6 June 1797 (*ibid.*, R², VII, 394), the thenceforward so-called Ligurian Republic (reorganised in 1802) in May-June 1805 was itself also annexed by France in the form, then usual, of a "réunion" (*ibid.*, R², VII, 685-700), as a result of which Corsica, in so far as it could be held still to be legally a part of Genoa, finally fell completely under French sovereignty. This new status of the island was not altered when, in spite of the—unauthorized and therefore invalid[2]—promise of the British Commander-in-Chief Lord William Bentinck at the capitulation of Genoa to the British forces in the spring of 1814 that her independence would be restored, the former Republic was, by the Congress of Vienna (Articles 2-4 of the multilateral Convention of 20 May 1815, with Annex, *ibid.*, N.R., II, 298, confirmed by Articles 86 *et seq.* and Annex 14 of the Final Act of 9 June 1815, *ibid.*, II, 379), incorporated into the Kingdom of Sardinia. Corsica, which had in fact remained in the hands of France, continued in that status.[3]

2. In the same sense: Verdross in Hatschek-Strupp's *Wörterbuch des Völkerrechts und der Diplomatie* (Berlin-Leipzig, 1924), I, 128, *in voce* "Bentinck, Versprechen an Genua".
3. Comp. on this island: Paul Arighi, *Histoire de la Corse* (Paris, 1966).

A very peculiar instance, the final liquidation of which was, on the contrary, carried out by a formal procedure, was another pledge dating from the same period, namely, that made by Sweden to the Grand-Duchy of Mecklenburg-Schwerin in 1803 by their treaty of 26 June 1803 (Martens, R², VIII, 54). On that occasion Sweden pledged to her partner the town and seigniory of Wismar (with two dependent baili-wicks), which had been a Swedish enclave in Mecklenburg territory since the treaty of Osnabrück of 24 October 1648 (K. Zeumer, *Quellen-sammlung zur Geschichte der Deutschen Reichsverfassung in Mittelalter und Neuzeit*, II, 395, at p. 418; Dumont, VI¹, 450), Article X, § 6, as a security for the reimbursement of a loan of 1.250.000 *Reichsthaler* granted to her by Mecklenburg-Schwerin. The pledge was given for a period of one hundred years, at the expiry of which the capital could be reimbursed.

> It is worth-while from a legal-historical point of view to quote the exact terms in which the transaction was couched. Whereas the preamble described it as a "cession conditionnelle et hypothécaire" of the Swedish possessions concerned, Article 1(2) detailed it as a cession "à titre d'hypothèque (anti-chresis) et moyennant une rétribution ... (de leur) pleine et entière posses-sion usufructuaire ... pour en jouir sans interruption pendant la durée du terme précité",—a cession accompanied, however, pursuant to Article 2, by a transfer by the king of Sweden to the person of the duke of Mecklenburg-Schwerin and his successors of "tous ses droits de souveraineté sur Wismar, son territoire et ses dépendances, sans en excepter aucun ..." and by his divesting himself "de toute l'autorité politique, militaire, civile, ecclésias-tique et judiciaire", thus far exercised over the possessions pledged and their inhabitants.

When the date of the expiry approached, the two States concerned agreed upon a formal cancellation of the pledgor-pledgee relationship: Wismar was to fall definitively under Mecklenburg sovereignty and the Swedish debt was to be annulled. A Convention to that effect was formally entered into by the two States on 20 June 1903 (Martens, N.R.G.², XXXI, 572) and was the same day, in conformity with the German *Reichsverfassung*, formally confirmed by a Convention between Sweden and the *Reich* (*ibid.*, 574).

> The same treaty of 1903 mentioned in its Article 5 an older pledge, granted in 1714 by the then Princess, later Queen, Ulrika Eleonora of Sweden in the name of King Charles XII to the then reigning duke of Mecklenburg Karl Leopold, of Sweden's right to a river toll at Warnemünde, but for the sole purpose of deleting the right of redemption (*droit de reluition*) which was attached to that pledge.

All these pledges used to imply the authorization of the pledgee to exercise sovereign rights in the territory pledged.

There are many more instances of such territorial grants in pledge, both in earlier and in more recent times, for example in connection with princely marriage treaties.

390

Thus, the Shetland islands were in the 15th century pledged by King Christian I of Denmark, Norway and Sweden to King James III of Scotland in lieu of a dowry owed by the former to the latter on the occasion of the marriage of his daughter Margaret to the Scottish Crown prince. The dowry was never paid and the pledge was gradually converted into full territorial sovereignty. A few details, also relating to the parallel case of the Orkney islands, follow below.

The Orkney islands were conquered about 900 by the Norse King Harald Hårfager, who granted them in fief to one of his nobles. After the then also Norwegian Hebrides had been overrun by the Scots under King Alexander III and King Haakon of Norway had in vain attempted to recapture them in 1263, an agreement was reached, by the Treaty of Perth of 1266 (confirmed in 1312 at Inverness by Robert de Bruce and Haakon V), to the effect that the Orkney and Shetland islands were to remain Norwegian but the Hebrides were ceded to Scotland, subject to the latter's obligation to make a direct payment to Norway of 4000 Marks and to follow that up by further annual payments of 100 Marks under a heavy financial penalty in every case of failure to pay the amount due. The increasing arrears in the payment of this tribute—the "annual of Norway"—eventually led to the pledging of the Orkneys and Shetlands to Scotland. When, namely, in 1460 the Scottish debt to Norway had become so great that King Christian of Denmark resolved to claim its payment, King Charles VII of France as a mediator negotiated a settlement, 8 September 1468, in the then familiar shape of a marriage contract between crown prince James (later King James III) of Scotland and Margaret, daughter of King Christian I of Denmark-Norway-Sweden, subject to the following stipulations: (a) remission of the arrears of the "Annual" by Norway; (b) award by the King of Norway to his daughter Margaret of a dowry of 60.000 Rhineland guilders, 10.000 of which were to be paid within a year; (c) pledge of the then Norwegian Orkney islands as a security for the remainder in the following terms:
"damus, concedimus, impignoramus, ac sub firma hypotheca et pignore imponimus, atque hypothecamus omnes et singulas terras nostras Insularum Orcadensium".
When on the expiry of the one year's term only 2000 of the 10.000 guilders had been paid, a further agreement was reached to the effect that payment of the arrears of the dowry would be secured by an additional pledge of the Shetland islands, on the understanding that they should be returned to Norway after settlement of the debt (without any fixed term) with the formula: "terrae insularum Regi nostro Jacobo impignoratae ad Norvegiae Reges revertantur", and that the islanders should preserve their traditional laws and customs under Scottish rule. As was to be expected, Scotland's grip on the islands gradually tightened and was finally transformed into full sovereignty by an Act sanctioning their annexation to the royal family. Redemption of the debt has since then repeatedly been offered by Norway during the second half of the 16th and around the middle of the 17th century, even as late as about 1750, but all attempts to this end were skilfully evaded, inter alia in 1585, when a special Norwegian embassy was sent to Scotland.
Comp. for further details of this development: Gilbert GOUDIE's The Celtic and Scandinavian Antiquities of Shetland (Edinburgh, 1904), pp. 213-229, and

for the text of the marriage treaty of 1468: FORFFAEUS, *Orcades seu rerum Orcadinensium historia* (Copenhagen, 1715).

Even very recently, in 1967, the Norwegian Ministry of Foreign Affairs still claimed the islands from the Foreign Office in London (see *R.G.D.I.P.* 1968 (72), p. 1097).

Another example on the British isles is that of the frontier town of Berwick-upon-Tweed, which was also, in the course of its stormy history, at some period given in pledge by Scotland to England. See p. 439.

Other examples of ancient international pledges are the two successive cessions of the town of Emden on the river Ems in pledge by Hamburg to the then *Häuptling* (later Count) of Norden in East-Friesland, and that of the Reiderland, adjacent to, and to the west of the Ems mouth, to the Count of Emden by the bishop of Münster.

The first pledge had a complicated history.

> After the forces of Hamburg had conquered in 1431 the town of Emden from its bailiff as a reprisal against the latter's assistance to the so-called *Viktualienbrüder,* notorious for their acts of piracy in the adjacent waters, the city of Hamburg in 1439 ceded the town for a certain period to two *Häuptlinge* in East Friesland by means of a medieval type of pledge (cession "auf Schlossglauben"). This temporary cession-in-pledge, revoked in 1447 after new disputes had arisen, was renewed in the same form in 1453 for a term of sixteen years. Attempts on the Hamburg side in 1469, repeated in 1480, to recover the town of Emden failed owing to a resolute refusal by Count Ulrich of East-Friesland and the break-down of an action, brought by Hamburg before the Emperor and his *Reichskammergericht* in 1483 and following years. The dispute was in 1493 terminated by an agreement between Hamburg and the Count by which Emden was definitively awarded to East-Friesland, conditional upon the redemption of the loan. Comp. E. FRIEDLÄNDER, *Ostfriesisches Urkundenbuch* (Emden, 1878-1881), I, Nos. 509, 658; II, Nos. 1133, 1361.

The second pledge was redeemable and still in existence in 1584 according to a report submitted by certain bishops to the English envoy Herle, charged with an enquiry into the quarrels in respect of the mouth of the river Ems in the days of Leicester's Lieutenant-Governorship of the Netherlands. This appears from the report which Herle presented at the time to Queen Elizabeth I and which I found in the Bodleyan Library in Oxford (MS. Rawlinson, C, 424).

For the rest, diplomatic history is full of other pledges of territory by their princes.

Other early instances of the pledging of territory to secure the repayment of a debt were those of

Maastricht in the beginning of the 13th century on behalf of the Count of Loon for a loan given to the Emperor;

parts of the duchy of Guelder in 1406 on account of a debt to the duke of Cleves;

392

the whole duchy of Guelder, pledged by Duke Arnoud to duke Charles the Bold in 1473, and the county and town of Zutphen pledged by the Emperor Frederick III to the bishop of Münster in 1475. Comp. on these events H. G. HARKEMA, *Historie van Gelre 1472-1492*;

the so-called "Anholter pandschap" of 1562-1612, established on the *Amt* of Bredevoort. Comp. F. SCHMIDT, *Die Bredevorter Fehde* (of 1325) (1910; *Veröffentlichungen des historischen Vereins für Gelder und Umgegend*, No. 25).

The examples cited above from Germany were only a few of the many *oppignerationes Imperiales* which in earlier centuries occurred within the ambit of the Holy Roman Empire. In order to prevent disputes over their existence or continuation, which obviously often arose in later periods, the Emperors were obliged expressly to confirm existing grants-in-pledge in the Capitulations which they used to endorse on their election as King of the Romans. Charles V undertook in § 4 of his *Wahlkapitulation* of 1519 (Zeumer, *Quellensammlung zur Geschichte der deutschen Reichsverfassung*, 2nd ed., II, p. 309)

> "(den Reichsfürsten) ire Regalia, Oberkait, Freiheiten, Privilegien, *Phandschaften* und Gerechtigkeiten, auch Gebrauch und guete Gewonheiten, so sie bisher gehebt oder in Übung gewesen sein, in gueter, bestendiger Form on all Waigerung (zu) confirmiren und bestetigen".

This clause was repeated in subsequent Capitulations, *inter alia*, in chapter 3 of that of Ferdinand III of 1637, to which in turn reference was made in Article V, § 26 (b), of the Peace Treaty of Osnabrück o 24 October 1648 (*ibid.*, II, no. 197, pp. 395 *et seq.*), paralleled by Article 47 of the Peace Treaty of Münster of the same date (*ibid.*, II, no. 198, pp. 434 *et seq.*):

> "Quod ad Oppignerationes Imperiales attinet, cum in Capitulatione Caesarea dispositum reperiatur, quod electus Romanorum Imperator Electoribus, Principibus caeterisque Statibus immediatis Imperii eiusmodi oppignerationes confirmare atque in earundem tranquilla et quieta possessione defendere ac manutenere debeat: conventum est, hanc dispositionem, donec consensu Electorum, Principum et Statuum aliter statutum fuerit, observandam esse".

This clause implied, in particular, the restitution of the towns of Lindau (on the Bodensee) and of Weissenburg ("in Noricis"). Should any territory have been pledged "ante hominis memoriam", then no redemption of the underlying debt would be permitted unless the merits of the case were thoroughly examined.—On the other hand, the Emperor Charles VI, in Article X of the "beständige Wahlkapitulation" of 1711 (draft in Zeumer, *ibid.*, II, no. 205, pp. 474 *et seq.*) undertook not only to abstain in the future from pledging any part of the Empire without the knowledge and consent of the Electors, Princes and Estates, but also to do his utmost to achieve the restitution to the Empire of all those areas which had been pledged in the past and had illegally fallen into the hands of foreign nations,—especially in Italy and Switzerland.

An historically famous mutual pledge was that between Spain and Portugal, following their continual clashes in the East Indies and Portugal's successes there, by their Treaty of Zaragoza of 22 April 1529 (Martens, S., I, 398; NAVARRETE, *Colección de los viajes y descubrimientos, etc.*, Madrid, 1837, Imprenta Nacional, IV, 389). By that treaty Spain pledged the Moluccan islands with the whole area up to 17° eastward to Portugal for the sum of 350.000 ducats, but Portugal undertook to have the legal situation elucidated by experts from both countries: should the islands appear to belong to the Spanish half of the globe, then the treaty would be changed accordingly and the debt repaid. Owing to the return home of the last Spaniards in 1536, this latter clause has never been implemented. The old controversy was, however, finally liquidated a century and a half later when, by Article 21 of their treaty of San Ildefonso of 1 October 1777 (Martens, R[2], II, 545), Portugal ceded to Spain all rights which she might have to the Philippines and the Marianes, and renounced any claim which she might have in virtue of the Treaty of Zaragoza without demanding the reimbursement of the sum she had paid at the time for what was now called a "sale".

Pledges of territory have occurred even in more recent times. I refer to two instances from the middle of the 18th century.

By a convention of 1750 the City of Hamburg granted to the House of Holstein a loan under the pledge to the City, "cum superioritate territoriali" and for a period of twenty years, of certain *pertinentia* of two Holstein *Ämter*. By Articles 5, 6 and 14 of a treaty of 27 May 1768 (Martens, R[2], I, 597), concluded on the Holstein side by the Russian Tsaritsa Catherine II in the name of her son, duke of Holstein-Gottorp and heir to the Russian throne, and the King of Denmark and Norway Christian VII, duke of Holstein-Glückstadt, some of the said *pertinentia* were definitively transferred to Hamburg in full sovereignty, whilst others were restored to the House of Holstein, subject to remission by the City of the debt of 1750 and of a much older debt owing to it since 1644.

The other example is that of the County of Bentheim.

This county, which had until 1729 also comprised the counties of Tecklenburg and Lingen (see the protests by the ruling counts of Bentheim-Bentheim and Bentheim-Steinfurt against their cession, made in that year to Friedrich Wilhelm I of Prussia, in Martens, N.S., III, 41 under the date of 4 December 1814), was in 1752 pledged by the then Count to the Elector of Hanover for a period of thirty years. This pledge should, consequently, have run out in 1782, but in fact it had been tacitly continued without a formal renewal, without the approval of the feudal successor and without ratification by the Emperor. On the death of the last Count of Bentheim-Bentheim (19 February 1803) the pledge-relationship came *ipso jure* to an end. This entitled the nearest agnate, the ruling Imperial Count of Bentheim-

Steinfurt, to take possession of the county against reimbursement of the debt. As France was at the time the actual possessor of Hanover, the First Consul of the French Republic and the Count agreed by their convention of 12/22 May 1804 (*ibid.*, R², VIII, 201) upon the repayment of the original debt to the Hanoverian treasury with the help of Prussia and Denmark and the consequent installation of the Count in his county with all the formalities customary in Germany (16 July 1804). However, when the Confederation of the Rhine was created in 1806, Bentheim was made part of the Grand Duchy of Berg (Article 24). This course of events had an epilogue in Article 32 (2) of the Final Act of the Congress of Vienna of 9 June 1815 (*ibid.*, N.R., II, 379) pursuant to which the traditional relations between Hanover and Bentheim under the pledge treaties would provisionally remain as they stood, but the county would after their final expiration be degraded to the status of a mediatized territory under Hanover in accordance with the new confederal Constitution of Germany.

Other historical instances of international pledges are those given to the States General of the Republic of the United Netherlands on

the (revenues of the) Austrian Low Countries as a security for the payment of certain subsidies by Austria to the Republic in virtue of Article 19 of the (third) Barrier Treaty of 15 November 1715 (Rousset, *Recueil* I, 56, 59, 62; 71, 408);

on East Friesland in virtue of older agreements with that princedom; when it devolved upon the King of Prussia in 1745, the latter assumed the obligations incurred by the Prince vis-à-vis the Netherlands under the pledge, but an arrangement was made for the reimbursement of the East-Frisian debts by Prussia (*ibid.*, XIX, 147, 153).

A new mortgage was still by Article 101 of the Final Act of the Congress of Vienna of 9 June 1815 (Martens, N.R., II, 379) established in favour of the ex-Empress of France, Marie Louise, duchess of Lucca, on certain Bavaro-Palatine seigniories in Bohemia as a security for the payment of an additional annuity, promised to that duchess by the Emperor of Austria and the Grand Duke of Tuscany.

A more modern form was the continued occupation of the Turkish Dodecanese by Italy as an (informal) pledge for the fulfilment of the Ottoman commitments under Article 2 of the Peace Treaty of Ouchy-Lausanne of 18 October 1912 after the Tripolitanian war (*ibid.*, N.R.G.³, VII, 7). This pledge, also, showed a marked tendency in the course of time to be converted into full sovereignty. The islands were not, in fact, returned to the Ottoman Empire, owing, *inter alia*, to the outbreak of World War I, but remained under Italian occupation until 1923, when the "pledge" was transformed into full sovereignty. The extremely complicated history of the Dodecanese can be summarized as follows.

At the close of the Balkan Wars the Balkan States, by Article 5 of their Peace Treaty of London of 30 May 1913 (*ibid.*, VIII, 16), maintained by Article 15 of the Greco-Turkish Peace Treaty of Athens of 14 November 1913 (*ibid.*, VIII, 93) entrusted the six Great Powers of that period with

395

the task of deciding the fate of all the Ottoman islands in the Aegean Sea, except Crete. Carrying out that mandate, the Conference of Ambassadors, by a decision reached in London and notified to Greece on 13 February 1914 (*British Documents on the Origins of the War* (1898-1914), vol. X, Part I, pp. 231-232; *Documents diplomatiques français* (1871-1914), 3rd series (1911-1914), t. IX, 1 Jan.-16 March 1914) decided to assign to Greece all the islands in the Aegean Sea actually occupied by her (except Imbros and Tenedos off the entrance to the Dardanelles and the island of Castellorizo near the coast of Asia Minor, all three to be restored to Turkey)—in particular: Lemnos, Samothrace, Mitylene, Chios, Samos and Nikaria. This decision implied that the Dodecanese—Stampalia, Chalki, Scarpanto, Casos, Tilos, Nisyros, Kalymnos, Leros, Patmos, Lipsos, Symi and Kos—and Rhodos, which were all still occupied by Italy, were also excepted from cession to Greece. Italy was thereupon promised by France, Great Britain and Russia, when they brought over Italy to their side, in Article 8 of their secret treaty of London of 26 April 1915 (*ibid.*, X, 329), that she would after the war obtain complete sovereignty over the Dodecanese which she continued to occupy. When in the summer of 1919 the Italian and Greek Governments decided to present a common front at the Peace Conference in order to achieve their national aims in the Eastern Mediterranean and the Balkan peninsula, as far as Italy was concerned, especially in Albania and Asia Minor, and as far as Greece was concerned, in Thrace, Northern Epiros and also in Asia Minor, the two Powers agreed in para. 5 of their secret Tittoni-Venizelos Agreement of 29 July 1919 (*ibid.*, R², XII, 575), that Italy would cede to Greece the Dodecanese which she still occupied, but that Rhodos would, under certain guarantees for the Greek population, remain under her sovereignty. This overall agreement was, however, in para. 7 made conditional upon both parties obtaining satisfaction at the Peace Conference of their respective aspirations: if not, either party "reprend pleine liberté d'action par rapport à tous les points du présent accord". This was what actually happened in the summer of 1920: as Italy failed to achieve her aims in Asia Minor and the Albanian people's national aspirations won the day, the Italian Government by a note of 22 July 1920 (text in *I documenti diplomatici della pace orientale*, a cura di Amedeo Giannini, Rome, 1922, series I, p. 26) denounced the Tittoni-Venizelos Agreement. This was, as far as the islands in the Aegean Sea were concerned, replaced three weeks later at Sèvres by the Bonin Longare-Venizelos treaty of 10 August 1920 (Martens, N.R.G.³, XII, 792). This treaty was ancillary to the main document of the Peace Conference at Sèvres, *viz.*, the Peace Treaty of Turkey of the same date (*ibid.*, XII, 664), by Article 122 of which Turkey renounced in favour of Italy possession of Rhodos, the Dodecanese and Castellorizo. At the same time, however, the Treaty made provision for a through-cession of the Dodecanese to Greece, thus leaving Italy in the possession of Rhodos, only subject to the prospect of a future plebiscite (not to be held until after fifteen years) should Great Britain decide to cede Cyprus to Greece. However, this second Italo-Greek Agreement also miscarried owing to the Nationalist revival in Turkey led by Kemal Ataturk and the breakdown of the peace settlement of Sèvres. The Italian Government, on 8 October 1922, notified Greece that it considered this Agreement also as lapsed. What thereupon emerged from the peace negotiations of Lausanne was the following arrangement. Pursuant to Article 12 of the Peace Treaty of 24 July 1923 (*ibid.*, XIII, 342) the decision of the Conference of Ambassadors of February 1914 concerning the sovereignty of Greece over the islands of the Eastern Mediterranean—

396

especially Lemnos, Samothrace, Mitylene, Chios, Samos and Nikaria (= Ikaria)—was maintained[4] (except as regards islands less than three miles from the Asian coast, *inter alia*, Paspargos). Pursuant to Article 15, on the contrary, Italy was definitively to acquire Rhodos and the Dodecanese in full sovereignty and also to obtain Castellorizo. This cession, which at last transmuted Italy's original status, ever since 1912, of a *de facto* pledgee of the archipelago into complete sovereignty, did not, however, produce its desired final effects. At the close of World War II Greece ultimately achieved her national aims in respect of the Aegean islands, and defeated Italy was forced to cede to her Rhodos, the Dodecanese and Castellorizo by Article 14 of the Peace Treaty of Paris of 10 February 1947 (*U.N.T.S.*, vol. 49, p. 3).

A similar pledge-like relationship was repeatedly established on behalf of Russia with regard to the Danubian principalities of Moldavia and Wallachia. The military occupation which constituted the pledge was always meant (at least asserted to mean) to serve as security for the compliance by Turkey of her treaty obligations towards Russia. Comp. further on this subject Part VI of this publication in the section relating to the guarantees for the performance of treaties.

Section 2. INTERNATIONAL LEASES

Leases of one State respecting land situated in another may be of different natures.

Just as a State (or in the terminological and legal variant of past centuries: a Prince) may have rights of property in respect of real estate in another State (or: in the country of another Prince) on a simple private law footing, so can a foreign lease to which a State is entitled be entirely subject to the municipal private law system of the foreign State concerned and thus present no special interest for public international law, apart from a possible claim of the lessee to sovereign immunity in respect of his lease. The situation would of course be directly governed by international law if specific treaty provisions should extend their protection even to such a lease of a private law nature.

What is discussed in this section is, however, the existence of genuine international leases, established by treaty and endowed with an international legal regime, including a more or less extensive number of sovereign rights for the benefit of the lessee State, or even a formal transfer of the exercise of all sovereign rights to the lessee. The lessor State in this variant retains its territorial sovereignty, but this is in part largely nullified by the rights of the lessee State, so that the case presents the picture of two layers of sovereign territorial rights, one superimposed

4. The curious thing is that, whereas the text of 1914 made an exception for Imbros, Tenedos and Castellorizo, the recital of that text in Article 12 of Lausanne mentions instead Imbros, Tenedos and the Rabbits islands (also off the entrance of the Dardanelles). These were to remain under Turkish sovereignty.

397

on the other. The rights of the lessee State may in actual fact all but eliminate those of the lessor and thus reduce the latter to a merely nominal territorial sovereignty. They may, on the other hand, be strictly defined and, in particular, lay down in express terms what the lessee is not allowed to do with regard to the territory leased. It is not always clear, sometimes even sharply controversial, whether the lease is of the first private law type or includes the exercise of sovereign rights.

In the days of feudalism and patrimonial State conceptions the existence of such leases was to a certain extent normal, but under modern conditions they are generally abnormal and destined to be in the event liquidated as an unpalatable survival of the past. If the discussion of this subject is further limited to modern international law, it appears that the best known cases of international leases date from the period of the colonization of the African continent, subsequent to the Congo Conference of Berlin of 1885, and from the beginning of the 20th century, when the "unequal" treaties with China were entered into. International leases occasionally occur also elsewhere, but they are more isolated instances.

A perusal of the available examples of international leases reveal their varying contents, the various precautions taken to prevent their gradual transformation into real and unfettered sovereignty, and the resistance which they subsequently provoked from the lessor State.

The historical examples of international leases served in the main five purposes: 1) to provide access to the big rivers or lakes of Africa; 2) to acquire suitable ports and additional establishments on the coast of China; 3) to assure the possibility of constructing a railway, a road or a canal across the territory of another State which was to remain under its sovereignty; 4) to secure free zones in foreign seaports with the object of remedying an unfavourable situation caused to a State by being cut off from the high seas; 5) to provide army, naval or air bases on foreign territory. These aims were not always pursued by means of leases; they could also be attained by means of the creation of State servitudes (comp. on this subject section 4 below), by the request for, and the granting of, other privileges, such as "concessions" and "settlements"[5]

5. The "concessions" in Chinese towns, such as Tientsin, being "locations en perpétuité" (perpetual rents), bear a different character. Comp. for example the Belgo-Chinese Convention of 6 February 1902 concerning a plot of land at Tientsin alongside the river Pei-ho (Martens, N.R.G.³, VIII, 215). Similar "concessions" already existed there: British, German, French, Russian. These "concessions" have gradually been rescinded and the areas concerned restored to China. Germany, Austria and Hungary were forced to give up their concessions after World War I: Article 132 Versailles; Article 116 St.Germain; Article 100 Trianon, under the formula "abrogation of the leases under which the Concessions are now held". Comp. the restoration by the United Kingdom of her Han-kow concession by an agreement of 19 February 1927 (ibid., XVIII,

or a right of "occupation and administration" (comp. on this latter right: section 3 below), or by a delimitation of colonial frontiers in such a manner that they included the access to a river, a lake, or the sea by the traditional method of the acquisition of territorial sovereignty. Famous examples of the latter solution date from the days of colonialism: the "Caprivi-Zipfel", which linked and still links South-West Africa with the river Zambesi, the "Kongo-" and "Ubanghi-Zipfel", which since 1911 had given the German Cameroons access to those rivers but which were returned to France in 1919, and the "Entenschnabel" between the rivers Logone and Shari, which linked the African possessions, first of Germany and since 1911 of France, with Lake Chad. Curiously enough, these colonial remains still dominate the African scene.

1°. Leases of the African type were aimed at supplementing, or at remedying certain untoward consequences of, colonial territorial adjustments or delimitations of spheres of influence between colonizing Powers. They operated in an area of the world so sensitive politically that they were sometimes capable of causing strained relations between the Great Powers. This was the case, for example, of Germany, on the one hand, and Great Britain and the Congo Free State, on the other, in 1894, as a consequence of the fact that the latter two States had granted each other, by their Agreement of 12 May 1894 (Martens, N.R.G.², XX, 805), the lease of certain areas within their respective zones of influence in East and Central Africa. The British lease to the Congo Free State, regulated in Article 2, was to extend over a vast area: starting from the western bank of Lake Albert, its boundary would run along the watershed between the Nile and the Congo to the parallel of long. 25° East, along this to its intersection with the meridian of lat. 10° South and from there back to Lake Albert through the thalweg of the Nile. This lease was curious in that (a) its life-time was bound up with the life of King Leopold II, after whose demise it would only remain valid for a reduced area, and (b) a special flag should be flown in the area as a token of its exceptional legal status.—The dispute arose, however, from the other lease, that granted, inversely, by the Congo Free State to Great Britain— regulated in Article 3—and concerning a strip of territory 25 kilometres in breadth, extending from the most northerly port on Lake Tanganyika to the southernmost point of Lake Albert (Edward). Germany considered this Article as being at variance with the commitments entered into by the Congo Free State towards herself in their treaty of 8 No-

668), of the Chin-kiang concession by an exchange of notes of 31 October 1929 (*ibid.*, XXII, 13), of the A-moy concession by an exchange of notes of 17 September 1930 (*ibid.*, XXIII, 705), etc. The International Settlement at Shang-hai also was returned to the jurisdiction of China in virtue of an agreement of 17 February 1930 (*ibid.*, XXIII, 220), prolonged on 8/12 February 1933 (*ibid.*, XXVII, 660).

vember 1884 (*ibid.*, N.R.G.², X, 367) wherein the boundaries between the German possessions and the Congo Free State in East and Central Africa had been fixed, and asserted, in my opinion incorrectly, that the strip of land concerned could not be handed over to Great Britain without her consent. The diplomatic correspondence concerning this dispute is inserted in Martens, N.R.G.², XXI, 531 *et seq.* The result of Germany's protests to the Congo Government was, however, that the latter requested the British Government for their consent—which was granted—to the cancellation of Article 3 (comp. the declaration of 22 June 1894, *ibid.*, N.R.G.², XX, 809). The other lease, established by Article 2, remained in force for nearly twelve years until it was in the event also annulled by Article 1 of a treaty of 9 May 1906 (*ibid.*, XXXIV, 387 = XXXV, 454), but even then King Leopold was still allowed to continue to occupy the so-called Lado enclave during his reign on the understanding that after his death or the end of his reign it was to be returned to the Government of the Sudan.

Other examples of African leases were those granted:

by Great Britain to France by Article 8 of their Convention of 14 June 1898 (*ibid.*, N.R.G.², XXIX, 116 = XXX, 249), for the objects and on the conditions specified in an annexed form of a thirty years' lease, as respects two pieces of ground, one on the right bank of the Niger between Leaba and its junction with the Moussa (Moshi) and the other on one of the mouths of the Niger, with an additional agreement of 21 March 1899 (*ibid.*, N.R.G.², XXIX, 387 = XXX, 264);

by Ethiopia to the British Government and the Sudan on 15 May 1902 (*ibid.*, N.R.G.³, II, 826) for the establishment of a commercial (non military) station on the Baro river; this grant forms in its wording an intermediate form between a lease and the type of grant dealt with in section 3 *infra*, because the territories are said, in Article 4, to be "*leased* to the Government of the Soudan to be *administered and occupied* as a commercial station so long as the Soudan is under the Anglo-Egyptian Government";

by Great Britain to Italy by an exchange of notes of 13 January 1905 (*ibid.*, N.R.G.², XXXIV, 505) in respect of a strip of land on the east side of Kismayu in the British East Africa Protectorate (now Kenya), for the erection of a bonded warehouse and a pier, with a corresponding right of way to the river Juba, and a conditional right for Italy to land troops at Kismayu *en route* to the Italian sphere. This Benadir bail was to remain in force for 33, 66 or 99 years according to the amount spent by Italy on the erection of the pier and buildings.

2° Leases of the Chinese type were successively established by treaties between China and

Germany on 6 March 1898 in respect of the bay of Kiao-Chou in the province of Shantoung (*ibid.*, N.R.G.², XXX, 326);

Russia on 27 March 1898 in respect of Port Arthur and Ta-lien-wan (ALBIN, *Les grands traités politiques* (Paris, 1912), p. 476);

France on 9/10 April 1898 in respect of Kwang-chou-wan in the province of Kwangtoung (G.E.P. HERSLET, *China Treaties* (London, 1908), vol. 1, p. 327);

Great Britain on 1 July 1898 in respect of the bay of Wei-hai-wei (Martens, N.R.G.², XXXII, 90), together with an extension of insular Hong-kong with an area on the opposite mainland Kow-loon (*ibid.*, XXXII, 89).

Since the contents and the fate of these four leases have differed, I will insert some details regarding each of them.

The German lease was described in Article 2 of the treaty concerned as the "pachtweise Überlassung" of both sides of the entrance of the bay of Kiao-chou (in the province of Shantung), encompassing pursuant to Article 3 the northern and the southern tongue of land, the whole surface of the bay up to the highest water level, two islands in the bay and all islands in the sea located in front of it. The lease was to be for 99 years and was subject to a number of additional stipulations, such as: Germany's undertaking to build fortifications for the defence of the bay, to install the necessary seamarks, and not to re-lease the territory to any other Power; and China's undertaking to place another area at Germany's disposal should her partner wish to restore the Kiao-Chou region to her in the future. The lease was moreover accompanied by an undertaking by China (Article 1) to allow the passage of German troops through the territory and not to take any action without the previous consent of Germany in a zone of 50 kilometres around the bay at high water level, under the express reservation, however, by the Emperor of China of all rights of sovereignty there. The most characteristic clause of this type of lease convention was the stipulation in Article 3 to the effect that the Imperial Chinese Government should not, during the time of the lease, exercise sovereign rights *(Hoheitsrechte)* in the leased area, but should delegate the exercise thereof to Germany. This clause, typical for the new type of international lease, has given rise to very divergent theoretical constructions of the rights thus acquired by the lease. Whereas some writers—VON LISZT, *Das Völkerrecht, systematisch dargestellt*, 6th ed. (Berlin, 1910), p. 99; MERIGNHAC, *Traité de droit public international* (Paris, 1905), I, 393; STRUPP, *Urkunden zur Geschichte des Völkerrechts* (Gotha, 1911), II, 128, note—listed this type of international agreement under the modes of acquisition of territory, as being nothing else than a "disguised cession", others—REHM, *Allgemeine Staatslehre* (Freiburg i.B., 1899), pp. 81-82, 142;[6] ULLMANN, *Völkerrecht* (Tübingen, 1908), p. 298;

6. "Denn davon kann keine Rede sein, dass das Deutsche Reich dieses an der Kiautschou-Bucht belegene Gebiet in seine Gebietshoheit brachte und dieses Gebiet somit deutsches Gebiet wäre. Wohl sagt der kaiserliche Erlass vom 27.

JELLINEK in *Deutsche Juristenzeitung* 1879 (III), p. 253—maintained that it was a particular form of the establishment of exceptional rights of one State on territory which remained under the territorial sovereignty of the other. The truth of the matter would seem to be that such leases must initially certainly be deemed to be *jura in territorio alieno* and not to imply any cession of territorial sovereignty by the lessor to the lessee State, but that, the longer the situation thus created lasts—and a term of 99 years is significant in this regard—, the more certainly the "lease" threatens to be gradually transformed (novated) into full sovereignty. However, in the case of the bay of Kiao-Chou the opponents of the theory of a "disguised cession" were proved right by the course of political developments: after the first World War Germany was compelled, in Article 156 of the Peace Treaty of Versailles, to renounce all her rights, title and privileges—*inter alia* those concerning the territory of Kiao-Chou—which she had acquired in virtue of her treaty with China of 6 March 1898. This renunciation was, however, to be made in favour of Japan which thus succeeded in the lease, but in her turn only temporarily as the whole system of leases of Chinese territory was in the event liquidated, pursuant to the resolutions of the Conference of 1921-1922 on the Limitation of Naval Armaments and related problems (see below, p. 404).

The Russian lease (27 March 1898, *A.J.I.L.* 1910 (4), Suppl., p. 289) was of still shorter duration. The original lease of 1898, said to be necessary for the protection of the Russian fleet in the waters of Northern China, was expressly stated not to prejudice the sovereignty of China over the territory concerned, was to last for 25 years, subject to further prolongation in common accord, and was supplemented by an undertaking by China not to send troops into an adjacent zone to the north of the territory leased without the previous consent of Russia. The two ports of Port Arthur and Ta-lien-wan which Russia would be entitled (not obliged) to fortify, were reserved for the exclusive use of Russian and Chinese warships.—Russia was, however, already compelled, as a consequence of her defeat in her war with Japan, by Article 5 of the Peace Treaty of Portsmouth of 5 September 1905 (Martens, N.R.G.², XXXIII, 3) in her turn to "transfer and assign to the Imperial Government of Japan, with the consent of the Government of China"—a characteristic passage for an exact legal valuation of the relationship in respect of the leased territory—"the lease of Port Arthur, Ta-lien-wan and adjacent territory

April 1898, das betreffende Gebiet sei "in deutschen Besitz übergegangen", allein unter diesem Besitz ist nicht Besitz zu eigener Herrschaft, Eigenbesitz, sondern nur Besitz zur Ausübung fremder Herrschaft, Verwaltungs- und Nutzbesitz, zu verstehen ... [Pursuant to Articles 2 and 3 of the 1898 treaty, China has] keineswegs verzichtet auf die Hoheitsrechte über dieses Gebiet selbst. Dasselbe ist also chinesisches Staatsgebiet geblieben".

and territorial waters (including the new Russian-built town of Dalni) and all rights, privileges and concessions connected with or forming part of such lease", the Parties mutually engaging to obtain the required consent of the Chinese Government. This aim was achieved by the treaty of 22 December 1905 between Japan and China (*ibid.*, N.R.G.², XXXIV, 748), whereby the latter consented to all the transactions and assignments made by Russia to Japan.—This, originally Russian, lease of Japan in turn ended, simultaneously with her, originally German, lease after the Naval Armaments Conference of Washington of 1921-1922 (see below p. 404). These events were, however, partially reversed after World War II by a Sino-Soviet treaty of 14 August 1945, providing for the use of Port Arthur by China and the Soviet Union jointly for a period of 30 years (*U.N.T.S.*, vol. 10, p. 300).

The French lease (27 May 1898; *A.J.I.L.*, Suppl. 1910 (4), p. 293) related to the bay of Kwang-chou-wan in the province of Kwang-toun, an advanced post for the protection of the French protectorate of Ton-kin east of the Lei-chou peninsula. It was to last for 99 years and was accompanied by a few supplementary stipulations, *inter alia*, forbidding cession to any other State, even on lease, of any territory in Yun-nan, Kwang-si or Kwang-toun, or the Chinese island of Hai-nan off the coast (supplemented by some further clauses relating to the construction of railway lines). This French lease was of the same legal nature as the others and was liquidated with them as an aftermath of the Conference on the Limitation of Naval Armaments and related subjects of 1921-1922 at Washington.

The British lease of Wei-hai-wei (1 July 1898; *ibid.*, p. 297 and Martens, N.R.G.², XXXII, 90) in the province of Shan-toung, and the adjacent waters, said to be agreed in order to provide Great Britain with a suitable naval harbour in North China, and for the better protection of British commerce in the neighbouring seas, was to be for an indeterminate period, namely, for so long as Port Arthur should remain under the occupation of Russia. It was to comprise, with the bay proper, all the islands therein and the island of Liou-kung, and a belt of land, ten English miles wide along the entire coastline of the bay. Great Britain was to have sole jurisdiction in that area, except for the walled city of Wei-hai-wei, within which Chinese officials should continue to exercise jurisdiction, subject to naval and military requirements for the defence of the area. In addition, Great Britain was granted the right to erect fortifications, station troops or take any other measures necessary for defensive purposes at any points on or near the coast of the region east of the meridian 121° 41¹ east of Greenwich, on the condition that within that zone Chinese administration would not be interfered with, though no troops other than Chinese or British should be allowed therein. A characteristic clause of this lease was that Chinese vessels of war, "whether neutral or otherwise", would retain the right to use the waters leased. —Already a few weeks earlier, by a Convention of 9 June 1898 (Martens, N.R.G.[2], XXXII, 89), the territory of Hong-kong—which had itself come under the full territorial sovereignty of Great Britain in virtue of the Sino-British agreement of January 1841, somewhat peculiar in form[7] (*ibid.*, N.R.G.[1], II, 1, 6 and 7)—had been enlarged by an additional area, including the waters of Mirs Bay and Deep Bay, this time under a lease for 99 years, with corresponding clauses relating to Chinese jurisdiction within the city of Kow-loon and to the admission of Chinese warships to the bays.

The regulations summarized above were, as far as the relations between China and her partners France, Great Britain and Japan were concerned, and with the exception of that regarding the extension of Hong-kong territory in 1898, since rescinded pursuant to a mutual understanding by the Great Maritime Powers at their Conference of Washington of December 1921/February 1922 to return the territories concerned to China: Article 1 of the collective treaty of 6 February 1922 (*ibid.*, N.R.G.[3], XIV, 323), followed by, *inter alia*, a bilateral treaty between Great Britain and China of 18 April 1930 concerning Wei-hai-wei (*ibid.*, XXIII, 698), formally restituted to China on 1 October 1930.

The Portuguese territory of Macão has a different origin and a different legal status. It was already acquired by the Portuguese in 1557 on the condition of an annual payment of 500 taels, which were indeed duly paid until 1848. In 1845 the ports of the town were declared free ports by the Queen of Portugal (*ibid.*, N.R.G.[1], VIII, 613). In a detailed treaty of 13 August 1862 (*ibid.*, XVII[2], 205) Sino-Portuguese relations in general were put on a new basis, including those "entre le gouvernement de la ville de Macão (autrefois province de Canton) et les autorités chinoises" (Article 2), but it was only in 1887 that the "perpetual occupation and government of Macau and its dependencies by Portugal, as any other Portuguese possession" was confirmed by China, subject to an engagement by Portugal never to alienate Macão and dependencies without agreement with China: Articles 2 and 3 of the preliminary protocol of Lisbon of 26 March 1887 (*ibid.*, N.R.G.[2], XVIII, 635) and of the Treaty of Peking of 1 December 1887 (*ibid.*, XVIII, 787).

7. A circular of the British plenipotentiary in China, Charles Elliot of 20 January 1841 mentions the conclusion of preliminary arrangements between the Imperial Chinese Commissioner and himself to the effect that the island and the port of Hong-kong were ceded to the British Crown. A proclamation of that same Commissioner of 29 January 1841, issued from H.M.'s *Wellesley*, stated that the island had been ceded to the British Crown by an Act sealed by the Imperial Minister and High Commissioner Keshen. And the events were concluded by a common proclamation by the British Commander-in-chief Bremer and Commissioner Elliot of 1 February 1841 to the inhabitants of Hong-kong that they were now subjects of the Queen of England.

3°. Sometimes recourse was had to international leases with the object of constructing roads, railways, canals, or telegraph- or telephone lines across foreign territory, without the acquisition of the formal territorial sovereignty over the strip of land needed for that purpose. Neither was it always the legal form of a lease which was chosen: thus the area needed for the construction, maintenance, operation, sanitation and protection of the Panama Canal was in 1903 conceded to the United States neither in the form of a cession, nor in that of a lease or a servitude, but in that of a "grant in perpetuity of the use, occupation and control" thereof. Comp. on this subject Chapter II, Annex, section 3 above, pp. 235 *et seq.*

Formal leases of this type—side by side with servitudes—were established *e.g.*, in Africa by Germany and France in Article 8 of their Convention of 4 November 1911 relative to their possessions in Equatorial Africa (Martens, N.R.G.³, VI, 328) in respect of an area along the rivers Bénoué and Mayo Kébi and in the direction of the Logone. This lease was intended to enable France to establish supply posts and storehouses destined to constitute a *route d'étapes*. The Convention was complemented by a detailed draft-lease contract, which has given rise to doctrinal discussion concerning its legal nature. Whereas some authors regarded this agreement as a simple lease, others qualified it as a clear limitation of German sovereignty *quoad usum*, or were even inclined to construe its terms as implying a disguised cession.

> The lease was to last for 99 years, for a nominal rent of one franc *per annum*. The lease areas remained subject to the laws of the German Cameroons. Elaborate provisions dealt with such subjects as: the specific purposes of the lease, limitations upon durable inhabitation of the zone, the fencing-in of its area, import restrictions, the erection of buildings, possible sub-leases, and an arbitration procedure.

4°. Other leases serve(d) the purpose of providing enclaved States, or States otherwise cut off from a particular seacoast, with a free zone in a foreign port. To this category belonged, for example:

the lease by Germany to the Czechoslovak State, for a period of 99 years, of areas in the ports of Hamburg and Stettin, which were placed under the general regime of free zones (Article 363 of the Peace Treaty of Versailles of 9 June 1919, further detailed in Article 364);

the lease by Italy to Czechoslovakia of a similar zone in the port of Trieste (treaty of 23 March 1921, *ibid.*, N.R.G.³, XXXIII, 564);

corresponding leases by Greece to Bulgaria—"in perpetuity"—in the port of Dedéagach, treaty of Sèvres between the Allied Powers and Greece of 10 August 1920 relative to Thrace (*ibid.*, N.R.G.³, XII, 779), Article 5, and to the Serb-Croat-Slovene State in the port of Saloniki (treaty of 10 May 1923, *ibid.*, XXI, 691) with subsequent protocols of 11 October 1928 and 17 March 1929 (*ibid.*, N.R.G.³, XXI, 708 and 710).

Certain clauses in the Convention of 9 November 1920 between Poland and the Free City of Danzig (*ibid.*, XIV, 45)—Articles 25 (3) and 30— are also suggestive of leases for public purposes.

A very peculiar type of lease was that, granted by Romania to the Serb-Croat-Slovene State by their treaty of 4 June 1927 (*ibid.*, XXXVI, 804) in respect of a strip of territory in the Banate of Temesvar (= Timi-şoara). After the boundary line between the two States in the Banate had been determined by their treaty of 24 November 1923 (*ibid.*, XVII, 342), Romania, pursuant to a *procès-verbal* of 13 June 1926, formally (retro-)ceded to the Serb-Croat-Slovene State in sovereignty a strip of land allotted to her in 1922, but at the same time in actual fact received it back from the Serb-Croat-Slovene State on lease for a term of 99 years, to be automatically renewed for another period of 99 years, save for denunciation six months prior to its expiry. According to the text of the 1927 treaty the Serb-Croat-Slovene State "reconnaît au Royaume de Roumanie la libre et entière disposition du terrain ainsi cédé et lui transmet de fait l'exercice de la souveraineté sur ce territoire, avec la responsabilité qui en découle",—a singular instance of shadow boxing in the field of international law.

Another isolated case occurred in April 1920 when India granted to France the lease of the French Loge at Balasore (HERTSLET's *Commercial Treaties*, XXX, p. 227).

5°. Various other leases, scattered all over the world, have been resorted to, in particular to secure military, naval or air bases on foreign territory. See for example the following cases of this type:

the Cuban lease of naval and whaling stations to the U.S.A. under two agreements of 16/23 February and 2 July 1903 (Martens, N.R.G.², XXXIV, 338, 340) in connection with Article 7 of the treaty of 22 May 1903 (*ibid.*, XXXII, 79). As appears from the agreement of 16/23 February 1903, this lease, granted by Cuba in accordance with the American Act of Congress of 2 March 1901 and Article VII of an Appendix to the Constitution of the Republic of Cuba of 21 February 1901, adopted by its Constitutional Convention on 12 June 1901 and again embraced by its Constitution of 20 May 1902 (cited in the preamble of the treaty of 22 May 1903), originally encompassed the areas of Guantánamo on the south coast and of Bahía Honda in the northwestern part of the island, and was granted "for the time required for the purposes of coaling and naval stations", and for those only. The legal contents of the lease were described in Article III of the agreement of 16/23 February 1903 as follows:

"While on the one hand the United States recognize the continuance of the ultimate sovereignty of the Republic of Cuba over the above described

406

areas of land and water, on the other hand the Republic of Cuba consents that during the period of the occupation by the United States of said area under the terms of this agreement the United States shall exercise complete jurisdiction and control over and within said areas with the right to acquire (under conditions to be hereafter agreed upon by the two Governments) for the public purposes of the United States any land or other property therein by purchase or by exercise of eminent domain with full compensation to the owners thereof".

The additional agreement of 2 July 1903 laid down some further details, *inter alia*, the undertaking of the U.S.A. to pay to Cuba for this lease the annual sum of $ 2.000 in gold coin of the United States.—The treaty of 22 May 1903 was revised by that of 29 May 1934 (Martens, N.R.G.³, XXIX, 326) by which the lease was limited to the bay of Guantánamo and surroundings.

The Finnish lease of the peninsula of Hangö to the U.S.S.R. under the Soviet-Finnish Peace Treaty of 12 March 1940 (*ibid.*, N.R.G.³, XXXVIII, 323) was, in accordance with the Armistice Agreement of 19 September 1944 (*A.J.I.L.* 1945 (39), suppl., p. 85), renounced by the Soviet Union by Article 4 of the Finnish Peace Treaty of Paris of 10 February 1947 (*U.N.T.S.*, vol. 48, p. 203), in order to be replaced by a lease of the use and administration of territory and waters for the establishment of a Soviet naval base in the area of Porkkala-Udd. This new lease included the use of the railways, waterways, roads and air routes necessary for the transport of personnel and freight dispatched from the Soviet Union to the base and the right of unimpeded use of all forms of communication. It was to be for 50 years at an annual rent payable by the Soviet Union of 5.000.000 Finnish marks. The Porkkala Peninsula was, however, given back to Finland by the treaty of 19 September 1955 (*U.N.T.S.*, vol. 226, p. 187). See Whiteman, vol. 3, pp. 165 *et seq.*

The lease of naval and air bases in Newfoundland, Bermuda, Jamaica, St. Lucia, Antigua, Trinidad and British Guiana, granted by Great Britain to the United States by a treaty of 27 March 1941 (Martens, N.R.G.³, XXXIX, 561), was to last for 99 years. It gave the lessee only a few limited rights of jurisdiction, in particular against treason and espionage (arrests for which need the assent of the lessor), but it did not include any further renunciation of sovereign rights or the exercise thereof. The jurisdiction clauses were modified in 1950 (*A.J.I.L.* 1951 (45), suppl., p. 97). A completely new treaty of 10 February 1961 has abrogated the treaties of 1941 and 1950; most bases were given back to the islands (*U.N.T.S.*, vol. 409, p. 67).

The Portuguese lease of an air base on the Açores, indirectly granted to the United States by an Anglo-Portuguese treaty of 17 August 1943 (*B.F.S.P.*, vol. 146, p. 447), was to last for an undeterminate period of years (it ended in 1946); that of a Polaris submarine base at Roda near Cadiz by Spain to the United States by a treaty of 26 September 1953

(*U.N.T.S.*, vol. 207, p. 83) for a period of 10 years, but the latter was recently (June 1969) prolonged in Washington for a period of two more years.

The legal fate of such bases became more often than not precarious in cases in which they had originally been established in common accord between a western Power and a young independent State just emerged from its former colonial status to independence. One has only to call in mind the leases of bases in Morocco to the United States, of the naval base of Bizerta in Tunisia and of that of Mers-el-Kebir in Algeria to France. They were all later given up, comp. the following data:

U.S.A. bases in Morocco, given up 16 December 1963 (see *Documents on American foreign policy* 1959, p. 1107, and 1963, p. 639; and *R.G.D.I.P.* 1964 (68), p. 513);

French naval base in Bizerta (see article by Ch. Debbasch, *La base militaire de Bizerte* in *A.F.D.I.* 1961 (VII), pp. 870-903);

United States and British bases in Libya, request for evacuation, 15 June 1967 (original treaties of respectively 9 September 1951—until 1971—and 29 July 1953—until 1973), eventually promised, November 1969;

French bases in Algeria (Colomb-Béchar, Reggane, Mers-el-Kébir), evacuation in 1967-1968, although the agreements of Evian (*R.G.D.I.P.* 1962 (66), pp. 686 *et seq.*) permitted the use of Mers-el-Kébir until 1977 (see *R.G.D.I.P.* 1967 (71), p. 1053).

Section 3. OCCUPATION AND ADMINISTRATION

The two best known historical examples of this particular type of *jus in territorio alieno*, in German legal literature sometimes adequately called *Verwaltungscession*, date from the days of the Congress of Berlin of 1878 and relate to Bosnia-Herzegovina (1878-1908) and Cyprus (1878-1914).

Turkish Bosnia-Herzegovina, with the exception of the sandjak of Novi-Bazar,[8] was placed under a newly invented[9] regime of "occupation and administration" by the Dual Monarchy of Austria-Hungary by Article 25 of the Treaty of Berlin of 13 July 1878 (Martens, N.R.G.[2], III, 449). The details of this territorial arrangement were agreed upon

8. Austria-Hungary only reserved the right to keep a garrison in this sandjak and to have at their disposal military and commercial roads all over this part of the old Bosnian vilayet. The details of these rights were laid down in Articles 7-10 and an Annex of the treaty of 21 April 1879, quoted in the text. The sandjak was, however, evacuated in 1909, when Bosnia and Herzegovina were annexed by the Dual Monarchy.

9. This regime had been hammered out as a possible solution by the Emperors of Russia and Austria in a conference at Reichstadt in 1876: no annexation, no cession; waiver of the capitulatory rights; special regulation of the status of the subjects.

by Austria-Hungary and the Ottoman Empire in their subsequent treaty of 21 April 1879 (*ibid.*, IV, 422), in the preamble of which it was expressly stated that "le fait de l'occupation de la Bosnie et de l'Herzégovine ne porte pas atteinte aux droits de souveraineté de Sa Majesté Impériale le Sultan sur ces provinces". The Dual Monarchy was to exercise the exclusive administration of the two provinces with the use of such Turkish officials, found in office, as should prove apt therefore and, in case of replacement, of natives from the areas. The name of the Sultan would continue to be pronounced in the public prayers of Moslims as in the past, and in so far as it was customary to fly the Ottoman flag from the minarets, this usage would be respected. The revenues from the provinces should be reserved exclusively for their own benefit and Turkish money should continue to have free circulation.—This artificial cession of Bosnia-Herzegovina in "occupation and administration" lasted for thirty years, but was in the event, as was to be expected, terminated as such: three *Handschreiben* (personal hand-writings) of Emperor Franz Joseph of 5 October 1908, addressed to his Ministers Von Beck, Von Aehrenthal and Burián (*ibid.*, N.R.G.[3], II, 657) announced his decision "die Rechte Seiner Souveränität auf Bosnien und die Herzegowina zu erstrecken und die für Sein Haus geltende Erbfolgeordnung auch für diese Länder in Wirksamkeit zu setzen...". This violation by Austria-Hungary of the treaties of 1878 and 1879, accompanied by another violation of the treaty of Berlin, *viz.*, Bulgaria's declaration of independence of the same date, 5 October 1908 (STRUPP, *Urkunden zur Geschichte des Völkerrechts* (Gotha, 1911) II, p. 12), provoked a major international crisis, which was however resolved by the conclusion of a new treaty between Austria-Hungary and the Ottoman Empire of 26 February 1909 (*ibid.*, N.R.G.[3], II, 661) whereby the Sublime Porte recognized in express terms the new state of affairs in Bosnia and Herzegovina, and by the ensuing exchange of diplomatic notes between the foreign Ambassadors in Vienna and the Austrian-Hungarian Government from 31 March to 19 April 1909, expressing the consent of the other Powers to the suppression of Article 25 of the Treaty of Berlin (*ibid.*, II, 6, 65; IV, 41 *et seq.*).

About the same time, but outside the deliberations of the Berlin Congress proper, in fact ten days before that Congress met, the Sultan had, in the general context of a defensive alliance between England and Turkey with the object of making the Ottoman territories in Asia secure against further conquests by Russia, consented to assign the island of Cyprus to be "occupied and administered" by Great Britain: Convention of 4 June 1878 (*ibid.*, N.R.G.[2], III, 272).[10] It was expressly laid down in

10. The status of Cyprus under this Convention was erroneously described as a British protectorate by the Anglo-Turkish Mixed Arbitral Tribunal in a judgment of 16 December 1929 (*A.D.* 1929-1930, Case No. 11).

Article VI of a subsequent Annex to that Convention, dated 1 July 1878 (*ibid.*, III, 274) that "if Russia restores to Turkey Kars and the other conquests made by her in Armenia during the last war, the Island of Cyprus will be evacuated by England, and the Convention of the 4th of June, 1878, will be at an end." As G. Noradounghian relates in his *Recueil d'actes internationaux de l'Empire Ottoman* (Paris, 1897-1903, III, 524) a message from the Queen of Great Britain on the occasion of the exchange of the instruments of ratification of the Convention, on 15 July 1878, declared that it was not intended in any way to impair the sovereign right of the Sultan.—The legal situation remained as it was established in 1878 until Cyprus was annexed by Great Britain by her *Cyprus (Annexation) Order* of 5 November 1914 (*B.F.S.P.*, vol. 108, p. 165) as soon as Turkey had entered the war on the side of the Central Powers against the Allied Powers. The preamble and the operative part of that Order combined showed a remarkable lack of logic in that they failed to infer from the outbreak of hostilities and the consequential lapse of all treaties in force between Great Britain and the Ottoman Empire the ineluctable conclusion that both the alliance of 1878 and the ancillary cession of Cyprus in "occupation and administration" to England in connexion therewith fell to the ground, but, on the contrary, proceeded by a curious *non sequitur* to the unilateral transformation of that regime into full sovereignty on grounds of expediency.[11] However this may be, Turkey was forced, first by Article 116 of the Peace Treaty of Sèvres of 10 August 1920 (Martens, N.R.G.³, XII, 664) and subsequently by Article 20 of that of Lausanne of 24 July 1923 (*ibid.*, XIII, 342), to acquiesce in Great Britain's unilateral action of 1914.

The particular international device of transfer into "occupation and administration", as initiated in Europe in 1878, was imitated in the following year in an arrangement made by the British Government with Afghanistan. In virtue of Article 9 (1) of their treaty of 26 May 1879 (*ibid.*, N.R.G.², IV, 536), by which Great Britain retained control over the Khyber and Michmi passes, certain Afghan districts were placed under a similar regime, which was emphatically declared not to imply their severance from the State of Afghanistan.

In 1892 the Sultan of Zanzibar ceded the Benadir coast of Somalia to

11. The text ran indeed as follows:

"Whereas, by virtue of the Convention of Defensive Alliance etc. ..., the Sultan assigned the Island of Cyprus to be occupied and administered by England ...;

And whereas by reason of the outbreak of war between His Majesty and His Imperial Majesty the Sultan the said Convention etc. ... have become annulled and are no longer of any force or effect;

And whereas it has, for the reasons hereinbefore appearing, *seemed expedient* [italics supplied] to His Majesty that the said Island should be annexed to and should form part of His Majesty's Dominions, etc. ..."

410

Italy in administration: treaty of 12 August 1892 (*ibid.*, N.R.G.², XXII, 298) with an additional agreement of 15 May 1893 (*ibid.*, 456), amended 1 September 1896. This transfer to foreign administration was only transformed into a genuine cession by a convention of 13 January 1905 (*ibid.*, XXXIV, 505).

The legal situation of the Peruvian provinces of Tacna and Arica between the Río Sama and the Río Camarones, which after the War of the Pacific were to remain in possession of Chile for a period of ten years in virtue of Article 3 of the Peace Treaty of Lima of 20 October 1883 (*ibid.*, N.R.G.², X, 191), can also be mentioned in this connection.

Quite a different expedient was Great Britain's consent to the temporary occupation by Italy, in case of military emergency, of Egyptian Kassala and the adjoining territory up to the river Atbara until the Egyptian Government should be in a position to reoccupy the district: Protocol of 15 April 1891 (reproduced no less than three times in Martens, N.R.G.², XVIII, *viz.*, pp. 176, 178 and 737). More such agreements have occurred elsewhere in the past.

Situations similar to those created by the transfer of a territory into "occupation and administration" by another State have been the result of, or have been planned by, other international agreements under differing verbal cloaks, *e.g.*, that concerning Smyrna pursuant to Article 69 of the (abortive) Turkish Peace Treaty of Sèvres of 10 August 1920 (*ibid.*, N.R.G.³, 664):

> "The city of Smyrna and the territory defined in Article 66 remain under Turkish sovereignty. Turkey however transfers to the Greek Government the exercise of her rights of sovereignty over the city of Smyrna and the said territory. In witness of such sovereignty the Turkish flag shall remain permanently hoisted over an outer fort in the town of Smyrna . . .".

On the complicated history of the Danube island Ada Kaleh ("fortress island"), also called New Orsova, 2 km below Orsova, which after various changes of fortune pursuant to the Austro-Turkish peace treaties of 1699 (Carlowitz), 1718 (Passarowitz), 1739 (Belgrade) and 1791 (Sistov), and a brief mention in Article 3 of the Russo-Turkish peace treaty of San Stefano of 3 March 1878 (*ibid.*, N.R.G.², III, 246), prescribing its evacuation and razing, was more or less "forgotten" in the final peace treaty of Berlin of 13 July 1878 (*ibid.*, III, 449), see: *R.G.D.I.P.* 1914 (21), pp. 379 *et seq.* Although legally having remained part of the Ottoman Empire until 1913, it was in the period 1878-1913 in actual fact occupied by the Dual Monarchy. The island, Romanian since 1919, is still exclusively inhabited by Turks, but is doomed to disappear because of the formation of a lake as a result of the hydraulic works at the Iron Gates (see p. 156).

In former centuries occupation of foreign towns and fortresses, for example for national security purposes, repeatedly occurred, often without any fixed term of duration. The Low Countries offer a number of instances thereof. Thus the Republic of the United Netherlands has for long periods maintained garrisons in:

the East-Frisian towns of Emden and Leer from 1595 to 1744.
The States General were often called upon to mediate in the disputes between the Count of East-Friesland, the town of Emden and the Estates (*Stände*) of East-Friesland. This resulted at the end of the 16th century in a Resolution of the States General—accepted by the parties in dispute and commonly referred to as the Treaty of Delfzijl—of 15 July 1595 (Dumont, V[1], 516), in virtue of which they would be entitled to station a garrison of the Republic in the towns of Emden and Leer. As the Emperor was reluctant to recognize the validity of such an agreement negotiated by a foreign State between powers subordinate to the Empire, he formally endorsed its contents in an Imperial Decree of 13 October 1597. These instruments were followed by a series of further documents, the concordat of 29 September 1599 (Rousset, *Suppl.*, II[1], 242), endorsed by a *Revers* of the town and Estates of 7 November 1599; the "pacification" of the States General between Count Enno and Emden, The Hague, 8 April 1603, ratified by the nobility and other Estates of East-Friesland on 29 November 1603 (*ibid.*, II[1], 251); a new Agreement of 1606, the Convention of Osterhusen of 1610, and another award of the States General of 1620. The right of guarantee and garrisoning, thus assumed by the United Netherlands in 1595, has survived during a century and a half without any serious challenge. It was, it is true, at the end of the 17th century (1686), when new controversies had arisen, disapproved in a Decree of the *Reichshofrat*, but by a compromise of 1693, reached through the mediation of the Electors of Brandenburg and Brunswick-Lüneburg and confirmed by the Emperor in 1699, the parties renounced all legal effects which might result for them from the Decree of 1688. The guarantee of law and order, supported by Netherlands garrisons, has continued to work and only ended after the conquest of East-Friesland by Prussia in 1744. The history of the termination of this old right of occupation and its financial liquidation in an agreement with Prussia has been described in detail by Rousset in his *Recueil*, vol. XIX, pp. 122-154;
certain fortress-towns on the Rhine in Germany—Rees, Wesel, Rheinberg—, whose occupation was occasioned by the War of the Jülich-Cleves Succession and lasted until 1672. This occupation had no other basis than a military intervention in the duchies in support of the hereditary claims of the margrave of Brandenburg against other pretenders. *Comp.* on this case Chapter V, section 1 below, pp. 434 *et seq.*;
the so-called "frontier- or barrier towns" in the southern Low Countries. They were, after the combined military action of the British and Netherlands forces in the southern provinces during the War of the Spanish Succession (1702-1713), destined at the Peace Congress of Utrecht to serve as a line of defence against a possible new French onslaught. Since these provinces were assigned at the Peace Congress to the House of Austria, it was this latter State which was loaded with this burden of military occupation. The arrangement lasted until the 1780's when the Emperor Joseph II made a clean sweep of this memento of old power politics. I will deal further with this important case of European concern under the heading of State servitudes *infra* in section 4, p. 420.

In other parts of Europe there have been similar instances of international agreements authorizing a State to keep one or more foreign towns or fortresses occupied in peace time, witness the garrison rights of France in the Imperial town of Philippsburg (in Baden, north of Karlsruhe) in virtue of Article 78 of the Peace Treaty of Münster of 24 October 1648 (Zeumer, *Quellensammlung*, 2nd. ed., II, no. 198, p. 434), and of Austria in the towns of Ferrara and Comacchio in the Papal States of northern Italy (Article 103 of the Final Act of Vienna of 9 June 1815, Martens, N.R., II, 379).

Section 4. STATE SERVITUDES

Why is it that the heated controversy over the existence or non-existence of State (or international) servitudes has never been finally solved? Is this problem inherent in the nature of the institution and does it arise from the irreconcilability of the varying doctrinal approaches to positive international law? Or is it the consequence of differing interpretations of the factual data provided by a somewhat disparate State practice and international case law? Or is the persisting theoretical skirmishing over this important problem of international law only due to a more innocent cause, *viz.*, an inadequate posing of the legal problem at issue?

What is the real meaning of a statement that international servitudes do, or do not "exist"? And why does the doctrine of international law attach so much importance to this problem: does the solution involve weighty legal consequences, or are we rather faced with a doctrinal "disputing for the love of it" as is so often the case where juridical discussions or inflated legal theories are concerned? Before entering into the merits of the problem one must therefore attempt to state clearly what precisely are the issues at stake.

If there is scope for singling out from the aggregate of international obligations of various kinds a special category called "international (or State) servitudes", there must be a practical reason for this and one must be thinking of a parallel with private law, for it cannot find its origin elsewhere, nor is it a case of spontaneous generation in the law of nations. It would hardly be sensible to advocate the introduction of the concept of servitudes into public international law from the domain of private law if the distinction made there between easements or servitudes and mere (contractual) obligations did not attribute to the former certain characteristics or legal effects which it is thought desirable to establish likewise for a specific group of inter-State engagements.

The concept itself, as a doctrinal notion, would seem to be of "continental" civil law—as opposed to Anglo-Saxon common law—origin and is, in the last resort, firmly rooted in Roman law. In what respects is a

413

"servitude" distinguishable from a (contractual) obligation? In the limitation of its possible legal contents? In the oppostion of a *praedium dominans* and a *praedium serviens*? In its "real", as opposed to "personal", nature? In its effects *erga omnes*? Or in its being equipped with a "droit de suite"? These various characteristics, which in part overlap each other or are different formulations for the same thing, imply the following traditional ideas and legal consequences. A servitude can never consist *in faciendo* (the most usual content of a contractual obligation), but only *in non faciendo* or *in patiendo*, *i.e.*, the burden resting on the owner of the *praedium serviens* consists of a duty to abstain from doing something, or to endure something, both being for the benefit of the owner of the *praedium dominans*. This legal relationship is "impersonal", "qualitative" in the sense of existing between the owners of the two *praedia* as such, so that neither the alienation of the *praedium serviens*, nor the dispossession of its owner, nor his demise affect it. As a result a servitude guarantees to the relationship a more durable existence, independent of the person momentarily entitled.

Is there, then, any justification or compelling reason for transplanting this notion of servitude into the domain of inter-State law and is it necessary, in order that the reasonableness of borrowing this legal concept from private law can be admitted, that the parallel should be complete and that all the essentials of a servitude in private law are mirrored in public international law? As far as the latter question is concerned, the answer must certainly be in the negative. The reasonableness of adopting the notion of servitudes also in inter-State relations is by no means dependent upon a complete identity between the two concepts, provided that there are sufficient similarities between them in their operation in either domain: essential characteristics of the international legal order may, in fact, exclude the transplantation of the corresponding notion of servitudes from the municipal legal order lock, stock and barrel into the body of inter-State law. Moreover, and this answers the first question posited above: the situation in this respect is not such that the traditional principles concerning servitudes in private law must be held to have been more or less automatically incorporated into public international law in their capacity of "general principles of (national) law recognised by civilized nations"—a juridical myth which many writers, in my opinion erroneously, have woven around the cryptic point 3 of paragraph 1 of Article 38 of the Statute of the Permanent Court of International Justice and its successor. It is rather that international lawyers are justified in elaborating in this field of inter-State relationships an independent doctrinal notion, with legal characteristics of its own, which they have chosen to call an "international (or State) servitude" because of its similarity with concepts developed from the days of Roman law onwards in the field of interindividual relationships concerning real property. Even if there is no compelling reason to borrow this *appellation* from private law—international lawyers might have preferred to call this legal phenomenon, for example, "durable burdens on State territory"—the *notion* which it stands for may have so firm a footing also in inter-State relations and may be an expression of juridical phenomena so clearly evidenced by international treaties that not only are there no reasonable grounds for objecting to the adoption of the legal concept of international servitudes, but its introduction into the doctrine of public international law may also be fully justified by the utility or even necessity to designate a typical institution of the law of nations by an appropriate name.

After having thus made a clean sweep of a number of existing prejudices against, or misapprehensions about, the use of the concept of servitudes in international legal relations, I must now turn to the central problem: does public international law actually accredit an institution closely comparable to servitudes under private law, and to what extent does it attribute to this kind of inter-State commitment legal consequences comparable to those attached to servitudes under private law?

There are good grounds for singling out at once from the field of State servitudes proper those charges on State territory which are universal in character and which are habitually not treated as servitudes under private law either, such as the rights and duties between owners of neighbouring estates in general. Such legal relationships do not need any specific act in law to be brought into being: they simply spring from the mere fact of individuals or States living together in a legal order and are, therefore, universal in character *ex lege*. Just as in private law between owners of neighbouring plots of land (the duty not to obstruct the natural flow of water downwards, to refrain from polluting a river or the air by infecting refuse or fumes, to grant access to and exit from enclaved estates, and so on), there exist, as between neighbouring States also, universal legal standards of behaviour. I may be allowed to refer to what I observe about this type of international obligation in Part VI of this publication. In order to merit qualification as a State servitude, a charge on State territory must, consequently, present the characteristics of an exceptional legal burden, deviating from the general legal situation of non-encumbrance,—it must, that is, have its origin in a specific international undertaking or, much more rarely, in a specific local custom. I eliminate, therefore, from the discussion rules of common vicinal law, the fundamental rules on freedom of navigation for riparian States on common rivers, freedom of transit under the Barcelona Convention of 1921, etc.

By singling out such general legal burdens on State territory, and assigning them for discussion to other chapters in the system of the law of nations the field of State servitudes is already narrowed considerably.

415

What remains, however, still presents a rather wide variety of burdens resting on State territory in favour of one or more foreign States. But there are reasons for narrowing the field still further.

Occasionally States are prevented from acting in a specific way with regard to the use of the whole of their territory, for example because of their compulsory permanent neutrality, or their obligatory demilitarization. Whereas treaty obligations of this type obtaining in respect of specified portions of the national territory can appropriately be listed among State servitudes, a supposed general burden must preferably be considered as a general curtailment of the State's sovereignty and thus find a place in the chapter on limitations exceptionally imposed upon the normal capacity of a State to perform juridical acts or to display territorial sovereignty as it thinks fit. I may refer here to section 2A of Chapter VI in Part II of this publication, pp. 455 *et seq.*

Moreover, the legal burden resting upon a portion of the State's territory must be a burden created by a genuine international treaty, and imply some form of diminution of the normal sovereign rights of a State (servitudes consisting *in non faciendo*), or of subjection to the exercise of some sovereign right by another State (servitudes consisting *in patiendo*). An international arrangement which does not bring about any such diminution or subjection cannot properly create a State servitude. There have been some international agreements of this type in Africa where a State granted to another the use of a strip of land alongside a river, for example, for transit purposes, without any accompanying sovereign rights attached to it, thus rather remaining within the orbit of private law.

There must certainly be a *praedium serviens*. Must there also necessarily be a *praedium dominans*? Or are there instances of international charges on specific portions of a State's territory that have been established not for the benefit of one or more individual States acting as a *praedium dominans*, but for the common weal of the international community, or at least of a wider region, or of a whole continent, and if so, would such a charge also qualify for recognition as a State servitude? There would seem to be in fact such charges on State territory, but this type of phenomenon is more remote from the usual type so that it is doubtful if there is still scope for the qualification thereof as State servitudes.

This latter observation leads on to a survey of the different doctrinal constructions put upon the occurrence of servitude-like phenomena as described above.

In addition to those international lawyers who accept the notion of State (or international) servitudes with all, or at least the main, legal implications thereof by analogy of those attached to them in private law, there are three other groups who construe the phenomena differently according to other theories.

416

Firstly: there is the theory that recognizes the existence of localized international obligations firmly linked with the territory concerned and forming an integral part of its status despite all political and territorial changes. In this theory there is no need for the designation of a *praedium dominans*, and nevertheless it explains the "real" and "successory" effects of the charge. I personally do not see much difference between the construction of the phenomena as a State servitude and that as a localized international obligation, which latter is usually treated in the doctrinal system under the heading of State succession in treaties.

Secondly: there is the theory that sees at least a number of such territorial charges as inherent parts of "European public law". According to those who propound it the treaties which created the obligation in question were intended by their authors to bring into being "objective law" ("droit objectif"), in contradistinction to "droits subjectifs", claims of right, thus creating true legal rules binding, in the first instance, on the contracting States, inclusive of the burdened State, but widening their purport at a later stage to all other States which might join the contracting parties in recognizing such a "rule of objective law". This doctrine, developed by the Committee of Lawyers in the Aaland Islands case of 1920, may well fit that particular case, and some similar cases, but ignores other bilateral treaties creating "servitudes", and consequently would seem to be incapable of explaining the latter cases, or would deny their legal existence. I quote, as an authoritative formulation of this theory the following passages from the report of the Committee of Lawyers, of 5 September 1920 (*L. of N., Off. Journal*, spec. suppl. No. 3, pp. 16-18):

> "(a) Sweden has put forward the theory that the Convention of 1856 definitely created a "real servitude" attaching to the territory of the Aaland Islands. A similar opinion was expressed by several eminent jurists. But the existence of international servitudes, in the true technical sense of the term, is not generally admitted; in particular, it was contested by the Court of Arbitration in its sentence of 7th September, 1910, in the case of the North Atlantic coast fisheries.
>
> Those who maintain that real servitudes, similar to those in civil law, can exist between States meet with the difficulty of naming a "*praedium dominans*" in relation to the "*praedium serviens*" represented by the Aaland Islands. At all events, Sweden can hardly be considered as the "*praedium dominans*", since it is neither a party to the Convention nor to the Treaty of 1856, nor is it even mentioned in these documents ...
>
> It is certain that the provisions agreed upon at Paris between the Powers and Russia went beyond purely Swedish interests. As a matter of fact there was a general European interest arising out of the strategic importance of the Aaland archipelago. The European character of the Convention can be clearly seen in the wording of the 5th point in the preliminary proceedings of the Treaty of 1856, which contains the words "The belligerent Powers reserve the right of creating, in the interests of Europe, special conditions ..." ...

The intention was to make the Convention concerning the demilitarization of the Aaland Islands into "European law" just as other provisions did in the case of the Treaty of 1856. Lord Clarendon, on his return from the Peace Congress, made a definite statement on this point in the House of Lords.

Indeed the Powers have, on many occasions since 1815, and especially at the conclusion of peace treaties, tried to create true objective law, a real political status the effects of which are felt outside the immediate circle of contracting parties ...

Thus admitting that the provisions of 1856 relating to the Aaland Islands bear the character of a settlement regulating European interests, it becomes obvious that such a settlement cannot be abolished or modified either by the acts of one particular Power or by conventions between some few of the Powers which signed the provisions of 1856, and are still parties to the Treaty".

Thirdly: there is the theory that admits the persistence of such "local" commitments throughout whatever changes in sovereignty the territory concerned may be subjected to in the course of the years, but only as between the Contracting Parties themselves. Since both France and Sardinia were parties to the treaty provisions which in 1815 created neutralized and customs-free zones around Geneva for the benefit of the Swiss Confederation, it was, pursuant to that theory, quite normal that the localized obligations remained in force when Sardinia ceded its possessions in Haute Savoie to France after the war of 1859 (Treaty of Zürich). This would seem to imply that, if not France, but, say, Spain had succeeded in the zones, there would have been no legal ground on which the local burden created earlier should have continued to exist. If this is indeed the implication of the theory (which perhaps was not intended by its defenders), then it must be rejected on the ground that all successor States must be held to succeed in local burdens assumed by their predecessors.

The Permanent Court has refrained from taking sides in the controversy over international servitudes and whittled down the dispute to a simple question of treaty construction.

Apart from the doctrinal aspects of the problem summarized above, some further survey of the actual or possible variants of State servitudes and of the legal implications of their existence is apposite.

I have already mentioned above the most famous historical instances of a State servitude, viz., those of the establishment of neutral and free zones around Geneva and of the demilitarization of the neutralized Åland Islands, which I personally have no objection whatsoever to classify as State servitudes. Other examples are many other demilitarizations or neutralizations, and the Netherlands mine servitude near Aachen.

When grouping the instances of territorial stipulations of this kind we can comfortably apply the classic distinction between servitudes consisting (i) *in patiendo* and those consisting (ii) *in non faciendo*. Among group (i) can be listed, *e.g.*, the international burden obliging the State concerned to allow (*a*) the passing of foreign troops across the national territory; (*b*) a temporary or lasting presence of foreign military, police or other civil authorities on it; (*c*) its use for varied specific purposes such as mining, fishing, water diversion, the establishment of means of communication, etc.; (*d*) the free use of a maritime port by another, especially an enclaved, foreign State. Among group (ii) mention can be made of the international obligation to abstain from (*a*) fortifying specific parts of the national territory; (*b*) maintaining armed forces, warships etc. therein; (*c*) levying import or export duties in specific areas; (*d*) alienating specific territories, etc. Examples of these various types of territorial burden are given below.

ad (i). Servitudes consisting *in patiendo*.

(*a*) *Transit by foreign troops*
on behalf of France over the roads and waterways connecting her territory with the French-garrisoned town of Philippsburg in Baden, north of Karlsruhe, in virtue of Article 78 of the Peace Treaty of Münster between France and the Empire of 24 October 1648 (Parry, vol. 1, pp. 296 and 341):

> "Patere etiam debebit Regi liber transitus per terras et aquas Imperii ad inducendos milites, commeatum et caetera omnia, quibus et quoties opus fuit";

on behalf of the communications between Saxony and Poland through Prussian Silesia: Article 10 of the Peace Treaty of Dresden of 25 December 1745 (Wenck, II, 194) and Article 9 of that of Hubertsburg of 15 February 1763 (Martens, R², I, 146);

France-Austrian Low Countries, Article 34 of the treaty of 16 May 1769 (*ibid.*, R², I, 661);

mutually on Santo Domingo, Article 8 of the Franco-Spanish treaty of 3 June 1777 (*ibid.*, R², II, 519);

on behalf of Austria-Hungary throughout the sandjak of Novi Bazar between Serbia and Montenegro, extending in a southeasterly direction, on the strength of Article 25 of the Peace Treaty of Berlin of 13 July 1878 (*ibid.*, N.R.G.², III, 449):

> "... l'Autriche-Hongrie se réserve le droit de tenir garnison et d'avoir des routes militaires ... sur toute l'étendue de cette partie de l'ancien vilayet de Bosnie",

and Articles 7-10 of the Agreement between Austria-Hungary and Turkey of 21 April 1879 (*ibid.*, IV, 422) laying down, *inter alia*, (Article 8) that

> "La présence des troupes de S.M. l'Empereur et Roi dans le sandjak de Novi-Bazar ne portera aucune entrave au fonctionnement des autorités,

administratives, judiciaires ou financières ottomanes de tout ordre, qui continuera à s'exercer, comme par le passé, sous les ordres exclusifs et directs de la Sublime Porte";

over certain rivers and possible future railways in Equatorial Africa, in virtue of mutual undertakings by France and Germany in Article 13 of their Convention of 4 November 1911 (*ibid.*, N.R.G.[3], V, 651).

(*b*) *Foreign garrisons*

in the so-called "barrier towns" in the southern Low Countries from 1713 to 1781, already mentioned above in section 3. The persisting military occupation of these towns by the States General during three quarters of a century has played a major rôle in European diplomacy since the War of the Spanish Succession.

> The final regulation of this occupation only took place by the Austro-Anglo-Netherlands treaty of Antwerp of 15 November 1715 (Dumont, VIII[1], 458; Rousset, *Recueil* I, 37). It had been preceded by two other, Anglo-Netherlands treaties of 29 October 1709 (Dumont, VIII[1], 243) and 30 January 1713 (*ibid.*, 322) which had different contents.
>
> (1709) Concluded for the fulfilment of the promise made to the States General by Article 5 of the Grand Alliance Treaty of The Hague of 7 September 1701 (Dumont, VIII[1], 89). The States General were to obtain possession of a number of fortified places in the then still Spanish Southern Low Countries as a barrier against France; the garrisons of the Republic would be paid from the regional revenues. Separate Articles held out a prospect of certain territorial acquisitions by the Republic, especially in Upper Guelder, and contained a promise of Netherlands support for the Protestant succession in Britain.
>
> (1713) Amending the earlier treaty to the effect of reducing the number of the contemplated barrier towns and dropping the promise concerning Upper Guelder because this had meanwhile been promised to Prussia.
>
> (1715) The final, this time tri-partite treaty of Antwerp, guaranteed by England, was to the following effect. The Republic undertook to transfer both the originally Spanish-held part of the Low Countries and the part ceded on this occasion by France to Austria, subject to the latter's engagement vis-à-vis the Netherlands and Great Britain to allow them to remain under Austrian sovereignty and never to cede them to France or any other Power. A force of 30.000 men was to be maintained in the country, for two thirds Austrian, for one third Netherlands. The Republic reserved to itself the right of maintaining exclusively Netherlands garrisons in Namur, Tournai, Menin, Furnes, Ypres, Warneton and the fortress of Knocke, and of sharing with Austria the garrisoning of Dendermonde.[12] The Republic was authorized to repair and fortify existing forts, but would require the consent of the Emperor for the erection of any new ones. In the case of enemy invasion the Republic would be empowered to occupy all the necessary forts and, in addition, to cut the necessary trenches and to operate the required inundations. Austria's contribution to the costs of maintenance of the troops of the Republic would amount to 1.250.000 Netherlands guilders, secured by a mortgage on the revenues of the Southern

---

12. Whereas the appointment of the governor of this town was reserved for the Emperor, he would be obliged to take an oath to the States General.

Netherlands. Additional clauses provided for the cession to the Republic of Venlo on the river Maas and a few other places in Upper-Guelder and for the maintenance of the existing tariff of import and export duties for ships and cargoes in the traffic between England and the Netherlands, on the one hand, and the Austrian Low Countries on the other, until this matter should be regulated by a treaty of commerce.[13]

The Barrier Treaty of 1715, which had also (in Article 17) laid down a detailed new frontier delimitation between the Austrian provinces and the Zeeland part of Flanders, diverging from an earlier one of 20 September 1664 (Dumont, VI[3], 25), was subsequently modified by a new treaty of 22 December 1718 (*ibid.*, VII[1], 551; Rousset, *Recueil*, I, 400), presented as an "explanation" of that of 1715: the boundary was altered once again; new provisions were laid down in respect of the existing mortgage and its extension, also as a security for the increasing arrears, and granted the States General a right of "real execution" on the pledges; etc.

The whole Barrier System collapsed in the last part of the 18th century, when the Emperor, in a note of 7 November 1781, abruptly notified the States-General of his decision to demolish the fortresses (Martens, R[2], III, 364) and the Republic could do nothing but acquiesce in the *fait accompli*;

in the neutralized provinces of Chablais and Faucigny and other Savoy territory north of Ugine, in virtue of Article 92 of the Final Act of the Congress of Vienna of 9 June 1815 (*ibid.*, N.R., II, 379):

"... toutes les fois que les puissances voisines de la Suisse se trouveront en état d'hostilité ouverte ou imminente, les troupes de S.M. le Roi de Sardaigne qui pourraient se trouver dans ces provinces, se retireront et pourront à cet effet passer par le Valais, si cela devient nécessaire; aucunes autres troupes armées d'aucune autre puissance ne pourront traverser ni stationner dans les provinces et territoires susdits, sauf celles que la Confédération Suisse jugerait à propos d'y placer; bien entendu que cet état de choses ne gêne en rien l'administration de ces pays, où les agents civils de S.M. le Roi de Sardaigne pourront aussi employer la garde municipale pour le maintien du bon ordre".

This famous servitude was, as a matter of course, transferred on the passive side by Sardinia to France in virtue of Article 2 of their treaty of cession, concluded in Turin on 24 March 1860 (*ibid.*, N.R.G.[1], XVI[2], 539), in the terms of which

"Il est également entendu que Sa Majesté le Roi de Sardaigne ne peut transférer les parties neutralisées de la Savoie qu'aux conditions auxquelles il les possède lui-même",

with the resulting conclusion that

"il appartiendra à Sa Majesté l'Empereur des Français de s'entendre à ce sujet, tant avec les puissances représentées au congrès de Vienne qu'avec la Confédération Helvétique ..."

The servitude was, however, abolished by Article 435 of the Peace Treaty of Versailles after World War I (1919) (with Annex *sub* I, 1°), in the terms of which

13. Austria later considered the whole Barrier Treaty as annulled on the ground that such a treaty of commerce was never concluded.

"The High Contracting Parties ... declare ... that the provisions of (the treaties of 1815) concerning the neutralized zone of Savoy ... are no longer consistent with present conditions",

and for that reason took note of the agreement reached between the two Governments

"for the abrogation of the stipulations relating to this zone which are and remain abrogated".

(c) *Various uses of foreign territory*

The Netherlands mining servitude under German soil near Kerkrade (Limburg) since 1815, comp. Chapter II, section 2 *supra*, p. 49;

the use of the Kunene falls in Portuguese Angola for the generation of electric power on behalf of neighbouring South West Africa in virtue of the Convention between Portugal and the Union of South Africa (as Mandatory) of 1 July 1926 (Martens, N.R.G.³, XXIII, 30);

the building or maintenance of telegraph lines or railways, *e.g.*, across British, respectively Portuguese zones of influence in Africa, Article XI (5) of the Convention of 11 June 1891 (*ibid.*, N.R.G.², XVIII, 185) and across German, respectively French possessions in Equatorial Africa, Articles 6 and 7 of the Convention of 4 November 1911 (*ibid.*, N.R.G.³, V, 651);

the construction and maintenance of oil pipelines, *e.g.*, from Iraq and Persia to Mediterranean ports, which was begun in the period of the Mandates System. See Articles 9-12 of the Anglo-French Memorandum of Agreement of San Remo of 24 April 1920 (*ibid.*, N.R.G.³, XII, 579): two separate pipelines through French spheres of influence;

the laying of cables for the transport of electricity *(houille blanche)* from one State across the territory of another: multilateral Convention of 9 December 1923 (Geneva) relating to the transmission in transit of electric power (*ibid.*, N.R.G.³, XIX, 276);

fishing rights on a foreign coast.

There have been cases in the past when two States mutually granted to their respective subjects the right to fish in their territorial sea. Comp. e.g. Article 3 of the Franco-Spanish Convention of 2 January 1768 (Martens, R², I, 479) "for the better understanding of Article 24 of their Family Pact of 15 August 1761":

"Les pêches sur les côtes de France et d'Espagne seront également communes aux deux nations, à condition que les Français et les Espagnols s'assujettiront respectivement dans les endroits où ils se détermineront de pêcher, aux lois, statuts et pragmatiques qui se trouveront établis pour les pêcheurs nationaux, conformément à ce qui a été décidé et prescrit par Sa Majesté Catholique dans ses ordonnances du 12 mai 1742, pour la pêche des tartanes françaises sur la côte et baie de Cadix, et du 27 janvier 1766, pour la pêche des côtes de Catalogne et de Provence."

The French *Compagnie royale d'Afrique* had a fishing privilege on the coasts of Tunis; it was restored in that privilege by Article 3 of the preliminary peace treaty between France and Tunis of 25 August and Article 2 of their definitive peace treaty of 13 September 1770 (*ibid.*, R², I, 700, 702).

On the other hand, France and the United States expressly mutually forbade under penalty of confiscation fishing by their respective subjects in the other's "harbours, bays, creeks, roadsteads, coasts and other places" under their sovereignty: treaty of 6 February 1778 (*ibid.*, R², II, 587), Article 9.

An asserted fishing servitude of old standing, localized on the coasts of Newfoundland, has in the beginning of this century given rise to international arbitral proceedings, centred, *inter alia*, on the question as to whether such a servitude implied the right of its holder to legislate with respect to the interests which it was designed to safeguard. This dispute had arisen between Great Britain and the United States, but was closely related to a much older one between France and Great Britain, which dates back to as early as 1713. This fishing servitude was later the object of a series of treaties of 1763, 1783, 1814, 1815, 1857 and 1904. The prolonged Franco-British controversies which arose on this subject had their roots in Article 13 of the Franco-British Peace Treaty of Utrecht of 11 April 1713 (Dumont, VIII¹, 339) in the terms of which the cession of Newfoundland by France to Great Britain was accompanied by the following stipulation:

"... Il ne leur [*i.e.*, to the King of France or his subjects] sera pas permis ... d'y [*i.e.*, on the island] établir aucune habitation en façon quelconque, si ce n'est des échafauts et cabanes nécessaires et usitées pour sécher le poisson, ni aborder dans ladite isle dans d'autres temps que celui qui est propre pour pêcher[14] et nécessaire pour sécher le poisson". (A further clause limited their right to fish and dry their catch to a well-defined area north of the line Pointe Riche-Cape of Bonavista.)

When after the Seven Years' War France lost her last American possessions in Canada to Great Britain, Article 5 of their Peace Treaty of Paris of 10 February 1763 (Martens, R², I, 104) disposed in favour of the French fishermen as follows:

"Les sujets de la France auront la liberté de la pêche et de la sécherie sur une partie des côtes de l'îsle de Terreneuve, telle qu'elle est spécifiée par l'article XIII du traité d'Utrecht, lequel Article est renouvellé et confirmé par le présent Traité", with the exception of the island of Cap Breton and the islands and coasts of the St. Lawrence Bay, with regard to which fishing would only be permitted at a distance of fifteen miles, respectively three miles from the coasts.

14. The word *pêcher* was a first and early cause of controversy, as the Newfoundlanders asserted that French fishers were not entitled to catch the valuable lobsters, which were said not to be "pêchés" (fished), but "capturés" (caught).

Certain new territorial adjustments were made in Article 5 of the Franco-British Peace Treaty of Versailles of 3 September 1783 (*ibid.*, R², III, 519): the limits of France's fishing rights were shifted from the coastline between Cape Bonavista and Pointe Riche to that extending from Cape St.Jean to Cape Raye:

> "Les pêcheurs français jouiront de la pêche[15] qui leur est assignée par le présent Article comme ils ont eu droit de jouir de celle qui leur est assignée par le Traité d'Utrecht".

As to the right of Frenchmen to fish on the grand bank of Newfoundland, on the coasts of this island and on the adjacent islands in the St.Lawrence Gulf the *status quo* of 1792 was after the Napoleonic wars restored by Article 13 of the first Peace Treaty of Paris of 30 May 1814 and Article 11 of the second of 20 November 1815 (*ibid.*, N.R., II, 1 and 682). Comp. already Article 15 of the Treaty of Amiens, 1802 (R², VII, 404).

After nearly a century and a half, on 14 January 1857, an elaborate new Convention in 21 Articles was concluded by France and England for the purpose of defining exactly the rights and obligations of their respective subjects (*ibid.*, N.R.G.¹, XVII¹, 202), to the following effect.

> (1) (8) A fishing monopoly for French fishermen between 5 April and 5 October in three precisely defined areas on the east, north and west coasts of Newfoundland.
> (2) (3) A concurrent right for English and French fishermen to fish on precisely defined parts of the west coast of Newfoundland and on the coasts of Labrador and Belle-île du Nord, and to dry and prepare their catch on the latter.
> (2) (4) (10) An exclusive right for the French, respectively the English to use specific parts of the coasts of Newfoundland for their trade.
> (11) (12) A restriction of the right to build fences or constructions in the respective reserved zones.
> (16) A concession for the French to cut wood for repairs.

A last convention in the series was that of 8 April 1904 (*ibid.*, N.R.G.², XXXII, 57), in section I of which France waived her fishing monopoly on the "Treaty shore", but retained the right for her citizens, on a footing of equality with English subjects, to fish and catch in the territorial waters bordering the north coast of Newfoundland between Cape Saint Jean and Cape Raye any kind of fish, included crustaceans (§§ 1-4). French fishermen who suffered damage as a consequence of this restriction of the treaty rights, would receive pecuniary compensation from the British Government (§ 3).[16]

---

15. The old controversy remained unsolved: did the *pêche* also extend to the catching of lobsters and other crustaceans? Moreover, did this clause grant the French fishermen a monopoly or only a concurrent right?
16. This compromise was part of a package deal by which France was granted in return territorial compensation elsewhere, *viz.*, in the form of certain fron-

Corresponding disputes had meanwhile developed between Great Britain and the new independent United States under Article III of their Peace Treaty of Paris of 3 September 1783 (Martens, R², III, 553), which defined the right of American fishermen to continue to fish and to dry and cure fish on the Grand bank and all the other banks of Newfoundland, in the Gulf of St.Lawrence, and in the unsettled bays, harbours and creeks of Nova Scotia, Magdalen islands, and Labrador. These Anglo-American disputes in the event led to an arbitration between the two States, agreed upon by a *compromis* of 27 January 1909 (*ibid.*, N.R.G.³, II, 742) and terminated by an award of the Permanent Court of Arbitration of 7 September 1910 (*ibid.*, IV, 89).

Among the many interesting questions raised in these proceedings[17] there was one which touched directly on the existence and content of the asserted fishing servitude.

In their third allegation regarding Question I submitted to the Arbitral Tribunal (see Martens, N.R.G.³, IV, at p. 93), the United States alleged

"that the liberties of fishery granted to the United States constitute(d) an international servitude in their favour over the territory of Great Britain, thereby involving a derogation from the sovereignty of Great Britain, the servient State, and that therefore Great Britain (was) deprived, by reason of the grant, of its independent right to regulate the fishery".

The Tribunal rejected this argument on various grounds, *inter alia*, because there was no evidence that the doctrine of international servitudes was one with which either American or British statesmen were conversant in 1818, no English publicists employing the term before 1818; because a servitude in international law predicates an express grant of a sovereign right and involves an analogy to the relation of a *praedium dominans* and a *praedium serviens*, whereas by the treaty of 1818 one State grants a liberty to fish which is not a sovereign right, but a purely economic right, to the inhabitants of another State; because the doctrine of international servitude in the sense which is now sought to be attributed to it originated in the peculiar and now obsolete conditions prevailing in the Holy Roman Empire of which the *domini terrae* were not fully sovereigns; because this doctrine being but little suited to the principle of sovereignty which prevails in States under a system of constitutional government such as Great Britain and the United States, and to the present international relations of sovereign States, has found little, if any, support from modern publicists. It could, therefore, in the general interest of the Community of Nations, and of the Parties to this treaty be

tier rectifications in Senegambia, to the east of the Niger and on Lake Chad, and of the cession to her of the group of the Los islands (Islas de los Idolos) vis-à-vis Conakry on the coast of French Guinea (§§ 4-8).

17. Relating, in particular, to the legal status and the closing-line of bays.

affirmed by the Tribunal only on the express evidence of an international contract.

The Tribunal, consequently, did not deny the possible existence of
State servitudes completely, but it rightly dismissed the American conclusion drawn from its asserted existence *in casu*, namely, that the servitude would imply a limitation in principle of British legislative power.
This latter conclusion was indeed unfounded, but such limitation, on
the other, hand, is not essential for the admission of a local burden as a
servitude.

(*d*) *Free transit via foreign seaports*

Servitudes of this type were established on behalf of Czechoslovakia,
Bulgaria, Bolivia and other enclaved countries and were often secured by
a concession in lease of a zone in the port concerned (see *supra*, section 2,
pp. 405 *et seq.*).

ad (ii) Servitudes consisting *in non faciendo*:

(*a*) and (*b*) On the frequent instances of demilitarization comp.
Chapter V, section 10 below;

(*c*) the customs-free zones south of Geneva, established by Article 79
of the Final Act of the Congress of Vienna of 9 June 1815 (Martens,
N.R.², II, 379):

> "... S.M. très-chrétienne [*i.e.*, France] consent à faire placer la ligne des
> douanes de manière à ce que la route qui conduit de Genève par Versoy en
> Suisse, soit en tout temps libre, et que ni les postes, ni les voyageurs, ni les
> transports de marchandises n'y soient inquiétés par aucune visite de douane,
> ni soumis à aucun droit",

a provision which was subsequently elaborated in a number of other
instruments of 1815 and 1816 and has ever since been observed during
more than a century.

The Peace Conference of Versailles has later (1919) opened the way
to an abolition of this regime of free customs zones, but it has done so in
a form which put France and Switzerland at loggerheads in the 1920's
and caused them to engage in a dogged juridical fight, which in the
course of three proceedings before the Permanent Court of International
Justice in 1929, 1930 and 1932 resulted in a legal victory for Switzerland.

> Unlike the case of the neutralized zones discussed above *sub* (i) (*b*), the
> Contracting Parties of the Peace Treaty of Versailles, though agreeing also
> with respect to the free zones of Upper Savoy and the Gex district that they
> "(were) no longer consistent with present conditions", in the same Article
> 435, with Annex *sub* I, 2°, nevertheless only laid down
> "that it is for France and Switzerland to come to an agreement together
> with a view to settling between themselves the status of these territories
> under such conditions as shall be considered suitable by both countries",
> thus clearly declining to make any statement to the effect that they had
> already legally lapsed.

426

The French Government nevertheless attempted to demonstrate that the territorial burdens, which it qualified in so many words as servitudes (see the passage quoted at p. 126 of the Judgment cited below: "la caducité des servitudes imposées à la France en 1815"), had already come to an end in principle. However, the arguments alleged to that effect by France found no favour in the eyes of the Court. While on its side abstaining from construing the territorial burdens as a State servitude, the Court held, on the contrary, in its Judgment of 7 June 1932 (*Publications P.C.I.J.*, series A/B, No. 46, p. 171),

> "that, as between France and Switzerland, Article 435, paragraph 2, of the Treaty of Versailles, with its Annexes, neither has abrogated nor is intended to lead to the abrogation of the provisions of the Protocol of the Conference of Paris of November 3rd, 1815, of the Treaty of Paris of November 20th, 1815, of the Treaty of Turin of March 16th, 1816, or of the Manifesto of the Sardinian Court of Accounts of September 9th, 1829, regarding the customs and economic régime of the free zones of Upper Savoy and the Pays de Gex."

Only further negotiations between France and Switzerland could, therefore, lead to an alteration or an abrogation of the existing servitude. The controversy has in the event been liquidated by a *Réglement sur les importations en Suisse des produits des zones franches de la Haute-Savoie et du Pays de Gex*, drawn up by three arbitrators on 1 December 1933 (Martens, N.R.G.[3], XXIX, 70), and later modified on 4 June 1937 (*ibid.*, XXXIV, 51) and 31 December 1938 (*ibid.*, XXXVI, 732). See *R.G.D. I.P.*, 1969 (73), p. 465.

(*d*) On the frequent cases in which alienation of any, or of a specific part of the national territory was prohibited in virtue of an international title comp. Chapter V, section 6 below, pp. 478 *et seq.*

Many examples of these various limitations of the free exercise of State sovereignty in particular areas of the national territory have already been, or will still be discussed elsewhere. That is why I do not go into each of them here, the less so because the justification of the qualification of an international burden on part of the national territory as a State servitude does not depend on its specific substantive content, but only on the legal implications or effects of its existence. Irrespective of what a particular territorial burden consists in, its characterization as an international servitude is, as I have already argued above, only justified theoretically, if the burden produces legal effects which offer a reasonable similarity with corresponding phenomena in the sphere of private law, in particular, its automatic transmission, or rather transition, to successor States, either on the side of the burdened State, or on that of the State(s) entitled to claim its observance. It may even make its effects felt, outside the case of a transfer of territorial sovereignty, in that of a temporary enemy occupation of the territory concerned. In how far this automatic transition really takes place in a given case of locally-bound international undertakings is a matter, *inter alia*, of treaty interpretation: the special features of inter-State relations caution against assuming such transition too readily. That is also the reason why my summary survey of local burdens must not be understood as claiming for each of them the irrefutable character of an international servitude.

Sometimes it is doubtful whether a particular burden on foreign territory is not rather of a private law nature, but protected by a treaty provision. Comp. Article 2 of the treaty of Lima between Chile and Peru of 3 June 1929 (*L.N.T.S.*, vol. 94, p. 402), by which Chile ceded to Peru all her rights to certain irrigation channels without prejudice to her sovereignty over those parts of the aqueducts concerned as might come within Chilean territory, over which, however, she granted to Peru a "perpetual and absolute easement". The original Spanish text has the following wording: "Respecto de ambos canales Chile constituye en la parte que atraviesan su territorio, el más amplio derecho de servidumbre a perpetuidad en favor del Perú." That easement (servidumbre) was to comprise the right to widen the channels, to change their course and to utilize all the waters that might be collected in their passage through Chilean territory, except those flowing into the river Lluta and those which were used in the Tacora sulphur mines.

Comp. further on this controversial subject my discussion of the problem of State succession in Part VII of this publication, and the following literature: I. CLAUSS, *Die Lehre von den Staatsdienstbarkeiten, historisch-dogmatisch entwickelt* (Tübingen, 1894); A. D. McNAIR, *So-called State servitudes* in *B.Y.I.L.* 1925 (VI), pp. 111-127; G. CRUSEN, *Les servitudes internationales* in *R.d.C.* 1928 (II), t. 22, pp. 1-79; Miss H. D. REID, *Les servitudes internationales* in the same *R.d.C.* 1933 (III), t. 45, pp. 1-73; X. VON MOOS, *Zur Lehre von den Staatsservituten*, acad. thesis Berne, 1933; Cl. MERCIER, *Les servitudes internationales*, acad. thesis Lausanne, 1939; F. A. VÁLI, *Servitudes of international law*, London, 1st ed. 1933, 2nd ed. 1958; and L. HERBST, *Staatensukzession und Staatsservituten*, acad. thesis Munich, 1960.

OTHER EXCEPTIONAL TERRITORIAL SITUATIONS

Section 1. CO-SOVEREIGNTY (CO-IMPERIUM)

This now rare phenomenon already betrays in its more usual name "condominium" its ancient origin and its association with old patrimonial concepts. Today it is better designated with the term co-imperium or co-sovereignty. This form of collective territorial supremacy over one and the same portion of the surface of the earth has its roots far in the past. It was already familiar to ancient Hellas where arbitrations between Greek cities have occurred which had precisely such situations for their subject, *e.g.*, the arbitration case between Corinth and Corcyra (now Corfú) concerning the Ionian island of Leukas (480 B.C.), in which the Athenian arbitrator Themistocles ruled that the island and town should remain a common colony. A dispute of 435 B.C. between the same cities concerning their common colony Epidamnos (now Durazzo) on the Illyrian coast could not be peaceably solved in the same manner: a proposal made by Corcyra to have the dispute decided either by a Peloponnesian town or by the oracle of Delphi was rejected by Corinth, and a war followed.[1]

Co-sovereignty was likewise in fairly frequent use during the centuries of European feudalism, or was employed by European dynastic houses as a device for holding together their ancient family possessions. Almost all those co-imperia of the past have in the course of time been liquidated, after having persisted for a very long time and having exhibited throughout their life the legal difficulties inherent in their existence. A very few have survived. Rare new instances of co-imperia have emerged during the last century, but they were nearly always of a temporary or transitional character and designed to be dissolved as soon as they had fulfilled their purpose.

Before attempting to illustrate this type of territorial supremacy by specified examples and grouping them in some logical order, I will make a few general remarks as an introduction.

---

1. A. RAEDER, *L'arbitrage chez les Hellènes* (Kristiania, 1912), pp. 24 and 33.

(*a*) The origin and the termination of a condominium. Its origin is far from uniform. It may have, or has had its inception in a dynastic pact, in an agreement between feudal rulers, in the judgment of a feudal court, in an international convention entered into with this particular purpose in view, in a judgment or award of an international tribunal, in a lack of clarity in a factual situation or treaty provision, in a conquest in common, or in the need of a provisional political solution of an otherwise insoluble problem. Its termination may be brought about by an express agreement between the co-sovereigns, by a coup-de-main by the stronger of the two partners, by a gradual factual dissolution of the original relationship of genuine co-sovereignty into two separate sovereignties each over part of the territory, by the emancipation of the object of the co-imperium as an independent political entity, or by its merger in a third State.

(*b*) The varying intentions of the authors of a co-imperium with respect to its duration. In earlier days it was often intended to be a durable relationship, for example, between a secular and an ecclesiastical ruler, or held indispensable as being the best possible or least dangerous solution of a controversy which presented lasting geopolitical features, or practised as a guarantee against the dismemberment of cohering possessions. It can, however, also be adopted as a merely provisional measure pending a final solution which is likely to emerge in the not too distant future, or it can even be nothing more than a purely technical juridical device designed to bridge a gap between an existing political situation and a new one already agreed upon, for example the provisional transfer by a vanquished State of part of its territory to its victors jointly, with the object of enabling them to effectuate the final juridical solution, such as the transformation of the territory concerned into a Free City.

(*c*) The internal regulation and delimitation of the respective public powers to be exercised by the co-sovereigns. The most normal arrangement is that those powers are equal, but special circumstances which led up to the establishment of the co-imperium may entail an unequal division of public authority. In the first case, the sovereign authority may be exerted by common organs set up on a footing of equality, or be conferred on either of the co-sovereigns alternately, or divided among different organs depending respectively on one and on the other co-sovereign. In the second case, the most singular variants of distribution of public authority are conceivable. Comp. on this internal division of governmental powers between the co-sovereigns below, pp. 440 *et seq.*

Condominia have occurred throughout the centuries. Very old examples are the legal condominium of the Count of Holland and the Bishop of Utrecht, established over Friesland by a judgment of the Emperor Frederick I (Barbarossa) of November 1065 (*Oorkondenboek van Holland en Zeeland tot het einde van het Hollandsche Huis (1299)*, edition

OBREEN (1937), pp. 90-92)[2] and the at least *de facto* condominium of the Counts of Holland and Flanders over the Zeeland islands of Walcheren and Beveland pursuant to their treaty of 7 March 1167[3] (*ibid.*, p. 94),[4] which remained in force until the islands concerned were ceded to Holland by the subsequent treaty of 18 March 1322 (?) (extract in Dumont, I[2], 52), by which the Count of Flanders renounced all homage which the Count of Hainault might owe him with regard to the islands of Zeeland and all claims to them, and the Count of Hainault in return relinquished in favour of the Count of Flanders all claims to the lands of Alost, Wass (Waes) and the Four Ambachten (Métiers).

The status of Andorra, a still existing co-imperium-like feudal fossile common to France and the Bishop of Urgel, dates back to a *pariage* of 1278. Comp. on this medieval institution *supra*, Chapter III, A, § 4, p. 324.

Another instance of a co-imperium created by a *pariage* is that of the town of Chatillon-sur-Seine: see the Convention of 1206 between Odo (Eudes), duke of Burgundy, and the bishop of Langres (Dumont, I, 235) by which they defined their respective seigniorial rights in the town, provided for the distribution of jurisdiction over the citizens, especially in penal matters, and divided in equal parts possible *vantae* and *forefacta* (fines and forfeits).

The centuries-old regime of "tweeherigheid" (subjection to two seigniors) of the now Netherlands town of Maastricht, which was established in the 13th century and only liquidated at the end of the 18th century, dates back to an instrument, called the "Alde Caerte" (the Old Charter) of 1283, drawn up by four arbitrators under an agreement between duke John of Brabant and the bishop of Liège John of Flanders and revised by another arbitral award of 1297. Comp. for the text of this Charter and on the legal regime of the town E. JASPAR, *De tweeheerigheid der stad Maastricht en het volkenrecht* in *Publ. de la Soc. hist. et archéol. dans le Limbourg (Maastricht)* 1938 (vol. 74), pp. 11 *et seq.*

Of feudal origin are also the Hispano-Portuguese condominium of

2. "Statuimus igitur, ut ęque participent prędicto comitatu Frisonum, episcopus (Traiectensis) videlicet et comes (Hollandię), et neuter eorum maiorem habeat in hoc comitatu commodum vel profituum; ambo concorditer sibi eligent comitem, qui vices eorum gerat in prędicto comitatu, qui presentatus ab eis domino imperatori bannum et potestatem iudicandi a manu domini imperatoris accipiat ..."
3. The dating 27 or 28 February 1168 which is sometimes found is not correct.
4. Article 3: "Quicquid pecunia in terra praefata acquisitum fuerit, inter comites aeque dividetur". The same applies, pursuant to Article 4, to that which "quis pro excessu suo hereditatem vel terram suam perdiderit". According to Article 12 neither of the Counts shall be allowed to erect, or buy, or maintain, or permit anybody else to erect, any fortifications.—This part of Zeeland remained, however, under feudal law a fief, held by the Count of Holland from the Count of Flanders.

La Contienda, which has since shrunk into the continued co-sovereignty of a road between the northern and southern halves of the territory, allotted to Spain and Portugal respectively by their treaty of 27 March 1893 (Martens, N.R.G.^{2}, XXII, 440), and the curious Franco-Spanish territorial intertwinements in the Pyrenees, where side by side with certain enclaves, there are also remnants of old condominia (comp. the chapter on State frontiers), pp. 516 and 535.

A fairly large number of condominia in Germany, which testify to the frequency and variety of this institution, have survived from the feudal era until late into the 19th century and have been only gradually liquidated:

waiver by Baden of "Mitansprüche" to sovereignty over Birkenau and Kallstadt in favour of Hesse (Article 2 of their Convention of 6 October 1806, *ibid.*, R^2, VIII, 520);

dissolution of the "communautés indivises" of old Hesse (Hesse-Westphalian treaty of 3 June 1810, *ibid.*, N.R., I, 264);

an *interimisticum* established by Lippe-Detmold and Lippe-Schaumburg on 5 July 1812 concerning the *Amt* Blomberg in virtue of which the right of legislation was provisionally suspended, but the other sovereign rights were to be exercised in part by Lippe and in part by Schaumburg (agreement mentioned in the second of the two *Austrägalentscheidungen*, rendered by the Court of Appeal of the Grand Duchy of Baden on 25 January 1839, *ibid.*, N.R., XVI^2, 470 *et seq.*, at pp. 472-473); see Part II of this publication, pp. 279 *et seq.*;

customs administration by Baden in the locality of Kürnbach common to her and Hesse-Darmstadt: convention of November 1835 (*ibid.*, N.R., XIII, 433);

special regulations on taxes and jurisdiction for the "Kommunion-Besitzungen" of Brunswick and Hanover of 14 March 1835 and 16 October 1845 (*ibid.*, N.R., XIII, 221 and N.R.G.^{1}, VIII, 539);

exchange of the "Mengdörfer" on both sides of the Weser mentioned in Article 1 of the Prusso-Hanoverian treaty of 25 November 1837 (*ibid.*, N.R., XIV, 468);

criminal jurisdiction in appeal by the Supreme Court of Kassel from judgments rendered in the districts under the co-sovereignty of Bavaria and Electoral Hesse: Law of the latter of 26 August 1841 (*ibid.*, N.R.G.^{1}, II, 167);

the municipalities of Widdern and Edelfingen under the common sovereignty of Baden and Württemberg, abolished by a Convention of 28 June 1843 (*ibid.*, N.R.G.^{1}, IX, 104), supplemented in 1846 (7 March, *ibid.*, IX, 110);

cession by Lippe to Prussia of its co-sovereignty over the town of Lippstadt by their treaty of 17 May 1850 (*ibid.*, N.R.G.^{1}, 316);

certain villages in the Lower Harz ("Kommunion-Unterharz"),

divided between Prussia and Brunswick by their treaty of 9 March 1874 (*ibid.*, N.R.G.², I, 277).

Certain condominia were already dissolved in the course of the 18th century by France in her border areas with

the duchy of Lorraine: partition of a wood—the "Bois du différend"—, which had been left undivided by an earlier convention of 1584, by Article 22 of their treaty of 21 January 1728 (Rousset, *Recueil*, I, 103);

the Elector of Trier (Trèves): partition of the "pays indivis" of Mertzig and Saargau along the river Saar (Sarre) by Article 3 of their treaty of 29 October 1773 (Martens, R², II, 260).

On the other hand, by Article 17 of her treaty with the Emperor of Austria in his capacity of ruler of the Southern Low Countries of 16 May 1769 (*ibid.*, R², I, 661) France expressly ceded to the Emperor her share in all her "possessions indivises" with Luxembourg.

The Helvetian Confederation also had its "gemeine Herrschaften", *viz.*, Toggemburg in the Canton of Thurgau and the Italian *Vogteien*. All these, and other cases of co-sovereignty throw some light upon the many practical questions which such condominia occasion, but many others may conceivably have arisen.

A peculiar sort of co-sovereignty once existed over a small enclave near the Swiss village of Neufchâtellois de Lignières which was placed under the "dépendance" of the (Prussian, monarchical) Canton of Neuchâtel as to civil jurisdiction, but under that of the bishopric of Basel as to criminal jurisdiction. However, in virtue of Article 76, *sub* 2 of the Final Act of the Congress of Vienna of 9 June 1815 (*ibid.*, N.R., II, 379) the village was ultimately transferred in full sovereignty to the principality of Neuchâtel.

Subsequently to the Netherlands-Spanish peace treaty of Münster of 30 January 1648 (Dumont, VI¹, 429), a large number of enclaves were created or maintained in existence, especially in the lands of Overmaze (Trans-Meuse), the former Spanish area "beyond", *i.e.*, east of the river Maas, by the "Partage-tractaat" (Partition Treaty) of 26 December 1661 (*ibid.*, VI², 399), and among those enclaves there were two which have continued their existence as condominia for a long time (1661-1785), *viz.*, Berneau and Elsloo. Berneau, situated in what is now the Belgian province of Limburg, and Elsloo, situated more to the north on the eastern bank of the river Maas (Meuse) were thus initially Netherlands-Spanish condominia, but they changed into Netherlands-Austrian ones in 1714, in the complicated manner described in Chapter III *supra*, p. 336, on the strength of the agreements reached at the Peace Congress of Utrecht (1713) after the war of the Spanish Succession. This co-sovereignty was dissolved by the definitive Austro-Netherlands treaty of Fontainebleau of 8 November 1785 (Martens, R², IV, 55) whereby the

433

States General renounced their claims to Berneau and the Emperor his claim to Elsloo. Prior to the Partition Treaty of 1661 the whole of "Overmaze" had provisionally continued to be treated as an interim condominium of Spain and the Netherlands: a convention of 13 December 1659 (Dumont, VI², 295) had laid down a number of financial arrangements.

The war of the Jülich-Cleves-Berg succession in the first quarter of the 17th century after the death of duke Johann Wilhelm, in which four pretenders[5] contested each other's claim to the triple[6] ducal throne, successively led to the establishment of condominia. In 1609 the duchies, though formally granted in fief by the Emperor to the duke of Saxony, were by the Recess of Dortmund of 31 May 1609 (*ibid.*, V², 103) placed under the actual collective administration of two of the pretenders, then *de facto* in power, *viz.*, the Elector of Brandenburg and the Count Palatine of the Rhine. By the tripartite treaty of Jüterbock of 21 March 1611 (*ibid.*, V², 160; Rousset, *Recueil*, VII, 417) the Elector of Saxony provisionally participated in an arrangement of co-sovereignty with the two others—possession *pro indiviso*—pending the ultimate solution of the dispute. By the treaty of Xanthen of 12 November 1614 (Dumont, V², 259) the administration of the duchies was in fact divided between the Elector (Cleves, Mark, Ravensberg and Ravestein) and the Count (Jülich and Berg), subject to the maintenance of a legal condominium. This latter treaty was never fully carried into execution owing to the international complications which the conflicting hereditary claims had conjured up from the outset, and which had resulted in an invasion by Imperial, Spanish and Netherlands troops, each in support of another pretender.—The struggle for the Jülich succession had an echo in Article IV of the Peace Treaty of Osnabrück of 24 October 1648 (Zeumer, *Quellensammlung* (Tübingen, 1913, 2nd ed.), vol. II, pp. 395 *et seq.*),

5. 1. The duke of Saxony, to whom the duchies of Jülich and Berg had been promised, first by the Emperor Frederick III in 1485, and subsequently again by the Emperor Maximilian in 1495; 2. the margrave Johann Siegmund, Elector of Brandenburg, married to a daughter of the eldest sister of the late duke, Maria Eleonore, on the strength of the marriage-contract entered into by the latter in 1573 with another member of the house of Brandenburg; 3. the Count of Pfalz-Neuburg in virtue of his marriage to the second daughter of the late duke, Anna; and 4. the Count of Pfalz-Zweibrücken on account of his marriage to the duke's third daughter Magdalena. See on this collision between hereditary claims the table of pretenders in Rousset, *Recueil*, VII, 300, and their individual "deductions" of 1732 and 1736: *ibid.*, VIII, 1 (Pfalz-Neuburg), VIII, 64 (Prussia), VIII, 134 (Sulzbach), XII, 6 (Pfalz-Zweibrücken), VII, 301 and XII, 4 (Saxony).
6. At first only the two duchies of Jülich and Berg were united under a common duke, but in 1511 the successor designate to the crown of Cleves (actual duke since 1521) succeeded in the two united duchies despite the "expectative" of Saxony.

434

§§ 11 (reversal of vacant Jülich fiefs to the Counts Palatine) and 57 (the succession conflict to be peaceably settled either by the Emperor or by *amicabilis compositio*). The duchies thereupon became a condominium proper in virtue of the first treaty of Düsseldorf of 11 May 1624 (Dumont, V^2, 446): the two occupant Powers were provisionally to hold the three duchies in common under a collective regency and to request from the Emperor, as their supreme feudal lord, a simultaneous investiture for both of them.

A provisional partition between the same Powers was decided upon on the strength of a second treaty of Düsseldorf of 9 March 1629 (*ibid.*, V^2, 569), Jülich and Berg to remain under the government of the Count Palatine; Cleves, together with the three related territories of Mark, Ravensberg and Ravestein, under that of the Elector of Brandenburg. However, a final formal dissolution of the condominium on the basis of the *status quo* only took place by the treaty of Cleves of 9 September 1666 (*ibid.*, VI^3, 117), which, moreover, provided for mutual succession in case either of the two houses should become extinct in the male line. Even on that occasion (Article 5) the seigniory of Ravestein still remained in common between the two, until 1668/1670, when it was definitely assigned to the Count Palatine. The Netherlands troops only evacuated the fortresses in the duchy of Cleves in 1672. This complicated war of succession still had an epilogue in the first half of the 18th century, when the extinction of the male line of the house of Pfalz-Neuburg became in fact imminent. Comp. the postscript to Chapter III, *supra* p. 334, *sub* (*a*).

A curious historical type of co-sovereignty was that established on 19 June 1774 by the Electors of Bavaria and the Palatinate (Martens, R^2, II, 284). The operation of this *Constitutum mutui possessorii* was to be that it would have the full effect of a "compossessio" vis-à-vis any third Power, but no effect at all *inter compaciscentes* as long as in both countries the male line should remain in office. Comp. also the *Vergleich* between the Emperor and the Elector of the Palatinate of 3 January 1778 (*ibid.*, R^2, II, 582), with an Act of accession by the duke of Pfalz-Zweibrücken (*ibid.*, 585).

The harbour of Vlissingen (Flushing) constituted a temporary condominium of France and the Netherlands (Batavian Republic) from 1795 to 1798 under Article 14 of their treaty of The Hague of 16 May 1795 (*ibid.*, R^2, VI, 88).

A peculiar condominium of Austria and the then duchy of Warsaw was in 1809 created over the salt-mines[7] of Wieliĉka, which had always up to the first partition of Poland in 1772 belonged to Poland, but this condominium also was shortlived: established by Article III, 4), para. 3

7. Quite a different affair was the old agreement of 4 February 1781 between Bavaria and Salzburg (dating back to conventions of the 16th century) concerning the salt *regale* of Hallein near Salzach: Martens, N.S., I, 102, 115, 118, 124, 143.

of the Austro-French Peace Treaty of Vienna (Schönbrunn) of 14 October 1809 (*ibid.*, N.R., I, 210), it was soon dissolved by Article 3 of the Final Act of Vienna of 9 June 1815 (*ibid.*, N.R., II, 379), in virtue of which the area concerned was placed under the exclusive sovereignty of Austria.

From the middle of the 19th century the following instances of co-imperia, even outside Europe, can be cited:

the island of Sakhalin was maintained, as before, under the co-sovereignty of Russia and Japan by Article 2 of their treaty of Simoda of 26 January 1855 (*ibid.*, N.R.G.[1], XVI[2], 454), until this "possession en commun" was terminated by their treaty of 7 May 1875 (*ibid.*, N.R.G.[2], II, 582) by which Japan ceded her share in the sovereignty over Sakhalin to Russia in exchange for the then Russian Kurile islands.

> Russia, however, lost the southern part of the island, along the 50th degree lat.N., with the adjacent islands, to Japan in virtue of Article 9 of their Peace Treaty of Portsmouth of 5 September 1905 (*ibid.*, N.R.G.[2], XXXIII, 3), but this acquisition by Japan was in its turn reversed by Article 2 (c) of the Peace Treaty of San Francisco of 8 September 1951 (*U.N.T.S.*, vol. 136, p. 45), by which Japan was forced to renounce all right, title and claim, not only to that southern portion with the adjacent islands, but also to the Kurile islands, acquired in 1875;

the Maritime Province in the Far East, made a (temporary) co-imperium of Russia and China by their treaty of Aigun of 28 May 1858 (Martens, N.R.G.[1], XVII[1], 1) until it fell to Russia pursuant to their subsequent treaty of Peking of 14 November 1860 (*ibid.*, XVII[2], 181);

the twin-duchies of Schleswig and Holstein and the duchy of Lauenburg ceded by Denmark after the short German-Danish war of 1864 to her opponents jointly by her peace treaty of Vienna with the German Bund of 30 October 1864 (*ibid.*, N.R.G.[1], XVII[2], 474, 485) to form a co-imperium of Prussia and Austria. This regime only lasted for a very short time: after the co-sovereigns had at first *de facto* divided the duchies between themselves, but only as far as the exercise of sovereignty was concerned, by placing Schleswig under Prussian and Holstein under Austrian administration, and Austria had ceded Lauenburg to Prussia, both by their treaty of Gastein of 14 August 1865 (Martens, N.R.G.[1], XVIII, 2), the co-imperium was after the ensuing brief war of 1866 between the two co-sovereigns finally abolished by the Austro-Prussian peace treaty of Prague of 23 August 1866 (*ibid.*, XVIII, 344), whereby Austria was forced to renounce her rights of co-sovereignty over the two duchies in favour of Prussia. Nemesis or Kleio intervened again at the close of World War I when the Northern, Danish-populated part of Schleswig was, after a plebiscite, awarded by the Principal Allied and Associated Powers to Denmark by the Treaty of Paris of 5 July 1920 (*ibid.*, N.R.G.[3], XIV, 881).

A new form of condominium—under a different name—emerged in the Samoa archipelago when Germany, Great Britain and the United States, after having first placed the town and district of Apia under their joint administration by a Convention of 2 September 1879 (*ibid.* N.R.G.², VI, 409 = X, 605), subsequently supplemented by a Convention of 29 September 1883 (*ibid.*, X, 608) (comp. Part II of this publication, p. 507), finally established a collective "protectorate" over the whole Samoa group by a General Act of 14 June 1889 (*ibid.*, N.R.G.², XV, 571), result of the Samoa Conference of Berlin (*ibid.*, XVI, 301). This co-protectorate was in the event wound up by an agreement of 2 December 1899 (*ibid.*, XXX, 683); comp. also *ibid.*, XXX, 652 and XXXII, 408. Comp. on such protectorates Part II, pp. 412 *et seq.*

On the organization of the zone of Tangier in Morocco comp. p. 488.

A very peculiar type of condominium was established after the defeat of the Mahdi by Great Britain and Egypt jointly over the Egyptian Sudan south of 22° lat. S. by the Cromer-Ghali Agreement of 19 January 1899 (*B.F.S.P.*, vol. 91, p. 19). This condominium was unusual because of the ill-balanced powers of the partners, and was, moreover, of dubious validity because Egypt was not entitled to enter into such international conventions. This condominium was in fact in its turn terminated in 1914 when Great Britain established her protectorate over Egypt.

The co-imperium over the New Hebrides, created by France and Great Britain by their Convention of 16 November 1887 (Martens, N.R.G.², XVI, 820), was well balanced and successful, but it has been repeatedly amended. It is in operation up to the present day.

The legal history of the Franco-British co-sovereignty over the New Hebrides began in 1887 after the British Government had protested against the establishment of French military posts on these islands for the protection of French colonists from New Caledonia. A compromise was reached in the Franco-British Convention of 16 November 1887 (*ibid.*, N.R.G.², XVI, 820) by which (*a*) Great Britain under certain conditions consented to the abrogation of an earlier Franco-British declaration of 19 June 1847 (*ibid.*, N.R.G.¹, XVI¹, 1) which prevented France from extending her existing protectorate over the Society Islands (especially Tahiti and the islands windward of that island), established in September 1842 (*ibid.*, N.R.G.¹, III, 566), to the islands of that archipelago leeward of Tahiti; (*b*) France undertook to withdraw her military posts from Sandwich and other islands of the New Hebrides; and (*c*) France and Great Britain agreed upon the constitution of a Joint Naval Commission charged with the duty of maintaining order and protecting the lives and property of British subjects and French citizens in the New Hebrides.[8] After the Franco-British negotiations at the beginning of the 20th century over a large number of disagreements between the two States in different parts of the world had led to their

8. The Declaration of 1847 ceased to exist on 15 March 1888 at the withdrawal of the French military posts (Martens, N.R.G.², XVI, 825). On the composition and powers of the Joint Naval Commission see the Declaration, with Annex, of 26 January 1888 (*ibid.*, 822).

famous *Entente cordiale*, embodied in the Cambon-Lansdowne Arrangement of 8 April 1904 (Conventions concerning Egypt and Morocco, and concerning Newfoundland and several African possessions; Declaration concerning Siam, Madagascar, and the New Hebrides, Martens, N.R.G.[2], XXXII, 29-39), the original rudimentary joint naval control of the New Hebrides was replaced by an elaborate system of joint administration, laid down in a Protocol of 27 February 1906, confirmed by a Convention of 20 October 1906 (*ibid.*, N.R.G.[3], I, 523-564, with Annexes, 564-589), which were rendered necessary by the difficulties resulting from the absence of jurisdiction over the natives of the archipelago and the persistent disputes of their respective nationals with regard to landed property.

Comp. on the organization of this condominium below, p. 440.

A condominium is sometimes designated under the wrong appellation of "neutral" territory. This was the case of "neutral" Moresnet, which came under the *de facto* co-sovereignty of the (enlarged) Kingdom of the Netherlands and Prussia in 1815 as a consequence of a faulty treaty provision (Article 66 of the Final Act of Vienna of 9 June 1815). It was originally administered by a common organ, set up by the two sovereign Powers in 1816. After Belgium's severance from the Netherlands in 1831/1839 this part of Moresnet provisionally remained under the common government of Belgium and Prussia, but in 1841 separate communal administrations were introduced in accordance with the wishes of the population. This co-imperium came to an end in 1919 in virtue of Article 32 of the Peace Treaty of Versailles which finally allocated "the contested territory of Moresnet (called Moresnet neutre)" to Belgium.

> The term "neutral territory" can also be found in other treaties as designating a special territorial situation, but then in a different sense. Comp. *e.g.*, Article 2 of the separate Convention, added to the Austro-Turkish peace treaty of Sistov of 4 August 1791 (*ibid.*, R[2], V, 254), where the term is applied to a small plain vis-à-vis the fortress of the island of Orsowa in the sense that "la souveraineté n'en appartiendra ni à l'un ni à l'autre", thus meaning, instead of a condominium, a *terra nullius*.

Condominia set up in the 20th century, were more often than not of a merely transient character, because they were specifically intended to form an interim stage on the way to a final settlement, which had already been decided upon.

A clear case of making the best of an almost unsoluble tangle was the creation of two so-called "neutral zones" in the desert west of the Persian Gulf, where Saudi Arabia, on the one hand, and Iraq and Kuwait, on the other, were unable to agree upon the exact *tracé* of their frontier. The difficulty was provisionally solved by making the two disputed zones each a condominium, that between Saudi Arabia and Iraq by treaties of 2 December 1922 (*ibid.*, N.R.G.[3], XXXII, 22) and of 19 May 1938 (*ibid.*, N.R.G.[3], XXXIX, 435), that between Saudi Arabia and Kuwait, also extending into the adjacent Persian Gulf, by a treaty of

438

2 December 1922 (*B.F.S.P.*, vol. 133, p. 646). See H. M. AL-BAHARNA, *The legal status of the Arabian Gulf States* (Manchester, 1968), pp. 264 *et seq.*

In another deserted area, in Africa, where the frontier delimitation was left very vague, France (for French Equatorial Africa) and Great Britain (for the Anglo-Egyptian Sudan) established a kind of condominium *de facto* by declaring a lake, a wad and a valley in the border zone "common to the tribes on either side": convention of 10 January 1924 (Martens, N.R.G.³, XVII, 406).

Situations such as that of the "neutral zones" just mentioned have also already occurred elsewhere in the remote past. I refer for an example to the status of the Anglo-Scottish borderzone from Berwick-upon-Tweed westward, where according to John SCOTT, *Berwick-upon-Tweed. The history of the town and guild* (London, 1888), p. 13, the parties, in their attemps in the first half of the 13th century, to fix a boundary between England and Scotland, ended by "leaving for centuries a part called the "debatable land" which could be assigned to neither country". Comp. also John FULLER, *History of Berwick-upon-Tweed* (Edinburgh, 1799). The legal status of this town, which seems to have changed hands thirteen times between 1147 and 1482, has, even after its final annexation by England, remained a singularity by its separate mention, as a territory endowed with a special regime, in many later Acts of Parliament, *inter alia*, the *Habeas Corpus Act* of 26 May 1679 (31 Ch. II, c.2), Articles XI and XII.[9]

A formal joint administration and control was established, for a period of fifty years, by the United Kingdom and the United States with regard to the Islands of Canton and Endenbury, belonging to the group of the Phoenix Islands in the Pacific, at approximately 3° lat. S. and 172° long.W. by their Agreement of 6 April 1939 (*ibid.*, N.R.G.³, XXXVII, 371). The administration was entrusted to two Commissioners.

Again quite different was the quasi-cosovereignty exercised by Austria and Hungary over Bosnia and Herzegowina after their cession in "administration and occupation" to the Dual Monarchy by Article 25 of the Peace Treaty of Berlin of 13 July 1878 (*ibid.*, N.R.G.², III, 449),— comp. Chapter IV, section 3, p. 408.

There is à certain similarity with a condominium also in the federal

9. The sources which I have been able to consult appeared to be not very enlightening with regard to Berwick-upon-Tweed. Comp., apart from the specific books of FULLER and SCOTT, cited in the text, the following works: John Hill BURTON, *The history of Scotland*, 2nd ed. in 8 vols. (Edinburgh-London, 1873); Allen Orr ANDERSON, *Early sources of Scottish history A.D. 500 to 1286* (Edinburgh, 1922); Andrew LANG, *A history of Scotland from the Roman occupation* (Edinburgh-London, 1929). Comp. also Samuel LEWIS, *Topographical Dictionary of England*.

district which is often established in federations as the seat of the federal government, outside the territory of any of the member States.

The variety of the methods by which the exercise of sovereignty over a territory subject to a co-imperium can be arranged or apportioned is exemplified by the following instances.

Already in the old examples quoted above from the 11th and 12th centuries the joint powers of the two rulers concerned were regulated in wholly different ways. Whereas in 1065 the common authority of the Count of Holland and the Bishop of Utrecht over Friesland (Frisia) was reflected in a joint administration of the country by two "schouten" (aldermen), each appointed by one of the co-sovereigns, the case of "Zeeland west of the Scheldt" showed quite a different picture in that the Count of Holland, who formally remained a vassal of the Count of Flanders, was, from 1167 onwards, to share the proceeds of the region with his nominal suzerain.

The co-imperium of the duke of Brabant (but at a later stage: the States General of the United Netherlands) and the Prince-Bishop of Liège over the town of Maastricht, which has lasted from 1283 to 1793, was initially (pursuant to the Old Charter of 1283) exercised partly *pro indiviso* (in matters of finance, the administration of justice, and police), partly on a personal basis (all those belonging to the "familia" of a number of specified churches to be considered subjects of the Prince-Bishop, all others of the duke of Brabant), and partly on a geographical basis (the seigniory of St. Pieter being reserved to the Bishop). In the course of time, however, this distribution of powers among the two sovereigns was changed to a considerable extent by a new Convention of 1297, again prepared by arbitrators under the mediation of the duke of Luxembourg; by a new "doghter Caerte" of 9 September 1356; an Edict of the co-sovereigns jointly of 1372, and a new Charter of 1379, etc. Comp. *supra* p. 431.

The condominium regime of the New Hebrides which was organized on a footing of complete equality in conformity with the Franco-British Declaration of 8 April 1904 (*ibid.*, N.R.G.[2], XXXII, 37) by a detailed Protocol of 27 February 1906, confirmed by a Convention of 20 October 1906 (*ibid.*, N.R.G.[3], I, 523), exhibited the following features.

> Each of the two Powers was to retain jurisdiction over its own nationals and neither was to exercise a separate control over the archipelago. Nationals of third Powers were to choose between the legal systems of one or the other of the two Powers, failing which the High Commissioners were instructed to decide. Those commissioners, appointed one by each government, would be provided with a police force of two divisions of equal strength. A number of essential services were to be undertaken in common. Each Power should defray its own administrative expenses, but share in the defrayment of the expenses of those common services and of the Joint Court

to be established. This Court was to consist of three judges, one appointed by each of the co-sovereigns and the third, to be its President, by the King of Spain. The High Commissioners were to issue jointly local regulations for the peace, order and good government of the islands. Aboriginals should remain under their native chiefs and not become subjects or *protégés* of either of the Powers. Elaborate provisions dealt with the jurisdiction conferred upon, the law to be applied by, and the procedure to be conducted before, the Joint Court (Articles 10-21), land suits (Articles 22-27), supervision of shipping (Articles 28-30), the recruitment and treatment of native labourers (Articles 31-56), arms, ammunition and intoxicating liquors (Articles 57-61), and elective municipal councils (Articles 62-67).

The judicial system, summarized above, was, however, altered eight years later by a Protocol of 6 August 1914 (*ibid.*, N.R.G.³, XII, 198-240) on the strength of which the Joint Court only maintained jurisdiction over natives, but was replaced by a system of separate jurisdiction by each of the two Powers over their own nationals.

Other minor alterations followed in the period 1927-1931 (*ibid.*, N.R.G.³, XXIII, 279-283, 696 and 392; XXVI, 312).

During the short co-imperium of Austria and Saxony over Wielička in Galicia and its saltmine, from 1809 to 1815, justice was administered in the name of the municipal authority and there was only a police force in equal numbers (Article III, (4), para. 3 of the Peace Treaty of Vienna of 14 October 1809, *ibid.*, N.R., I, 210). By an additional convention between Austria and Saxony of 19 November 1811 (*ibid.*, N.R., IV, 74) Austria assumed the sole technical-economic administration of the common salt-mine for a period of eight years. This regime was, however, already terminated in 1815 by Austria's acquisition of Wielička in virtue of Article 3 of the Final Act of Vienna.

The *co-imperium pro indiviso* of France and Spain over the Isle of the Pheasants (Isle of the Conference), which dates back to a treaty of 2 December 1856 (*B.F.S.P.*, vol. 47, p. 765) is by a Convention of 27 March 1901 (Martens, N.R.G.³, V, 737) organized as follows: the two States exercise the right of police by turns for a period of six months; the respective subjects are justiciable in respect of criminal law by their own national tribunals; foreigners are so justiciable by the tribunals which exercised the right of police at the time of their offence, or if they are involved in the same offence jointly with French or Spaniards, by the same tribunal as are the latter; and the authorities of the two States shall accordingly mutually hand over without formality any offenders in their custody.

The modern transitional co-imperia, *e.g.*, of the Principal Allied Powers pursuant to the Peace Treaty of Versailles of 28 June 1919 (Martens, N.R.G.³, XI, 323), were governed as separate entities by a body composed of representatives of those Powers. This form of organization entailed the legal consequence that, for instance, in their capacity of temporary co-sovereigns of the territory to be organized as the Free City of Danzig, they concluded an agreement with themselves in their capacity of temporary co-sovereigns of the territory of Memel prior to its incorporation into Lithuania as an autonomous unit.

A special problem arose in this context in respect of the temporary co-sovereignty of the Principal Allied (and Associated) Powers established over certain parts of the Ottoman Empire after the first War of the Balkans in 1913. The Peace Treaty of London of 30 May 1913 (*ibid.*, N.R.G.[3], VIII, 16) disposed in two different ways of the territories which Turkey was forced to give up. By Articles 2 and 4 of that treaty joint sovereignty of the four then allied Balkan States, Bulgaria, Greece, Montenegro and Serbia was established over the greater part of European Turkey (west of the line Enos-Midia, with the exception of Albania) and the island of Crete. A different legal situation was created by Articles 3 and 5 of the same treaty with respect to three other parts of the Ottoman possessions in Europe, namely Albania, the Ægean Islands other than Crete, and the Mount Athos peninsula. This latter situation cannot be properly labelled as a temporary co-imperium because sovereignty over the territory and islands concerned was not expressly transferred to the then six Great Powers and the latter were only empowered to decide of the ultimate fate thereof. I mention this particular instance of a joint right of disposal of territory because it has given rise to a special problem of considerable legal importance.

The exercise of this joint right of disposal was delegated in 1913 by the Supreme Council to the Conference of Ambassadors as a subordinate body. Owing to the outbreak of World War I, however, that body was only able on 6 December 1922 to take the last remaining decisions in the performance of the task entrusted to it under the Treaty of London, in particular the frontier delimitation between Albania and the Serb-Croat-Slovene Kingdom and the allocation of the Monastery of Saint Naoum. Meanwhile, the composition of the group of six pseudo-condomini, which were *nominatim* mentioned in the Peace Treaty of 1913, had changed as a consequence of World War I: Germany and Austria-Hungary were no longer considered members of the group, whereas Japan had been admitted to it. The decision of 6 December 1922 was taken by the Conference of Ambassadors in its new composition, not identical, therefore, with the agency initially authorized to discharge the function of fixing the frontiers of the State of Albania. The Permanent Court of International Justice, in its Advisory Opinion of 4 September 1924 (*Publications P.C.I.J.*, series B, No. 9), referring to a preceding Opinion of 6 December 1923 (*ibid.*, No. 8) concerning the closely analogous affair of Jaworzina between Poland and Czechoslovakia, recognized the validity of the decision of 6 December 1922, taken by the group of Great Powers in despite of the change in its composition, without however paying any attention to the problem involved. Comp. on this case my *The Jurisprudence of the World Court*, vol. I, pp. 38-39.

Section 2. ENCLAVES

Enclaves and, seen from the other side, exclaves are of some importance in international law because of the special difficulties which they sometimes cause.

By enclaves I mean here only those, often widely scattered, smaller parcels of territory which are dependencies of a larger international unit and are surrounded on all sides by territory of one or more other international entities. I exclude, consequently, those self-contained international persons which are themselves entirely encircled by territory of other States, and are therefore at present called landlocked States, such as Czechoslovakia, Ecuador, Laos, Lesotho, Chad, San Marino.[10] Their probleme are, for the rest, much the same as those of enclaves proper. The interests of those landlocked States, cut off from the high seas, have recently been safeguarded first by certain provisions in Article 3 of Convention II of Geneva (1958) on the High Seas, and more recently by a Convention on Transit Trade of Landlocked Countries, concluded at New York on 8 July 1965 (*I.L.M.* 1965 (IV), p. 957). Neither do I have in view here the legal difficulties which may befall a State which consists of two separate, geographically unconnected halves, such as is the situation of (West and East) Pakistan. Nor do I intend to pay special attention, by expatiating on their legal history and status, to those smaller areas, belonging to a State but severed from its mainland, which, although on the whole surrounded by foreign territory, are not enclaves proper because part of their area borders on the open sea. Quite a number of these areas—which in a sense constitute or constituted *corpora aliena*, of feudal, colonial or military origin, within another body politic—have or have had in the past a somewhat stormy existence and have been the object of foreign military or diplomatic attacks:
Calais.

> This town was captured by the English in 1347 and has remained under British sovereignty until its recapture by the French in 1558. The preliminary Peace Treaty of Cateau Cambrésis of 12 March 1559 between Henri II of France, the Dauphin François and his wife Mary of Scots, on the one hand, and Elizabeth of England, on the other (Dumont, V, 28) laid down that Calais would remain in the hands of the King of France for a period of eight years and would after the expiry of that term be handed back to

10. Napoleon has in vain suggested, in the days of his Cisalpine Republic, that San Marino should be given an outlet to the Adriatic; the tiny republic has, however, declined the offer.

England. The town has, however, remained in French hands. Its temporary conquest by Spain at the end of the 16th century was reversed by the Franco-Spanish Peace Treaty of Vervins of 2 May 1598 (Dumont V¹, 561).

Gibraltar (as from 1704 *de facto*, from 1713 *de jure*).

On Gibraltar see Chapter V, section 6 on the right of re-emption, below, p. 482.

Portuguese, Dutch and French possessions on the Malabar and Coromandel coasts of India;
Monaco, once an exclave of Piedmont; and
Pemba, once a continental appendix of the Sultanate of Zanzibar.

Naturally I do not deal either with the "domaine public" of a State on foreign territory and still less with private property of a foreign dynasty. Comp. on these subjects: SCHMELZER, *Das Verhältnis auswärtiger Kammergüter* (Halle, 1819), pp. 48, 179 *et seq.*, and KLÜBER, *Droit des gens*, §§ 124, 128.

Enclaves were particularly frequent in earlier centuries when the great many smaller, and often minute, territorial units of those days had still to merge in modern States. Nowadays they are very much more exceptional than they were in the era of feudalism and patrimonial conceptions of the State, although several of them continued to exist even until the middle of the present century, as two proceedings before the International Court of Justice have shown, respectively in the *Case concerning right of passage over Indian territory* (*I.C.J. Reports* 1957, p. 125; 1960, p. 6) and in that *concerning sovereignty over certain frontier land* (*ibid.*, 1959, p. 209). The situation of such enclaved plots of land was sometimes further complicated by the fact that they were placed under the co-sovereignty of two States (comp. section 1, *supra* p. 433).

Since Professor Ed. BAUER of Neuchâtel wrote his exhaustive study concerning the historical cases of enclaves recorded from 1648 onward and intended to support the defence of Portugal against India in the case just mentioned of her right of passage between littoral Damão and her enclaved territories of Dadrá and Nagar-Aveli (Annex 25 to the Portuguese observations in the *Pleadings etc.*, vol. 1, pp. 762 *et seq.*), it will probably not be easy to adduce many more instances of, and particulars about, this gradually vanishing, legally abnormal relic of the past. The analogy between the legal status of these international enclaves and that of the comparable enclosed plots of land under private law has, moreover, been analysed on the same occasion by Professor Max RHEINSTEIN (*ibid.*, Annex 20, pp. 714 *et seq.*). I will not, therefore, go here into much detail.

When further confining the subject chiefly to enclaves proper, I will first give some particulars regarding those which have existed in great number in the past in my own country, mainly because they present a standard example of the complicated procedure by which these remnants of the feudal system were in the event wound up.

The present territory of the Kingdom of the Netherlands in Europe has in the days when that Kingdom was still the (confederal) Republic of the United Netherlands remained for more than two centuries dotted with a large number of enclaves belonging to foreign rulers, in particular along the rivers Maas (Meuse) and Rhine, and has moreover itself consisted for a minute part of exclaves in foreign territory. All of them have persisted up to the turn of the 18th century, when in the days of the French Revolution the foreign enclaves were, save for a few (Baerle-Hertog), incorporated into the new unitary State and its few exclaves were, except for one, part of Baarle-Nassau, engulfed by its southern neighbour.

The whole of what is now the Netherlands province of Limburg, stretching along the river Maas from South to North, was for some centuries nothing but a picturesque patchwork of enclaves. Bordered in the South by the independent bishopric of Liège and the old duchy of Limburg, and in the West by the County of Looz,[11] it has in the course of its history been composed of a great number of self-contained isolated units and of parts of adjoining States: the Republic of the United Netherlands; Spain, respectively Austria, in their Belgian appendix of the Low Countries,[12] the duchies of (southern) Limburg, Jülich,[13] Guelder,[14] and

11. This county, whose rulers, of the branch Looz-Corswarem, were collateral descendants of the Counts of Hainault, only lost its old status at the end of the 18th century. The then duke and duchy were still mentioned as members of the German College of Princes in § XXXII of the *Reichsdeputations-Hauptschluss* of 25 February 1803 (Martens, R², VII, 435 *et seq.*, at pp. 494 and 497, under No. 127), but in their new capacity of duke and duchy of Rheina-Wolbeck, with which they had been compensated for their loss in the Netherlands.
12. The formerly Spanish (southern) Low Countries were at the close of the War of the Spanish Succession in 1713-1715 allotted to the House of Austria by way of their delivery by France into the possession of the Republic of the United Netherlands with the specific object of their further transfer by the latter to Austria. See Article 7 of the Franco-Netherlands Peace Treaty of Utrecht of 11 April 1713 (Dumont, VIII¹, 366) and Article 1 of the (third) Barrier Treaty of 15 November 1715 (Dumont, VIII¹, 458; Rousset, *Recueil*, I, 37).
13. The duchies of Jülich and Cleves became the object of successive international transactions as a consequence of the War of the Jülich-Cleves Succession in the beginning of the 17th century. After a prolonged interim period of co-sovereignty (comp. section 1 *supra*, p. 435), the first duchy finally fell to the palsgrave of the Rhine (Pfalz-Neuburg), whereas the second was annexed by the margrave of Brandenburg (Prussia).
14. The southernmost part of the old duchy, namely Upper Guelder, had remained after the Eighty Years' War a Spanish possession. By far the largest part of this Upper-Guelder (with the capital Gelder) was in 1713 excepted from transfer to Austria and allotted instead to Prussia. A smaller part—Venlo and surroundings—fell to the Republic of the United Netherlands. Only Roermond

445

Cleves;[13] the Imperial county of Horn; a number of scattered, in part *reichsunmittelbare*, territories—Wittem, Eys, Rijkholt, Gronsveld, Petersheim, Reckheim, Wijnandsrade, Rimburg, Stein—,[15] and the "tweeherige" (bi-seigniorial) town of Maastricht, subject to the (unequal) co-imperium of the States General and the princely bishopric of Liège.[16]— Further down the same river Maas, where it turns westward towards the sea, there was another chain of foreign-ruled enclaves: Boxmeer, Grave and the land of Cuyck, Ravenstein, the tiny county of Megen, the seigniory of Lith, the minuscule County of Bokhoven, and the small seigniory of Nieuwkuik. See on these enclaves S. J. FOCKEMA ANDREAE, *De Nederlandse Staat onder de Republiek* in *Verhand. der Kon. Ned. Akad. v. Wetensch. afd. Lett.*, Nieuwe reeks, vol. LXVIII, No. 3, p. 84.

> The seigniory of Boxmeer was mentioned in § 10 of the *Reichsdeputations-Hauptschluss* of 1803: feudal rights in it appertained to the Prince of Hohenzollern-Sigmaringen.
>
> On Grave and the Land of Cuyck see D. PARINGET, *Memoriael* (Utrecht, 1752).
>
> The seigniory of Ravenstein had, after a prolonged co-imperium (comp. p. 435), ultimately (1668) fallen to the Elector of Brandenburg as a consequence of the War of the Jülich-Cleves Succession. He was dislodged from it in 1803 and was compensated for this and other losses by the allocation of certain areas in Germany (§ 2 of the *Reichsdeputations-Hauptschluss*).
>
> The duchy of Megen belonged to the Count of Schall, see § 6 of the *Reichsdeputations-Hauptschluss*.

The seigniories of Lith and Nieuwkuik were tacitly absorbed by the Netherlands.

The county of Bokhoven was a possesion of the bishopric of Liège.

Near the lower course of the Rhine from where it enters the present territory of the Netherlands, there were a few other foreign enclaves, parts of the duchy of Cleves, especially Zevenaar, Huissen and Malburg.

> On these enclaves of Zevenaar, Huissen, Malburg and other places (Wehl, Hulhuizen, de Lijmers), which belonged to the duchy of Cleves, see Article 10 of the secret provisions, additional to the Peace Treaty of Campo Formio between France and the Emperor of 17 October 1797 (Martens, R², VI, 426), Article 1 of the Franco-Netherlands treaty of Paris of 5 January 1800 (*ibid.*, VII, 37), Article 1 of the Franco-Prussian treaty of Berlin of 14 November 1802 (*ibid.*, VII, 426), § 3 of the *Reichsdeputations-Hauptschluss* of 1803, Article 2 of the Franco-Netherlands treaty of Fontainebleau of

and surroundings were transferred to Austria. See Article 7 of the Franco-Netherlands Peace Treaty of Utrecht (Dumont, VIII¹, 366).

13. See note 13 on page 445.

15. Some of these small territories are, in connexion with their mediatization about 1800, mentioned by name in § XXIV of the *Reichsdeputations- Hauptschluss* of 25 February 1803 (Martens, R², V, 443, at pp. 473 *et seq.*): Reckheim, belonging to the Count of Aspremont-Lynden; Wittem and Eys, belonging to the Count of Plettenburg; Gronsveld, belonging to the Count of Törring; also the territory of Slenaken, belonging to the Count of Goltstein.

16. Comp. on this curious condominium section 1 *supra*, pp. 440 *et seq.*

11 November 1807 (*ibid.*, VIII, 718), Article 66, last paragraph, of the Final Act of the Congress of Vienna of 1815, and the Netherlands-Prussian Convention of 25 May 1816 (Lagemans, No. 43).

The present Netherlands province of North Brabant, governed for a long time by the States General as a *Generaliteitsland*, under the direct confederal administration of the "Generalty", still encompassed at the time a few foreign-ruled enclaves, such as Gemert, Bergen op Zoom, Thorn, and Baarle-Hertog.

Gemert was a Commandery of the Teutonic Order. Comp. the Convention between the States General of the United Netherlands and Leopold of Austria in the name of that Order of 14 June 1662 (Dumont, VI², 421).

The marquisate of Bergen op Zoom had in the course of time been a possession of different foreign margraves of high standing, among others, Hohenzollern, de la Tour d'Auvergne, Pfalz-Sulzbach, Pfalz-Zweibrücken. At the time of its final liquidation (*Reichsdeputations-Hauptschluss* of 1803, § II) it belonged to the Elector of Bavaria, Count Palatine of the Rhine, who then lost it to the Netherlands. See on the history of this marquisate— combined with the seigniory of Breda—up to 1287: A.G. KLEYN, *Geschiedenis van het Land en de Heeren van Breda tot het tijdstip der afscheiding van Bergen op Zoom* (Breda, 1861) and up to 1567: W. MOLL, *De rechten van den heer van Bergen op Zoom* (Groningen, 1915).

Thorn was a sovereign ecclesiastical unit, an abbey under the rule of a *reichsunmittelbare* Abbess. It was secularized in the Napoleonic period.

The two territories of Baarle: Baerle-Hertog (belonging of old to the dukes of Brabant and enclaved in the Netherlands province of North Brabant) and the hamlet of Castelre, part of Baarle-Nassau (belonging to the Prince of Nassau, in his capacity of baron of Breda, for a minute part enclaved in Belgium) have up to the present time escaped all attempts of the Governments concerned to wind them up. As a result, they alone remain as apparently indestructible feudal fossils on the Netherlands-Belgian frontier. Comp. my paper in *The Jurisprudence of the World Court*, vol. II, pp. 353 *et seq.* An elaborate account of the origin and fortunes of these enclaves has since been given by F. A. BREKELMANS, *De Belgische enclaves in Nederland. Bijdragen tot de rechtsgeschiedenis van Baerle-Hertog en Baarle-Nassau* in *Bijdr. tot de geschied. van het zuiden van Nederland*, vol. IV (Tilburg, 1965).

Mutual claims to yet other enclaves, in the duchy of Guelder, have in the 17th century contributed to the recrudescence of the controversies existing between the Netherlands, on the one hand, and the archbishop of Cologne and the bishop of Münster, on the other, and even led to two wars, the first from 1665 to 1666, and the second from 1672 to 1674. The enclaves concerned were those of Borculoo and Bredevoort.

See on these two territories: H. G. HARKEMA, *De betrekkingen van het bisdom Munster tot de Nederlanden, inzonderheid tot Gelderland, tot aan den vrede van Kleef, 18 April 1666* (in *Gelre*, 1904 (VII), p. 1); on Bredevoort: J. N. BAKHUIZEN VAN DEN BRINK and B. STEGEMAN, *Het Ambt Breedevoort tijdens het*

447

Anholter pandschap, 1562-1612 (Werken Gelre, No. 19, Arnhem, 1933). Comp. also under section 1 on Pledges, p. 393 *supra.*

Another enclave was that of Anholt in the border area between Guelder and Prussia, a seigniory which was given to the Count of Salm-Salm as a compensation for the loss of his original county of Salm-Salm in the Ardennes. Anholt was *nominatim* enumerated in Article 1 of the treaty of Paris between France and the Batavian Republic of 5 January 1800 (Martens, R², VII, 37) among the territories which, having been earlier ceded by Prussia to France, should be further transferred by the latter to the Batavian Republic. Prussia, however, maintained that Anholt had never been so ceded and has in actual fact retained the seigniory (see the Prussian-Netherlands Boundary Treaty of Cleves of 7 October 1816 in Martens, N.R., III, 45).

> Anholt was mediatized in 1815 and its former rulers simply became subjects of Prussia within the German Bund. Since, however, the mediatized German princes were in Article 14 of the *Bundes-Acte* granted special privileges, the Count of Salm-Salm has after World War II attempted in Netherlands Courts to achieve exemption from the confiscation of his possessions in the neighbourhood of Anholt as enemy property, but without success. See *I.L.R.* 1957, p. 893, and p. 10 *supra.*

And even one of the Frisian islands, Ameland, has lived a more or less independent existence as a curious enclave under the local dynasty of the Camminga's.

> This island used to be respected as neutral territory in a war in which the Republic of the United Netherlands was involved. See the relevant decisions of the Archduchess Isabella (Spanish Governess of the Low Countries) of 23 February 1629 and of Cromwell of 20 February 1654, kept in the General State Archives (*Nass. Dom.*, Nos. 10313 and 10226, VI). Comp. further on this island: J.HOUWINK, *De staatkundige en rechtsgeschiedenis van Ameland tot deze eeuw* (Leyden, 1899).

The legal status of many of these enclaved territories was already controversial in the 17th century; the question of sovereignty over some of them has been discussed by the Netherlands Council of State, as appears from its Archives in the General State Archives under No. 2162, relating to Megen, Ravestein, Gemert and Boxmeer.

Almost all of these enclaves have in the period of their final deletion as separate units been the object—*nominatim* or anonymously—of international treaties between Napoleonic France, the Empire, Prussia and the Netherlands (in its successive guises of the Batavian Republic and the (Napoleonic) Kingdom of Holland). The general course of events amounted to the following.

> After France and the Emperor had stipulated in Article 10 of the secret provisions additional to their Peace Treaty of Campo Formio of 17 October 1797 (Martens, R², VI, 426) that, should Prussia cede to France or to the Batavian Republic her small possessions on the left bank of the Meuse or

the enclaves of Zevenaar and other territories near the river Yssel, the Emperor would employ his good offices to have those cessions endorsed by the Empire, France by Article 1 of her treaty of Paris with the Batavian Republic of 5 January 1800 (*ibid.*, VII, 37) renounced in favour of the latter all claims to the acquisitions which she had just made on the left bank of the Rhine so far as these were situated in the Batavian Republic, *viz.*, Ravenstein; Megen; Boxmeer; Anholt; Huissen, Malburg and Hulhuizen; certain villages in the Land of Cuyck, and in a general description, all further former possessions of German princes in the Batavian Republic (among them, *inter alia*, the old abbey of Thorn). Prussia thereupon by Article 1 of her treaty of Berlin with the Batavian Republic of 14 November 1802 (*ibid.*, VII, 426), implementing a preceding treaty with France of 23 May 1802, indeed renounced her enclaves along the lower Rhine. The *Reichsdeputations-Hauptschluss* of 25 February 1803 (*ibid.*, VII, 435 *et seq.*, 443 *et seq.*) confirmed a number of those cessions *nominatim* in §§ II (Ravenstein, Bergen op Zoom), III (Zevenaar *c.a.*), VI (Megen), X (feudal rights of German princes in Boxmeer, Berg, Gendringen, Elten, Wisch, Pannerden, Millingen) and XXIV (Reckheim, Wittem and Eys, Gronsveld, Slenaken). The transfer of Zevenaar *c.a.* was again confirmed by Article 2 of the treaty of Fontainebleau between France and the then (Napoleonic) Kingdom of Holland of 11 November 1807 (*ibid.*, VIII, 718).

Pari passu with this French action the Netherlands authorities proceeded to a formal annexation of the new territories by Decree, and the early 19th century Netherlands constitutions incorporated the enclaves and a series of other *vrije heerlijkheden* (free seigniories), in the Betuwe and in Groningen,[17] into the public structure of the country, first by allocating them to the French-inspired *Départements*, as established by the Basic Laws of 1801 (Article 21) and 1805 (Article 10), and ultimately by embodying them in its traditional provincial system (Constitution of 1814, Article 51).

Also in other parts of Europe and the world many enclaves have succeeded in tenaciously prolonging their often useless existence until late in the 19th and even the 20th century, especially in Germany, Switzerland, Italy and the southern Low Countries. I refer to exclaves of one member State of Germany, in her successive constitutional phases since 1815, within the territory of another, such as certain areas of Saxe-Weimar and Anhalt-Bernburg in Prussia, with regard to whose commerce conventions concerning the levying of taxes at the outer frontier of Prussian territory were required (1823, Martens, N.R., VI, 269 and 344); the same applies to parts of the principality of Lippe, *viz.*, Cappel, Lipperode and Grevenhagen, and to the Saxe-Coburg-Gotha bailiwick

17. See on the "free seigniories" in the border area between the provinces of Gelderland, Holland and Utrecht (Ysselstein, Buren, Leerdam, Culemborg and Vianen): R. FRUIN, *De vrije heerlijkheden, gelegen in het grensgebied etc.* (*Verslagen en Mededelingen der Vereeniging tot uitgaaf der bronnen van het Oud-Vaderlandsche Recht*, 1934 (VIII), p. 352).—See on Westerwolde: R. FRUIN, Th. Azn., *Overzicht der staatsgeschiedenis van het landschap Westerwolde tot op zijn vereeniging met de XVII Nederlanden* (Leiden, 1886).

of Volkenrode, all of them also surrounded by Prussian territory: conventions of 9/17 June 1826, renewed 18 October 1841 (*ibid.*, N.R., VI, 1023 and N.R.G.¹, II, 222), respectively 4 July 1829 and 26 June 1833 (*ibid.*, N.R., VIII, 118 and IX, 649); the enclave of Vogesack (Bremerhafen): convention between Bremen and Hanover of 20 December 1828 (*ibid.*, N.R., VII, 772); several areas of Baden in Württemberg and *vice-versa*, objects of corresponding customs regulations in 1831 and 1835 (*ibid.*, N.R., X, 373 and XIII, 431); certain enclaved bailiwicks of Saxe-Weimar, respectively Saxe-Coburg-Gotha, which were admitted in 1831 into the customs system of Bavaria-Württemberg (*ibid.*, N.R., IX, 193 respectively 369);

of a foreign prince or State within the Swiss (Con)federation, such as: the Baden municipality of Büsingen, still enclaved within the Swiss Canton of Schaffhausen, with regard to which certain customs arrangements were made in the German-Swiss treaty of 21 September 1895 (*ibid.*, N.R.G.², XXI, 569);

the still existing Italian enclave of Campione within the Canton of Ticino (Lake of Lugano):

> In the treaty of Varese, concluded on 2 August 1752 between the Empress Maria Theresia and the twelve cantons of the "Lega Elvetica dominante di quà dai monti" (Wenck, III, 35), which was specifically intended to fix the boundary between the former Duchy of Milan and the former baliaggi of Locarno, Lugano and Mendrisio, the enclaved Lombardian comune of Campione was disregarded. Hence the insertion by Italy and Switzerland of an express agreement on the frontiers of this enclave in their treaty of 5 October 1861 (*ibid.*, N.R.G.¹, XX, 186) *sub* XI (*ibid.*, 198-200), which fixed not only the land frontier of Campione, but also the boundary line in the lake, Italy renouncing on that occasion her sovereignty over the opposite "costa di San Martino" and retreating towards a line through the middle of the lake. Comp. on the legal status of this curious enclave and the national frontiers in this border lake Chapter VI, section 3, on State frontiers, below p. 578;

the seigniory of Tarasp in the Canton of Grisons, once, prior to its mediatization, belonging to the prince of Dietrichstein, and the secularized bishopric of Chur (Coire) also in Grisons (see §§ XI and XXIX of the *Reichsdeputations-Hauptschluss* of 1803); and the former Austrian enclave, the seigniory of Rhäzuns, in the same Canton, which was only given up by the Emperor in Article III, *sub* 2 *in fine*, of the Peace Treaty of Vienna (Schönbrunn) with France of 14 October 1809 (*ibid.*, N.R., I, 210) and ceded to Grisons by his Declaration of 20 March 1815, confirmed by Article 78 of the Final Act of the Congress of Vienna of 9 June 1815 (*ibid.*, N.R., II, 379). Comp. also the strange enclave of Lignières under the condominium of the Canton of Neuchâtel and the archbishopric of Basel, mentioned in section 1 *supra*, p. 433;

of Austrian Carniola on the Gulf of Trieste, and of Austrian Bohemia in Saxony, both groups of exclaves given up by Austria in the same Peace Treaty of Vienna (Schönbrunn) of 1809 (Article III, *sub* 2 and 3), a waiver which, as far as the former was concerned, was *expressis verbis* confirmed by Article 18 (3) of the Final Act of Vienna (1815);

of Spain in the French Pyrenees, such as the Llivia enclave (near Puigcerda in the North West), which has played a rôle in the execution of Article 42 of the Treaty of the Pyrenees of 7 November 1659 (Dumont, VI², 264): the transfer of thirty-three villages of La Cerdagna to France was refused with regard to Llivia by Spain on the ground that Llivia was a town and not a village (*ibid.*, p. 283).

The southern (first Spanish, since 1714 Austrian) Low Countries, now Belgium, were equally thronged with enclaved territories. These have been successively and systematically wound up by Conventions entered into

between France and Austria. See the extensive exchange, effected by their treaty of 16 May 1769 (*ibid.*, R², I, 661), in Article 27 of which the intention of the parties was declared to abolish all enclaves still existing between the Moselle and the sea, and by an authorization of their respective commissioners in Article 27 of their subsequent treaty of 18 November 1779 (*ibid.*, R², II, 730) to proceed to the exchange of all further small enclaves which they might still discover;

between France and the bishopric of Liège. See the wiping-out by exchange of a number of enclaves by a series of conventions entered into between 1772 and 1778 (*ibid.*, R², II, 44-83);

between France and the electoral bishopric of Trier. See the cession of certain enclaves, in exchange for other lands, by Articles 2 and 3 of their supplementary Convention of 29 October 1773 (*ibid.*, R², II, 265);[18]

between Austria and the Netherlands. See their conventions of 20 September and 8 November 1785 (*ibid.*, R², IV, 50, 55, 62).

All these exchange operations have at the time been described in detail by P. M. DE NÉNY, *Historische en staatkundige gedenkstukken*, vol. II, (Amsterdam-Antwerpen, *c.* 1784).

A similar operation has been carried through in Germany under the motto of "epuration" or "purification", systematically and thoroughly by the *Reichsdeputations-Hauptschluss* of 1803 and more haphazardly by subsequent agreements.

I refer to the conventions entered into to that effect between Baden and Württemberg by their "treaty of exchange and epuration" of 17 October 1806 (Martens, R², VIII, 521) and between Hanover and Oldenburg by the "purification" of their respective possessions in certain parishes

18. See on certain disputes over enclaves in the county of Hainault: Article 15 of the preliminary Peace Treaty of Aachen of 30 April 1748 (Wenck, II, 310): they were referred to the Congress.

pursuant to the treaty of Bremen of 4 February 1817 (*ibid.*, N.R., III, 373).

A famous enclave in France was the Papal possession of Avignon (with Venaissin). Comp. Part II of this publication, Chapter I, p. 21.

In Italy there have also existed numerous enclaves: many data concerning these can be collected from Marten's N.R.G.[1], XV, pp. 1 *et seq.*, from where it appears, however, that in Italy no similar systematic operation of their winding-up has been undertaken.

Some western States have in former centuries acquired areas on the coasts of India with inland dependencies, which can equally well be called enclaves, *viz.*, the Republic of the United Netherlands, through conventions concluded by the United East Indian Company with native princes in the 17th century, later wrested from her by Great Britain: Negapatnam on the Coromandel coast by Article IV of their peace treaty of Paris of 20 May 1784 (*ibid.*, R[2], III, 560), Cochin and its dependencies (Bernagore) on the Malabar coast in exchange for the island of Banka, by Article II of a Convention of 13 August 1814 (*ibid.*, N.R.[2], II, 57), and the last remaining possessions of Tuticorin, Kutuk and Sadras by the Convention of 17 March 1824 (*ibid.*, N.R., VI, 415 = N.S., I, 628);

France, similarly through conventions with indigenous princes in the 18th century on the coasts of Coromandel, Orissa and Malabar in Bengal, restored to her, after her defeat in the Seven Years' War, by Great Britain by Article XI of their Peace Treaty of Paris of 10 February 1763 (*ibid.*, R[2], I, 104), but eventually voluntarily surrendered by France to independent India in 1951 (treaties of 2 February 1951, *U.N.T.S.*, vol. 203, p. 155, and 28 May 1956).

Portugal acquired form the Mahrattas—pursuant to the legal construction given to the original transaction by the International Court of Justice in 1960[19]—initially in the legal form of a lease, which was, however, subsequently imperceptibly transmuted into full sovereignty; they were eventually lost to the Union of India in 1962 as a result of the latter's aggressive action condoned by the United Nations.

> Comp. on the relations between the Mahratta Empire and Portugal with regard to these enclaves the treaties of Poona of 29 January 1741 and 4 May/17 December 1779 (extracts, respectively text, in *I.C.J. Pleadings Passage case*, 1960, I, 293, respectively 233) and the *Sanads* of 29 May 1783 and 22 July 1785, complementary to the 1779 treaty (*ibid.*, I, 37, 38; 41, 43).

Portugal still possesses in Africa an exclave, Cabinda, to the north of the river Congo, as a dependency of her overseas province of Angola, now enclaved within the independent State of Congo (Brazzaville), once a French colony. Comp. on this enclave Article X of the Anglo-Portuguese

19. *I.C.J. Reports*, 1960, pp. 37 *et seq.*; my *The Jurisprudence of the World Court*, vol. II, pp. 359 *et seq.*

Treaty of Friendship of 19 February 1810 (Martens, N.R., I, 245).

Other well-known enclaves, of long historical standing, have been those of Venice on the coast of Albania—Préveza, Vónitsa, Butrinto and Parga—, on which comp. the Act of ratification of the Sublime Porte relative to the cession of the Ionian Islands to Great Britain of 24 April 1819 (Martens, N.R. V, 387), and

that of Gwadar, on the coast of Beluchistan on the northern shore of the Gulf of Oman, once a dependency of the Sultanate of Muscat, but in the event sold by the latter to Pakistan by a convention of 4 September 1958 (*The Middle East and North Africa 1966-67* (Europa Publ. London, 13th ed. 1966, p. 515).

The most important question regarding the international status of enclaves is, of course, apart from their situation in respect of commerce and customs, whether the State under whose sovereignty they are placed has a right of free transit for its civil officers and police and military forces between its main land and its exclaved portions. There are old examples of the recognition of such a right granted by an international agreement, *e.g.*, the Partition Treaty concluded between the Republic of the United Netherlands and Spain, in implementation of Article 3 of their Peace Treaty of Münster of 30 January 1648 (Dumont, VI¹, 429), on 26 December 1661 with regard to their respective scattered possessions in the Land of Overmaze (Trans-Meuse), the territories of Daalhem, Valkenburg and Rolduc (*ibid.*, VI², 393). In that treaty the parties indeed agreed upon a mutual right of transit between their own exclaves across the other's territory (postscript to the treaty: transit freedom from Maastricht and Navagne to Daalhem and from the Monastery of St. Gerlach to the highroad to Heerlen). In the same way a right of transit was guaranteed in 1714 to the Emperor of Austria from his new possessions in the Low Countries to his exclave of Roermond in Limburg (Dumont, VIII¹, 415; Rousset, *Recueil*, I, 1).

It has often been argued, on the analogy of comparable private law situations, that such a right of transit is sanctioned by international customary law or by general principles of law, in my opinion rightly so, although certain precautions are reasonable as regards the movements of troops. When this argument was advanced by Portugal in her dispute with India over her asserted right of passage between littoral Damão and the enclaves of Dadrá and Nagar-Aveli, the International Court of Justice avoided an examination of this general question by holding that this particular Indian-Portuguese relationship was governed by specific rules of local customary law which prevailed over any supposed general rule.

Comp. on the permission given to the Portuguese Armed Police Force to travel across British-Indian and to enter Portuguese territory, and *vice versa*, the agreements between the Government of Bombay and that of Portuguese

India of 21 January/20 February 1913, 31 August/25 September 1920 and 30 July/5 August 1940 (*I.C.J. Pleadings, Passage* case, 1960, I, pp. 462/463; p. 471, and pp. 479/480); on the conclusions drawn by the International Court of Justice: *I.C.J. Reports* 1960, p. 6, and my analysis in *The Jurisprudence of the World Court, vol. II*, p. 359 *et seq.*

The Belgian enclave of Baerle-Hertog in Netherlands North-Brabant has during World War I given rise to a very special question of neutrality law: could the Netherlands without violating their neutrality allow the operation within their boundary of a radio emission station of belligerent Belgium? The solution then reached was that the Netherlands could not legally interfere inside the Belgian enclave, but that they were free, if not obliged, to forbid the transport across their own territory of material necessary for the constant operation of the station. Comp. the Netherlands Orange Book of 1916.

Other disputes arising from this Belgian enclave have related to the operation of a gambling hall in the Belgian part of Baerle.

To conclude, it may be remembered that enclaves are specially mentioned in the Statute of Barcelona (1923) on Waterways of International Concern (Martens, N.R.G.³, XIX, 250). Article 23 thereof lays down that the Statute must not be interpreted as regulating in any way rights and obligations *inter se* of territories forming part of or placed under the protection of the same sovereign State, whether or not these territories are individually contracting States.

Section 3. MANDATED AND TRUST TERRITORIES

As I have explained in the introduction to section 5 of Chapter VI of Part II of this publication (p. 545), a systematic theoretical approach to the novel institution of Mandates under the League of Nations Covenant since 1919 raises certain difficulties owing to the varying legal nature of the Territories under an A-Mandate as compared with those under a B- or a C-Mandate, in particular in view of the doctrinal controversy which had arisen concerning the seat of the territorial sovereignty over them. In that respect hardly any real problem could arise in respect of the countries under an A-Mandate since the existence of those countries or "communities", formerly belonging to the Ottoman Empire, as independent nations was provisionally recognized in Article 22 (4) of the League Covenant subject to the rendering of administrative advice and assistance by a Mandatory until such time as they would be able to stand alone. It was clear that these "communities" fell, from a systematical legal point of view, within the category of not yet fully sovereign subjects of international law, vested as such with territorial supremacy over the area comprised within their borders. The situation was, however, different as regards the territories under one of the Mandates B, established under Article 22 (5) over peoples, especially in Central Africa, whose actual stage of development was still too backward to allow them to stand alone, and C, such as South-West Africa and certain of the Southern-Pacific islands, which pursuant to Article 22 (6) could for various reasons be best administered under the laws of the Mandatory as integral portions of its territory. These latter two groups of communities were certainly not yet subjects of international law and with regard to them it was very doubtful with whom territorial sovereignty rested. There is one international document in existence in the preamble of which it is asserted that sovereignty belonged to the Mandatory, *viz.*, the Boundary Agreement between the Union of South Africa and Portugal (for Angola) of 22 June 1926 (Martens, N.R.G.³, XXIII, 299), according to which "en vertu d'un mandat à lui conféré par le Conseil de la Société des Nations,...le Gouvernement de l'Union Sud-Africaine... possède la souveraineté sur le territoire du Sud-Ouest Africain", but this assertion was obviously incorrect, as clearly results from an analysis of the status of the Territory concerned by the International Court of Justice in 1950 (*I.C.J. Reports* 1950, p. 128).

In view of this basic difference between the Mandates *inter se* I decided at the time to split up the subject by dealing with the A-Mandates in Part II on International Persons and referring the B- and C-Mandates to this Part III on Territory. Since, however, all three types had certain features in common and as I wished to offer also a general assessment of the legal aspects of the Mandates regime as a coherent system, I preceded my separate descriptions of the three A-Mandates: Palestine-Transjordan, Syria-Lebanon and Mesopotamia-Iraq under sub-section B, §§ I, II and III, at pp. 556-573 of Part II, by a general analysis of that system as a whole in an introductory sub-section A at pp. 545-556. One of the conclusions reached in that analysis was that the specific conditions peculiar to the status of the territories under a B- or C-Mandate prevented any clear-cut allocation of territorial sovereignty to anybody in particular because of its dissection into different components and the resulting division of the totality of public powers among different authorities. This conclusion naturally led to the classification of these Mandates among the subjects dealt with in this Chapter VI concerning exceptional territorial situations.

However, as a consequence of this splitting-up of the subject over Parts II and III, I have to face the fact that not very much is left to be discussed in the present section, the less so because I have also already analysed in my *The Jurisprudence of the World Court*, vol. II, pp. 47-64, 217-229 and 231-239, the three Advisory Opinions delivered in 1950, 1955 and 1956 by the International Court of Justice with regard to

455

various legal uncertainties in the present regime of the C-Mandate of South-West Africa, and at pp. 497-521 of the same volume the first, preliminary Judgment of the Court in the cases, brought against the Republic of South Africa by Ethiopia and Liberia in 1961 and adjudicated on 21 December 1962 (*I.C.J. Reports* 1962, p. 319). Since, however, I have been unable still to insert in my publication on the case law of the Court a paper on the "second phase" preliminary Judgment in the same cases—said by (a majority in) the Court to be a judgment on the "merits"—of 18 July 1966 (*ibid.*, 1966, p. 6), this section is the obvious place to incorporate it as yet below (under (*b*).

I will further confine myself in this section to inserting under (*a*) a paper which I wrote in 1933 on an earlier dispute relating to the Mandates system, namely, that concerning the impact of Japan's rupture with the League of Nations after her illegal invasion of Manchuria upon her C-Mandate over certain islands in the Pacific Ocean, and to adding under (*c*) a few words on the Trusteeship status which is much less complicated than the diversified status of the Mandated territories.

(a) *The Japanese mandate over certain islands in the Pacific* (1933).*

The silence which has prevailed in Geneva with regard to the Manchurian conflict after the unanimous resolution of the League of Nations Assembly in its recent extraordinary session (1933) which bears far from comforting witness to the degree of zeal with which the Members of the League are prepared, in a difficult case, to effectively uphold the principles of the Covenant, also extends to cover the legal fate of the islands north of the Equator placed under a Japanese Mandate: the Marian Islands (Ladrones), Carolines, Marshall and Palau Islands, and Yap.

Yet, the rupture between the League of Nations and Japan gives rise to a series of important problems which touch on the root of the Mandates System and the solution of which the League will perhaps in the long run be unable to evade without further serious prejudice to its prestige.[20]

I do not allude here so much to what will actually befall the mandated islands, for in the light of the experience gained up to the present there is no ground whatever for illusion in this respect.[21]

* This Article was originally published in Dutch in the *Telegraaf* of 16 April 1933.
20. The legal problems involved have in fact only been partially considered by a qualified organ of the international community after the replacement of the Mandate by the Trusteeship system after World War II, when the legal status of South-West Africa was analysed by the International Court of Justice.
21. Japan has in fact remained in undisturbed possession of the archipelagos, until she was finally dislodged from them, in fact in the last stages of World War II and in law by Articles 2 and 3 of the Peace Treaty of San Francisco of 8 Septem-

Apart from the political situation, however, there remains the legal position, which cannot be impaired by international inaction and the general unwillingness to take effective steps against an aggressor, and that legal position is certainly worthy of a short analysis. In order to form a considered opinion concerning the extent to which in respect of these islands the Members of the League will probably again ignore the basic principles of the Covenant, it is first of all necessary to make a correct analysis of the juridical situation and of what the League accordingly *ought* to do.

The opinion is sometimes expressed that the termination of Membership of the League automatically entails the termination of a Mandate. This opinion, however, is generally speaking assuredly incorrect. The capacity of a Mandatory Power is not, under the rules of the Covenant, insolubly linked with Membership of the League. Thus, it might be desirable for political reasons to confer a specific Mandate upon a State not a Member of the League, for example, the United States. From a juridical point of view there would be no objection to such a conferment, should the State envisaged as Mandatory be prepared to accept it. For, of course, in such a case that State should also be prepared to submit its administration to the normal control of the Mandates Commission, in conformity with the provisions of the Covenant, and be bound vis-à-vis the League of Nations to fulfil its obligations under the Mandate Agreement, *inter alia*, as concerns the prohibition to establish military or naval bases, or to build fortifications in the Mandated Territory.

But if this is so, as a corollary a Mandatory does not either *ipso jure* lose that capacity as a consequence of the termination of its Membership of the League of Nations. The Covenant envisages three cases of such a termination: expulsion by a unanimous resolution of the Council because of a violation of obligations under its provisions, voluntary withdrawal from the League subject to two years' notice, and the automatic cessation of Membership in the case of non-acceptance of possible alterations of the Covenant. Only in the first of these three cases would the continuation of a Mandate seem to be inconsistent with the spirit of the Covenant, but even in that case the Mandate does not automatically come to an end, but must be terminated by a deliberate decision to that effect.

Now, what procedure is designated for that purpose and which authority is empowered to conduct it?

This question is closely related to the juristic nature and the genesis of the Mandate. Is this institution a unilateral mandate conferred by the League, which, as a result, is to be held to be likewise unilaterally revocable? Or is it rather a convention between the League and the

ber 1951 (*U.N.T.S.*, vol. 136, p. 45) in favour of the United States, which was then entrusted with a trusteeship over them.

Mandatory which is insusceptible of unilateral denunciation, or at least a juridical act which, though in essence unilateral, yet only becomes complete by the acceptance of the mandate by the opposite number, and the legal consequences of which cannot, therefore, be reversed without the latter's co-operation? Or is the matter perhaps wholly outside the competence of the League and is some other authority—for example, the Principal Allied Powers jointly—competent?

The curious thing is that the Covenant is completely silent on the question of the termination of a Mandate and on the designation of a new Mandatory. One Mandate, that regarding Iraq, has already ceased to exist. In that case the League was forced, on the advice of the Mandates Commission, to lay down new rules by improvisation, *inter alia* that the admission of a Mandated Territory to Membership of the League automatically puts an end to the Mandate, which is a reasonable new legal rule. For all other possible cases, however, any specific provisions are still lacking, so that one can only deduce them from the general principles which underlie the Mandates system.

These general principles are, however, fairly uncertain. Hence the wide divergence of views on the problem as to whether the juridical tie between the League and the Mandatory can be unilaterally denounced, either by the Mandatory Power itself, or by the League. An arbitrary dissolution of the legal bond, once voluntarily established, is in my opinion inadmissible. What, however, can be granted is that on reasonable grounds, on the one hand, a Mandatory has the right to surrender its Mandate to the League, and on the other, the League has the right to withdraw a Mandate. As far as revocation by the League is concerned, the ground for this can consist either in the fact that a Mandatory Power has ceased to deserve its maintenance as such (for example, owing to neglect of its specific obligations as a Mandatory, or to the violation of its duties as a Member of the League in general), or in considerations of a general political nature (for example, the undesirability of a continuation of the Mandate in the case of a Mandatory's voluntary withdrawal from the League).

It is again uncertain which of the main organs of the League is in such a case competent to terminate the Mandate. For the sake of juridical security the action should in this case emanate not from the Council (which has nowhere been explicitly granted this authority), but from the Assembly, and this, if possible, by a unanimous vote. The lack of any explicit direction in the Covenant on this point indeed opens the way for juristic quibbling, against which a unanimous resolution of the Assembly would constitute the most solid juridical defence.

This latter question is closely connected with one of the most thorny and still unresolved puzzles of the law on international Mandates: who was in 1919 or 1920 the competent authority for the appointment of the

458

Mandatory Powers? A problem which can also be projected into the future: who is entitled to designate a new Mandatory Power in the case of the one earlier designated falling out? Mainly there are three authorities which came and come into consideration: the Principal Allied Powers, the Council and the Assembly. On this point, too, the Covenant is absolutely mute, which can be easily explained from a politico-historical point of view, but which from the juridical angle is proof of unforgivable negligence.

What tells in favour of the Principal Allied Powers is, *inter alia*, the argument that Germany has been forced to cede to them her former colonies (Article 119 of the Peace Treaty of Versailles) and that any express provision for the throughtransfer thereof by them to the League is lacking. What further tells in favour of their competence is the fact that in the—unratified—Peace Treaty of Sèvres with Turkey the conferment of the ex-Ottoman territories as Mandated areas has been expressly entrusted to the Principal Allied Powers. And finally, there is the fact that the appointment of all the Mandatory Powers was in 1919 and 1920 actually made by them, albeit with subsequent confirmation by the Council.

What, however, pleads in favour of the competence of the League of Nations is the entire system established by Article 22 of the Covenant, which is basically inconsistent with the thesis that the Principal Allied Powers reserved for themselves, in future also, the right to appoint a Mandatory. Article 22 indeed lays down in so many words that the countries charged with the administration of the territories concerned shall exercise their powers of government in the capacity of Mandatories and in the name of the League, a capacity with which a right of appointment reserved in the future for the Principal Allied Powers is hardly compatible. Of the two chief organs of the League, the Council would come into consideration if decisive importance is attached to the argument of analogy: since in other respects (for example, the determination of the extent of the Mandatory's powers) it is the Council which was expressly made competent, there is ground for regarding it as also competent in matters for which no express provision has been made. The Assembly, however, would be more appropriately entitled on the strength of the argument *a contrario*: should the Covenant have intended, also for the future to leave the appointment of the Mandatories to the Council, it would have expressly laid this down; as matters stand, such an appointment therefore requires, because of its overriding importance, a resolution of the Assembly as the representative body of all the Members.

These theoretical controversies are of the greatest practical importance also in connection with the desire of Germany and Italy to hold colonial Mandates. I do not intend to enter here into the further knotty question of unanimity or (simple or qualified) majority in the voting on the decision to award or terminate a Mandate, either of the Principal Allied Powers, or of one or the other principal organ of the League.

It has already become obvious that Japanese diplomacy takes full advantage of these juristic controversies in order to stick firmly to her Mandated archipelagos. Certain articles in the press have contended that Japan basically rejects the League Mandate as being the legal foundation of her present power of administration of the islands, on the ground that they had already been allotted to her by the Supreme Allied Council prior to the juridical birth of the League of Nations. Should these press reports be correct (which I will not assume without reserve), then Japan would be attributing wrong legal effects to an, in itself undeniable, historical fact. It is indeed true that the Principal Allied Powers had already apportioned the future Mandates *inter se* prior to the birth of the League of Nations: Japan received her Mandate assigned to her by the Supreme Council on 7 May 1919, even before the Peace Treaty with Germany had been signed. This historical fact can indeed be held to throw some weight into the scales when an answer is required to the question as to who is in law the competent authority to appoint the Mandatory for a specific territory, but it cannot do away with the fact that the first appointment, also, has been made subject to the territory's future status as a Mandated territory and to the Mandate provisions in the Covenant as drafted. The juridical foundation of Japan's administration is, therefore, doubtless Article 22 of the Covenant, albeit in connexion with the conferment of the Mandate by the Supreme Council which, although made prior to the coming into force of that Article, was nevertheless indissolubly linked with it. Even if there should remain a juridical doubt, any possibility for Japan to invoke in her favour this notorious juristic controversy would be debarred by her own attitude since 1920: not only has she, without any relevant reservation, concurred in the resolution of 17 December 1920 by which the Council definitively confirmed her Mandate, but she has also since then consistently behaved as the Mandatory Power. It is therefore juridically beyond all question that even after Japan's withdrawal from the League Article 22 and the resolution of the Council of 17 December 1920 continue to govern the situation and that in the case that Japan's Mandate is maintained, her position as a Mandatory does not undergo any basic change. Also with respect to the position of the United States all remains juridically as before: the special treaty of Washington of 11 February 1922 between the Governments in Tokyo and Washington relating to the Mandated islands (Martens, N.R.G.³, XII, 841) remains in force unchanged.

It is in my opinion also beyond doubt that Japan's withdrawal from the League does not bring about either now, or after the lapse of two years, the automatic termination of the Mandate, but that the League is

460

competent in the case under consideration to end it by an *ad hoc* resolution. In order to be armoured as strongly as is feasible against possible juristic attacks, such a resolution should be adopted by the Assembly of the League unanimously, thus including the votes of the members of the Council and of the Principal Allied Powers, which might conceivably, as rivalling authorities, claim to be entitled to act.

Finally, the designation of a new Mandatory Power is, also from the juridical point of view, the most crucial issue. A reasonable construction of the Covenant requires in my view that this task be considered for the future to fall outside the sphere of competence of the Principal Allied Powers and to rest with the League of Nations. Which of the latter's two main organs is competent, it is scarcely possible to determine owing to the serious lacunae in the Covenant. On this point it will be necessary to cut the knot: the important function of appointing a new Mandatory Power should to my mind fall to the Assembly.

(b) The South West Africa Cases (second phase)*

In order to form a fair opinion on the juridical merits of the latest judgment of the International Court of Justice of 18 July 1966 in the *South West Africa Cases (Second Phase)*, as they are officially called,[22] it is necessary to place it in its historical context which leads us back to 1950. In that year, by an Advisory Opinion of 11 July,[23] the Court found:

unanimously, that South West Africa is a territory under the international Mandate assumed by the Union of South Africa on 17 December 1920;

by a large majority (12-2)[24] that South Africa continued to have the international obligations stated in Article 22 of the Covenant of the League of Nations and in the Mandate, as well as the obligation to transmit petitions from the inhabitants of that territory, the supervisory functions to be exercised by the United Nations, to which the annual reports and the petitions are to be submitted, and the reference to the Permanent Court of International Justice to be replaced by a reference to the International Court of Justice, in accordance with Article 7 of the Mandate and Article 37 of the Statute of the Court;

again unanimously, that the provisions of Chapter XII of the Charter

* This Article was originally published in *International Relations* of October 1966, vol. III, no. 2, p. 87.
22. *International Court of Justice Reports*, 1966, p. 6.
23. *Ibid.*, 1950, p. 128.
24. Judges McNair and Read dissenting. These Judges found that although, in their opinion also, South Africa's substantive international obligations arising under the Mandate continued, her former accountability to the League of Nations and the latter's supervision had lapsed and had not been transferred to the United Nations.

461

(International Trusteeship System) are applicable to the Territory in the sense that they provide a means by which it *may* be brought under the Trusteeship System, but

by a small majority (8-6)[25] that they do not impose on South Africa a legal *obligation* to place it under that System;

again unanimously, that South Africa acting alone has not the competence to modify the international status of the Territory, and that the competence to determine and modify that status rests with South Africa acting with the consent of the United Nations.

The General Assembly accepted this Advisory Opinion by a Resolution of 13 December 1950,[26] and subsequently, on 28 November 1953[27] and 11 October 1954,[28] further implemented the 1950 resolution by first establishing a Committee on South West Africa with the task of continuing the supervisory functions, as far as possible in accordance with the procedure of the former main organs of the League of Nations and the Permanent Mandates Commission, and by thereupon adopting a group of six special rules prepared by the said Committee, including a Rule F which prescribed the two-thirds majority rule for decisions on questions relating to reports and petitions concerning the Territory, held to rank amongst "important questions" within the meaning of Article 18 (2) of the Charter. Since some elucidation was desirable, in particular as to whether the said Rule F corresponded to a correct interpretation of the 1950 Opinion—in particular, to the passage obtaining therein according to which "The degree of supervision to be exercised by the General Assembly should not therefore exceed that which applied under the Mandates System, and should conform as far as possible to the procedure followed in this respect by the Council of the League of Nations"—the General Assembly on 23 December 1954[29] requested the International Court (*sub* a) to give an advisory opinion on that specific question. The answer of the Court, in its Opinion of 7 June 1955,[30] again unanimously, was to the effect that Rule F was indeed a correct interpretation of the 1950 Opinion. This second Opinion was also adopted by the General Assembly.

However, as it happened that the 1950 Opinion, in the same passage quoted above, later proved to be ambiguous on a further specific point of practical importance, the General Assembly thought it necessary to approach the Court for a third time[31] to request its opinion on the ques-

25. Judges Alvarez, Badawi, Guerrero, Krylov, De Visscher and Zoričić dissenting.
26. Resolution 449 A (V).
27. Resolution 749 A (VIII).
28. Resolution 844 (IX).
29. Resolution 904 (IX).
30. *I.C.J. Reports* 1955, p. 67; my *The Jurisprudence etc.*, vol. II, pp. 218-229.
31. Resolution 942 A (X) of 3 December 1955.

tion as to whether "it (was) consistent with the (1950 Opinion) for the Committee on South West Africa...to grant oral hearings to petitioners on matters relating to the Territory..." This question, which had been raised in the Committee itself, hinged on a controversy concerning the correct construction of the italicised word in the second half of the passage quoted: "should conform as far as possible to the procedure *followed* (in French, *appliqué*) in this respect by the Council of the League of Nations": did that word refer only to measures which had in actual fact been applied by the League or also to measures which it would have been entitled to apply? In its Opinion of 1 June 1956,[32] the Court by a majority of 8-5,[33] found in the latter sense and thus considered the grant of oral hearings to petitioners permissible.

Although this sequence of judicial assessments of the legal situation of South West Africa under the Mandate in the period 1950-1956 is in part extraneous to the issues involved in the contentious proceedings of 1960-1966, they are nevertheless still to a high degree relevant for the evaluation of the legal position as it has since developed, despite the final negative outcome of the latter proceedings in 1966. Both the formal final contents of the answers given in the successive advisory opinions and the statement of reasons underlying them offer a clear idea of what the International Court, unanimously on the main issues and with a large majority on a further essential point, considered in the fifties the legal situation to be. The consecutive answers together form a coherent legal picture and there is no inner contradiction between them. True, these Opinions are not in their own right binding pronouncements, but they have been to all intents and purposes unanimously accepted by the General Assembly—the authority which by the quasi-unanimous finding of the World Court had been declared to be competent to act in this field.

The first[34] of the two Judgments in the contentious proceedings which were more recently started by two parallel unilateral applications introduced in November 1960 by Ethiopia and Liberia against South Africa, in no way detracted from the advisory findings of the Court in the earlier period. This Judgment which was exclusively concerned with a number of preliminary objections to the applications, in particular relating to the asserted inapplicability of the jurisdictional clause inserted in Article 7 (2) of the Mandate, clearly took exactly the same road as had been followed by the Court since 1950, and did so in precisely the same spirit: the Court, in its preliminary Judgment of 1962, obviously confirmed its preceding basic findings on all points and gave not the

32. *I.C.J. Reports* 1956, p. 23; my *The Jurisprudence etc.*, vol. II, pp. 231-239.
33. Judges Badawi, Basdevant, Hsu Mo, Armand-Ugón and Moreno Quintana dissenting.
34. 21 December 1962 (*I.C.J. Reports* 1962, p. 319) *loco cit.*, pp. 497-521.

slightest hint of any alteration of its earlier legal assessments. On the contrary, in many passages it expressly referred to its preceding advisory pronouncement of 1950, and to the statement of reasons on which it was based, including a passage concerning precisely the issue of the continued validity of the adjudication clause which South Africa sought to discard in the contentious proceedings. There is, therefore, not a shadow of a doubt that the Court in its Judgment of 1962 pursued its earlier argument without any sign of wavering.

I say "the Court", but I mean by that the majority of the Judges, and on this occasion even the smallest possible majority. For in the meantime a most remarkable shift had taken place in the relative positions of the members of the Court and in the relative strengths of the majority and the minority. Whereas, indeed, eight of the Judges still clung to the legal evaluation of the situation as originally analysed in 1950, a powerful minority of seven Judges had emerged[35] who proved to be strongly opposed to the basic findings reached by the Court in 1950 and confirmed in 1955 and 1956. This opposition, as stated above, was formally only directed against the applicability of the jurisdictional clause of Article 7 (2) of the Mandate to the contentious proceedings in course, but it was in actual fact based on a statement of reasons which flew in the face of the main juristic construction adopted by the (quasi-unanimous) Court in 1950. During the preliminary proceedings of 1960-1962, only three of all the thirteen ordinary Judges responsible for the Opinion of 1950 (Badawi, Basdevant and Winiarski) were still in office; all the ten others were new. In any case, the majority still remained in favour of the original construction, and the decision thus reached on South Africa's preliminary objections in contentious proceedings was this time, unlike the preceding advisory opinions, vested in its proper field with the force of *res judicata*. Now, the curious thing is that in the latest Judgment of 1966 this character of *res judicata* was, it is true, not expressly denied and indeed apparently respected, but so much reduced in scope that the minority of 1962[36] succeeded as a new "majority", by dint of a number of procedural fortuities and technicalities,[37] in imposing as yet its own

35. When the two Judges *ad hoc*, who were as usual of contrary opinions, are eliminated, the result of the voting was 7-6. No such Judges had sat on the bench in the advisory proceedings of 1950-1956.

36. The "majority" of 1966 (7-7, or without the votes of the Judges *ad hoc*, 6-6), was identical with the minority of 1962 with one exception, *viz.* that Judge Basdevant had been replaced by Judge Gros, both of French nationality. The other members of this majority are Judges Spender (President), Winiarski, Spiropoulos, Fitzmaurice and Morelli.

37. The illness of one Judge; the abstention of another, too recently elected to sit on the bench; the maintenance on the bench of one Judge considered by the Respondent as being too prejudiced to sit, in virtue of an express Order of the Court of 18 March 1965 by a majority of 8 votes to 6 (*I.C.J. Reports* 1965, p. 3); the semi-voluntary withdrawal from the bench of one other Judge, held by the

legal vision upon the old majority, thus in fact reversing the earlier decision by resuming and substituting for it the contrary juridical reasoning which had been defeated in 1962, and thus to all intents and purposes flatly contradicting the legal arguments which had won the day three and a half years ago.

To a continental lawyer there is, of course, nothing particularly strange in the fact that a tribunal on a later occasion reverses an interpretation of the law which it has professed earlier but which it has since become convinced was incorrect, although such an occurrence in the field of inter-state adjudication casts a doubtful light on the intrinsic value of a provision such as Article 38 (1) sub *d* of the Statute of the Court which enjoins the latter to apply "judicial decisions" as one of the sources of the positive law of nations—albeit only "as subsidiary means for the determination of rules of law". However, in order to be admissible, such a reversal of earlier case law must not come into conflict with the general principle of international as well as national procedural law that a judicial decision duly rendered by a competent tribunal has the force of *res judicata* between the parties and is also final in respect of the tribunal itself which has rendered it. There is indeed a profound theoretical chasm between, on the one hand, the thesis that a court is empowered to modify its earlier construction of the law if it deems this necessary for the good administration of justice, and on the other, the assertion that, in so doing, it is also entitled to reverse an earlier judgment which has once become vested with the force of *res judicata* between the same parties in the same suit. The juristic assessment of the intrinsic worth of the latest Judgment of 18 July 1966 consequently entirely hinges on the following question. Did the Court in 1966 still have freedom to in actual fact reverse its earlier preliminary finding of 1962 "that it ha(d) jurisdiction to adjudicate upon the merits of the dispute"—meaning, of course, the dispute that was then pending between two specific Applicants and the Respondent since no other Applicant had brought a dispute before the Court—by the device of unexpectedly introducing into the discussion as an assertedly entirely new and separate element the necessity for the Applicant States to establish, in addition to the jurisdiction of the Court and their own *locus standi* under the jurisdictional clause, a legal right or interest of their own in the case, and of representing this requirement as completely divorced from the competence of the Court under the same clause, already finally determined in 1962, to adjudicate upon the

President, with the support of a majority in the Court, to be disqualified to participate on the ground of his having accepted in an interlude between two periods of membership of the Court an invitation of the Applicants to sit as a Judge *ad hoc*—as revealed in an official communiqué circulated by the Embassy of Pakistan in the Netherlands shortly after the Judgment—; and the casting vote of the President.

(real) merits of the dispute. Was this device, viewed in the light of the obvious purport of the first, preliminary Judgment, juristically justifiable —as the Court, in the persons of the new "majority" of 1966, attempted to make plausible, and as Judge Morelli, one of that majority, evidently felt it necessary to argue more convincingly than did the official statement of reasons? Or was this surprising splitting-off of a further, in reality adjectival issue—the asserted inadmissibility of the claims of the Applicants because of their failure to establish any legal right or interest appertaining to them in the subject-matter thereof—from the issue, already judicially decided, of the Court's competence to adjudicate upon the merits of the same dispute, and the incorporation of that further preliminary issue in the real merits, nothing more than an after-thought or after-wit, having presented itself to the defeated minority of 1962 as the only possible remaining escape from the otherwise ineluctable obligation to adjudicate upon the *real* merits of the dispute or, in other words,—as Judge Jessup forcefully argued—a highly artificial juristic construction *ex post*? The validity of this device can only be assessed by a comparison of what the Court—the majority of 1962—alleged in favour of its finding that it had jurisdiction to adjudicate upon the merits of the dispute between the Applicant States and South Africa, with what the Court—the minority of 1962, having become the "majority" of 1966— now advanced in an effort to turn the original reasoning upside down.

As it requires the greatest care not to misrepresent by a free paraphrase, however close, the subtle reasoning of the Court in its Judgment of 1966 on the so-called "merits"[38]—a Judgment which is in fact to all intents and purposes a reproduction of the views of the defeated minority of 1962—in comparison with its preliminary Judgment of 1962, it is recommendable to juxtapose and contrast the two on essential points by a series of literal quotations.

In 1962 the Court found:

> (p. 334) "The unanimous holding of the Court in 1950 on the survival and continuing effect of Article 7 of the Mandate continues to reflect the Court's opinion to-day. Nothing has since occurred which would warrant the Court reconsidering it".
>
> (p. 335) "The validity of Article 7, in the Court's view, was not affected by the dissolution of the League, just as the Mandate as a whole is still in force ...".
>
> (pp. 336-338) "... judicial protection of the sacred trust in each Mandate was an essential feature of the Mandates system ... The only effective recourse for protection of the sacred trust would be for a Member or Members of the League to invoke Article 7 and bring the dispute as also one between them and the Mandatory to the Permanent Court for adjudication. It was for this all-important purpose that the provision was couched

38. As remarked above, the title of the Judgment avoids this completely misleading word by using the term "second phase".

466

in broad terms embracing 'any dispute whatever ... between the Mandatory and another Member of the League of Nations relating to the interpretation or the application of the provisions of the Mandate ...'" (p. 343) "The language used is broad and clear and precise: it gives rise to no ambiguity and it permits of no exception. It refers to any dispute whatever relating not to any one particular provision or provisions, but to 'the provisions' of the Mandate, obviously meaning all or any provisions, whether they relate to substantive obligations of the Mandatory toward the inhabitants of the Territory or toward the other Members of the League or to its obligation to submit to supervision by the League under Article 6 or to protection under Article 7 itself. For the manifest scope and purport of the provisions of this Article indicate that the Members of the League were understood to have a legal right or interest in the observance by the Mandatory of its obligations both toward the inhabitants of the Mandated Territory, and toward the League of Nations and its Members".

(p. 338) "... the Court sees no valid ground for departing from the conclusion reached in the Advisory Opinion of 1950 to the effect that the dissolution of the League of Nations has not rendered inoperable Article 7 of the Mandate".

The operative clause ran as follows: "the Court finds that it has jurisdiction to adjudicate upon the merits of the dispute".

To what extent the "majority" of the Court in 1966 has felt justified in watering down or completely reversing most of its earlier findings in 1962—either by "vaporizing" positive pronouncements into mere hypothetical propositions, or by flatly contradicting them—appears from the following observations. The Court opens its reasoning by a general exposition of the various controversial issues raised by the parties and the discovery amongst them of two "questions which had such a character that a decision respecting any of them might render unnecessary an enquiry into other aspects of the matter". These two questions were: (1) "whether the Mandate still subsists at all, as the Applicants maintain that it does"; (2) the "antecedent question", said to be "even more fundamental", "of the Applicants' standing in the present phase of the proceedings—not, that is to say, of their standing before the Court itself, which was the subject of the Court's decision in 1962, but the question, as a matter of the merits of the case, of their legal right or interest regarding the subject-matter of their claim" (pp. 18-19). When accordingly first engaging in this latter question, the Court precedes its enquiry by the amazing statement that it does so "without pronouncing upon, and wholly without prejudice to, the question of whether the Mandate is still in force". The Court, in 1966, attempts to justify this device by the argument that, in 1962 also, the "decision on the question of competence was equally given without prejudice to that of the survival of the Mandate which is a question appertaining to the merits of the case", and asserts that this question "was not in issue in 1962, except in the sense that survival had to be assumed for the purpose of determining the purely jurisdictional issue which was all that was then before the Court".

467

What "the Court" does here is to ascribe to the preliminary Judgment of 1962 a purport and intention which are in the most obvious contradiction with those of its authors.

It was in this rarefied air of purely hypothetical assumptions that the Court in 1966 embarked upon the "antecedent" question under (2) above, *viz.* as to whether the Applicants had demonstrated an individual legal right or interest relative to the subject-matter of their claim. There would, of course, be no sense in such an enquiry unless the Applicants were *bound*, as a precondition of the admissibility of their claim, to demonstrate that they had such a special legal right or interest of their own under the jurisdictional clause, but that was just what the Court had emphatically *denied* in 1962 on the very ground that a correct interpretation of the clause implied that any Member of the League of Nations did as such have a legal right or interest in the observance by the Mandatory of its obligations toward the inhabitants of South West Africa and to the League and its Members (see the quotation above *ad* p. 343). The new thesis of the Court in 1966 that the Applicants had to show a special legal right or interest of their own apart from that implied in the grant of a right of action against the Mandatory under the jurisdictional clause, was therefore diametrically opposed to its thesis of 1962 and urgently needed a plausible justification. The attempt to supply an acceptable explanation of this reversal of an earlier finding and of the Court's complete *volte-face* in general was made by means of a combination of the following juristic contrivances.

As appears from one of the quotations above, the first thing was to draw a distinction between the Applicants' standing before the Court "(in) itself" and their standing with regard to the merits, which latter standing was—without any convincing argument—declared to be itself a question appertaining to the merits. In order to be able to deny the Applicants' "standing" in the latter sense, the Court had first to reverse the contrary finding of 1962 to the effect that such standing was implied in the jurisdictional clause. This was achieved by making a new distinction between provisions in the Mandates generally, relating to the "conduct" of the Mandatory *vis-à-vis* the inhabitants of the Mandated Territory and the League of Nations, and provisions relating to "special interests" of the Members of the League—such as those concerning the principle of the "open door", freedom for missionaries, etc.—and by postulating as an *a priori*, more than proving, that that distinction was decisive for the correct interpretation of the jurisdictional clause. Thus, in flat contradiction to the finding of 1962, this clause was held to apply only to the "special interests" provisions of the Mandates and not to their "conduct" provisions and simply to belong to the category of ordinary jurisdictional clauses the operation of which is dependent upon the existence of a special legal right or interest in the person of the plaintiff. This conclusion was drawn, on the one hand, from an abstract reasoning regarding the general "system" of the Mandates regime in the framework of the structure of the League of Nations—which, it was said, excluded the idea of judicial action against a Mandatory by individual Member States for the purpose of ensuring the performance of its duties towards the inhabitants under the Mandate—and, on the other hand, from the Court's new conception of the genesis of the jurisdictional clause.

As to the first reasoning *in vacuo*, the argument was devoted partly to an analysis of the basic ideas said to underlie the Mandatory regime and the structure of the League which, it was argued, laid the supervision of the Mandatories' duties exclusively in the hands of the organs of the League, and partly to an exposition of the untoward consequences which, in the Court's opinion, would follow from the acceptance of the contrary view, advocated by the Applicants (and, for that matter, already clearly expressed by the Court in 1962). In the course of this argument much stress was laid on a new thesis, quite foreign to that adopted in 1962, *viz.* that a jurisdictional clause can never create by itself substantive rights, but that its activation presupposes the existence of substantive rights, to be sought for elsewhere than in that clause. It is clear that this latter thesis again is in direct contradiction with the findings of 1962. In this context the Court dismisses all arguments derived from comparable clauses obtaining *e.g.* in the Minority Treaties after World War I, a fair number of which are discussed in detail in Judge Jessup's dissenting opinion.

As to the genesis of the jurisdictional clause in particular, the Court is remarkably brief (paragraphs 77-79 of its Judgment). It evidently attaches far more weight to its theoretical speculations *in vacuo* than to the actual historical data afforded by a minute research into that genesis. It would, for the rest, in my conviction have been very difficult for the Court to build up a convincing refutation of the conclusions drawn by the same dissenting Judge from an extremely thorough analysis of the historical data, which in fact unravels piece by piece the conclusions reached in the doctrinal exposition of the Court.

The Court is equally brief and equally unconvincing in dealing with the "suggestion" (of the "minority"?)—one of the highest legal importance, but no more than "glanced at, though only as a digression" (paragraphs 74-76)—that the question "of what rights, as separate Members of the League, the Applicants had in relation to the performance of the Mandate" was not a question appertaining to the merits of the claim, but was really one of its admissibility, and that as such it was disposed of by the 1962 Judgment. The Court denies this, with the obvious purpose of rendering it plausible that the 1962 Judgment, despite its operative clause upholding the Court's jurisdiction under Article 7 (2) of the Mandate to adjudicate upon the merits of the dispute—in the view of the authors of the 1962 Judgment undoubtedly its *real* merits—left the Court still free to avoid adjudicating upon those merits. This object was achieved by what I cannot but see as a juristic stratagem. In order to bar a decision on the real issues at the last moment, the "majority" of 1966 unexpectedly introduced into the legal argument the above-mentioned element of an, in essence, adjectival nature, which was represented as an, assertedly still open, question belonging to the (real) merits—namely, that of the Applicants' individual legal right or interest in the subject-matter of their claim, or, in other words, of their admissibility in the proceedings—and that, on the strength of a (different) construction of the same jurisdictional clause which had been clearly rejected in 1962. However ingeniously this was argued, and however strongly—and in their opinion rightly—the minority of 1962 may have disliked the preliminary decision, this distortion of the 1962 Judgment cannot be accepted as an honest construction of it, and as due respect shown to the *res judicata* of that year. Whatever one may personally think about the correctness, or otherwise, of that preliminary Judgment, and irrespective of whether one regrets that decision or not, it is there as an unambiguous decision of the Court which should have been respected, instead of explained away. That decision was final in its limited field of upholding the jurisdiction of the Court to adjudicate, in accordance with its quite manifest opinion in 1962, upon the real merits of the dispute between the Applicant States and South Africa on the strength of a jurisdictional clause which in itself, and *without* further need of demonstrating any additional individual legal right or interest, vested the Applicants with the right to ask for a judgment of the Court on the legal question as to whether the Respondent acts in conformity with its substantive obligations under the Mandate. There is no possibility of arguing one's way out of that *res judicata* by any reasoning, however skilful, without doing violence to its patent purport. This can certainly not be done by substituting for the textual construction of Article 7 (2) in the 1962 Judgment (comp. above *ad* p. 343) the diametrically opposed construction laid down in the following passages (paragraph 72): "The Court does not however consider that the word 'whatever' in Article 7, paragraph 2, does anything more than lend emphasis to a phrase that would have meant exactly the same without it; or that the phrase 'any dispute (whatever)' means anything intrinsically different from 'a dispute'; or that the reference to the 'provisions' of the Mandate, in the plural, has any different effect from what would have resulted from saying 'a provision'. Thus reduced to its basic meaning, it can be seen that the clause is not capable of carrying the load the Applicants" —what about the Court in 1962?—"seek to put upon it...". Neither can it be done by the assertion that the authority of *res judicata* is ex-

470

clusively confined to the operative part of a Judgment, and that this can be construed in isolation without regard to the essential juridical arguments on which it is based, nor by denying the authority of *res judicata* to a preliminary decision in the further proceedings on the merits, nor by a distinction, artificial in this case, between *locus standi* "(in) itself" and *locus standi* with regard to the merits. I may be allowed to quote in this respect one single paragraph from Judge Jessup's dissenting opinion which would seem to contain a slashing criticism of the Court's latest attitude (p. 382):

> "The Judgment of the Court rests upon the assertion that even though—as the Court decided in 1962—the Applicants had *locus standi* to institute the actions in this case, this does not mean that they have the legal interest which would entitle them to a judgment on the merits. No authority is produced in support of this assertion which suggests a procedure of utter futility. Why should any State institute any proceedings if it lacked standing to have judgment rendered in its favour if it succeeded in establishing its legal or factual contentions on the merits? Why would the Court tolerate a situation in which the parties would be put to great trouble and expense to explore all the details of the merits and only thereafter be told that the Court would pay no heed to all their arguments and evidence because the case was dismissed on a preliminary ground which precluded any investigation of the merits?"

The defence which the Court puts up against this reproach in paragraph 5, *viz.* that it was not at an earlier stage in a position to decide on the issue of the Applicants' legal right or interest, is wholly unsatisfactory and as artificial as its entire juristic edifice of hypotheses and distinctions.

The extraordinary size of the volume which contains the (twice) 50 pages of the Judgment itself and the accompanying (twice) 450 pages of personal declarations and dissenting opinions makes it impossible in a short analysis to do justice to the various views. I am personally most impressed by the elaborate dissenting opinion of Judge Jessup which would seem to tear the latest Judgment to pieces.

Should the Court in its new "majority" have respected the *res judicata* of 1962 and, consequently, have engaged in an examination of the real merits of the dispute, it would, of course, have found itself placed before one of the most tricky controversies of the present time. As a judicial body however—not being a political organ, nor a body with pseudo-legislative competences—the Court would then, in my view, have met with serious difficulties in finding against South Africa on strictly legal grounds. For not only does the Mandate in express terms give her freedom to administer and legislate over South West Africa as an integral portion of South Africa and to apply her own laws to it, but moreover she cannot be held to be bound by stricter obligations than she was under the League of Nations, and at that period the system of separate development was not yet anathema as it is now. This principle of retrospective assessment also follows from the earlier analysis by the Court in 1955, although it then only applied to the degree of supervision. Not to submit to that supervision at all remains, however, a breach of the law by South Africa which might entail for her grave legal consequences.

For the rest, the substantive findings of the Court in its series of advisory opinions are not invalidated by the latest Judgment on an adjectival issue of pseudo-merits.

Postscript to (b).

After the Court had thus declined to enter into the real merits of the dispute concerning South West Africa under the cloak of a rejection of the joint claims of Liberia and Ethiopia on their pseudo-merits, the United Nations General Assembly intervened to do what in any case ought to be done, *viz.*, to divest the Republic of South Africa of its legal position as a Mandatory Power. This decision, laid down in a Resolution of the General Assembly of 27 October 1966 (2145 (XXI), was in any case, if not for other reasons, fully justified on the ground that the Republic had already for a long time refused to submit the compulsorily prescribed annual reports to the United Nations and to acknowledge its legal status as a Mandatory Power vis-à-vis South West Africa. As a matter of principle this termination of the Mandate should already have been decided much earlier, and it could have legally been done so on the grounds developed in my exposition of 1933 under *(a)* above relative to the Japanese Mandate. The assumption of supreme control over the Territory concerned by the General Assembly was also entirely in consonance with the principles of the Mandates System. See further p. 474.

(c) The Trusteeship System

After what I have set out concerning the essence of the Mandates System little remains to be said about that of its successor, the Trusteeship System. Its juristic features are indeed in general identical with those of the Mandates System, variants B or C. The territories under Trusteeship were or are no subjects of international law, but territorial areas subordinate to a complex system of international supervision. Comp. on the Trusteeship system: R. N. CHOWDHURI, *International mandates and trusteeship systems* (The Hague, 1955); Ch. E. TOUSSAINT, *The trusteeship system of the U.N.* (London, 1956), and N. VEÏCOPOULOS, *Traité de territoires dépendants;* tome 1, *Le système de tutelle* (Athens, 1960).

Section 4. TERRITORY UNDER THE GOVERNMENT OF THE
INTERNATIONAL COMMUNITY

It is possible that a particular portion of the surface of the earth is occasionally placed under the territorial sovereignty or government, not of one or more individual States but under that of the international society of States as a whole, either legally linked together in such organizations as the League of Nations or the United Nations, or, hypothetically, even not so linked, but conceived as a kind of mythical all-embracing international Person, the *societas generis humani*.

The latter construction is, however, nothing more than a doctrinal cobweb. It might be held to apply to the high seas or to their bed, or to space and heavenly bodies, but it has no real substance and is wholly unnecessary to explain the legal rules applying, or to be applied in future, to such areas of common use, *res communis omnium*.

The former variant of collective sovereignty or government is not merely a theoretical construction, but susceptible of juridical realization since the Charter of the United Nations, in its Article 81, expressly foresees the possibility that a specific area is placed under the trusteeship of the Organization itself. And what applies to a collective trusteeship may in common accord be adapted by improvisation to apply to other forms of international administration.

The idea, once considered with regard to the former colonies of Italy in North Africa, taken from her by Article 23 and Annex XI of the Peace Treaty of Paris of 10 February 1947 (*U.N.T.S.*, vol. 49, p. 3), of placing them under the trusteeship of the United Nations was never realized.

In another variant it has, however, found an unexpected materialization in the temporary, very short government of the United Nations over the former Netherlands West New Guinea (West Irian) as an intermediary form of collective "sovereignty" to bridge the period between the abandonment of Netherlands sovereignty over that country as from 1 January 1963 and the establishment of Indonesian sovereignty as from 1 May 1963. The Netherlands-Indonesian Agreement of New York of 15 August 1962 (*U.N.T.S.*, vol. 437, p. 273) had on this point, briefly summarized, the following tenor (Articles 2-13).

(2) The Netherlands was to transfer administration of the territory to a United Nations Temporary Executive Authority (UNTEA) established by and under the jurisdiction of the Secretary-General upon the arrival of a United Nations Administrator. The UNTEA was thereupon in turn to transfer the administration to Indonesia.

(3) The Netherlands Governor of West New Guinea (West Irian) was, after a brief consultation with a representative of the Secretary General, to depart prior to the arrival of the United Nations Administrator.

(4) (5) The latter was to be acceptable to Indonesia and the Netherlands

and to be appointed by the Secretary-General. He was to have full authority under the latter's direction to administer the territory for the period of the UNTEA administration as its chief executive officer.

(6) The United Nations flag was to be flown during the period of United Nations administration. The flying of the Indonesian and Netherlands flags could only be determined by agreement between the Secretary-General and the respective Governments.

Further articles provided for the necessary security forces to supplement existing Papuan police in the task of maintaining law and order (7), for the replacement of top Netherlands officials with non-Netherlands, non-Indonesian officials during the first phase of United Nations administration (9) and for the gradual transfer of administrative control to Indonesia during the second phase (12). Article 11 left existing laws and regulations in effect in principle, but vested UNTEA with the power to promulgate the necessary new laws and regulations or to amend the existing ones.

On the future exercise by the Papuan people of its rights of self-determination (Articles 14 *et seq.*), see Part V of this publication.

The present situation of South West Africa, which was once a Mandated Territory of the C-type under the League of Nations Covenant, entrusted to the then Union of South Africa, and which had remained in that status under the Charter of the United Nations (comp. on this controversial issue the Advisory Opinion of the International Court of Justice of 11 July 1950, *I.C.J. Reports* 1950, p. 128), can also be considered as falling, at least on paper, under the category of cases dealt with in this section after the now Republic of South Africa was deprived of her Mandate by the United Nations General Assembly on the ground of its continual violation by the Mandatory. Comp. G.A. Resolution 2145 (**XXI**) of 27 October 1966, culminating in the following verdict *sub* (3):

"Declares that South Africa has failed to fulfil its obligations in respect of the administration of the Mandated Territory and to ensure the moral and material well-being and security of the indigenous inhabitants of South West Africa and has, in fact, disavowed the Mandate,"

and in the decisions *sub* 4 and 5, according to which:

"the Mandate conferred upon His Britannic Majesty to be exercised on his behalf by the Government of the Union of South Africa is therefore terminated; South Africa has no other right to administer the Territory, and henceforth South West Africa comes under the direct responsibility of the United Nations;

in these circumstances the United Nations must discharge those responsibilities with respect to South West Africa".

These responsibilities of the organized international community were to be discharged by a fourteen Member States Committee for South West Africa (*sub* 6), but, as is well known, the Resolution is completely disregarded by the former Mandatory which, on the contrary, continues illegally to consider itself to be the lawful sovereign of the Territory.

The Saar Territory has also been placed, between 1920 and 1935, in the legal situation of being administered by an international Commission on behalf of the organized society of nations, in this case the League of Nations. Comp. on this case Article 49(1) of the Peace Treaty of Versailles which ruled that

> "Germany renounces in favour of the League of Nations, in the capacity of trustee (*fidéicommissaire*), the government of the territory ...".

This special status came to an end in 1935 as a result of a plebiscite in favour of Germany. Comp. on this exercise of the right of self-determination Part V of this publication.

The Saar-regime was regulated by Articles 45-50 of the Peace Treaty of Versailles, with an Annex, divided in 3 Chapters (on the Cession and exploitation of mining property, the Government of the Saar Basin and the Plebiscite); see Martens, N.R.G.³, XI, pp. 360-380. Chapter II of the Annex provided for an international Governing Commission (Articles 16-18) of 5 persons (a Frenchman, an inhabitant of the Saar and three other persons) chosen by the Council of the League. This Commission had the full powers of government, though Germany retained the *nuda proprietas* of sovereignty and the inhabitants of the Saar retained their German nationality. The Commission was charged with the protection abroad of the interests of the inhabitants (entrusted on 7 July 1920 to the French government), it rendered justice in its own name, legislated after consultation with the elected representatives of the inhabitants and levied taxes (Articles 21, 23, 25 and 26). The Commission had also the power to decide all questions arising from the interpretation of the provisions of Chapter II (Article 33).

Section 5. SUPERIMPOSED LAYERS OF PUBLIC POWER OVER THE SAME TERRITORY

The juridical phenomenon of a territory placed under two superimposed layers of public power can take different forms.

Apart from the instances which I have already dealt with above in Chapter IV, sections 1-4, as more or less typical, distinct legal institutions—international pledges, international leases, transfer into foreign "occupation and administration" and State servitudes—and from the otherwise typical Mandate and Trusteeship institutions analysed in Part II of this publication, pp. 545-573, and in a complementary section 3 of this Chapter, pp. 454-472 above, reference can be made to the following examples of the situation envisaged in this section.

(i) Enemy occupation. In this case, belonging systematically to the laws of war, there is a division of powers between the occupant and the authorities of the occupied country.

An encampment of foreign forces and the accompanying presence of administrative officers, which began as enemy occupation but gradually blended into the type of occupation mentioned under (ii) below, was that of Germany from 1945 to 1954 and that of Austria from 1945 to 1955.

Comp. on the former:

> Occupation Statute of 8 April 1949, operative as from 21 September 1949 (*U.N.T.S.*, vol. 140, p. 196);
>> Charter of the Allied High Commission of 20 June 1949 (*ibid.*, vol. 128, p. 141);
>>> Revision of the Occupation Statute, 6 March 1951 (*ibid.*, vol. 141, p. 400);
>>> Convention No. I of Bonn of 26 May 1952 on relations between the Three Powers and the Federal Republic of Germany (*ibid.*, vol. 331, p. 327);
>>> Protocol of Paris on the termination of the Occupation Regime in the Federal Republic of 23 October 1954 (*ibid.*, vol. 331, p. 253);

and on the latter:

> Agreements between the Governments of the United Kingdom, the United States, the U.S.S.R. and France concerning control machinery and zones of occupation in Austria and the administration of the City of Vienna of 9 July 1945 and 28 June 1946 (*ibid.*, vol. 160, p. 359 and vol. 138, p. 85).

(ii) Peace time occupation. This type of essentially temporary unilateral infringement of the normal rights of the territorial sovereign can have different purposes. It can serve as a guarantee for the fulfilment of treaty engagements (comp. Part VI of this publication). Or it can be employed as a means of compulsion short of war in order to bring pressure to bear upon another State; one of the most repulsive instances of this means of coercion is the recent occupation of Czechoslovakia by Soviet and allied satellite troops (1968).

(iii) The situation arising from the stationing of troops on allied territory in common consent for military exercises or defensive purposes, as practised by NATO forces, troops of the Warsaw Pact, SEATO, etc.

(iv) The peculiar regime sometimes established in favour of surrounding States as a burden on the precarious life of "free cities", such as Cracovia (1815-1846), Danzig (1919-1939), Fiume (1920-1924) and Trieste (1947-1954). Comp. on these international entities and their limitations Part II of this publication, Chapter VI, section 5, pp. 305 *et seq.*

(v) Other exceptional cases, such as those

of Smyrna, under Articles 69 and 83 of the (abortive) Peace Treaty of Sèvres of 10 August 1920 (Martens, N.R.G.³, XII, 664), see *supra*, Chapter IV, section 3, p. 411;

of U.S.A. forces in the Dominican Republic under the conventions of 27 December 1924 and September 1940 (*ibid.*, XXXIX, 492, 499); comp. on this type of military control also Part II of this publication, Chapter VI, section 2A, *sub* (*i*), 3, p. 481;

of Greenland during World War II under a convention between the

476

United States and a Danish diplomat without the otherwise required authorization of his Government in Copenhagen under German occupation, for the defence of Greenland against the Germans: 9 April 1941, with Notes (*ibid.*, XXXIX, 26);

of Iceland during World War II under a Convention between the United States and the Icelandic Government of 1 July 1941 (*ibid.*, XXXIX, 398);

of the many air or naval bases accorded to the United States by Great Britain during World War II: Conventions of 2 September 1940 (*ibid.*, XXXVIII, 360) and 27 March 1941 (*ibid.*, XXXIX, 361).

In the cases alleged as examples a delimitation between the jurisdiction of the territorial sovereign and that of the occupant, ally or supervising power(s) is necessary and has indeed repeatedly been regulated in detail. Comp., *e.g.*, the provisions obtaining on this subject—among others, relative to the activity of foreign courts on the national territory and the immunity of members of foreign forces from trial by local criminal courts—

on the stationing of French troops on Corsica: the agreement with Genova of 16 August 1764 (Martens, R², I, 265);

on the occupation of the Rhineland: Articles 428-432 of the Peace Treaty of Versailles of 28 June 1919, with annexed Agreement of the same date (*ibid.*, N.R.G.³, XI, 659);

on the visiting armed forces of the Brussels Treaty Powers: Agreement of London of 21 December 1949 (Cmd. 7868), which however has never become operative;

on the North Atlantic Treaty forces: Treaty of London of 19 June 1951 (*U.N.T.S.*, vol. 199, p. 67);

on the stationing of Allied forces in Germany after World War II: the Occupation Statute of 8 April 1949, cited above, revised 6 March 1951, and Convention II of Bonn of 26 May 1952 on the rights and obligations of foreign forces and their members in the Federal Republic of Germany (*U.N.T.S.*, vol. 332, p. 3). Comp. on Germany under Allied occupation Part II of this publication, Chapter III, section 1, Annex A, *sub* (c), pp. 109 *et seq.*

See further on the subject of conflicts of jurisdiction in this field, among others: VAN PANHUYS in *Netherlands International Law Review* 1955 (II), pp. 253-278 and KALSHOVEN, *ibid.* 1958 (V), pp. 165-194.

In view of the extreme political importance and prolonged existence of the control machinery in Allied-occupied Austria and Vienna from 1945 to 1955 I follow up the above list of instances of what I called the superimposition of two layers of public power over the same territory by a summary of the legal status of that country and capital between the end of World War II and the ultimate conclusion of the so-called Austrian State Treaty of 15 May 1955 (*U.N.T.S.*, vol. 217, p. 223).

The Moscow Declaration of 6 November 1943 had stated that the *Anschluss* was to be considered null and void, and that Austria was to be treated as a liberated country. Later on, however, the Allied Powers decided on an occupation regime for Austria and signed two agreements on the control machinery and the occupation zones in July 1945 (*U.N.-T.S.*, vol. 160, p. 359 and *Cmd.* 6958). Under the first agreement the "ultimate and supreme power" was laid in the hands of the four Occupying Powers; decisions of the Allied Council (concerning the whole country) had to be unanimous; each zone was ruled by its Commander-in-Chief.

In the meantime the leaders of the Austrian political parties on 27 April 1945 had proclaimed the independence of their country and set up a provisional Government. After elections had been held in November 1945, this Government was officially recognized by the Allies. On 28 June 1946 the Government obtained a new agreement on control machinery (*U.N.T.S.*, vol. 138, p. 85) which was much more favourable to Austria. Apart from constitutional laws, which still needed the unanimous approval of the Allies, all other legislative acts and international agreements would be considered approved unless unanimously rejected by the Allies. Thus, almost complete liberty was achieved, and this situation lasted until the signing of the State Treaty in 1955.

See on this subject R. E. CLUTE, *The international legal status of Austria 1938-1955* (The Hague, 1962) and Whiteman, vol. 3, p. 425.

Section 6. LIMITATIONS UPON THE FREEDOM TO ALIENATE
NATIONAL TERRITORY. PRE-EMPTION OR RE-EMPTION

Limitations upon the normal freedom of a State to alienate the national territory can be of different kinds. I have already briefly alluded to this type of limitation of national sovereignty in Part II of this publication, Chapter VI, section 2A, under (*h*) 1, p. 477, but it deserves some further analysis also in the context of this Part and Chapter.

A prohibition to alienate any part of the national territory can be based either in a municipal constitution or in an international treaty.

If it is a purely national prohibition, this cannot affect the validity of a treaty of cession which is entered into by the State concerned, for example after a lost war, in defiance of the constitutional interdiction. The merits of this potential controversy between the ceding and the cessionary State are dealt with elsewhere (in Part VI of this publication).

What I have in view here is, however, an international prohibition. This can either be of a general nature legally excluding any alienation of territory, or only bar a cession to a specific State or prevent a cession to any State, other than a specific State.

478

Apart from such cases of real inalienability, absolute or relative, a State can also be fettered in its freedom of action by the less far-reaching international commitment not to proceed to the alienation of a specified part of its territory[39] without having first offered it either to its former sovereign who has reserved the "right of re-emption", or to another State which has stipulated for itself a "right of pre-emption", preferential to possible offers by other interested States. These latter types of international commitment belong almost completely to the feudal-patrimonial or to the colonial past. In so far as a right of re-emption or pre-emption is still formally in existence, the State which benefits from it will no longer be in a position politically to enforce it. Only very exceptionally it may still be capable of present-day application.

An old example of the reservation of the right of re-emption is that concerning the territory of Draheim, based on the Prusso-Polish Treaty of Bydgošć (Bromberg) of 6 November 1657 (Lünig, *Part. Spec., Cont.*II, *Forts.* I, p. 114, 116—*Part. Spec., Theil* III, p. 171), renounced by Poland in Article 5 of her treaty with Prussia (first partition) of 18 September 1773 (Martens, R², II, 149), the same Article in which she also renounced a certain right of reversion (comp. *supra* Chapter III, section 1, § 2, (*e*), p. 322).

Famous examples of the grant of a right of pre-emption are those relating to Gibraltar (1713), Malacca and parts of Sumatra (1824) and Timor (1893). Comp. on these cases below, pp. 481 *et seq.*

International prohibitions of these different types can be the outcome of the temporary pressure of particular international events. This was the case during the Crimean War, when France and Great Britain obtained an undertaking from Sweden-Norway not to cede to, nor to exchange with, nor to allow the occupation by, Russia of any portion of the united kingdoms, in exchange for a promise by France and Great Britain to assist them, if need be, against Russian claims of that nature. See their Treaty of 21 November 1855 (*ibid.*, N.R.G.¹, XV, 628). It was only much later, after the dissolution of her real union with Sweden in 1905, that Norway, in view of the existing political tension in Europe, again entered into a similar engagement, but on that occasion vis-à-vis France, Germany, Great Britain and Russia indiscriminately (treaty of 2 November 1907, Martens, N.R.G.³, I, 14). However, under the changed conditions of the inter-war period the latter treaty was in its turn cancelled by a new treaty of 8 January 1924 (*ibid.*, N.R.G.³, XIII, 493).

More often than not, however, a prohibition of one of the types distinguished above was either (i) peculiar to the general status of a particular State as an international person, or (ii) connected with

39. What is said here about State territory proper equally applies to leased or pledged territory, or to colonial zones of influence.

colonial rivalries, or (iii) imposed as a condition of the cession or adjudication of a disputed territory.

(i) A typical instance of the first variant is provided by the principality of Monaco which in the additional Articles of the Franco-Monégasque treaty of 2 February 1861 (*ibid.*, N.R.G.¹, XVII², 55), confirmed by Article 3 of their treaty of 17 July 1918 (*ibid.*, N.R.G.³, XI, 313), undertook "de ne point aliéner la Principauté, soit en totalité, soit en partie, en faveur d'aucune autre Puissance que la France."

Another example of this type can be seen in Article 8 of the Treaty of Paris of 12 July 1806 establishing the (Napoleonic) Confederation of the Rhine (*ibid.*, R², VIII, 480): the Members of that confederation were empowered to alienate their sovereignty entirely or in part, but only among themselves, obviously in order to prevent their upsetting the political balance in disfavour of the Confederation's "protector".

When in 1904 Spain was awarded a sphere of influence in Mediterranean Morocco, she gave an undertaking, in Article 7 of her secret treaty with France of 3 October 1904 (*ibid.*, N.R.G.³, V, 666), that she would not alienate or cede any of the territories comprised in that zone, nor "her establishment at Santa-Cruz-de-Mar-Pequeña (Ifni)", nor her spheres of influence in West-Africa on the coasts of the Sahara and the Gulf of Guinea, in any form, even temporarily. On Ifni see already 26 April 1860 (*ibid.*, N.R.G.¹, XVI², 590).

(ii) Instances of the second variant are the following,

Article 8 of the Anglo-Spanish Peace Treaty of Utrecht of 13 July 1713 (Dumont, VIII¹, 393) forbidding the cession of any part of America to France or other countries.

An arrangement made by Great Britain and the Netherlands in their treaty of 17 March 1824 (*ibid.*, N.R., VI, 415 = N.S., I, 628) relative to a number of territories or establishments in East Asia, *viz.* (Articles 8-12): the remaining Netherlands establishments on the Indian continent, ceded on that occasion to Great Britain; Great Britain's possession on the island of Sumatra (fort Marlborough), then ceded to the Netherlands; the Netherlands town and fortress of Malacca, then ceded to Great Britain; the island of Billiton and its dependencies, to the occupation of which by the Netherlands Great Britain would no longer object; and the island of Singapore, to the occupation of which by Great Britain the Netherlands would no longer object (subject to the former's undertaking to renounce any territorial aspirations with respect to the Carimon islands and any islands south of the straits of Singapore). None of these territories was, pursuant to Article 15, to be at any time transferred to any other Power. And the Article added that

"in case of any of the said possessions being abandoned by one of the Contracting Parties the right of occupation thereof shall inmediately pass to the other",

480

a provision which was intended to operate automatically.

A corresponding arrangement made by the Netherlands and Portugal regarding the Timor and Solor archipelago in a Declaration of 1 July 1893, supplementary to their Demarcation Convention of 10 June 1893 (Martens, N.R.G.², XXII, 463, 465) was to the effect that they

> "se reconnaissent réciproquement, en cas de cession, soit en partie, soit en totalité, de leurs territoires ou de leurs droits de souveraineté dans l'archipel de Timor et Solor, le droit de préférence à des conditions similaires ou équivalentes à celles qui auraient été offertes".

This provision consequently created a mutual right of pre-emption.

Another prohibition by treaty to cede colonial territory to a third State without the consent of the co-contracting party was that laid down in the Anglo-Portuguese treaty of 20 August 1890 (*ibid.*, N.R.G.², XVI, 929 = XVIII, 154), Articles 1-4, relative to territories to the south of the Zambesi. In their original wording the provisions burdened Portugal unilaterally (Article 2):

> "Portugal engages not to cede her territories to the south of the Zambesi to any other Power without the previous consent of Great Britain".

However, after a new arrangement concluded on 14 November 1890 (*ibid.*, XVI, 492 = XVIII, 160) the (separate) provisions of Articles 1-4 were deleted in a third Convention of 11 June 1891 (*ibid.*, XVIII, 185) and replaced by a new, non-discriminatory provision (Article 7²) in the terms of which

> "The two Powers agree that in the event of one of them proposing to part with any of the territories to the south of the Zambesi assigned by these Articles to their respective spheres of influence, the other shall be recognized as possessing a preferential right to the territories in question, or any portion of them, upon terms similar to those proposed".

France in 1884 acquired a "droit de préférence" to the possessions of the International Association of the Congo (letters between President Ferry of France and the President of that Association of 23/24 April 1884 (*ibid.*, N.R.G.², XVI, 582, 583), confirmed by a Decree of the Independent State of the Congo of 1 August 1885 and letters of 22/29 April 1887 (*ibid.*, 584, 585). The right was later by way of substitution recognized by Belgium in the Belgo-French agreements of 5 February 1895 (*ibid.*, XX, 698 = XXI, 622) and 23 December 1908 (*ibid.*, N.R.G.³, VI, 336).

As regards the Spanish possessions of Río Muni and the islands of Elobey and Corisco on and in the Gulf of Guinea a preferential right was established in favour of France by Article 7 of the Franco-Spanish treaty of 27 June 1900 (*ibid.*, N.R.G.², XXXII, 59). It was this right which France, on the occasion of her colonial arrangement with Germany pursuant to their exchange of Notes of 4 November 1911 (*ibid.*, N.R.G.³, VI, 323), declared herself prepared to renounce in favour of

481

Germany should the latter wish to acquire the Spanish possessions concerned. This renunciation, however, lost its effect after Germany's defeat in World War I (Article 125 of the Peace Treaty of Versailles, 1919).

Other preferential rights of this kind were still established with respect to a piece of colonial territory in Africa between Great Britain and Italy by Article 5 of their treaty of 15 July 1924 (Martens, N.R.G.³, XVII, 585).

Such rights of preference or pre-emption were especially familiar in colonial affairs, but neither were they unknown in other contexts, comp. *infra sub* (iii) (Gibraltar).

The prohibition of alienation of territory (as, for that matter, of the granting of leases), thus established in the colonialist era, was after World War I extended to certain Mandated Territories. Comp. Article 5 of the Mandate for Palestine (*ibid.*, N.R.G.³, XV, 297).

(iii) Old examples of this variant were those documented in Article 2 of the Barrier Treaty between the Emperor, the Netherlands and Great Britain of 15 November 1715 (Dumont, VIII¹, 458; Rousset, *Recueil* I, 37) for the cession of the southern Low Countries to Austria on the understanding that they should not be alienated by Austria to the Crown of France or to any prince who was not a successor to the House of Austria in Germany, and in Article IV, para. 2, of the treaty between Denmark and Hamburg of 27 May 1768 concerning the *Elb-Pertinentiën* in the mouth of the river (Martens, R², I, 597).

Another old example is the right of pre-emption or re-emption that was established in favour of Spain in a stipulation added to the cession of Gibraltar by her to England by the elaborate Article X of their Peace Treaty of Utrecht of 13 July 1713 (Dumont, VIII¹, 393). Pursuant to the final clause of that Article

> "Quod si vero Coronae Magnae Britanniae commodum olim visum fuerit donare, vendere, aut quoquo modo ab se alienare dictae urbis Gibraltaricae proprietatem, conventum hisce concordatumque est ut prima ante alios ejus redimendae optio Coronae Hispanicae semper deferatur".

Spain has often in the course of time attempted to regain Gibraltar by force or by diplomatic devices—*inter alia* by a siege in 1779; by the insertion of a clause in Article 2 of her Treaty of Alliance with the Emperor of 30 April 1725 (Dumont, VIII², 106; Rousset, *Recueil*, II, 178) by which however the latter undertook no more than to abstain from opposing the restitution of Gibraltar if that could be achieved peacefully, and, if need be, to lend his good offices or mediation, and by demands laid before the Congress of Cambrai in 1729. But all these attempts have been in vain: the status of the town, as established in 1713, inclusive of the right of (p)re-emption, has remained unchanged, in particular since the Anglo-Spanish treaty of Sevilla of 9 November 1729 (Dumont, VIII²,

482

158; Rousset, *Suppl.*, II², 288), by which all preceding treaties were emphatically confirmed (Article 1). It is true that one of the objections of the twenty-four Protestant Peers in Great Britain against this treaty—comp. Rousset, *ibid.*, V², pp. XXXIII *et seq.*, at p. XXXVI, *sub* 8—was that the right of Great Britain to Gibraltar was not confirmed in so many words and only implicitly, but this does not affect the true legal situation.

The other clauses of Article X of the treaty of Utrecht relate to such matters as: the prevention of smuggling between Gibraltar and the Spanish mainland, a prohibition to allow Jews and Moors to establish themselves in Gibraltar, a prohibition to admit Moorish warships into the harbour, and freedom for the inhabitants to practice Roman-Catholic worship.

More recent examples of a ban on the alienation of specific parts of a national territory are those

of the Spitsbergen archipelago, allotted by the Powers to Norway in their treaty of 9 February 1920 (Martens, N.R.G.³, XIII, 473) with the express recognition in Article 1 of the "full and absolute sovereignty of Norway over the Archipelago of Spitsbergen". A Draft Statute of 26 January 1912 (*Jahrbuch des Völkerrechts* 1913 (I), p. 412; *R.G.D.I.P.* 1913 (20), p. 282), which was never adopted because of the outbreak of World War I, still tried to internationalize the territory:

> Article 1. "Le Spitsbergen demeurera *terra nullius*. Il ne pourra, ni en tout, ni en partie, être annexé par aucun Etat, ni être soumis, sous quelque forme que ce soit, à la souveraineté d'une Puissance quelconque",

and of the territory of Northern Schleswig, transferred to Denmark by her treaty with the Principal Allied Powers concluded in Paris on 5 July 1920 (*ibid.*, N.R.G.³, XIV, 881) under the express stipulation (Article 2) that that territory was to be inalienable except with the consent of the Council of the League of Nations.

A special case was that of Cyprus in the inter-war period: successive Franco-British arrangements to appease their friction over certain aspects of the new political situation in the Middle East also implied a prohibition for Great Britain to cede Cyprus to another Power without the consent of France: comp. Article 4 of the Sykes-Picot agreement of 9/16 May 1916 (*ibid.*, N.R.G.³, X, 351):

> "Le gouvernement de Sa Majesté, de son côté, s'engage à n'entreprendre à aucun moment des négociations en vue de la cession de Chypre à une tierce puissance sans le consentement préalable du gouvernement français."

Article 4 of the Paris treaty of 23 December 1920 (*ibid.*, N.R.G.³, XII, 583) used almost the same words.

The regimes which I have in view here are of two types.

(a) Regimes intended for the protection of specific minority groups of the population

As I have stated above in Part II of this publication, Chapter VI, section 2A *sub* (*d*), 3, p. 466, the international protection of minorities has in various cases taken the form of the establishment of regional regimes of autonomous government.[40] Amongst the fairly frequent instances of this phenomenon the following are worth mentioning.

The Lebanon. After the Egyptian Vice-Roy Muhammad 'Ali had been ousted from his temporary pashalik of Syria in 1840, the Great European Powers demanded from the Sultan, as a condition for its restitution to the Ottoman Empire, that in the Lebanon region separate administrations under two kaimakams should be set up, for the Maronites in the North and for the Druses in the South. This form of government has remained in force until the massacres of 1860 forced the Great Powers to authorize a military intervention by France (protocol of 5 September 1860, Martens, N.R.G.[1], XVIII, 224) and to impose upon the Sultan a new regime for the Lebanon, severed from Syria as a separate pashalik under the control of their envoys and under a Christian Governor, to be appointed for successive periods of three (later five) years. This was laid down in the first *Règlement relatif au Liban* of 9 June 1861 (*ibid.*, N.R.G.[1], XVII[2], 101), issued by an Imperial firman, with an annexed protocol (*ibid.*, 107) by which the Sultan undertook to come to an agreement on each occasion with the Great Powers on the person of the Governor to be appointed. A new protocol with annexed revised *Règlement* was adopted by the Porte and the five Powers on 6 September 1864 (*ibid.*, N.R.G.[1], XVIII, 227); it has since functioned regularly, *inter alia*, through the periodic appointment of a Governor, and had only to be supplemented much later by a new protocol of 23 December 1912 (*ibid.*, N.R.G.[3], VIII, 656). The whole system was changed after World War I as a result of the emancipation of Syria-Lebanon to an A-Mandate of the League of Nations entrusted to France.

40. Such regional regimes can also be established without any international obligation. Comp. for example the regime of Puerto Rico, analysed by Ramírez DE ARELLANO in three lectures during the XXIIIth course of the University of Valladolid en Victoria, 1968, on *El estatuto político de Puerto Rico.*—Other examples are the gradually developing autonomy of French Canada within the federal Dominion of Canada; the decentralization in unitary States such as Italy (*regioni autonome*) and temporarily—before the civil war which upset the whole situation —Spain (for the Basques and Cataluña); and lately in Belgium (a Flemish part, a Walloon part, and Brussels). The latter decentralization according to the linguistic frontier has already given rise to international proceedings before the Strasbourg Court of Human Rights (see *I.L.M.* 1969(8), p. 825).

The Walach Communities of the Pindus (Koutzo-Walachs). Their legal status was to comprise local autonomy in regard to religious, charitable and scholastic matters under the control of the Greek State. After an initial exchange of notes annexed to the Peace Treaty of Bucharest of 10 August 1913 between the four Balkan Allies in their second war and Bulgaria (*ibid.*, N.R.G.[3], VIII, 61,75), the regime was confirmed by Article 12 of the special treaty between the Principal Allied and Associated Powers and Greece of 10 August 1920 (Sèvres) (*ibid.*, N.R.G.[3], XII, 801), put into force by Protocol XVI annexed to the Peace Treaty of Lausanne of 24 July 1923 (*ibid.*, N.R.G.[3], XIII, 338 *et seq.*, at p. 448).

Communities of the Saxons and Czekler in Transylvania. Local autonomy was granted to them on the same footing with the Walachs of the Pindus: Article 11 of the special treaty between the Principal Allied Powers and Romania of 9 December 1919 (Paris) (*ibid.*, N.R.G.[3], XIII, 529).

The Ruthene Territory south of the Carpathians. Here an autonomous, fully self-governing unit within the Czechoslovak Republic was created, possessed of a special Diet with limited powers of legislation, placed under a Governor, to be appointed by the President of the Republic and responsible to the Diet, and entitled to equitable representation in the Legislative Assembly of the State. This special regime for the Carpatho-Russians of Eastern Galicia has never as it was planned materialized. See Article 57 of the Peace Treaty of St.-Germain with Austria of 10 September 1919 (*ibid.*, N.R.G.[3], XI, 691) and Chapter II, Articles 10-14, of the special treaty between the Principal Allied and Associated Powers and Czechoslovakia of 10 September 1919 (*ibid.*, N.R.G.[3], XIII, 512).

Memel Territory. This was organized as an autonomous territory within the boundaries of Lithuania in virtue of Article 99 of the Peace Treaty of Versailles (1919) and a detailed Convention between the Principal Allied Powers and Lithuania of 8 May 1924 (*ibid.*, N.R.G.[3], XV, 106). Controversies concerning the functioning of that Convention led in 1932 to proceedings between the parties to it before the Permanent Court of International Justice, judgments of 24 June and 11 August 1932, series A/B, Nos. 47 and 49 (comp. on this case my papers in *The Jurisprudence of the World Court*, vol. I, pp. 294 and 299, 300).

Eastern Carelia. This country should have become, under the Finno-Russian Peace Treaty of Dorpat of 14 October 1920 (*ibid.*, N.R.G.[3], XII, 37), an autonomous territory within the U.S.S.R., in conformity with the real wishes of the population of Finnish extraction. The whole scheme soon came to grief on a difference of interpretation of the clauses concerned, the Soviet Government contending that they had already been

485

implemented by the Soviet way of granting autonomy, namely, by the establishment of a "labour commune" there. Requested by the Council of the League of Nations to give its advisory opinion on that dispute, the Permanent Court of International Justice felt unable to accede to the request on the ground that the Soviet Union had opposed this procedure: Advisory Opinion of 23 July 1923, series B, No. 5 (comp. on this case my observations in *The Jurisprudence of the World Court*, vol. I, pp. 50-52).

The Turkish islands of Imbros and Tenedos. These islands also were to be endowed with a special administrative organization composed of local elements, assisted by an indigenous police force. See Article 14 of the Peace Treaty of Lausanne of 24 July 1923 (*ibid.*, N.R.G.³, XIII, 342), by which the transfer of the islands to Greece—already once in the past denied to her by the decision of the Conference of Ambassadors of 13 February 1914 (*British Documents on the origin of the war (1898-1914)*, vol. X, part I, pp. 231/2), but promised to her in Article 84 (3) of the (abortive) Peace Treaty with Turkey of Sèvres of 10 August 1920 (*ibid.*, N.R.G.³, XII, 664)—was definitely rejected.

Adrianople. This town would, under Article 86 of the same Peace Treaty of Sèvres and Article 15 of the ancillary special treaty with Greece (Martens, N.R.G.³, XII, 779), have obtained an organization including a municipal council in which the various racial elements habitually resident in it would have been represented, if the town had not been attributed to Turkey by the operation of Article 2 (2°) of the definitive Peace Treaty of Lausanne of 24 July 1923 and the said Article 15 had not been cancelled, as henceforth without object, by Protocol XVI (Article 2) annexed to that Peace Treaty (*ibid.*, N.R.G.³, XIII, 448).

Smyrna. An elaborate section (Articles 65-83) of the (abortive) Turkish Peace Treaty of Sèvres (1920) has set up a fantastic scheme for the provisional organization of the city of Smyrna (Izmir) and an adjacent area as a territory which was to remain formally under Turkish sovereignty, but substantively, as to the actual exercise of the rights of sovereignty, under Greece, and for its final adjudication by the Council of the League of Nations to either Turkey or Greece in accordance with a majority vote by a local parliament to be set up. Comp. Chapter IV, section 3, p. 411.

Kurdistan. See on this territory Part II of this publication, pp. 45-46.

Southern Tyrol. Autonomy in legislative and executive matters was promised to the populations of the Bolzano Province and the neighbouring bilingual townships of the Trento province of Italy south of the Brenner Pass in the Gruber-de Gaspari Agreement of 5 September 1946, referred

486

to in Article 10 (2) of the Italian Peace Treaty of Paris of 10 February 1947 (*U.N.T.S.*, vol. 49, p. 3) by reference to its Annex No. IV. This promise was in the Italian view fulfilled by the establishment, in conformity with the new republican Constitution of Italy of 27 December 1947, of the *Regione Autonoma di Trento-Alto Adige*. This was not, however, the view of Austria which objected to the constitutional union of the two areas concerned in one single autonomous region on the ground that this union gave an overall majority in the whole *regione* to the Italian elements of the population who had flocked into the area in large numbers and had been given privileges by the Italian authorities. What Austria hopes for is not, therefore, the achievement of an—in itself improbable—judicial decision which denies the legality of the action taken by Italy, but a change in the existing juridical situation in her favour. Consequently, it is easy to understand that Austria does not exhibit any great interest in a submission of the controversy to the International Court of Justice. See A. FENET, *La question du Tyrol du Sud* (Paris, 1968). A new agreement has just been concluded (November 1969).

(b) Other special regional regimes

Special regional regimes occasionally result from other considerations or developments. I will allege here as examples three very different instances.

(i) Autonomous regime of Mount Athos. The multinational, preponderantly Greco-Russian community of monks on the Haghion Oros, the easternmost of the three landtongues of the Chalcidian Peninsula, has for centuries enjoyed a regime of selfgovernment, thanks to a grant by Sultan Murad II. The monasteries date in part already from the end of the 9th century, the big Lavra Monastery from the second half of the 10th. The community is traditionally governed by an autonomous Synod, consisting mainly of representatives of each of the monasteries. Both the Russo-Turkish preliminary Peace Treaty of San Stefano of 3 March 1878 (Martens, N.R.G.², III, 246), Article 22, § 2, and the Peace Treaty of Berlin of 13 July 1878 (*ibid.*, III, 449), Article 62 *in fine*, maintained the monks, irrespective of their country of origin, in their rights and prerogatives on an equal footing. Threatened after the Balkan Wars with political internationalization of their community under the collective secular protection of all six orthodox States—Russia, Bulgaria, Montenegro, Serbia, Romania and Greece—and under the spiritual jurisdiction of the Oecumenical Patriarch, the Superiors and Primates of the seventeen Greek convents out of the total of twenty—the three others being Slav—protested fiercely against that "changement fondamental, laïque et d'un caractère international" on the grounds that it was directly contrary both to the traditional autonomy of the community and to its preponderantly Greek character. See the notes of protest in *Jahrbuch des Völkerrechts*,

II², pp. 48-69; Karl Strupp in his *Ausgewählte diplomatische Aktenstücke zur orientalischen Frage* (Gotha, 1916), pp. 46 *et seq*. The Greek convents won their point. The status quo was maintained: the Great Powers, entrusted by the Balkan Powers (Article 5 of the Peace Treaty of London of 30 May 1913) with the mandate of deciding the fate of Mount Athos, attributed it to Greece by their decision of 13 February 1914, subject to her obligation to maintain the traditional rights and liberties enjoyed by the non-Greek monastic communities under Article 62 of the Treaty of Berlin. This obligation of Greece was restated and confirmed by Article 13 of the special treaty between the Principal Allied Powers and Greece of 10 August 1920 (Sèvres), put into force by Article 1 of Protocol XVI annexed to the final Peace Treaty of Lausanne of 24 July 1923 (*ibid.*, N.R.G.³, XII, 779 and XIII, 448).

(ii) Municipal regime in settlements on the grounds of the Eastern Chinese Railway. The origin and organization of these settlements have already been described *supra*, p. 271.

(iii) International regime of the Tangier zone.

A special regional regime of an international character has in the course of time been imposed upon Tangier, the seat of Morocco's Ministry of Foreign Affairs and the diplomatic corps. Morocco was for the first time drawn into concerted international action in connection with the right of diplomatic protection which certain powers had acquired by treaty with respect, in particular, to Moroccan subjects being in their service. Those treaties dated from long ago:

France-Morocco, 28 May 1767, *ibid.*, R¹, VII, 27;
Spain-Morocco, 1 March 1799, *ibid.*, R², VI, 349;
Great Britain-Morocco, 9 December 1856, N.R.G.¹, XVII¹, 128.

They were extended to other powers in 1863 and made the subject of the multilateral Convention of Madrid of 3 July 1880 (*ibid.*, N.R.G.², VI, 624)[41] which laid down the definitive basis of the right of protection.

Further collective intervention in Moroccan affairs followed in the beginning of this century when the Moroccan police had shown itself unable to protect foreigners and the Moroccan finances were insufficient to defray the costs of the necessary reforms. On the invitation of the Sultan an international Conference in 1906 convened at Algeciras for the purpose of organizing the reforms. Article 61(5) of the Act of that Conference of 7 April 1906 (*ibid.*, N.R.G.², XXXIV, 3) already foresaw the setting-up of a municipal organization. This idea was further

41. Parties to that convention were—with Morocco itself—the following twelve: Austria-Hungary, Belgium, Denmark, France, Germany, Great Britain, Italy, the Netherlands, Portugal, Spain, Sweden-Norway and the United States.

488

pursued in Article 1 of the Franco-Moroccan Protectorate Treaty of 30 March 1912 (*ibid.*, N.R.G.[3], VI, 332) and Article 7 of the Franco-Spanish treaty of 27 November 1912 (*ibid.*, VII, 323), but it was only worked out in detail after World War I by the tripartite Anglo-Franco-Spanish Convention in 56 Articles concluded in Paris on 18 December 1923 (*ibid.*, XIII, 246), complemented by an Annex (Regulations for the *gendarmerie*—a native police force—of the Zone) and two draft *dahirs* recommended for adoption by the Sultan and dealing, respectively, with the administration of the Zone in accordance with the provisions of the Convention, and with the organization of an international jurisdiction at Tangier.

The main lines of the Convention were the following:

The Sultan delegated his legislative and administrative powers, and also jurisdiction over foreigners to the International Administration of Tangier (Articles 1, 5 and 48). The foreigners were subject to the Mixed Court; the capitulations were abrogated.

A representative of the Sultan, the Mendoub, administered directly the native population (Article 29), saw to it that they payed their taxes to the International Administration and, as president of the Legislative Assembly, promulgated its laws in the name of the Sultan.

The Moroccan subjects of the Tangier Zone remained under the protection of France; foreign Powers were only represented by consuls (Articles 6 and 49). Within the limits of the autonomy of the Zone, local authorities could directly negotiate with the consuls.

Treaties concluded by the Sultan only extended to Tangier with the consent of the Legislative Assembly (Article 8). This Assembly consisted of 26 members: 17 foreign and 9 Moroccan members; it was presided by the Mendoub. It had to approve the annual budget and vote new laws. It also appointed the Administrator (a subject of one of the Signatory Powers of the Statute of Tangier), who was the head of the administration and carried out the decisions of the Assembly (Article 35). Ultimate control over the Zone rested with the Committee of Control, composed of the consuls of the Signatory Powers. This Committee could veto the laws passed by the Assembly (Article 31), dissolve the Assembly, remove the Administrator, etc.

The whole Zone was placed under a regime of permanent neutrality (Article 3). The surveillance of contraband traffic in the territorial waters was exercised by British, Spanish and French naval forces (Article 4).

Comp. on this subject: R. Ruse, *L'organisation du statut de la Zone de Tanger* in *Rev. de dr. intern.* 1924, pp. 590 *et seq*; K. Fr. von Grävenitz, *Die Tangerfrage* (Berlin, 1925) and M. Ydit, *Internationalised territories* (Leiden, 1961), pp. 163-171.

The Convention, which was presented for accession to the other

Powers,[42] signatories of the Treaty of Algeciras, was owing to Italian complaints amended by a quadripartite treaty of 25 July 1928 by which Italy was put on an equal footing with France, Great Britain and Spain (*ibid.*, XXI, 70). This treaty was the poor result of Primo de Rivera's exacting demand in August 1926 that the Tangier Zone be incorporated into the Spanish zone of Morocco, in which Tangier was enclaved. The 1928 treaty provided only for some minor alterations. A further agreement of 13 November 1935 gave Spain more rights.

Tangier and the International Zone have continued in the status thus defined until in June 1940 Spain saw her chance of achieving her aim by having them invaded and occupied by General Franco's troops. The other Powers ended by after World War II accepting the *fait accompli* and abrogating the international regime subject to certain guarantees. See the Convention of 29 October 1956 (*U.N.T.S.*, vol. 263, p. 165). Tangier and its Zone now form part of independent Morocco. See Whiteman, vol. 1, p. 595.

Section 8. INTERNATIONAL PROTECTION OF SACRED PLACES

Apart from the special regime which may apply to well-defined areas of a national territory, set out in section 7 above, such a special international regime can also attach to particular real property—or, for that matter, even to personal property, choses in action, etc.—present on that territory.

I only refer here in passing to the protection, as a general principle, of immovables belonging to, or occupied by, foreign States, such as embassies or consular premises, or to, or by, inter-state organizations with an international personality of their own: the United Nations, the European Coal and Steel Community, the European Economic Community, Euratom, the Pan-American Union, etc.

What I have in view is the special protection accorded by international law to such real property as the Holy Places of Jewry, Christianity and Islam in the Near East, or other religious places of pilgrimage.

The Holy Places of Christianity in Jerusalem, Bethlehem and Nazareth have always occupied a prominent place in this international protection. After the successive waves of the Crusades for the reconquest of the Holy Land had ebbed without leaving any lasting imprint, and the Turks had finally made themselves absolute masters of it, the Ottoman Sultans have gradually granted Christian pilgrims access to the Holy Places. Those grants, laid down in capitulations and treaties with Christian nations, were part of a system of general protection of foreigners profes-

42. See for example Sweden's accession 4/19 October 1928 (Martens, N.R.G.³, XXI, 94).

sing the Christian faith, and were accompanied by permission to found churches in Constantinople and elsewhere, and to administer their Holy Places. Diplomatic protection of Roman Catholics was exercised by France and Austria, of orthodox Christians by Russia. The concurrence of different Christian denominations in the Church of the Holy Sepulchre in Jerusalem gave rise, at first to a continuous struggle between Roman-Catholics and others, and in the end to an extremely complicated system of partition of the building amongst them.

In his *Geschichte der orientalischen Angelegenheit im Zeitraume des Pariser und des Berliner Friedens* (Berlin, 1892) Felix BAMBERG has reproduced between pp. 22 and 23 two ground-plans of the Church of the Holy Sepulchre before and after the fire of 1808. From those plans it appears (with minor variations) that certain central parts of the Church were held by the various denominations in common, whereas others were, sometimes in minute parts, parcelled out amongst Catholics, Orthodox, Armenians, Kopts, Syrians and Abyssinians.[43]

Frederick II's treaty (armistice agreement) with the Egyptian ruler of 18 February 1229 already provided for an allocation of the Holy Places according to religion: those of Christianity to the revived kingdom of Jerusalem, the Omar Mosque to the Moslems. The first Capitulation between Turkey and France of 1535 (Noradounghian I, 83; STRUPP, *Urkunden zur Geschichte des Völkerrechts* (Gotha, 1911), I, 11) did not yet mention the Holy Places specifically, but it did accord to French merchants and other subjects freedom of religious worship in the Ottoman Empire. Free access to Jerusalem was only expressly granted to them by subsequent, to a certain extent cryptic, confirmations and extensions of the original Capitulation.[44] Special importance attached to its renewal on 5 June 1673 (Noradounghian I, 136), extorted from a reluctant Sultan, on the orders of Louis XIV, by a special envoy, backed by four French warships. This was a blow to the Greek and the Armenian Christians who also laid claim to parts of the Church of the Holy Sepulchre, because the Sultan allotted the whole of it to the Roman-Catholics. Although the rival groups succeeded in causing this allocation to be reversed, it was only for a short period since a new firman of 1690

43. There is an official note in existence in which the various hatt-i-sheriffs for the protection of Christians of the orthodox religion and their properties in Jerusalem, in particular against infringements by Armenians and "Papists", are enumerated, covering the period 636-1840: see Martens, N.R.G.¹, XV, 491. Documents of 1852 and 1853 deal with disputes over the Holy Places between Greeks and "Latins" (*ibid.*, XV, 494 and 497) and documents of 1853 and 1862 with the necessary repairs of the cupola of the Church of the Holy Sepulchre (*ibid.*, XV, 499 and XVIII, 226, the latter being a French-Russian-Turkish protocol of 5 September 1862 providing for its reconstruction on joint account). 44. See note 2) at p. 21 of BAMBERG's *Geschichte der orientalischen Angelegenheit*, cited in the text.

reinstated the Roman-Catholics; the subsequent Capitulation of 28 May 1740 (*ibid.*, I, 277) was a confirmation of that of 1673.[45] After a long introductory preamble it opened with an Article 1 which, in the official French translation of the Turkish original, laid down that

> "L'on n'inquiétera point les Français qui vont et viendront pour visiter Jérusalem, de même que les religieux qui sont dans l'Eglise du Saint Sépulchre, dite camamat",

and further introduced, in Articles 32 *et seq.*, detailed provisions concerning the paramount position of France in the mechanism of diplomatic protection and the legal status of the Holy Places. Article 32 provided, in effect, that at the request of the "emperor" of France on behalf of other Christian nations which had until then been forbidden to carry on trade in the Ottoman Empire but had been in fact allowed access to Jerusalem "sous la bannière de France", the Sultan confirmed them in that customary privilege and made a possible future grant of freedom of commerce to them dependent on the condition that "elles iront et viendront pour lors sous la bannière de l'empereur de France." Article 33, which was the first of a series of additional provisions, laid down (in its translated text) that

> "Les religieux francs, qui, suivant l'ancienne coutume, sont établis dedans et dehors de la ville de Jérusalem [46] dans l'église du Saint Sépulchre, appelée camamat, ne seront point inquiétés pour les lieux de visitation qu'ils habitent et qui sont entre leurs mains, lesquels resteront encore entre leurs mains comme par ci-devant, sans qu'ils puissent être inquiétés à cet égard ..."

This French protection of Christians did not apply to Christian subjects of the Ottoman Emperor himself, however ambitiously the King of France strove for that concession also. France's capitulatory rights, which had usually been granted by unilateral firmans of the Sultan, were finally confirmed in the form of a synallagmatic treaty of 25 June 1802 (Martens, R², VII, 416), Article 2.

The rival Orthodox and other non-Roman Catholic religious communities, whose claims to the Holy Places even dated back to older titles,[47] gradually drew Russia into the struggle. Austria, moreover, did not acquiesce in the preponderant position of France in the protection of Roman Catholics and advanced claims of her own.

As to Austria comp. Article 13 of the Austro-Turkish Peace Treaty of Carlowitz of 26 January 1699 (Dumont, VII², 448), providing for the protection of Roman Catholic subjects of the Sublime Porte by Austria: "Moreover, let it be permitted for the Most Serene and Most Powerful

45. Comp. for further details BAMBERG, *loco cit.*, pp. 18-20.
46. A list of the sanctuaries involved was, according to BAMBERG, *loco. cit.*, pp. 20/21, only dressed in 1757.
47. BAMBERG, *loco. cit.*, pp. 21 *et seq.*

492

Emperor of the Romans to set forth to the Sublime Porte the matters entrusted to him concerning the religion and the places of Christian pilgrimage in the Holy City, Jerusalem,...", a privilege confirmed by Article 13 of the Peace Treaty of Passarowitz of 21 July 1718 (Dumont, VIII[1], 524; Rousset, *Recueil*, II, 411) and Article 9 of that of Belgrade of 18 September 1739 (Wenck, I, 326).

Russia entered onto the scene in 1720 when Tsar Peter the Great and Sultan Ahmed III, in Article 12 of their treaty of Constantinople of 16 November of that year (Noradounghian, I, p. 227, No. 21), agreed upon the freedom for Russian subjects to make pilgrimages to Jerusalem.[48] This privilege was later confirmed or enlarged by Article IX of the Russo-Turkish Peace Treaty of Belgrade of 18 September 1739 (Wenck, I, 326), Articles 7, 8 and 14 of that of Küçük Kaynarca of 21 July 1774 (Noradounghian I, 319; Martens, R[2], II, 286), which also gave permission for a Russo-Greek church to be built in the Constantinopolitan suburb of Galata, and Article 2 of that of Yassy of 9 January 1792 (Martens, R[2], V, 291).

The steadily increasing rivalry between the Western Powers and Russia with respect to the diplomatic protection of Christians in the Ottoman Empire and the legal situation in the Holy Places came to a head in the 1850's when the insolent behaviour of the Russian Ambassador Menshikov in the Sublime Porte was the direct occasion for the outbreak of the Crimean War in 1853. A detailed account of this crucial period in European history can be read in BAMBERG's book. The conflagration ended by a compromise solution on this point, embodied in Article 9 of the Peace Treaty of Paris of 30 March 1856 (Martens, N.R.G.[1], XV, 770).

So long as the status of the Church of the Holy Sepulchre and the other places of Christian worship only remained an apple of discord between the Christian communities *inter se*, or between the innerly divided group of their protectors and the Sublime Porte, the situation was still relatively uncomplicated. This changed however when the Ottoman Empire was dislodged from its outer Arabic possessions at the end of World War I and the twin Territory of Palestine-Transjordan was placed under the Mandate of a Christian power. The Palestinian Mandate dealt with the Holy Places in its Articles 13 and 14, according to which

(Article 13) "All responsibility in connection with the Holy Places ... is assumed by the Mandatory ...",
(Article 14) "A special Commission shall be appointed by the Mandatory to study, ... the rights and claims in connection with the Holy Places ...",

and it became even more complicated when after World War II Great Britain abandoned its Mandate and Palestine was divided between

48. Comp. BAMBERG, *loco cit.*, p. 282.

Jordan (which ruled the old city of Jerusalem) and the new sovereign State of Israel, which had its own aspirations in respect of the Holy City (see Part II of this publication, pp. 560-561). From that moment onwards, the three world religions confronted each other in a limited and politically disrupted area, equally holy to each one of them. The internationalization of Jerusalem and the other places of pilgrimage would have been the best solution if it had been politically realisable, but this proved impossible in the inter-war period. Comp. further on this thorny problem J. LUCIEN-BRUN, *Les lieux-saints* in *A.F.D.I.* 1968 (XIV), p. 189.

It was, for the rest, not exclusively the most renowned Holy Places of Christianity in Palestine which have formed the object of international concern and regulation.

Mecca and Medina, for a long period also dominated by Turkey, since 1918 by the Hedjaz and since 1926 by Saudi Arabia, have also played a certain part in international law in that pilgrimages to those towns dear to Islam have also been placed under international protection of some kind.

Other places of Islamic worship have likewise found treaty protection. See, *e.g.*, Article 10 of the treaty of Saint-Germain between the Great Powers and the Serb-Croat-Slovene State of 10 September 1919 (Martens, N.R.G.³, XIII, 521) for the protection of mosques, cemeteries and other Musulman religious establishments, and the *Protocole de Signature* of the Italo-Egyptian Treaty of 6 December 1925 (*ibid.*, XXX, 58) relating to free access to all Musulman holy places in Jaghbub.

The Austro-Turkish Peace Treaty of Carlowitz of 26 January 1699, quoted above, imposed upon the Hungarians the obligation to keep in repair and to respect the mausoleum of the Mohammedan priest Gül Baba on the Hill of the Roses in Budapest. See E. DRIAULT, *La question d'Orient* (Paris, 1917), p. 43.

Article 10 of the Serbo-Turkish Peace Treaty of Constantinople of 14 March 1914 (*ibid.*, VIII, 643) demanded equal respect for the tomb of Sultan Murad the Hudavendiguar at Kosovo.

Christian churches have also required protection in the Far East, *e.g.*, in the days of Emperor Tü-Düc of Annam who inflamed public feeling against the Christians and thus provoked a common Franco-Spanish war against his country, which was terminated by the Peace Treaty of Saïgon of 5 June 1862 (*ibid.*, N.R.G.¹, XVII², 169).

Section 9. ZONES OF INFLUENCE OR INTEREST

From a doctrinal point of view a special place must be allotted to what has been called "zones of influence" or "spheres of interest". This name was given in the imperialist era to those territories which a State unilaterally proclaimed to be an area which it intended to bring under its sovereignty by gradually appropriating it through actual occupation, or which two (or more) States delimited *inter se* with the same purpose. Such zones or spheres did not thereby become State territory proper, but as far as they were concerned an inchoate title was vested in the proclaiming or delimiting State(s) that could gradually develop into full sovereignty. Third States were not, in principle, bound by such international acts and were fully entitled to make reservations and to act in the same area with the same object in view. However, as between the parties to such treaties of delimitation of the respective zones the delimitation was binding.

From a systematic point of view, there is reasonable doubt where exactly this type of territorial acquisition must be placed in the theoretical system. It can be argued that its proper place is in the section on occupation of *terra nullius*, in the context of the subject of "inchoate territorial rights", on the ground that such zones or spheres do not definitely constitute State territory and that their establishment is consequently only a means for the gradual acquisition of territorial sovereignty. One could also feel inclined to deal with these zones in a separate section concerned with the various elements of State territory in the border area between this and Stateless domain (comp. the legal status of the continental shelf). In the event, however, I have decided to place them in this section of a Chapter devoted to various exceptional territorial situations, in which they are at home in any case.

A great many of such zones of influence have been established and mutually delimited on the African Continent, especially in the period of the Congo Conference of Berlin of 1885, but they have also been created elsewhere, in particular in the archipelagos of Oceania. The zones of interest which have been established on the Asian mainland, however, had as a rule another purpose, *viz.*, of securing exclusive commercial, industrial and even political influence in well-defined areas of less developed and weaker sovereign fellow States, if not of gradually subjecting the latter to a protectorate, witness the history of Siam, China and Persia.

The substantive content of this peculiar kind of territorial relationship therefore varies from one group of cases to another.

In so far as it related to parts of continents or archipelagos where no State authority proper in the European sense was in existence and which were, consequently, at that period considered as *terra nullius*, the bilateral establishment of zones of influence by colonizing powers functioned in fact as a prelude to their acquiring territorial sovereignty by means of occupation and as the conclusion of provisional colonial boundary treaties.

The usual formula of a stipulation of this type was the following, obtaining in Article 3 of the Anglo-German arrangement concerning East Africa of 1 November 1886 (Martens, N.R.G.², XII, 298 *et seq.*, at p. 301):

> "Both Powers agree to establish a delimitation of their respective spheres of influence on this portion of the East African Continent of the same character as that to which they have agreed as regards the territories on the Gulf of Guinea.
>
> The territory to which the arrangement applies is bounded on the south by the Rovuma River, and on the north by a line ... starting from the mouth of the Tana River ...
>
> The line of demarcation starts from the mouth of the River Wanga or Umbe ... to a point on the Eastern side of Lake Victoria Nyanza ...
>
> Great Britain engages not to make acquisition of territory, accept protectorates, or interfere with the extension of German influence to the south of this line; and Germany makes the same engagement as regards the territories to the north of this line".

See for a case of consolidation of spheres of influence by their assignment to a Chartered Company the Conditions on extending the field of the operations of the British South Africa Company to the North of the Zambesi, February 1891 (*ibid.*, N.R.G.², XX, 828).

In so far as imperialist powers created them with the object of obtaining exclusive or preponderant influence in countries possessed of international personality, but being still in a condition of underdevelopment, they intended more often than not to give them a double function, namely, both vis-à-vis the country itself and vis-à-vis their rival(s). The latter spheres of interest did not, however, nor were they intended to operate as titles of acquisition of territorial sovereignty.

See for an example of a stipulation of this type the Anglo-Russian Arrangement concerning Persia of 31 August 1907 (Martens, N.R.G.³, I, 8), Articles 1-3 of which, after a preamble professing respect for the integrity and independence of Persia and acceptance of the principle of the open door with regard to commerce and industry of all other nations, divided the country into three zones, a northern Russian, a southern British, and a central "neutral" one, in the following formula:

> (Article 1) "La Grande Bretagne s'engage à ne pas rechercher pour elle-même et ne pas appuyer en faveur de sujets britanniques, aussi bien qu'en faveur de sujets de puissances tierces, de concessions quelconques de nature politique ou commerciale, telles que les concessions de chemin de fer, de banques, de télégraphes, de routes, de transport, d'assurance, etc. au delà d'une ligne allant de Kasri-Chirin par Ispagan, Iezd, Khakh, et aboutissant à un point sur la frontière persane à l'intersection des frontières russe et afghane, et à ne pas s'opposer, directement ou indirectement, à des demandes de pareilles concessions dans cette région soutenues par le Gouvernement russe".

Article 2 determined a similar (British) zone between the Afghan frontier and Bender-Abbas and Article 3 stipulated equal opportunities for British and Russian subjects in the central zone.

Bilateral treaties of the first type, creative of zones of influence and mutually delimiting them, could in the absence of international personality of the people passively involved, only be disputed by third colonizing powers, which, as a matter of principle, were not bound by such *res inter alios actae*. The sudden upsurge of colonial expansion in Africa in the 1880's and the political dangers arising therefrom led to the convening by Bismarck of the Congo Conference of 1885 in Berlin which laid down certain basic rules on colonial occupation (comp. Chapter III, supra, p. 354). These rules did not apply to areas outside the African continent, *e.g.*, Madagascar and the archipelagos of Oceania where the danger of corresponding conflicts arose.

Treaties of the second type could of course be freely entered into by two or more rival imperialist States, but they were, again as a matter of principle, not binding upon the underdeveloped country concerned without its consent. This basic juridical truth was quite rightly invoked by the Emperor of Ethiopia in 1906 when three rival powers, France, Great Britain and Italy, notified him of their tripartite agreement on a partition of his country into three zones of influence (Martens, N.R.G.³, V, 733). Comp. Part I of this publication, pp. 518-519.

First variant

Colonizing powers have concluded scores of such treaties for the delimitation of their respective zones of influence or interests. They can better be dealt with elsewhere, partly (as to Africa) in the context of State land frontiers (Chapter VI below), partly (as to Oceania) in that of the drawing of lines of demarcation in the open sea (Part IV-A of this publication). Since, however, such boundary treaties, although dating from the imperialist-colonialist era, still to a large extent dominate the territorial divisions between the new independent African States and in Oceania, I will also pay some attention to them here by giving below for the purpose of consultation a list of the most important of them, dating from the latter part of the 19th century with the places where their text can be found in Martens, N.R.G.²

Africa
Germany-Great Britain
West Coast on the Gulf of Guinea, April/May 1885, XI, 471; July/August 1886, XI, 503; 14 April 1893, XX, 235, and 15 November 1893, XX, 276.
East Africa, October/November 1886, XII, 298.
East and West Africa, 1 July 1890, XVI, 894.
East Africa, 25 July 1893, XX, 271.
area of Lakes Nyasa and Tanganyika, 11 November 1898, XXXII, 399; 23 February 1901, XXX, 492.

France-Germany

West coast (Biafra Bay, Slave Coast, Senegambia), 24 December 1885, XI, 497.

Dahomey, Soudan, Togo, 9 July 1897, XXV, 415.

France-Great Britain

Somali coast, 2/9 February 1888, XX, 757.

West coast, 10 August 1889, XVI, 738, 853.

area between Niger and Lake Chad, 5 August 1890, *sub* 2 (2), XVI, 928 = XXI, 760.

area of the Central and Upper Niger, 26 June 1891, XVIII, 596.

Gold Coast, 12 July 1893, XX, 265, 273.

Sierra Leone, 21-22 January 1895, XXIII, 3, 7; XXXIV, 385.

Fashoda incident 1895, XXIX, 166.

Central Africa west and east of the Niger, 14 June 1898, XXIX, 116 = XXX, 249, complemented 21 March 1899, XXIX, 387 = XXX, 264.

France-Portugal

West Africa, 12 May 1886, XIV, 108.

Great Britain-Portugal

East Africa north and south of the Zambesi, and Central Africa, 20 August 1890, XVI, 929 = XVIII, 154; 11 June 1891, XXVIII, 185,[49] and May/June 1893, XX, 256.

Amatongaland, September/October 1895, XXIII, 150, and December 1898/January 1899, XXIX, 273.

Association internationale du Congo-Germany, 8 November 1884, X, 367.

Congo Free State-Great Britain

East and Central Africa, 12 May 1894, XX, 805.—Comp., however, Germany's objections in XXI, 531, 676 and XX, 809; *supra* p. 399.

Congo Free State-France

area of Manyanga, 22 November 1885, XVI, 587; Oubanghi, 29 April 1887, XVI, 588 = XX, 701; Haut-Oubanghi, 14 August 1894, XX, 702 = XXI, 674.

Great Britain-Italy

Somalia, 24 March/15 April 1891 (Giuba frontier), XVIII, 175, 177, 737, complemented 5 May 1894, XX, 803.

Oceania

France-Germany, 24 December 1885, XI, 497, *sub* IV.

Germany-Great Britain, West Pacific between 15° lat. N. and 30° lat. S. and between 165° long. W. and 130° long. E., 6 April 1886, XI, 505.

49. This zone of influence has led to arbitral proceedings between the two countries in 1895: award of the Italian lawyer Vigliani of 30 January 1897 (*ibid.*, N.R.G.², XXVIII, 275 *et seq.*).

States which have fallen victim to such agreements concluded to their detriment by imperialist third States have, apart from Ethiopia on which comp. above p. 497, been China, Persia, Siam and Turkey.

The establishment of zones of influence in China dates from the days of the construction of the Chinese Eastern or Manchurian railway by Russia and the extortion of lease territories from China after the Boxer revolt of 1900 by four European Powers, later followed by Japan. Comp. on that railway the section on railways above, at p. 269, and on the Chinese leases Chapter IV, section 2 above, pp. 400-404.

Since the privileges wrung from China by Russia in Manchuria in support of her railway project alarmed other governments, that project led to the delimitation of zones of influence between Russia, on the one hand, and Great Britain and Japan, on the other:

Great Britain-Russia, 28 April 1899 (Martens, N.R.G.^{2}, XXXI, 9);

Japan-Russia, correspondence of 1903-1904 relative to the pre-ponderating interests of Japan in Korea and of Russia in Manchuria (*ibid.*, XXXI, 613-641).

The same method was followed on the establishment and extension of the lease territories on the Chinese coast. The zones created at that time proved in later years to be liable to profound change as a consequence of shifts in the respective power positions: Russia being thrown out after her defeat in the Russo-Japanese war, Germany after hers in World War I.

Persia was the object of rival claims of Russia and Great Britain to preponderant economic and industrial influence in the north and the south of the country respectively. This political antagonism was reconciled *inter partes* by their Arrangement of St. Petersburg of 31 August 1907, from which I quoted already above (p. 496) the text of Article 1.

Siam narrowly escaped partition in the form of subjection to international "protection" by the concerted action of Great Britain pressing toward her from the West (India) and France from the east (Indochina) in the early years of this century. This action led first (1893) to delimitation agreements relative to the region of the Upper Mekong: *ibid.*, N.R.G.^{2}, XX, 188 = 273, and resulted later in the Franco-British *entente* of 8 April 1904 (*ibid.*, XXXII, 37) under I, where the respective zones of influence were *inter partes* delimited by the basin of the river Meinam.

The old Ottoman Empire has been in continual danger of either forthright partition or creeping dismemberment by way of the establishment of zones of interest in various periods of her harassed political history. She ultimately only escaped this fate as far as her national Turkish territory was concerned, because all her other non-Turkish territories have in consecutive stages been transformed into, or ceded to, new independent Balkan States or Arabic nation-States. Without going into any detail here with regard to the notorious partition plans of a number of Great European Powers with respect to the dominions of the "Sick Man" of Constantinople in the last quarter of the 18th and the beginning of the 19th century (comp. Part II of this publication, p. 373-374)—which proved abortive, not least owing to mutual rivalry—, or to the progressive lapse of Ottoman rule on the Balkan Peninsula, I will only recall the Tripartite Agreement of Sèvres of 10 August 1920 between the British Empire, France and Italy (Martens, N.R.G.³, XII, 785) for the delimitation of traditional zones of interest in Anatolia, pursuant to which the special interests of France were recognized in the south-east and those of Italy in the south-west.

Section 10. DEMILITARIZATION AND NEUTRALIZATION

These two institutions must be sharply distinguished. Demilitarization is a technical term to designate a situation—or the creation of a situation—in which the sovereign of a territory is obliged by an international title to abstain from introducing or maintaining there any, or specific, military forces or installations. Such an obligation burdens the State concerned—or, in case the burden bears the exceptional nature of a State servitude, the territory itself—, irrespective of whether there exists a state of peace or of war.—Neutralization, on the other hand, is a technical term to designate (the creation of) an entirely different situation, namely, that in which a territory is placed by the fact that belligerent Powers are bound by an international title to abstain from committing acts of war within the territory concerned. This obligation is thus confined to the time of war and has in principle nothing to do with the presence of fortifications, troops, naval bases, etc. in the territory concerned. However, it often happens that a territory is at the same time both demilitarized and neutralized with the combined legal effects of both regimes.

Attempts have occasionally been made in international treaties to define the two regimes with respect to specified cases, i.e., without any pretention to claim for it a general validity in international law. Thus a definition of demilitarization was inserted under D in Annex XIII to the Italian Peace Treaty of Paris of 10 February 1947 (*U.N.T.S.*, vol. 49, p. 225):

> "For the purpose of the present Treaty the terms "demilitarisation" and "demilitarised" shall be deemed to prohibit, in the territory and territorial waters concerned, all naval, military and military air installations, fortifications and their armaments; artificial military, naval and air obstacles; the basing or the permanent or temporary stationing of military, naval and

military air units; military training in any form; and the production of war material. This does not prohibit internal security personnel restricted in number to meeting tasks of an internal character and equipped with weapons which can be carried and operated by one person, and the necessary military training of such personnel",

and, much earlier, in Articles 13 and 14 of the Soviet-Finnish Peace Treaty of Dorpat of 14 October 1920 (Martens, N.R.G.³, XII, 37) where, under the misleading name of "neutralisation militaire", it is defined as follows:

"l'interdiction de construire ou d'établir des fortifications, batteries, postes d'observation militaires, radiostations d'une puissance supérieure à un demi-kilowatt, ports de guerre et bases de flottes, dépôts d'objets militaires et de matériel de guerre, ainsi que d'y faire stationner plus de troupes qu'il n'en faudra pour le maintien de l'ordre."

This definition applied to the demilitarization of a number of islands in the Finnish Gulf and, with a very slight alteration, of the island of Hogland (Suursaari).

Instances of demilitarization, neutralization or a combination of both can be found in the following survey.

Comp. for further particulars on neutralization Part IX of this publication on War and Neutrality.

As already alluded to above, the precise content of a demilitarization can vary considerably according to whether it is general or local, more or less intense, relative to either material defences, or armed forces, warships, or otherwise, etc.

It can either be a mutually agreed regime on a footing of equality, especially for the better preservation of peace along a common frontier, or be unilaterally imposed upon one of the parties, in particular after a lost war. The first variant promises better prospects of durability than the latter, which political history proves is often set aside at the first disturbance of the original power position.

In the course of history the device has developed from the primitive form of laying a strip of territory waste (comp. on this expedient Chapter VI on State frontiers, p. 514) to up-to-date plans for the denuclearization of large areas of the world.

In the following survey I will confine myself to dealing with the demilitarization of a more or less accurately defined part of the territory of a State—as opposed to military restrictions imposed upon a State in general—,[50] coupled or not with neutralization. Since it is obviously wholly unfeasible to list all historical instances, I will only allege a

50. Demilitarization of an entire State belongs more appropriately to Part II of this publication dealing with International Persons. Comp. in that Part Chapter VI, Excursus to section 2A, sub (l), pp. 488-490.

number of them, chosen from different historical periods and different parts of the world, and of different contents, in order to give an idea of their frequency, their geographical spread and their variety. I will arrange them by continents and under each heading in chronological order without, however, insisting upon the many instances of demilitarization of rivers or straits which are dealt with elsewhere. The abundance of examples taken from Europe is not fortuitous but a reflection of the fact that demilitarization is in origin a typically European device and that it has already been put into practice there in an early period. I therefore begin with

Europe

A very old example is offered by paragraph 12 of the treaty of Bruges of 7 March 1167 between Count Philip of Flanders and Count Floris III of Holland (*Oorkondenboek van Holland en Zeeland tot het einde van het Hollandsche huis* (1299), 2nd ed. (OBREEN), p. 94) laying down

> "Quod neuter comitum in sępedicta terra munitionem faciet, nec factam emet nec in perpetuum habere debet, nec aliquis hominum eorum in prędicta terra ab eis fęodabitur, ut in illo fęodo munitio ędificetur ..."

See also Article 12 of the peace treaty of Câteau Cambrésis of 3 April 1559 (Dumont, II, 287): the area of Thérouanne and Yvoix.

A prohibition to erect fortifications was not unfamiliar in the Holy Roman Empire: thus in 1378 it was forbidden to build fortresses at a distance of less than a mile from the city of Nürnberg. The Great Privilege of the Elbe of 3 June 1628, granted by the Emperor Friedrich II (Rousset, *Recueil* VIII, 335), prohibited the building of forts on islands in the river.

At the end of the Eighty and Thirty Years' Wars in 1648 certain demilitarization clauses were inserted in the peace treaties:

in respect of the border area between the Spanish and the Netherlands part of Flanders the parties agreed upon the mutual demolition of fortifications there and on the river Scheldt, and a more general ban was put on the building of new strongholds or even of strategic defensive canals—Articles 68, resp. 58 of the Spanish-Netherlands Peace Treaty of Munster of 30 January 1648 (Dumont, VI[1], 429);

pursuant to Article 8[3] of the other Peace Treaty of Munster, between France and the Emperor, of 24 October 1648 (*ibid.*, VI[1], 450) the fortifications of Rheinau and of Benfeld (in the Lower Alsace) were to be demolished.[51]

---

51. On the other hand, certain provisions (Articles X, 6 and XI, 8) of the parallel Peace Treaty of Osnabrück between the Empire and Sweden (Zeumer, *Quellensammlung*, pp. 332-370) expressly granted (as to Wismar) or maintained (as to Magdeburg) the right of fortification.

Other instances of demilitarization, which give an impression of the wide spread and variety of this expedient, are the following.

Banate of Temesvar: destruction of specified fortified places and a prohibition on Austria

"ne in posterum prope ripas fluviorum Marusii (Maros) atque Tibisci (Thisza, Theiss) alia vel majora vel minora loca, quae possunt speciem fortificationis exhibere, exstruantur,"—

Austro-Turkish Peace Treaty of Carlowitz of 26 January 1699 (Dumont, VII², 448), Article 2;

banks of the Dniepr and Turkish area surrounding the Russian fortress of Azov on the Black Sea: destruction of, and/or interdiction to (re)build, fortifications.—Russo-Turkish Peace Treaty of Constantinople of 13 June 1700 (Noradounghian, I, 197), Articles 2 and 7;

destruction of certain fortresses on the northern bank of the Black Sea near the river Saman: Russo-Turkish Peace Treaty of the Pruth of 21 July 1711 (F. BAMBERG, *Geschichte der orientalischen Angelegenheit* (Berlin, 1892), p. 281), Article 2;

Dunkerk (after a short period of English domination—from its conquest in 1658 and the ensuing Peace Treaty of the Pyrenees of 1659 until its re-purchase by Louis XIV in 1662—French again): dismantling of its fortifications and filling-up of its port for good—Article 9 of the Franco-British Peace Treaty of Utrecht of 11 April 1713 (Dumont, VIII¹, 339).

Keeping to the letter of this provision, Louis XIV very shortly afterwards, in 1714, ordered the construction of a new port at a distance of a mile from Dunkerk by digging an enlarged Mardik canal, ostensibly for drainage and local trading purposes. Since, however, this canal was equipped with high-class locks, the British Government protested. Their protest resulted in the conclusion at Hampton Court on 30 September 1716 of an agreement to the effect that the new big sluice should be demolished and the width of a smaller one reduced, that the jetties of the new canal gulling into the sea should be razed, and that the jetties and remaining forts of the old port should also be levelled. This agreement was thereupon inserted in Article 4 of the Triple Alliance Treaty of The Hague of 4 January 1717. (Comp. on this episode: Rousset, *Recueil*, I, 83-88 and 93-97; for the text of the Treaty also: Dumont, VIII¹, 484.) Dunkerk re-appeared in Article 17 of the Peace Treaty of Aachen of 18 October 1748 (Wenck, II, 310; Rousset, *Recueil*, XX, 179) which allowed it to remain fortified on the landward-side, but left it on the seaward-side on the footing of the old treaties, and Article 13 of that of Paris of 10 February 1763 (Martens, R², I, 104; Wenck, III, 329). However, Great Britain ultimately consented, by Article 17 of the Peace Treaty of Versailles of 3 September 1783 (Martens, R², III, 519), to the abrogation and suppression of all the earlier treaty provisions concerning Dunkerk in force as from 1713;

certain fortresses built during the war by France on the right bank of, or on islands in, the Rhine, *e.g.*, opposite Hüningen, were to be demolished; no garrison would be admitted in Bonn in peace-time.—Peace

Treaty of Baden between France and the Empire of 7 September 1714 (Dumont, VIII¹, 436; Rousset, *Recueil*, I, 1), Articles 6 and 8, respectively 15(4);

no fortress building by Austria near Stevensweert on the river Maas after its cession to the United Netherlands; dismantling of the fortifications of Liège and Huy further upstream—Netherlands-Austrian-British Barrier Treaty of 15 November 1715 (Dumont, VII¹, 458; Rousset, *Recueil*, I, 37), Articles 18(1) and 27. The fortifications of Liège have, however, been left in existence under a new convention between the States General and the elector of Cologne, bishop of Liège, of 22 June/ 28 July 1717 (Rousset, *Recueil*, I, 442). Protracted quarrels later, in 1726, developed between Austria and the Netherlands over the fortification by the latter of the St. Pietersberg near Maastricht (*ibid.*, III, 179 *et seq.*);

frontier region between the Ottoman Empire and Venice in Herzegowina, Dalmatia and Albania: ban on the (re)building of fortresses— Peace Treaty of Passarowitz of 21 July 1718 (Dumont, VIII¹, 520; Rousset, *Recueil*, II, 437), Article 12;

new frontier area between Austria and Turkey: mutual commitment to demolish the newly built fortresses near Belgrade, on the banks of the Danube and the Save, and in Austrian Wallachia—Articles 1, 2, 4 and 5 of the Austro-Turkish Peace Treaty of Belgrade of 18 September 1739 (Wenck, I, 326);

area of Azov on the north-eastern bank of the Black Sea: destruction of its fortress, coupled with permission for Russia to build a new fortress near the island Cherkask in the Don, and for Turkey on the river Kuban; interdiction to Russia to rebuild the demolished fortress of Taganrog, and to have a fleet on the *mer de Zabache* (Sivaš) (*pars pro toto* for the Sea of Azov) and the Black Sea—Article 3 of the Russo-Turkish Peace Treaty of Belgrade of 18 September 1739 (Wenck, I, 326) (comp. below, 1856);

Alpine border area in Grisons near the Laghetto and Scalottola, ceded by Maria Theresia in her capacity of duchess of Milan to the three *Bünde* in Upper Rhätia, Article 6 of their treaty of 8 February 1763 (Martens, R², I, 175): no erection of fortifications and no transit of foreign troops against Milan, in conformity with older *Capitulate* of 1639 and 1726;

certain islands in the mouth of the Elbe, ceded by Denmark to Hamburg: no building of entrenchments or batteries, nor any other employment for war purposes—treaty of 27 May 1768 (*ibid.*, R², I, 597), Article 4, § 2;

banks of the river Scheldt near Mortagne: demilitarization—Franco-Austrian treaty of 16 May 1769 (*ibid.*, I, 661), Articles 7 and 8;

Old Orsowa on the river Cerna and certain districts on the left bank of the river Unna (southern affluent of the river Save) not to be fortified by Austria—pursuant to Articles 2 and 3 of the Separate Convention additional to the Peace Treaty with Turkey of Sistov of 13 August 1791 (*ibid.*, R², V, 255);

boundary region between Bavaria and Italy: no fortifications in the whole of Italian Tyrol to the south, nor in a strip of 500 ells to the north, of the military line drawn in Article 2 of Napoleon's treaty with Bavaria of 11 February 1806 (*ibid.*, R², VIII, 447), Articles 1 and 3;

demolition of the newly built Turkish forts—Article 8 of the Russo-Turkish Peace Treaty of Belgrade of 28 May 1812 (*ibid.*, N.R., III, 397);

demilitarization of the Free City of Cracow—Articles 8 and 9 of the Final Act of the Congress of Vienna of 1815 (*ibid.*, N.R., II, 379);

special arrangement regarding the Savoy provinces of Chablais and Faucigny and the Savoy territory to the north of Ugine in connection with their neutralization—Article 92 (2) of the same Final Act:

> "En conséquence, toutes les fois que les Puissances voisines de la Suisse se trouveront en état d'hostilité ouverte ou imminente, les troupes de S.M. le Roi de Sardaigne qui pourraient se trouver dans ces Provinces, se retireront ...; aucunes autres troupes armées d'aucune autre Puissance ne pourront traverser ni stationner dans les Provinces et territoires susdits, sauf celles que la Confédération Suisse jugerait à propos d'y placer ...";

Hüningen in the Alsace was on the orders of Louis XIV of France transformed by Vauban into a fortress as "a pistol on the breast of Basel" in 1690. Repeated requests for the demolition of its fortifications in the last decade of the 17th century were unsuccessful (comp. A. HUBER, *Geschichte Hüningen's von 1679-1698*, academic thesis Basel, 1894). Its demilitarization was only achieved by Article 3 (1) of the (second) Peace Treaty of Paris of 20 November 1815 (Martens, N.R., II, 682):

> "Les fortifications d'Huningue ayant été constamment un objet d'inquiétude pour la ville de Bâle, les hautes parties contractantes, pour donner à la confédération helvétique une nouvelle preuve de leur bienveillance et de leur sollicitude, sont convenues entre elles de faire démolir les fortifications d'Huningue; et le gouvernement français s'engage, par le même motif, à ne les rétablir dans aucun temps, et à ne point les remplacer par d'autres fortifications à une distance moindre que trois lieues de la ville de Bâle".

This demilitarization is a typical example of what may be called an international servitude (comp. Chapter IV, section 4, pp. 413 *et seq.*);

Danube delta: no fortifications—Article 3 of the Russo-Turkish Peace Treaty of Adrianople of 14 September 1829 (*ibid.*, N.R., VIII, 143);

Moldavia and Wallachia: no rebuilding of Turkish fortifications in the principalities on the left bank of the Danube: additional treaty of Adrianople of 14 September 1829 (*ibid.*, VIII, 152);

Samos: no troops on the island—Article 5 of the diplomatic Note of the Porte of 10 December 1832 (Noradounghian, II, 216);

Black Sea: new interdiction to Russia, under quite different circumstances from those prevailing in 1739 *(supra)*, to have warships or maritime military arsenals on that sea, which was at the same time "neutralized"—Articles 11 and 13 of the Peace Treaty of Paris of 30 March 1856 (Martens, N.R.G.[1], XV, 770). Article 11 ran as follows:

"La mer Noire est neutralisée; ouverte à la marine marchande de toutes les nations, ses eaux et ses ports sont formellement et à perpétuité interdits aux pavillons de guerre soit des Puissances riveraines, soit de toute autre Puissance (save certain exceptions)".

This "perpétuité" has for the riparian States lasted fourteen years: Articles 11 and 13 were indeed (with a connected Article 14) struck out by Article 1 of the Pontus Treaty of London of 13 March 1871 (*ibid.*, N.R.G.[1], XVIII, 303), pursuant to Article 2 of which the access of warships of other States to the Black Sea remained governed by the regime of the Straits, comp. Part IV-A of this publication;

Åland Islands: interdiction of fortification and of the maintenance or creation of military or naval establishments—Franco-British-Russian treaty of 30 March 1856, annexed to Article 33 of the Peace Treaty of Paris of the same date (*ibid.*, N.R.G.[1], XV, 788), renewed in a much more elaborate form in the ten-Power treaty of 20 October 1921 (*ibid.*, N.R.G.[3], XII, 65), entered into on a recommendation of the Council of the League of Nations, placed under its supervision as "part of the actual rules of conduct among governments", and expressly endowed with a lasting character "in spite of any changes that may take place in the present *status quo* in the Baltic Sea", thus exhibiting the typical features of a State servitude (comp. *supra*, p. 417). This Convention was in its turn replaced by a Russo-Finnish Convention of 11 October 1940 (*ibid.*, N.R.G.[3], XXXIX, 456), put into force again by Article 9 of the Armistice Agreement with Finland of 19 September 1944, *A.J.I.L.*, suppl. 1945 (39), p. 85. Article 5 of the Finnish Peace Treaty of Paris of 10 February 1947 (*U.N.T.S.*, vol. 48, p. 203) ultimately evaded any precise statement on the legal position by simply laying down that "the Åland Islands shall remain demilitarised in accordance with the situation as at present existing". Comp. N.R.G.[3], X, 733 (Brest Litovsk, 1918), Art. 6[4];

Ionian Islands: neutralized and demilitarized at their cession to Greece by Articles 2 and 3 of the treaty of 14 November 1863 (Martens, N.R.G.[1], XVIII, 55): no naval or military armed force; demolition of the fortifications of Corfu and its immediate dependencies;

a ten kilometres area around Samakov in Bulgaria near the Serbian border: no construction of new fortifications; demolition of ancient Turkish forts in Bulgaria, not to be rebuilt by her—Articles 2 *in fine* and 11 of the Peace Treaty of Berlin of 13 July 1878 (*ibid.*, N.R.G.[2], III, 449);

banks of the Danube: after a provision for the total demolition of all Danube fortresses in Article 12 of the preliminary Russo-Turkish Peace Treaty of San Stefano of 3 March 1878 (*ibid.*, III, 246), that demolition was restricted, by Article 52 of the Treaty of Berlin of 13 July 1878 (*ibid.*, III, 449), to the fortifications between the Iron Gates and the mouth of the river, but even these have not been in fact demolished;

different parts of independent Montenegro: prohibition of the construction of fortifications along the river Boyana between Austrian Dalmatia and Montenegro, barring those which might be necessary for the local defence of Skutari over a distance of not more then six kilometres; demolition of the fortifications between the Lake of Skutari and the coast; closure of the port of Antivari (now: Bar) and of all Montenegrinian waters for warships of all nations; prohibition for Montenegro to have any vessels of war herself —Article 29 of the Peace Treaty of Berlin of 13 July 1878 (*ibid.*, III, 449). These restrictions on Montenegro's sovereignty were, however, lifted by an exchange of notes between Austria-Hungary, on the one hand, and the other Great Powers, on the other, of April/May 1909 (*ibid.*, N.R.G.³, IV, 41), save for the demilitarization of the banks of the Boyana and subject to Antivari not being transformed into a military port;

the Gulf of Arta in Northern Greece under the treaty of 24 May 1881 between the mediating Powers and Turkey (*ibid.*, N.R.G.², VI, 744, 753): disarmament of the fortifications commanding the entry to the Gulf, but only in time of peace (Article 2);

the Suez Canal; no stationing of warships in the waters of the canal, inclusive of Lake Timsah and the Bitter Lakes, subject to a saving clause in favour of Egypt for the country's defence—Articles 7 and 10 of the Convention of Constantinople of 29 October 1888 (*ibid.*, N.R.G.², XV, 557); comp. for more details *supra*, pp. 228 *et seq.*;

part of the Norwegian-Swedish frontier area between the sea and the 61st parallel: demilitarization, combined with neutralization; dismantling of existing fortifications and prohibition to concentrate armed military forces, and to establish new fortifications, naval ports, or repositories of provisions destined for the army or the navy—Convention II of Karlstad of 26 October 1905 (*ibid.*, N.R.G.², XXXIV, 703);

different areas on the Balkan Peninsula, *viz.*, the Bulgarian bank of the Danube between upstream of Turtukaya and the Black Sea: dismantling of existing fortifications and interdiction of new such constructions at Ruschuk (= Ruse), Shoumla, the country in between, and a twenty kilometres zone around Balchik—Article 2 of the Peace Treaty of Bucharest of 10 August 1913 (*ibid.*, N.R.G.³, VIII, 61);

Spitsbergen: no naval base or fortifications, Article 9 of the treaty of 9 February 1920 (*ibid.*, N.R.G.³, XIII, 473).

A great many areas were endowed with a regime of demilitarization in one form or another by the main Peace Conferences of 1919-1920 after World War I.

Versailles (Martens, N.R.G.³, XI, 323):

all German territory on the left bank of the Rhine and a strip of a breadth of 50 kilometres on its right bank: disarmament and dismantling of all fortified works, fortresses and field works, and prohibition of the construction of any new fortification, whatever its nature and importance (Articles 42 and 180); prohibition of the maintenance and the assembly of armed forces and military manoeuvres, and of the upkeep of all permanent works for mobilization (Article 43).—The system of fortified works of the southern and eastern frontiers shall be maintained in its existing state (Article 180, last paragraph);[52]

Saar Basin: no military service nor fortifications; only a local gendarmerie (§ 30 of the Annex following Article 50);

islands of Heligoland and Dune: destruction and prohibition of the reconstruction of all fortifications, military establishments and harbours (Article 115 and Additional Protocol *sub* 1°);

northern region of Germany, up to 50 kilometres from the coast, divided into two zones: (*a*) the area between latitudes 53° 27' and 54° N and longitudes 9° and 16° E (*i.e.*, encompassed by the west coast of Sleswig, its northern and southern borders and their prolongation eastward, and a line in the east well beyond Stettin): demolition of existing, and prohibition of the erection of new, fortifications and gun installations (Article 195); (*b*) the rest, inclusive of the islands off the coast: maintenance in their actual existing condition, but prohibition of the construction of new fortified works (Article 196).

St. Germain and Trianon (*ibid.*, N.R.G.³, XI, 692 and XII, 423):

Czechoslovak territory on the right bank of the Danube to the south of Bratislava (Pressburg): no erection of any military works by the Czechslovak State (Article 56 St. Germain = Article 51 Trianon);

Danube: surrender by Austria and Hungary of all Austro-Hungarian warships, except three river police patrol-boats each (Article 136 St. Germain = Article 120 Trianon).

Neuilly (*ibid.*, N.R.G.³, XII, 661):

Danube and Bulgaria's sea-coast: restriction of warships to four torpedo-boats and six motorboats for police and fishery duties.

Sèvres and Lausanne:

Zone of the Straits, defined in detail in Article 179 of the (abortive) Peace Treaty of Sèvres of 10 August 1920 (*ibid.*, N.R.G.³, XII, 664) (with annexed map) and comprising, apart from the Dardanelles, the Sea of Marmora and the Bosporus themselves, their north and south coasts, the islands of the Sea of Marmora, and those of Lemnos, Imbros,

---

52. See on this latter provision the subsequent agreement of 5 February 1927 between Belgium, France, Great Britain, Italy, Japan and Germany (*ibid.*, XVIII, 661).

Samothrace, Tenedos and Mytilene: besides the neutralization of the Straits proper (no blockade, no acts of hostility) by Artcile 37 of the same treaty, Articles 177 and 178 provided for its demilitarization by the disarmament and demolition of all fortifications in the entire zone, and a ban on their reconstruction, coupled with the prohibition of the unauthorized construction of new roads and railways on, and the use for military purposes of, the latter group of islands, where, except for military and air forces deemed necessary by France, Great Britain and Italy, only Greek respectively Turkish gendarmerie was allowed to be employed.—These demilitarizations were, after the lapse of the treaty of Sèvres, upon the whole upheld in Convention II, annexed to the Peace Treaty of Lausanne of 24 July 1923 (Martens, N.R.G.³, XIII, 338 et seq., at p. 401). (Comp. on this Straits Convention Part IV-A of this publication.) Mytilene was, as to its regime, severed in 1923 from the group of five islands and formed together with Chios, Samos and Nikaria into a new group where, pursuant to Article 13 of the Peace Treaty itself, no naval base or fortifications should be erected and only limited military forces maintained;

Russo-Finnish southern border area under the provisions of the Peace Treaty of Dorpat of 14 October 1920 (ibid., N.R.G.³, XII, 37): "neu-tralisation militaire" of eight islands in the Finnish Gulf (Article 13), the island of Hogland (Suursaari) (Article 14), parts of the coast of the Gulf to a maximum depth of 20 kilometres inland (Article 15), Lake Ladoga with its banks and tributaries, and part of the river Newa (Article 16);

Finnish coastal waters of the Arctic Ocean in Petchenga under Article 6 of the same treaty of 1920: no armed vessels above a certain tonnage, nor submarines or armed airplanes; no naval ports or bases.—After the Russo-Finnish winter war of 1939/1940 these demilitarizations lapsed, partly as a consequence of a shift of the boundary in the area of the Finnish Gulf westward to the west of Viborg and the lease of Hangö to the Soviet Union as a naval base by the Peace Treaty of 12 March 1940 (ibid., N.R.G.³, XXXVIII, 323), and partly of the retrocession of Petchenga to the Soviet Union, in virtue of Article 7 of the Finnish Armistice Convention of 19 September 1944 (A.J.I.L., 1945 (39), suppl., p. 85), by Article 2 of the Finnish Peace Treaty of Paris of 10 February 1947 (U.N.T.S., vol. 48, 203). The lease of Hangö, on the other hand, was by Article 8 of the said Armistice Convention abandoned by the Soviet Union in exchange for the area of Porkkala-Udd more to the east;

border regions between Greece and Turkey and between Bulgaria and Turkey: demilitarization of a zone 30 kilometres wide from the Aegean to the Black Sea—Article 24 of the Peace Treaty of Lausanne of 24 July 1923 and Convention III annexed thereto; Bulgarian territory to the north of the frontier with Greece: no permanent fortifications where weapons capable of firing into Greek territory can be placed, nor ancillary military installations—Article 12 of the Bulgarian Peace Treaty of Paris of 10 February 1947 (*U.N.T.S.*, vol. 41, p. 21);

large parts of Italian territory pursuant to the Italian Peace Treaty of Paris of 10 February 1947 (*U.N.T.S.*, vol. 49, p. 3):

the islands of Pantellaria, Pianosa and the Pelagian Islands in the Adriatic (Article 49);

the Italian side of the Franco-Italian and Italo-Yugoslav frontier areas: destruction and ban on the reconstruction of all Italian permanent fortifications and military installations (Articles 47 and 48);

a coastal area 15 kilometres deep, stretching from the Franco-Italian border to the meridian of 9° 30′ E., and the Apulian peninsula east of longitude 17° 45′ E: no construction of new, and no expansion of existing permanent military, naval or military air installations (Articles 47 (5) and 48 (6));

Sardinia: removal or demolition of all permanent coast defence artillery emplacements and all naval installations located within a distance of 30 kilometres from French territorial waters, and (this also on Sicily) of all permanent installations and equipment for the maintenance and storage of torpedoes, sea mines and buts (Article 50);

the Dodecanese Islands after their cession to Greece by Article 14 of the same Italian Peace Treaty of 1947;

the Yugoslav island of Pelagosa off the Adriatic coast—Article 11 (2) of the same Peace Treaty of 1947;

the Free Territory of Trieste—Article 3 of the Permanent Statute, defined in Annex VI to the same treaty.

The device of demilitarization is much less widely used on other Continents.

Asia

Yaska (near the river Argun): demolition of a Russian fortress—Article 2 of the Russo-Chinese Treaty of Nerchinsk of 1689 (Martens, N.R.G.[1], XVII[2], 173);

French possessions in British Bengal: neither fortifications nor troops—Article 11 of the Peace Treaty of Paris of 10 February 1763 (*ibid.*, R[2], I, 104);

no fortifications to be built in the establishments which the Netherlands will recover on the Indian subcontinent within the compass of British India and limitation of troops to the necessary police force—Article 4 (2) of the Anglo-Netherlands colonial convention of 13 August 1814 (*ibid.*, N.R., II, 57);

Eastern part of Siam: no Siamese armed vessels on the Great Lake, the river Mekong and its tributaries; no fortifications or military establishments nor armed forces in the (then) Siamese provinces of Battambang and Siem-Reap, or within a radius of 25 kilometres on the right bank of the Mekong—Articles 2-4 of the Franco-Siamese treaty of 3 October 1893 (*ibid.*, N.R.G.², XX, 172), the latter Article amended by Article 6 of the Convention of 13 February 1904 (*ibid.*, XXXII, 130);

Sakhalin and adjacent islands: mutual undertaking by Japan and Russia not to fortify their respective halves—Article 9 of their Peace Treaty of Portsmouth of 5 September 1905 (*ibid.*, N.R.G.², XXXIII, 3);

Turkish territory adjacent to the frontier of the projected Armenian State: Article 89 of the (abortive) Peace Treaty of Sèvres of 10 August 1920 (*ibid.*, N.R.G.³, XII, 664);

border area between Transjordan and Nejd: no fortifications, nor a military centre at Qaf—Article 2 of their treaty of 2 November 1925 (*ibid.*, N.R.G.³, XXI, 684);

border area between Israel and Jordan and Syria: a defensive force only (Art. VII), resp. prohibition of the presence of any armed forces (Art. III)—armistice agreements of 4 April and 20 July 1949 (*U.N.T.S.*, vol. 42, pp. 303 and 327);

Palestine, Article 17 of the Mandate Agreement of 24 July 1922 (Martens, N.R.G.³, XV, 296): only voluntary recruitment of security forces.

Africa

Apart from the general neutralization of the Conventional Congo Basin by the General Act of Berlin of 26 February 1885 (Martens, N.R.G.², X, 414), special demilitarization commitments have been assumed in respect of the following areas:

Stanley Pool: apart from the placing of the island of Bamu under the regime of perpetual neutrality, ban of any military establishment by the Franco-Belgian declaration of 23 December 1908 (*ibid.*, N.R.G.³, VI, 334);

colonial convention of exchange between France and Germany of 4 November 1911 (*ibid.*, N.R.G.³, V, 651): ban on the construction of fortifications in the Equatorial-African areas exchanged (Article 9), but on the other hand mutual freedom to transport troops over the large rivers and over railways still to be built (Article 13).

America

Islands of St. Pierre and Miquelon: no French fortifications or troops after their cession to France by Great Britain by Article 6 of the French-British-Spanish Peace Treaty of 10 February 1763 (*ibid.*, R², I, 104);

Bay of Honduras: demolition of all British fortifications in the British establishments in Spanish Belize—Article 17 of the same Peace Treaty;

part of the border area between the Portuguese and Spanish colonies: no construction of fortresses nor stationing of guards or troops in a river zone and on the mountains—Article 6 of the Preliminary Treaty of San Ildefonso of 1 October 1777 (*ibid.*, R², II, 545);

Lake Ontario, Upper Lakes and Lake Champlain: limitation of the respective naval forces to a few light vessels—British-American Rush-Bagot Arrangement of April 1817 (*ibid.*, N.R., V, vol. suppl., 395).

Antarctica

See on this area Part IV-A of this publication.
On outer space and heavenly bodies see Part IV-B of this publication.

CHAPTER VI

LAND FRONTIERS

Prefatory

At the end of my general introduction to Chapter II at p. 16 above, I have explained the considerations which induced me to devote in an Annex a separate exposition to the details regarding the legal status of the different elements of the land territory of a State with which I was going to deal more in general in section 1 of that Chapter itself. The reason for that arrangement—not wholly satisfactory from a systematic point of view—was simply that the source material collected, systematized and analysed had grown to such an extent that I felt the need for singling it out from the main body of the text, in order not to overload Chapter II to too great an extent. For systematic reasons, however, I maintained in that Annex (pp. 94-296) a division in sections entirely parallel to that in §§ applied in section 1 of that Chapter.

Exactly the same considerations have led me to present the subject matter of the frontiers of the land territory of a State, as far as necessary, separately. This subject also is so varied and complicated that it deserves such separate treatment. The need for it did not exist with respect to the other territorial elements dealt with in sections 2-5 of Chapter II, namely, the subsoil, the territorial sea, the air column and the continental shelf, because a discussion of the boundary problems concerning those elements could easily be woven into the systematic texture of my general exposition of their legal status.

In this Chapter, after a general introduction, attention will successively be paid to boundary situations with regard to mountains, rivers, inland seas or lakes, and bays or estuaries.

General introduction

The frontier is the principal line of demarcation between State sovereignties. It has become more and more precise in the course of the centuries: from a borderzone, a natural or artificially created desert, a mountain, a wood, a swamp, a river or a lake it has gradually narrowed to a definite line through the zone or the desert, over the mountain, through the wood or the swamp, in the river, or across the lake, thus shrinking from two dimensions into one.

Examples of desert border zones, artificially created or intentionally maintained in that state, are particularly well known from the Balkans and southern Russia.

Thus, Article 5 of the Russo-Turkish Peace Treaty of Constantinople of 13 June 1700 (Noradounghian, I, p. 197) laid down with regard to the isthmus of Perekop which separates the Crimea, at that time still under the suzerainty of the Ottoman Empire as the land of the Crimean Tartars, from the mainland of Russia, that the whole twelve miles stretch of territory was to be left deserted and uninhabited, and a corresponding provision was inserted in Article 3 of the Peace Treaty of Belgrade of 18 September 1739 between the same powers (*loco cit.*, I, p. 258; Wenck, I, 368) in respect of the area of the fortress of Azov which was to serve in its deserted state as a barrier between the two empires.—Similar provisions obtained in later treaties, *e.g.*, concerning the Danube delta and some adjacent mainland strips up to a certain distance from either the northern or the southern channel of that river-delta. Comp. the stipulation laid down in Article 4 of the Russo-Turkish Peace Treaty of Bucharest of 16/28 May 1812 (Martens, N.R., III, 397) relating to the small and large islands in the Danube delta opposite Ismail and Kilia, which were likewise to remain, at least in part, deserted and uninhabited. However, as appears from Article 2 of the supplementary treaty of Akkerman of 7 October 1826 (*ibid.*, N.R., IV, 1053), the implementation of the stipulation of 1812 had been soon acknowledged to be impossible and it had therefore been replaced by a new arrangement of 21 August 1817. Another provision of the same nature was embodied in Article 3 of the subsequent Russo-Turkish Peace Treaty of Adrianople of 2/14 September 1829 (*ibid.*, N.R., VIII, 143), by which Russia extended her sovereignty over the whole delta, forbidding any habitation within a distance of two hours from the right bank of the southernmost St. Georges mouth of the Danube, that is, on Turkish territory.—Austria also took similar precautions in her relationship with the Ottoman Empire. Most curious of all is the provision obtaining in Article 2 of the Separate Convention supplementary to the Peace Treaty of Sistov between the two Empires of 4 August 1791 (*ibid.*, R^2, V, 244 *et seq.*, especially p. 256) pursuant to which the small plain vis-à-vis the Danube island of Orsova between the river Cerna and the Danube (comp. Article 5 of the earlier Austro-Turkish Peace Treaty of Belgrade of 18 September 1739, Wenck, I, 368) was not only to remain unfortified, but "pour toujours, dans le sens le plus strict, neutre entre les deux dominations, c'est à dire, que la souveraineté n'en appartiendra ni à l'une ni à l'autre", *i.e.*, was to remain *terra nullius*, which the parties undertook "à laisser absolument déserte, sans jamais permettre à personne d'y bâtir, d'y demeurer, ni d'y exercer la culture."

Faint echoes of these old practices can occasionally still be heard in modern international agreements.

Comp. for example the clause obtaining in Article 4 of the agreement between the Government of the Union of South Africa (in its capacity of Mandatory of the Territory of South-West Africa) and Portugal (for Angola) of 22 June 1926 (Martens, N.G.R.³, XXIII, 299) for the solution of a dispute concerning the identification of the falls of the river Kunene, mentioned in an earlier treaty between Germany and Portugal of 30 December 1886 (*ibid.*, N.G.R.[2], XV, 479): "L'ensemble de la ligne de démarcation sera dégagé et maintenu exempt de buissons et d'arbres".

The desert of Acatamá between Bolivia and Chile was divided in 1866 (treaty of 10 August of that year, *ibid.*, N.R.G.[1], XX, 609) along the 24th degree of latitude south with a view to the exploitation of guano deposits, with the further stipulation, however, that the exploitation of those deposits would be carried out in common by the two States between the 23th and the 25th degree. The treaty laid down a detailed regulation of this form of cooperation, which could not, however, serve to prevent the cropping-up of further controversies which in 1873/1874 led to the cancellation of the 1866 treaty and in 1879 to the outbreak of war between the parties.

A marsh was still to constitute the frontier in America between Portugal and Spain pursuant to Article 5 of their preliminary Treaty of Peace and Delimitation of San Ildefonso of 1 October 1777 (*ibid.*, R[2], II, 545), which also in other respects made a very extensive use of "stateless" buffer zones, comprising not only rivers and lakes, but even mountains (Article 6).

> Article 5 laid down that "... on réservera entre les territoires des deux Couronnes, les marais de Merim et de Manguiera et les langues de terre qui se trouvent entre eux, et la côte de la mer; sans qu'aucune des deux nations les occupe, ils serviront seulement de séparation, de sorte que ni les Portugais passent le torrent de Tahim, en ligne droite à la mer, jusqu'à la partie méridionale, ni les Espagnols le torrent de Chui et de St. Michel, jusqu'à la partie septentrionale."—Article 6 added a similar provision in respect of "un espace de terrain", less wide than the marshes, to serve as a dividing strip in which no colonies, fortresses, guards or troops were to be maintained, "de sorte que cet espace n'appartiendra ni à l'un, ni à l'autre...".

Gigantic protective walls are well known from earlier centuries, such as those erected by the Chinese, and by the Romans in the north of England (the walls of Hadrian between the Tyne and the Solway and of Antoninus between the Firth of Forth and the Clyde) and in the Dobrudja near Constanţa (Trajan's wall, still mentioned in Article 20 of the Peace Treaty with Russia of 30 March 1856, Martens, N.R.G.[1], XV, 770), and their series of fortifications along the 9000 kilometres long *limes romanus*. There is also the old Danish Danewerk (Dannewirke) north of the river Eider, dating from the beginning of the 9th century, which, however, even after a systematic refortification in the middle of the 19th century, definitely proved its ineffectiveness as a military barrier in the Danish-German war of 1864.

Main roads were occasionally favoured as State frontiers, witness the old Roman Watling Street (*stratum Vatellianum*) running from the Channel coast via London and Verulamium (St. Albans) to the west, which was adopted at the end of the 9th century as the boundary between the Danish Empire in England and the English by Alfred the Great's treaty of 886 with the Danes.—Roads acting as international frontiers are still not unknown. They are interesting, in particular, when they are the last shrivelled remains of old and larger *condominia*, such as the Pyrenean road between the region of the Aldudes (Quinto-Real) and Val-Carlos, and the Spanish-Portuguese border road in the area of La Contienda. Comp. *supra* pp. 431-432 and *infra*, p. 535.

The concept of "natural" frontiers, in one sense, only denotes a particular type of boundary. It then relates to the choice of rivers, mountains, deserts, and so on as State frontiers and such "natural" boundaries are sometimes expressly declared by the parties themselves to be desirable: Article 18 of the Franco-Prussian Peace Treaty of Tilsit of 9 July 1907 (*ibid.*, R^2, VIII, 661) concerning the frontier between Russia and the Duchy of Warsaw. In another sense, however, the concept of "natural" frontiers is highly political. Such "natural" frontiers constitute *desiderata* the attainment of which has often been appraised in the course of history as being worthy of all the efforts of diplomacy, if need be reinforced by warlike operations. The sustained struggle of France in a certain period of her history to reach the "natural" Rhine boundary is notorious. This *desideratum* was temporarily completely realized by Article VI of the Peace Treaty of Lunéville of 9 February 1801 between the German Emperor and the First Consul of the French Republic (*ibid.*, R^2, VII, 296), supplemented by Article VI of the Treaty of Paris between France and the Napoleonic Kingdom of Holland of 16 March 1810 (*ibid.*, N.R., I, 327).[1]

Although writers on international law have occasionally emphasized the desirability or necessity of changing the traditional conception of the frontier as a rigid dividing line between nations[2] into a line of amicable contact connecting them, political reality shows *ad nauseam* how much weight is still up to the present time attached to the frontier as a strict line of separation between territorial sovereignties and how necessary it remains to keep arms at the ready with the object of defending the national territory against treacherous foreign invasions, intrusion of spies, infiltration of subversive propaganda, etc. Frontiers as defensive partitions remain indispensable so long as the cry for "peaceful co-

---

1. The French policy in this respect was expressed in the latter Article VI in the following words: "Etant de principe constitutionnel en France que le Thalweg du Rhin est la limite de l'Empire Français".—Charles ROUSSEAU denies any historical tendency of France to reach this political goal: *Droit International Public* (Paris, 1953), p. 259.

2. Comp. for example George SCELLE, in the general framework of his theory of "le dédoublement fonctionnel": "Obsession du territoire" in *Symbolae Verzijl* (Leyden, 1958), p. 347.

existence" is not much more than a deceitful catchword designed to induce others into a trap.

As a result international law has gradually elaborated a detailed set of rules governing the precise *tracé* of State frontiers where they are defectively or not at all defined by treaty or otherwise, *e.g.*, in State documents dating from colonial times, by arbitral awards, or by judgments of a tribunal.

The great majority of State boundaries—with the exception of maritime frontiers both towards the high seas and towards the maritime territory of adjacent States—are at present determined in more or less detail by international treaties. A considerable number have, however, in the course of time been fixed by awards or judgments of international tribunals. Many in the last resort still rest up to the present day on old legal instruments, such as: bills of enfeoffment; agreements between the minor political entities of former centuries; old ecclesiastical divisions; colonial charters or their modern descendants: Mandates of the League of Nations and Trusteeship Agreements under the United Nations Charter; territorial circumscriptions originally internal, and domestic judicial findings; even on custom and tradition, on immemorial possession or prescription, or on a specific *status quo* evidenced by historical research to have existed at a crucial date. Without engaging here in a detailed analysis of all such sources of present day boundary situations, I will briefly sketch the overall development in different parts of the globe.

Europe is the continent on which the actual *tracé* of many boundaries still dates back to feudal times. Enfeoffments or judgments of feudal courts have left their traces all over Europe: in the Pyrenees, at the mouth of North-German rivers, in Swiss lakes and Alpine regions, in the wide-spread enclaves or rare condominia. They appear to display a curious character of sacrosanctity which forbids their elimination even today. Europe is also the continent on which present State frontiers often are nothing other than a concatenation of shorter, originally regional or even local, stretches of boundary lines agreed upon in the past by the then existing smaller or even minute political units, and maintained and respected ever since.

Latin America, on the contrary, is a part of the world where present State frontiers still mainly rest on old colonial charters in connection with the principle of *uti possidetis* as existing in 1810 and 1821[3] respectively.

3. 1810 was the year of the South-American, 1821 that of the Central-American *uti possidetis*. Haiti and the Dominican Republic happened to develop a long-drawn controversy over the real meaning of an agreed special *uti possidetis*, peculiar to their common island of Santo Domingo, namely, either that of 1874 or that of 1856. Haiti asserted that this *uti possidetis* referred to the "possessions occupées à l'époque de la signature du traité du 9 novembre 1874" (Martens,

Such colonial charters were often so vague in their wording and so often lent themselves to widely divergent construction that they urgently needed interpretation by impartial judgment. Those charters also not seldom proved in subsequent centuries to be entirely incorrect owing to defective geographical knowledge which resulted in boundary limitations along non-existent mountain ranges or rivers. Hence the series of international arbitrations which have in the course of time terminated many disputes that had arisen between the Spanish-American States after their emancipation from the colonial rule of Spain. And even so it happened more than once that one of the contesting parties refused to acquiesce in an award thus obtained. Sometimes the solution of the controversy was entrusted to the former mother country, especially qualified to construe the old colonial instruments; sometimes a fellow State of the Spanish-American community or a group of such States was called upon to decide on the correct *tracé* of the boundary of the former *capitanías* or *virreinatos*; once the Central-American group set up a permanent Court of Justice with the task of solving, *inter alia*, frontier disputes between them; in other cases again, outsiders were called in, such as the President of the United States or other, European, Heads of State, the Pope, or private lawyers.

> The determination of the *status quo* of 1810 has, for that matter, met with many difficulties, as was proved, *e.g.*, by the boundary arbitration between Bolivia and Perú pursuant to their special agreement of 30 December 1902 (Martens, N.R.G.[3], III, 50). Under this agreement the boundary was to be determined on the one hand (Article 1) according to whether the disputed territory in 1810 belonged either to the old Audiencia de Charcas, part of the Virreinato of Buenos Aires, or to the Virreinato of Lima, but on the other (Article 3), in conformity with the Recopilación de Indias, Cédulas y Órdenes Reales, the Ordenanzas de Intendentes, etc., whilst (Article 4) "siempre que los actos o disposiciones reales no definan el dominio de un territorio de manera clara, el árbitro resolverá la cuestión equitativamente" and (Article 5) "la posesión de un territorio ejercida por una de las Altas Partes Contractantes no podrá oponerse ni prevalecer contra títulos o disposiciones reales que establezcan lo contrario". The *status quo* of 1810 was, consequently, considered as a *status quo* existing *de jure*, not one existing merely *de facto*. The arbitrator, the President of Argentina, in his award of 9 July 1909 (*ibid.*, III, 53; *A.A.*, XI, 141), reached the conclusion that the Royal Acts and other provisions in force in 1810 "no definían de manera clara el domino del territorio disputado", and that neither had any decisive document been produced to locate the "provincias no descubiertas" in question. He consequently proceeded to determine the frontier "equitativa-

N.R.G.[2], XXVII, 3); the Dominican Republic maintained that the expression "possessions actuelles" in Article 4 of that treaty could reasonably only have in view "les possessions fixées par le *status quo post bellum* in 1856". Comp. the introduction to their treaty of 3 July 1895 (Martens, N.R.G.[2], XXVII, 17). The dispute was to be submitted to the Holy See. It was eventually solved by the Haiti-Dominican boundary treaty of 21 January 1929 (Martens, N.R.G.[3], XXX, 337). See p. 614 below.

mente", along a line, however, which the parties concerned replaced, a few months later (treaty of 15 September 1909, *ibid.*, III, 59), by a different frontier, better adapted to the geographical conditions and to their mutual convenience. In his award, President Figueroa Alcorta expressly alluded to the possibility that "el criterio de demarcación vigente en 1810 hubiera modificado el de las leyes de la Recopilación de Indias [1st complete edition of 1680; 5th edition of 1841, 6th and last edition of 1890], con arreglo a las Ordenanzas de Intendentes de 1782 y 1803."

In the partition of South America into a Spanish and a Portuguese part the eye of the imagination can still see the lasting effect of a Papal Bull of 1493, as modified by the Treaty of Tordesillas of 1494.

In North America the scene was also, at least in part, dominated by old colonial charters from the days of British rule, both towards Canada and between the individual states of the Union. As far as Canada is concerned, those charters were vis-à-vis the United States rapidly supplemented or altered by international treaties, which in their turn needed construction by arbitration; but a boundary dispute between Canada and Newfoundland in respect of Labrador was, still in 1928, solved by the Judicial Committee of the Privy Council in London (137 *Law Times Reports*, p. 187 and *A.D.* 1927-1928, No. 81; see also Part II of this publication, p. 286). As far as the inter-state disputes within the United States are concerned, the task of interpreting old British charters for the determination of boundaries between the individual member states of the Federation fell to the Supreme Court from its inception in 1776.[4]

The picture is again entirely different on the African continent. There the frontier *tracé*'s between the many new independent States are still in principle identical with the boundaries which the colonizing Powers: Portugal, Spain, France, England, Germany, Italy and the Sovereign of the Free Congo State of 1885 or (since 1908) his successor Belgium have successively either agreed upon between themselves with respect to their respective territorial acquisitions under the, now practically obsolete, principle of occupation of *terra nullius*, their "spheres of influence" and a few exceptional territorial "leases", or unilaterally determined in their sovereign capacity between different parts of their colonial empire without taking into account any ethnological considerations. This general basis of the actual system of State frontiers in Africa has scarcely been disputed by the new independent States and has been provisionally

---

4. In the first short period under the Articles of Confederation of 1775 (Article IX) the dispute was to be referred to Commissioners or Judges to be chosen by the parties themselves or to be appointed by Congress. In those days eleven of the thirteen States were involved in boundary disputes, but only one was definitely decided: *Pennsylvania v. Connecticut*, both claiming the Wyoming Valley. Comp. on these inter-state disputes my separate paper in Part II of this publication, at p. 283.

recognized by the Conference of African States, held in 1963 at Addis Ababa, although the Charter of the Organization of African Unity created by it does not mention this informal understanding. This basic recognition of the *status quo* for practical reasons naturally includes the few arbitral boundary settlements which have taken place in the colonialist era and a couple of frontier adjustments which certain Mandatory Powers under the League of Nations Covenant or Trustees under the United Nations Charter have after World Wars I and II carried out. Thus many river boundaries in Africa, too, still date back to the colonial period.

There are rare cases in which an ethnical limit was expressly considered. Thus after World War I, the frontier between the French and the British zone of the former Mandated Territory of Togo was in 1929 so traced that, among several other factors (waterways, mountain-crests, watersheds and roads), regard was also had to the ethnical limit between certain tribes—see the Franco-British Delimitation Convention of 21 October 1929 (Martens, N.R.G.³ XXV, 452/453), replacing that of 10 July 1919 (*ibid.*, XV, 246).-⁵ The same applies to the corresponding Convention for the French and British Cameroons of 9 January 1931 (*ibid.*, XXV, 478). Ethnic considerations had already played a part in the correspondence between Great Britain and Belgium of 27 April/28 August 1923 (*ibid.*, XV, 232) and in their protocol of 5 August 1924, followed by an exchange of notes of 17 May 1926 (*ibid.*, XXIII, 288, 292), relating to the boundary line between the large British and the small Belgian part of the former German East-African Protectorate, transformed in 1922 into two separate Mandated Territories: Tanganyika and Ruanda-Urundi (see for this Belgian Mandate of 29 July 1922: *ibid.*, XV, 272), —a delimitation which has survived their new transformation into Trust Territories (G. A. Res. 63 (I) of 13 December 1946, approving the terms of trusteeship for the two territories) and their recent emergence as three sovereign States on 9 December 1961 and 1 July 1962 respectively (G. A. Res. 1642 (XVI) and 1746 (XVI)).

Before World War I, however, certain international arrangements between colonial powers had already taken tribal realities into account. Comp. *e.g.*, the Conventions of Ethiopia with Great Britain (for Uganda) of 6 December 1907 (*ibid.*, N.R.G.³, II, 832) and with Italy (for the country of the Somalis) of 16 May 1908 (*ibid.*, II, 121). The first of these two Conventions presents a peculiar feature in that it not only provides expressly for a demarcation of the limits between the tribes concerned, the Borana and the Gurré, in concert with their chiefs and in accordance with their customs, but also confirms their right to use the grazing grounds on the other side of the tribal limit as in the past, in which case they shall temporarily, during their migrations, be subject to the jurisdiction of the territorial authority. The second of the Conventions is a warning example of the pitfalls which

5. The frontier between French and British Togoland has since become the frontier between the independent State of Togo (the former French Trust Territory) and independent Ghana: after a plebiscite, held in the British Trust Territory of Togoland, had resulted in a pronouncement in favour of a union with an independent Gold Coast, their merger into the new sovereign State of Ghana was approved by General Assembly Resolution of 13 December 1956 (G.A. Res. 1044 (XI)).

may be hidden in boundary arrangements: the dangerous Wal-Wal incident between Ethiopia and Italy in 1934, with the ensuing arbitral proceedings of 1935 (*A.A.*, vol. III, p. 1657), exist to prove that boundary delimitation exclusively along tribal lines without any further demarcation on the ground is far from being recommendable.

Even outside the colonial sphere, State frontiers occasionally coincided with boundaries between tribes: comp. for example the description of the new boundary of Montenegro in Article 28 of the Treaty of Berlin of 13 July 1878 (Martens, N.R.G.², III, 449).

Hence many of the political convulsions which beset the decolonized African world at the present time and presumably will still continue to bedevil the situation for a long period to come since, no matter what the new States may detest in their colonial past as victims of "colonialism", they are only too keen to follow the example of their foreign masters in a resolute display of imperialist tendencies in their mutual relations.

Occasionally the novel transitional Mandate and Trusteeship regimes under the League of Nations and the United Nations supervision have also left their marks on the political physionomy of Africa and, in consequence, on the present State boundaries.

See on this subject the thesis (Aix-Marseille) of F.J. de França Dias van Dunem, *Les frontières africaines* (1969) and the article by I. W. Zartman in *The Journal of Modern African Studies* 1965 (3), p. 155.

Part of Asia is in the same position. Certain frontiers in South-East Asia still rest on conventions concluded many decades ago by colonial powers, such as France in her relation to Siam, whereas there are others, in the Near East, which owe their present *tracé* to the action of the former Mandatory Powers and the competent organs of the League of Nations or the United Nations. Elsewhere the delimitation is a typical result of the power positions existing in the past and usually determined by natural frontiers, such as mountain ranges and rivers. Thus the Russo-Chinese boundary dates back to the Treaty of Nerchinsk of 1689 (Martens, N.R.G.¹, XVII², 173), later modified by the Treaty of Aigun of 28 May 1858 (*ibid.*, XVII², 1) and an additional convention of 14 November 1869 (*ibid.*, XVII¹, 181; comp. p. 192).[6] The Sino-Indian frontier is pre-

---

6. The boundary was in 1689 fixed along the Kerbetchi and Ergoni (Argun), both tributaries of the river Saghalien-Oula, leaving uncertainty in respect of the easternmost section of the frontier (in the area of the Maritime Province), but laying down that the basin of the river Amur was to remain Chinese. The long middle section of the borderline between south of Lake Baikal (Turkestan) and the river Argun was later delimited by the Convention of Kiachta (or Kuldja) of 21 October 1727/14 June 1728 (*ibid.*, N.S., I, 711), with a supplementary treaty of 18 October 1768 (*ibid.*, N.S., I, 75/79). The Amur frontier between China and Russia was only established by the treaty of Aigun of 16/28 May 1858 (*ibid.*, N.R.G.¹, XVII¹, 1): the left (northern) bank was to be Russian up to the Okhotsk Sea, the right (southern) bank up to the Ussuri to be Chinese, whereas the area on the right bank between the Ussuri and the sea

dominantly traditional and customary, although a few treaties are recorded, among others, the British-Chinese convention of 17 March 1890 (*ibid.*, N.R.G.², XVI, 888) delimiting the boundary between Sikkim and Tibet, confirmed by a later treaty of 27 April 1906 (*ibid.*, XXXV, 447). The Russo-Afghan, respectively Russo-Indian borderlines find their origin in Russo-British agreements, namely, as concerns Afghanistan, a treaty of 12 November 1873, followed by the Protocols of St. Petersburg of 25 August 1887 (*ibid.*, N.R.G.², XIV, 180) and a treaty of 12 November 1893 (*ibid.*, XXXIV, 645), and as concerns India, a convention of 11 March 1895 for the delimitation of the Russian and British spheres of influence in the region of the Pamirs (*ibid.*, XXIII, 25).

A treaty boundary line may be drawn in great detail with the help of the most variegated objects: geodetical points, church towers, railway tracks, ditches, pools, bridges, canals, roads, river banks, sources, locks, dykes, hills or mountain tops, vulcans, farms, cemeteries, swamps, oases, trees, monuments, and so on. Striking examples of such detailed boundary *tracés* are the old circumstantial description of the Eastern frontiers of the Netherlands with Germany northward from the former county of Bentheim (Prussia) to the bay of the Dollard, as inserted in the Netherlands-Hanoverian Treaty of Meppen of 2 July 1824 (*ibid.*, N.R., VII, 379), which itself referred back to earlier regional or even local arrangements of 1801, 1784, 1779, 1778, 1764, 1723, 1706, 1659 and 1636, and even one dating as far back as 1548 (between the then existing seigniory of Overijssel, acquired by Emperor Charles V in 1528, and the county of Bentheim), and the determination of the southern Netherlands frontier with Belgium between the river Meuse and the sea by the Boundary Treaty of Maastricht of 8 August 1843 (Netherlands *Staatsblad* 1844, No. 12; *B.F.S.P.*, vol. 35, p. 1202), with only one interruption (Article 14, § 5) in the region of the two Baarle's, mentioned above at p. 447.

Other boundary lines are drawn much more summarily or do not need such minute description because they simply follow the course of one of the banks, the middle, or the thalweg of a river, or are indicated by a meridian or a parallel of latitude,[7] or by other straight lines. A look at

was to remain provisionally "as it had been up till then", that is, a condominium. Comp. below, p. 538.

7. Even a demarcation along a parallel or a meridian may occasionally cause trouble. This was the case between the American states of Maryland and West Virginia in 1910, when the astronomical borderline, which was designated as the frontier in old documents, but which was initially, in 1788, incorrectly demarcated, had appeared after correction not to coïncide with the actual borderline as it had been observed during a long series of years. In that case the Supreme Court held that long usage, even if contrary to an official delimitation, must prevail. Comp. J. Brown SCOTT, *Judicial Settlement of controversies between*

an atlas reveals how many State frontiers are drawn along straight lines.

Amongst the boundaries defined by parallels of latitude the most conspicuous are:

a very large stretch of the Canadian-American border from the Rocky Mountains near the waters which separate the island of Vancouver from the American mainland to the Lake of the Woods (49° lat. N.) (treaty of 9 August 1842, Martens, N.R.G.[1], III, 456, Article 2 *in fine*),

and south of the Quebec province between the rivers Connecticut and Saint Lawrence (or Iriquois) (45° lat. N.) (treaty of 3 September 1783, *ibid.*, R[2], III, 553, Article II);

two sections of the boundary between the United States and Mexico to the west of the Río Grande near El Paso (treaty of 30 December 1853, *ibid.*, N.R.G.[3], I, 1);

part of the northern frontier of Guatemala with Mexico (treaty of 27 September 1882, *ibid.*, N.R.G.[2], XIII, 670, Article III, *sub* 4°, 6°, and 7°);

the frontier between Bolivia and Chile (24° lat. S.) (treaty of 10 August 1866, *ibid.*, N.R.G.[1], XX, 609);

the boundary between Egypt and the Sudan (22° lat. S.) (agreement of 19 January 1899, *ibid.*, N.R.G.[3], IV, 791);

various other sections of the borderlines between colonial possessions and/ or new independent States in Africa: Río de Oro (treaty of 27 June 1900, *ibid.*, N.R.G.[2], XXXII, 59, Article I); Río Muni (same treaty, Article IV); Angola-Southwest Africa (treaty of 30 December 1886 between Portugal and Germany, *ibid.*, N.R.G.[2], XV, 479, Article 1); agreement of 22 June 1926 between Portugal and the Union of South Africa as Mandatory Power (*ibid.*, N.R.G.[3], XXIII, 299); Angola-(ex-Belgian) Congo (treaty of 25 May 1891, *ibid.*, N.R.G.[2], XVIII, 30); across the waters of Victoria Nyanza (Anglo-German arrangement of 1 July 1890, *ibid.*, N.R.G.[2], XVI, 894),

and the frontier between Syria and Jordan (Anglo-French agreement of 23 December 1920, *ibid.*, N.R.G.[3], XII, 582).

The urgent necessity of arriving at some agreement forced the Great Powers to adopt the same system in respect of the delimitation between North and South Korea (38° lat. S.) (military occupation line of 1945, see Whiteman, vol. 2, pp. 180-181) and between North and South Vietnam (17° lat. S.) (Geneva Conference of 1954, see Whiteman, vol. 2, pp. 234-238).

The boundary between the northern Russian and the southern Japanese part of the island of Sakhalin from 1905 (Article IX of the Peace Treaty of Portsmouth of 5 September 1905, *ibid.*, N.R.G.[2], XXXIII, 3) to 1951 (Article 2(c) of the Peace Treaty of San Francisco of 8 September 1951, *U.N.T.S.*, vol. 136, p. 45) also ran along a parallel of latitude (50° lat. N.)

Meridians play a similar part in the delimitation of State frontiers. Apart from the famous circle of longitude of the past, once fixed as the frontier between the colonial possessions, existing and future, of Portugal and Spain by the Bull *Inter Caetera* of Pope Alexander VI of 4 May 1493 (100 miles west of the Açores and the Cabo Verde Islands), as modified by the two Powers concerned through their Treaty of Tordesillas of 7 June 1494 (Martens, S. I, 372, 389; Strupp, *Urkunden*, I, 4) (370 miles west of the Cabo Verde Islands), recognized by Pope Julius II on 24

States of the American Union (New York, 1918), vol. II, pp. 1619 *et seq.* Something similar occurred in Somaliland between the Italian and the British zone.

June 1506 (Rousset, *Suppl.*, I², 10) and subsequently supplemented for the East Indies by their treaty of Zaragoza of 22 April 1529 (Martens, S. I, 398) relating to the Moluccas, mention can be made here of

the boundary between Canada and Alaska (141° long. W.) (Russo-British treaty of 28 February 1825, Martens, N.R., VI, 684 and N.S., II, 426, Article III; Russo-American treaty of 30 March 1867, *ibid.*, N.R.G.², I, 39, Article I);

the western frontier of British Honduras with Guatemala, from the Garbutt's Falls "due North" until it strikes the American frontier (notes of 25/26 August 1931, *ibid.*, N.R.G.³, XXVI, 42);

the borderline between Chile and Argentina in the South across the Tierra del Fuego (treaty of 23 July 1881, *ibid.*, N.R.G.², XII, 491, Article 3);

by far the largest part of the divisory line between western and eastern New Guinea (141° long. E.) (treaty of 16 May 1895, *ibid.*, N.R.G.², XXIII, 53);

and again various frontier sections in Africa: Río de Oro (treaty of 27 June 1900, *ibid.*, N.R.G.², XXXII, 59, Article I) and Río Muni (same treaty, Article IV); between Togo and Dahomey (declaration of 12/28 September 1912, *ibid.*, N.R.G.³, VII, 381), and between Libya (Cyrenaica) and Egypt (treaty of 6 December 1925, *ibid.*, N.R.G.³, XXX, 58: the southern section following 25° long. E.); parts of the eastern boundaries of Angola with Rhodesia, determined on the basis of an arbitral award concerning the kingdom of Barotse, given by the King of Italy on 30 May 1905 (*ibid.*, N.R.G.², XXXV, 542), by a British-Portuguese protocol of 5 March 1915, confirmed by an exchange of notes of 3 November 1925 (*ibid.*, N.R.G.³, XVIII, 211/213), and with the Mandated Territory of South-West Africa, originally by an agreement of 1 July 1890 between Germany and Great Britain (*ibid.*, N.R.G.², XVI, 894: successively 20° long. E., 22° lat. S., 21° long. E. and 18° lat. S.).

The British and Italian spheres of influence in Somaliland, too, were partly separated by parallels and meridians (protocols of 24 March and 15 April 1891, *ibid.*, N.R.G.², XVIII, 175, 176) before the regions concerned merged into the new independent Somali Republic.

Besides parallels of latitude and circles of longitude other straight boundaries are legion everywhere:

between the states of Arizona (U.S.A.) and Sonora (Mexico) from 111° long. W. to the river Colorado (treaty of 30 December 1853, *ibid.*, N.R.G.², I, 1);

between Ecuador and her neighbours Colombia (treaty of 15 July 1916, *ibid.*, N.R.G.³, XXI, 193), Brazil (treaty of 6 May 1904, *ibid.*, N.R.G.², XXXIV, 519) and Perú (treaty of 29 January 1942, *A.J.I.L.*, Suppl., 1942 (36), p. 168),

and between Bolivia and Paraguay across the Chaco Boreal (arbitral award of the Presidents of Argentina, Brazil, Chile, Perú, Uruguay and the United States of 10 October 1938 (*A.A.*, vol. III, p. 1817), in virtue of a *compromis* of 21 July 1938 (Martens, N.R.G.³, XXXVI, 692);

between the former French Equatorial Africa and Libya (agreement of 12 September 1919, *ibid.*, N.R.G.², XXI, 196);

between the former French Equatorial Africa and the Sudan (treaty of 10/21 January 1924, *ibid.*, N.R.G.³, XVII, 406/408, from 24° long. E. to 19°30′ lat. N.); between Libya and the Sudan (exchange of notes between the United Kingdom, Italy and Egypt of 20 July 1934, *ibid.*, N.R.G.³, XXIX, 672: 25° long. E., 20° lat. N., 24° long. E.), and between Libya (Cyrenaica) and Egypt (agreement of 6 December 1925, *ibid.*, N.R.G.³, XXX, 58: from 25° long. E. to 22° lat. N.); between Kenya and Tanganyika (agreement of 1 July 1890 between Great Britain and Germany, *ibid.*, N.R.G.², XVI, 894, later confirmed and specified by a protocol of 11 November 1898, *ibid.*, N.R.G.², XXXII, 399, and an arrangement of 23 February 1901, *ibid.*, N.R.G.², XXX, 492);

between Israel and Egypt: the old traditional frontier between Turkey and Egypt, starting from the northern tip of the Gulf of Aqaba between Taba and Aqaba in northwesterly direction, as confirmed in 1906 by an Anglo-Turkish exchange of notes of 14/15 May concerning the *status quo* in the Sinaï peninsula (*ibid.*, N.R.G.³, V, 880) and the Turkish-Egyptian arrangement of 1 October 1906 concerning the administrative delimitation between the Hedjaz and Jerusalem vilayets and the said peninsula (*ibid.*, V, 882);

between Israel and Jordan and between Jordan and Saudi Arabia: frontiers converging in straight lines to the top of the Gulf of Aqaba, on the strength of the Israel-Jordan armistice agreement of 3 April 1949, *U.N.T.S.*, vol. 42, p. 303 (see Part II of this publication, pp. 565-566), respectively the treaty between Great Britain and the Hedjaz, with notes of 19/21 May 1927, Martens, N.R.G.³, XVIII, 343 and *B.F.S.P.*, vol. 134, p. 275 (amended by the treaty of 8 August 1965 between Saudi Arabia and Jordan (see *R.G.D.I.P.* 1965 (69), p. 1103).

The delimitation of the so called "neutral zones" between Saudi Arabia and Iraq (protocol between Nejd and Iraq of 2 December 1922, *B.F.S.P.*, vol. 133, p. 648), respectively Kuwait (2 December 1922, *B.F.S.P.*, vol. 133, p. 726) to the southwest of the Persian Gulf equally follows in part geometrical straight lines. The first of these two zones thus forms a lozenge-shaped desert area, provisionally held in common by Saudi Arabia and Iraq. The second, for the time being under a Saudi Arabian-Kuwaiti coïmperium, extends over part of the waters of the Persian Gulf. See H. M. AL-BAHARNA, *The legal status of the Arabian Gulf States* (Manchester, 1968), pp. 264, 317 and 324.

Treaties sometimes mention unusual boundary delimitations, such as that by means of arcs of circles around a fortress, a town or a harbour.

When France, by Article 2 of her secret preliminary convention of Leoben with the Emperor of 18 April 1797 (Martens, R², VI, 385, 387) waived her claim to the three *legazioni* of Romagna and Bologna, ceded to her by the Treaty of Tolentino, she reserved to herself the fortress of Castelfranco with a surrounding district, the radius of which should not be less than the range of a cannon-shot.

A similar arc of a circle was agreed upon, with a ten kilometres radius around Beacon-Point, in the Italo-Egyptian convention of 6 December 1925 concerning Egypt's boundary with Cyrenaica (*ibid.*, N.R.G.³, XXX, 58).

Frontiers need not necessarily be absolutely stable: they may be subject to automatic changes. This applies almost exclusively to river boundaries which may shift together with a shift of the thalweg and even, though more rarely, with a displacement of the river-bed. It may, however, theoretically but very exceptionally, also apply to mountain frontiers, *e.g.*, when natural causes bring about a change of the watershed. See below, at p. 533.

Existing trade or caravan routes have occasionally played a rôle in the determination of the exact frontier line between colonial possessions or zones of influence in Africa.

> Comp. for example Article 8 of the great diplomatic Convention of 8 April 1904 between Great Britain and France (Martens, N.R.G.², XXXII, 29), in which the borderline was primarily determined by the trade routes (see paragraph 4: "the boundary shall ... be traced at a distance of 5 kilometres to the South of the caravan route from Zinder to Yo"), subject to such modifications elsewhere as might prove desirable, regard being had to "the present political divisions of the territories" from the tribal point of view (see paragraph 6).
>
> Similarly, Italy and France had in their protocol of 24 January 1900 for the delimitation of their possessions on the coasts of the Red Sea and the Gulf of Aden (*ibid.*, N.R.G.³, II, 830/831) expressly laid down that the boundary line should in any case leave the caravan routes from Assab to Aussa on the Italian side.
>
> Comp. also the Italo-Egyptian Arrangement of 7 December 1898 (*ibid.*, N.R.G.³, II, 821) for the delimitation of the Eritrean-Sudanese boundary between Ras Casar and the Barca, in compliance with the Kitchener-Baratieri understanding of 7 July 1895: it included the design to induce Ethiopia to consent to a territorial exchange which should bring the trade route from Gondar to Eritrea under Ethiopian sovereignty.

A State frontier may be finally demarcated in detail so as to follow closely the boundaries of private estates situated on either side. This was stated as a principle in Article 5 of the Prussian-Hanoverian treaty of 25 November 1837 (Martens, N.R., XIV, 468)—"unter Berücksichtigung des Grundsatzes "die Landesgrenze möglichst die Grenze der Privatbesitzungen folgen zu lassen"—, and it was also applied in practice by the Commissioners appointed in the middle of the 19th century to fix the exact boundary line between Austria (Bohemia) and Prussia (Silesia), as it existed in 1742 (Peace Treaty of Breslau of 11 June 1742 after the first Silesian War, Wenck, I, 734), but taking into account the many exchanges and reallotments which had since been made by or between the private landowners concerned (see the Austro-Prussian Delimitation Treaty of Vienna of 1869, Martens, N.R.G.¹, XX, 301).

A special problem is raised by the contingency of "relative" boundaries, different vis-à-vis one State and vis-à-vis another. This cannot happen between two adjacent States, but may occur in respect of the delimitation of the territorial sea towards the high seas. Comp. on this problem my *The Jurisprudence of the World Court*, vol. II, pp. 101-102.

Demarcation of a frontier, being an activity on the spot, must be distinguished from delimitation by treaty or judgment. It is often formally

526

prescribed by a boundary agreement as an indispensable means of complementing the more schematic delimitation by a map line or in terms of verbal description by the placing of boundary columns, stone heaps, and so on in the field, but even when there is no such formal prescription, experience often proves the necessity of further demarcation on the spot.

The setting-up of boundary commissions was already prescribed in old treaties:
between Russia and Turkey, Constantinople, 13 June 1700 (Noradounghian I, p. 197), Article 7, with respect to Azov and the Kuban;
between Spain and Portugal, San Ildefonso, 1 October 1777 (Martens, R², II, 554), Articles 15 and 16, with respect to their possessions in South America;
between Austria and Turkey, Sistov, 4 August 1791 (*ibid.*, R², V, 245).

Such demarcations, usually described in protocols drawn up by the respective commissioners and subsequently ratified by the competent authorities, are mostly very detailed. See for an example of this type of international instrument the "procès-verbal de limites" concerning the demarcation of the frontier between the Pays de Gex (France) and the baillage of Nyon (Canton of Bern), from the Lake of Geneva to the foot of the Jura, of 15 November 1774 (Martens, R², II, 331-363). This demarcation operation was carried out with a view to making more precise the earlier demarcations effected in execution of the Treaty of Lausanne of October 1564 in the period 1750-1761, but which were held to be insufficient for practical purposes because the boundary stones were too few and too far apart: the original 25 landmarks were therefore replaced by 64 new ones.

There are cases, however, in which particular—and probably decisive—importance was attached to a boundary map annexed to the treaty, rather than to its text, or in which the frontier was not described in words at all.

Franco-Spanish Boundary Treaty concerning the island of Santo Domingo of 3 June 1777 (Martens, R², II, 519), Article 3, laying down that a certain topographical plan on which all the 221 pyramids placed by the respective Commissioners were marked "doit être considéré comme partie très essentielle du présent traité" and was to be signed by both parties.

No verbal description was given at all in the Convention between Prussia and Oldenburg of 16 February 1864 (*ibid.*, N.R.G.², I, 265) whereby the latter ceded to the former a strip of land and water bordering or in the Jahde-bay, only delimited on an annexed map, to establish the naval base of Wilhelmshaven. The boundaries of the area were altered in 1873, again by a map (*ibid.*, I, 276). Comp. also the agreement between Great Britain and Afghanistan entered into at Kabul on 12 November 1893 (Martens, N.R.G.², XXXIV, 646), *sub* 1

527

and 4, as to the eastern and southern Afghan frontier from Wakhan to the Persian border, which simply refers to an attached map.

Boundary marks have been known from of old to have been under the special protection of the gods. But also in later centuries strong protection was provided for them in treaties in the form of the threatening of severe punishment to those who would venture to remove, displace or destroy them. Thus, Article 6 of the Hispano-Portuguese Treaty of 3 June 1777 relative to their boundary on the island of Santo Domingo (Martens, R², II, 519) even exposed them, as guilty of "rebellion", to the death penalty, to be imposed by a court martial.

The material and shape of the boundary marks were often prescribed in detail. Comp. for example

> mounds (*kurgans*) on a substratum of coal (agreement between Russia and the Sultan of 4 April 1775, Martens, R², II, 396), and
> a beacon made of a heap of stones about five metres high (Anglo-French protocol of 10 January 1924, Martens, N.R.G.³, XVII, 408) on the frontier between French Equatorial Africa and the Anglo-Egyptian Sudan.

From the point of view of international law the only interesting question here is whether, and to what extent, the Commissioners entrusted with the task have discretion to deviate from the map line or the verbal description in view of unforeseen geographical—mainly hydrographical or orographical—discoveries. Sometimes specific elements in the treaty description appear *a posteriori* simply not to exist, such as the "highlands" mentioned in Article II of the British-American Peace Treaty of 3 September 1783 in its definition of the boundary between the United States and Nova Scotia (Martens, R², III, 553), and the Río del Rey supposed, in the Anglo-German treaty of April/May 1885 for the delimitation of zones of influence, to run eastward from the coast of Guinea inland (Martens, N.R.G.², XI, 471), but stated in their subsequent treaty of 1 July 1890 (*ibid.*, XVI, 894) only to exist as a creek.

A second, cognate question relates to the legal consequences to be attached to a discrepancy which, during the demarcation operations, may be discovered between the verbal description of the boundary in the text of the treaty and an accompanying map such as is sometimes appended to that text. In most of the cases where the frontier is both described in words and shown on an annexed map the treaty itself expressly lays down which of the two shall have priority: this is usually the treaty text.[8] The same must therefore, save possible proof of a contrary

8. It sometimes occurs that a treaty does not contain any territorial description but only refers to an annexed map: apart from the above-mentioned convention between Oldenburg and Prussia of 1864 concerning the cession of certain territory on the Jahde Bay to Prussia, special importance was attached to an appended map in the Austro-Turkish treaty of 7 May 1775 relating to the cession of the Bucovina to Austria (*ibid.*, N.R.G.¹, XV, 448), implemented by a further delimitation treaty of 12 May 1776 (*ibid.*, N.R.G.¹, XV, 452).

intention, be admitted in cases where the parties to the Convention have not bothered to take this precaution.

See, for example, Article 1 of the Italian Peace Treaty of Paris of 10 February 1947 (*U.N.T.S.*, vol. 49, p. 3):

> "... In case of a discrepancy between the textual description of the frontiers and the maps, the text shall be deemed to be authentic".

See, however, the second remark after Article 2 of the Russo-Finnish Peace Treaty of Dorpat of 14 October 1920 (Martens, N.R.G.³, XII, 37):

> "En cas de contradiction entre les cartes et le texte concernant les presqu'îles des Pêcheurs et de Srednij, la carte maritime No. 1279 fera foi; mais pour les autres parties de la frontière le texte seul décidera".

The authentic character of a map was doubted in the Advisory Opinion of the Permanent Court of International Justice in the Albanian frontier question (Monastery of Saint-Naoum) of 4 September 1924 (*Publications, series B, No. 9*), p. 21.

It is also possible that the Commissioners charged with the task of demarcation on the spot in the performance of their duty *bona fide* commit errors. Such a mistake formed one of the elements which recently composed the substance of the extremely involved Thai-Cambodian dispute concerning the Temple of Preah Vihear (comp. *I.C.J. Reports* 1962, p. 6, and for further particulars the analysis of this case in my *The Jurisprudence of the World Court*, vol. II, p. 425).

In another case of discrepancy between relevant documentary evidence—this time between a set of partly contradictory descriptive protocols relating to the same stretch of frontier between the Netherlands territory and a Belgian enclave therein—priority was, curiously enough, given by the International Court of Justice to the supposed text of a protocol which could not be produced over a text which could be, and in actual fact was, produced (comp. *I.C.J. Reports* 1959, p. 209, and for further particulars of this case my exposition *loco cit.*, vol. II, p. 353).

The boundary commissions set up by the Peace Treaties following the First World War were vested with a fairly wide competence. Thus, it was laid down in Article 29 of the Treaty of St. Germain, that "they shall have power, not only of fixing those portions which are defined as a line to be fixed on the ground, but also, where a request to that effect is made by one of the States concerned, and the Commission is satisfied that it is desirable to do so, of revising portions defined by administrative boundaries", under the proviso, however, that this shall not apply in the case of "international boundaries existing in August 1914, where the task of the Commissions will be confined to the re-establishment of signposts and boundary-marks".

A considerable measure of discretion was also granted to the Commissioners entrusted in 1906 with the determination of the boundary

between the French and the German colonial possessions in the region of
Lake Chad (Martens, N.R.G.², XXXV, 463).

Among the boundaries, only roughly described by tradition, charter,
treaty or judgment, it is in particular the frontiers over mountains or in or
along rivers which are famous for the uncertainties to which they have
given rise and for the concrete solutions which the disputes thereover
have found. But not less thorny is the problem of the (lateral) State
boundary in bays and estuaries. The delimitation in inland seas and
lakes does not, generally, cause so many conflicts. A special problem has
arisen as an aftermath of the Judgment of the International Court of
Justice in the *Fisheries* case between the United Kingdom and Norway
and the endorsement of its findings in a generalized form by the United
Nations Conference of 1958 on the Law of the Sea (Article 4 of Convention I). I will deal with these frontier problems in the following
sections 1 to 4.

Section 1. MOUNTAIN FRONTIERS

A mountain frontier usually follows one of three main lines: along its
foot, along its highest crests and peaks, or along the watershed, but other,
more unusual *tracés* are also possible and in actual fact occur.
    The first main method of delimitation mentioned is relatively rare,
although it was more often adopted in earlier times. Instances are:
    the Austro-Turkish Peace Treaty of Belgrade of 18 September 1739
(Wenck, I, 326), Article 4: "Sa sacrée Majesté cède à la Porte Ottomane
toute la Valachie autrichienne (*i.e.*, the Banate of Kraiova), en y com-
prenant les montagnes";
    the Greco-Turkish Peace Treaty of 4 December 1897 (Martens,
N.R.G.², XXVIII, 630), Article 1: parts of the new frontier will run
along "le bas des pentes" of certain mountains.
    The other two main delimitations are rival *tracés* which were not even,
until fairly recently, consciously distinguished. A large number of late
18th century and of 19th century treaties—even certain 20th century
conventions—still used both boundary lines indiscriminately or jointly
as if they were naturally identical. This was the underlying idea of
provisions such as the following:
    Article 4 of the Peace Treaty of Utrecht of 11 April 1713 between
France and Savoy (Ghillany, vol. I, p. 139): boundary of the Alps along
"la crête des eaux pendantes";
    Article 2 of the British-American Peace Treaty of Paris of 3 Septem-
ber 1783 (Martens, R¹, III, 553): the boundary is described as following certain "highlands which divide those rivers that empty them-

selves into the river St. Lawrence from those which fall into the Atlantic Ocean";

Article 1 of the Franco-Spanish Boundary Treaty of 27 August 1785 (*ibid.*, R², IV, 26); borderline "par les cimes des montagnes qui versent les eaux dans les vallées de Baigorri, des Aldudes et de Bastan";

Article 7 of the Franco-Spanish Peace Treaty of Basel of 22 July 1795 (*ibid.*, R², VI, 124), instructing the boundary commissioners to base their demarcations of the territories disputed before the war in the region of the Pyrenees as much as possible upon "la crête des montagnes qui forment les versants des eaux en France et en Espagne";

Article 4 of the Russo-Turkish treaty of Turkmantchai of 22 February 1828 (*ibid.*, N.R., VII, 564): boundary over "les crêtes des montagnes... séparans de part et d'autre le versant des eaux";

Article 28 of the Peace Treaty of Berlin of 13 July 1878 (*ibid.*, N.R.G.², III, 449): boundary between Turkey and Montenegro over "la chaîne principale et la ligne du partage des eaux entre le Lin et le Drin";

Article 3 of the Boundary Convention between France and the International Association of the Congo of 5 February 1885 (*ibid.*, N.R.G.², X, 377 = XX, 700): "crête de partage des eaux du Niadi Quillou et du Congo";

Article 1 of the Anglo-Chinese Convention of 17 March 1890 (*ibid.*, N.R.G.², XVI, 888), confirmed 27 April 1906 (*ibid.*, XXXV, 447): the boundary between Sikkim and Tibet from the Bhutan to the Nepal frontier along "the crest of the mountain range separating the waters flowing into the Sikkim Teesta and its affluents from the waters flowing into the Tibetan Mochu and northwards into other rivers of Tibet";

Article 2 of the Peace Treaty between Bolivia and Chile of 20 October 1904 (Martens, N.R.G.³, II, 174): "las cumbres divisorias de aguas".

Although evidence of the adoption of both these lines is handed down to us from antiquity, the history of modern international law proves that the older of the two is certainly the orographical line, following the crests and the summits. This line was, however, often too uncertain, owing to a lack of topographical knowledge, to give a reliable delimitation and, consequently, repeatedly gave rise to serious dispute. At a later stage international practice began to adopt, and by so doing brought more into prominence, the watershed (water-parting, *divortium aquarum, displuvio, spartiacqua, ligne de partage des eaux, divisoria de las aguas*), although often alternating it with the line along the crests and mountain summits even in the same instrument for different sections of the frontier. See for example:

the frontier in the region between Burma and Tibet, as defined in the Anglo-Chinese boundary treaty of 1 March 1894 (*ibid.*, N.R.G.², XX, 794), revised by that of 4 February 1897 (*ibid.*, XXV, 288), where it jumps from crests of mountain ranges via river courses to the line of

531

water-parting between the basins of the Salween and the Mekong;
the boundary *tracés* in Article 27 of the Austrian Peace Treaty of
St. Germain of 10 September 1919 (*ibid.*, N.R.G.[3], XI, 691) are generally
lines of watershed (between the basins of Inn and Adige; Drave and
Adige; Drave and Piave; Raab and Mur, etc.), but an exception is made
in the Klagenfurt area for the crests of the Karavanken;
    the frontier between Bulgaria and the Serb-Croat-Slovene State
pursuant to Article 27 of the Bulgarian Peace Treaty of Neuilly of
27 November 1919 (*ibid.*, N.R.G.[3], XII, 323) changes from one watershed to others via the crest lines of the Kom Balkan and the Ruj Planina;
    the Pyrenees boundary—maintained without variation in 1792 by
Article 3 of the (first) Peace Treaty of Paris of 30 May 1814 (*ibid.*, N.R.,
I, 13)—also shows an alternation between crest and watershed.
    Whereas the boundary treaty between France and the Association
internationale du Congo of 5 February 1885 (*ibid.*, N.R.G.[2], X, 377 =
XX, 700) had opted for the watershed between the basins of the Niadi
Quillou and the Congo, the supplementary Franco-Belgian treaty of
23 December 1908 (*ibid.*, N.R.G.[3], VI, 335) filled the gap which had
been left uncertain between the northernmost source of the Shiloango
river and the said watershed range by a "ligne de faîte comprise entre
pic Kiama et pic Bembo".
    The hydrographical line has progressively gained in prestige and
frequency of use so as to warrant the conclusion that in the case of the
silence of the treaty concerned—which, however, becomes increasingly
unlikely—a mountain frontier should rather be held to follow the watershed than the line of the crests and summits.
    It would take me too far afield to try to draw up a more or less ex-
haustive list even of the most important mountain boundaries according
to whether the treaties which have determined them chose the orographical or the hydrographical solution. I hope it may suffice therefore to
give only a few examples from different continents. It is hardly necessary
to recall that, just as in the case of boundary rivers, many mountain
ranges which were State or (originally) administrative or colonial boundaries in the past no longer fulfil that function in the present political
division of the world. This does not exclude the possibility, however, that
new territorial changes may revive the old delimitation issues.
    In other cases the orographical and hydrographical lines were sharply
distinguished, witness the delimitation of the frontier between Siam and
the then protectorate of France, Cambodia, in the Franco-Siamese
treaties of 13 February 1904 (Martens, N.R.G.[1], XXXII, 130) and
23 March 1907 (*ibid.*, N.R.G.[2], II, 38). Not only was the northern
boundary line of Cambodia in 1904 fixed in its western section along the
watershed of the Dangrek range, and further eastward along the crests
of the Pnom Padang, the prolongation of that range towards the east, but

moreover the latter *tracé* over the crest was in 1907 expressly replaced by the line of the watershed.—The recent proceedings between Cambodia and Thailand before the International Court of Justice (1959-1962) respecting the borderline in the area of the Temple of Preah Vihear in the eastern section of the Dangrek chain have meanwhile adumbrated two curious novel problems of mountain boundary law, namely: (*a*) what would be the legal consequences for a watershed boundary if the watershed itself shifted in consequence of natural causes (comp. the parallel, but not novel, question regarding a river *thalweg*), and (*b*) what should the legal solution be if a watershed, adopted in a boundary treaty, subsequently appears to be unstable and to change from one period to another owing to a difference in the quantity of water involved in the wet and in the dry season? Comp. the dissenting opinion of Judge Wellington Koo in the *Temple of Preah Vihear case* (*I.C.J. Reports* 1962, p. 6, at p. 75) and my *The Jurisprudence of the World Court*, vol. II, p. 425.

The boundary question only began to be viewed more in accordance with the factual situation after geographers had made it clear that the line of the crest or the highest mountain summits—the orographical—and that of the watershed—the hydrographical line—need not necessarily, and in fact often fail to, coincide. This geographical phenomenon is attributable to different causes. Convulsive movements of the earth's crust may cause part of a mountain range to crumble and open a gap through which the water may henceforth flow down more easily than it could in the past on the opposite side of the range. Erosion by mountain rivers themselves may also produce similar results. Often also, a watershed is in no way connected with any real mountain range, running, as it may, through a relatively flat, for instance swampy, plateau from which the water flows down haphazardly in opposite directions, as was once the case of the Pinsk marshes from which part of the water flowed down to the Baltic Sea through the Vistula and the other part to the Black Sea through the Dniepr.

This possible divergence of the orographical and the hydrographical line became an issue at the end of the 19th century in a controversy between Chile and the Argentine over the correct *tracé* of their boundary in the Cordilleras de los Andes which was defined in Article 1 of their Boundary Treaty of 23 July 1881 (Martens, N.R.G.[1], XII, 491) as running "de Norte a Sur hasta el paralelo 52 de latitud"..."por las cumbres más elevadas de dichas Cordilleras que dividen las aguas" and passing "por entre las vertientes que se desprenden a un lado y otro". In that case also, the two lines were consequently still considered as being identical, although the provision concerned further foresaw that difficulties "pudieran suscitarse por la existencia de ciertos valles formados por la bifurcación de la Cordillera" which might render "la línea divisoria de las aguas" uncertain, in which case the controversy should be referred to experts. In the course of the subsequent operations of demarcation the two lines eventually appeared indeed to diverge over a distance of some 300 miles and the practical importance of the question thus became very considerable. In that case the arbitrator, the King of Great Britain, on 20 November 1902 solved the problem more *ex aequo et bono* than juridically, by drawing the boundary between the two lines in such a manner that somewhat less than half of the disputed territory, including the fertile Patagonian valleys, fell to Argentina and the rest to Chile (award in *A.A.*, vol. IX, p. 29). This Andes boundary delimitation has had an epilogue in a new arbitration over the southern-most part of the mountain range in 1965 (*A.J.I.L.* 1976 (61), p. 1071).

Clear cases of a frontier along the watershed are, *e.g.*, those between

China and Russia, 7 October 1864 (*B.F.S.P.*, vol. 67, p. 174): traditional delimitation following the watershed;

French Indochina and China, 20 June 1895 (Martens, N.R.G.², XXIII, 94);

Netherlands Surinam and Brazil, 5 May 1906 (*ibid.*, N.R.G.³, III, 70): between the basin of the rivers flowing towards the Atlantic Ocean and the basin of the Amazon, respectively;

Brazil and Peru, 8 September 1909 (*ibid.*, N.R.G.³, VI, 849): different water-partings;

Bolivia and Peru, 15 April 1911 (*ibid.*, N.R.G.³, VII, 899), Arts. 5ᵉ and 20;

France (for Equatorial Africa) and Great Britain (for the Sudan), 10 January 1924 (*ibid.*, N.R.G.³, XVIII, 408): between the basins of the Nile and the Congo;

Great Britain and Portugal, 3 November 1925 (*ibid.*, N.R.G.³, XVIII, 211): between the basins of the Congo and the Zambesi.

Exceptionally other *tracés* have been either suggested or adopted.

A border line halfway up the side of a mountain range
This solution was suggested by the Prussian Commissioners in the course of the protracted operations on the spot for the precise delimitation of the northern frontier of Bohemia between Prussia and Austria (comp. their boundary settlement of 9 February 1869 in Martens, N.R.G.¹, XX, 301). Their suggestion to fix the boundary line "an der halben Berglehne" was, however, rejected by the Austrian Commissioners (comp. *sub* I of that settlement).

A similar mountain frontier has in fact existed in the Barga district in Northern Italy where the boundary was, pursuant to Article 2 of the treaty of 28 November 1844 between Tuscany, Parma/Lucca and Modena (*ibid.*, N.R.G.¹, XII, 425 = XV, 5), to be transferred "du versant oriental sur le dos de la montagne".

534

Under the Agreement of 3 February 1922/7 March 1923 between Great Britain (for Palestine) and France (for Syria and the Lebanon) (*ibid.*, N.R.G.³, XVII, 208) the frontier was to follow the white cliffs on the western slopes of the plateau of the Jaulan.

An escarpment line

In the Thai-Cambodian dispute of 1959-1962 concerning the Temple of Preah Vihear Thailand argued for the adoption of an escarpment line, but this was not accepted by the International Court of Justice (comp. my *The Jurisprudence of the World Court*, vol. II, p. 425).

An escarpment *tracé* was agreed upon by Italy (for Eritrea) and Egypt (for the Sudan) on 7 December 1898 (Martens, N.R.G.³, II, 821): "i contrafforti che limitano da nord la parte inferiore di quest'ultima valle", or "l'orlo settentrionale di un altopiano".

"Contrafuertes" were also chosen as the border line in parts of the mountainous frontier area between Bolivia and Chile: Article 2 of their treaty of 20 October 1904 (*ibid.*, N.R.G.³, II, 174), which for the rest referred to *cumbres, volcanos, cerros*, etc.

Comp. also the delimitation by Great Britain and Russia of their respective spheres of influence in the region of the Pamirs by their convention of 11 March 1895 (*ibid.*, N.R.G.², XXIII, 25, 27), where mention is made, first of a line over the crest, and later of a line along the spur (contrefort) of a mountain range south of Hindukush east of Lake Victoria (Zor Koul). Several rocky escarpments also form part of the new Franco-Italian frontier, fixed by Annex II to the Italian Peace Treaty of Paris of 10 February 1947 (*U.N.T.S.*, vol. 49, p. 3).

A promontory is referred to in the Italo-French protocol of 24 January 1900 (*ibid.*, N.R.G.³, II, 830, 831) for the delimitation of the respective zones of Assab and Tadjourah on the coast of the Red Sea and the Gulf of Aden.

Mountain roads or paths

Occasionally mountain roads or paths play a part in the delimitation of frontiers. They are either themselves designated as the State boundary, or expressly left to one of the parties, so that the frontier runs alongside them. Examples of these varying solutions can be found, *e.g.*, in Article 27 of the Hungarian Peace Treaty of Trianon of 4 June 1920 (*ibid.*, N.R.G.³, XII, 423) where on the border with Czechoslovakia a road on a mountain crest remained on Hungarian territory,—or in Annex II, just mentioned, to the Italian Peace Treaty of Paris (1947), describing the new Franco-Italian frontier: "it follows the mule-track"; "along the ridge road (or path) which is left in French territory"; "it skirts the road"; "following the summit path", etc. In one case I found a mountain path (in the Pyrenees), expressly declared to be "common" to the adjacent States, France and Spain.

Part of the State boundary there indeed follows neither the watershed nor the crest line but a mountain road of very long standing, which was declared to be common to both countries for their respective subjects to drive their cattle over; a number of watercourses and fountains along that road were included (Article 2 of the treaty of 27 August 1785 (Martens, R², IV, 26) respecting the State boundary between the area of the Aldudes or Quint-Royal and Val-Carlos between the Col d'Yzpeguy and Irriburieta). Comp. on these curious *condominia* and the larger ones for which they were substituted *supra*, pp. 431-432.

A mountain range as territorium nullius

One of the best known instances is that offered by Article 6 of the (preliminary) Hispano-Portuguese Treaty of San Ildefonso of 1 October 1777 (Martens, R², II, 545) pursuant to which certain of the highest mountains, "du pied jusqu'au sommet seront regardées comme des bornes n'appartenantes à personne, et où aucune des deux nations n'osera bâtir, envoyer des Colonies, ou élever des forts".

Sometimes arbitrators have been faced with a choice between a "dry" and a "wet" frontier. This occurred in the Austro-Hungarian arbitration of 1902 relating to the Meerauge-Morskie Oko-Halastó—, a lake in the Galician Tatra mountains (award of 13 September 1902, *ibid.*, N.R.G.³, III, 71 *et seq.*). In that case Austria favoured, in respect of the boundary between the Meeraugenspitze and the confluence of the Poduplaski- and the Fischseebach into the Bialkabach, a dry frontier over the Zabiegrat, Hungary on the contrary a wet frontier along the Fischseebach. The arbitral tribunal observed (*ibid.*, pp. 81-82):

> "Als natürliche Grenzen qualifizieren sich ... alle natürlichen Hindernisse: in der Tiefe, das ist in der Niederung, die Wasserläufe ...; im Gebirge ... die Berggrate. Wo der Wasserlauf nach Beschaffenheit des Rinnsales und nach Wasserfülle seinen Charakter als Hindernis verliert, geht die Grenze natürlicherweise auf den Berggrat über, und zwar immer entschiedener, je höher man kommt. Auf der einen Seite nehmen die Wasserlinien an Bedeutung als Hindernis ab, die Grate dagegen zu. An irgend einer Stelle wird die Grenze überspringen vom Flusse zum Grate, von der Rinne zum Rücken"

and referred in support to Article 2 of the Treaty of Berlin of 13 July 1878 (*ibid.*, N.R.G.², III, 449).

Boundaries across mountain ranges also present great variety in detail, but they are more stable than river boundaries, although, as I have already remarked earlier, even mountain frontiers are susceptible of shifts by merely natural causes, comp. *supra*, p. 533.

The determination of mountain frontiers has repeatedly been referred to arbitration. On the other hand, boundary treaties have gradually become more detailed, so as to prevent future controversies arising over their exact *tracé*.

Well-known cases of arbitration or adjudication of disputes relating to mountain boundaries are those concerning certain highlands in Nova Scotia (1831), sovereignty of the Alpe Cravairola (1874), the Cordilleras de los Andes (1902) and the Thai-Cambodian case of the Temple of Preah-Vihear (1961). Comp. for further references the Excursus on arbitral or judicial adjudication of territory *infra* pp. 610 *et seq.*

Section 2. RIVER BOUNDARIES

When surveying *in vacuo*, but in the light of the general historical development the different possibilities respecting the precise *tracé* of State frontiers in the case of boundary rivers, one can easily draw up the following list:

(*a*) the river is exempt from the territorial supremacy of the riparian rulers as it is reserved to a common superior authority, the King or the Emperor;

(*b*) it is exempt from any territorial supremacy whatsoever, being considered as *territorium nullius*;

(*c*) the whole river belongs to one of the riparian States up to the farther bank;

(*d*) it belongs to one of the riparian States inclusive of both banks;

(*e*) the river forms a *condominium*;

(*f*) it belongs *pro diviso* to the riparian States either (i) along its median line, or (ii) along its deepest channel;

(*g*) very exceptional geographical or political conditions may entail a corresponding very exceptional frontier regime.

I begin with a few general observations.

The variant under (*a*) is inseparably linked with the medieval conception of the Holy Roman Empire and the feudal system, which, however, have left their traces up to the present time long after their disappearance. Comp. my historical survey *infra*, pp. 540 *et seq.*

The variant under (*b*) has completely vanished from actual State practice. The idea of a boundary river being exempt from the territorial supremacy of both riparian States is of very ancient origin. It would seem to be mirrored in the old practice of rulers negotiating with one another in the middle of a river. Thus, as early as 921 two royal descendants of Charlemagne, Charles III of Western Francia and Henry I of Eastern Francia met on the river Rhine for the conduct of treaty negotiations. See *Oorkondenboek van Holland en Zeeland tot het einde van het Hollandsche huis (1299)*, ed. OBREEN (The Hague, 1937), p. 11, first column:

537

"Convenerunt enim ambo illustres reges, sicut inter se discurrentibus legatis convenerant, II nonas Novembris, feria prima; dominus enim Karolus super Rhenum flumen ad Bonnam castrum et strenuus Heinricus ex altera parte Rheni. Et ea tantum die mutuis se visibus intuentes super ripas eiusdem fluminis huc et ultra, ut sui fierent fideles innoxii sacramento, quo hanc eorum conventionem fuerant polliciti. Verum feria IV, VII idus Novembris, in medio Rheni fluminis saepius dicti principes in navibus quisque suis in tertiam ascenderunt quae ancorata in fluminis media gratia eorum colloquii fixa erat, ibique in primo hanc sibi vicissim convenientiam ob statum pacis juramento sanxerunt ita:"

Late reminders of this old diplomatic device under wholly changed conditions can be recorded from 1659 when the Treaty of the Pyrenees between France and Spain (7 November 1659, Dumont, VI², 264) was concluded in a house specially built on the Island of the Pheasants in the boundary river the Bidassoa "aux confins des deux Royaumes", and from 1807, when Napoleon and Tsar Alexander I met on a raft in the river Niemen for the conclusion of their peace treaty of Tilsit (7 July 1807, Martens, R², VIII, 637).

It is, however, often doubtful whether a specific frontier delimitation was meant to leave the river concerned in the status of a *flumen nullius* or, rather, to make it a *condominium*, especially when the text confined itself to drawing the boundary line along the left and the right bank. Comp. *e.g.*, the treaties between Russia and China of Nerchinsk of 1689 (Martens, N.R.G.¹, XVII², 173) and Aighoun of 28 May 1858 (*ibid.*, XVII¹, 1) with respect to the rivers Kerbetchi, Ergoni (Argun), Amur, Sungari and Ussuri, and the Austro-Turkish peace treaty of Passarowitz of 21 July 1718 (Dumont, VIII¹, 524) with respect to the Aluta (Oltu): "ita ut praedicti fluvii ripa occidentalis ad Romanorum, ripa vero orientalis ad Ottomanorum Imperatorem pertineat." Comp. further *sub (e)*.

The variants under (c) and (d), exemplified by many treaty provisions of past centuries, still exist to-day, but they are seldom found. Present-day instances of these unusual river boundary *tracés* often have their roots in the feudal past, but these variants have also occurred in the Balkans area, in Eastern Europe, in America and in the colonial division of Africa. Some details are given below, pp. 543 *et seq.*

The variant under (e) is rare under present-day conditions, but it still obtains in some places.

The use in a treaty of the expression that a particular stream is "common to the two countries" may, however, be misleading as it often does not convey in actual fact the idea of a *condominium* proper, but is simply meant to indicate that that stream forms the boundary between the countries concerned, or that its use—for example, as in the case just cited of the Aluta—is "utriusque partis subditis communis, quoad potationem pecorum et piscationes, aliosque hujusmodi perquam neces-

538

sarios usus". Comp. *e.g.*, the term "rivière de la Versoix qui sert de limite commune entre les deux Etats" (France and Bern), employed in their *procès-verbal de limites* of 15 November 1774 (*ibid.*, R², II, 331 *et seq.*, at p. 344). The Peace Treaty of Teschen between Maria Theresia and the Elector of the Palatinate of 13 May 1779 (*ibid.*, R², II, 669) contains another such doubtful provision in Article 5:

"Les rivières mentionnées dans l'Article précédent (*viz.*, the Danube, the Inn and the Salza) seront communes à la Maison d'Autriche et à l'Electeur Palatin, en tant qu'elles touchent les pays cédés; aucune des deux parties contractantes ne pourra y altérer le cours naturel des rivières, ni empêcher la libre navigation et le libre passage des sujets, des marchandises, denrées et effects de l'autre, et il ne sera permis à aucune d'elles d'y établir de nouveaux péages et aucun autre droit, quel nom qu'il puisse avoir ..."

Did this Article constitute in fact a case of fluvial co-sovereignty proper, or was it, rather, simply a definition of the legal status of an international river, as conceived at the time?

A clear case of co-sovereignty was, however, that of the river Saar (Sarre) pursuant to Article 3 of the Convention of 27 April 1780 between France and the Electorate of Trier (Trèves) (*ibid.*, R², II, 268): "Cette rivière restera indivise entre les deux Souverainetés". The specific legal effects of the attribution of the character of an undivided "common river" to the Saar are defined as implying that either of the riparian States was empowered, without the other's cooperation and without a preceding demand to the other, to proceed to the pursuit of smugglers, deserters and criminals on the whole course of the river.

Another section of the same river Saar, between French and Nassau-Weilburg territory, was on the contrary divided along the median line: Article 5 of the treaty of 24 January 1776 (Martens, R², II, 429).

Comp. further Article 25 (4) of the Final Act of the Congress of Vienna of 9 June 1815 (*ibid.*, N.R., II, 379) in the terms of which the rivers Saar (Sarre), Moselle, Sauer (Sûr) and Our on their boundary stretches "appartiendront en commun aux Puissances limitrophes".

Genuine *condominia* over rivers are at present very rare, but they still exist in places, for example, on the frontier between the Netherlands and Germany in virtue of the Netherlands-Prussian boundary treaties of Aachen of 26 June 1816 (*ibid.*, N.R., III, 24) and Cleves of 6 October 1816 (*ibid.*, III, 45), and the Netherlands-Hanoverian treaty of Meppen of 2 July 1824 (*ibid.*, N.R., VII, 379), which declare the (small) boundary rivers to be common to both adjacent States, a quality, for the rest, which they share with frontier roads and, curiously enough, even with boundary hedges. Yet, here also, some caution is called for about the real legal meaning of the provisions.

Certain (unnavigable) rivers are specifically called "mitoyennes", *e.g.*, in the treaty of 27 November 1886 between Belgium and Luxembourg (*ibid.*, N.R.G.², XII, 534). The Lys (a navigable tributary of the Scheldt) had already been declared "mitoyenne" in Article 6 of the Franco-Netherlands boundary treaty of Courtray of 28 March 1820 (*B.F.S.P.*, vol. 55, p. 395).

To all intents and purposes the problem is nowadays confined to the two variants of the attribution of territorial sovereignty to both riparian States *pro diviso*, mentioned under (*f*).

Comp. for a few instances of a quite extraordinary boundary *tracé* as alluded to under (*g*), below, p. 552.

Before surveying in the following pages in more detail the diverse river frontier situations outlined above, I must state that the rules governing the exact territorial delimitation between States in the case of boundary rivers exhibit different and entirely independent lines of development in Europe—and in different parts of Europe at that—, on the American Continent and in Asia and Africa. I therefore begin with a brief historical exposition, which I will intersperse with a few instances of the older boundary settlements distinguished above.

A large part of Europe, being subject to the rule of that grand medieval structure the Holy Roman Empire, was also governed by its river laws. At the base of those laws lay the *Constitutio de regalibus* of the Emperor Frederick I, 1158,[9] pursuant to which "regalia sunt...viae publicae, flumina navigabilia et ex quibus fiunt navigabilia". The Görlitzer Landrecht accordingly laid down in its Article 34, § 1: "Iegelich vlizinde wazzir heizet des riches sträze". The legal regime of the main rivers of the Empire as "stratae regiae" could thus correctly be described by one of the most authoritative writers on German legal history[10] as follows:

> "Als "des Reiches Strasse" blieben die schiff- und flossbaren Flüsse nicht bloss dem Privatrecht entrückt, sondern wurden auch von der Territorial-bildung nur so weit ergriffen, als eine ausdrückliche Verleihung, sei es der Stromhoheit überhaupt oder der einzelnen stromhoheitlichen Rechte, seitens des Reiches stattgefunden hatte. Ohne eine solche Verleihung endigte die landesherrliche Gewalt am Ufer, und der Strom selbst, bis zu den Grenzen seines gewöhnlichen Inundationsgebietes, stand ausschliesslich dem Reiche zu, das darüber unabhängig von der territorialen Zugehörigkeit der Ufer verfügt".

Among the different "stromhoheitliche" rights, which could thus be granted separately and which constituted together the overall "Strom-

9. *Monumenta Germaniae Historica. Legum sectio IV. Constitutiones et acta publica imperatorum et regum, tomus I* (edidit L. WEILAND, Hanover, 1893), p. 244. This particular *Constitutio* was originally only destined for Italy, but it was later "received" in Germany together with the *libri feudorum*.

10. Richard SCHRÖDER, *Lehrbuch der deutschen Rechtsgeschichte*, (Berlin, 1932), 7th ed.

hoheit", were: jurisdiction on the river, the right of convoy and of towing, the right to construct and exploit harbours, ferries, bridges, mills and similar river installations, fishing rights and the so-called "Grundruhrrecht" (corresponding to the right of salvage on the seashore). There are plenty of historical instances which bear witness to the fact that separate royal or imperial rights were successively granted on the same river either to the same ruler who was thus enabled gradually to acquire legally or by further usurpation the entire "Stromhoheit", or to different rival powers. The great rivers of Northern Germany, in particular, have been the scene of an incessant and stubborn struggle for exclusive power over them between the rulers of adjacent areas or other powers: secular princes, ecclesiastical dignitaries and large commercial towns. Those rivers, especially the Trave (Lübeck), the Elbe (Hamburg), the Weser (Bremen) and the Ems (Emden), formed the boundary between the smaller political units of those days. Such rivalry was not, however, confined to units facing each other on either bank, but extended to the relations between those situated upstream and downstream, for example in connection with the usurpation of river tolls and the so-called staple-right (the right to force passing shipping to unload their cargo for a certain time in the port concerned in order to secure for the local citizens a right of preemption). Striking historical evidence of the practical importance of the feudal theory of *stratae regiae*[11] in respect of rivers is, among others, the fact that, when in the 13th century fierce competition developed in respect of the supremacy over the Weser between the (arch)bishop of Bremen, the city of Bremen and the duke of Oldenburg, the latter two, who were themselves rivals and both unwilling to recognize their opposite number's claim to authority over the river, inserted in their peace treaty of 2 October 1221, as a common defence against a similar claim of Archbishop Gerhard II of Bremen to the "dominium Visurgis", the express statement that the Weser had continued to be a *strata regia*.[12]

In the course of their prolonged battle for territorial supremacy over a river, rival rulers did not even shrink from using the well known medieval device of forging originally genuine feudal grants or of forthrightly fabricating spurious instruments; for this procedure both the Weser and the Ems are notorious.[13]

11. *Bremisches Urkundenbuch*, I, No. 233. Comp. also Joh. Geo. SPIER, *Geschichte der bremischen Strom-, Schiffahrts- und Hafenpolizei* (academic thesis Göttingen, 1960, p. 23).
12. The idea that navigable rivers originally remained *regalia, stratae regiae* is reflected in the old tradition that the riparian ruler could only exercise his authority as far as he could enter the river and reach with his sword, or throw a plough-share into it, and similar traditions.
13. Comp. on the Weser my exposition at p. 159.—As far as the Ems is con-

The big commercial towns of Northern Germany naturally strove for an extension of their rule over the territory on the opposite bank of the river which was their very life-line. This self-evident ambition caused the rivers to fall entirely, with both their banks, under the sovereignty of the influential trading-towns and thus traces from earlier centuries are still left in the boundary regime and the distribution of competences prevailing in the lower sections of the rivers Elbe and Trave and their estuaries.[14]

Most of the rivers of the Holy Roman Empire to which such exceptional and often controversial border regimes applied are no longer international boundaries: they have since become internal rivers, or at the utmost frontiers between member units of a federal State, but they still present considerable interest for the student of the history of the development of international fluvial law.

> This statement is equally true, for that matter, for many other rivers which once constituted the frontier between separate States; such as the Po from a very remote past to the middle of the 19th century, the Niemen, the Bug, the Dniepr, the Dniestr, the Save, the Mississippi and many others.
> On the other hand, the political transformation of Latin America in the first part of the 19th century and of Africa in the decolonization era of the middle of our century exhibits many instances of the inverse development by which originally internal-colonial rivers have become boundary rivers between independent States.

The history of international fluvial law outside the Holy Roman Empire shows an entirely different picture.

On and directly north of the Balkan Peninsula and in southern Russia near the Black Sea, rivers have also played an important part in the delimitation of State territory. In those areas, however, the river boundaries generally mirrored in their consecutive stages the incessantly shifting military power situation between the Ottoman Empire, on the one hand, and the Austrian and Russian Empires, on the other, and the modalities attached to their fixation—*e.g.*, the compulsory demolition of fortresses on, and the accompanying further demilitarization of, their banks, the creation of deserted buffer zones or even of strips of *terra nullius*—were inspired by the need of preventing as far as possible a new

cerned, the old controversy between the Counts of East Friesland and their western neighbour over the exact tracé of the frontier in the estuary has remained unresolved up to the present day. Germany still claims, without foundation, that her territorial sovereignty extends over the entire breadth of the Ems estuary right up to its bank under the smoke of the Netherlands town of Delfzijl. Comp. on this dispute p. 4, *supra*.
14. Comp. on the Elbe also my exposition at pp. 162-164. The Trave and the Bay of Lübeck have given rise to proceedings before the German federal courts. Comp. on that case section 4 *infra*, p. 592, and Part II of this publication, at p. 282.

outbreak of hostilities in the river area. Apart from such varying modalities, the frontier *tracés* themselves also were not identical. Although the wording of the treaty provisions concerned was often unclear, it must be inferred from them that boundary rivers either were a kind of no man's land between adjacent States each extending their territorial supremacy only to the river's bank, or fell entirely under the sovereignty of one of them. I did not find much indication which could support the conscious acceptance in early times of the idea of a river condominium proper, and the express partition of a river into two strips divided by its median line, let alone divided along its *thalweg*, was still very rare. Nearly all the examples which can be drawn from the territorial provisions in the series of peace treaties or other territorial adjustments between Austria and Turkey and between Russia and Turkey from the end of the 17th to the first quarter of the 19th century relate to the Danube, its many tributaries: the Save, the Theiss, the Maros, the Olta, the Bug, and the ramifications of its delta: the Kilia, Sulina and St. Georges branches, and to the Dniestr and the Dniepr. A brief survey of the relevant frontier provisions reveals the following picture.

The three rival Powers from the end of the 17th century until the beginning of the 19th, often used the device of fixing the State frontier in such a way that the boundary river fell up to its opposite bank under the supremacy of one of the parties, dependent upon their existing relative military strength. Thus, the Austro-Ottoman peace treaty of Carlowitz of 26 January 1699 (Dumont, VII², 448) introduced this regime for the Hungarian rivers Maros and Theiss (Tisza) and the Bosnian rivers Bossut and Unna by drawing the new boundary lines "citerioribus (or: ulterioribus) ripis" of the rivers concerned—in contradistinction to the river Save whose "altera quidem pars, pertinens ad ditionem Caesaream, possideatur ab ejus Majestate, altera vero pars possideatur ab Imperatore Ottomannorum". Twenty years later, however, in virtue of Article 3 of the peace treaty of Passarowitz (Požarewac) of 21 July 1718 (*ibid.*, VIII¹, 524) the Save also fell under the sole territorial supremacy of Austria.— Whereas the Russo-Ottoman peace treaty of Yassy of 9 January 1792 (Martens, R², V, 291) would seem to warrant the conclusion that it made the left (eastern) bank of the Dniestr the frontier between the two empires, their peace treaty of Bucharest of 28 May 1812 (*ibid.*, N.R., III, 397), confirmed by those of Akkerman of 7 October 1826 (*ibid.*, N.R., VI, 1053) and Adrianople of 14 September 1829 (*ibid.*, N.R., VIII, 143), Article 3, fixed the new boundary line along the river Pruth through its middle (replaced by the *thalweg* in the peace treaty of Berlin of 13 July 1878, Article 45, *ibid.*, N.R.G.², III, 449).

In the series of Balkan peace treaties from 1699 to 1878 the Danube played an increasingly important rôle, changing with the relative military successes and failures of the three rival Powers in their successive wars. The struggle in the event focussed on the domination of the Danube delta. Comp. the Annex to Chapter II, pp. 143 *et seq.* above.

Other rivers that have temporarily functioned as boundary rivers in that period in southeastern Europe and southern Russia are the Timok, the Cerna, the Oltu (Aluta), the Dniepr, the Don and the Kuban, and—in Russia's preliminary peace treaty with Turkey at San Stefano of 3 March 1878 (*ibid.*, N.R.G.[2], III, 246), which proved abortive owing to the intercession of the other Great Powers and the Congress of Berlin—*inter alia*, the Boyana, the Drina, the Lim, the Morava and the Arda, sometimes with express mention of their *thalweg*.

For the rest, an examination of the numerous territorial adjustments between States in other parts of Europe in earlier centuries—for example, on the Iberian and Appennine peninsulas, in France, in eastern Europe—does not testify to the adoption of any fixed general customary rule in this respect. It would even seem to have more often than not been the outcome, in each particular case, of more or less fortuitous or arbitrary considerations, no longer historically retraceable, or of obvious military preponderance, which specific solution was accepted: that of a factual condominium, the establishment of a *territorium nullius*, an exclusive one-sided right to the whole river, or a strict partition thereof along its median line.

Thus the frontier agreements of Austria, Prussia and Russia with their victim Poland, or *inter se*, in the days of the three partitions (1772-1795) were as follows:

Whereas Russia did not show any particular wish to annex entire boundary rivers, Austria—and to a lesser extent also Prussia—did.

Thus, on the first partition of Poland in 1772 (comp. the treaties of 25 July 1772 in Martens, R[2], II, 89 and 97) the whole breadth of the Vistula from the frontier of Silesia to its junction with the Save was brought under Austrian sovereignty by Article 2 of the Austro-Polish treaty of 18 September 1773 (*ibid.*, R[2], II, 109). In virtue of Article 4 of a subsequent treaty of 9 February 1776 (*ibid.*, R[2], II, 124), however, half of its bed was allotted to the newly created Free City of Cracow. By Article 1 of the same treaty, by which Austria retroceded to Poland certain areas on the right bank of the Bug, that part of the river remained under Austrian sovereignty over its whole breadth. Prussia on her side secured to herself the entire width of the river Netze by Article 2 of her treaty with Poland of 18 September 1773 (*ibid.*, R[2], II, 149). Russia obviously did not follow the example of the other two in respect of the Dwina and the Dniepr: according to Article 2 of the Russo-Polish treaty of 18 September 1773 (*ibid.*, R[2], II, 129) the rivers concerned would be the natural limit, without further specification.

On the second partition of Poland, in 1793, to which Austria was not a party, Article 2 of the Prusso-Polish treaty of 25 September 1793 (*ibid.*,

R², V, 544) simply extended the respective frontiers to the right and the left bank of the river Pilica, thus suggesting the status of a *flumen nullius* for the river itself.

On the third and final partition of 1795, the Austro-Russian Declarations of 3 January 1795 (*ibid.*, R², VI, 168), *sub* 2, again stipulated a boundary *tracé* along the right bank of the Pilica and the Vistula and along the left bank of the Bug. The three parallel conventions of St. Petersburg of 24 October 1795 (*ibid.*, R², VI, 171) would seem to be silent on these frontier details.

England and Scotland have also had their frontier problem at the mouth of the river Tweed, where sovereignty over the town of Berwick has for a long time been disputed. See Chapter V, section 1, p. 439.

In addition to what I have already remarked above, I will follow up the survey by a number of cases in which the boundary of a State was drawn along the opposite bank of a river, so that the river itself became part of its territory (variant *c*).

Amazon: in its frontier stretch both banks came under the sovereignty of Portugal pursuant to Article 10 of her peace treaty of 11 April 1713 with Spain (Dumont, VIII¹, 353);

Chiers, a tributary of the Meuse: cession of the whole course of the river to France by Article 21 of her treaty with Austria of 16 May 1769 (*ibid.*, I, 661);

Othe in Wallachia: cession of the "superiority" over the river to Austria by Article 2 of a (non-ratified) treaty of 6 July 1771 with the Porte (*ibid.*, II, 21);

Maas (Meuse): renunciation by the Prince-Bishop of Liège in favour of France of his half of a certain stretch of the course of the river, but cession of another stretch, below Givet, by France to Liège, Articles 5 and 17 of their treaty of 24 May 1772 (*ibid.*, II, 44);

Netze: cession of the whole course of the river by Poland to Prussia, Article 2 of their above-mentioned treaty of 18 September 1773 (*ibid.*, R², II, 149);

Bug: the "property" of the whole boundary stretch of the river will remain Austrian together with all the islands in it, Article 1 of the Austro-Polish treaty of 9 February 1776 (*ibid.*, II, 124);

Río de la Plata and Uruguay, certain sections of these rivers will appertain exclusively to Spain, Article 3 of her treaty with Portugal of San Ildefonso of 1 October 1777 (*ibid.*, II, 545);

Adige, Tartaro and Po: delimitation of the Venetian territory which falls to Austria by the left bank of those rivers, Article 6 of the Peace Treaty of Campo Formio of 17 October 1797 (*ibid.*, VI, 420);

Flossgraben between Weisse-Elster and Saale entirely Prussian: Article 15 (9) of the Final Act of Vienna of 9 June 1815 (*ibid.*, N.R., II, 379);

Sabina, Red River and Arkansas entirely under the sovereignty of the United States in virtue of Article 3 of its treaty of 22 February 1819 with Spain relative to the cession of the Floridas (*ibid.*, N.R., V, 328);

Danube: the northern frontier of Bulgaria will follow the right bank of the river, Article 2 of the Peace Treaty of Berlin of 13 July 1878 (*ibid.*, N.R.G.², III, 449); in 1879, however, the thalweg became the frontier (see p. 555);

Río del Rey (coast of Guinea): entirely German, arrangement with Great Britain of April-May 1885 (*ibid.*, N.R.G.², XI, 471);

Orange River (South-West Africa) and Volta (West Africa): German sphere of influence limited by their northern, respectively left bank, Articles 3 and 4 of the Anglo-German Agreement of 1 July 1890 (*ibid.*, N.R.G.², XVI, 894);

Arda: *tracé* of the Bulgaro-Turkish frontier along its right bank, Article 1 (8) of the Peace Treaty of Constantinople of 29 September 1913 (*ibid.*, N.R.G.³, VIII, 78).

Even arbitrators have sometimes drawn a frontier along one of the banks of a river, namely E.P.Alexander in his award of 30 September 1897 relative to the San Juan del Norte, attributed over its full width to Nicaragua (LA FONTAINE, *Pasicrisie internationale*, p. 529), and King Victor Emanuel III in his award of 30 May 1905 (*ibid.*, N.R.G.², XXXV, 542), by which he determined as between Great Britain (for Rhodesia) and Portugal (for Angola) the territory over which the king of Barotse had been Paramount Ruler in June 1891: the eastern edge of the high water bed of the river Cuando. This award was later implemented by a treaty of 3 November 1925 (*ibid.*, N.R.G.³, XVIII, 211).

I also refer to the inter-colonial Agreement of 1799 concerning the mouth of the Guyanan river Corantijn, below p. 551.

The latest instance of a claim by one of the riparian States to sovereignty over the full breadth of a boundary river is that of the German Federal Republic in respect of the river Elbe (see *Bulletin of Legal Developments* 1966 (1), p. 121).

Variant (*d*)—appurtenance of a river with both its banks to one of the riparian States—is much more rare. Apart from the natural tendency of big commercial towns to extend their authority in this way, referred to above, p. 542, I mention the cases of the rivers

Save, according to Article 3 of the Austro-Turkish peace treaty of Passarowitz of 21 July 1718 (Dumont, VIII¹, 524): "integer fluvius Savus cum suis ripis ad Sacram Caesaream Regiamque Maiestatem pertinent", and

Oder, in virtue of Article 8 of the peace treaty of Hubertsburg between Prussia and Saxony-Poland of 15 February 1763 (Martens, R², I, 146), which attributed to Prussia sovereignty over a certain stretch of the river and over both its banks.

See also the case of the Lauter, the Franco-German boundary river between the Lower Alsace and the Palatinate. Exception was made for the town of Weissenburg, traversed by the river, which would remain French in its entirety up to a radius on the left (German) bank not exceeding thousand *toises* (of 1949 metres). See the (2nd) Peace Treaty of Paris of 20 November 1815 (Martens, N.R., II, 682), Article 1, and the Franco-Bavarian boundary treaty of 5 July 1825 (*ibid.*, N.R., VIII, 1 = N.S., II, 439), Article II, 3.

I now turn, in particular, to North America, whose Mid- and Far-Western areas have for a long time after the final discovery of the New World and its colonization continued to be empty regions from the point of view of territorial sovereignty, and which exhibits a development entirely of its own. This was dominated at first by the struggle between the three main colonizing powers on the eastern coast: Spain (since 1519, Cortéz in Mexico), France (since 1533, Cartier in Canada) and England (since 1584, Sir Walter Raleigh in Virginia), by England's desperate battle to break the revolt of her thirteen colonies and by the final liquidation of the French and Spanish colonies in the deep south, and at a later stage by the power entrusted to the new United States Supreme Court to solve any legal disputes, amongst others on boundaries, which might arise between the component States (see Part II of this publication, at p. 283). Thus it was, during the early colonial era, in particular the rivers St. Croix and St. Lawrence in the north, and the Mississippi in the south, and following the war of independence a series of other rivers in addition to them: the Ohio, the Missouri, the Columbia, the Potomac, the Savannah, the Delaware, which gave rise to frontier disputes. Further controversies arose in the middle of the 19th century over the Río Grande del Norte, the new boundary between the United States and Mexico. Whereas those boundary problems were typically international in the north and the south, they were internal-federal in the centre and towards the west, and closely connected with old colonial charters or with special conditions attached to the admission of new member States to the Union. The development, internationally and internally, has as a consequence followed different and independent lines.

Even the United States has, though exceptionally, applied the method of fixing the State boundary along the far bank of a river. Thus, in its treaty with Spain of 22 February 1819 (Martens, N.R., V, 328) concerning the cession of Florida, it secured for itself the sovereignty over the entire breadth of the future boundary rivers concerned: the Sabine, the Red River and the Arkansas. This was a deviation from what it had done earlier in 1783 with regard to the rivers Connecticut and St. Lawrence (= Iriquois) in the north (treaty of Paris with Great Britain of 3 September 1783, *ibid.*, R², III, 553, Article 2) or in 1795 with regard to the Chattahoochee and St.Mary's rivers (towards Spanish Florida) and the Mississippi (towards French Louisiana) in the south (treaty of San Lorenzo with Spain of 27 October 1795, *ibid.*, R², VI, 142, Article 2). It did not follow that method either at a later stage in 1848, in respect of the rivers Río Grande and Gila (treaty of Guadelupe Hidalgo of 2 February 1848, *ibid.*, XIV, 7, Article 5). The same delimitation alongside the opposite bank of a river was, however, sanctioned by the United States Supreme Court in a few cases with regard to the boundary between individual States of the Union. On the case law of the Supreme Court in this field see below, pp. 556 *et seq.*

In Central and South America the frontier situation was, except for (*a*) the relation between the Spanish and Portuguese areas, (*b*) the colonial enclaves of other European Powers in Guyana and (*c*) one single territory on the Central-American isthmus, entirely internal-colonial in origin. As a consequence of the principle of *uti possidetis*, generally adopted by the new independent Latin-American States in the first quarter of the 19th century, their international frontiers, inclusive of their river boundaries, were to remain identical with the former borderlines between the *capitanías* and *virreinatos* under the old colonial charters, on the basis of which many boundary disputes have had to be resolved. Comp. on this latter principle below, p. 552.

ad (*a*). After their original delimitation by Pope Alexander VI (1493) and the Treaty of Tordesillas (1494) nothing much would seem to have occurred with regard to the boundaries between these areas for a considerable period. A more precise demarcation was, however, undertaken in the Spanish-Portuguese treaty of Madrid of 13 January 1750 (Martens, S., I, 328) and that of San Ildefonso of 1 October 1777 (*ibid.*, R², II, 545) by which the borderline was in part fixed along rivers, such as the Río de la Plata and the River Uruguay.

In a later period the frontiers of independent Brazil towards her independent Spanish-speaking neighbours have also been fixed on the basis of the *uti possidetis*, by separate treaties with Venezuela (5 May 1859, N.R.G.¹, XVII², 161), Bolivia (27 March 1867, *ibid.*, N.R.G.¹, XX, 613), Paraguay (9 January 1872, *ibid.*, N.R.G.², IV, 573), Argentina (28 September 1885, *ibid.*, N.R.G.², XII, 584, and 6 October 1898, *ibid.*, XXXII, 397) and Ecuador (6 May 1904, *ibid.*, N.R.G.², XXXIV, 519).

ad (*b*). Whereas the southern (west-to-east) boundaries of the Guyanas, on the one hand, and Brazil, on the other, are mainly mountain boundaries (see section 1, above, p. 534), all north-to-south frontiers—barring that between Venezuela and British Guyana which is of a mixed nature —are river boundaries, from west to east respectively: between the northwesternmost tip of Brazil and British Guyana, along the Ireng

(Mahui) and the Tacutu; between British and Netherlands Guyana (Surinam), along the Corantijn; between Surinam and French Guyana, along the Maroni (Marowijne); and between French Guyana and Brazil, along the Oyapoc (Yapoc or Vincent-Pinçon).

Of these frontiers of the Guyanas no less than four have been determined by arbitral awards:

the Venezuelan-Guyanan boundary by the famous arbitration of 1897-1899, organized under the mediation of the United States Government and terminated by the award of a five members' arbitral tribunal under the presidency of F. de Martens of 3 October 1899 (Martens, N.R.G.², XXIII, 316; XXVIII, 328; XXIX, 581). Venezuela has, however, up to the present time continued to dispute the legal validity of this award.[15]

> On the other hand, the arbitrator in the dispute between Great Britain (for British Guyana) and Brazil, 1904 (see below) denied any legal effect to this award of 1899 between Great Britain and Venezuela as against Brazil, which in its turn laid claim to part of the same disputed territory;

the Netherlands-French (Maroni or Marowijne river) boundary by an award of Tsar Alexander III of Russia of 25 May 1891 (*ibid.*, N.R.G.², XVIII, 100 = XXVII, 136), which recognized as the frontier in the upper reaches of the Maroni the eastern tributary the Awa (or Lawa) in accordance with the Netherlands claim, and rejected as such the western tributary, the Tapanahoni, defended by France. However, this award and the subsequent Marowijne treaty with France of 30 September 1915 (*ibid.*, N.R.G.³, XII, 269) have not yet finally disposed of the matter since it was discovered at a later stage that the Awa river further upstream bifurcated again into the Litani (west) and the Mariwiri (east) and thus formed another triangle of territory, the appurtenance of which to either Surinam or French Guyana is controversial.

> In his turn, this arbitrator denied any legal effect as against the Netherlands to the Franco-Portuguese Convention of 28 August 1817, which was invoked as a basis of decision in the following Oyapoc arbitration;

the eastern (Oyapoc river) and the southern (interior) boundary of French Guyana towards Brazil by an award of the Federal Council of Switzerland of 1 December 1900 in virtue of a special agreement of 10 April 1897 (*ibid.*, N.R.G.², XXV, 335; N.R.G.³, X, 153), partly on the basis of the Franco-Portuguese Peace Treaty of Utrecht of 11 April

---

15. Comp. the repeated expositions of the Venezuelan Minister of Foreign Affairs to the Chamber of Deputies: see the publications by the Ministry of Foreign Affairs of Venezuela *Reclamación de la Guyana Esequiba* (Caracas, 1967) and *Report on the boundary question with British Guiana ... by the Venezuelan experts* (Caracas, 1967).

1713 (Dumont, VIII[1], 353) and partly on that of another old treaty of 28 August 1817 (Martens, N.R., IV, 490).

The river Yapoc or Vincent-Pinçon formed the traditional frontier between French and Portuguese Guyana pursuant to Article 8 of the Franco-Portuguese Peace Treaty of Utrecht of 11 April 1713. After French forces had overrun Portuguese Guyana in 1792, the Franco-Portuguese boundary was shifted southeastward to the river Arawari or Araguary by Article 8 of a separate Franco-Portuguese peace treaty of 20 August 1797 (*ibid.*, R[2], VII, 203), later confirmed by Article 7 of the Peace Treaty of Amiens of 25/27 March 1802 (*ibid.*, R[2], VII, 404). After a successful military counteraction by Portugal in 1809 it was stipulated in Article 10, in connection with Article 8 of the (first) Peace Treaty of Paris of 30 May 1814 (*ibid.*, N.R., II, 1) that Portugal should restore to France her colony, as it existed on January 1st, 1792. As Portugal found difficulty in carrying the said Article 10 into execution, this was later cancelled and replaced by Articles 106 and 107 of the Final Act of the Congress of Vienna of 9 June 1815 (*ibid.*, N.R., II, 379), pursuant to which Portugal was to return to France her part of Guyana up to the river Oyapoc (which had always been considered by Portugal to be the line of the Peace Treaty of Utrecht). The frontier was subsequently described somewhat more precisely (*viz.*, by a specification of the location of its mouth between 4° and 5° lat. N.) in Article 1 of the Franco-Portuguese convention of 28 August 1817. However, the identity of the river Yapoc or Vincent-Pinçon of 1713 later proved doubtful: hence the arbitration concerning this point, entrusted after a lapse of eighty years to the Swiss Federal Council, which was at the same time invited to fix the interior boundary from the river Yapoc, as it should be identified, westward to the frontier of Netherlands Surinam. As regards this interior frontier, the same Franco-Portuguese convention of 1817 had accepted the meridian of 2° 24′ lat. N., but this again could not affect the rights of the Netherlands with regard to their interior frontier with Brazil.

The complicated state of affairs, reviewed above, explains the arbitration mandate, given to the Swiss Federal Council.

As to the (eastern) river boundary the Arbitrator was empowered to identify the Yapoc or Vincent-Pinçon of the Treaty of Utrecht (1713) as being the Oyapoc which flows into the Ocean to the west of Cape Orange (Brazilian thesis) or the Araguary which empties into it to the south of Cape North (French thesis) or to choose any river between those two.

As to the (interior) frontier the Arbitrator was given power to fix it either starting from the Oyapoc, along the parallel of 2° 24′ lat. N. (Brazilian thesis), or starting from the main source of the main branch of the Araguary first parallel to the Amazonas and further on along the left bank of the Río Branco up to the outer point of Mount Acarary (French thesis), or—again—to choose for the stretch between the Yapoc, as identified, and the Netherlands Surinam boundary as an intermediary solution the watershed of the Amazon basin, constituted here almost entirely by the crest of the Tumuc Humac Mountains.

The Swiss Federal Council decided that the Oyapoc is identical with the Yapoc of 1713, and adopted the watershed line;

the southern (mountain) boundary between British Guyana and Brazil by an award of King Victor Emanuel III of Italy of 6 June 1904, in virtue of a *compromis* of 6 November 1901 (Martens, N.R.G.[2], XXXII,

413, 485), followed by a treaty and a convention of 22 April 1926 (*ibid.*, N.R.G.³, XXIII, 268, 272).

As to the remaining frontiers of the Guyanas

that between Surinam and Brazil has been determined along the watershed between the Amazonas basin and the rivers flowing down to the Atlantic Ocean: treaty of 5 May 1906 (*ibid.*, N.R.G.³, III, 70);

that between British Guyana and (Netherlands) Surinam has never been precisely delimited. The Anglo-Netherlands colonial treaty of 13 August 1814 (*ibid.*, N.R., II, 57) simply restored the Netherlands in the sovereignty over the territory which they possessed on 1 January 1803, with the exception of Demerary, Essequibo and Berbice (British Guyana). The only agreement relative to the boundary dates from 1799, when the Governors of Berbice and Surinam, at that time both in British hands, provisionally adopted the river Corantijn as the boundary, without any express authorization by their Government (text in *The Laws of British Guiana, chronologically arranged from the year 1773 to 1870* (Georgetown, 1870) and in BENJAMINS, *De grenzen van Nederlandsch Guyana* in *Tijdschrift v.h. Kon. Ned. Aard. Gen.*, December 1898, pp. 797 *et seq.*, note 17). That agreement, in which the boundary *tracé* in the mouth of the Corantijn river was recognized by the Berbice side to be Surinam territory over its full width, gave no answer to the question where the boundary was to run in the upper reaches of the Corantijn, and quite naturally so because the existence of a westerly tributary, the New River, flowing into the easterly Coeroeni, was only discovered in 1871—a problem similar to that of the Maroni solved by the Tsar in 1891. The boundary problem is still unresolved between Surinam and independent Guyana because the British Government declined to seek an agreement with the Netherlands or with Surinam in time before the transfer of sovereignty to Guiana in 1965.

ad (*c*) The colony of British Honduras or Belize is up to the present day a subject of dispute between the United Kingdom and Guatemala (and to a certain extent also Mexico). Apart from the basic controversy concerning the sovereignty over this territory (comp. Chapter III, section 2, § 8, p. 385) there is no real dispute about its frontiers: initially fixed between the Río Hondo and the Río Belice by the peace treaty between England and Spain of 3 September 1783 (Martens, R², III, 541), three years later the boundaries were, by a treaty of 14 July 1786 (*ibid.*, IV, 133), on a *do ut des* basis (against Britain's renunciation of her claims to the Mosquito coast) shifted towards the south from the Río Belice to the Río Jabón (or Sibún), and by a subsequent treaty of 30 April 1859 (*ibid.*, N.R.G.³, XXVI, 45) again shifted southward to the Río Sarstún (or Sarstoon). Comp. on the connection between the latter treaty and the Clayton-Bulwer treaty of 19 April 1850 the subsection on the Panama Canal, *supra* p. 232.

As I remarked above, the *uti possidetis* principle has played a major rôle in boundary disputes in Latin America, not only, for that matter, in cases where international rivers were concerned. Arbitrators have often experienced great difficulty in determining the colonial boundaries of the past, both as regards their *de facto* possession and as regards their *de jure* status. Comp. for example, the arbitration by the President of Argentina in the boundary dispute between Bolivia and Peru (special agreement of 30 December 1902, *ibid.*, N.R.G.³, III, 50; award of 9 July 1909, *ibid.*, III, 53), and the dispute between Peru and Ecuador concerning the basin of the river Marañón, terminated by the Protocol of Río de Janeiro of 29 January 1942 (*A.J.I.L.* 1942 (36), Suppl., p. 168), which, however, was again denounced by Ecuador in 1960. See *A.J.I.L.* 1969 (63), pp. 28-46.

Comp. on the operation of the "principle"—not a rule of international law proper—: G. IRELAND, *Boundaries, possessions, and conflicts in South America* (Cambridge, Mass., 1938), pp. 321-329.

Alongside all the variants of possible river boundary *tracés* referred to above, there still occasionally occur (*g*) other, very uncommon delimitations, obviously caused by special geographical conditions.

As an example I quote the fixing of the frontier in the river Rovuma between Tanganyika and Mozambique in an unusually detailed provision of an agreement between the United Kingdom and Portugal of 11 May 1936/28 December 1937 (Martens, N.R.G.³, XXXV, 370). By that provision the river boundary was made dependent primarily upon the existence of islands in the river, to the effect that all islands in the upper part of its course were to belong to Tanganyika and all islands in its lower part to Mozambique, and that, as a corollary, the thalweg, which was generally designated as the borderline, especially in stretches of the river without islands, was to be locally replaced by subsidiary channels in order to allow the islands concerned to fall under the sovereignty of the State to which they were respectively allotted. This elaborate provision is also interesting from other points of view, as it equally bears on such connected practical problems as: the definition of the thalweg, the distinction between islands and shifting sandbanks, and possible future changes of the position of the thalweg caused by a natural alteration in the bed of the river. Comp. on these particular problems below pp. 563 *et seq.*

Another uncommon older example is the boundary regime established by Article 25, para. 4, of the Final Act of the Congress of Vienna of 9 June 1815 (*ibid.*, N.R., II, 379) in respect of the Franco-Prussian frontier stretches of the rivers Sarre, Moselle, Sauer (Sûr) and Our, to the effect that, whereas those river stretches themselves were to "appertain in common" to the adjacent States, the places traversed by them would remain undivided and were attributed with their *banlieue* to the Power on whose territory their longest course was situated.

On the diverse variants of intra-federal river boundary delimitation, see the case law of the United States Supreme Court, reviewed *infra* pp. 556 *et seq.*

Eliminating further the older, now obsolete or rare river frontier delimitations, listed above, p. 537 under (*a*)-(*e*) and (*g*), one can state that the issue is nowadays to all intents and purposes reduced to the delimitation *sub* (*f*), *viz.*, according to which the river belongs *pro diviso* to the adjacent States either (i) along its median line, or (ii) along its deepest channel, two variants of partition which have for a very long time been rivals.

A survey of the history of the river boundary demonstrates that the competition between the (older) median line and the (more recent) thalweg came to a head at the beginning of the 19th century, first in Europe and later in North America. Comp. on this subject the elaborate study of N. KERCEA, *Die Staatsgrenze in den Staatsflüssen* (dissertation Berlin, 1916).

The median line, very frequent in former times, but still obtaining in more recent days, was adopted as the frontier, *e.g.*, in respect of the following rivers:

Mississippi, Iberville river and Maurepas and Pontchartrain Lakes on to the sea: Anglo-Franco-Spanish Peace Treaty of Paris of 10 February 1763 (Martens, R², I, 104), Article 7;

Scheldt (Escaut): Austro-French boundary treaty of 16 May 1769 (*ibid.*, I, 661), Article 7;

Saar river: treaty France-Nassau Weilburg of 24 January 1776 (*ibid.*, R², II, 429), Article 5;

Vistula along the Free City of Cracow: Austro-Polish Treaty of 9 February 1776 (*ibid.*, R², II, 124);

Connecticut and Iroquois rivers and further waterways westward and through the Great Lakes: Peace Treaty of Paris of 3 September 1783 (*ibid.*, R², III, 553), Article 2;

Chattahoochee and St.Mary's river (frontier with the Florida's): treaty of San Lorenzo el Real between Spain and the United States of 27 October 1795 (*ibid.*, R², VI, 142), Article 2: "along the middle of the river"; more doubtful as regards the Mississippi (frontier with Louisiana) in Article 4: "in the middle of the channel or bed of the river";

Gila: peace treaty of Guadelupe Hidalgo between the United States and Mexico of 2 February 1848 (*ibid.*, N.R.G.¹, XIV, 7), Article 7; more doubtful as regards the Río Grande in Article 2: "from thence up the middle of that river following the deepest channel, where it has more than one" and Article 7;

Bidassoa, Franco-Spanish boundary treaty of Bayonne of 2 December 1856 (*B.F.S.P.* vol. 47, p. 765), Article 1;

Faro River and lower section of the Benue, near Lake Chad: Anglo-German Agreement of 19 March 1906 (Martens, N.R.G.^{3}, II, 691), Article 1;

Stanley Pool (Africa): Franco-Belgian treaty of 23 December 1908 (*ibid.*, VI, 334);

Marowyne (Guyana): Franco-Netherlands treaty of 30 September 1915 (*ibid.*, XII, 269): "ligne médiane des eaux ordinaires";

Kagera river (Rwanda): treaty modifying the boundary between the Belgian and British Mandated Territories of Ruanda-Urundi and Tanganyika, approved by the League of Nations Council on 31 August 1923 (*ibid.*, N.R.G.^{3}, XV, 232);

Río Madeira, treaty between Bolivia and Brazil of 25 December 1928 (*ibid.*, N.R.G.^{3}, XXXII, 221), Article 1: "la frontera correrá por la línea de la media distancia entre las márgenes";

Ríos Chingo and Paz, treaty between Guatemala and El Salvador of 9 April 1938 (*ibid.*, XXXVIII, 50) Article 1, *sub* b;

the *O.i.C.* of 1 January 1964 relative to the separation between North and South Rhodesia made an express reservation in respect of the median line in the Zambesi (*Newsletter Southern Rhodesia* of 3 January 1964, No. 1/64).

The river with regard to which the principle of the thalweg was first adopted was the Rhine. The first secret Article of the Peace Treaty of Campo Formio of 17 October 1797 (Martens, R^2, VI, 426) still kept to a boundary *tracé* which granted to France only the left bank of the Rhine between the Swiss frontier and Andernach (inclusive of the bridge-head of Mannheim and the town and fortress of Mainz), though combined with the freedom of navigation on the river for France from the Swiss border to the frontier of the Batavian Republic. However, following an understanding, already reached at the Congress of Rastadt of 1797-1799, convened pursuant to Article 20 of that Peace Treaty, the thalweg principle was still adopted for the Rhine in Article 6 of the Peace Treaty of Lunéville of 9 February 1801 (*ibid.*, R^2, VII, 296), as for that matter for the Adige (Article 3). This basic rule concerning the Rhine[16] has not only been confirmed by subsequent treaties: Article III, 5 (2) of the first Peace Treaty of Paris of 30 May 1814 (*ibid.*, N.R., II, 1), and Article 1, § 2 of the second Peace Treaty of Paris of 20 November 1815 (*ibid.*, N.R., II, 682), but has in the first decades of the 19th cen-

---

16. The principle adopted in 1801 by France and the Empire was in 1808 extended to the section of the Rhine between Baden and the Swiss canton of Aargau: treaty of 17 September 1808 (Martens, N.R., I, 139). Comp. also section II of the treaty of 30 January 1827 between France and Baden (*ibid.*, N.R., VII^1, 123).

tury also spread to other European waterways, such as: the Bug, the Bobra and the Narew: Article 9 of the Franco-Russian Peace Treaty of Tilsit of 7 July 1807 (*ibid.*, R², VIII, 637): the Torneå and the Muonio: Article 5 of the Russo-Swedish Peace Treaty of Fredrikshamn of 17 September 1809 (*ibid.*, N.R., I, 19); the Save: Article III, 2) of the Austro-French Peace Treaty of Vienna of 14 October 1809 (*ibid.*, N.R., I, 210); the Dniestr: Austro-Russian treaty of Leopol, 19 March 1810 (*ibid.*, N.R., I, 252); the Elbe: Article 4 of the treaty of 14 May 1811 between Prussia and the then Kingdom of Westphalia (*ibid.*, N.R., I, 382); the Vistula and the Po: Articles 4 and 95 (2) of the Final Act of the Congress of Vienna of 9 June 1815 (*ibid.*, N.R., II, 379). Later instances of the very frequent adoption of the thalweg as the river boundary in Europe are those of

(1879) Danube between Romania and Bulgaria. In deviation from Article 2 of the Peace Treaty of Berlin of 13 July 1878 (Martens, N.R.G.², III, 449), which determined Bulgaria's northern frontier along the right bank of the Danube, the European Commission charged with a more detailed delimitation of her boundary, in its session of 29 July 1879 (Protocol No. 23, *ibid.*, V, at p. 628), unanimously decided to replace that frontier *tracé* by that of the thalweg;

(1881) Arta, Article 1 of the Final Act fixing the new Greco-Turkish frontier, 27 November 1881 (*ibid.*, N.R.G.², VIII, 44);

(1913) Timok, protocol annexed to Article 4 of the Peace Treaty of Bucharest of 10 August 1913 relative to the old Serbo-Bulgarian frontier (*ibid.*, N.R.G.³, VIII, 71);

Maritza, Article 2, last paragraph, of the Bulgaro-Turkish Peace Treaty of Constantinople of 29 September 1913 (*ibid.*, VIII, 78).

Although there would seem to be little sense in adopting a thalweg as the State boundary in what amounts to a brook, the arbitral tribunal in the *Meerauge* dispute between Austria and Hungary of 1902 (*ibid.*, N.R.G.³, III, 71) drew that boundary through the *Rinnsal* of the Fischseebach.

Development in North America has been slower. There the competition between the rival principles lasted over some decades, witness the striking fact that the frontier regime of the St. Lawrence river between Great Britain (Canada) and the United States is in this aspect different for its eastern and its western stretch between Lake Ontario and the Lake of the Woods. Article 2 of the Peace Treaty of Paris of 3 September 1783 (*ibid.*, R², III, 519), when describing the northern frontier line of the new independent United States of America in the boundary rivers Connecticut and Iroquois (= St. Lawrence), the boundary lakes Ontario, Erie, Huron, Superior and Long Lake, and the water communications between the latter and with the westernmost Lake of the Woods, only mentioned "the middle" of the said rivers, lakes and communications, just as, for that matter, it did in respect of the western and southern boundary rivers Mississippi, Apalachicola, Flint and St. Mary's. The subsequent Peace Treaty of Ghent of 24 December 1814 between the same powers (*ibid.*, N.R., II, 76) did not, in its Articles 6 and 7, define the water frontier more accurately, but referred the demarcation of the northern boundary to two separate commissions, formed on the basis of parity, which were to fulfil their task one after the other, first for the trajectory from the eastern end to the Neebish Falls (in the water communication between Lakes Huron and Superior) and subsequently from there westward to the Lake of the Woods. The first commission duly performed its task by an award of 18 June 1822 in which it drew the borderline in the geometrical middle of the waterways concerned (DE LAPRADELLE-POLITIS, *Recueil des arbitrages internationaux*, vol. I, p. 314). When, however, the second—in fact the same—commission continued the work of demarcation, differences of opinion arose between the commissioners owing to the fact that the American commissioner had realized that a further drawing of the frontier along the median line would in many places render navigation impossible for one of the neighbouring States unless the territorial settlement was accompanied by a simultaneous agreement on the mutual freedom of navigation which was lacking in the treaties of 1783 and 1814. The final solution reached was that the two States concerned, while upholding the purport of the arbitral award of 1822, in a later treaty—the Webster-Ashburton Treaty of 9 August 1842 (Martens, N.R.G.[1], III, 456)—adopted for the second (western) section of the boundary the thalweg principle ("the middle of the channel") and for the whole river the principle of freedom of navigation for their subjects (Articles 2 and 7). This solution had, for that matter, already been adopted much earlier by the United States and Spain with regard to the lower course of the Mississippi in their peace treaty of San Lorenzo el Real of 27 October 1795 (*ibid.*, R[2], VI, 142, Article 4). It is interesting to note that the American Member of the second Commission (1824-1827) made detailed suggestions concerning the manner in which the thalweg boundary should be fixed in the case of a waterway splitting into two or more separate channels. Comp. on this particular subject below, p. 565.

As regards the intra-federal boundaries, the cases decided by the United States Supreme Court show a rather varied picture. This is not, however, attributable to a wavering attitude of the Court but to the fact that it was bound to solve particular inter-state disputes on the basis of either old colonial charters or concessions, or conventions concluded between individual States of the Union. In such cases it was unable to decide them on the strength of general principles. When, however, there were no such special considerations to observe, the Court founded its judgments on what it deemed to be the accepted rule of public international law, applicable also, in its view, to controversies between states of the Federation. It adopted, that is, for navigable rivers the *thalweg* and for non-navigable rivers the median line. Thus, the following results emerge from a perusal of the judgments. Reference is, as to the older decisions (until 1918), made to the collection in J.Brown SCOTT, *Judicial settlement of controversies between States of the American Union*, cited Scott (Washington, 1918-1919, 3 vols.).

In some cases the boundary river was held to belong entirely to one of the riparian States, namely:

the *Chattahoochee* (1859) to Georgia, to the normal level of the water on the opposite bank of Alabama, in accordance with an old concessionary contract (23 Howard, 505; Scott, II, 975);

the *Ohio* (1890) to Kentucky, equally in virtue of an old concession, but in this case to the low water line on the opposite bank of Indiana (136 U.S. 479; Scott, II, 1070, with sequels of 1895-1897, 159 U.S. 275, 163 U.S. 520 and 167 U.S. 270; Scott, II, 1155, 1235 and 1264);

the *Potomac* (1910) to Maryland to the exclusion of West Virginia, pursuant to an old charter of King Charles I of 1632 (217 U.S. 1; Scott, II, 1619, with sequels of 1910 and 1912, 217 U.S. 577 and 225 U.S. 1; Scott, II, 1645 and 1670);

the section of the *Mississippi* between Arkansas and Tennessee (1940), on the ground that the former had acquiesced in the actual exercise of State authority by the latter since 1826 (310 U.S. 563; *A.D.* 1938-1940, Case No. 43; *A.J.I.L.* 1941 (35), p. 154).

In one case (1922) a boundary river, the *Savannah*, was divided along the median line between the two adjacent States Georgia and South Carolina on the ground that there was no deepest channel because the river was unnavigable (257 U.S. 516; *A.D.* 1919-1922, Case No. 60).

In all other cases the Supreme Court adopted as a matter of principle the thalweg as the border line, in particular for the following rivers:

Mississippi. In 1893 a number of bridges across it were, for tax purposes, held to belong *pro diviso* to the riparian states Iowa and Illinois respectively, each to just above the middle of the *thalweg* (147 U.S. 1; Scott, II, 1120). The thalweg rule was held to be a customary rule of positive international law, based on sound legal principle, applicable also to internal American rivers, subject only to strong historico-legal indications to the contrary:

"When a navigable river constitutes the boundary between two independent States, the line defining the point at which the jurisdiction of the two separates is well established to be the middle of the main channel of the stream. The interest of each State in the navigation of the river admits of no other line. The preservation by each of its equal right in the navigation of the stream is the subject of paramount interest. It is, therefore, laid down in all the recognized treaties on international law of modern times that the middle of the channel of the stream marks the true boundary between the adjoining States up to which each State will on its side exercise jurisdiction. In international law, therefore, and by the usage of European nations, the term "middle of the stream", as applied to a navigable river, is the same as the middle of the channel of such stream ... The middle of the channel of a navigable river between independent States is taken as the true boundary line from the obvious reason that the right of navigation is presumed to be common to both in the absence of a special convention between the neighbouring States, or long use of a different line equivalent to such a convention. ... The reason and necessity of the rule of international law as to the mid-channel being the true boundary line of a navigable river separating independent States may not be as cogent in this country, where neighbouring States are under the same general government, as in Europe, yet the same rule will be held to obtain unless changed by statute or usage of so great a length of time as to have acquired the force of law".

The same partition along the mid-channel was held to obtain in respect of other stretches of the Mississippi: in 1918 between Arkansas and Tennessee (246 U.S. 158; Scott, II, 1741, with sequel 247 U.S. 461; Scott, II, 1774; *A.J.I.L.* 1918 (12), 654); in 1919 between Arkansas and Mississippi (to the express exclusion of the line of equidistance between the two banks) (250 U.S. 39; *A.J.I.L.* 1920 (14), 260); in 1920 between Minnesota and Wisconsin even with respect to its upper course (252 U.S. 273; *A.D.* suppl. vol. 1919-1942, Case No. 51), as it had already been admitted in 1906 for its mouth, the Mississippi Sound, where Louisiana won its case against Mississippi in a dispute in which certain oyster banks in the estuary were involved (202 U.S. 1; Scott, II, 1481, with sequel 202 U.S. 58; Scott, II, 1515; *A.J.I.L.* 1907 (1), 204);

Missouri, in 1904, between Missouri and Nebraska (196 U.S. 23; Scott, II, 1403; *A.J.I.L.* 1907 (1), 203);

Columbia, in 1908, between Washington and Oregon (211 U.S. 127; Scott, II, 1600; *A.J.I.L.* 1912 (6), 904);

Delaware, in 1934, between Delaware and New Jersey, even as regards bays and estuaries (291 U.S. 361; *A.D.* 1933-1934, Case No. 48).

Several of these cases presented interesting features of detail:

in the case of avulsion or the formation of a new bed elsewhere the old frontier is maintained, as was held with regard to the river Missouri in Nebraska *v.* Iowa, 1892 (143 U.S. 359; Scott, II, 1904) and Missouri *v.* Nebraska, 1904 (196 U.S. 23; Scott, II, 1403, with sequel in 1905, 197 U.S. 577; Scott, II, 1412; *A.J.I.L.* 1907 (1), 203);

in the case of gradual accretion the boundary line shifts accordingly, as was held in principle in Missouri *v.* Nebraska, 1904 (Scott, II, 1403); Washington *v.* Oregon, 1908 (Scott, II, 1600); Arkansas *v.* Tennessee, 1918 (Scott, II, 1741); Arkansas *v.* Mississippi, 1919 (250 U.S. 39; *A.J.I.L.* 1920 (14), 260), and Kansas *v.* Missouri, 1943 (322 U.S. 213; *A.J.I.L.* 1945 (39), 122);

even if another channel becomes more important, the axis of the old principal thalweg remains the state boundary, as was held in respect of the river Columbia in Washington *v.* Oregon, 1908 (Scott, II, 1600, with sequel II, 1611);

prolonged *de facto* possession can prevail over other, strictly legal considerations, such as were advanced in Maryland *v.* West Virginia, 1910, where the boundary was originally fixed along an astronomical line (217 U.S. 1; Scott, II, 1619; *A.J.I.L.* 1912 (6), 517). In the case of New Jersey *v.* Delaware, 1934, the parties had constantly been engaged in a dispute as to the boundary between them so that there was no question of acquiescence (291 U.S. 361; *A.D.* 1933-1934, Case No. 48; *A.J.I.L.* 1935 (29), 331-345): "There can only be a question of prescription in the case of peaceful and continuous display of sovereignty".

The Court has, however, on the whole, also in respect of land boundaries, attached great importance to acquiescence by one of the parties in the exercise of state authority by the other: 1893, Virginia *v.* Tennessee (148 U.S. 503; Scott, II, 1134); 1906, Louisiana *v.* Mississippi (Scott, II, 1481); 1926, Oklahoma *v.* Texas (272 U.S. 44); 1940, Arkansas *v.* Tennessee (310 U.S. 563; *A.D.* 1938-1940, Case No.43; *A.J.I.L.* 1941 (35), p. 154).

On the special subject of the allocation of river islands comp. below, p. 569.

After the thalweg principle had been applied, as set out above, to a steadily increasing number of European rivers since roughly 1800 and had also been adopted by the British and American Governments for the western section of their boundary of the Great Lakes in 1842, it has further been extended to the colonial possessions of the European Powers in Latin-America, Africa and Asia, to the frontier relations of the Latin-American States *inter se*, and, as I have already set out above by anticipation, on the federal level to those between the various states of the United States of America. The following particulars may suffice to substantiate this statement.

As to the colonial possessions in Latin-America see:

British Honduras-Guatemala, treaty of 30 April 1859 (Martens, N.R.G.[1], XVI[2], 366 = N.R.G.[3], XXVI, 45): "beginning at the mouth of the river Sarstoon in the Bay of Honduras, and proceeding up the mid-channel thereof to Gracias a Diós Falls", subsequently after an inspection *in loco* detailed by an agreement of 25/26 August 1931 (*ibid.*, N.R.G.[3], XXVI, 42);

British Honduras-Mexico, treaty of 8 July 1893 (*ibid.*, N.R.G.[2], XXV, 331): the river Hondo "in its deepest channel".

In regard to the frontier between French Guyana and its neighbours, Netherlands Surinam and Brazil, the thalweg principle was at the end of the 20th century also recognized in arbitral proceedings, *viz.*, by the Tsar of Russia for the river Maroni in his award of 25 May 1891 (*ibid.*,

559

N.R.G.², XVIII, 100 = XXVII, 136) and by the Swiss Federal Council for the river Oyapoc in that of 1 December 1900 (*ibid.*, N.R.G.², X, 153).

As to European colonies or spheres of influence in Africa comp.:

Independent State of the Congo-France, 29 April 1887 (*ibid.*, XVI, 588 = XX, 701): thalweg of the Oubanghi;

Great Britain (Central and South Africa)-Portugal (Angola), treaties of 20 August 1890 (*ibid.*, N.R.G.², XVI, 929) and 11 June 1891 (*ibid.*, XVIII, 185): "centre of the (main) channel" of the Upper Zambesi, the Kabompo, the Ruo, the Shiré and the Sabi,—as far as the latter is concerned, detailed by an arbitral award of Vigliani of 30 January 1897 (LA FONTAINE, *Pasicrisie internationale*, p. 485; Martens, N.R.G.², XXVIII, 294);

Great Britain-Italy (East Africa), protocol of 24 March 1891 (Martens, N.R.G.², XVIII, 175, 177): thalweg of the river Juba;

Congo Free State-Portugal (Angola), treaties of 25 May 1891 (*ibid.*, N.R.G.², XVIII, 28 and 30 = XXVII, 137 and 152): thalweg of the rivers Cuango, Cassaï and Congo, as to the latter (Article 3): "la ligne moyenne du chenal de navigation généralement suivi par les bâtiments de grand tirant d'eau";

Spain (Río Muni)-France (West Africa), treaty of 27 June 1900 (*ibid.*, N.R.G.², XXXII, 59): thalweg of the Río Muni;

Italy (Eritrea)-Sudan: "il corso principale dell'Atbara", agreement of 16 April 1901 (*ibid.*, N.R.G.³, II, 823);

Italy-France, coastal region of Red Sea and Gulf of Aden: thalweg of the Weima: protocol of 10 July 1901 (*ibid.*, N.R.G.³, II, 831);

Great Britain (for Uganda)-Ethiopia: thalweg of the rivers Dawa and Kibish, arrangement of 6 December 1907 (*ibid.*, N.R.G.³, II, 832);

Germany (for Togo)-France (for Dahomey and Sudan), Declaration of 28 September 1912 (*ibid.*, N.R.G.³, VII, 392), Article 5, as a general rule in respect of all boundary waterways: the thalweg will be the frontier, but the median line will act as such where no thalweg proper can be identified or where there are rapids.

Comp. further on the Tanganyika-Mozambique boundary in the river Rovuma the complicated detailed *tracé* of 1936/1937, summarized above, p. 552.

As to river frontiers in Asia and Oceania, see:

Great Britain-The Netherlands, treaty of 16 May 1895 (*ibid.*, N.R.G.², XXIII, 53) concerning their boundary in New Guinea: thalweg of the Fly river;

Great Britain (for five Malay States)-Siam, treaty of 10 March 1909 (*ibid.*, N.R.G.³, II, 685): the thalweg of the main stream of the Singei Golok.

Comp. further on the Burmese-Siamese boundary in the river Meh-

Sai (Meh Sye), the special convention of 1931/1932 (*ibid.*, N.R.G.³, XXVI, 48), mentioned below, p. 568.

Regarding the frontier relations between Latin-American States *inter se*, comp.:

Argentina-Paraguay, treaty of 3 February 1876 (*ibid.*, N.R.G.², IX, 748): "por la mitad de la corriente del canal principal del Río Paraná", which was no longer controversial at the time of the arbitral proceedings of 1878, conducted by President Hayes of the United States (LA FONTAINE, *Pasicrisie internationale*, p. 223; Martens, N.R.G.², XII, 472);

Guatemala-Mexico, 27 September 1882 (*ibid.*, N.R.G.², XIII, 670), Article 3: "la línea media del canal más profundo";

Brazil-Perú, treaty of 8 September 1909 (Martens, N.R.G.³, VI, 849), *sub* 1 (5°): "el medio del canal más hondo del Purús";

Bolivia-Perú, protocol of 30 March 1911 (*ibid.*, VII, 897), Article 23, general clause: "Siempre que un río constituya la frontera entre los dos países, el thalweg de dicho río será la línea divisoria";

Colombia-Perú, treaty of 24 March 1922 (*ibid.*, N.R.G.³, XXV, 669): thalweg of the Ríos Putumayo and Amazonas;

Dominican Republic-Haiti, treaty of 21 January 1929 (*ibid.*, N.R.G.³, XXX, 337): thalweg of the mouths (not of the inner stretches) of the rivers Massacre (Dajatan or Danabon) in the north (Manzanilla Bay) and Pedernales in the south.

In this part of the world, however, one still comes across frontier delimitations along "la línea de la media distancia entre las márgenes", *e.g.*, as regards the Río Madeira between Bolivia and Brazil, treaty of 25 December 1928 (*ibid.*, N.R.G.³, XXXII, 221).

The above summary survey entirely upholds the conclusion that the *thalweg* principle must nowadays be considered to be a general rule of customary international law. This rule, however, is not mandatory, does not bear the character of *jus cogens*, since nothing prevents two States adopting for special reasons a different solution for their particular neighbourly relations. But it may be held to govern all those cases where treaties are silent and no contrary tradition of long standing clearly attests to a different legal regime. Especially in earlier periods the exact *tracé* in a river was often left unspecified. This was still the case, for instance, of the Shiloango (Chiloango) and the Congo as regards their frontier stretch between the territories of France and the International Association of the Congo (5 February 1885, N.R.G.², XX, 70) and of the Lucula, Congo and Cuango as regards theirs vis-à-vis Portugal (Angola) (14 February 1885, *ibid.*, X, 381), and much later, that of the Pilcomayo (Argentina-Bolivia 9 July 1925, *ibid.*, N.R.G.³, XXXVI, 802).

The change in actual State practice has been mirrored in the views of writers, who have also shifted their preference from the median line

see GROTIUS, *De jure belli ac pacis*, l. II, c. iii, § 18: "... in dubio ... imperia ad medietatem fluminis utrinque pertingunt"; VATTEL, *Le Droit des Gens* (Leyden, 1758), l., ch. xxii, § 266,

to the thalweg. A striking proof of this shift is, for instance, that HEFFTER's remark in the earlier French editions of his *Europäisches Völkerrecht* that, in deviation from the median line, "quelquefois le chenal dit "Thalweg" a servi de limite", was corrected by the editor of the fourth French edition of 1883 (p. 157 note 7), GEFFCKEN, to the effect that "Ce n'est pas quelquefois, mais régulièrement que ce procédé a été suivi".

The victory of the thalweg was again confirmed by an identical provision in all five peace treaties after the first World War: Article 30 of the Treaties of Versailles, St. Germain, Neuilly, Trianon and Sèvres (= Article 6 Lausanne) which laid down the following rule:

"In so far as frontiers defined by a waterway [Article 6 of the Peace Treaty of Lausanne intercalates here the words "and not by its banks"] are concerned, the phrases "course" or "channel" used in the description of the present treaty signify, as regards non-navigable rivers, the median line of the waterway or of its principal branch, and, as regards navigable rivers, the median line of the principal channel of navigation".[17]

This identical clause applied to the following boundary rivers:

(Versailles): Netze, Küddow and Piasnitz (with Poland); Nogat, Vistula, Skottau, Neide and Niemen or Memel (East Prussia); Scheidebek or Alte Au, Süder Au and Wied Au (Schleswig);

(St. Germain): Drave, Mur, Danube, Morava, Thaya, Glanfurt, Glan and Gurk (Klagenfurt area);

(Neuilly): Timok, Lukaviča, Jablaniča, Maritsa, Danube;

(Trianon): Landva, Mur, Drave, Kigyos, Tisza or Theiss,[18] Maros, Batar, Csaronda, Ronyva, Hernad, Eipel, Danube;

(Sèvres): Djaihun Irmak, Tigris, Smyrna river;

(Lausanne): Maritsa, Arda;

17. This was not the first time that the principle was thus formulated. It was already put forward in Article 4 of the Protocol which was drawn up, on 11 November 1898, by the British and German Commissioners, charged with the demarcation of the possessions of the two countries between Lakes Nyasa and Tanganyika (Martens, N.R.G.², XXXII, 399), and in part adopted by the Governments concerned in their official Agreement of 23 February 1901 (*ibid.*, XXX, 492) in the following words: "In all cases when a river or stream forms the boundary it is said to be understood that the boundary line is the "thalweg" of the stream; but in cases where the "thalweg" is indeterminate, the centre line of the bed is to be taken as the boundary". It was adopted only in part, because the Governments struck out the second paragraph of the said Article 4, relating to the case of any boundary river changing its course in the future (comp. on this subject below in the text, p. 568).

18. In the backwater of this river it is, of course, again the median line which is decisive.

(complementary treaty of Sèvres of 10 August 1920 between the Principal Allied and Associated Powers and Poland, Romania, the Serb-Croat-Slovene State and the Czecho-Slovak State relative to certain frontiers of those States, Martens, N.R.G.[3], XII, 815): Batar, Tisza, Nera, Danube, Dniestr.

In the light of these data, gathered from international practice all over the world, there would seem to be no shadow of a doubt as to the customary rule applicable to boundary rivers.

The median line does not generally give rise to many questions of detail. A solution must, of course, be sought for the eventuality that, owing for example to the irregularity of the banks, the middle of the river automatically shifts with the rise or fall of the level of the water in the riverbed; this possible cause of future dispute can be eliminated by agreeing upon a standard level of the water as the basis of the boundary delimitation. There is also the more general question of the attribution of islands to one or the other of the adjacent States; different understandings on this point are possible in theory and adopted in practice. Comp. *infra*, p. 569.

The thalweg principle, on the other hand, entails a number of more serious and intricate problems which urgently require solution either in a general sense or in specific cases by treaty or by arbitral or judicial settlement. (*a*) What exactly is meant by the term thalweg? (*b*) What is the legal boundary position in the case of different channels running alongside each other in the bed of the same river? (*c*) Is the frontier subject to automatic displacement together with a shift of the thalweg and does it make any significant difference whether the shift of the thalweg is due to avulsion or to erosion? (*d*) Does the principle of changeability, if recognized, also apply to the case of the river concerned cutting out an entirely new bed elsewhere?

In a number of instances these questions have been at least partly considered in bilateral treaties, but in presumably many more they have not found any specific solution. In such unregulated cases an arbitration tribunal or an international court can be forced to adopt a solution of its own choosing, should it refrain from pronouncing a *non liquet*, which might conceivably be the most correct finding on the basis of strict positive international law.

ad (*a*). *Definition of the thalweg*

The thalweg notion itself is ambiguous, as it can convey three different meanings, *viz.*:

1) the line which connects the deepest points in the river;
2) the line which connects the deepest points in the channel (as in a treaty between France and Baden of 5 April 1840, De Clercq, IV, 516:

"axe du talweg", being "la ligne de son cours qui est déterminée par la suite non-interrompue des sondes les plus profondes");

3) the center of the normal principal navigation channel (Article 30 of the Peace Treaty of Versailles 1919), or further specified: the line drawn in the middle between the double row of buoys (Article 9 of the Netherlands-Belgian boundary treaty of 5 November 1842, Martens, N.R.G.[1], III, 613), or in the terms of Article 3 of the treaty between the Independent State of the Congo and Portugal of 25 May 1891 (*ibid.*, N.R.G.[2], XVIII, 30): "la ligne moyenne du chenal de navigation généralement suivie par les bâtiments de grand tirant d'eau".

Article 2 (1) of Protocol No. 33 of the European Commission for the Delimitation of Bulgaria of 20 September 1879 (*ibid.*, N.R.G.[2], V, 680 *et seq.*), *sub* 1 (Danubian frontier) defined the thalweg frontier as follows:

> "Le thalweg du Danube est la ligne continue des plus grands sondages, qui correspond généralement à la voie la plus propre à la navigation d'aval durant les plus basses eaux ordinaires".

Sometimes the thalweg is further specified by such details as "at low water" (Netherlands-Belgian treaty of Maastricht of 8 August 1843, *Nederl. Staatsblad* 1844, No. 12, Article 4, § 2, relative to the boundary in the river Maas; *B.F.S.P.*, vol. 35, pp. 1202 and 1220). In view of the changeability of the thalweg of the Elbe, dependent on its water-level, a survey was ordered by Articles 2 and 4 of the Prusso-Westphalian treaty of 14 May 1811 (*ibid.*, N.R., I, 382) with the object of determining the thalweg more exactly.

Where there are, or come into existence, two or more separate navigable channels, it is reasonable to adopt the principal navigation channel as the river boundary. Comp. on this case *infra ad* (*b*).

ad (*b*). *Different channels*

The fact that it does happen (and especially because this was the case of the Rhine), that a river has two *Thalwege* was for early writers a ground of dissatisfaction with the new idea of the thalweg as the State boundary. Comp. for example KLÜBER in the French edition of his work (*Droit des gens moderne de l'Europe* (Stuttgart, 1819), I, 207 and note *d* at p. 208), referring to JOLLIVET, *Du thalweg du Rhin* (Mainz, 1801).

Local geographical situations differ so widely *inter se* that it is hardly possible to lay down any general rule apt to cover all possible cases in which a river has two or more navigable channels, especially so when this complication is accompanied by the presence of islands in it. On the latter complication see below, p. 569. I can therefore only adduce a few instances of regulation of the problem of different channels.

St. Lawrence and Great Lakes. One of these instances is the situation in the waterways which link the Great Lakes in the border area between the United States and Canada. The decision of the commissioners under Article 6 of the Anglo-American Peace Treaty of Ghent of 24 December 1814 (Martens, N.R., II, 76), dated 18 June 1822 (DE LAPRADELLE-POLITIS, *Recueil des arbitrages internationaux*, I, p. 314; Martens, N.R., VI, 45), was implicitly based on the following principles: a) even in the case of islands the boundary must be a water *tracé*; b) if there is only one navigable branch, this must be followed, irrespective of its volume and its nearness to one or the other of the banks; c) if there are two, the boundary must follow the channel that offers the greatest quantity of water; d) if there are three or more, the frontier must pass through the channel which is nearest to the centre and permits good navigation to both riparian States; e) where there is no navigation, the boundary *tracé* must ensure an exact partition and good distribution of the territory (comp. DE LAPRADELLE—POLITIS, *loco cit.*, p. 320).

Rhine, Article 9 of the boundary treaty between France and Baden of 30 January 1827 (Martens, N.R., VII[1], 123):

> "Der Thalweg des Rheins ist der während des gewöhnlichen niedrigsten Wasserstandes für die Thalschiffahrt geeigneteste Weg. Im Fall dass über zwei Aerme des Flusses Streit entstehen sollte, so wird derjenige der beiden Aerme, welcher im Lauf der Achse seines eignen Thalwegs die fortlaufende grösste Tiefe hat, als ein Arm des Hauptthalwegs angesehen".

Danube. The solution adopted for the Danube by Article 2 (1) of Protocol No. 33 of the European Commission for the Delimitation of Bulgaria of 20 September 1879 (*ibid.*, N.R.G.[2], V, 680 *et seq.*) was negatively worded:

> "Dans le cas où le fleuve forme deux bras navigables, celui des deux qui dans le cours de l'axe de son thalweg particulier offrira la sonde la moins profonde ne pourra être considérée comme le bras du thalweg du fleuve".

Faro-Benué (Central Africa, between Yola and Lake Chad), Anglo-German Agreement of 19 March 1906 (*ibid.*, N.R.G.[3], II, 691): "At the junction (of the Faro) with the Benué the line shall follow the centre of the middle one of the three channels".

Maritsa. The frontier between Bulgaria and Turkey at the lower end of the river near the Aegean Sea was to follow the thalweg of the right branch, Article 1 *in fine* of their Peace Treaty of 29 September 1913 (*ibid.*, N.R.G.[3], VIII, 78).

ad (c). Shift of the thalweg

It has gradually become an established treaty practice to lay down the rule that in the case of a shift of the thalweg in a boundary river—unlike the case of a shift of the whole river bed, whereupon comp. below *ad (d)*—the State boundary shifts together with the thalweg (on the effect of such a shift upon the sovereignty and ownership of islands see below, p. 569). Comp. the following instances:

Rhine: implied acceptance of the principle of an automatic shift of the frontier in Article III, 5, 2nd paragraph of the (first) Peace Treaty of Paris of 30 May 1814 (Martens, N.R., II, 1) and Article I, 2, 2nd sentence, of the (second) Peace Treaty of Paris of 20 November 1815 (*ibid.*, N.R., II, 682). This rule was in Articles 10 to 12 of the treaty between France and Baden of 30 January 1827 (*ibid.*, N.R., VII[1], 123) qualified to the effect that the thalweg was to be examined every year in October and demarcated afresh by poles, but that in the period between two such examinations it would remain stable irrespective of possible interim changes;

Po: the same implied acceptance in Article 95, last paragraph, of the Final Act of the Congress of Vienna of 9 June 1815 (*ibid.*, N.R., II, 379);

> *Elbe*. The Prusso-Westphalian treaty of 14 May 1811 (*ibid.*, N.R., I, 382) had still adopted the opposite solution in respect of the Elbe: pursuant to Article 4 the State boundary would remain unaltered, both if the whole course of the river and if only the thalweg should shift. An express exception to this rule was, however, made for the case that the change would bring both banks of the new principal current under the sovereignty of one and the same State: in that case the new thalweg was to constitute the new State boundary.
>
> And there are other instances, still at present, of a basic immutableness of the river frontier even in the case of a simple shift of the thalweg, comp. for example the treaty between Guatemala and El Salvador of 1938, cited under (*d*).

Schelde: Article 9 of the Netherlands-Belgian treaty of The Hague of 5 November 1842 (*ibid.*, N.R.G.[1], III, 613) laid down in express words that the boundary between the Belgian province of Antwerp and the Netherlands province of Zeeland would be continuously formed by the changeable thalweg of the river.

Maas: again implied acceptance of the principle in Article 11, § 5 of the subsequent boundary treaty of Maastricht of 8 August 1843 (Netherlands *Staatsblad* 1844, No. 12; B.F.S.P., vol. 35, pp. 1202 and 1220).

Article 30 of the Peace Treaty of Versailles (1919) and the corresponding Articles of the other peace treaties left it to the Boundary Commissions "to specify in each case whether the frontier line shall follow any changes of the course or channel which may take place or whether it shall be definitely fixed by the position of the course or channel at the time when the present Treaty comes into force".

Rio Grande, Rio Gila and Rio Colorado: Major difficulties in this field have induced the United States and Mexico to lay down special rules for these rivers in Articles 1 and 2 of their treaty of 12 November 1884 (Martens, N.R.G.[2], XIII, 673), which make a sharp distinction between the cause of the changes:

(Article 1) "The dividing line ... shall follow the center of the normal channel of the rivers named, notwithstanding any alterations in the banks or in the course of those rivers, provided that such alterations be effected by natural causes through the slow and gradual erosion and deposit of alluvium and not by the abandonment of an existing river bed and the opening of a new one.

(Article 2) Any other change, wrought by the force of the current, whether by the cutting of a new bed, or when there is no more than one channel by the deepening of another channel than that which marked the boundary at the time of the survey (1852), shall produce no change in the dividing line ..., but the line then fixed shall continue to follow the middle of the original channel bed, even though this should become wholly dry or be obstructed by deposits".

Article 3, in addition, expressly forbade the making of any artificial changes in the navigable course of the river.[19]

The parties subsequently set up an International Boundary Commission for this purpose, treaty of 1 March 1889 (Martens, N.R.G.[2], XVIII, 553). At a later stage, after new conflicts had arisen, *inter alia*, relative to the Chamizal District between Ciudad Juárez and El Paso (*A.J.I.L.*, 1911 (5), 782) they laid down new regulations in their treaty of 1 February 1933 (Martens, N.R.G.[3], XXXVI, 175) in order to relieve the towns and agricultural lands located within the El Paso-Juárez Valley from flood dangers, and to ensure "the stabilization of the international boundary line, which, owing to the present meandering nature of the river (Río Grande), it has not been possible to hold within the mean line of its channel".[20]

ad (d). *Shift of the entire bed*

Unlike the case of a shift of the thalweg in an existing river bed (*ad (c)*) which as a rule causes the State boundary to shift together with the thalweg, the diversion of a river into a new bed usually leaves the existing boundary unaffected. This was already GROTIUS' theory (*De jure belli ac pacis*, l. II, c. 3, §§ 16 and 17) and is instanced by many treaties, but there are exceptions. One of these exceptions is that of the river

Maas (Meuse). Detailed rules are contained in the above-mentioned Netherlands-Belgian boundary treaty of Maastricht of 8 August 1843 (Netherlands *Staatsblad* 1844, No. 12) with regard to the river Maas (Meuse). Article 11, § 1, stipulates, contrary to what is usual, that should

19. The prohibition specifically extended to the building of jetties, piers, or obstructions which may tend to deflect the current or produce deposits of alluvium; to dredging to deepen another than the original channel under the Treaty when there is more than one channel; and to the cutting of waterways to shorten the navigable distance. The prohibition did not apply to the protection of the banks on either side from erosion by facings of stone or other material not unduly projecting into the current of the river.

20. See on this subject N. HUNDLEY Jr., *Dividing the waters. A century of controversy between the United States and Mexico* (Univ. of California Press, 1966).

the river abandon its bed and overflow into another, the State boundary is to follow the thalweg of this new bed. In that case, however, the damaged State will be entitled at its own expense to execute the necessary works to cause the river to return to its abandoned bed; should this not have taken place within the term of four years, then the severed territory will definitively fall to the State which benefits by the new thalweg.

Asia. Other—more recent—exceptions to the rule are those of two boundary rivers of Burma, the Meh-Sai and the Pakchan River.

Meh-Sye. This boundary river between Burma and Siam caused trouble by forming a new bed. Great Britain (for Burma) and Siam by a convention of 12 May 1931—14 March 1932 agreed to adopt the new channel of the river as the boundary between Siam and Kengtung "on the understanding that, in the future, should the Meh-Sye River again change its course, the two Governments would be prepared to always hold the "deep-water channel" of the river as the boundary, irrespective of any territorial loss that may be incurred thereby" (Martens, N.R.G.[3], XXVI, 48).

Pakchan River. A similar solution was adopted by Burma and India with respect to the Pakchan River, after it had cut off a couple of bends: amending their boundary treaty of 8 September 1868, the parties accepted the new deep channel as their new frontier, also for future occurrences of the same type in that stretch of the river that was liable to change its course: agreement of 1 June 1934 (*ibid.*, N.R.G.[3], XXX, 107).

International practice has, however, as a rule continued to maintain the old abandoned river bed as the State boundary. I will cite a few examples at random.

Africa. Anglo-German Boundary Protocol of 11 November 1898 (*ibid.*, N.R.G.[2], XXXII, 399) relative to the area of Lakes Nyasa and Tanganyika, general rule in Article 4:

> "If any river forming part of the boundary should change its course in the future, the "thalweg" or centre line of the old bed, as it exists on this date, shall still be the boundary line".

America. Guatemala and El Salvador in Article 2 of their treaty of 9 April 1938 (N.R.G.[3], XXXVIII, 50) agreed that whatever changes might occur in the rivers Chingo and Paz, the frontier would remain as fixed, irrespective of the natural or artificial causes of the changes in the river bed, even if the existing bed should be totally abandoned.

This solution is, however, not so readily acceptable as a general rule when the change of the river bed is not due to natural causes but the result of hydrotechnical works. In such a case it stands to reason that the co-operating parties themselves will make out what the effects of the works on the State boundary will be. The parties are as a matter of

568

course entirely free to regulate those effects as they think fit. Thus the historical Austro-Swiss boundary between Brugg and the Bodensee was expressly maintained in the old bed of the Rhine and demarcated afresh: protocols of 19 May 1903, 14/17 May 1909, 13/26 February 1913, 28 April 1914 and 20 April 1915 in *ibid.*, N.R.G.[3], IX, 754-763.

Mississippi. The United States Supreme Court drew a distinction between the cases of avulsion and accretion, comp. *supra* p. 558. In Arkansas *v.* Tennessee (judgment of 3 June 1940, 310 U.S. 563; *A.J.I.L.* 1941 (35), p. 154; *A.D.* 1938-1940, Case No. 43) the Court was confronted with an old avulsion case, in which the river, which had run prior to 1821 in a large bend around a peninsula (Moss Island), had shortened its course by cutting right through its neck, and the original bed had since been filled up completely.

In this case the dispute was decided in favour of Tennessee on the grounds of prescription and acquiescence by Arkansas:

> "The rule of the *thalweg* yields to the doctrine that a boundary is unaltered by an avulsion, and in such case, in the absence of prescription, the boundary no longer follows the *thalweg* but remains at the original line, although now on dry land because the old channel has filled up. And, in turn, the doctrine as to the effect of an avulsion may become inapplicable when it is established that there has been acquiescence in a long-continued and uninterrupted assertion of dominion and jurisdiction over a given area. Here that fact has been established and the original rule of the *thalweg* no longer applies".

River islands

Treaty regulations dealing with the State frontier in the case of the existence of islands in a boundary river are legion and many of them date of a much earlier period.

In the majority of cases it was the median line or is at present the thalweg of the river which is decisive for the appurtenance of islands to one or the other of the riparian States. This was admitted as far as the thalweg was concerned at an early stage. It is more rare that, inversely, the exact *tracé* of the water frontier is dependent upon the existence or the location of islands to the effect that the thalweg boundary is locally abandoned in places where the presence of islands is of primary importance. I have already referred to the case of the river Rovuma between British East Africa (now Kenya) and Mozambique (p. 552). The allocation of islands can also be made more difficult by the presence of more than one main channel in the river. This is the case of the great waterways between Lake Huron and the Lake of the Woods, mentioned above p. 565.

The occurrence of treaty regulations governing the frontier *tracé* in the case of islands, sometimes very elaborate, is so frequent and varied that I can only give a limited sample of the different solutions agreed upon.

569

They are of three types: they either attribute the islands to one of the riparian States or parcel them out between them or qualify them as "neutral", whatever this latter expression may mean in clear juridical language. I cite from different periods and parts of the world the following instances.

Maros and Theiss (Tisza): Austro-Turkish Peace Treaty of Carlowitz of 26 January 1699 (Dumont, VII², 448), Article 2:

"... Insulae quaecumque in praedictis fluviis, cum actu sint in potestate Caesarea maneant, uti possidentur".

Bug: Austro-Polish boundary treaty of 9 February 1776 (Martens, R², II, 124), Article 1:

"... bien entendu que la propriété de toute la rivière dans cette partie ensemble avec les isles demeurera à Sa Majesté l'Impératrice-Reine ...".

Vistula: same treaty, Article 4, by which Austria returns the town of Casimir, situated on an island in the old Vistula vis-à-vis Cracow (Kraków), to Poland, in exchange for half the bed and all the islands of the river within her new boundaries.

all Spanish-Portuguese boundary rivers in South America: treaty of San Ildefonso of 1 October 1777 (*ibid.*, R², II, 545), Article 14:

"Toutes les isles qui se trouveront dans les fleuves que traversera la ligne en conséquence de ce Traité préliminaire, relèveront du territoire, duquel elles approcheront le plus dans les saisons les plus sèches; celles qui se trouveront à une distance égale des deux rives, resteront neutres à moins qu'elles ne fussent d'une grande étendue et utilité, car alors on les partagera en traçant par le milieu une ligne de séparation qui marquera les limites des deux nations".

Save: Franco-Austrian Peace Treaty of Vienna, 14 October 1809 (*ibid.*, N.R., I, 210), Article 11:

"les isles de la Save qui doivent appartenir à l'une ou à l'autre puissance, seront déterminées d'après le thalweg de la Save".

Rhine: France-Allied Powers, (first) Peace Treaty of Paris of 30 May 1814 (*ibid.*, N.R., II, 1), Article III *sub* 5:

"Quant au Rhin, le thalweg constituera la limite, de manière cependant que les changemens que subira par la suite le cours de ce fleuve n'auront à l'avenir aucun effet sur la propriété des isles qui s'y trouvent; l'état de possession de ces îles sera rétabli tel qu'il existait à l'époque de la signature du traité de Lunéville (1801)",

a provision repeated in Article I, *sub* 2 of the (second) Peace Treaty of Paris of 20 November 1815 (*ibid.*, N.R., II, 682) and further implemented by a treaty between France and Baden of 30 January 1827 (*ibid.*, N.R., VII¹, 123), which made a sharp distinction between their future boundary from the point of view of ownership and that of sovereignty (*Eigentumsgränze* and *Hoheitsgränze*). This *status quo* clause with

570

respect to the ownership of islands in case of a change of sovereignty as a consequence of possible shifts in the course of a river has since become a standard clause in many other boundary treaties. See already as regards the river

Po: Article 95[2] of the Final Act of the Congress of Vienna of 9 June 1815 (*ibid.*, N.R., II, 379).

Exceptionally adjacent States have made the attribution of sovereignty over islands in a river dependent upon their existing appurtenance to owners under private law.

Moselle: partition of the islands between the Netherlands and Prussia by Article 28 of their Boundary Treaty of Aachen of 26 June 1816 (Martens, N.R., III, 24).

Danube: separate Russo-Turkish treaty of Adrianople of 14 September 1829 (*ibid.*, N.R., VIII, 152), paragraph 3: assignment of all islands adjacent to its left bank to the Danubian principalities of Moldavia and Wallachia.—Article 2 (2) of Protocol No. 33 of the European Commission for the Delimitation of Bulgaria of 20 September 1879 (*ibid.*, N.R.G.[2], V, 680 *et seq.*, *sub* 1, at p. 682):

> "Toutefois, pour ne porter aucune atteinte aux droits précédemment établis, toutes les îles situées à droite du thalweg qui, dans la délimitation de 1829 ont été attribuées aux Principautés, resteront comme enclaves à la Roumanie; toutes celles qui, situées à gauche du thalweg, ont été attribuées aux provinces de la rive droite du Danube feront partie de la Bulgarie".

Maritsa: the attribution of the islands was *sub* B of Protocol No. I, annexed to the Bulgaro-Turkish Peace Treaty of Constantinople of 29 September 1913 (*ibid.*, N.R.G.[3], VIII, 78, 85), entrusted to a special commission.

Mekong: Article 1 of the Franco-Siamese treaty of 3 October 1893 (*ibid.*, N.R.G.[2], XX, 172 = 752): attribution of all the islands to France.

Stanley Pool: comp. below p. 573.

Uruguay and Iguassu: Article 4 of the treaty between the Argentine and Brazil of 6 October 1898 (*ibid.*, N.R.G.[2], XXXII, 397):

> "The islands of the Uruguay and Iguassu shall belong to the country indicated by the thalweg of each of these rivers. The Boundary Commissioners, however, shall have the power to propose such exchange as they may consider advisable in the interests of both countries, which exchange shall depend on the approval of the respective governments".

Río Madeiro: Article 1 of the Bolivian-Brazilian treaty of 25 November 1928 (*ibid.*, N.R.G.[3], XXXII, 221).

A rule which gave further freedom of decision was adopted by Germany and Great Britain with regard to their possessions between Yola and Lake Chad by an agreement of 19 March 1906 (*ibid.*, N.R.G.[3], II, 691), Article 9:

"Where islands occur in the rivers, the local officers are further authorized to determine their ownership (sic) by mutual agreement on equitable principles, subject to ratification (by the Governments concerned)".

Zambesi: On the dissolution of the Federation of Rhodesia and Nyasaland, the *O.i.C.* of 1 January 1964, sanctioning it, also laid down certain rules relative to the islands in the Zambesi river, in particular the Livingstone islands near the Victoria Falls. While making a reservation as regards the median line of the river as the future boundary between Northern and Southern Rhodesia, the Order stipulated that the islands in the Zambesi river would be attributed to the State with the bank nearest to the islands (to be decided for each island separately). See *Newsletter Southern Rhodesia* of 3 January 1964, No. 1/64, and A. O. CUKWURAH, *The settlement of boundary disputes in international law* (Manchester, 1967), p. 56.

It is more rare that a river boundary in the case of islands does not follow the (main) channel, but passes across one or more islands. In that case different solutions can be adopted.

The British Member of the Commission set up by Article 7 of the Peace Treaty of Ghent of 24 December 1814 (Martens, N.R., II, 76) for the determination of the river boundary between Lake Huron and the Lake of the Woods in 1827 proposed with regard to the island Saint Georges in the waterway Sainte Marie between Lake Huron and Lake Superior, that it should in principle be divided into two equal portions but that, if this were not possible, the State which obtained the largest portion was allowed to keep it entirely, conditional upon its obligation to give its counterpart a territorial *quid pro quo* (DE LAPRADELLE-POLITIS, *Recueil des arbitrages internationaux*, I, p. 320).

Kunene: Article 6 of the Agreement between the Union of South Africa (on behalf of its then Mandated Territory of South-West Africa) and Portugal (for Angola) of 22 June 1926 (*ibid.*, N.R.G.[3], XXIII, 299):

"... chaque fois que la ligne médiane de la rivière ... traversera une île située dans le lit de la rivière, cette ligne médiane constituera la frontière".

The United States Supreme Court has held that a shift of the river bed or of the thalweg leaves the sovereignty over the islands unaffected:

Ohio river, 1890 (136 U.S. 479; Scott, II, 1070, with sequels in 1895-1897): an island of Kentucky that as a result of the shift southwards of the main bed of the river Ohio came to be situated to the north of that river and was in actual fact united with Indiana, nevertheless continues to appertain to Kentucky.

Missouri river, 1908 (213 U.S. 78; Scott, II, 1607): an island belonging to the State of Missouri has remained part of that State despite a shift of the thalweg towards Kansas as a consequence of erosion.

There are exceptional cases in which the allotment of an island to one of the riparian States is accompanied by its demilitarization or/and neutralization: this was stipulated on the assignment of the island of

572

Bamu in the Franco-Belgian boundary river Stanley Pool to France in the agreement of 23 December 1908 (*ibid.*, N.R.G.[3], VI, 334).

Comp. also the demilitarization of certain Rhine islands, stipulated in Articles 6 and 8 of the Franco-German Peace Treaty of Baden of 7 September 1714 (Dumont, VIII[1], 436; Rousset, *Recueil*, I, 1): demolition of the fortresses built by France during the war, *inter alia*, on islands in the Rhine.

River deltas

Special difficulties are sometimes created by river deltas. The most notorious example from the point of view of boundary delimitation in the past was the delta of the Danube which has successively shown five different State frontiers in its area. Comp. Part II of this publication, pp. 372-373.

Many river deltas are situated within the territory of one single State, as are the deltas of the Rhine, the Wolga, the Dniepr, the Rhône, the Po, the Nile, the Huang-Ho. These are not likely to cause international friction, although even they may theoretically give rise to the question as to whether a clause on the freedom of fluvial navigation necessarily extends to all the branches of the delta. This point has arisen, *e.g.*, in respect of the Rhine (comp. Chapter II, Annex § 2). Others are, or have been at some period, divided between two States, *e.g.*, those of the Scheldt, the Vistula, the Ganges (Bramaputra), the Shatt-al-Arab (Euphrates and Tigris), the Saigon, the Mississippi, the Niger, the San Juan del Norte, the Amazonas, the Río Grande and the Congo.

One can still at present, as one could in the past, come across boundary deltas which belong over their whole breadth to one of the adjacent States. This has been the case of the Danube between 1829 and 1856 and is again the case since the Soviet-Romanian exchange of notes of 26-29 June 1940 (see *Soviet Documents on Foreign Policy* 1917-1941, London, 1953; vol. III, pp. 458 *et seq.*), as confirmed by the Peace Treaty of 10 February 1947 (*U.N.T.S.*, vol. 42, p. 3). In the same way the delta of the San Juan de Nicaragua falls under the sole sovereignty of Nicaragua by virtue of the boundary treaty between the latter and Costa Rica of 15 April 1858 (*B.F.S.P.*, vol. 48, p. 1049), which fixed the frontier as following the right bank of that river below Castillo. The river became a source of dispute between Costa Rica and Nicaragua owing to the fact that the level of the water is exposed to considerable changes. Arbitrator E. P. Alexander, in his third award of 22 March 1898 (LA FONTAINE, *Pasicrisie Internationale*, p. 533), which defined the frontier line more precisely, ruled that the boundary line follows the lowest watermark of a navigable stage of the river.

I will further confine myself to quoting here a few examples of deltas which have given rise to international friction.

The exact boundary line in the Shatt-al-Arab and its delta has long been a bone of contention between Persia (Iran) and Turkey (later: Iraq). See the Protocol of 4(17) November 1913, modified by Article 2 of a Convention between Iran and Iraq of 4 July 1937 (Martens, N.R.G.³, XXXVII, 684). These instruments define the boundary line partly along the low-water line and partly along the thalweg, and grant freedom of navigation to the ports of both countries on a footing of equality. See also p. 603 *infra*.

The delta of the river Wanks (or Coco) at the easternmost extremity of the frontier area between Honduras and Nicaragua near Cape Gracias a Diós has played a part in the controversy which has opposed the two States for many decades. An arbitral award of the King of Spain of 23 December 1906 (Martens, N.R.G.², XXXV, 563) found for Honduras in her dispute with Nicaragua in which the former claimed a frontier following the river Wanks and the latter a mountain boundary north of that river. The arbitrator, however, left undecided where the exact borderline in the Wanks delta runs. The Nicaraguan Government refused at a later stage to acquiesce in the award, alleging different grounds of nullity. In the event, this new dispute was submitted to the International Court of Justice which in its turn decided against Nicaragua (Judgment of 18 November 1960, *I.C.J. Reports* 1960, p. 192; comp. on this judgment my paper in *The Jurisprudence of the World Court*, vol. II, pp. 408 *et seq.*). As, however, the boundary line in the Wanks delta was once again left undecided, the States concerned, which both accepted the Judgement, have since entered into negotiations on the precise *tracé* of their frontier in the delta area, which have been successfully concluded: see Whiteman, vol. 3, pp. 633-648, at p. 648.

River bridges

Bridges across rivers cause only minor boundary problems. Apart from the conceivable solution that a bridge, especially over a "common river" proper, is made a condominium, the choice will be between a State frontier across the middle of the bridge or above the middle of the thalweg.

As far as I have been able to verify, it is customary to adopt as the State frontier the middle of the bridge. This is sometimes said to be the case even where the boundary in the river itself follows the thalweg.

France-Nassau Weilburg, 24 January 1776 (Martens, R², II, 429), Article 5: although a bridge across the Saar was said to be "common", it would nevertheless be divided between the parties with regard to ownership, sovereignty (*Hoheit*) and upkeep; a boundary stone was to be placed on the middle of the bridge, and neither of the parties was allowed to levy a bridge toll on it.

France-Holy Roman Empire, Peace Treaty of Lunéville of 9 February

1801 (*ibid.*, R², VII, 296), Article 3 relative to the Adige frontier between Austria and the Cisalpine Republic:

"... comme par cette ligne de délimitation (*i.e.*, the thalweg of the river Adige) les villes de Vérone et de Porto Legnano se trouveront partagées, il sera établi sur le milieu des ponts des dites villes des ponts levis qui marqueront la séparation".

Franco-Allied Powers, (second) Peace Treaty of Paris of 20 November 1815 (*ibid.*, N.R., II, 682), Article I, *sub* 2 *in fine*: half of the bridge between Strasbourg and Kehl will belong to France, the other half to the Grand Duchy of Baden.

Baden-France, 10/26 January 1861 (*ibid.*, N.R.G.[1], XVII[1], 305), Articles 1-3, concerning Rhine bridges: middle of the bridge between Strasbourg and Kehl; this rule equally applicable to future bridges, independently of the boundary line in the river along the thalweg. However, under Article 66 of the Peace Treaty of Versailles, 1919, the ownership of all the bridges across the Rhine within the limits of Alsace-Lorraine would belong to France.

By a declaration of 30 October 1760 (*ibid.*, N.S., I, 5) for the interpretation of Article 3 of the Franco-Sardinian boundary treaty of 24 March 1760 (Wenck, III, 220):

"si le torrent sortoit du nouveau lit qui lui aura été assigné, et abandonnoit le pont de Saint Genis, ce cas n'apporteroit aucun changement à la limitation établie par le milieu de ce pont".

In the same sense N.S., I, p. 7: "les bornes ... posées sur les autres ponts...n'ont d'autre objet que d'indiquer le point de division de ces mêmes ponts, sans influer sur la limitation des rivières qui coulent au dessous d'iceux, lesquelles...doivent toujours se diviser par le milieu de leur plus grand cours".

The United States Supreme Court has, however, on various occasions fixed the intra-federal State boundaries on bridges across the Mississippi above the thalweg: comp. Iowa *v.* Illinois, 1893 (147 U.S. 1; Scott, II, 1120), 1894 (151 U.S. 238; Scott, II, 1150) and 1906 (202 U.S. 59; Scott, II, 1516). The Court was "of opinion that the controlling consideration in this matter is that which preserves to each State equality in the right of navigation in the river." It therefore held "that the true line in navigable rivers between the States of the Union, which separates the jurisdiction of one from the other, is the middle of the main channel of the river ... and, if there be several channels, ... the middle of the principal one, or rather, the one usually followed", and from these basic considerations it drew the conclusion that the same must apply to the state boundary on bridges. Comp. p. 557 *supra*.

Comp., however, the older lawsuit between the Mississippi & Missouri Railroad Company and James Ward, in which the latter, as owner of a

575

shipping company, complained of obstructiou of the river by a bridge built across it, and asked for the removal of half of the bridge by one of the states concerned (Iowa). The District Court rendered a decree in favour of the complainant, but he failed in the appeal proceedings (67 U.S. 485; 1863). The Supreme Court, it is true, found that "the Constitution of Illinois calls for the middle of the Mississippi River as the western boundary of that State, and as Iowa was admitted into the Union after Illinois, a line in the middle of the river is the dividing line between the States . . . and as the western half of the river is undeniably within the jurisdiction of Iowa, it follows that the bridge is a clear nuisance within that district to the extent of half its length", but it nevertheless dismissed the claim that the bridge be destroyed.

River frontiers are often difficult to determine *in concreto* because the contracting parties, owing to their geographical ignorance, only mentioned in their boundary treaties the name of the river in its lower course without being aware of the fact that that lower stretch was fed by the confluence of two or more tributaries higher upstream, each of which might be considered as the origin of the main river. This fact has played a major rôle in the relations between the Guyanas in South America, especially between Netherlands and French Guyana (Maroni or Marowyne) and between British and Netherlands Guyana (Corantijn). Comp. *supra* pp. 549 *et seq.*

Section 3. FRONTIERS IN INLAND SEAS AND LAKES

As I have remarked earlier, an inland lake or sea surrounded by two or more riparian States may theoretically form a *condominium* between them, but there is none in existence. Or it may belong exceptionally entirely to one of them, as in the case of the Central-American Lake of Nicaragua, mentioned above, p. 19, and the Lake of Tiberias in Israel. Some African lakes were also placed in the latter position: see, for example, Lakes Abbé and Alli where the frontier between Ethiopia and the French possessions was drawn along one of their banks: treaty of 20 March 1897 (Martens, N.R.G.[3], II, 120); Lakes Chiuta and Chilwa, with regard to which Great Britain (for Nyasaland, now Malawi) and Portugal (for Mozambique) agreed on 20 August 1890 (*ibid.*, N.R.G.[2], XVI, 929 = XVIII, 154) that the boundary should follow their eastern shore (comp. also the *modus vivendi* of 31 May/5 June 1893, *ibid.*, XX, 256). Lake Rudolf and Lake Stefanie, on the other hand, differ from those just mentioned in that almost the whole of them belongs to one of the two adjacent States—Kenya and Ethiopia, respectively—, Lake Rudolf to the former and Lake Stefanie to the latter, but that their extreme tip just crosses the border and thus falls under the sovereignty of the other

State (British-Ethiopian boundary agreement of 6 December 1907, *ibid.*, N.R.G.[3], II, 832).

Unless such exceptional conditions prevail in frontier lakes, the border line will as a rule, and in the simplest cases, run either along a curved or broken median line or line of equidistance, or along a straight line between the two shores—namely, when the land frontier happens to meet an oval or oblong lake at both ends—, or straight across it—namely, when that frontier cuts the lake somewhere between two more distant ends.

The first variant occurs, for example, in the large lakes which separate the United States from Canada: Lakes Ontario, Erie, Huron and Superior, and in the chain of smaller lakes bordering the Republic of Congo (Kinshasa) on the east: Lake Mwera between Katanga and Zambia (formerly Northern Rhodesia), Lake Kivu in the borderzone with Rwanda, and Lakes Edward and Albert in that with Uganda. It is, however, often difficult to draw a correct median line or line of equidistance in a lake, the shores of which encompass an irregular geometrical figure: in such cases it sometimes becomes necessary to fix the "middle" of the lake along a repeatedly broken line, zigzagging across its surface. Comp. as an example the boundary line through Lakes Edward and Albert *infra*, p. 586.

The second variant occurs, *e.g.*, in Lago Maggiore and occurred in the past in Lago di Garda before its northern tip was lost to Italy in 1919, and in Lake Victoria (Victoria Nyanza) when a boundary line was first drawn in 1890 between the colonial possessions of Germany and Great Britain. Comp. on these lakes *infra*.

In many cases, however, the situation is not as straightforward as that, or has since become more complicated as a consequence of later developments. This applies, *inter alia*, to the Lakes of Lugano and Geneva and to Lakes Chad and Nyasa. Comp. on these lakes *infra*.

The boundary *tracé* across a lake has also sometimes been affected by the presence of islands in it and the wish to reserve one or more of them to one of the adjacent States, as was the case of Lakes Nyasa and Mweru. On the former comp. *infra*, p. 586. As to Lake Mweru Great Britain (for Northern Rhodesia, now Zambia) and the then Congo Free State agreed by Article 1 (*b*) of their treaty of 12 May 1894 (Martens, N.R.G.[2], XX, 805) that the boundary in that lake, instead of being drawn along a straight or a median line from one end to the other, was "deflected toward the south of the lake so as to give the island of Kilwa to Great Britain".

After these general introductory remarks I will now enter into some detail in a brief survey of the history of a number of inland seas or lakes and the criteria of their partition between or among the adjacent States, grouped according to Continents.

577

Bodensee (Lake of Constanz). Comp. on this lake *supra*, p. 19. It is at present divided among the Member States of three federations, *viz.*, the *Länder* Baden-Württemberg and Bavaria of the German Federal Republic, the Austrian *Land* of Vorarlberg and the Swiss Cantons of Turgau and Sankt Gallen. See G. Riva, *L'exercice des droits de souveraineté sur le Lac de Constance* (*S.J.I.R.* 1967 (XXIV), pp. 43-66). In 1969 the three States mentioned above have opened negotiations on the division of the lake (*Bulletin of Legal Developments* 1969 (4), p. 38).

Lake of Geneva (Lac Léman). French territorial sovereignty penetrated into the, otherwise Swiss, lake between Hermance and Saint Gingolph, forming at first a French riparian belt, bordered to the west and the east by a perpendicular drawn from the French bank, and extending to a median line between the northern and southern shores. However, the parties later agreed to alter the frontier so as to replace the quadrangular French water area by a hexagonal one : Convention of 25 February 1953 (*S.J.I.R.* 1954 (XI), pp. 193-194 and 1967 (XXIV), p. 49). See also the article by Ch. Rousseau in the *R.G.D.I.P.* 1954 (58), pp. 211 and 364.

Lago Maggiore. Divided into a large Italian and a small Swiss part by a west-east boundary line: treaty between Switzerland and (originally) Austria of 2 August 1752 (Wenck, III, p. 35).

Lake of Lugano. This lake, though Swiss in its central basin, is Italian in the farther end of its eastern and southwestern branches, towards Porlezza and Porto Ceresio, divided between Switzerland and Italy in its northwestern branch leading to Ponte Tresa, and moreover bordered at the centre by the small Italian land enclave of Campione with its corresponding stretch of lake. As a result, the State frontier crosses the lake between Gandria (confine) and Santa Margherita in the east and runs in the middle between the western Italian shore and the Morcote peninsula from midway between Brusino and Poncia to Ponte Tresa in the northwest, whereas a further boundary line runs at mid distance between the Campione enclave and the opposite bank of San Martino, which became Swiss only in 1861: treaty of 5 October 1861 (Martens, N.R.G.[1], XX, 186, *sub* XI). Comp. on this curious enclave Chapter V, section 2, *supra*, p. 450.

Wörthersee. This lake escaped becoming an Austrian-Yugoslav frontier lake as a result of the plebiscite held in October 1920 in the Klagenfurt area pursuant to Article 50 of the Austrian Peace Treaty of St. Germain of 10 September 1919 (*ibid.*, N.R.G.[3], XI, 691). According to that Article the said area was divided into two zones, separated by a transversal median line across the lake from its western extremity south of Velden in an easterly direction to the outlet of the Glanfurt from the lake. The plebiscite would first be held in the southern zone, occupied by Serb-Croat-Slovene troops, under the control of an international commission, and only be followed by a plebiscite in the northern zone, occupied by Austrian troops, in case the first result would be in favour of the Serb-Croat-Slovene State. Since, however, this plebiscite held in October 1920 resulted in favour of Austria, the whole Klagenfurt area, including the whole of the Wörthersee, remained Austrian territory.

Neusiedler See. This inland lake (in Hungarian: Fertö Tava) in the Burgenland, the border area between Austria and Hungary, was historically part of Hungary. When, however, the Dual Monarchy of Austria-Hungary was dissolved in 1918 as a consequence of World War I, this West-Hungarian land was ceded to Austria and the frontier line drawn through the Neusiedler See, starting south of Panhagen and passing south of a certain island to a point on its southern bank between Holling and Hidegseg: Article 27, *sub* 5, St. Germain (*loco cit.*) = Article 27, *sub* 1, Trianon (Martens, N.R.G.[3], XII, 423). A plebiscite which was subsequently organized for the West-Hungarian area of Sopron (Oedenburg) by the Austro-Hungarian Protocol of Venice of 13 October 1921 (*ibid.*, XIX, 763), resulted in the said town and environs being retroceded to Hungary, but it did not effect any change in the lake frontier.

Lago di Garda. This lake was divided between Austria and her southern neighbour, then the Cisalpine Republic, in virtue of Articles 6 and 8 of the Austro-French Peace Treaty of Campo Formio of 17 October 1797 (*ibid.*, R[2], VI, 420), but it returned to Austria at the Peace Congress of Vienna of 1815: Final Act of 9 June (*ibid.*, N.R., II, 379), Articles 85 (referring to an older treaty of 4 October 1751, *ibid.*, N.S., I, 746) and 93. It was, however, divided again in virtue of the Austro-Franco-Sardinian Peace Treaty of Zürich of 10 November 1859 (*ibid.*, N.R.G.[1], XVI[2], 531), Article 3, between the Lombardo-Venetian kingdom (Austria) and Sardinia, which gave Sardinia half of the lake from the southern limit of Tyrol via Bardolino and Manerba to Peschiera. The Italian part of Lake Garda was considerably extended northward by the Austro-Italian Peace Treaty of Vienna of 3 October 1866 (*ibid.*, N.R.G.[1], XVIII, 405; comp. in particular the Final Act on boundary delimitations of 22 December 1867, *ibid.*, 421 *et seq.*, at pp. 423-424), up to a roughly west-east line which only left the northernmost tip of the lake south of Riva in Austrian territory. And when ultimately by Article 27, *sub* 2, of the Peace Treaty of St. Germain (*loco cit.*), the Austro-Italian boundary was once again shifted far to the north, the whole of Lake Garda became part of Italian territory.[21]

21. As a plaque of marble, affixed in 1921 to a wall of the castle of Tirolo near Merano in memory of the day of Dante's death six centuries ago, reminds us, this great poet sang as a legal historian a remarkable feature of this Lago

Russia

Lake Ladoga. Since Finland was conquered by Sweden at the end of the 13th century and was formally integrated into its territory in virtue of the Peace Treaty of Nöteborg with the principality of Novgorod in 1312, this lake has been situated in the border area between Sweden and Russia as a frontier lake under Swedish sovereignty.[22] By the Russo-Swedish Peace Treaty of Nystad of 10 September 1721 (Dumont, VII[1], 36), however, the boundary was shifted northwestward as a result of the cession of the southeastern districts of Sweden, including the lake, to Russia. It remained, of course, an internal Russian lake when Sweden was forced by the Peace Treaty of Fredrikshamn of 17 September 1809 (Martens, R[2], I, 19) to renounce all her rights to Finland, which on that occasion was incorporated into Russia as a Grand Duchy under the Tsar. However, when more than a century later, after World War I and the Bolshewik Revolution, Finland achieved national independence from the Soviet State, sanctioned by their Peace Treaty of Dorpat of 14 October 1920 (*ibid*, N.R.G.[3], XII, 37), Article 2 (2) of that treaty moved the Finnish frontier forward again to the Lake of Ladoga, which it was to cross in a northeastern—southwestern direction towards the Carelian isthmus and the Finnish Gulf. This situation changed again after the Russo-Finnish Winter War of 1939-1940, which resulted in the Peace Treaty of Moscow of 12 March 1940 (*ibid.*, N.R.G.[3], XXXVIII, 323), by Article 2 of which the frontier was shifted towards the north-west between Vyborg and Virolahti, and the whole of Lake Ladoga fell again under Soviet-Russian sovereignty. No further change on this point was made by the Finnish Peace Treaty of Paris of 10 February 1947 (*U.N.T.S.*, vol. 48, p. 203).

Lakes Peipus and Pskov. These two lakes south of the Finnish Gulf, once border lakes between the possessions of the Teutonic Order and the principality of Novgorod, have later (17th century) shared the fate of the Baltic area, disputed between Sweden, Poland and Russia. They became exclusively Russian lakes as a consequence of the Peace Treaty of Nystad between Sweden and Russia of 10 September 1721 (*supra*).

Benaco: there was a spot in the middle of the lake where three bishops could exercise jurisdiction (Canto XX of his *Inferno*, verses 61-63, 67-69):
  Suso in Italia bella giace un laco
  Appiè dell'Alpe che serra Lamagna
  Sovra Tiralli ch'ha nome Benaco
  ...
  Luogo è nel mezzo là, dove il Trentino
  Pastore, e quel di Brescia e il Veronese
  Segnar potria, se fesse quel cammino.
22. Comp. on Finland's older history, *inter alia*, ERICH's *Das Staatsrecht des Grossfürstentums Finnland (Suomi)* in *Das öffentliche Recht der Gegenwart*, vol. XVIII (Tübingen, 1912), pp. 1 *et seq.*

When, however, after World War I the Soviet Government "renounced voluntarily and forever" all sovereign rights over the Baltic peoples and territories, in particular by the Peace Treaty with the newly constituted republic of Estonia, concluded at Dorpat on 2 February 1920 (Martens, N.R.G.[3], XI, 864), the two lakes became boundary lakes with Russia again, divided between Estonia and Russia by roughly northsouth lines. This frontier situation has presumably continued in a federal variant after the incorporation of the short-lived sovereign republic of Estonia as a member state into the U.S.S.R. in 1940.

Balkan Peninsula
Lake Scutari (Skadar). Lake Scutari was Turkish until 1878, when the Congress of Berlin, following to a certain extent the example set by Article 1[23] of the preliminary peace treaty of San Stefano between Russia and Turkey (*ibid.*, N.R.G.[2], III, 246), extended Montenegro's territory towards the southeast, *inter alia* with Antivari, and divided the lake between Turkey and Montenegro in a north-south direction by a line crossing it near the island of Gorice Topal: Article 28 of the Peace Treaty of 13 July 1878 (*ibid.*, III, 449). The alterations, made in Article 29 of the same treaty in 1880 under the threat of a naval demonstration by the Great Powers against Turkey—further cession of Dulcigno to Montenegro in exchange for certain Albanian-populated districts by a bilateral treaty between Montenegro and Turkey of 25 November 1880 (*ibid.*, N.R.G.[2], VI, 510)—and in 1909 after the annexation of Bosnia-Herzegowina by Austria-Hungary—the freeing of Montenegro from certain restrictions of her sovereign rights by an, again multilateral, exchange of notes of April/May 1909 (*ibid.*, N.R.G.[3], IV, 41)—had no influence upon the lake boundary. Neither has this boundary changed when, as a consequence of the emergence of an independent Albania after the Balkan Wars—delimitation by a Protocol of the Conference of Ambassadors of 11 August 1913 at London (*Publ. P.C.I.J.*, series C, No. 5-II, p. 265)—, the lake became a border lake between Montenegro and Albania. If the secret treaty of London between France, Great Britain and Italy of 26 April 1915 (Martens, N.R.G.[3], X, 329), intended to lay down their concessions in favour of Italy, should she join the war against the Central Powers, had been carried out, Albania would have been dismembered into four parts: a small autonomous Moslem State under Italian protection in the center, a southwestern tip around Valona under full Italian sovereignty, a southeastern part south of Lake Ochrida to be added to Greece, and a northern part to be added to Montenegro, including Lake Scutari which would thus have become an entirely Montenegrinian lake. The implementation of that secret treaty

23. The frontier delimitation of Berlin differed from that of San Stefano.

was, however, wrecked in particular on President Wilson's refusal to recognize its validity in the peace settlement. The frontier of 17 December 1913 between Albania and Montenegro after World War I was first left undefined (Article 4, *sub* 1, of the treaty of Sèvres of 10 August 1920 relative to certain frontiers (Martens, N.R.G.³, XII, 815) and the reservation made on the occasion of Albania's admission to the League of Nations in December 1920), but ultimately, by a decision of the then Great Powers of 9 November 1921 (*Publ. P.C.I.J.*, series C, No. 5-II, p. 77), confirmed as the frontier between Albania and the Serb-Croat-Slovene Kingdom, subject to a few minor alterations, *sub* II and IIIᵃ, thus leaving Lake Scutari divided between the two States.

Lake Ochrida (Ohridsko Jezero). This lake became the subject of a lengthy controversy after the Balkan Wars when a new Albanian State was established and its frontiers had to be fixed. Should its southeastern boundary with Serbia (Serb-Croat-Slovene Kingdom) be drawn west of the lake, somewhere across it, or between it and Lake Prespa? Both the Albanians and the Serbians claimed the area, and other countries, also the Great Powers, were interested. The Conference of Ambassadors, entrusted with the task of fixing the boundaries of Albania as the executive organ of the Principal Allied Powers (Article 3 of the Peace Treaty of London of 30 May 1913, Martens, N.R.G.³, VIII, 16), and the Delimitation Commission set up for that purpose by the Conference, decided in their sessions of August-December 1913 at London and Florence (*Publ. P.C.I.J.*, series C, No. 5-II, pp. 265-267) that "the western and southern shore of Lake Ochrida, from the village of Lim as far as *(jusqu'à)* the Monastery of Saint-Naoum would form part of Albania". This would imply a boundary line across the lake from Lim to the area of the Monastery. See for the final Protocol of Florence of 17 December 1913 also Martens, N.R.G.³, IX, 650. Had the secret treaty of London of 26 April 1915 *(ibid.,* X, 329)—comp. above under Lake Scutari—been carried out, then Greece would have been entitled to an area south of Lake Ochrida, but it was not implemented after World War I. The Great Powers instead continued, with the unanimous consent of the Assembly of the League of Nations of 2 October 1921, to exercise their powers under Article 3 of the Peace Treaty of 1913 by confirming the *tracé* of the frontiers established in 1913, subject to a few "rectifications", implying—under III *d)* of their Decision of 9 November 1921 (*Publ. P.C.I.J.*, series C, No. 5-II, p. 77)—an alteration in the district of Lim in order to assure the economic communications between Elbasan and Koritza on the borders of Lake Ochrida. This reconsideration of the boundary question led to a further resolution of the Conference of Ambassadors of 6 December 1922 (*Publ. P.C.I.J., loco cit.,* p. 268), simply informing the Serbo-Albanian Boundary Commission and the Albanian and Yugo-Slav Governments that it had agreed to allocate the Saint-Naoum Monastery to Albania, which in turn implied a somewhat changed *tracé* of the boundary between Lim and the southern shore. The Conference based its power to make this decision on the thesis that the 1913 Protocol had not stated explicitly to which of the two States the Monastery should be attributed. As the Serb-Croat-Slovene Government disputed both that thesis and the validity of the decision, the Conference of Ambassadors submitted the controversy to the Council of the League of Nations in the following formulation:

> "Have the Principal Allied Powers, by the decision of the Conference of Ambassadors of December 6th, 1922, exhausted, in regard to the frontier between Albania and the Kingdom of the Serbs, Croats and Slovenes at the Monastery of Saint-Naoum, the mission, such as it has been recognized by the interested Parties, which is contemplated by a unanimous Resolution of the Assembly of the League of Nations of October 2nd, 1921?
>
> Should the League of Nations consider that the Conference has not exhausted its mission, what solution should be adopted in regard to the question of the Serbo-Albanian frontier at Saint-Naoum?"

The Council in its turn in June 1924 brought the first of these two questions before the Permanent Court for an Advisory Opinion. The Court by its Opinion of 4 September 1924 (*Publ. P.C.I.J.*, series B, No. 9) answered the question in the affirmative mainly on the ground that the allocation to Albania of an area "jusqu'au monastère" in 1913 was not sufficiently precise in its terms (whether inclusive or exclusive) to indicate how the frontier at Saint-Naoum should run, so that the question was still open in 1921/1922, and could be validly decided by the Conference of Ambassadors. Comp. on this dispute, in particular on the question whether the Great Powers of 1920 were indeed entitled simply to continue the work of the, quite different, group of Great Powers of 1913, my *The Jurisprudence of the World Court*, vol. I, pp. 62 *et seq.*

Lake Prespa (Prespansko Jezero). This lake, to the southeast of Lake Ochrida, has also, but not to the same extent, given rise to difficulties between the adjacent States. Its northern half already belonged to Serbia along a west-east line in virtue of a boundary treaty of 10 August 1913 (Martens, N.R.G.[3], VIII, 61), but its southern shore was still in 1921-1922 controversial between Greece and Albania which claimed the Suhagora peninsula between Lakes Prespa and Mala-Prespa. The Albanian claim was, with the support of the Turkish authorities, upheld (comp. Publ. *P.C.I.J.*, series C, No. 5-II, pp. 114, 260, 284, 328, 331), to the effect that a small southwesternmost part of the lake was together with the peninsula attributed to Albania, thus leaving the rest of the southern half to Greece.

Lake Dojran would seem to have remained entirely under Yugoslav sovereignty. Its importance for Greece, however, appears from the *procès-verbaux* of the Greek and Yugoslav delegations of 31 March 1956 and 1 September 1957 and Article 1 of the Greco-Yugoslav Agreement of 18 June 1959 (*U.N.T.S.*, vol. 363, p. 133), inserted in *Legislative texts and treaty provisions concerning the utilization of international rivers for other purposes than navigation* (U.N. Document St/Leg/Ser.B/12), pp. 811, 813 and 818, dealing with the level of the lake, the use of its waters for irrigation, and various other hydro-economic questions.

Africa

The main cause of the phenomenon that there are so many international lakes in Africa lies in the fact that all colonizing Powers alike strove for access to the main lakes, and that, as far as possible, they delimited their zones of influence accordingly. And their action in the past is still effective for the benefit of the new independent nations.

Lake Chad (= *Tchad*). This lake was surrounded in the colonial era by the territorial possessions or zones of influence of three European States: France (Niger and Equatorial Africa), Great Britain (Nigeria) and Germany (Cameroons). The boundary line between the French and British zones of the lake (with a corresponding allocation of islands) was defined in Article IV of a Convention of 14 June 1898 (Hertslet, No. 241, p. 785; Martens, N.R.G.², XXIX, 116 = XXX, 249) and confirmed in the last paragraph of Article I of a Franco-British Protocol of 9 April 1906 (Hertslet, No. 256, p. 843), inserted with an annexed map in a subsequent treaty of 29 May 1906 (Martens, N.R.G.², XXXV, 463). It was to run from the mouth of the river Komodugu-Yobe eastwards along the parallel of latitude to its intersection with the meridian of 35′ east of the centre of a certain town Kukawa, and from there southwards along that meridian to its intersection with the southern shore of the lake.—The boundary line between the French (Congo) and German (Cameroon) zones of the lake (also with a corresponding allotment of islands) was described in detail in Article I, under K, of a Convention of 18 April 1908 (Hertslet No. 379, p. 1215; Martens, N.R.G.³, I, 612): it was to run from the mouth of the main navigable branch of the river Shari into the lake to the intersection of the meridian of 14° 28′ long. E. with the parallel of 13° 5′ lat. N., along which it was then to run westwards to the Franco-British boundary as fixed by the Conventions of 1898 and 1906 above.— With regard to the same lake, however, a special paragraph (7) was later inserted in Article 8 of the Franco-British treaty of 16 February 1910 (*ibid.*, N.R.G.³, VII, 362) for the delimitation of the area extending between the Niger and the lake, and providing for a future modification, if necessary, of the frontier-line as fixed, "so as to assure to France a communication through open water at all seasons between her possessions on the northwest (now the Republic of Niger) and those on the southeast of the lake (now the Republic of Tchad), and a portion of the surface of the open waters of the lake at least proportionate to that

assigned to her by a map annexed to the above-mentioned treaty of
14 June 1898". The "nappe d'eau" of the lake had in 1910 appeared to
be quite different from what was thought in 1898 (comp. Martens,
N.R.G.², XXXII, p. 50/51).

The territorial situation was altered in 1911 as a consequence of the
Franco-German Convention (Cambon-Kiderlen Wächter) of 4 November of that year concerning the respective possessions in Equatorial
Africa (*ibid.*, N.R.G.³, V, 651), by which Germany ceded to France the
so-called *Entenschnabel* between the rivers Shari and Logone, being a
strip of territory connecting the existing French possessions with Lake
Chad. The area more to the south which France on that occasion ceded
to Germany as a *quid pro quo* (the Congo- and Ubanghi-*Zipfel* and a
narrow strip of territory between Spanish Río Muni and French Gabon,
connecting German Cameroon with the Atlantic Ocean), returned to
France after World War I in virtue of Article 125 of the Peace Treaty of
Versailles.

The number of three surrounding States in 1919 changed into two
(France and Great Britain) and a British-Mandated Territory.

As a consequence of Africa's decolonization after World War II Lake
Chad has now become the meeting place of the frontiers of four new
sovereign African States—*viz.*, the Republics of Niger and Tchad, the
Federation of Nigeria and the ex-French Mandated and Trust Territory
the Republic of Cameroun, which meant a further splitting-up of the
lake among those four instead of the earlier three surrounding States.
Their present "national" territory is, consequently, simply the result of
imperialist and colonial barters of the past.

Victoria Nyanza. The frontier of this lake was first drawn as a straight
west-east line across it by the Anglo-German treaty of 1 July 1890
(Martens, N.R.G.², XVI, 894; Hertslet, No. 270, p. 899). The situation
changed twice in later days, first in 1919 when Germany was ousted
from the African Continent after World War I and Victoria Nyanza
became surrounded partly, in the north, by British possessions (Uganda
and Kenya Protectorates), and partly, in the south, by the Territory of
Tanganyika under a British Mandate, and again subsequently when,
after World War II, those territories developed into three different
sovereign States: Uganda, Tanganyika (later Tanzania) and Kenya.
The original boundary line of 1890 was maintained as the lake frontier
between the then Kingdom of Buganda and Kenya to the north and
Tanganyika to the south, whilst the originally colonial frontier between
the Uganda and the Kenya Protectorate under the Boundary Agreement of 10 March 1900 (Hertslet, No. 89, p. 397) through the northern
part of the lake, which kept closely to the Kenya shore, became the
international boundary between the independent States of Buganda and
Kenya.

Lakes Edward and Albert. The boundary line through these two lakes was originally fixed by an agreement between Belgium (on behalf of her then colony of the Congo) and the United Kingdom (on behalf of its Uganda Protectorate[24]) of 3 February 1915 (Martens, N.R.G.[3], XV, 539), where part of the boundary in East Africa from Mount Sabinio to the Congo-Nile watershed, after first being described (Article 2, *sub* 4) as following a straight line across lake Edward from the mouth of one river (Ishasha) to that of another (Lubilia-Chako), is later (Article 2, *sub* 10) said to continue along "a succession of straight lines across Lake Albert, passing through points situated midway between the shores of that lake on the parallels of 1° 30', 1° 45' and 2° latitude N., to a point midway between the shores of the lake on the parallel 2° 7' latitude N., and from that point northwards" along the meridian of that point.[25]

A similar problem has arisen in respect of pluristatal bays (see *infra* section 4, at p. 606).

Lake Tanganyika. The approximately north-south boundary line through Lake Tanganyika belongs to the normal, though slightly complicated, type of lake frontier, running as it does along a median line between its opposite western (Congo) and eastern (Tanganyika) shores over its entire length, save for a small northeasternmost strip where the western frontier of Burundi, and for a similar southernmost tip where the northern frontier of Zambia runs into the lake. This boundary dates from the Convention between the Independent State of the Congo and Great Britain of 12 May 1894 (Martens, N.R.G.[2], XX, 805) and continued to be the frontier under the subsequent Mandate and Trust regimes in East Africa and the emergence of the sovereign States of Tanzania, Congo, Uganda and Zambia.

Lake Nyasa. The frontier *tracé* in this lake is also complicated. In respect of its northern part Germany and Great Britain stipulated in their treaty of 1 July 1890 (*ibid.*, N.R.G.[2], XVI, 894; Hertslet, No. 270, p. 899) for the delimitation of their zones of influence in East Africa (Article I, 2) that Germany's sphere of influence in East Africa (Tanganyika) should be bounded to the south by a line which in part followed the eastern, northern and (north)western shores of Lake Nyasa. The same would seem at first sight to follow from Article I (2) of the treaty of 20 August 1890 between Great Britain (for Nyasaland, now Malawi) and Portugal

---

24. At the time when Great Britain concluded her agreement with the Kabaka, Chiefs and People of Uganda on 10 March 1900, Lake Albert was still held to be entirely within the boundaries of the Uganda Protectorate, of which the Kingdom of Uganda was only a part. Comp. HERTSLET, *The map of Africa by treaty*, 3rd ed. (1909), vol. I, No. 89, p. 397).

25. It was along the western bank of this Lake Albert that the once diplomatically famous Belgian Lado enclave was situated (1894). See on this enclave Chapter IV, section 2, *sub* 1°, *infra* p. 400.

(for Mozambique) (Hertslet, No. 308, p. 1006; Martens, N.R.G.², XVI, 929 = XVIII, 154)—with a new version of 11 June 1891 (Hertslet, No. 310, p. 1016; Martens, N.R.G.², XVIII, 185)—in which Great Britain recognized as being within the dominion of Portugal in East Africa the territories bounded in part by the eastern shore of (the central part of) the lake. Article IV of the same treaty, however, delimited a frontier running through the middle of the lake from north to south, while leaving to the British protectorate a few islands in the eastern part of the lake. The curious combined result of these delimitations, which remained in force under the Mandates system after World War I and also at first under the Trusteeship system after World War II, was that Lake Nyasa, where it faced Tanganyika, *i.e.*, in its northernmost stretch belonged wholly to Nyasaland; that it then, in its central stretch, became equally divided between Nyasaland and Mozambique, except for the islands of Chisamulo and Likome in the Portuguese half, allotted to Nyasaland; and that it finally became again wholly Nyasaland territory in its southernmost part from the point where the Mozambique land frontier bends off from the lake towards the southeast.

This frontier delimitation lasted until 1954 when the United Kingdom for Nyasaland and Portugal for Mozambique, by a new convention of 18 November 1954 (*U.N.T.S.*, vol. 325, p. 307), implemented by an agreement of 29 November 1963 (*U.N.T.S.*, vol. 534, p. 441), shifted their shore boundary westward to the median line, to the effect that the frontier then ran through the middle of the lake over its entire north-south length. The islands remained as British insular enclaves in the Portuguese half of Lake Nyasa together with a belt of water, two sea miles in width, surrounding each of these islands.

Asia

Caspian Sea. By Article 8² of the Russo-Persian Peace Treaty of Turkmanchai of 22 February 1828 (Martens, N.R., VII, 564), this inland sea was placed in the special position of being reserved to Russia for navigation by warships (a monopoly only deleted by Article 11 of the treaty between the Soviets and Persia of 26 February 1921, *ibid.*, N.R.G.³, XIII, 173). It is not clear from the text of the 1828 treaty nor from those of the subsequent treaties of 21 December 1881 and 8 June 1893 (*ibid.*, N.R.G.², IX, 228 and XXXIII, 561), whether the Caspian Sea itself was divided between Russia and Persia from a territorial point of view: Article 4, *in fine* of the Treaty of Turkmanchai indeed described the Russo-Persian frontier as ending at the mouth of the river Astara flowing into the Caspian Sea, which gives the impression that that sea was considered as a *mare nullius* reserved for the two adjacent States.

Lake Tiberias was already mentioned as a border lake in the Separate

587

Act annexed to the Quadruple Treaty of London of 15 July 1840 (*ibid.*, N.R.G.¹, I, 156, 160) for the liquidation of the political crisis, provoked by the Egyptian Pasha Muhammad 'Ali: the pashalik of Acre which the Great Powers were prepared to place under his rule was to be limited by the western shore of the lake.

At a later stage, after World War I, Lake Tiberias was, pursuant to Article 1 of a Franco-British Convention of 23 December 1920 on certain points connected with the Mandates for Syria/Lebanon and Palestine/ Mesopotamia (*ibid.*, N.R.G.³, XII, 582), divided into two by a boundary line running from Samakh across the lake to the mouth of the Wadi Massadyie.

This delimitation was, however, altered by a new Franco-British Agreement of 7 March 1923 on the basis of the report of a Commission, dated 3 February 1922 (*ibid.*, N.R.G.³, XVII, 208), which fixed the frontier by "a line on the shore parallel to and at ten metres from the edge of the lake following any alteration of level consequent on the raising of its waters owing to the construction of a dam on the Jordan south of the lake", that is, a boundary gradually receding eastward.

According to the United Nations General Assembly Resolution 181 (III) of 29 November 1947, embodying a "Plan of Partition with Economic Union", the Jewish State was to include, among others, the whole of the Hula Basin and Lake Tiberias.

After the birth of the State of Israel in 1948 the Syrian Armistice Agreement of 20 July 1949 (*U.N.T.S.*, vol. 42, p. 327) again determined the frontier between Israel and Syria in such a way that it was to run at a distance of 10 metres from the eastern bank of Lake Tiberias.

On the contrary, the *Dead Sea*, which would equally have lain outside the boundaries of the pashalik of Acre promised to Muhammad 'Ali in 1840, is at present, pursuant to the Armistice Agreement of Rhodes of 3 April 1949 (*U.N.T.S.*, vol. 42, p. 303), divided between Israel and Jordan along a line which leaves only the western part of the southern half of the Sea to Israel and all the rest to Jordan. Under the Mandate for Palestine the Dead Sea still formed part of Palestine proper, whereas under the "Plan of Partition" of 1947 the boundary would have followed about the same line as under the Armistice Agreement of 1949.

America

Great Lakes. Most famous for its legal-historical importance in the New World is the chain of lakes, extending from East to West in the border area between Canada and the United States, marked by the river Saint Lawrence. As I have already dealt with that river in section 2 *supra*, pp. 555 *et seq.*, I will confine myself here to giving some particulars relative to the border lakes through which its waters flow, *viz.*, Lakes

Ontario, Erie, Huron and Superior and the Lake of the Woods. Lake Michigan is wholly American.

The *tracé* of the long boundary in the Great Lakes and the connecting waterways (from east to west: the rivers Niagara, Detroit, Sainte Claire, Sainte Marie (Neebish Falls) and Pigeon), as fixed by the mixed commissions established under Articles 6 and 7 of the Peace Treaty of Ghent (1814) and subsequently by the Webster-Ashburton Treaty of 1842, can hardly be studied without the help of a series of maps illustrating its verbal description. This series consists of twenty-five maps relating to the eastern sector between 45° lat. N. and the communication between Lake Huron and Lake Superior (Article 6) and thirty-six relating to the western section between the said communication (Neebish Falls) and the northwesternmost point of the Lake of the Woods (Article 7); they are printed in MOORE, *International Arbitrations*, vol. VI; a limited number is reproduced in DE LAPRADELLE-POLITIS, *Recueil des arbitrages internationaux*, after p. 762 of vol. I (map)2. These maps also show the division of the islands between the two countries. Whereas, for example, in the easternmost stretch of the St. Lawrence Waterway the boundary sometimes runs between two of them (Sheik and Barnhart islands), it mostly follows closely one of the banks, thus leaving them either to Canada (Cornwall island), or to the United States (Upper and Lower Long Sault islands). The greatest difficulty of the partition was caused in the section up-stream the Neebish Falls. In this sector there were three islands, by far the largest Saint Joseph, allotted to Great Britain, the smallest, Saint Tammany, to the United States, and Saint Georges. Great Britain wished this island to be divided by a land boundary across it "in the middle of the river" according to Article 2 of the Peace Treaty of Paris of 3 September 1783. The United States claimed it for itself by advocating a frontier *tracé* in the middle of the only navigable channel near its own bank. The two commissioners were unable to agree and referred their disagreement to their governments. These only resolved the controversy, in favour of the United States, by the Webster-Ashburton Treaty of 9 August 1842 (Martens, N.R.G.[1], III, 456).

On the delimitation in the Lake of the Woods see the treaty of 24 February 1925 (Martens, N.R.G.[3], XXVI, 912).

Comp. on the legal regime of the Lakes in general: Charles BÉDARD, *Le régime juridique des grands lacs de l'Amérique du Nord et du Saint-Laurent* (Quebec, 1966).

Lake of Nicaragua. In Central America it is, in particular, the Lake of Nicaragua which deserves attention in this context. It is not a frontier-lake proper because it is over its entire surface Nicaraguan and Costa Rica is even separated from its southern shore by a narrow strip of land. It was precisely a controversy over this southern boundary situation which in 1899 gave rise to an international arbitration. The territorial

589

extent of Nicaragua vis-à-vis her southern neighbour was originally fixed by a treaty of 15 April 1858 (*B.F.S.P.*, vol. 48, p. 1049). Its validity was disputed many years later by Costa Rica, but upheld in arbitral proceedings by an award of President Cleveland (U.S.A.) of 22 March 1888 (LA FONTAINE, *Pasicrisie internationale*, p. 299; *B.F.S.P.*, vol. 79, p. 555). The new disagreement related precisely to the exact location of the above-mentioned strip of land alongside the southern shore. The new arbitrator, E. P. Alexander, gave a decision on the *tracé* of this frontier—which, consequently, is not a lake-frontier proper—in the fourth of his five successive awards between the two countries, rendered on 26 July 1899.[26] The southern boundary of Nicaragua was to run, under the treaty of 1858, at a distance of 2 miles from the lake. As the arbiter set out in detail, he had a choice between five possible *tracés* of the base line from which the boundary should thus be measured, dependent upon the different levels of the water in the lake. He opted for the mean high water line, considering that the parties had obviously intended in 1858 to allocate a strip of dry land along the southern bank of the lake to Nicaragua. This intention would be frustrated if the otherwise customary low water line were chosen since Nicaragua would then be left in times of high water with a strip of inundated territory.

Lake Titicaca. In South America the most important lake from an international law point of view is Lake Titicaca, a border lake between Peru and Bolivia. It is divided between these two countries by a border line running from north to south. See their treaty of 15/17 September 1909 (Martens, N.R.G.[3], III, 59, 61), concluded on the basis of an arbitral award by the President of Argentina of 9 July 1909 (*ibid.*, III, 53). For some further details on this lake I may refer to the Annex to Chapter II, section 1, *supra* p. 98, where I have summarized its main contents.

Section 4. BOUNDARIES IN BAYS AND ESTUARIES

The problem of the *tracé* of the State frontier in inlets from the sea— bays, gulfs, fjords, estuaries, etc., further to be generally called "bays"— is particularly difficult in respect of pluristatal bays where the question of the "closing line" towards the territorial sea (approximately following the general direction of the coastline) is coupled with that of the (lateral) boundary inside the bay between the adjacent States, especially where more than two riparian States are involved, as in the Arabian Gulf of Aqaba and the Central-American Gulf of Fonseca. In such cases the problem may become as a matter of law almost insoluble when the

26. LA FONTAINE, *ibid.*, p. 535.

States concerned are unwilling to cut the Gordian knot either by treaty or by arbitration *ex aequo et bono* or otherwise.

The first Conference of Geneva on the Law of the Sea (1958) afforded no help towards the solution of this problem. On the one hand, its terms of reference excluded dealing with the subject of delimitation of the borderline in "internal waters" extending on the land-side of the "closing line" of a bay towards the territorial sea; on the other, it avowed its inability to give any ruling whatsoever on the legal regime of pluristatal bays, even in so far as that closing line was concerned.

The general problem of delimitation in pluristatal bays is, consequently, up to the present moment, left to be decided by *ad hoc* agreements between the adjacent States, or by arbitrators or courts of justice. These cannot really solve it on the basis of existing generally accepted customary law or of "general principles of (international) law" and are, therefore, compelled, if they do not wish to pronounce a *non liquet*, to muster all their available force of creative imagination in order to compose a judgment which can be more or less justified. As examples of arbitral awards or judicial decisions which have been instrumental in terminating international controversies of this particularly thorny type, I will report in brief below three famous cases of international adjudication, *viz.*, those relating to the Gulf of Fonseca just mentioned and the Bay of Salinas (on the Pacific and the Atlantic Ocean coast of Central America respectively), and to the Bay of Oslo (the Grisbådarna case),[27] and two well known examples of intra-federal judgments, *viz.*, that concerning the Mississippi Sound and that relative to the Bay of Lübeck in the inter-war period.

In a fairly large number of other cases adjacent States have fixed their boundary in bays by an express amicable agreement, whereas occasionally State frontiers in bays have been imposed by a peace treaty. Such bilateral or multilateral instruments show a wide variety of solutions, due, for example, to a difference in the main function of the bay concerned (commercial navigation, fishing, naval defence, *etc.*), or to local geographical circumstances, such as the complicating factor that it is fringed or scattered with islands. Comp. on various solutions so adopted, below, p. 592.

The issue remains doubtful in cases where the States concerned have never delimited their bay frontier by agreement, nor entrusted arbitrators or an international tribunal with the task of fixing it. The uncertainties in this respect are mainly due to four causes.

There is, firstly, (*a*) the general controversial question as to whether a

27. Another example is that of the boundary in the bays of Fundy and Passamaquoddy between the United States and Canada. Comp. on those bays *infra*, p. 604.

bay which, owing to the relative narrowness of its entrance, would have to be considered "internal" water in case of its being bounded by one single State, must equally be so considered if it is surrounded by two or more States, or whether such a pluristatal bay must not rather be held, barring a narrow belt of territorial sea closely following the coastline, to form in its central area part of the high seas. In 1928, the German *Staatsgerichtshof* expatiated on the legal uncertainty with respect to such bays on this basic point in a judgment, rendered in a dispute between Lübeck and Mecklenburg-Schwerin concerning the respective rights of sovereignty over the Bay of Lübeck (Travemünde Bay). The *Staatsgerichtshof* (*Entscheidungen des Reichsgerichts in Zivilsachen,* vol. 122, Appendix, p. 1; *Z.a.ö.R.V.* 1929 (I (2)), p. 180; *A.D.* 1927-1928, Cases Nos. 3, 76 and 88) rejected Mecklenburg-Schwerin's contention that according to international law pluristatal bays belong *pro diviso* to the adjacent States. The Court rejected that contention, not because this cannot be the case, but because there are no clear general rules on the subject in force; the question is controversial and must rather be decided on the merits of each particular case in the light of the historical development and the needs of the States concerned. There are different possible legal situations. A bay enclosed by the territory of more than one State can form part of the open sea, but this is certainly not a general mandatory rule, either. Such a bay may be territorially divided; it may be placed under the co-sovereignty of the adjacent States; it may in its entirety possess the status of territorial sea; the whole bay may appertain to one of the adjacent States; and finally it is possible that sovereignty is divided functionally. I fully agree with this reasoning of the Court: the only rule in force is that there is no general rule and that all depends on the particular features of the case in question. In this Bay of Lübeck case the Court resolved the controversy on the basis of a partly geographical, partly functional division, comp. below p. 599; see also Part II of this publication, p. 282.

Then there is (*b*) the presence or absence of an island or a chain of islands in the opening of the bay towards the high seas, a geographical feature which may influence the legal issue.

A further factor of decisive importance might be (*c*) the geographical difference between bays through which a river flows to the sea and those into which no river runs.

Added to these three elements there is (*d*) the possibility that a bay— also when surrounded by two or more States—may be correctly claimed to bear the, somewhat enigmatic, character of an "historical bay", a species, and certainly the most striking one, of the—still more problematical—group of "historical waters", intentionally left floating in the air by the Conference on the Law of the Sea of 1958.

ad (*a*). If the theory is adopted that a bay, even with a "narrow"

592

entrance, when it is surrounded by two or more States, constitutes, at least as to its centre, part of the high seas, then there are the usual problems of delimitation: (i) between the conterminous strips of territorial sea along the inner coast of the bay, on the one hand, and the pocket of open sea in its centre, on the other, and (ii) between such strips of coastal belt *inter se*. Both boundary questions belong to the section on the territorial sea (Chapter II, section 3, *sub* C and D, *supra*, pp. 60 and 66). If, however, that theory is rejected—*i.e.*, if such a bay is considered to be territorial—, then real new problems arise, first that of the possible regime of co-sovereignty over the waters of the bay, or otherwise, if the bay must be held to belong to the riparian States *pro diviso*, that of the exact delimitation between them inside its internal water area. The solution of these problems may depend on historical data, or on the factors mentioned under (*b*), (*c*) and (*d*). Personally I deny the validity of any general theory according to which a wide bay with a narrow entrance should be considered as comprising a central pocket of open sea on the sole ground that it is surrounded by more than one State; there is indeed no convincing authority for such a general theory. The riparian States are completely free to agree upon a solution of this sort but there is no mandatory rule to this effect in force. It is up to them to regulate the question as they think fit.

ad (*b*). This factor is only an *ad hoc* instance of the difficulties implied in the more general problem of the "closing line" of bays. The Conference on the Law of the Sea of 1958 only dealt with bays surrounded by one State and gave a ruling for that case alone. Must the criterion adopted for the "territoriality" of such bays (Article 7 (4) of Convention I: a maximum closing line of 24 miles) henceforward be deemed likewise to apply to pluristatal bays? Or have these rather remained subject to the pre-existing customary law, whatever its content may be, or to the free decision of the riparian States concerned? I personally favour the latter alternative on the understanding that 24 miles form the maximum of a permissible closing line also in respect of pluristatal bays.

ad (*c*). There is good reason to contradistinguish in this respect bays into which no navigable river discharges and bay-like river estuaries. Whereas the latter will ordinarily show one or perhaps more deeper channels through which the river flows into the sea, this is not characteristic for ordinary bays; these also may be intersected by deeper channels, but this is rather a chance phenomenon. This contradistinction permits a provisional conclusion, namely, that in the case of river estuaries there is good ground for presuming that the boundary between the adjacent States continues to run along the river thalweg, unless there is proof to the contrary, but that in ordinary bays there is much more ground for the inverse presumption, namely, that the median

593

line or line of equidistance constitutes the boundary, likewise subject to proof of the contrary. Such contrary proof can in both cases follow either from geographical or geological, or from legal and historical considerations.

ad (*d*). The whole doctrine of "historic bays"—let alone that of "historic waters" in general—has never emerged from the mist shrouding that somewhat obscure notion, and an attempt of the Japanese delegation at the Conference on the Law of the Sea of 1958 to get the concept at least summarily defined by confining the classification of "historic waters" to those which fulfil certain minimum requirements failed:[28] this proposal was not put to the vote because Japan withdrew it in view of the acceptance by the Conference of a resolution charging the Secretary General with a study of the problem (comp. A/Conf. 13/C1/L 158 at p. 252 of vol. III of the Official Records of the 1958 Conference, and also pp. 145, 147 and 198). Keeping the fog surrounding certain notions of international law as dense as possible is for States indeed often an effective means of reserving the opportunity of invoking them in future to cover further international claims, however shaky.

The majority of writers would seem to be of the opinion that it is possible to state a general rule applicable to all bays surrounded by two or more States, *viz.*, that there cannot with regard to them be any question of a closing line across their entrance to the effect that the enclosed area would constitute a body of internal waters; they hold, on the contrary, that the respective coasts of such bays are washed by a corresponding number of belts of territorial sea, which may in the case of wider bays even leave a pocket of open sea in their center. The "simple and decisive" reason why the idea of a transverse line across the entry to a pluristatal bay must be rejected is according to G. GIDEL, *Le droit international public de la mer* (Paris, 1934), vol. III, pp. 595-596, that any of the adjacent States might otherwise be in a position to put an absolute bar on the maritime communications of the other(s):

> "En écartant la construction d'une ligne transversale dans le cas de pluralité de riverains, on ne laisse au-devant des territoires respectifs des Etats riverains et de leurs laisses de basse mer qu'une bande de mer "territoriale" (et non pas d'eaux intérieures); or il est de la nature juridique de la mer territoriale de comporter le droit de "passage inoffensif". La liberté des communications maritimes avec la mer ouverte des Etats riverains de la baie se trouve ainsi juridiquement assurée".

28. The text, in the form of an amendment to Article 7, para. 4, ran as follows (Doc. A/Conf. 13/C1/L 104): "The foregoing provisions shall not apply to historic bays. The term "historic bays" means those bays over which coastal State or States have effectively exercised sovereign rights continuously for a period of long standing, with explicit or implicit recognition of such practice by foreign States". See p. 241 of the above quoted vol. III.

594

This motive of protection of the interests of one or more riparian States further inside the bay against possible encroachments on their freedom of passage by a State at the bay's entrance is fully justified and, for that matter, honoured by Article 16 (4) of the Geneva Convention No. I (1958) on the Territorial Sea (*U.N.T.S.*, vol. 516, p. 205). Yet, I for one doubt whether it is possible to state any imperative general rule on this subject. What, in fact, will be the position if the adjacent States agree *inter se* to close the bay by a transverse line, while guaranteeing one another complete freedom of access? An agreement to this effect would certainly be valid and could not be challenged by third States which would desire to have free access to the bay contrary to the common decision of the adjacent States. The general rule, enunciated by Gidel with a view to protecting the interests of one or more less favourably situated riparian States, would therefore seem to need qualification to the effect that it ceases to operate when the riparian States themselves collectively agree on a closing line, on the understanding that this line does not exceed the length of twenty-four miles, just as in the case of a unistatal bay. The bay would then contain internal waters instead of forming an area of contiguous belts of territorial sea plus, if any, a pocket of open sea in its center. In this case the bay might further constitute either an area under co-sovereignty (as in the case on the Gulf of Fonseca) or belong to the adjacent States *pro diviso*.

As it is impossible to handle the subject by formulating general principles from which deductions can be made for individual boundary situations, I will further in this section pass in review a limited number of bays surrounded by two or more States, with the solutions reached with respect to them. There is the more reason not to go into too many details in this publication, because the general subject of *The regime of bays in international law* has already been analysed in great detail in this same series *Nova et Vetera Juris Gentium* (series A, No. 1) by Dr. L.J. Bouchez, a distinguished member of the staff of our Institute, in 1963.

I will arrange my exposition by continents, but stress again that these individual solutions do not permit one to draw conclusions from them in support of any postulated general principles applicable to other, unregulated bay situations. Such general principles might theoretically be deduced from such case law or treaty solutions either on a merely statistical basis, or on that of an assessment of their relative validity by abstract standards of justice, or—if a *non liquet* was to be avoided—they might, apart from any legal precedents, be based on general considerations relative, for example, to the main function of the bay concerned, or to what was equitable in regard to countries situated higher up the bay, etc.

Europe. The very complicated Franco-Spanish frontier in the Bay of Higuera (baie du Figuier) at the western end of the Pyrenees, through which the river Bidassoa flows into the sea, was determined by a Declaration of Bayonne of 30 March 1879 (Martens, N.R.G.[2], IV, 364), supplementary to an earlier treaty of delimitation of 2 December 1856 (*B.F.S.P.*, vol. 47, p. 765; *Archives diplomatiques* 1869, II, 664), with additional Acts of 31 March 1859 and 11 July 1868 (*B.F.S.P.*, vol. 59, p. 430; *Arch dipl.*, II, 700, 764), in such a way that the waters of the bay were divided "from the point of view of jurisdiction" into three zones, one under the exclusive jurisdiction of Spain, one under that of France and one forming the "zone of common waters". The bay was "closed" towards the Bay of Biscay by a transverse line of about three kilometres connecting the extreme point of Cape Higuera (Spain) and the Pointe du Tombeau (France). A meridian passing through the middle of that line northward was to form the boundary between the respective territorial seas (comp. Chapter II, section 3, *sub* D, above p. 70.), whereas the three inward zones were delimited by two lines, precisely drawn on an annexed map and running in the opposite direction from the same transverse line at points situated on exactly one third of its length from either side, the water between the transverse closing line and those two lines to form the "zone of common waters". Subsequent conventions have regulated special matters of common concern, such as fishing—18 February 1886 (Martens, N.R.G.[2], XII, 687)—and the suppression of smuggling—10 May 1890 (*ibid.*, XVIII, 72).

The *Grisbådarna* case between Norway and Sweden, decided in virtue of a special agreement of 14 March 1908 (*ibid.*, N.R.G.[3], II, 761) by the Permanent Court of Arbitration by an award of 23 October 1909 (*ibid.*, III, 85; *A.A.*, vol. XI, p. 155), commented upon by Strupp in Schücking, *Das Werk vom Haag*, 2nd Series, 1st Band, 2nd Teil, p. 47 *et seq.*, at pp. 100-140, concerned the most seaward part of the *tracé* of their maritime frontier in the Bay of Oslo. These arbitral proceedings were only started after the dissolution of the Real Union between the two States in 1905; earlier arbitration proposals laid before the parliaments of the united countries in 1904 by the common King were wrecked on Sweden's claim to superiority over Norway in their relationship (comp. Part II of this publication, Chapter IV, Excursus B, p. 290, note 151). There was no real clash of opinion between the two countries with regard to the landward part of the borderline which was, therefore, simply determined by the Court in accordance with the common view of the parties. For the rest, the line was drawn by the Tribunal, after a "descente sur les lieux"—a rare event in arbitral practice—, in such a way as to assign the Grisbådarna to Sweden. The award is remarkable, *inter alia* for its observations concerning the principles of intertemporal law in their application to the thalweg rule.

One of the issues was whether the tribunal was bound to determine the frontier in accordance with present-day principles of delimitation or with the rules in force at a crucial date in the past, namely, in the middle of the 17th century—peace treaties of Röskilde (1658) and Stockholm (1660), by which Sweden acquired (and kept) Bohuslän from Denmark and thereby became Norway's neighbour in the maritime area concerned, and boundary treaty of 1661. In conformity with what has repeatedly been held in comparable cases—*e.g.*, the Russo-American case of the *Cape Horn Pigeon and other vessels* of 1902 (*A.A.*, IX, 51), the *Anglo-Brazilian boundary* case of 1904 (*A.A.*, XI, 11) and the Netherlands-American *Island of Palmas* case of 1928 (*A.A.*, II, 829)—the tribunal decided the dispute on the basis of the rules of law considered to have been in force about 1660, when the principle of the median line between neighbouring islands and rocks had not yet been demonstrably adopted. Comp. STRUPP's analysis of the award in SCHÜCKING's *Das Werk vom Haag*, 2nd series, 1st Band, 2nd Teil, pp. 47 *et seq.*, at pp. 113 *et seq.*

The division of Ireland into the Irish Free State (Eire) of the twenty-six Counties and Northern Ireland of the six, effected by the tripartite Boundary Agreement of 3 December 1925, in which the United Kingdom Government also took part—comp. F. GALLAGHER, *The Indivisible Island* (London, 1957), p. 175—created two new international bays, Lough Foyle (in the northwest near Londonderry) and Lough Carlingford (in the southeast near Newry). I can only presume that the boundary line in these loughs was drawn along the median line, but I have been unable to verify this even by a visit to the Irish Embassy and the Northern Ireland Office in London. See BOUCHEZ, cited above, at pp. 135-137.

Owing to a territorial reshuffle after World War I by the provisions of the Peace Treaty of Versailles (1919) three new boundaries were drawn through bays. Thus the Flensburg fjord was divided between Denmark and Germany by a median line (Article 109 and Treaty of 5 July 1920 between Denmark and the Principal Allied Powers, Martens, N.R.G.³, XIV, 881); the Frische Haff was divided between the Free City of Danzig and Germany (Eastern Prussia) by a straight line across it from the mainland to the Frische Nehrung (Article 28), and the Kurische Haff was divided between Germany (Eastern Prussia) and Lithuania (Memel Territory) also by a straight line between the mainland and the Kurische Nehrung (Article 28 *in fine* and German-Lithuanian Boundary Treaty of 29 January 1928, *ibid.*, N.R.G.³, XXI, 400). The latter two boundaries have since been wiped out as a result of political developments.

Similar events after World War II led to new delimitations. Since the situation on the Baltic coast (*e.g.*, in regard of the Bay of Lübeck) is still too unsettled, I confine myself here to mentioning the solutions adopted for the coast of the Upper Adriatic. When the Free City of Trieste was

created on paper at the Peace Conference of Paris (1947), its boundaries
had to be fixed both towards the northwest (Italy) and towards the
south (Yugoslavia), which involved determining the borderline between
the respective maritime zones in the Gulf of Trieste. This was done by
Article 4, respectively Article 22 of the treaty. However, these boundaries were also superseded by later developments after the Free City had
proved to be non-viable. The solution agreed upon by the Peace Conference was in a distinctly irregular manner replaced by a new solution
embodied in the so-called "Memorandum of Understanding" of 5 October 1954 (U.N.T.S., vol. 235, p. 99), and expressly or tacitly accepted
by all the Powers directly concerned. (Comp. on these developments
Part II of this publication, Chapter VI, section 3, p. 504.) This new
solution, which perpetuated the original military occupation zones A
and B as final territorial divisions, produced a new Italo-Yugoslav
boundary, ending in the San Bartolomeo Bay, without any supplementary *tracé* of that boundary into the Gulf of Trieste.

Further bay delimitations have taken place in
—the Gulf of Finland between Finland and Soviet-Russia: Article 3 of
their Peace Treaty of Dorpat of 14 October 1920 (Martens, N.R.G.[3],
XII, 37), which was rather a complicated mutual delimitation of territorial seas of varying breadths. It was later replaced by a new delimitation in the Virolahti area by a treaty of 12 March 1940 (*ibid.*, XXXVIII,
323), maintained in this respect by the subsequent Finnish Peace
Treaty of Paris of 10 February 1947 (U.N.T.S., vol. 48, p. 203); see for
the latest boundary delimitation the treaty of 20 May 1965 (U.N.T.S.,
vol. 566, p. 31);
—the Varanger Fjord between Norway and the Soviet Union: convention of 15 February 1957 (U.N.T.S., vol. 312, p. 322);
—the area south of the mouth of the Torneå between Sweden and
Finland: convention of 8/20 November 1810 (Martens, N.R., I. 313 =
IV, 33);
—the Frische Haff between the Soviet Union and Poland: treaties of
16 August 1945 (U.N.T.S., vol. 10, p. 200) and 5 March 1957 (U.N.T.S.,
vol. 274, p. 139).

The Netherlands still have two unresolved centuries-old boundary
problems in estuaries, *viz.*,—

in the Wielingen (mouth of the river Schelde), where the main
(southern) channel passes through the territorial sea of Belgium. This
fact is the principal foundation of the Belgian claim that the Wielingen
fairway is Belgian territory whereas the Netherlands claim it on historical grounds as theirs as an essential part of the river. A compromise
solution, never arrived at, might be the joint adoption of Belgian sovereignty, subject to a State servitude in favour of the Netherlands. This
old controversy still flares up occasionally; it became fairly serious in

World War I, when Belgium was a belligerent and the Netherlands neutral;

in the Ems estuary, where the legal situation has also been extremely controversial for centuries (comp. *supra*, Chapter I, p. 4). This dispute has to all intents and purposes been laid to rest in 1960-1962 by the Convention of Bennekom between the Netherlands and the German Federal Republic of 14 May 1962 (*U.N.T.S.*, vol. 509, p. 140), additional to their general treaty of 8 April 1960 (*ibid.*, vol. 509, p. 64): the parties agreed to leave the sovereignty boundary in abeyance, but on the one hand, to regulate practically all possible controversial questions which might spring from the continued dispute over the State frontier in the estuary, and on the other hand, to draw an exploitation boundary regarding the continental shelf under it, subsequently supplemented by a further delimitation across the continental shelf under the territorial sea up to 54° lat. North (*U.N.T.S.*, vol. 550, p. 123).

The intra-federal dispute, already mentioned above, p. 592, between Lübeck and Mecklenburg-Schwerin regarding sovereignty over the Bay of Lübeck, which arose in the inter-war period and was then settled by means of federal jurisdiction, had very peculiar features, which were reflected in the judgment of the German *Staatsgerichtshof* of 6/7 July 1928.[29] The decision was based on documentary and other evidence which convinced the Court that Lübeck had for centuries possessed exclusive rights of fishery and of navigation in the disputed parts of the Bay of Lübeck. There was, however, no such evidence of immemorial possession in other respects, and therefore the Court proceeded to a division of the Bay between the two States in matters other than fisheries and navigation. The result of this judgment was, consequently, a peculiar division of the Bay, partly on a territorial, partly on a functional basis.

A special case was that of the Jahde-Bucht, divided in Germany's confederal period between Prussia and Oldenburg with the particular destination of this water area as a naval base (Wilhelmshaven) for Prussia in view. See their conventions of

20 July 1853 (Martens, N.R.G.[1], XVI[2], 457), complemented 1 December 1853 (*ibid.*, 467): protection of the Oldenburg flag and coasts by Prussia and cession to her of part of the bay;
5 November 1854: Prussian Incorporation Decree (*ibid.*, 469), followed by a *Grenzrezess* of 31 March 1856;
16 February 1864 (*ibid.*, N.R.G.[2], I, 265): development of the relations created by the treaty of 1853;
January/February 1873 (*ibid.*, N.R.G.[2], I, 276): new alteration of the boundary.

29. *Entscheidungen des Reichsgerichts in Zivilsachen*, vol. 122, Appendix, p. 1, digested in *A.D.* 1927-1928, Cases Nos. 3, 76 and 88; comp. also *loco cit.*, 1925-1926, Case No. 85.

Alongside real State boundaries in bays and delimitations of continental shelf areas under the waters of a bay, as in the above-mentioned case of the Ems estuary, there are also cases in which limits have been agreed upon by coastal States bordering on a bay specifically for fishery purposes: comp. the treaty of 20 December 1928 between Great Britain, Ireland and France regarding the Bay of Granville (*ibid.*, N.R.G.[3], XXIII, 216).

Africa

The waters of Corisco Bay, which was still at that juncture a bay bordered by the colonies of only two States, namely Spanish Río Muni Territory and the French Congo (Gabon), were not themselves intersected by a boundary line in Article 4 of the Franco-Spanish Convention of 27 June 1900 (*ibid.*, N.R.G.[2], XXXII, 59; HERTSLET, *The map of Africa by treaty* 3rd ed., III, 1166), which only determined a frontier, departing landinwards from the point of intersection of the thalweg of the river Muni with a straight line connecting two projecting points on the coast (Coco Beach and Diéké). However, the islands of Elobey and Corisco, lying in that bay off the coast of French Congo were recognized in Article 7 as being subject to the sovereignty of Spain. This probably meant that the bay itself, apart from a belt of territorial sea around the islands, was to remain open sea; if not, the regulation implied that the land frontier was to be carried forward from the point of intersection fixed in Article 4 into the bay so as to continue in a sharp bend to the south and to leave the islands lying in the Spanish zone.

The bay was later transformed into one bordered by the colonies of three States as a consequence of the Convention between Germany and France of 4 November 1911, known under the name of the Kiderlen Wächter-Cambon Agreement (Martens, N.R.G.[3], V, 651), whereby the frontier of the German Cameroons was advanced in three directions: eastward to include the "Ubanghi-Zipfel", southward to reach the river Congo in a "Kongo-Zipfel" and westward to give the Cameroons another access to the Ocean through a narrow strip of territory between the southern boundary of Spanish Río Muni and French Gabon. This famous colonial arrangement would seem to have had no consequences for the legal status of Corisco Bay proper; anyhow, the territory concerned was soon (1919) returned to France.

Due south of Corisco Bay lies Monda Bay. The Kiderlen Wächter-Cambon Agreement just mentioned described the narrow strip of territory, sandwiched between Spanish Río Muni (north) and French Gabon (south), as extending along the sea coast from the Río Muni southward to halfway along the eastern shore of Monda Bay. The detailed supplementary Franco-German Declaration of 28 September 1912 (*ibid.*, VII, 135) contained, among many others, further partic-

600

ulars on the delimitation of the frontier in that bay. Article 9, para. 3, of the first of the three arrangements of which that Declaration consisted laid down that

"à partir du point de rencontre des limites territoriales maritimes de la France et de l'Allemagne en face des côtes du Gabon et du Cameroun, la limite entre les eaux territoriales des deux pays dans la baie de Monda sera constituée par la ligne médiane entre les côtes occidentale et orientale de cette baie jusqu'à une ligne perpendiculaire à la direction de la côte et aboutissant au point de départ de la frontière terrestre sur la rive orientale de la baie de Monda".

Seldom, however, was such an elaborate diplomatic instrument so short-lived. In August 1914 World War I broke out, the German colonies were overrun and Article 125 of the Peace Treaty of Versailles made a *tabula rasa* of all that the epochmaking agreements of 1911 and 1912 had stipulated in favour of the German Reich. The present sovereign successors to the former colonial possessions, French Gabon and German Cameroon, were consequently never in any way concerned with those agreements.

Delagoa Bay had already much earlier formed the subject of an old boundary dispute between Great Britain and Portugal. This related especially to the appurtenance of certain islands in the Bay. The controversy was resolved in favour of Portugal by an arbitral award of the French President Mac Mahon of 25 September 1872 (LA FONTAINE, *Pasicrisie internationale*, p. 170; Martens, N.R.G.², III, 517). The Arbitrator held that the island of Inyack and the Elephant Islands had always, together with the Northern coast of the bay, belonged to the tribal kings of Tembe and Mapooto, from whose authority they had fallen to Portugal on her colonial occupation of the bay in the 17th century, and that a British explorer had in 1823 erroneously assumed that the chieftains of the local tribes were still independent, so that new conventions could lawfully be concluded by them with Great Britain. The latter had, moreover, already earlier (1817) recognized that the entire bay belonged to Portugal.

Asia

Bi- or pluristatal bays which have caused, still partly unresolved, international disputes in this continent are, in particular, the Gulf of Aqaba, the estuary of the Shatt-al-Arab and the Rann of Kutch. Others have given rise to delimitation by treaty.

The Gulf of Aqaba is surrounded by two States at its entrance and adjacent coasts, Egypt and Saudi Arabia, and two others at its farther end, Israel and Jordan. The only thing which is certain about this Gulf is that innocent passage through the Straits of Tiran at its entrance towards and from the ports of Eilat and Aqaba is legally free (comp.

Part IV-A of this publication, Chapter I on the High Seas, under the heading Maritime Straits), despite the narrowness of that entrance and the presence of islands in it. For the rest, it is uncertain what exactly is the legal regime of the Gulf from the point of view of territorial sovereignty: is it subject to a regime of co-sovereignty, or does it belong to the riparian States *pro diviso* and then presumably along the line of equidistance, or is it perhaps, after all, to be considered part of the open sea? The qualification of "international waters", often applied to this Gulf in connexion with the Arab-Israeli conflict, need not necessarily relate to the question of territorial sovereignty; it would, rather, seem to bear upon the freedom of navigation through it for all nations alike, including of course Israel. The idea of co-sovereignty would certainly not be out o place in this case, seeing that the Gulf was once entirely surrounded by Ottoman territory and a partition of its surface among the successor States has never since taken place. There would then be a striking analogy with the Gulf of Fonseca (see below).

Although other juridical constructions are possible, the Gulf of Aqaba must in my opinion be considered to be a bay of the Red Sea, divided mainly into four zones of territorial sea, respectively belonging to Egypt and Saudi Arabia from the straits of Tiran at its entrance inward, and to Israel and Jordan at its far end. As long as the adjacent States held to a territorial sea of three miles, there remained a long pocket of open sea in its center, but this changed when they successively extended their coastal belt as a rule to six miles:

> Saudi Arabia, by a decree of 28 May 1949 (*A.J.I.L.* 1949 (43), Suppl., p. 154); a royal decree No. 23 of 16 February 1958 extended the belt to 12 miles (see M.I. KEHDEN and M.-L. HENKMANN, *Die Inanspruchnahme von Meereszonen durch Küstenstaaten*, Hamburg, 1967, p. 178);
> Egypt, by a law of 15 January 1951 (Anglo-Norwegian *Fisheries* case, *I.C.J. Pleadings*, vol. III, p. 678);
> Israel, by a law of 23 October 1956 (*U.N. Legislative Series ST/LEG/SER. B/6*, p. 26; and
> Jordan, by a law of 1960 (Article 7^2: territorial sea of 5 kilometres; see KEHDEN-HENKMANN, *loc. cit.*, p. 108).

The Gulf is, therefore, now an area consisting of four territorial belts—apart from a reduced pocket of open sea where its breadth exceeds twelve miles—and, as was for that matter explicitly recognized by Egypt in 1950, freely accessible for innocent passage through the Straits of Tiran, passing the islands of Tiran and Sanafir. If the international relations between the four riparian States concerned were good, the Gulf might also be considered, on historical grounds (their former subjection to one and the same State, the Ottoman Empire), as an historical bay under co-sovereignty, but this construction as an area appurtenant to the riparian States *pro indiviso* is under the existing circumstances impossible.

Comp. on this Gulf *inter alios*: L. M. BLOOMFIELD, *Egypt, Israel and the Gulf of Aqaba in international law* (Toronto, Canada, 1957); CH. B. SELAK, *A consideration of the legal status of the Gulf of Aqaba* in *A.J.I.L.* 1958 (52), pp. 660-698; A. MELAMID, *Legal status of the Gulf of Aqaba* in *A.J.I.L.* 1959 (53), pp. 412-413; R. LAPIDOTH, *Le passage par le détroit de Tiran* in *R.G.D.I.P.* 1969 (73), pp. 30-51; H. F. VAN PANHUYS, *De golf van Akaba en de vrije doorvaart* in *Ned. Jur. Blad* 1967, pp. 637-649, 796; LEO GROSS, *The Geneva Conference on the Law of the Sea and the right of innocent passage through the Gulf of Aqaba* in *A.J.I.L.* 1959 (53), pp. 564-594.

The exact State boundary in the estuary of the Tigris and the Euphrates in their confluence in the Shatt-al-Arab and its delta has long been a bone of contention between Persia (Iran) and Turkey (later: Iraq). See the Turkish-Persian Protocol of 4/17 November 1913 (reproduced in GEHRKE-KUHN, *Die Grenzen des Irak, Historische und rechtliche Aspekte des irakischen Anspruchs auf Kuwait und des irakisch-persischen Streites um den Schatt al-Arab*, Stuttgart, 1963, Dokumenten-Anhang, p. 53), for the implementation of the Anglo-Turkish Declaration of London of 29 July 1913 (*ibid.*, p. 67), as modified by the Iraqi-Iranian Boundary Treaty of 4 July 1937, with Protocol (*ibid.*, p. 72; Martens, N.R.G.³, XXXVII, 684). These instruments also define the boundary line in the Shatt-al-Arab, partly along the low-water line and partly along the thalweg *(medium filum aquae)*, and past Abadan, and apportion the islands in the river partly to Iraq and partly to Iran. The treaty, moreover, grants freedom of navigation to the ports of both countries on a footing of equality. Iran, however, recently (April 1969) denounced the treaty of 1937 on the pretext that Iraq had violated its provisions (*I.L.M.* 1969 (VIII), p. 478). See also Whiteman, vol. 3, p. 904.

The Rann of Kutch, a marshy area in the border zone between West Pakistan and India, being the estuary of the Sir Creek, has up till recently occasioned serious conflicts between these neighbours. When British India was split into two sovereign States in 1947, the Punjab Boundary Commission delimited their boundary according to the previously existing district frontiers (Report Radcliffe Award, *Select Documents on Asian affairs, India 6947-6950*, vol. I, p. 66, no. 16, 12 August 1947, annexure A). This boundary delimitation was however, obviously insufficient. The dispute, which thus arose, led to armed clashes, but was in the event settled by an award of 19 February 1968, which attributed the greater part to India, and allotted the rest to Pakistan (*I.L.M.* 1968 (7), p. 633). See BEBLER, "The Indo-Pakistan western boundary case" in *Yugoslav Review of International Law* 1968 (XV), pp. 55-71, with map.

The boundary in the estuary of the *Pakchan River* between Burma and Thailand, which is separated from the Indian Ocean by an extensive fringe of islands, was originally delimited by the British (Indian)-

Siamese treaty of 8 September 1868 (*B.F.S.P.*, vol. 59, p. 1146). This boundary was, however, altered by a Thaï-Burmese agreement of 1 June 1934 (Martens, N.R.G.[3], XXX, 107) by which two plots of land on either side of the river boundary that had become separated from their own bank by avulsion were exchanged. This agreement is remarkable for a further provision inserted in it to the effect that, should similar avulsions repeat themselves in the future, the same solution will be adopted.

Contrary to what is customary, the State boundary between British North Borneo and the Netherlands part of Borneo in the area of Sibuko Bay, where different rivers or creeks flow between a number of islands, has not, in the Anglo-Netherlands treaty of 20 June 1891 (*ibid.*, N.R.G.[2], XVIII, 644), been determined through one or the other of those waterways, such as the Cowie Bay, but along a straight line across the largest of those islands, Sibetik. This boundary was further detailed in an Anglo-Netherlands boundary protocol of 28 September 1915 (*ibid.*, N.R.G.[3], XII, 264) and a subsequent convention of 26 March 1928 (*ibid.*, N.R.G.[3], XXIII, 283).

Comp. further on the boundaries in

the Khor Abdullah (Iraq-Kuwait): exchange of letters of 4/19 April 1923 (Arnold TOYNBEE, *Survey of International Affairs* (1927), p. 336; Rupert HAY, *The Persian Gulf States* (Washington, 1959), p. 98; H.M. AL-BAHARNA, *The Legal Status of the Arabian Gulf States* (Manchester, 1968), pp. 256-7; *I.C.L.Q.* 1962 (XI), pp. 113-114 and 121-122);

the Sundarbans (Hariabhanga and Raimangal Rivers) near their outlet into the Bay of Bengal (India-East Pakistan): *Report Bengal Boundary Commission* 1947, Annexures A and B, subsections 7-8, the so-called Radcliffe Award. See: *Select documents on Asian affairs* (S.L. Poplai), India 1947-1950, vol. I, Internal Affairs, p. 59, no. 14 (12 August 1947);

the estuary of the Naaf River (East Pakistan-Burma): agreement of Rawalpindi between President Ayub Khan and General Ne Win of May 1966 (Burmese *Guardian* of June 1966, p. 5);

the Deep Bay and the Mirs Bay between British Hongkong Territory and the Chinese mainland: convention of 9 June 1898 (Martens, N.R.G.[2], XXXII, 89).

America

In North America it was, in particular, the Bays of Fundy and Passamaquoddy which have caused difficulties from the aspect of frontier delimitation (comp. DE LAPRADELLE-POLITIS, *Recueil des arbitrages internationaux* I, 298 *et seq.*, 303). Pursuant to Article 4 of the British-American Peace Treaty of Ghent of 24 December 1814 (Martens, N.R., II, 76) a Mixed Commission was set up to decide whether, under Article 2 of the preceding Peace Treaty of Paris of 3 September 1783 (*ibid.*, R², III, 553), the Great Manan Island in the Bay of Fundy and a chain of islands in the Bay of Passamaquoddy belonged to Great Britain or to the United States. The award of 24 November 1817, which gave no reasons, adjudicated Great Manan Island to Great Britain and divided the other islands in dispute between the two countries, but it abstained from further delimiting the water boundary through the Bay of Passamaquoddy. This was only fixed much later, in virtue of Article 2 of a Convention of 22 July 1892 (*ibid.*, N.R.G.², XX, 221 = XXII, 296). The boundary in the bay was eventually further detailed and retouched by two supplementary agreements of 11 April 1908 and 20/28 May 1910 (*ibid.*, N.R.G.³, IV, 191 and 205): it winds between the various islands in the bay.

Another water boundary dispute between the United States and Canada, on the west coast, related to the San Juan de Fuca Straits between Vancouver's Island and the continent. A treaty of 15 June 1846 (*ibid.*, N.R.G.¹, IX, 27) had determined the boundary through the middle of the Fuca Straits, but this tracé left two interpretations open, *viz.*, that the line should follow either the Rosario or the Haro Channel. The German Emperor as Arbitrator found in favour of the United States in his award of 21 October 1872 (LA FONTAINE, *Pasicrisie internationale*, p. 149).

A further dispute of the same type arose between the same countries over the water frontier situation in the area of the Portland Channel and the Prince of Wales Island (Alaska), which had not been sufficiently clearly determined in the Anglo-Russian treaty of 28 February 1825 (Martens, N.R., VI, 684 = N.S., II, 426) and in that between the United States and Russia of 30 March 1867 (*ibid.*, N.R.G.², I, 39). It was referred for decision to a five-member arbitral tribunal by a special agreement of 24 January 1903 (*ibid.*, N.R.G.², XXXI, 494 = XXXII, 418) and resulted in a not-unanimous award of 20 October 1903 (*ibid.*, N.R.G.², XXXII, 423-479).

Further south, other bays have been involved in doubts about their exact partition between adjacent states on the federal level. They also, although their regime is not based on a real international title, deserve mention here in view of the close analogy between "inter-State" and "inter-state" bays.

First the case of the bay of Hudson River. In that case the boundary line was fixed by a convention between the two adjacent states of the Union: New York and New Jersey, entered into on 16 September 1833, and approved by Congress on 28 June 1834 (*ibid.*, N.R., XI, 713, 717). This very detailed convention laid down that from a certain point in the middle of the Hudson River to the main sea the boundary line between the two states should successively be the middle of the said river, that of the Bay of New York, that of the waters between Staten Island and New Jersey, and that of Rariton Bay, and further elaborated on various questions of jurisdiction.

An intra-federal controversy relative to a frontier estuary arose in 1906 between the American States of Louisiana and Mississippi over their boundary in the Mississippi Sound. It derived its (economic) interest from the fact that the estuary contained oyster banks. The Supreme Court, called upon to settle the dispute, found for Louisiana (202 U.S. 1) on the ground that the deep-water channel of the river Mississippi also remained the boundary line in its estuary. See J. Brown Scott, *Judicial Settlement of Controversies between States of the American Union* (New York, 1918), vol. II, p. 1481. Comp. section 2 *supra*, p. 558.

See also the judgment of 5 February 1934 between New Jersey and Delaware (291 U.S. 361; *A.D.* 1933-1934, No. 48; *A.J.I.L.* 1935 (29), pp. 341-345), and the restatement of the principle in Wisconsin *v.* Michigan (295 U.S. 455, 461; *A.D.* 1935-1937, No. 54), which related to the Great Lakes.

In Central America State boundaries in bays have been determined partly by treaties, partly by arbitral or judicial adjudication.

A curious example of frontier delimitation in a bay by treaty is that between British Honduras (Belice) and Mexico: it zigzags through Chetumal Bay in a broken line with a number of right angles: British-Mexican treaty of 8 July 1893 (Martens, N.R.G.², XXV, 331), supplemented 7 April 1897 (*ibid.*, 333). Another boundary line was drawn through Honduras Bay between British Belice and Guatemala: treaties of 30 April 1859 (*ibid.*, N.R.G.¹, XVI², 366 = N.R.G.³, XXVI, 45) and 25/26 August 1931 (*ibid.*, N.R.G.³, XXVI, 42).

It was again by way of arbitration that Honduras and Nicaragua finally terminated a long-standing dispute between them, that neither the King of Spain as Arbitrator (award of 23 December 1906, *ibid.*, N.R.G.², XXV, 563; *A.A.*, vol. XI, p. 101), nor the International Court of Justice (Judgment of 18 November 1960, *I.C.J. Reports* 1960, p. 192) had succeeded in finally resolving. Comp. my *The Jurisprudence of the World Court*, vol. II, pp. 408-424. It related to their exact boundary *tracé* in the delta estuary of the river Wanks (or Segovia, or Coco) on the Atlantic coast. See the report of the Mixed Commission set up for that purpose, dated 16 July 1963 (*Organization of American States*, Document OEA Ser. L/III/II.9). See also Whiteman, vol. 3, p. 633.

An arbitral award was likewise required to end a dispute over the Bays of San Juan del Norte and Salinas, and a judgment of the Central American Court of Justice to settle another over the Gulf of Fonseca.

The latter case of the Gulf of Fonseca is characterized by the facts that (i) it has a wide entrance (approximately 19 miles) and would, therefore, at least according to the standards accepted in the first quarter of this century, in its centre normally form part of the high seas; (ii) it is bordered by three States (El Salvador, Honduras and Nicaragua); (iii) its surface is dotted with a number of islands which belong to only two of the three States concerned, El Salvador and Honduras respectively. The dispute concerning the legal status of the Gulf originated in the conclusion by Nicaragua of a treaty with the United States (5 August 1914; Martens, N.R.G.³, IX, 350), allowing the latter to construct an interoceanic canal through Nicaraguan territory which would terminate in Nicaragua's portion of the Gulf, and to build a naval base there. Since the other two riparian States concerned denounced the conclusion of this treaty as being an encroachment upon their collective right to the waters of the Gulf, the consequent dispute was brought before the newly created Central American Court of Justice. In its judgments of 30 September 1916 (Costa Rica-Nicaragua) and 9 March 1917 (El Salvador-Nicaragua) this Court came in substance to the following conclusions in respect of the legal status of the Gulf (*A.J.I.L.* 1917 (11), pp. 181 *et seq.*, 674 *et seq.*):

The bay must be considered to be an "historical bay" which can, consequently, in its capacity of territorial waters, be dominated by the riparian States in common without any violation of the principle of the freedom of the seas. Inside this territorial bay each of the three surrounding States has full sovereignty over a littoral belt of a breadth of three miles along its land territory and, as far as El Salvador and Honduras are concerned, also around the islands in the bay under their sovereignty. The remaining part was declared to be a condominium of all three riparian States.

Whereas the central part of the Gulf of Fonseca was thus held to be subject to the co-sovereignty of the three riparian States by an, on that point declaratory, judgment of the Central American Court of Justice, unsupported by any express conclusive treaty provision, the co-imperium of two other bays in Central America was explicitly established by treaty. Article 4 of the Boundary Treaty of 15 April 1858 between Costa Rica and Nicaragua (LA FONTAINE, *Pasicrisie*, p. 298), laid down in effect that "the Bay of San Juan del Norte (on the Atlantic Coast), as well as that of Salinas (on the Pacific Coast) shall be common to both Republics and consequently their advantages and the obligation to unite for their defense shall be common also". The validity of that treaty was at one time disputed between the contracting Parties, but this dispute was settled by an arbitral award of the United States President Cleveland of 24 December 1886 in the sense of its validity (LA FONTAINE, *loco cit.*, pp. 299 *et seq.*). The provision concerned was thus made the foundation of two subsequent arbitral awards by Umpire E. P. Alexander of 30 September/20 December 1897 and 22 March 1898 (*ibid.*, pp. 529, 532, 533). The Umpire found against an award which should determine

607

a boundary, declared in advance to be changeable according to future shifts of the banks or the channels in the inundation area of the river, and confined himself to indicating the frontier as it was at the time:

"La exacta línea de división entre la jurisdicción de los dos países es el borde de las aguas sobre la márgen derecha, cuando el río se halla en su estado ordinario, navegable por las embarcaciones y botes de uso general".

The entire water surface of the delta was held to be under the sovereignty of Nicaragua.

The case of the Bay of Salinas was not strictly a case of frontier delimitation in the usual sense since it centered on a very special question: the exact determination of the location of the "centre" of that common bay. The umpire declined in his 5th award of 10 March 1900 (*ibid.*, p. 537) to apply the method, employed in mechanics, of fixing the "centre" of the bay by determining its "point of gravitation" (obviously by experimenting with a model of the bay) and found the "mid position of its area" through an ingenious mathematical operation.

On South America see below.

The delimitation in the Gulf of Paria between Venezuela and Trinidad, agreed upon by the Governments concerned in 1942 (*L.N.T.S.*, vol. 205, p. 121), was not a delimitation of State frontiers proper. It related only to a division of the continental shelf under the waters of the Gulf (see Chapter II, section 5 above, p. 84). It resembles in this respect the situation in the Ems estuary, mentioned above p. 599.

Just as do estuaries, by which I understand river mouths which widen so much on nearing the open sea that they take on the character of bays, deltas also present special features. By deltas I mean the lower stretches of rivers which flow into the sea through different arms, one of which must be designated as the real river boundary. The most famous specimen, from the international law point of view, of a delta is that of the Danube in which a number of varying frontier *tracés* have in the course of time been drawn successively. Comp. on this delta Part II of this publication, pp. 372-373.

Other examples are those of the maritime boundary

between Bulgaria and Turkey in the delta of the lower end of the river Evros (Maritsa): Article 1 *in fine* of their Peace Treaty of 29 September 1913 (Martens, N.R.G.[3], VIII, 78);

between Perú and Ecuador, where a river empties into the sea through different branches: fruitless arbitrations in virtue of special agreements of 2 May 1890 (see G. IRELAND, *Boundaries, Possessions and Conflicts in South America* (Cambridge, Mass., 1938), pp. 222-224) and 21 June 1924 (Martens, N.R.G.[3], XX, 616): arbitration by the President of the United States), followed by a war in 1941-1942 and a provisional boundary treaty of 16 July 1945, once again followed by military clashes (1951-1955);[30] and

between Nicaragua and Costa Rica in the delta area of the river San Juan del Norte (comp. *supra*, p. 607).

An often complicating factor is the fact that a river boundary reaches the sea, not through an estuary or a delta proper, but at a point on the coast where a number of islands fringe it and leave as possible accesses to it only a corresponding number of narrow creeks. Such is the local situation in the case of the river Mataja on the maritime frontier between Colombia and Ecuador near the Bay of Ancón de Sardinas. In such a case the boundary must be determined so as to run through one of the creeks concerned. In this case the solution proved to be very difficult. A treaty between the two countries of 24 May 1908, complemented 21 July 1908, failed to be ratified by Ecuador (see: A.J. URIBE, *Colombia-Venezuela-Costa Rica-Ecuador-Brazil-Nicaragua y Panama, Cuestiones de límites etc.*, pp. 238 *et seq.*). A subsequent treaty of 15 July 1916 (Martens, N.R.G.³, XXI, 193) was, however, accepted; Article 3 provided for a mixed demarcation commission, which finished its work in 1919 (see IRELAND, *loco cit.*, pp. 183-184).

A similar situation can be noted with regard to the maritime frontier at the mouth of the Río Kasset between Portuguese and (ex-French) Guinea, where it runs between the islands of Katak and Tristão, Convention of 12 May 1886 (*ibid.*, N.R.G.², XIV, 108).

Yet another variant is where the land boundary between two States ends in a right or an oblique angle at the side of a lagoon or a haff from where it either winds through it into the sea or crosses it to reach the sea via its narrow opposite bank. See for a lagoon boundary the frontier situation between French West Africa (now Ivory Coast) and the Gold Coast (now Ghana) at the mouth of the Tana river: Franco-British Agreement of 10 August 1889 (Martens, N.R.G.², XVI, 738), Article 3; and for a boundary running across a haff, that dividing into two the formerly (1919-1939) German-Danzig, now (since 1945) Polish-Soviet Frisches Haff on the Baltic Sea: Article 28 of the Peace Treaty of Versailles of 28 June 1919 (*ibid.*, N.R.G.³, XI, p. 353); treaties between the USSR and Poland of 16 August 1945 and 5 May 1957 (*U.N.T.S.*, vols. 10, p. 200 and 274, p. 139).

Comp. for the rest the study *A brief geographical and hydrographical study of bays and estuaries, the coasts of which belong to different States*, prepared by Commander R.H. KENNEDY on behalf of the Conference on the Law of the Sea of 1958 (Preparatory Document No. 12, A./Conf.13/15 of 13 November 1957); the elaborate study of BOUCHEZ cited above, p. 595;

30. See L.J. BOUCHEZ, *The regime of bays in international law* (Leyden, 1964), p. 168; and G. MAIER, *The boundary dispute between Ecuador and Peru (A.J.I.L.* 1969 (63), pp. 28-46).

Y. Z. BLUM, *Historic titles in international law* (The Hague, 1965), pp. 241-334, and Whiteman, vol. 4, pp. 207-258.

Frontier bays may be dammed in common accord. Comp. the endiking of the Zwin (frontier delimitation in this water area by a convention of 15 March 1869, Martens, N.R.G.[1], XX, 546) in virtue of the Belgo-Netherlands treaty of 24 May 1872 (*ibid.*, N.R.G.[2], I, 136) and that of parts of the Dollard in accordance with the Prusso-Netherlands treaty of 23 September 1874 (*ibid.*, IV, 340), to be reclaimed further subject to the conditions laid down recently in the Ems-Dollard Treaty between the Netherlands and the Federal Republic of Germany of 8 April 1960 (*U.N.T.S.*, vol. 509, p. 64), supplemented on 14 May 1962 by the treaty of Bennekom (*U.N.T.S.*, vol. 509, p. 140).

Annex. Arbitral or judicial adjudications of territory

Legal history displays an incessant stream of territorial adjudications by arbitral and, in a more recent period, judicial tribunals. They are, in accordance for that matter with territorial disputes in general, chiefly of three different types as they relate either (*a*) directly to disputed land boundaries, or (*b*) to disputed land areas the boundaries of which were not as such, or were only indirectly, the object of controversy, or (*c*) to disputed islands. Although the borderline between (*a*) and (*b*) is, it must be admitted, fluid, this distinction between three types gives at least some lead through the vast maze of territorial adjudications in the past.

It is well known from Ræder's research into international arbitration in Greece[31] that a surprising number of cases of arbitral settlement of territorial disputes has already occurred in Greek Antiquity. The same can be stated with respect to the Middle Ages during which such disputes have frequently been submitted to, or authoritatively decided by, third parties: the Pope, the Emperor, other secular or ecclesiastical authorities of a superior, or even of an equal rank, existing courts, mixed commissions, individual statesmen, diplomats or private lawyers. I will refrain from going so far back into the past in this context (comp. for further data Part VIII of this publication) and will here only give some brief historical data and references posterior to what has been called the "renaissance" of international arbitration in 1794, which may serve as a guide. Not all the special agreements, however, have led to a positive result.

Reference is made in the following survey to the collections of Martens (R[2], N.R. and N.R.G.); LA FONTAINE, *Pasicrisie internationale* (*Pas.*

---

31. A. RÆDER, *L'arbitrage international chez les Hellènes* (Kristiania, 1912) in *Publications de l'Institut Nobel Norvégien*, vol. I.

Int.); DE LAPRADELLE-POLITIS, *Recueil des arbitrages internationaux* (*Lapr.-Pol.*), and the *Reports of International Arbitral Awards* (*A.A.*).

I intend to offer a few more details on territorial arbitrations in a general systematic survey, to be inserted in Part VII of this publication on International Disputes and Arbitration.

Before entering into some detail concerning individual arbitration cases, there is reason to mention a few questions of a general nature which have from time to time arisen in arbitral or judicial proceedings.

One is that of the *onus probandi* in territorial disputes. The Austro-Hungarian tribunal in the *Meerauge* dispute of 1902 (award of 13 September; Martens, N.R.G.³, III, 71, at p. 75) was faced by the question in connection with certain Hungarian contentions concerning past events: the tribunal referred to "general procedural principles" to support its view that the burden of proof must be laid on Hungary. On other occasions arbitrators have claimed freedom to assess the evidence freely according to circumstances without holding themselves bound by any strict division of the *onus probandi.*

In his award of 6 June 1904 (Martens, N.R.G.², XXXII, 485, 487) the King of Italy, placed as arbitrator before the same doubtful position in a dispute between Brazil and Great Britain in respect of British Guyana, decided as follows:

"That it does not appear from the documents ... that there are historical and legal claims on which to found thoroughly determined and well-defined rights of sovereignty in favour of either of the contending Powers over the whole territory in dispute, but only over certain portions of the same;

That not even the limit of the zone of territory over which the right of sovereignty of one or of the other of the two Parties may be held to be established can be fixed with precision;

That it cannot either be decided with certainty whether the right of Brazil or of Great Britain is the stronger.

In this condition of affairs, since it is Our duty to fix the line of frontier between the dominions of the two Powers, We have come to the conclusion that, in the present state of the geographical knowledge of the region, it is not possible to divide the contested territory into two parts equal as regards extent and value, but that it is necessary that it should be divided in accordance with the lines traced by nature, and that the preference should be given to a frontier which, while clearly defined throughout its whole course, the better lends itself to a fair division of the disputed territory".

(There follows a frontier *tracé* along a watershed and the thalweg of two rivers.)

Another general question concerns the freedom of an arbitrator to decide a dispute *ex aequo et bono*, either because the finding would otherwise have to be a *non liquet*, or because a decision according to strict law would be unsatisfactory. On this point arbitral tribunals have also taken very different views. The majority of awards, however, tells against the

611

decision of the same *Meerauge* tribunal (at p. 73) which attributed a very wide competence to itself:

"(The arbitration agreement) enthält keine Bestimmung darüber, auf welche Art und Weise das Schiedsgericht die Feststellung der Grenze vorzunehmen habe: ob es sich namentlich darum handle, bereits in früherer Zeit fixierte Grenze zu erforschen, oder ob das Schiedsgericht ermächtigt sei, die Grenze nach eigenem gewissenhaften Ermessen zu bestimmen.

Beim Fehlen irgend welcher beschränkenden Bestimmung hierüber hat das Schiedsgericht den Standpunkt eingenommen, dass die Feststellung der fraglichen Grenze seinem freien auf eingehender Würdigung aller vorgebrachten Umstände beruhenden Ermessen überlassen sei."

For a further discussion of these basic questions I also refer to Part VII of this publication.

(a) Boundary adjudications proper

America

United States-Canada

Northeastern boundary between Maine and New Brunswick (arbitration under Article V, No. 1, of the Jay Treaty of 19 November 1794: R², V, 642): identification of the source of the river St. Croix, mentioned in Article 2 of the Anglo-American Peace Treaty of Paris of 3 September 1783 (R², III, 553)—award of a mixed commission with a neutral umpire of 25 October 1798 (*Lapr.-Pol.*, I, 11).

Islands in the Bay of Passamaquoddy and the Grand Manan Island in the Bay of Fundy; award of a mixed commission, under Article IV of the Peace Treaty of Ghent of 24 December 1814 (N.R., II, 76), of 24 November 1817 (N.R., V, vol. suppl., 397, 399; *Lapr.-Pol.*, I, 303).

Northwestern corner of Nova Scotia: identification of certain highlands, also mentioned in Article 2 of the same Peace Treaty of 1783, but impossible to retrace—statement of 4 October 1821 by a mixed commission under Article V of the same treaty of Ghent (*Lapr.-Pol.*, I, 309)—; followed by the reference of the dispute for final decision to King Willem I of the Netherlands (*compromis* of 29 September 1827, N.R., VII, 491), who, in the given circumstances, found no other way out than to give an award *ex aequo et bono* of 10 January 1831 (*Lapr.-Pol.*, I, 371), which was, however, repudiated by the United States (note of protest in N.R., X, 317) and ultimately set aside by a treaty of 9 August 1842 (N.R.G.¹, III, 456).

Eastern sector of the frontier of the Great Lakes from the point of intersection between the parallel of 45° lat. N. and the Iroquois River (= St. Lawrence) to Lake Huron (arbitration under Article VI of the treaty of Ghent)—award of a mixed commission of 18 June 1822 (N.R., VI, 45; *Lapr.-Pol.*, I, 314).

Western sector of the same frontier from Lake Huron to the Lake of the Woods: arbitration under Article VII of the treaty of Ghent, which was wrecked on a partial dissent between the Members of another (in fact the same) mixed commission, stated in their *procès-verbal* of 23 December 1826, and relating *inter alia* to the St. Georges Island(*Lapr.-Pol.*, I, 322).

Water frontiers on the Pacific side through one of the channels of the San Juan de Fuca Strait between Vancouver's Island and the Continent, either that of Rosario or that of Haro (arbitration under Articles 34 *et seq.* of the treaty of Washington of 8 May 1871, N.R.G.[1], XX, 698)— award of Emperor Wilhelm I of Germany of 21 October 1872 (Martens, N.R.G.[1], XX, 775; *Pas. Int.*, 150).

Alaska boundary in the Portland Channel—award of a six-member tribunal of 20 October 1903 (N.R.G.[2], XXXII, 423-479; *A.A.*, XV, 481).

United States-Mexico

Chamizal district in the bend of the Río Grande between El Paso and Ciudad Juárez—award by a three-member tribunal of 15 June 1911 (N.R.G.[3], VI, 66; *A.A.*, XI, 309). In this case the Joint Commission, established in virtue of the Convention of 24 June 1910 (N.R.G.[3], IV, 719) held that:

1) the boundary line established by the treaties of 2 February 1848 (N.R.G.[1], XIV, 7) and 30 December 1853 (N.R.G.[2], I, 1) along the Río Grande was not a fixed and invariable line;

2) the United States had not acquired title to the Chamizal district by prescription;

3) the treaty of 12 November 1884 (*ibid.*, XIII, 675) applied to all changes in the river subsequent to the survey of 1852;

4)-6) the Chamizal tract, as defined in the Convention of 1910, was formed by slow and gradual erosion and deposit of alluvion within the meaning of Article 1 of the Convention of 1884, as far as its formation was prior to 1864, but not of that character as far as it was caused by the flood of 1864 or during the succeeding years up to and including 1868.

The American member of the Commission not only delivered a dissenting opinion (N.R.G.[3], VI, 88 *et seq.*; *A.J.I.L.* 1911 (5), p. 832), but even went the length of contending that the award was void for various reasons (see his statement in Martens, pp. 105-106). The United States Government repudiated the award accordingly and was only prepared in 1962-1964 to revise its attitude and still to accept its implications. See *A.J.I.L.* 1964 (58), pp. 165 and 336; *D.S.B.*, 19 October 1964 (51), p. 545; Whiteman, vol. 3, p. 680.

Central America and the Caribbean

Honduras-El Salvador—special agreement of 18 December 1880 to submit their boundary dispute to arbitration by President Zavala of

Nicaragua (*Pas. Int.*, 647): probably without result; new *compromis* of 19 January 1895 (*Pas. Int.*, 505). See G. IRELAND, *Boundaries etc. in Central and North America and the Caribbean* (Cambridge, Mass., 1941), pp. 144-158.

Colombia (Panama)-Costa Rica—award given, after the decease of King Alfonso XII of Spain, first designated as arbitrator (1880), by President Loubet of France on 11 September 1900 (N.R.G.², XXXII, 411), followed by a fresh arbitration concerning its interpretation in 1910 (see *infra*).

Colombia-Venezuela—award of the Queen-Regent of Spain, Maria Cristina, of 16 March 1891 (N.R.G.², XXIV, 110; *Pas. Int.*, 513): on the basis of the *uti possidetis* of 1810.

Costa Rica-Nicaragua—award, on the strength of a special agreement of 24 December 1886 (*Pas. Int.*, 298), of President Cleveland (U.S.A.) of 22 March 1888 (*Pas. Int.*, 299) in favour of the validity of their boundary treaty of 15 April 1858; see further *infra* (1897).

Honduras-Nicaragua—arbitration treaty of 7 October 1894 (*Pas. Int.*, 478), only followed by actual arbitral proceedings in 1906. See *infra* (1906).

Guatemala-Honduras—convention of 1 March 1895 providing for arbitration in case of failure of direct agreement (*Pas. Int.*, 506), only followed by actual arbitration much later: award of 23 January 1933 (*A.A.*, II, 1307) by a three-member tribunal in virtue of a new *compromis* of 16 July 1930 (N.R.G.³, XXXI, 365).

Dominican Republic-Haiti—*compromis* of 3 July 1895 (N.R.G.², XXIII, 79 = XXVII, 17; *Pas. Int.*, 602)—see for the previous correspondence and documents of 1894-1895 N.R.G.², XXVII, 12-25, providing for arbitration by the Pope: choice for the construction of a treaty of 9 November 1874 (N.R.G.², XXVII, 3) between the *uti possidetis* of that year and the *status quo post bellum* of 1856. This *compromis* has never been implemented because the Pope has not delivered his award within a year, as he had been asked to do. The dispute was ultimately settled by a convention of 31 January 1938 (*L.N.T.S.*, vol. 187, p. 169). Comp. on the course of events G. IRELAND, *Boundaries etc. in Central and North America and the Caribbean* (Cambridge, Mass., 1941), pp. 61-68.

Costa Rica-Nicaragua—five consecutive awards of the Umpire E. P. Alexander of 30 September and 20 December 1897, 22 March 1898, 26 July 1899 and 10 March 1900 on the construction of the boundary treaty of 1858, cited above (*Pas. Int.*, 528-539).

Colombia-Costa Rica—award of President Loubet of France of 11 September 1900 (N.R.G.², XXXII, 243) in virtue of a special agreement of 4 November 1896 (*ibid.*, XXV, 62).

Honduras-Nicaragua—award of King Alfonso XIII of Spain of 23 December 1906 (*A.A.*, XI, 101), repudiated by Nicaragua much later, but upheld by the International Court of Justice in 1960 (*I.C.J. Reports* 1960, p. 192; comp. my *The Jurisprudence of the World Court*, vol. II, pp. 408-424, and Part I of this publication, p. 296).

Costa Rica-Panama—award of the Chief Justice of the United States, White, of 12 September 1914 (*A.A.*, XI, 519), in virtue of a new *compromis* of 17 March 1919 (N.R.G.³, V, 678), interpreting the earlier award of President Loubet of 1900, cited above.

South America

On the Guyana's see *supra*, p. 549.

France-The Netherlands: award, on the basis of a *compromis* of 29 November 1888 (N.R.G.², XVI, 730 = XVII, 124), complemented 28 April 1890 (*Pas. Int.*, 328), of the Emperor Alexander III of Russia of 25 May 1891 (N.R.G.², XVIII, 100 = XXVII, 136; *Pas. Int.*, 329).

Great Britain-Venezuela: award, in virtue of an arbitration treaty of 2 February 1897 (N.R.G.², XXVIII, 328; *Pas. Int.*, 554), of a five-member tribunal (Umpire: de Martens) of 3 October 1899 (N.R.G.², XXIX, 581; *Pas. Int.*, 556).

France-Brazil: award, in accordance with a treaty of 10 April 1897 (N.R.G.², XXV, 335; *Pas. Int.*, 563), of the Swiss Federal Council of 1 December 1900 (N.R.G.³, X, 153; *Pas. Int.*, 564).

Great Britain-Brazil: award of King Victor Emmanuel III of Italy of 6 June 1904 (N.R.G.², XXXII, 485; *A.A.*, XI, 11).

France-The Netherlands: special agreement of 30 September 1915 (N.R.G.³, XII, 269; Neth. *Staatsblad* 1916, No. 481), for the further delimitation in the upper reaches of the river Maroni-Awa, in accordance with the award of 1891, cited above.

Between Latin-American States

Argentina-Paraguay—award of President Hayes of the United States of 12 November 1878 (N.R.G.², XII, 472; *Pas. Int.*, 224), relative to a disputed territory between the Pilcomayo and Verde Rivers, on the basis of their boundary treaty of 3 February 1867 (*Pas. Int.*, 223).

Argentina-Brazil—award of President Cleveland (U.S.A.) of 5 February 1895, on the basis of an arbitration treaty of 7 September 1889 (*Pas. Int.*, 340), concerning the Territorio das Misiões (*Pas. Int*, 341).

Colombia-Venezuela—award, pursuant to a *compromis* of 14 September 1881 (*Pas. Int.*, 512), of the Queen-Regent of Spain of 16 March 1891 (N.R.G.², XXIV, 110; *Pas. Int.*, 513), followed by a new arbitration in virtue of a *compromis* of 3 November 1916 (N.R.G.³, XX, 371), see *infra* (1922).

Ecuador-Perú—convention to request an arbitral decision by the King of Spain: special agreement of 1 August 1887 (*Pas. Int.*, 323), only acceded to by Colombia in 1894 (*Pas. Int.*, 324). Comp. on the complicated further developments the elaborate article by G. MAIER in *A.J.I.L.* 1969 (63), pp. 28-46.

Argentina-Chile—*procès-verbal* of an arbitral tribunal with the Minister of the United States in Buenos Aires, Buchanan, as Umpire, drawn up on 24 March 1899 (*Pas. Int.*, 585, 587) relating to sovereignty over part of their frontier area, north of 26°52'45" lat.S. up to 23° lat.S., called Puna d'Atacama.

Argentina-Chile—award, in virtue of § 8 of an arbitration agreement of 17 April 1896 (*Pas. Int.*, 543; *B.F.S.P.*, 88, 553), of King Edward VII of 20 November 1902 concerning the southern part of their boundary in the Cordilleras de los Andes (*B.F.S.P.*, 95, 162; *A.A.*, IX, 29).

Bolivia-Perú—award of President Figueroa Alcorta of Argentina of 9 July 1909 (N.R.G.³, III, 53; *A.A.*, XI, 133).

Colombia-Venezuela—award of the Swiss Federal Council of 24 March 1922 for the implementation of the award of 1891 cited above (*A.A.*, I, 223).

Bolivia-Paraguay (Gran Chaco) 1938. See *infra sub* (*b*), p. 619.

Argentina-Chile—award of Queen Elizabeth II of 9 December 1966 (Official publication of the Foreign Office, 1966; *A.J.I.L.* 1967 (61), p. 1071; *R.G.D.I.P.* 1967 (71), p. 257, with commentary at pp. 151-173) concerning a small southern portion in a middle sector of the Andes boundary to the north of Lakes Palena and General Paz which had appeared not to have been described exactly enough in the preceding award of 1902.[32]

Argentina-Chile—special agreement of 12 June 1960 (*R.G.D.I.P.* 1960 (64), p. 619) to submit their water boundary dispute in the southernmost part of South America (frontier in the Beagle Canal: west, between or north of the Islas Lennox and Nueva?) to the International Court of Justice, repeated in a common declaration of 9 November 1964 (*ibid.*, 1965 (69), p. 442) which, however, kept a backdoor open to arbitration instead of adjudication by the Court. See also *R.G.D.I.P.* 1968 (72), pp. 392-401.

Africa

Orange Free State-Transvaal—award of the Lieutenant-Governor of Natal, R.W. Keate, of 19 February 1870 (*Pas. Int.*, 589; *Lapr.-Pol.*, II, 576) concerning the boundary in the mountainous area of the upper course of the Vaal River.

South-African Republic-Griqua and Bechuana Tribes—award of the same arbitrator of 17 October 1871 as Umpire (*Lapr.-Pol.*, II, 691) in a boundary dispute closely related to the existence of diamantiferous strata in West Griqualand. See, however, on the results *Lapr.-Pol.*, II, 693 *et seq.* (doctrinal note by J. WESTLAKE).

Great Britain-Portugal—award, in virtue of a Protocol of 25 September 1872 (*Pas. Int.*, 170), of President Mac Mahon of France of

32. J. C. PUIG, *El laudo arbitral británico en el Caso del Río Encuentro* in the *Revista de Derecho Internacional y Ciencias Diplomáticas* 1966/67 (XV, XVI), p. 30.

24 July 1875 (N.R.G.², III, 547; *Pas. Int.*, 172) recognizing Portugal's sovereignty over the northern bank of, and certain islands in, Delagoa Bay.

Great Britain-Transvaal—award of the Chief Justice of the Orange Free State, de Villiers, of 5 August 1885 (*Pas. Int.*, 245) concerning their southwestern frontier.

Congo Free State-Portugal—*compromis* of 7 February 1890 (*Pas. Int.*, 617), to confer a decision upon the Swiss Federal Council; arbitration avoided by a direct agreement of 25 May 1891 (N.R.G.², XVIII, 30 = XXVII, 152).

Great Britain-Portugal—award of the Italian judge Vigliani of 30 January 1897 relative to the delimitation of their spheres of influence south of the river Zambesi (Manica boundary) (N.R.G.², XXVIII, 294; *Pas. Int.*, 486).

Great Britain-Portugal—award of King Victor Emmanuel III of Italy of 30 May 1905 concerning the western frontier of the indigenous Kingdom of Barotse (Angola-Rhodesia) (N.R.G.², XXXV, 542; *A.A.*, XI, 59), followed by an exchange of notes of 5 March 1915/3 November 1925 for its implementation (N.R.G.³, XVIII, 211).

Germany-Great Britain—award of Don Joaquín Fernández Prida, appointed by the King of Spain, of 23 May 1911 (N.R.G.³, VI, 396; *A.A.*, IX, 263): boundary between Angola and South West Africa south of the Walfish Bay.

Ethiopia-Italy—award of a five-member tribunal of 3 September 1935 (*A.A.*, III, 1657) given on the occasion of the Wal Wal incident.

Europe

Italy-Switzerland—award of the Arbitrator G.P.Marsh of 23 September 1874 (N.R.G.², VIII, 560; *Pas. Int.*, 203) concerning their frontier on the Alpe Cravairola, pursuant to a *compromis* of 31 December 1873 (*Pas. Int.*, 201).

Austria-Hungary—award of a three-member tribunal of 13 September 1902 on their boundary in the Galician Meerauge region (N.R.G.³, III, 71).

Norway-Sweden—award of the Permanent Court of Arbitration of 23 October 1909 concerning their maritime boundary (Grisbådarna case) (N.R.G.³, III, 85; *A.A.*, XI, 147). See *supra* p. 596.

Estonia-Latvia—award of Colonel Tallent of 1/3 July 1920 (*Doc. de l'Ass. de la S.d.N.* 70, 20/48/70, *Mem. Secr. Gen.*, p. 21 Annex VII), followed by a boundary treaty of 19 October 1920 (N.R.G.³, XV, 686).

Czechoslovakia-Poland—frontier in the region of Spisz (Jaworzina district): Advisory Opinion of the Permanent Court of International Justice of 6 December 1923 (*Publications P.C.I.J.*, series B, No. 8; comp. my *The Jurisprudence of the World Court*, vol. I, pp. 36-39).

Albania-Serb-Croat-Slovene Kingdom—frontier at the Monastery of Saint-Naoum on Lake Ochrid: Advisory Opinion of the Permanent Court of International Justice (*Publications P.C.I.J.*, series B, No. 9; comp. my *The Jurisprudence of the World Court*, vol. I, pp. 37-39).

Hungary-Czechoslovakia and Hungary-Romania—pseudo-arbitrations by Hitler and Mussolini of 2 November 1938, respectively 30 August 1940 (N.R.G.[3], XXVI, 662, resp. XXXVIII, 338), followed by declarations of acceptance of the same dates, imposed upon the victim States (*ibid.*, XXXVI, 663 and XXXIX, 348).

Asia

Great Britain(Afghanistan)-Russia—recommendation by Commissioners, accepted by the parties; no real arbitration: July/August 1887 (N.R.G.[2], XIV, 180; *Pas. Int.*, 287).

The Netherlands-Portugal—award of the Permanent Court of Arbitration of 1 October 1914, concerning their boundary on the island of Timor (*A.A.*, XI, 481).

Saudi Arabia-Sultanate of Oman-Muscat—arbitration relative to the Buraimi oasis, wrecked on the attitude of Saudi Arabia in 1955. Comp. on the development of these arbitral proceedings H. M. AL-BAHARNA, *The legal status of the Arabian Gulf States* (Manchester, 1968), pp. 203-207; KELLY in *International Affairs* (London) 1956 (32), pp. 318 *et seq.*, and GOY in *A.F.D.I.* 1957 (3), pp. 188 *et seq.*

Cambodia-Thailand—Judgment of the International Court of Justice of 26 May 1961 (*I.C.J. Reports* 1961, p. 17; comp. my *The Jurisprudence of the World Court*, vol. II, p. 425) concerning sovereignty over the Temple of Preah-Vihear.

India-Pakistan—award of a three-member tribunal of 19 February 1968 (*I.L.M.* 1968 (7), 633) concerning sovereignty over the Rann of Kutch, based on an arbitration agreement of 30 June 1965 (*I.L.M.* 1968 (7), 635). See *supra* p. 603 and the articles by A. BEBLER, *The Indo-Pakistan western boundary case* in the *Yugoslav Review of International Law* 1968 (XV), p. 55, with map and by J. J. A. SALMON in *A.F.D.I.* 1968 (XIV), p. 217.

(*b*) *Disputed areas*

Chile-Perú—*compromis* of 16 April 1898 (*Pas. Int.*, 610), not ratified by Chile, ordering the organization of a plebiscite on the future sovereignty over the provinces of Tacna and Arica in accordance with the Peace Treaty of 20 October 1883 (N.R.G.[2], X, 191), followed in 1925 by a different award (see *infra*).

Great Britain-Nicaragua—award of Emperor Franz Joseph of 2 July 1881 (N.R.G.[2], X, 609; *Pas. Int.*, 385), relating to the measure of sovereignty of Nicaragua over the Mosquito Coast, attributed to the latter.

Great Britain (Iraq)-Turkey—decision of the Council of the League of Nations of 29 October 1924 concerning the allotment of Mosul to Iraq (*L.N.T.S.*, vol. 64, p. 389), further implemented by the treaty of 5 June 1926 (N.R.G.³, XVIII, 332; *L.N.T.S.*, vol. 64, p. 379).

Chile-Perú. By Article 3 of their Peace Treaty of Lima of 20 October 1883 (Martens, N.R.G.², X, 191) Chile and Perú agreed that Chile would keep the Peruvian provinces of Tacna and Arica under her administration for a term of ten years and that after the expiration of that term a plebiscite should be held there. When Chile proved unwilling to co-operate, Perú on 16 April 1898 achieved the conclusion of a special agreement with her (*Pas. Int.*, 610) to submit the dispute to arbitration by the Queen Regent of Spain, in particular as to the persons who would be qualified to take part in the plebiscite, and to the secret or public character of the voting; it was however, rejected by the Chilean parliament. A new attempt, much later, seemed to promise a better result: a second *compromis* conferred arbitral powers on President Coolidge of the United States, who by an award of 4 March 1925 (*A.A.*, II, 921; *A.J.I.L.* 1925 (19), pp. 393-433; *A.D.* 1925-1926, Case No. 269) found that there was no valid reason to cancel the plebiscite and that, therefore, it should be held. Its realization, however, proved impracticable of accomplishment, as the Plebiscitary Commission stated in its resolution of 14 June 1926 (*A.J.I.L.* 1926 (20), p. 624) because Chile had rendered impossible the creation and maintenance of conditions proper and necessary for the holding of a free and fair plebiscite. On this ground the Commission terminated the plebiscitary proceedings. The dispute was ultimately settled by a compromise of 3 June 1929 (*L.N.T.S.*, vol. 94, p. 401), allotting Tacna to Perú and Arica to Chile (against the payment of 6 million dollars to Perú). Comp. for an interim decision of the Arbitrator of 9 December 1925 on the question whether the authority of the Plebiscitary Commission derogated from the powers hitherto exercised by Chile in Tacna and Arica: *A.J.I.L.* 1926 (20), p. 614; *A.D.* 1925-1926, Case No. 83.

Canada-Newfoundland—judgment of the Judicial Committee of the (British) Privy Council of 1 March 1927, sanctioning the appurtenance of Labrador to Newfoundland (*Zeitschrift für Völkerrecht* 1928 (XIV), p. 569; *A.D.* 1927-1928, Case No. 81).

Bolivia-Paraguay—award of 10 October 1938, rendered by the Governments of the Argentine, Chile, Brazil, Peru, Uruguay and the United States jointly, dividing the Gran Chaco between the parties *ex aequo et bono* (*A.A.*, III, 1817). The work of a demarcation commission resulted in 1969, in the transfer of 800 sq.kms. of Chaco territory from Bolivia to Paraguay. See the *Bulletin of Legal Developments* 1969 (4), p. 194.

Belgium-The Netherlands—Judgment of the International Court of

619

Justice of 20 June 1959 (*I.C.J. Reports* 1959, p. 209) relative to sovereignty over certain plots of land, enclaved in the Netherlands.

(c) Disputed islands

The Netherlands-Venezuela—award of Queen Isabel II of Spain of 30 June 1865 (*Pas. Int.*, 152; *Lapr.-Pol.*, II, 412), attributing the Aves Island near Saba in the Caribbean to Venezuela.

Great Britain-Portugal—award of President Grant of the U.S.A. of 21 April 1870 (*Pas. Int.*, 83; *Lapr.-Pol.*, II, 612), allotting the island of Bulama on the West coast of Africa to Portugal.

Germany-Spain—findings by Pope Leo XIII of 22 October 1885 as mediator in favour of the sovereignty of Spain over the Carolines and Palaos in Oceania (*Pas. Int.*, 285; N.R.G.[2], XII, 292).

Germany-Great Britain—award of Baron Lambermont of 17 August 1889 (N.R.G.[2], XXII, 101; *Pas. Int.*, 335) relative to the island of Lamu (not strictly territorial).

France-Mexico—award of King Victor Emmanuel III of Italy of 28 January 1931, in virtue of a *compromis* of 2 March 1909 (N.R.G.[3], V, 8), attributing the Island of Clipperton (about 10° lat. N. and 110° long.W.) in the Pacific Ocean to France (*A.A.*, II, 1105).

The Netherlands-United States—award of Max Huber of 4 April 1928 in the Island of Palmas case (N.R.G.[3], XIV, 124; *A.A.*, II, 829).

Swan Islands. Since 1857 occupied by the U.S., but claimed by Honduras as from 1921. Recognized as Honduran on 12 November 1969, See Hackworth, I, pp. 516-520 and the *D.S.B.* of 15 December 1969 (LXI), p. 550.

(d) Unsolved territorial disputes

Some of the better-known territorial disputes which are still pending relate to

Sakhalin and the Kuriles, originally Japanese territory, after World War II occupied by the USSR and now claimed back by Japan; see Y. Takano in the *Japanese Annual of International Law* 1959 (3), p. 52, Whiteman, vol. 3, p. 477 and *R.G.D.I.P.* 1969 (73), p. 485; Haruhiko Shibuya, *Die territoriale Frage zwischen Japan und der Sowjetunion nach dem zweiten Weltkrieg* in *Macht und Recht im kommunistischen Herrschaftssystem* (Festschrift für Boris Meissner, Köln, 1965), pp. 207-245;

the Ussuri-region, claimed by the USSR and China; see p. 521 *supra*, and H. Pommerening, *Der chinesisch-sowjetische Grenzkonflikt* (Olten, 1968) and Ch. Rousseau in the *R.G.D.I.P.* 1969 (73), pp. 1083-1109;

the border between India and China: see S. P. Sharma in *A.J.I.L.* 1965 (59), p. 16 and G. N. Rao, *The India-China border; a reappraisal* (London, 1968);

Kashmir, a bone of contention between India and Pakistan since the *India Independence Act* of 11 June 1947; see on this problem P.LYON in *International Relations* 1966 (III), p. 111 and W.ABENDROTH in *Wörterbuch des Völkerrechts*, vol. II, p. 210;

the Shatt-al-Arab, after the one-sided abrogation of the 1937 frontier treaty by Iran, see p. 603;

Sabah (North Borneo), claimed by the Philippines; see M.LEIFER, *The Philippine claim to Sabah* (Zug, 1968) and *R.G.D.I.P.* 1969 (73), p. 488;

the boundary between Saudi Arabia and the People's Republic of South Yemen; see the article by A.HOTTINGER on p. 5 of the *Neue Zürcher Zeitung* of 11 December 1969;

the borderzone of Ethiopia, Kenya and Somalia, claimed by the latter to form a "Greater Somalia". Whereas the relations between Kenya and Somalia seem to have quietened down after the agreement of 28 October 1967, the Somali claims to part of Ethiopia are still fully alive. See J.DRYSDALE, *The Somali dispute* (London, 1964); D.J.L.BROWN in *I.C.L.Q.* 1961 (10), p. 167; ROUSSEAU in *R.G.D.I.P.* 1960 (64), p. 625, 1968 (72), pp. 434 and 454, and 1969 (73), p. 460, and Whiteman, vol. 3, pp. 661 and 668;

Belize (British Honduras), claimed by Guatemala from Great Britain, see *I.C.L.Q.* 1968 (17), p. 996; p. 385 *supra*;

the frontier between Venezuela and Guyana, see p. 549 *supra* and *R.G.D.I.P.* 1969 (73), p. 478;

the río Lauca between Chile and Bolivia, see Ministerio de Relaciones Exteriores de Chile, *La cuestión del río Lauca* (Santiago de Chile, 1963) and R.D.TOMASEK, *The Chilean-Bolivian Lauca River dispute and the O.A.S.* in the *Journal of Inter-American Studies* 1967 (9), p. 351;

the boundary in the río de la Plata between Argentina and Uruguay, see the articles of H. GROS ESPIELL in the *A.F.D.I.* 1964 (X), pp. 725-737 and Ch. ROUSSEAU in the *R.G.D.I.P.* 1969 (73), pp. 1068-1075;

the Falkland islands (islas Malvinas), claimed by Argentina; see p. 355 *supra* and J.C.J.METFORD in *International Affairs* (London) 1968 (44), p. 462 and

Gibraltar, claimed by Spain from Great Britain, see p. 482 *supra* and lately J.E.S.FAWCETT, *Gibraltar: the legal issues* in *International Affairs* (London) 1967 (43), p. 236.

PRINCIPAL COLLECTIONS CONSULTED
AND QUOTED

Besides the principal collections consulted and quoted, cited at pp. 593 *et seq.* of Part II of this publication, use was also made of:

Clercq, de, Recueil des traités de la France (Paris, 1864-1907).
Lagemans, E.G., Recueil des Traités et conventions conclus par le Royaume des Pays-Bas avec les Puissances étrangères, depuis 1813 jusqu'à nos jours (The Hague, 1858-1926).
Parry, C., The Consolidated Treaty Series (New York, 1969-   ).

ABBREVIATIONS

A.A.   Reports of International Arbitral Awards
A.D.   Annual Digest (and Reports) of Public International
                Law Cases
A.F.D.I.   Annuaire Français de Droit International
A.J.I.L.   American Journal of International Law
B.F.S.P.   British and Foreign State Papers
Cmnd   Command Paper of Great Britain
I.C.J. Reports Reports of the International Court of Justice
I.L.M.   International Legal Materials
I.L.R.   International Law Reports
L.N.T.S.   League of Nations Treaty Series
N.T.I.R.   Nederlands Tijdschrift voor Internationaal Recht
O.i.C.   Order in Council
P.C.I.J.   Publications of the Permanent Court of International
                Justice
R.D.I.   Rivista di Diritto Internazionale
R.E.D.I.   Revista Española de Derecho Internacional
R.G.D.I.P.   Revue Générale de Droit International Public
S.J.I.R.   Schweizerisches Jahrbuch für Internationales Recht-
                Annuaire suisse de droit international
U.N.T.S.   United Nations Treaty Series

INDEX

reed cutting, 216
regularization and maintenance, 201 *et seq.*
river commissions, 117 *et seq.*, 218 *et seq.*
river traffic, 197 *et seq.*
staple right, 108, 113-114, 193 *et seq.*
timber floating, 215 *et seq.*
tolls, 107 *et seq.*, 160 *et seq.*, 189 *et seq.*
watermills, 111
Irian, see (Netherlands) New Guinea
Islands, list of, 29-47
Islas Malvinas (Falkland Islands), 35, 355, 621
Italy, unification of, 363 *et seq.*
Izmir, 411, 476, 486

Jahde Bucht, boundaries, 599
Jerusalem, 491 *et seq.*
Judicial decisions in territorial disputes, 610 *et seq.*
Jülich, 345, 434, 445
  Eventual-Investitur, 312
  war of succession, 334
Jurisdiction over foreign forces, 477

Kashmir, 620
Kiel Canal, 237 *et seq.*
Kurile Islands, 37, 369, 371 *et seq.*, 436, 620

Lac Lanoux, 100-101
Lado enclave, 400, 586
Lago di Garda
  boundaries, 579
Lago Maggiore
  boundaries, 578
Lakes
  See also Inland lakes
  boundaries, 576 *et seq.*
  national and international, 18-19
Lake Chad
  boundaries, 584
Lake Dojran, 290
  boundaries, 583 *et seq.*
Lakes Edward and Albert
  boundaries, 586
Lake of Geneva, 101
  boundaries, 578
Lake of Konstanz, *See* Bodensee
Lake Ladoga, 102-103
  boundaries, 580

Lake of Lugano
  boundaries, 578
Lake of Nicaragua
  boundaries, 589 *et seq.*
Lake Nyasa, 98
  boundaries, 586 *et seq.*
Lake Ochrida
  boundaries, 582 *et seq.*
Lakes Peipus and Pskov, 103
  boundaries, 580
Lake Prespa
  boundaries, 583
Lake Scutari
  boundaries, 581 *et seq.*
Lake Tana, 18, 95
Lake Tanganyika
  boundaries, 586
Lake Tiberias
  boundaries, 587 *et seq.*
Lake Titicaca, 98, 288
  boundaries, 590
Lake Victoria (Victoria Nyanza)
  boundaries, 585
Landlocked countries, 244, 443
Lauter, river, 205, 547
Leases, 397 *et seq.*
Lebanon, 484
Liège (Luik), 346
  condominium over Maastricht, 431, 440
Livorno (Leghorn), free port, 24, 337
Louisiana, sale of, 374, 377 *et seq.*
Lucca, 320 *et seq.*, 360
Lübeck, Bay of, 592, 599
Luxembourg, 9

Maas (Meuse), 114, 168 *et seq.*
  boundaries, 566 *et seq.*
  lateral canals, 21
  tolls, 169 *et seq.*
Maastricht, *condominium* over, 114, 431, 440
Macao, 404
Manchurian Railway, 269-274
Mandates
  appointment of mandatory, 458 *et seq.*
  legal status of mandated territory, 454 *et seq.*
  Japanese-, 456
  South West Africa, 455-456, 461 *et seq.*
  termination of, 457 *et seq.*
Marowijne (Maroni) river, 459

633

COLOPHON

This book is a publication of the Institute for International Law of the University of Utrecht being volume 7 of the series Modern International Law, edited by Professor Dr. M. Bos.
Text set in Monotype Baskerville and printed and bounded by A. W. Sijthoff, Printing Division, Leyden in 1970.

DATE DUE

IL 86225636 sent 120130 due 120312			

DEMCO 38-297